Handbook of Research on Blockchain Technology and the Digitalization of the Supply Chain

Tharwa Najar
Gafsa University, Tunisia

Yousra Najar
Manar University, Tunisia

Adel Aloui
EM Normandie Business School, France

A volume in the Advances in Logistics,
Operations, and Management Science (ALOMS)
Book Series

Published in the United States of America by
    IGI Global
    Business Science Reference (an imprint of IGI Global)
    701 E. Chocolate Avenue
    Hershey PA, USA 17033
    Tel: 717-533-8845
    Fax: 717-533-8661
    E-mail: cust@igi-global.com
    Web site: http://www.igi-global.com

Copyright © 2023 by IGI Global. All rights reserved. No part of this publication may be reproduced, stored or distributed in any form or by any means, electronic or mechanical, including photocopying, without written permission from the publisher. Product or company names used in this set are for identification purposes only. Inclusion of the names of the products or companies does not indicate a claim of ownership by IGI Global of the trademark or registered trademark.
    Library of Congress Cataloging-in-Publication Data

Names: Tharwa, Najar, 1981- editor. | Yousra, Najar, 1980- editor. | Aloui,
   Adel, 1976- editor.
Title: Handbook of research on blockchain technology and the digitalization
   of the supply chain / edited by Najar Tharwa, Najar Yousra, Adel Aloui.
Description: Hershey, PA : Engineering Science Reference, [2023] | Includes
   bibliographical references and index. | Summary: "The book will present
   blockchain's basic concepts and pertinent methods that contributed to
   meet key supply chain management objectives such as supporting the
   digitalization process and electronic integration. It covers the issues
   inherent to most emergent topics and critical issues in blockchain
   adoption and diffusion from a supply chain perspective. It determines
   the current trends and challenges in the use of blockchain to enhance
   supply chain management. Moreover, the book defines solutions that
   hamper the adoption of blockchain in the supply chain field. It will be
   written for professionals who want to improve their understanding of the
   strategic role of this technology in improving problems related to fraud
   and trust in the supply chain"-- Provided by publisher.
Identifiers: LCCN 2022053590 (print) | LCCN 2022053591 (ebook) | ISBN
   9781668474556 (hardcover) | ISBN 9781668474570 (ebook)
Subjects: LCSH: Business logistics--Technological innovations. |
   Blockchains (Databases)
Classification: LCC HD38.5 .H35546 2023 (print) | LCC HD38.5 (ebook) |
   DDC 658.70285--dc23/eng/20221104
LC record available at https://lccn.loc.gov/2022053590
LC ebook record available at https://lccn.loc.gov/2022053591

This book is published in the IGI Global book series Advances in Logistics, Operations, and Management Science (ALOMS) (ISSN: 2327-350X; eISSN: 2327-3518)

British Cataloguing in Publication Data
A Cataloguing in Publication record for this book is available from the British Library.

All work contributed to this book is new, previously-unpublished material. The views expressed in this book are those of the authors, but not necessarily of the publisher.

For electronic access to this publication, please contact: eresources@igi-global.com.

Advances in Logistics, Operations, and Management Science (ALOMS) Book Series

John Wang
Montclair State University, USA

ISSN:2327-350X
EISSN:2327-3518

Mission

Operations research and management science continue to influence business processes, administration, and management information systems, particularly in covering the application methods for decision-making processes. New case studies and applications on management science, operations management, social sciences, and other behavioral sciences have been incorporated into business and organizations real-world objectives.

The **Advances in Logistics, Operations, and Management Science** (ALOMS) Book Series provides a collection of reference publications on the current trends, applications, theories, and practices in the management science field. Providing relevant and current research, this series and its individual publications would be useful for academics, researchers, scholars, and practitioners interested in improving decision making models and business functions.

Coverage

- Production Management
- Risk Management
- Marketing engineering
- Information Management
- Networks
- Computing and information technologies
- Decision analysis and decision support
- Services management
- Political Science
- Organizational Behavior

IGI Global is currently accepting manuscripts for publication within this series. To submit a proposal for a volume in this series, please contact our Acquisition Editors at Acquisitions@igi-global.com or visit: http://www.igi-global.com/publish/.

The Advances in Logistics, Operations, and Management Science (ALOMS) Book Series (ISSN 2327-350X) is published by IGI Global, 701 E. Chocolate Avenue, Hershey, PA 17033-1240, USA, www.igi-global.com. This series is composed of titles available for purchase individually; each title is edited to be contextually exclusive from any other title within the series. For pricing and ordering information please visit http://www.igi-global.com/book-series/advances-logistics-operations-management-science/37170. Postmaster: Send all address changes to above address. Copyright © 2023 IGI Global. All rights, including translation in other languages reserved by the publisher. No part of this series may be reproduced or used in any form or by any means – graphics, electronic, or mechanical, including photocopying, recording, taping, or information and retrieval systems – without written permission from the publisher, except for non commercial, educational use, including classroom teaching purposes. The views expressed in this series are those of the authors, but not necessarily of IGI Global.

Titles in this Series

For a list of additional titles in this series, please visit: http://www.igi-global.com/book-series/advances-logistics-operations-management-science/37170

Digital Supply Chain, Disruptive Environments, and the Impact on Retailers
Ehap Sabri (University of Texas at Dallas, USA)
Business Science Reference • © 2023 • 373pp • H/C (ISBN: 9781668472989) • US $250.00

Digital Entrepreneurship and Co-Creating Value Through Digital Encounters
Farag Edghiem (Manchester Metropolitan University, UK) Mohammed Ali (University of Salford, UK) and Robert Wood (University of Manchester, UK)
Business Science Reference • © 2023 • 312pp • H/C (ISBN: 9781668474167) • US $250.00

Principles of External Business Environment Analyzability in an Organizational Context
Bruno F. Abrantes (Niels Brock Copenhagen Business College, Denmark)
Business Science Reference • © 2023 • 318pp • H/C (ISBN: 9781668455432) • US $215.00

Entrepreneurship Ecosystems and Their Opportunities and Challenges
Mohammed El Amine Abdelli (University of Brest, France) Shajara Ul-Durar (University for Creative Arts, UK) and Hala Wasef Hattab (British University in Egypt, Egypt)
Business Science Reference • © 2023 • 300pp • H/C (ISBN: 9781668471401) • US $250.00

Change Management During Unprecedented Times
Kyla Latrice Tennin (College of Doctoral Studies, University of Phoenix, USA & Forbes School of Business, USA & World Business Angels Investment Forum (WBAF)-G20, USA & Lady Mirage Global, Inc., USA)
Business Science Reference • © 2023 • 413pp • H/C (ISBN: 9781668475096) • US $250.00

Perspectives on Women in Management and the Global Labor Market
Elisabete S. Vieira (GOVCOPP, University of Aveiro, Portugal) Mara Madaleno (GOVCOPP, University of Aveiro, Portugal) and João Teodósio (Polytechnic Institute of Santarém, Portugal)
Business Science Reference • © 2023 • 382pp • H/C (ISBN: 9781668459812) • US $240.00

Perspectives and Strategies of Family Business Resiliency in Unprecedented Times
Hotniar Siringoringo (Gunadarma University, Indonesia) and Ravindra Hewa Kuruppuge (University of Peradeniya, Sri Lanka)
Business Science Reference • © 2023 • 322pp • H/C (ISBN: 9781668473948) • US $240.00

701 East Chocolate Avenue, Hershey, PA 17033, USA
Tel: 717-533-8845 x100 • Fax: 717-533-8661
E-Mail: cust@igi-global.com • www.igi-global.com

List of Contributors

A. P., Prasanna Moorthy / *Vellore Institute of Technology, India*	431
A. V., Senthil Kumar / *Hindusthan College of Arts and Sciences, India*	86
Anbarasi, M. / *Vellore Institute of Technology, India*	431
Babei, Jean / *University of Douala, Cameroon*	327
Bansal, Vishesh / *Vellore Institute of Technology, India*	166
Bifulco, Francesco / *University of Naples Federico II, Italy*	310
Biloa, Serge Guy / *University of Douala, Cameroon*	327
C. R., Sriram / *Vellore Institute of Technology, India*	431
Chaâbane, Najeh / *University of Gafsa, Tunisia*	346
Chellatamilan, T. / *Vellore Institute of Technology, India*	431
Clemente, Laura / *Sapienza University of Rome, Italy*	310
Dahlborn, Åsa / *IOTA Foundation, Germany & INATBA, Germany*	207
de la Roche, Mariana / *IOTA Foundation, Germany & INATBA, Germany*	207
Deshmukh, Atharva / *Terna Engineering College, Navi Mumbai, India*	364
Elmalki, Anas / *University of Gafsa, Tunisia*	346
Ferreira, João C. / *ISCTE, University Institute of Lisbon, Portugal*	273
Galiautdinov, Rinat / *Independent Researcher, Italy*	454, 470
Helmer, Louis / *IOTA Foundation, Germany & INATBA, Germany*	207
Kajtazi, Laura / *IOTA Foundation, Germany & INATBA, Germany*	207
Kar, Dulal Chandra / *Texas A&M University, USA*	180
Kara, Karahan / *Artvin Coruh University, Turkey*	254
Krishnan, Santhi / *Independent Researcher, India*	431
Kumar, Sunita / *CHRIST University (Deemed), India*	15
Lassaad, Lakhal / *ISG Sousse, Tunisia*	1
Leila, Ennajeh / *Gabes University, Tunisia*	40
Lolit, M. Villanueva / *Xavier University, Philippines*	86
M., Kawsalya / *Hindusthan College of Arts and Science, India*	86
Manoharan, Abirami / *Department of Electrical and Electronics Engineering, Government College of Engineering, Srirangam, India*	399
Manoharan, Hariprasath / *Department of Electronics and Communication Engineering, Panimalar Engineering College, Chennai, India*	399
Martins, Ana Lúcia / *ISCTE, University Institute of Lisbon, Portugal*	273
Masadeh, Shadi Rasheed / *Isra University, Jordan*	86
Murpani, Varun / *Vellore Institute of Technology, India*	166
Ngassam, Martial Tangui Kadji / *University of Douala, Cameroon*	327

Önden, Abdullah / *Yalova University, Turkey*	254
Pal, Kamalendu / *University of London, UK*	137, 228
Patel, Sulaiman Saleem / *Durban University of Technology, South Africa*	287
Pawar, Pratap Dnyandeo / *Vellore Institute of Technology, Bhopal, India*	364
Putta, Bharathi / *Texas A&M University, USA*	180
Quazi, Tahmid Al-Mumit / *University of KwaZulu-Natal, South Africa*	287
Rawat, Anamika / *SAGE University, India*	86
Reaidy, Paul / *CERAG, Université Grenoble Alpes, Grenoble, France*	113
Riabova, Marianna / *CERAG, Université Grenoble Alpes, Grenoble, France*	113
Samar, Ben Slimene / *ISG Sousse, Tunisia*	1
Selvanambi, Ramani / *Vellore Institute of Technology, India*	57, 166
Selvarajan, Shitharth / *Department of Computer Science, Kebri Dehar University, Kebri Dehar, Ethiopia*	399
Sheth, Hariket Sukesh Kumar / *Vellore Institute of Technology, Chennai, India*	364
Sridharan, A. / *CHRIST University (Deemed), India*	15
Srivastava, Rohan / *Vellore Institute of Technology, India*	57
Tokkozhina, Ulpan / *ISCTE, University Institute of Lisbon, Portugal*	273
Tyagi, Amit Kumar / *Vellore Institute of Technology, Chennai, India*	364
V., Akash / *Hindusthan College of Arts and Science, India*	86
Venkatachalam, K. / *Department of Electronics and Communication Engineering, Audisankara College of Engineering and Technology, Gudur, India*	399
Yalçın, Galip Cihan / *Kırıkkale University, Turkey*	254

Table of Contents

Foreword xxii

Preface xxiv

Section 1
Technology Potential in the Supply Chain

Chapter 1
Communication Systems and the Evolution of the Supply Chain 1
Ben Slimene Samar, ISG Sousse, Tunisia
Lakhal Lassaad, ISG Sousse, Tunisia

Chapter 2
Strengthening Supply Chain Management Through Technology 15
A. Sridharan, CHRIST University (Deemed), India
Sunita Kumar, CHRIST University (Deemed), India

Section 2
Overview of Blockchain Technology

Chapter 3
Overview of Blockchain Technology Diffusion and Adoption: Theoretical Analysis Based on IDT Theory 40
Ennajeh Leila, Gabes University, Tunisia

Chapter 4
Blockchain and Governance Structure 57
Rohan Srivastava, Vellore Institute of Technology, India
Ramani Selvanambi, Vellore Institute of Technology, India

Section 3
Security and Blockchain Technology

Chapter 5
Blockchain-Based Secure Transactions 86
    Kawsalya M., Hindusthan College of Arts and Science, India
    Senthil Kumar A. V., Hindusthan College of Arts and Sciences, India
    Akash V., Hindusthan College of Arts and Science, India
    M. Villanueva Lolit, Xavier University, Philippines
    Shadi Rasheed Masadeh, Isra University, Jordan
    Anamika Rawat, SAGE University, India

Chapter 6
Blockchain Arbitration: A Supply Chain Perspective 113
    Marianna Riabova, CERAG, Université Grenoble Alpes, Grenoble, France
    Paul Reaidy, CERAG, Université Grenoble Alpes, Grenoble, France

Section 4
Blockchain Technology's Impact on the Supply Chain

Chapter 7
Managing Supply Chain Digitalization With Blockchain Technology 137
    Kamalendu Pal, University of London, UK

Chapter 8
Blockchain Supply Chain Integration Relation 166
    Vishesh Bansal, Vellore Institute of Technology, India
    Varun Murpani, Vellore Institute of Technology, India
    Ramani Selvanambi, Vellore Institute of Technology, India

Chapter 9
Enhancing Supply Chain Efficiency Through Blockchain Integration 180
    Bharathi Putta, Texas A&M University, USA
    Dulal Chandra Kar, Texas A&M University, USA

Section 5
Blockchain Technology and Supply Chain Sustainability

Chapter 10
Impact of Distributed Ledger Technology on Supply Chain Sustainability 207
    Mariana de la Roche, IOTA Foundation, Germany & INATBA, Germany
    Laura Kajtazi, IOTA Foundation, Germany & INATBA, Germany
    Åsa Dahlborn, IOTA Foundation, Germany & INATBA, Germany
    Louis Helmer, IOTA Foundation, Germany & INATBA, Germany

Chapter 11
Blockchain-Enabled Internet of Things Application in Supply Chain Operations Sustainability Management 228
    Kamalendu Pal, University of London, UK

Section 6
Blockchain Technology's Application in the Supply Chain

Chapter 12
Moderating Role of Supplier Coordination Level in Relation to Data-Driven Supply Chain and Supply Chain Coordination Capability 254
    Karahan Kara, Artvin Coruh University, Turkey
    Galip Cihan Yalçın, Kırıkkale University, Turkey
    Abdullah Önden, Yalova University, Turkey

Chapter 13
A New Panacea for Supply Chains? Experience Feedback From Blockchain Technology Adopters 273
    Ulpan Tokkozhina, ISCTE, University Institute of Lisbon, Portugal
    Ana Lúcia Martins, ISCTE, University Institute of Lisbon, Portugal
    João C. Ferreira, ISCTE, University Institute of Lisbon, Portugal

Chapter 14
Socio-Technical Systems Engineering Perspectives Towards a South African Halaal Blockchain System 287
    Tahmid Al-Mumit Quazi, University of KwaZulu-Natal, South Africa
    Sulaiman Saleem Patel, Durban University of Technology, South Africa

Chapter 15
Time Stamp and Immutability as Key Factors for the Application of Blockchain in the Cultural Sector 310
    Laura Clemente, Sapienza University of Rome, Italy
    Francesco Bifulco, University of Naples Federico II, Italy

Chapter 16
Deployment of Blockchain Technologies in Africa: Challenges and Conditions of Success for the Performance of the Supply Chains of Cameroonian Firms 327
    Martial Tangui Kadji Ngassam, University of Douala, Cameroon
    Jean Babei, University of Douala, Cameroon
    Serge Guy Biloa, University of Douala, Cameroon

Section 7
Cryptocurrencies, Market, and Blockchain Technology

Chapter 17
The Dynamics of the Relationship Between Price and Volume of Cryptocurrencies: A Wavelet Coherence Analysis 346
    Najeh Chaâbane, University of Gafsa, Tunisia
    Anas Elmalki, University of Gafsa, Tunisia

Chapter 18
A Survey on Blockchain and Cryptocurrency-Based Systems 364
    Atharva Deshmukh, Terna Engineering College, Navi Mumbai, India
    Hariket Sukesh Kumar Sheth, Vellore Institute of Technology, Chennai, India
    Pratap Dnyandeo Pawar, Vellore Institute of Technology, Bhopal, India
    Amit Kumar Tyagi, Vellore Institute of Technology, Chennai, India

Section 8
Perspectives on AI Technologies and Blockchain

Chapter 19
Implementation of Internet of Things With Blockchain Using Machine Learning Algorithm: Enhancement of Security With Blockchain 399
    Hariprasath Manoharan, Department of Electronics and Communication Engineering,
        Panimalar Engineering College, Chennai, India
    Abirami Manoharan, Department of Electrical and Electronics Engineering, Government
        College of Engineering, Srirangam, India
    Shitharth Selvarajan, Department of Computer Science, Kebri Dehar University, Kebri
        Dehar, Ethiopia
    K. Venkatachalam, Department of Electronics and Communication Engineering,
        Audisankara College of Engineering and Technology, Gudur, India

Chapter 20
Blockchain-Based Decentralized Documentation System... 431
    Sriram C. R., Vellore Institute of Technology, India
    Prasanna Moorthy A. P., Vellore Institute of Technology, India
    Santhi Krishnan, Independent Researcher, India
    T. Chellatamilan, Vellore Institute of Technology, India
    M. Anbarasi, Vellore Institute of Technology, India

Chapter 21
Brain-Machine Interface and Blockchain in Avatar-Based Systems 454
    Rinat Galiautdinov, Independent Researcher, Italy

Chapter 22
The New Approach to the Architecture of Smart Contracts: Its Impact on Performance,
Vulnerability, Pollution, and Energy Saving Optimization 470
    Rinat Galiautdinov, Independent Researcher, Italy

Compilation of References 488

About the Contributors 544

Index 552

Detailed Table of Contents

Foreword xxii

Preface xxiv

Section 1
Technology Potential in the Supply Chain

Chapter 1
Communication Systems and the Evolution of the Supply Chain 1
    Ben Slimene Samar, ISG Sousse, Tunisia
    Lakhal Lassaad, ISG Sousse, Tunisia

Under the pressure of the extremely complex and turbulent economic environment, mainly due to globalization and the strategies implemented by companies, logistics, like all the vital functions of the company, have undergone a real transformation redefining their role, mission, and field of action within the framework of an effort to adapt and restrict strategic dimensions. This chapter focuses on the evolution of the traditional supply chain to the notion of SCM. This evolution has taken place due to the emergence and use of information systems and IT. All this contributes to the achievement of overall organizational performance through the achievement of efficiency and effectiveness objectives. This technological advance certainly contributes to improving the links between the various partners in the chain through the sharing and exchange of information. This chapter highlights the prominent role of technological advances in making information reliable and accessible by all partners in the chain and also in achieving the organizational performance of all partners.

Chapter 2
Strengthening Supply Chain Management Through Technology 15
    A. Sridharan, CHRIST University (Deemed), India
    Sunita Kumar, CHRIST University (Deemed), India

The removal of trade barriers with the advent of WTO and which led to LPG (liberalization, privatization, and globalization) across the universe increased choices of brands for consumers and even the complexity of products within organization and the expectations of consumers rising daily. Organizations look for better management of their supply chain from "end to end," i.e., sourcing of raw materials from vendors to delivering finished products at the doorstep of consumers. This means businesses that used to be 'operations hubs' within the company have moved into the epicenter of business innovation, and this process can not be done manually or by few people within organizations, thus the need to back up business innovations and product complexities through advanced technologies. Using sensors like RFID, CRM, AI, and ML, organizations today collect information at every checkpoint from status of raw materials flow to the location of finished goods. Supply chain management is the process of planning and implementing the operations of the sourcing of quality materials at competitive cost. This chapter explores strengthening supply chain management through technology.

Section 2
Overview of Blockchain Technology

Chapter 3
Overview of Blockchain Technology Diffusion and Adoption: Theoretical Analysis Based on IDT Theory 40
    Ennajeh Leila, Gabes University, Tunisia

The main focus of the chapter is to study the diffusion of blockchain technology. Under the theoretical framework of innovation diffusion theory (IDT) analyses were conducted with the aim to localize blockchain technology in the adoption decision process and in the adoption curve. Thus, innovators and adopters of blockchain in different economic activities such as finance and banking, manufacturing, healthcare, education, and agriculture were presented. The purpose is to identify what economic sectors are reaping benefits from blockchain technology and what sectors are yet far away from its adoption. Furthermore, advantages of blockchain technology were also addressed because they are able to influence and accelerate its adoption. Insights are particularly relevant for future adopters and policy makers to enhance emergent technology adoption and reach economic benefits in the digitalization era.

Chapter 4
Blockchain and Governance Structure 57
    Rohan Srivastava, Vellore Institute of Technology, India
    Ramani Selvanambi, Vellore Institute of Technology, India

The rapid growth in the advancement of blockchain technology and its development has brought its usage in every field. Traditional legal frameworks, which depend on establishing central points of accountability and responsibility, have difficulties as a result of the characteristics of blockchain, such as decentralisation, transparency, integrity, and immutability, among others. A key challenge behind the adoption of blockchain is understanding the dynamics of blockchain governance. With the promise of an efficient network owing to the elimination of intermediaries, governance in blockchain may be understood as addition of standards and culture, laws and codes, people, and institutions that promote coordination and jointly decide a particular organisation. As a result, having a headquarters is not necessary; instead, development can rely on a globally dispersed network of programmers who create the software protocol, giving rise to the idea of a DAO (decentralized autonomous system).

Section 3
Security and Blockchain Technology

Chapter 5
Blockchain-Based Secure Transactions 86
    Kawsalya M., Hindusthan College of Arts and Science, India
    Senthil Kumar A. V., Hindusthan College of Arts and Sciences, India
    Akash V., Hindusthan College of Arts and Science, India
    M. Villanueva Lolit, Xavier University, Philippines
    Shadi Rasheed Masadeh, Isra University, Jordan
    Anamika Rawat, SAGE University, India

Traditional transactions have several issues, like physical cash, for instance, boarding fake bank notes and also building stock to use money significantly less complex. In this digital marketing world, hackers are using many ways and techniques to scam money. The three most common online transaction frauds in India are scam using QR codes, UPI frauds, remote access/screen sharing frauds. Protection and privacy are the main anticipated features in the field of online transactions, which can be fulfilled by blockchain technology. This proposal is crucial as it is the first attempt to apply blockchain technology to payment services. In the proposed system, due to high level of fraud, blockchain technology is used. Hackers attack one block and change their address, and hence, transaction is blocked and amount will also be refunded using blockchain approach hashing algorithms. The main steps of blockchain used in the proposed system are transaction data, changing blocks with a hash, and creating signature (hash) using cryptographic hash function.

Chapter 6
Blockchain Arbitration: A Supply Chain Perspective... 113
    Marianna Riabova, CERAG, Université Grenoble Alpes, Grenoble, France
    Paul Reaidy, CERAG, Université Grenoble Alpes, Grenoble, France

Blockchain technology offers substantial benefits to supply chains (SCs). Along with transparency and traceability and other undeniable advantages, blockchain technology enables smart contract integration. Blockchain and smart contracts are, however, not flawless and can create a new category of disputes. The recognition of these disputes by traditional legal institutions is questionable. This chapter presents the concept of blockchain arbitration that allows for smart contract and blockchain dispute settlement via a decentralized resolution platform. The chapter reveals that despite existing challenges, blockchain arbitration can enhance the resolution process in terms of flexibility, cost, and time reduction, increase trust among SC stakeholders, and boost overall SC performance.

Section 4
Blockchain Technology's Impact on the Supply Chain

Chapter 7
Managing Supply Chain Digitalization With Blockchain Technology... 137
    Kamalendu Pal, University of London, UK

Digitization of manufacturing supply chain operations is essential in changing management practices and enhancing business transparency-related aspects. The digitalization of supply chain business processes often exploits emerging technologies such as radio frequency identification (RFID), the internet of things (IoT), data analytics, cloud computing, and blockchain technology to reshape supply chain management. The IoT technology integrates various smart objects (or things) to form a network, share data among the connected objects, store data, and process data to support business applications. However, some of the IoT infrastructural components are a shortage of computational processing power and local data storing ability, and these components are very vulnerable to the privacy and security of collected data. This chapter presents an information system architecture consisting of IoT and blockchain technology to maintain data security and transparency and how this helps improve business operations.

Chapter 8
Blockchain Supply Chain Integration Relation.. 166
    Vishesh Bansal, Vellore Institute of Technology, India
    Varun Murpani, Vellore Institute of Technology, India
    Ramani Selvanambi, Vellore Institute of Technology, India

In this chapter, the authors aim to focus to integrate blockchain with the existing infrastructure, such that it works with the underlying core infrastructure to automate the supply chain integration as much as possible to decrease human intervention to the bare minimum level and solve the underlying problems that might occur due to the human factor in the supply chain integration. The authors will also shed light on the various regulatory issues associated with blockchain technologies. At the same time, one will also try to keep in mind that the newly proposed system can be well integrated with the existing and well-established system. The goal is to address problems that can arise from the human factor in supply chain management. The proposed system can be used in various industries requiring inventory management, the authenticity of goods, digital escrow services, etc. The authors have also discussed various regulatory issues as well as environmental concerns and procurement of raw materials associated with blockchain technologies.

Chapter 9
Enhancing Supply Chain Efficiency Through Blockchain Integration.. 180
    Bharathi Putta, Texas A&M University, USA
    Dulal Chandra Kar, Texas A&M University, USA

Blockchain technology offers several beneficial features that make it well-suited for supply chain management (SCM). Particularly, it can improve transparency, traceability, security, efficiency, and accountability in supply chains (SC). This chapter focuses on how blockchain technology can completely transform SC processes due to its inherent features. By implementing blockchain, businesses can cut costs, improve efficiency, and ensure accountability. The chapter explains the basics of blockchain technology and its potential benefits for SCM. The various beneficial features of blockchain technology such as trust, immutability, reliability, and security are discussed and highlighted in the chapter. The chapter showcases real-world uses of blockchain technology in SCM to depict the possible benefits. Benefits and challenges of incorporating blockchain into SC processes are also discussed in the chapter. Finally, this chapter emphasizes how crucial it is for companies to identify the factors that weaken their SC and to ensure that blockchain is applied to address such issues.

Section 5
Blockchain Technology and Supply Chain Sustainability

Chapter 10
Impact of Distributed Ledger Technology on Supply Chain Sustainability 207
    Mariana de la Roche, IOTA Foundation, Germany & INATBA, Germany
    Laura Kajtazi, IOTA Foundation, Germany & INATBA, Germany
    Åsa Dahlborn, IOTA Foundation, Germany & INATBA, Germany
    Louis Helmer, IOTA Foundation, Germany & INATBA, Germany

This chapter describes the challenges and vulnerabilities of current supply chain management and presents the benefits of implementing blockchain and DLT technology in the supply chain processes. For a more precise understanding, the chapter presents a summary of the characteristics of blockchain technology and an overview of the energy consumption of different blockchain protocols to demystify the negative criticism of blockchain technologies in terms of energy consumption. The purpose of analyzing the characteristics and energy requirements is to present the potential of DLTs to positively impact supply chains and make the blockchain industry more sustainable. After describing the sector's challenges and the technology's characteristics, the chapter presents case studies in which DLT has been successfully integrated into the supply chain of various products and goods. The chapter concludes by highlighting the necessary conditions to promote the adoption of DLT technology globally.

Chapter 11
Blockchain-Enabled Internet of Things Application in Supply Chain Operations Sustainability Management 228
    Kamalendu Pal, University of London, UK

In recent decades, sustainability and green supply chain management have played essential roles in business operations. This chapter examines how the textile and apparel supply chains can comply with the United Nations Sustainable Development Goals. In particular, verifying the source of raw materials and maintaining visibility of merchandise products and related services while moving through the value-chain network is challenging. The internet of things (IoT) application can help textile and apparel supply chain operation managers observe, monitor, and track products and relevant business processes within their respective value chain networks. However, the IoT infrastructural components have a shortage of computational processing power and local saving capability, and these components are vulnerable to the privacy and security of collected data. This chapter presents blockchain technology with IoT-based infrastructural elements and service-oriented computing architecture as a solution for information processing for apparel supply chain management.

Section 6
Blockchain Technology's Application in the Supply Chain

Chapter 12
Moderating Role of Supplier Coordination Level in Relation to Data-Driven Supply Chain and Supply Chain Coordination Capability 254
    Karahan Kara, Artvin Coruh University, Turkey
    Galip Cihan Yalçın, Kırıkkale University, Turkey
    Abdullah Önden, Yalova University, Turkey

Big data and big data analytics have contributed to the collection of large amounts of data. This has led to the transformation to data-driven supply chain (DDSC) structures. The supply chain coordination capability (SCCC) has also been strengthened in DDSC. In this study, the effect of DDSC on SCCC and the moderator effect of supplier coordination (SCO) have been investigated. The research was carried out in the manufacturing firms. Three hundred eighty-three pieces of data were obtained between August and December 2021 by the simple random sampling method. Two hypotheses were developed. Simple regression analysis was used to test the first hypothesis, and moderator effect analysis was performed with the SPSS process to test the second hypothesis. It has been determined that the DDSC has a significant effect on the SCCC. In addition, SCO has a moderating effect, and when there is a high SCO, the DDSC has a greater effect on the SCCC.

Chapter 13
A New Panacea for Supply Chains? Experience Feedback From Blockchain Technology Adopters 273
    Ulpan Tokkozhina, ISCTE, University Institute of Lisbon, Portugal
    Ana Lúcia Martins, ISCTE, University Institute of Lisbon, Portugal
    João C. Ferreira, ISCTE, University Institute of Lisbon, Portugal

Blockchain technology (BCT) is being actively discussed for application in business contexts to digitalize supply chains (SCs). The current nascent level of BCT adoption in businesses creates resistance for further scalability in the industry. This study explores real pilot cases and experiences of BCT pioneers from various continents and industries, revealing the intentions behind the adoption, feasible improvements, and challenges that need to be further addressed. Findings reveal the business incentives of decentralizing trust constituent and efficiency improvements of data sharing. However, the challenges remain in scaling the adoption to a broader level and guaranteeing the accurate input of data.

Chapter 14
Socio-Technical Systems Engineering Perspectives Towards a South African Halaal Blockchain System 287
    Tahmid Al-Mumit Quazi, University of KwaZulu-Natal, South Africa
    Sulaiman Saleem Patel, Durban University of Technology, South Africa

Blockchain is an emerging technology and part of the fourth industrial revolution. Its ability to improve transparency and traceability has found many supply chain applications, including the Halaal supply chain (defining a Halaal blockchain system). The religious roots of the Halaal status makes the Halaal blockchain system inherently socio-technical. This chapter first conceptualises the Halaal blockchain system using a socio-technical systems framework, and then analyses the system in the South African context. The analysis discusses the interconnected relationships between people, culture, goals, infrastructure, technology, and processes within the external environment of stakeholders, regulatory frameworks, and financial/economic circumstances. Challenges towards implementing a Halaal blockchain system in South Africa are discussed along with potential impacts for the communities. The study concludes by identifying open research areas that require further investigation to realise a Halaal blockchain system implementation in South Africa.

Chapter 15
Time Stamp and Immutability as Key Factors for the Application of Blockchain in the Cultural Sector 310
    Laura Clemente, Sapienza University of Rome, Italy
    Francesco Bifulco, University of Naples Federico II, Italy

In recent years, blockchain, a new and potentially disruptive technology, has come to the fore. Despite its widespread use in several fields, it is in the cultural sector that it can offer numerous advantages. The implementation of a blockchain system could make the traditional art market less opaque by recording data on an encrypted and immutable register, and its use could also improve the circulation of works of art, encourage their collection, and promote a new form of ownership. This chapter highlights the features of blockchain that make it suitable for the management and enhancement of cultural heritage, considering the different fields of application as well as the way in which it can be integrated to support the sale and management of cultural assets and to develop new business models for cultural and creative firms.

Chapter 16
Deployment of Blockchain Technologies in Africa: Challenges and Conditions of Success for the Performance of the Supply Chains of Cameroonian Firms 327
    Martial Tangui Kadji Ngassam, University of Douala, Cameroon
    Jean Babei, University of Douala, Cameroon
    Serge Guy Biloa, University of Douala, Cameroon

The problem of this chapter is to understand how technological developments, in particular blockchain applications, affect the performance of the supply chains of companies based in Cameroon. This work will allow us to analyze the conditions for the success of the deployment of the supply chain in Cameroon in a dynamic of improving its performance. The empirical research carried out consisted in carrying out 18 semi-structured interviews lasting an average of 60 minutes with actors in the supply chain sector in Cameroon. The researchers adopted a qualitative type methodology based on a thematic content analysis. The results obtained are of two kinds: on the one hand, the results related to the challenges and conditions of success of the blockchain; and on the other hand, the results related to the contribution of the blockchain to the performance of the supply chains in Cameroon.

Section 7
Cryptocurrencies, Market, and Blockchain Technology

Chapter 17
The Dynamics of the Relationship Between Price and Volume of Cryptocurrencies: A Wavelet Coherence Analysis 346
    Najeh Chaâbane, University of Gafsa, Tunisia
    Anas Elmalki, University of Gafsa, Tunisia

In this study, the authors investigate the volume as the pricing driver of the top three cryptocurrencies (Bitcoin, Ethereum, and Binance) based on a wavelet analysis from January 1, 2019 to December 31, 2021. The dynamics of the relationship between price and volume in the cryptocurrency market could have valuable market implications for stakeholders and investors and contribute to making optimal investment decisions via portfolio diversification strategies. The results reveal that the relationship between price and volume is positive in the medium and long term and that price is the leading volume for both Bitcoin and Binance markets. The findings suggest that the COVID-19 pandemic significantly affected the cryptocurrency price and volume series links. Indeed, these results contribute to the emerging and growing literature on cryptocurrencies in the time of COVID-19, which has received limited attention during the pandemic compared to the classical asset financial classes.

Chapter 18
A Survey on Blockchain and Cryptocurrency-Based Systems 364
    Atharva Deshmukh, Terna Engineering College, Navi Mumbai, India
    Hariket Sukesh Kumar Sheth, Vellore Institute of Technology, Chennai, India
    Pratap Dnyandeo Pawar, Vellore Institute of Technology, Bhopal, India
    Amit Kumar Tyagi, Vellore Institute of Technology, Chennai, India

Projects, facilities, services, and gadgets are attracting more people as life speeds up. Blockchain and cryptocurrency systems are trending worldwide. Blockchain interests everyone with technology. They make an interesting transaction medium because they have no single powerful source. Cryptocurrencies are vital financial software platforms. Mining is crucial to its decentralised information ledger dataset. Mining adds transaction data to the chain, a decentralised ledger that lets users securely agree on actions. In 2008, Santoshi Nakamoto tried to use blockchain as a restricted ledger for bitcoin, the most successful cryptocurrency. It's unlike the internet. This chapter will discuss blockchain security, cryptocurrency fraud, cyberattacks, etc. This chapter identifies cryptocurrency blockchain threats and proposes solutions. This chapter reviews and analyses top-cited articles to reach a conclusion. In this chapter, strengths and threats of cryptocurrency and their emergence in the internet-connected financial payments in the futuristic economic world will be discussed.

Section 8
Perspectives on AI Technologies and Blockchain

Chapter 19
Implementation of Internet of Things With Blockchain Using Machine Learning Algorithm:
Enhancement of Security With Blockchain 399
    Hariprasath Manoharan, Department of Electronics and Communication Engineering,
        Panimalar Engineering College, Chennai, India
    Abirami Manoharan, Department of Electrical and Electronics Engineering, Government
        College of Engineering, Srirangam, India
    Shitharth Selvarajan, Department of Computer Science, Kebri Dehar University, Kebri
        Dehar, Ethiopia
    K. Venkatachalam, Department of Electronics and Communication Engineering,
        Audisankara College of Engineering and Technology, Gudur, India

In recent days, all networks are connected by internet and all people around the world are able to control things in their remote locations. Even though these technologies have been used only by selected people, it is definite in the future that all people will use this technology and they will move towards building smart cities, homes, and industries. However, when advanced technologies are created, people always worry about security when they move towards smart environment. If the internet is connected to their home then much valuable information in their home can also be sent through smart devices. Therefore, for this IoT-based technology, a blockchain-based method can be introduced where more security for data transfer process can be provided. Also, these technologies have to work efficiently by integrating a new artificial intelligence-based machine learning algorithm. Therefore, for this, a deep learning model will be integrated, thus providing effective data transfer from transmitter to receiver.

Chapter 20
Blockchain-Based Decentralized Documentation System 431
    Sriram C. R., Vellore Institute of Technology, India
    Prasanna Moorthy A. P., Vellore Institute of Technology, India
    Santhi Krishnan, Independent Researcher, India
    T. Chellatamilan, Vellore Institute of Technology, India
    M. Anbarasi, Vellore Institute of Technology, India

Property enrolment is a salient process. There are several escape clauses and issues. The existing system endures the fabrication of land documents which results in a loss of revenue to the government. So, developing a decentralized online registration using blockchain (BC) makes it comfortable for citizens to transfer property, prevents the touting of the same property to various buyers, and also helps the government to monitor and keep track of property movement to prevent money laundering on real estate. The process of automation eliminates the need for more humans to employ and also reduces the need for storage building which is required for storing physical documents. In this chapter, interplanetary file system (IPFS) is used for connecting all computing devices or nodes with the same system files and storing large files effectively. The land is successfully transferred between users after the successful completion of payment. Moreover, the proposed hybrid system does not require nodes to solve complex puzzles and thus reduces the use of high computational energy.

Chapter 21
Brain-Machine Interface and Blockchain in Avatar-Based Systems 454
Rinat Galiautdinov, Independent Researcher, Italy

The main purpose of this research is to provide a solution that allows neuroscientists and developers to keep the track of the neurosignals of live beings or biologically simulated neural networks and store them having the ability to guarantee that output of neurosignal translation was correct and can be reproduced later on any other biologically simulated neuron. Such a situation is especially important for the case when producers of different equipment, which are based on the biologically simulated neurons, can predict its behavior and guarantee that it will have accepted level of output deviations. Such a situation can be used for tracking live neurosignals of a beings and then reproduce them on avatars or different types of robots, neural networks, etc.

Chapter 22
The New Approach to the Architecture of Smart Contracts: Its Impact on Performance, Vulnerability, Pollution, and Energy Saving Optimization 470
Rinat Galiautdinov, Independent Researcher, Italy

This research analyzes the problems of smart contracts and the whole concept of smart contracts and provides a solution that can resolve all such the issues in the current smart contract concept and additionally to this change the architecture used in smart contracts and blockchain. In this research, the author lists the issues, analyzes them, and provides the solution explaining how it will change the whole concept, performance, and what sort of positive impact it will have not only on the performance of smart contracts and their extensibility but also the impact on pollution and saving of energy.

Compilation of References 488

About the Contributors 544

Index 552

Foreword

With great pleasure, I introduce this timely and insightful book, "Handbook of Research on Blockchain Technology and Digitalization of the Supply Chain." This book is a comprehensive collection of 22 chapters, written by experts in their respective fields, that delve into the vast possibilities of blockchain technology and digitalization and its impact on the supply chain.

As we move further into the digital age, the supply chain is experiencing a rapid transformation, thanks to advancements in technology. Digitalization and the introduction of blockchain technology have brought a new level of security, efficiency, and transparency to the supply chain. The authors of this book have explored these possibilities and their potential to revolutionize the supply chain in the 21st century.

The book is divided into eight sections that cover a wide range of topics related to blockchain technology and the supply chain. The first two sections provide a broad overview of the evolution of the supply chain and how technology is strengthening supply chain management. The next sections delve into the various aspects of blockchain technology, such as adoption and diffusion, governance structure, and security in the supply chain.

The book offers a highly valuable section that provides practical contributions to the field. This section is particularly interesting as it presents a range of case studies demonstrating blockchain technology's potential in transforming the supply chain. These cases cover different regions and sectors, including supplier coordination, engineering perspectives of a South African *Halaal* blockchain system, blockchain adoption feedback, time stamp and immutability in the cultural sector, and blockchain deployment in African supply chains. These diverse case studies provide insightful and actionable information that can help practitioners, researchers, and decision-makers to understand the challenges and opportunities associated with implementing blockchain technology in the supply chain.

The book also explores the impact of blockchain technology on the supply chain, including the integration of blockchain technology, enhancing supply chain efficiency, and the role of blockchain technology in promoting sustainability. The book concludes with sections on cryptocurrencies, market dynamics, and the intersection between AI technologies and blockchain.

Overall, "Handbook of Research on Blockchain Technology and Digitalization of the Supply Chain" is an excellent resource for anyone interested in exploring the potential of blockchain technology in the supply chain. I would like to commend the authors for their contributions to the field and their efforts in bringing together such a comprehensive and informative book.

Finally, I would like to express my sincere gratitude to the authors of this insightful book. It was an honor to have the opportunity to write the foreword for this valuable contribution to the field. The authors have done an excellent job of bringing together a diverse range of topics and perspectives on blockchain technology and its potential impact on the supply chain. The book provides a comprehensive

Foreword

and practical overview of the current state of blockchain technology in supply chain management and offers valuable insights and recommendations for practitioners and researchers. Once again, thank you to the authors for their excellent work, and I hope this book will serve as a valuable resource for anyone interested in the intersection of blockchain technology and supply chain management.

Moacir Godinho Filho
Metis Lab, EM Normandie Business School, France

Preface

Blockchain is a recent technology promising to revolutionize how supply chains are designed and operated. Regarding its role in securing exchanges of data, this technology has remarkably changed the manner of governing the structure of the supply chain relationships and the way that transactions are made. Blockchain technology is likely to influence future supply chain practices by performing electronic integration, supporting partners' connections, and offering real-time information flows. Thus, blockchain technologies are gaining interest among both academicians and professionals. This interest concerns the conceptual level and the practical and concrete levels of the implementation of blockchain technology in supply chains.

Nowadays, the adoption of blockchain technology in the supply chain is gaining much attention and is considered very important. Blockchain is a distributed ledger system that provides secure and transparent exchanges between entities without the need for third parties. It has the potential to revolutionize the supply chain sector by increasing transparency, traceability, and efficiency while lowering costs and preventing fraud.

The incorporation of blockchain technology into supply chains is particularly significant in today's highly complex and globalized world, where there is an increasing demand for visibility and accountability. COVID-19 has also spotlighted the fragility and susceptibilities of global supply chains, thus creating more interest in blockchain technology as a possible answer to these issues.

While the adoption of blockchain technology in supply chains still lies in its infancy phase, several corporations and organizations have already started experimenting with blockchain solutions to enhance their supply chain management. Examples of such blockchain-empowered supply chain solutions include tracking the origin of products, checking on the temperature or condition of items during transportation, and verifying conformity with policies and standards.

Handbook of Research on Blockchain Technology and the Digitalization of the Supply Chain presents blockchain's basic concepts and pertinent methods that contributed to meeting key supply chain management objectives. It determines the current trends and challenges in the use of blockchain to enhance supply chain management. Covering topics such as communication systems, sustainability, documentation systems, and supply chain digitalization evolution, this premier reference source is an excellent resource for business leaders and managers, logistics professionals, IT managers, students and educators of higher education, librarians, researchers, and academicians.

Overall, the upcoming pages will present a diverse range of topics that have been explored by prominent scholars and professionals in 22 chapters. These topics span from the significance of science in computer sciences to business and operations management and portfolio management strategies in emerging economies. Furthermore, the following pages will also include detailed discussions and

Preface

instances related to supply chain management and emerging technology use (communication systems, blockchain, IoT, machine learning…).

Chapter 1 advances that SCCS (supply chain communication systems) is a strategic tool for enhancing cooperation between suppliers and retailers. Logistics has expanded its scope to cover the entire chain of product and service creation, from manufacturers and suppliers to carriers, warehouses, retailers and consumers. This has enabled the integration of the Supply Chain and allows consumers to react in real-time to market changes. The evolution of the traditional supply chain has necessitated the development of a global managerial approach through the creation and management of "business chains". This approach allows to manage a set of dispersed units in ensuring the definition of a global and common objective to which the various partners refer. Companies have been forced to seek solutions to grow and perform beyond their borders, necessitating the development of a global managerial approach through the creation and management of "business chains". To complement traditional indicators, modern chains must be reactive, agile, efficient, and intelligent.

Chapter 2 discusses the impact of technology on the business world, specifically in the context of supply chain management. It covers various technologies such as Artificial Intelligence, Machine Learning, robotics, Data Analytics, Cloud Computing, and Blockchain. The chapter also includes case studies to reinforce the theoretical concepts discussed. It highlights both the advantages and potential pitfalls of implementing these technologies in a business setting. Overall, it provides a comprehensive overview of how technology is transforming the industry and what businesses can do to adapt to these changes.

Chapter 3 provides an overview of Blockchain technology diffusion and adoption. It uses the Innovation Diffusion Theory framework to analyze the localization of Blockchain technology in the adoption decision process and curve. The chapter presents innovators and adopters of Blockchain in various economic activities, such as finance and banking, manufacturing, healthcare, education, and agriculture. The purpose is to identify what economic sectors are reaping benefits from Blockchain technology and what sectors are yet far away from its adoption.

Chapter 4 discusses the use of blockchain technology in the governance structure. It explains the background of blockchain in governance, its working and architecture, and its applications and use cases. The main contribution of this chapter is to make the government and its structure more efficient and reliable by implementing blockchain technology. The chapter concludes with a future assessment of the potential impact of blockchain on governance.

Chapter 5 focuses on how blockchain technology can be used to address the challenges associated with traditional transactions and online transaction frauds, providing a secure and efficient alternative for conducting transactions in the digital age.

The main ideas discussed are:

1. The issues with traditional transactions, such as physical cash and online transaction frauds.
2. The need for protection and privacy in online transactions, can be fulfilled by blockchain technology.
3. The use of blockchain technology in payment services to provide tamper-resistant and decentralized shared ledger content.
4. The advantages of using blockchain technology, such as increased security, transparency, and efficiency.
5. The potential applications of blockchain technology beyond payment services, such as property fraud detection and prevention.

Chapter 6 advances that Blockchain technology and Smart Contracts have the potential to provide advantages such as transaction transparency, security, and higher levels of trust. However, blockchain and Smart Contracts can also create a new category of disputes related to the adoption and usage of these technologies. Existing dispute resolution methods are not prepared for resolving disputes arising from Smart Contracts and decentralized blockchain transactions. This book chapter explores Blockchain Arbitration, an innovative dispute resolution method specifically designed for blockchain and smart contract disputes, and its potential for the Supply Chain domain. It explores the motivation of Supply Chain companies for blockchain and Smart Contracts adoption and the advantages these technologies bring, as well as the risk that SC disputes represent and the regulatory lacuna concerning blockchain and Smart Contract disputes. Trust among SC stakeholders is often lacking due to these issues. It is an important element in the Supply Chain partners' relationship, as it facilitates collaborative processes, positively impacts stakeholders' satisfaction, commitment, and loyalty, and contributes to better performance.

Chapter 7 supposes that new technologies come with different disruptions to operations and ultimate productivity, such as malicious threats that hinder the safety of goods and services. It discusses the importance of digitization in manufacturing supply chain operations and how emerging technologies such as RFID, IoT, data analytics, cloud computing, and blockchain technology can reshape supply chain management. The Internet of Things (IoT) system integrates heterogeneous objects and sensors which surround manufacturing operations and facilitates information exchange among business stakeholders. Despite the potential of blockchain-based technology, severe security issues have been raised in its integration with IoT to form an architecture for manufacturing business applications. This chapter presents different types of security-related problems for information system design purposes. It introduces the basic idea of digitation of manufacturing business process, presents the use of blockchain technology in IoT for the manufacturing industry, discusses future research directions, and presents the concluding remarks and future research directions.

Chapter 8 aims to integrate blockchain with the existing infrastructure to automate the supply chain integration and decrease human intervention. The proposed system can be used in various industries requiring inventory management, the authenticity of goods, digital escrow services, etc. The chapter also shed light on the various regulatory issues associated with blockchain technologies. The conclusion states that the integration of blockchain technology into the supply chain has the potential to revolutionize traditional supply chain management practices, increasing efficiency and reducing the need for human intervention. However, there are regulatory issues that need to be addressed to fully experience the benefits of this technology.

Chapter 9 explains that blockchain technology can improve transparency, traceability, security, efficiency, and accountability in supply chains. The chapter focuses on how blockchain technology can completely transform SC processes due to its inherent features. By implementing blockchain, businesses can cut costs, improve efficiency, and ensure accountability. It explains the basics of blockchain technology and its potential benefits for SCM. It also presents real-world uses of blockchain technology in SCM to depict its practical applications. The conclusion summarizes the benefits and drawbacks of integrating blockchain into a supply chain and highlights how it can address several issues in supply chain management such as inventory inefficiencies, counterfeit goods, and stakeholder engagement.

Chapter 10 discusses the potential of blockchain technology to positively impact supply chain sustainability. It describes the challenges and vulnerabilities of current supply chain management and presents the benefits of implementing blockchain in the supply chain processes. The chapter also provides a summary of the characteristics of blockchain technology and an overview of the energy consumption of

Preface

different blockchain protocols to demystify negative criticism. Additionally, it explores how blockchain can promote the circular economy by mapping the complete life cycle of food and products. Finally, it reviews supply chain use cases in different regions.

Chapter 11 explores how IoT can help supply chain managers track and monitor products and business processes within their networks, while also addressing the challenges of maintaining sustainability. Additionally, the chapter discusses how blockchain technology can enhance the security and privacy of collected data. It concludes by discussing how blockchain-enabled IoT can be used in supply chain operations sustainability management.

The main ideas discussed are:

1. Modern supply chains have evolved into highly value-proposing networks and are considered an essential source of sustainability for business operations.
2. Verifying the source of raw materials and maintaining visibility of merchandise products and related services while moving through the value-chain network is challenging and maintaining sustainability.
3. The Internet of Things (IoT) application can help supply chain operation managers observe, monitor, and track products and relevant business processes within their respective value chain networks.

Chapter 12 is a research study on the moderating role of supplier coordination in relation to data-driven supply chains and supply chain coordination capability. The study investigates the impact of big data and analytics on supply chain structures and how it strengthens coordination capability. The research was carried out in manufacturing firms, and 383 data were obtained between August and December 2021 by the simple random sampling method.

Chapter 13 is a study that explores the potential of blockchain technology (BCT) in supply chain management. It includes real pilot cases and experiences of BCT pioneers from various continents and industries, revealing the intentions behind the adoption, feasible improvements, and challenges that need to be further addressed. The study discusses the business incentives of decentralizing trust constituent and efficiency improvements of data sharing. Additionally, it highlights some challenges that still exist for full integration of BCT-based solutions into supply chain operations, including institutional, regulatory, technical issues, high cost of technology and technical support, organizational readiness for change, lack of technical expertise, and scalability threats.

Chapter 14 explores the potential of blockchain technology to improve transparency and traceability in the *Halaal* supply chain. It analyzes the system in the South African context, considering the interconnected relationships between people, culture, goals, infrastructure, technology, and processes. The article first conceptualizes the *Halaal* blockchain system using a socio-technical systems framework and then discusses challenges towards implementing a *Halaal* blockchain system in South Africa. The study concludes by identifying open research areas that require further investigation to realize a *Halaal* blockchain system implementation in South Africa.

Chapter 15 explores the potential uses of Blockchain technology in the cultural and creative industries. It discusses how Blockchain can help protect cultural heritage, ensure authenticity, and support the financial sustainability of cultural institutions. It also examines the benefits and limitations of Blockchain for managing transactions in the art industry, emphasizing the importance of immutability, traceability, and transparency. It provides examples of good practices implemented by start-ups and small digital-oriented companies active in the cultural sector that can serve as a benchmark for future studies. Finally, it highlights the need for further research to explore and analyze more empirical cases to better understand the direction the art market will take and the role Blockchain will play within it.

Chapter 16 is focused on understanding how blockchain technology can improve the performance of supply chains for companies based in Cameroon. The researchers conducted 18 semi-structured interviews with actors in the supply chain sector in Cameroon and used a qualitative methodology based on thematic content analysis. It is organized into three main topics: introducing yourself and theoretical concepts, deploying blockchain within the Cameroonian supply chain, and assessing supply chain performance. It aims to contribute to the literature on this subject and provide insight into how emerging technology can be implemented in supply chain management in Cameroon.

Chapter 17 investigates the relationship between the price and volume of three cryptocurrencies (Bitcoin, Ethereum, and Binance) based on a wavelet coherence analysis from January 1, 2019, to December 31, 2021. The results reveal that the relationship between price and volume is positive in the medium and long term and that price is the leading volume for both Bitcoin and Binance markets. The findings suggest that the COVID-19 pandemic significantly affected the cryptocurrency price and volume series links. Cryptocurrencies are a type of digital financial asset that uses blockchain technology and serves peer-to-peer financial transactions. The results provide investors and portfolio managers with additional information about the relationships between the prices and trading volumes of the most commonly traded cryptocurrencies, such as Bitcoin (over 1 trillion Dollars), Ethereum (540 billion Dollars), and Binance (100 billion Dollars). Wavelet coherence has the advantage of exposing associations between cause and effect over time and frequency, providing regions that show the direction and degree of dependence of prices and trading volumes. The "price-volume" concept is a bidirectional sense that involves either a linkage between volume and the magnitude of return or a linkage between volume and return.

Chapter 18 is a survey on blockchain and cryptocurrency-based systems. It explores the potential of these innovative technologies for revolutionizing transactions in various industries, including education, agriculture, and healthcare. It discusses the advantages of using blockchain for transactions and highlights the versatility and demand for these systems. However, it also acknowledges potential challenges and drawbacks to implementing blockchain and cryptocurrency systems, such as security and privacy concerns. The conclusion of the survey is that blockchain and cryptocurrency systems are still in the developing phase but have great potential to improve transaction-related services.

Chapter 19 introduces the implementation of blockchain technology in Internet of Things (IoT) systems. It discusses the advantages of using blockchain technology and machine learning algorithms for connecting IoT devices, and how this can enhance the security of data transfer processes. The investigation also proves that blockchain technology provides more security for transfer of data when it is integrated with IoT devices. The chapter also highlights the potential applications of this technology in various fields such as smart homes, transportation, agriculture, medical health care, and more.

Chapter 20 is an informative guide to blockchain technology. It covers the basics of blockchain, including its decentralized and immutable nature, as well as its various consensus mechanisms. It also discusses the role of hashing and cryptography in maintaining authenticity in blockchain and provides real-world examples of how blockchain is being used in industries such as finance, healthcare, and supply chain management. Overall, this chapter serves as a comprehensive overview to blockchain technology and its potential applications.

Chapter 21 analyzes the problems of smart contracts and proposes a solution that can resolve all the issues in the current smart contract concept. The paper also proposes a change in the architecture used in smart contracts and blockchain. The author lists the issues, analyzes them, and provides a solution

Preface

explaining how it will change the concept's performance and have a positive impact on the performance of smart contracts, their extensibility, and the environment by reducing pollution and saving energy. The chapter concludes by summarizing its findings and proposing future research directions.

Chapter 22 discusses the use of blockchain technology in tracking and storing neurosignals of live beings or biologically simulated neural networks. The goal is to ensure correct output translation and reproducibility, which is especially important for future producers of equipment based on biologically simulated neurons. It explores the use of blockchain technology to guarantee the behavior of these neurons and track live neurosignals, which can be reproduced on avatars or robots.

Finally, the "Handbook of Research on Blockchain Technology and the Digitalization of the Supply Chain" can have a significant impact on the field by providing insights and perspectives on the potential benefits and challenges of adopting blockchain technology in the supply chain. The book can contribute to the subject matter in several ways:

1. Providing a comprehensive overview: the "Handbook of Research on Blockchain Technology and the Digitalization of the Supply Chain" can provide a comprehensive overview of the topic, covering the basics of blockchain technology, its potential applications in the supply chain, and the challenges and opportunities associated with its adoption.
2. Sharing real-world examples: The book can share real-world examples of companies and organizations that have successfully implemented blockchain solutions in their supply chains, highlighting the benefits and lessons learned from these initiatives.
3. Analyzing the impact: The book can analyze the potential impact of blockchain technology on the supply chain industry, including the potential benefits in terms of improved transparency, traceability, and efficiency, as well as the potential challenges and limitations, such as the need for standardization and collaboration among stakeholders.
4. Providing guidance: The book can provide guidance for companies and organizations looking to adopt blockchain solutions in their supply chains, including best practices for implementation, key considerations for selecting a blockchain platform or solution provider, and strategies for managing the transition.

We believe these chapters will generate ideas for future research efforts as well as for the development of practical policies that will influence both global and national prosperity. All suggestions to improve this work for future publication efforts would be welcomed.

Tharwa Najar
Gafsa University, Tunisia

Yousra Najar
Manar University, Tunisia

Adel Aloui
EM Normandie Business School, France

Section 1
Technology Potential in the Supply Chain

Chapter 1
Communication Systems and the Evolution of the Supply Chain

Ben Slimene Samar
ISG Sousse, Tunisia

Lakhal Lassaad
ISG Sousse, Tunisia

ABSTRACT

Under the pressure of the extremely complex and turbulent economic environment, mainly due to globalization and the strategies implemented by companies, logistics, like all the vital functions of the company, have undergone a real transformation redefining their role, mission, and field of action within the framework of an effort to adapt and restrict strategic dimensions. This chapter focuses on the evolution of the traditional supply chain to the notion of SCM. This evolution has taken place due to the emergence and use of information systems and IT. All this contributes to the achievement of overall organizational performance through the achievement of efficiency and effectiveness objectives. This technological advance certainly contributes to improving the links between the various partners in the chain through the sharing and exchange of information. This chapter highlights the prominent role of technological advances in making information reliable and accessible by all partners in the chain and also in achieving the organizational performance of all partners.

INTRODUCTION

Under the pressure of the extremely complex and turbulent economic environment, mainly due to globalization and the strategies implemented by companies (relocation, innovation, cost, differentiation, etc.), logistics, like all the vital functions of the company have undergone a real transformation redefining its role, its mission and its field of action within the framework of an effort to adapt and restrict strategic dimensions (Jawab and Bouami, 2004). With technological development, the traditional definition of the

DOI: 10.4018/978-1-6684-7455-6.ch001

supply chain restricted it to a simple technique of operational optimization, generally linked to transport, has evolved to a new concept called "Supply Chain Management" (SCM).

Today, in order to optimise the vertical and horizontal links between the partners, the company is obliged to use outside expertise to build or reinforce the offer for the end customer. Indeed, the use of cooperation and coordination between several partners often seems to be a sine qua none condition for optimizing the company's value creation process. It is here that logistics skills present a source of differentiation and competitive advantage for the company (Brulhart, 2002).

It is in this same line that the eminent role of information systems is presented, where UCCnet[1] statistics show that 30% of data exchanged between suppliers and retailers do not correspond to their expectations. This is mainly due to the inefficiency[2] or even the lack of communication systems. This presents a huge problem for the industry, where the lack of data greatly influences the quantitative understanding between retailers/suppliers, especially in terms of the actual quantities placed either on shelves or in warehouses. This is where we needed to say that poor data translates directly into huge costs, missed revenues, and quite often, dissatisfaction with the end user or consumer (Ben Slimene and Lakhal, 2020).

Thus, it seems interesting to adopt tools that can cover both the intra- and inter- organizational aspect of the company. It was the "Supply Chain Communication System: SCCS" which has made it possible to restructure the relationship between suppliers and retailers. The SCCS supply chain communication system is a strategic tool for enhancing cooperation between them[3] (Kim and al. 2006).

It is at this level that it is interesting for any organization to integrate information systems (IS) to be more competitive and competitor. In this context, Silveira and Cagliano (2006) stipulate that the so-called Unilateral Inter-Organizational Systems have emerged to be more associated with the priorities of the so-called stable supply chain (in terms of cost, delivery and quality)., while the Multilaterals have emerged to be more associated with the priorities of the so-called dynamic chain (in terms of flexibility and quality).

In the context of this research, we are interested in the supply chain of a company that forms all the steps directly or indirectly involved in fulfilling the client's request (Jawab and Bouami, 2004). It includes not only manufacturers and suppliers but also carriers, warehouses, retailers and consumers. And it is thanks to the IS that the integration of the Supply Chain will be possible. This is an asset for consumers who will be directly linked to suppliers, who in turn will be able to react in real time to market changes. That's how they can match supply to demand (Ben SLimene and Lakhal, 2020).

Throughout the flows of products/services generate a great growth of information that can beused in the decision-making of the "Supply Chain Management". The latter is seen as an important mechanism that simplifies business processes and increases productivity (Ben SLimene and Lakhal, 2020).

FROM SUPPLY CHAIN TO SUPPLY CHAIN MANAGEMENT

After its success within the company, logistics has expanded its scope to cover the entire chain of product and service creation right down to the final consumer. We are therefore talking about the supply chain integrating all stakeholders (customers, suppliers, service providers, subcontractors, etc.) and whose management, tools, synchronization and optimization of flows are classified under the generic term "Supply Chain Management". This development can be explained, on the one hand, by the fact that the managers of the companies have become aware of the global dimension that must be accorded to the management of flows and, on the other hand, by which is recognized as a factor of competitiveness, both in terms of improving the level of customer service and in terms of reducing costs.. (Jawab and Bouami, 2004).

Evolution of the Traditional Supply Chain

Within the framework of a classic management approach that emphasizes the internal dimension of the company, and with an increasingly exorbitant reduction in the cost of manufacturing and an increasingly noticeable elimination of the main internal causes of inefficiency, further improvements will be more difficult to obtain. As a result, companies have been forced to seek solutions to grow and perform beyond their borders. This situation has necessitated the development of a global managerial approach through the creation and management of "business chains". Jawab and Bouami (2004) find in this respect the very purpose of "Supply Chain Management" which, through its cross-functional dimension, allows to manage a set of dispersed units in ensuring the definition of a global and common objective to which the various partners refer (Ben Slimene and Lakhal, 2020).

Under this approach, suppliers, service providers, customers and subcontractors must be considered as partners working together for the benefit of all. The initiative came from the large industrial organizations, which are only the leaders in their sectors of activity. Each has moved from being a stand-alone company to being a central link in the supply chain, from suppliers to customers.

Certainly, reducing logistics costs and delays as well as improving the quality of services, which are essential criteria for measuring the performance of companies' supply chain, are no longer sufficient. To complement these traditional indicators, modern chains will have to be reactive (creative capacity to identify and meet unexpected demands), agile (the company's ability to rapidly reconfigure its own system by effectively redeploying available resources), efficient (systematic elimination of all forms of waste) and intelligent (ability to make full use of all available information and an instant view of all physical and informational flows).

Figure 1. The chronological evolution of logistics and supply chain concepts

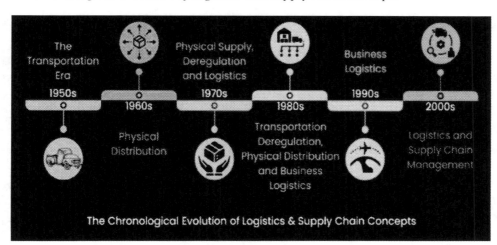

Restructuring of Organizations and Development of Information Systems

Generally, the international economic environment is characterized by three trends: the development of partnership relations, the development of reticular organizational forms and the growing role of new information and communication technologies (NTIC). Partnership relationships are underpinned by the expansion of relational strategies that are based not only on the law of competition, but also on privileged relationships that the company establishes with certain partners in its environment. It is here that the concept of competition is not totally absent, it is secondary compared to an agreement sealed over the counter, escaping the normal rules of the market. In short, these partnership relationships do not replace so-called competitive strategies, but the two can either combine or succeeded in time (Ben Slimene and Lakhal, 2020).

By extrapolation, the partnership can be considered as a business relationship based on mutual trust, openness, risk and benefit sharing (Lambert, 1996). The objective is to provide a better competitive advantage over what individual partners could have achieved. The development of this type of relationship has highlighted the notion of organizational networking. It is a new type of relationship between customers (clients) and suppliers (subcontractor), including a leader (pivot) who takes charge of one or more network activities, or simply ensures the articulation activities of specialized operators according to their skills. It is with Thorelli (1986) that this network is only one element consisting of two (or more) firms linked by trade relations strong enough to create a kind of contractual sub-market in the global market, where supply and demand are confronted. These exchange relations are part of the long-term, where their stability requires a minimum number of agreements and mutual trust between agents. A "network management" coordination effort is crucial. The use of reticular forms may be justified by competition beyond the firm to concentrate on the entire supply network.

However, companies no longer directly competing, but rather competing through the various supply networks to which they belong. In addition, the development of NICTs has had a decisive impact on the development of the supply chain. This is how we talk about inter-organizational information systems:

INTER-ORGANIZATIONAL INFORMATION SYSTEMS

Inter-organizational information systems (IOIS) are formed by a network of computers that support the exchange of information within the organization's borders (Choudhury and al, 2021). The main contribution of these systems in managerial operations is to provide coordination support between suppliers. Indeed, the ability to exchange information at a lower cost is considered to be one of the major determinants of the success of the supplier relationship. Generally, an effective SIIO is a system that allows for a rich exchange of information, fast and reliable data availability and easy access to chain's partners. From a transaction cost perspective, their adoption can simultaneously reduce coordination costs and transaction risks (Clemons and Row, 1992). However, realizing the potential benefits of SIIOs requires their adoption to provide the company's capacity and application needs. These are systems that in addition to provide communication benefit scan differ in their capabilities to provide superior reintegration (Choudhury and al, 2021).

In the context of this reflection, it seems interesting to note that the involvement of SIIOs in the realization of the performance of the chain has been explored by some researchers by proposing typological alternatives of said systems. Others are interested in studying the categories of SIIO which can be classified into three streams, namely: intra-organizational, inter-organizational and hybrid systems. At this level, Choudhury and al. (2021) focuses on another SIIO classification where he is interested in "Electronic dyads"4 and the multilateral SIIO. For the first, it supports a two-way communication that includes a seller and few suppliers. Indeed, this system has been treated by various researchers with the exception of Da Silveira and Cagliano (2006).

The latter have already presented dyadic systems as a means of supporting exchange relations between a small number of chain partners. Their points of use in building long-term collaborative networks are based on strong coordination. As for the second, the multilateral SIIO, it integrates multiple sellers and suppliers, to create electronic markets, where it allows firms to communicate with a large number of partners. This type of system is built on the Internet in the form of online auctions executing low-cost sales, private virtual markets creating transaction opportunities for sellers. In contrast to the dyadic system, there is considerable uncertainty about the role and benefits of multilateral systems. It is at this level that several researchers with respect to Stank and al. (2019) have presented the reduction of the cost of supplier change as a major benefit as well as the improvement of collaboration and integration of the Supply Chain.

It is in the context of this analysis that we try to focus our attention on the study of communication systems or "Supply chain communication system" while identifying their different types so that we proceed to a confrontation between what has been experienced theoretically and reality.

Supply Chain Communication Systems (SCCS)

In this context, Jawab and Bouami (2004) and Swatman (1994) consider that EDI5 constitutes the first fundamental factor leading to integrated supply chains. Among the integrative systems developed in this direction, we find the EDIFACT standard and its subset EANCOM, for the synchronization of databases and continuous replenishment, the Organization for the Development of Exchanges by Tele-transmission in Europe (ODETTE), the Group for the Improvement of Connections in the Automobile Industry (GAL-LIA), and the ALLEGRO system, which is a common language for manufacturers and large retailers.

The Different Software Packages of a Supply Chain

The IT solutions of the Supply Chain are based on a considerable and varied range of software packages which we quote:

- ERP (Enterprise Resource Planning), which is an integrated business management software package focused on managing internal processes (financial, commercial, human resources, inventory, purchasing management, etc.). It is one of the most promising ways to manage information flows by ensuring transversality at the company level. It develops new added value through their ability to manage all management processes between the company, its partners and its customers. Thanks to ERP, the planning of supply and the execution of demand are intimately linked by the instantaneous nature of the information. The consensus between the various decision-makers in the chain is progressing and constitutes where we are witnessing the end of the isolated company, which protects itself and the confidentiality of the data it produces (Jawab and Bouami, 2004).

Also, Laughlin (1999) defined ERP as "software that affects everything from order capture to accounting and purchasing to warehouse. ERP grows out with the need to plan, manage and account for resources in a predominantly discrete industrial environment". Furthermore, Slater (1999) defines ERP as "software that integrates key business and management processes to provide the highest level of many things that happen in the organization". ERP allows the efficient exchange of relevant data concerning production processes and the association of administrative tasks Rajagopal and al, (2018). The different information systems are as follows:

- The MES (Manufacturing Execution System) specialized in the management of the workshops, which ensure the follow-up of production, the maintenance and the management of the equipment and the personnel as well as the tools (Jawab and Bouami, 2004).
- The APS (Advanced Planning System) which allows advanced planning and scheduling. They presented themselves as a means of direct and real-time link between operations and planning. But also a means of connection between the databases of the planning and programming simulators and the "Supply Chain Execution" (SCE) (distribution logistics and management of customer orders). All this via radio frequency for warehouse management, satellite for transport management and Internet for customer order management (Jawab and Bouami, 2004).
- CRM (Customer Relationship Management), which connects customer management, from a marketing point of view, with business databases. It has two objectives, of which we find the development of a database common to marketing, sales and after-sales service, as well as the establishment of a common and coherent steering between customer management and product development in order to greatly improve the service (Jawab and Bouami, 2004).

In conclusion, it should be said that all of these software packages develop in a similar way to that of the Internet until we reach undeniable advantages for the Supply Chain. It is here that these software packages allow savings on the purchase costs resulting from increased competition between suppliers, improvements in the quality of operations, resulting from the automation of processes which significantly reduces error rates, and stock reductions as well as shortening of the supply cycle due to the substantial reduction in order processing time.

Therefore, the Intranet, a private enterprise network, allows the sharing of information or even communication on heterogeneous computer systems. It offers users the ability to easily produce and disseminate information through email or web servers. When the Internet becomes a non-public secure network, we are talking about of the Extranet which represents an open intranet used for quick and effective, private communication, between partners.

It is with the development of the Internet that important computer tools such as "groupware" and "workflow" have been developed, which are used for communication and collaboration through information sharing and coordination. They allow the partners of a Supply Chain to work together on the same documents, jointly organize agendas, automate the routing of forms, send purchase requests or cost information, etc.

Figure 2. Supply chain management software

SUPPLY CHAIN PERFORMANCE

The Supply Chain brings together all the tasks and actors that act on the physical and informational flows to enable the transformation of goods from the raw material to a finished product suitable to be marketed. The management tools and methods used to optimize this chain are referred to as "Supply Chain Management", whose approach consists in refocusing the organization, essentially, on the needs of the customer. The use of this approach can be explained above all by the substantial gains generated by its implementation (Morana & Paché, 2003). In a study conducted by the firm Benchmarking Partners, 90% of the companies surveyed benefited in qualitative and quantitative terms from the adoption of communication systems. In addition, 71% were able to achieve gains in inventory reduction and 54% were able to improve their forecasts. At that time, Jawab and Bouami (2004) saw an improvement in customer service of more than 4% and a reduction in transport costs of 25%.

Mastery of Interfaces in Search of a Global Optimum

At the operational level, one of the vocations of Supply Chain Management results in the management of company's internal and external interfaces. At the external level, the Supply Chain must use, upstream, to cross-functional process sourcing which is strongly linked to a network of available and responsive partners, providing raw materials, components and services, which correspond to the defined specifications, at the lowest cost and within the negotiated timeframes.

This sourcing contributes to redefine the boundaries of the company through the alliance and cooperation games it generates. It also stands out as a major strategic component for the company, because if they are involved in the product design process from the start, buyers can ensure a technology watch role and can help build a competitive advantage for this product. It is here that sourcing integrates as a key process of the Supply Chain within the framework of an increasingly extended and interdependent company of its environment and in particular of its suppliers (Jawab & Bouami, 2004).

As for the downstream interface, the Supply Chain covers both the physical, financial and informational flows related to customer and order management. The Supply Chain Management approach pushes the boundaries of this interface in order to bring it as close as possible to the customer, enabling them to find themselves at the very heart of the production planning process. It thus reduces the uncertainty that exists among the final consumer. Internally, the role of the Supply Chain manifests itself through the new function of the "Supply chain manager", whose content differs from one company to another but whose common feature the management of demand from the improvement of sales forecasts and reliability of replenishment plans until final distribution to customers. Its objective is to break down the barriers in the plant in order to completely review the acquisition processes, from the smallest component to the implementation of products (Jawab & Bouami, 2004).

After presenting a presentation of the supply chain and before proceeding to the analysis of its performance, it seems relevant and interesting to present some problems encountered by said chain.

Supply Chain Issues

Before anything else, it is interesting to say that the integrative aspect of the Supply Chain highlights two dimensions, on the one hand by focusing on the optimal composition of the chain, in terms of actors and distribution of roles in the execution of the activities, and on the other hand by focusing on the implementation of the means necessary to coordinate the various functions and activities of the company.

In this sense, the problems of companies with a weak supply chain are mainly due to strategic factors. It is here that Jawab and Bouami (2004) present three main difficulties encountered by these companies in terms of strategic implementation:

- Problems related to criteria for selecting partners at the level of the industrial chain.
- Communication problems related to the poor sharing of information between the various actors in the chain (implementation of different ERPs for example).
- Insufficient performance monitoring due to the lack of an agreement on the definition of key performance indicators between the industrial chain partners.

To overcome these limits, the strategy of Supply Chain can no longer be that of an isolated company, but that of the competitive industrial network, highlighting the interdependence and complexity of relationships. This strategy has three major advantages in terms of competitiveness:

- Set up a reliable, responsive and economical intermediary network.
- Create more value for the customer (faster and more efficient service).
- Constitute a lasting competitive advantage in that the network is composed of already efficient firms with highly integrated information systems either through communication between ERPs, or through the use of business hubs (marketplace) and organizational processes that become difficult to emulate.

The Strategies of a Successful Supply Chain

For this type of strategy, Jawab and Bouami (2004) highlight three broad principles:

- The development of partnership relations;
- Action on processes;
- Reduction of delays and stocks.

The relationships between these strategies are of great importance, which is why success depends not only on the correct formulation of each separate strategy, but also on the timing, formulation and implementation of the three strategies at once.

Developing Partnership Relationships

Through New Information and Communication Technologies (NICT), leading companies develop highly targeted segmentation models (micro markets) by maintaining deep and close relationships with customers. This type of relationship is growing and concerns a set of tools and practices. These include the use of standard packaging and barcodes, the sharing of forecasts, personalised sales to order, punctual delivery to the place of use, sharing planning information and production and inventory management with suppliers.

Similar to what is being detected, leaders are creating and managing supply chain networks to take advantage of the improved process efficiency achieved through partnership and the flexibility of alliances. However, the establishment of the Supply Chain network is based on three elements: firstly, the adoption and promotion of quality, performance and communication standards at the level of an activity sector; secondly, the replacement of contractual relations by relations of trust, based on the skills of each, directed towards a common objective and supported by a regular flow of business and finally, the establishment of balanced power relations between the different supply chain actors. All this to avoid the temptation to return to negotiation practices that favour individual interests (Mesnard & Dupont, 1999).

Action on the Process

In view of the requirements of micro-markets, the leading companies are delaying the configuration of products and services while delaying a number of production and/or distribution phases while achieving them out as late as possible. This means developing products with maximum modularity while facilitating assembly. In addition, to reduce costs, leaders are trying to turn part of the fixed costs into variable costs by outsourcing of non-strategic processes. To achieve this goal, companies use flexible labour, equipment sharing and the development of versatility, all while investing in training (Jawab & Bouami, 2004).

Reduction of Lead Times and Inventories

To achieve this objective, all supply channels must strive for an efficient and uninterrupted flow of products. This requires the control of internal processes and the precise management of interfaces, using the logistics of flows coordinated by managing deadlines and timing throughout the chain and by sharing forecast data between the various actors, planning and monitoring.

TYPES OF SUPPLY CHAIN MODELS

Continuous Flow Model

This is one of the most traditional supply chain models and is best suited for mature industries that operate with a certain degree of stability. It offers stability in high demand situations. Manufacturers producing the same goods repeatedly, and having a customer demand profile with little variation can benefit from this model.

This model relies on the stability of supply and demand. Its processes are scheduled in such a way that a continuous flow of information and products is ensured.

Agile Model

This model of supply chain is best suited for industries that deal with unpredictable demand and products that are made to order.

This model focuses on the supply chain's ability to amp up production on a moment's notice but can remain static when the demand is low. It demands excess production capacity, and the processes are designed for the smallest possible batches of products.

Fast Chain Model

This supply chain model is best suited for industries that manufacture a trendy product and has a short life cycle, such as fashion items. In addition to that, these businesses also need to get them out fast before the trend ends. This model offers a certain degree of flexibility.

For the said industry, a business' value proposals are evaluated by how quickly and efficiently they can update their product catalog in accordance with the latest trends.

The three main capabilities of this model are:

From concept to market in a short time
Highest forecast accuracy to reduce market mediation cost
End-to-end efficiency to ensure affordable costs for customers.

Flexible Model

This model is best suited for industries with no unexpected demands or relatively predictable demand peaks and long periods of low workload.

The flexible model provides businesses the freedom to meet high demand peaks and manage long periods of low volume work-load. The production can be switched on and off easily.

Four main capabilities of this model are:

Stock-pile of critical resources
Rapid-response capability
Technical strengths in process and product engineering
A process flow designed to be quickly reconfigurable.

Custom Configured Model

As the name suggests, this model's primary focus is on providing custom configurations, especially for assembly and production processes. It is a hybrid combination of the agile model and the continuous flow model.

Let us understand this with the example of an automobile manufacturing process. Usually, the processes involving intricate sub-assemblies such as assembling gears in a transmission box are complicated and very time consuming because of intricate interlinking of tiny parts. But attaching these multiple sub-assemblies into a final product is as easy as plug-n-play. For example, attaching an assembled transmission box to the car's drive-train. Just like that, in cases where final assembly is simpler compared to initial assembly and the other downstream processes, the final assembly is managed under an efficient, or a continuous-flow supply chain model. The intricate sub-assembly configurations and the later downstream processes then operate in an agile model.

Efficient Chain Model

This model is best suited for businesses operating in highly competitive markets wherein pricing plays a large part and businesses are fighting for the same group of customers. Markets, where customers may not perceive major differences in the value proposals of various competitors and end-to-end efficiency, are the premium goal.

For achieving this, management must maximize the utilization of machinery and other assets at their disposal to maintain high overall equipment efficiency and a resultant reduction in cost. Inventory management and order fulfillment are prime areas of focus for the profitability of the business.

Figure 3. Six types of supply chain models

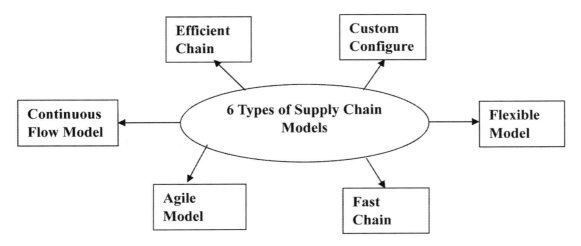

CONCLUSION

The companies have succeeded in their transaction, thanks to the implementation of an efficient logistics system, supported by well-controlled communication and information technologies. Companies have long understood that competition is no longer between companies, but rather between supply chains. The implementation of a communication system requires time and cannot be improvised (delay for product approval, for the development of the computer tool).

It requires the implementation of a product identification and information recording system, as well as an integrated logistics system (multi-level planning, inventory management, flow management, etc.). The complex problem posed by the use of a well-defined communication system is that it goes beyond the scope of the company since it covers the entire supply chain. There is no more place for a "weak" link in the chain. To succeed in this transition, it is necessary to coordinate efforts through the same "committee" which would cover each of the sectors. There is therefore organizational work to be done both in companies and at the level of all the stakeholders in the supply chain. The organizational culture of using communication systems is a major constraint. But it can be transformed at settlement (which requires significant investment) while significantly improving their performance.

REFERENCES

Ben Slimene, S., & Lakhal, L. (2020). The moderating effect of Technological readiness and the exchange of information on supply chain performance: An empirical study in the Tunisian context. *Journal of Business and Management Research*, *13*, 258–270.

Brulhart, F. (2002). Le rôle de la confiance dans le succès des partenariats verticaux logistiques: Le cas des coopérations entre industriels agro-alimentaires et prestataires logistiques. *Finance Contrôle Stratégie*, *5*(4), 51–77.

Choudhury, A., Behl, A., Sheorey, P. A., & Pal, A. (2021). Digital supply chain to unlock new agility: A TISM approach. *Benchmarking*, *28*(6), 2075–2109. doi:10.1108/BIJ-08-2020-0461

Clemons. Eric, K., & Row. Michael, C. (1992). Information Technology and Industrial Cooperation: The Changing Economics of Coordination and Ownership. *Journal of Management Information Systems*, *9*(2), 9–28. doi:10.1080/07421222.1992.11517956

Da Silveira, G., & Cagliano, R. (2006). The relationship between interorganisationnel information systems and operations performance. *International Journal of Operations & Production Management*, *26*(3/4), 232–253. doi:10.1108/01443570610646184

Jawab, F., & Bouami, D. (2004). La démarche Supply chain management enjeux et stratégies: Cas du commerce électronique. *La revue de sciences de gestion, Direction et Gestion Marketing, ABI/INFORM Global,* 208-209.

Kim, D., Cavusgil, S. T., & Calantone, R. J. (2006). Information System Innovations and Supply Chain Management: Channel Relationships and Firm Performance. *Journal of the Academy of Marketing Science*, *34*(1), 40–54. doi:10.1177/0092070305281619

Lambert, D., Emmehainz, M., & Gardner, J. (1996). Developing and implementing supply chain partnership. *International Journal of Logistics Management*, *7*(2), 1–18. doi:10.1108/09574099610805485

Stank, T., Esper, T., Goldsby, T. J., Zinn, W., & Autry, C. (2019). Toward a Digitally Dominant Paradigm for twenty-first century supply chain scholarship. *International Journal of Physical Distribution & Logistics Management*, *49*(10), 956–971. doi:10.1108/IJPDLM-03-2019-0076

Swatman. (1994). Efficient Consumer Response (ECR): A Survey of the Australian Grocery Industry. *ACIS'97 8th Australasian Conference on Information Systems*, 137-148.

Thorelli, H. B. (1986). Networks: Between markets and hierarchies. *Strategic Management Journal*, *7*(1), 37–51. doi:10.1002mj.4250070105

KEY TERMS AND DEFINITIONS

Information Systems and Information Technologies: The field of information systems works as the bridge between technology and people, whereas information technology focuses on helping them utilize and make sense of that system. The two disciplines are related, but have distinct sets of learnings and career paths.

Organizational Performance: Organizational performance is the ability of an organization to reach its goals and optimize results. In today's workforce, organizational performance can be defined as a company's ability to achieve goals in a state of constant change.

Supply Chain and Supply Chain Management: A supply chain is one of the core activities of the organization that is associated with the delivery of goods and services to customers. Supply chain management is defined as the management of flow of goods as well services and includes processes involved in transforming raw materials to final products.

Supply Chain Partners: A supply chain partner is also a company that will provide you with the product or service you'll need. The difference is that a supply chain partner has a full-service solution for sourcing, quality control, and logistics and consists of a network of multiple suppliers.

ENDNOTES

[1] Site which concerns suppliers and customers and presents all the necessary information for each part as well as their complaints.

[2] We mean by the inefficiency or lack of information systems, the frequent presence of manual data entry and convoluted processes (http://www.uccnet.org).

[3] This confirmation is accompanied by the importance that takes and firmly retains the concept of the "Supply Chain: SC" and its major role in the development of internationally renowned companies such as Dell Computer, Boeing Aircraft, Procter and Gamble, following the adoption of these information systems.

[4] We can say that electronic dyads is a system that includes the special case of monopolies when applied to a single product.

5   It is a one-dimensional language linking information systems of several organizations and having completely separate databases as well as an undeniable impact on the improvement of customer service and delivery conditions.

Chapter 2
Strengthening Supply Chain Management Through Technology

A. Sridharan
https://orcid.org/0000-0002-0753-3585
CHRIST University (Deemed), India

Sunita Kumar
https://orcid.org/0000-0002-0628-1873
CHRIST University (Deemed), India

ABSTRACT

The removal of trade barriers with the advent of WTO and which led to LPG (liberalization, privatization, and globalization) across the universe increased choices of brands for consumers and even the complexity of products within organization and the expectations of consumers rising daily. Organizations look for better management of their supply chain from "end to end," i.e., sourcing of raw materials from vendors to delivering finished products at the doorstep of consumers. This means businesses that used to be 'operations hubs' within the company have moved into the epicenter of business innovation, and this process can not be done manually or by few people within organizations, thus the need to back up business innovations and product complexities through advanced technologies. Using sensors like RFID, CRM, AI, and ML, organizations today collect information at every checkpoint from status of raw materials flow to the location of finished goods. Supply chain management is the process of planning and implementing the operations of the sourcing of quality materials at competitive cost. This chapter explores strengthening supply chain management through technology.

INTRODUCTION

The technologies like Artificial Intelligence, Machine Learning, robotics, Data Analytics, Cloud Computing and Blockchain are transforming how companies need to change their business activities. These

DOI: 10.4018/978-1-6684-7455-6.ch002

technologies are challenging but create enormous opportunities for businesses to reach more customers than in the past.

With the advent of LPG (Liberalisation, Privatisation and Globalisation), huge competition from multi-national companies and consumers' perceptions, tastes, and preferences are changing rapidly. For example, Zara Fashion keeps inventory for just one week as consumers prefer newer designs and fashionable clothes.

Supply Chain 4.0 is a new paradigm that connects vendors to facilities to distribution centres through sensors, devices and the internet. This rapid growth of technology has transformed the supply chain to become more effective and cost-effective. Today, supply chain managers source the best materials wherever it is available globally and at the right cost. The Internet of Things' ability to gather data and analyse them in real-time help the supply chain and the organisation to adapt to newer materials at a lesser cost, but very importantly, place materials just in time. The IoT helps in real-time data means the supply chain can track the market demand regularly and ensure raw materials reach the on time at the facility and, more importantly, the bullwhip effect has been eliminated.

Supply chain management is the coordination of different parts of a company to provide a product or service to customers. This includes everything from the sourcing of raw materials to the delivery of the final product (Galaskiewicz, 2011). Supply chain management is a system that businesses use to plan, create, and deliver products and services. SCM includes all the steps a product goes through, from when it is first made to when it is delivered to the customer (Shin et al., 2000).

The performance of the supply chain ensures benefits end-to-end, starting from vendors to the organisation to customers. The vendor gets information on supplies in a timely manner to produce and supply materials, and the organisation gets the right quality of materials the right quantity of materials at the right time, which will ensure the organisation meeting the demands of consumers in the marketplace. Moreover, this helps in the retention of existing customers and adding new customers at all times.

Every day morning, a street hawker brings vegetables and sells them in a particular area as he knows the demand. There will be no shortages to meet consumer demand or no wastages as the hawker knows the exact demand of the colony people. This may not be an earth-shaking event, nor will it shake the global economy. However, a modern organisation with 100s of brands and 1000s of SKUs will not have market information even with technology usage. This actually leads to bullwhip in the system and throws multiple challenges to Supply Chain Manager (Lee et al., 1997). Functions within organisations operated on a 'silo' system, where the exact market demand will not be known to the supply chain, how much material is being sent to facilities by SCM, or how much Finished Goods is being transported by the facility to Sales Depot / Wholesalers / Distributors.

SCM has to manage a web of businesses linked through upstream and downstream linkages that convert raw materials and packaging materials into valued added products for the end consumers. This means the supply chain manager gets involved in sourcing materials from vendors, sends them to the factory for conversion into value-added products, and then transports them to markets. There needs to be a "strategic fit" between Facilities, Inventory, Transportation, and, more importantly, "Information." Obviously, information plays a vital role in linking all stakeholders and creating a "strategic fit." Information is bi-directional flow that helps an organisation to create a dialogue with vendors as a backward linkage to the forward linkage to production, marketing, and, finally, reaching out to the consumers.

If there is a breakdown of production at the vendor's place and if the material is not going to reach facilities on time, and information is not given to the facility, it obviously will only lead to wastage of production time, resulting in making the market starving for the brand.

Strengthening Supply Chain Management Through Technology

Information Technology through "Enterprise Resource Planning" will lead to better management of inventories, better running of facilities without any stoppages and smooth transportation of finished goods to markets. One of the examples in business is the usage of technology for business processes like sourcing, inventory management, production and marketing through cyberspace. Information technology can bring a competitive advantage to firms by giving new ways to outperform rivals. Sourcing of material can be done through "Reverse Auction," which will be transparent as well as bring down costs as vendors compete on equal footing, but at the same time, try to corner maximum volume to enjoy economies of scale.

Dell Computers and Apple get connected to 100+ vendors globally but ensure inventory is kept at the lowest possible levels. In fact, Apple turns over their inventories 56 times a year and controls the cost of carrying inventories. Dell Computers did its growth strategy in the home-computer segment and delivered personal computers within 4-5 days though their vendors are separate all over the globe (Adam, 2019). Dell and Apple would not have succeeded, but for their digital connectivity to their vendors and consumer market. Organisations today look for a cost-efficient information system which will lead to an efficient supply chain with a focus on responsiveness to the market.

"ZARA", with multiple vendor locations, keeps very limited finished goods as fashion changes daily/weekly. Despite vendors spread globally, they manufacture fabrics to suit consumer needs. If a particular model is not sold within one week, the model dress is withdrawn immediately from the retail shelf of Zara. All these are possible because of technology accessed by Zara (Mhugos, 2022). Technology like "Radio Frequency Identification" helps organisations reduce inventories and look for opportunities for "Just In Time" and "Vendor Managed Inventory Systems," which greatly reduces inventory carrying costs and less pressure on warehousing space.

In terms of Logistics, the GPS helps in tracking the track movements and helps deliver materials on time in the marketplace, which will ensure brands are always available in the marketplace without the empty retail shelves and competitors filling up the space left void because of want of stocks. While technology brings many benefits to the supply chain, it also poses challenges to the organisation. First, the investment cost will have to be studied, and the organisation has to look at the return on investment and the period within which it can collect back the investment costs. Secondly, we should remember the tendency to overinvest in technology but under-utilize it either because technology is not understood properly or change to technology is painful. Thirdly, technology will have to bring in the close relationship between "purchase To Pay," i.e., all stakeholders, vendors, production, marketing, finance, sales depots and wholesalers should be aligned to the technology, without which the stakeholders will continue to be in 'silos '(Hippold, 2022).

OBJECTIVES

- To identify various technologies used in supply chain management
- To evaluate the impact of such technologies on the efficiency and effectiveness of supply chain operations

Supply Demand Network

The supply chain management operations are complex and dynamic, with supply- and demand networks constantly changing. Companies must adapt their supply chain strategies quickly and efficiently to remain highly competitive in the marketplace. The supply chain is the network of suppliers, manufacturers, warehouses, and distribution centres that produce, distribute, and deliver a company's products and services. The supply chain management field of operations manages this network and ensures it runs smoothly. The supply chain management field of operations is complex and dynamic, with supply- and demand networks constantly changing. Companies must adapt their supply chains quickly and efficiently to stay ahead of the competition. Several factors can impact the supply chain management field of operations, such as changes in customer demand, new technology, and global events. To be successful, companies need to have a good understanding of these factors and how they can impact the supply chain. Customer demand can fluctuate for a variety of reasons, such as changes in the economy, fashion trends, and seasonal changes. To meet customer demand, companies need to be able to adapt their supply-chains quickly. New technology can also impact the supply chain management field of operations. For example, the introduction of new manufacturing methods or the development of new logistics systems can have a significant impact on the way that the supply chain operates. Global events can also impact the supply chain management field of operations. For example, political instability in one country can lead to disruptions in the supply of goods from that country. Natural disasters can also impact the supply chain, as can changes in the global economy. To succeed in supply chain management operations, companies must quickly adapt to supply- and demand network changes. They also need to have a good understanding of the factors that can impact the supply chain.

Figure 1. Supply demand network
Source: Wieland and Wallenburg (2011)

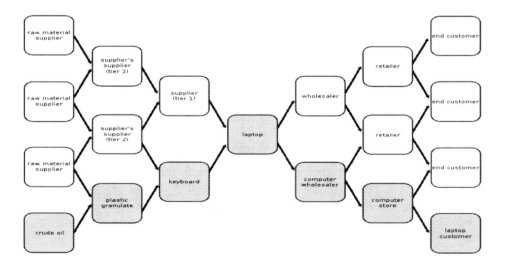

Literature Review

Supply chain management is not only growing and expanding beyond the borders of nations but also shifting its goal post due to significant technological changes, pushing the supply chain to adopt them for quicker and better movements of raw materials and finished goods.

The paradigm shift in the business world is much faster than in earlier decades due to significant discoveries like Artificial Intelligence, Machine Learning, RFID, and Robots. Supply chain 4.0, due to the faster pace of technology, is making both the organisation and supply chain management work on cost control measures while simultaneously delivering suitable quality materials at the marketplace.

Our research article, fine-tuned based on the case analysis method and inspired by inputs from various research papers published on technology, is bringing more nuances to readers on the impact of supply chain 4.0 on the profound impact on the industry and the benefits and pitfalls of using such technologies.

Apart from discussions on emerging technologies which will bring about a significant shift in supply chain operations, our research chapter also describes how the merger of technology and supply chain will be valuable to academicians and business practitioners. Our case study analysis could spark future research on the consolidation of supply chains and technology and its usefulness to organisations.

Bentaher (2022) did a comprehensive study on the motives and obstacles in the implementation of SCM Technology and its impact on the SCM processes in the long run. The researcher, in his research, analyses the relations between technology and a Lean supply chain (LSC) and an agile supply chain (ASC). He brought out the significant role of IT in these two strategies and concluded that if IT is to transform the performance of SCM, the organisation has to think differently and conceptualise the concept of IT in the supply chain.

However, these conceptualisations can affect the study's outcomes depending on the organisation's requirements. Hence, first, a theoretical development model has to be made on the significance of technology over the supply chain before embarking on research. (Oliveira-Dias et al., 2022).

While technology, as already mentioned, is still nascent stage, they are definitely gaining moment. Auto ID, RFID, AI, and Robots have already significantly contributed to the efficiency of supply chain operations.

The value addition that can happen to the supply chain through technology adoption can be related to four major areas, extended visibility, traceability, digitalisation and disintermediation. Very importantly, the value addition can only be effective if data security is ensured so that no theft occurs or hackers malign the organisation.

Wang et al. (2019) explored the opportunity provided by a blockchain-enabled supply chain from a design perspective and identified several challenges and gaps in implementing this technology in the supply chain.

Components of Supply Chain Management

Supply chain management practices are the ways that companies manage their supply chains. There are many different ways to do this, and companies can use different combinations of methods to manage their supply chains. Some of the ways that companies manage their supply chains include:

- Planning and control
- Forecasting

- Inventory management
- Transportation management
- Warehousing
- Packaging
- Distribution
- Customer service

Companies use different combinations of these methods to manage their supply chains. Some companies might use all of these methods, while others might only use a few. It depends on the company and what its supply chain looks like.

Table 1. Dimensions of SCM practices

No	Authors	Dimension
1	(Chin et al. 2011)	Information sharing, customer relationship, strategic supplier partnership, material flow management and corporate culture.
2	(Sukati et al., 2012)	Strategic partnership with suppliers, sharing of information, relationship with customers
3	(Chow et al., 2008)	Four elements are essential to managing a successful business: suppliers and customer management, information sharing, speed of communication, and supply chain features.
4	(Min & Mentzer, 2004)	Seven essential things to remember when practising supply chain management: 1. Having a clear vision and goals, 2 sharing information, 3—sharing risks and rewards, 4. Cooperating with others 5. Integrating processes 6. Having long-term relationships 7. Having a robust supply chain leader
5	(Chen & Paulraj, 2004)	The article discusses ways to improve buyer-supplier relationships. One way is to reduce the number of suppliers that a company uses. Another way is to develop long-term relationships with suppliers and communicate well with them. The article also suggests involving suppliers in cross-functional teams.
6	(Choon Tan et al., 2002)	Six elements of SCM are supply chain integration, information sharing, customer service management, geographical proximity, and JIT capability.
7	(Alvarado & Kotzab, 2001)	The inter-organizational system is a system where organisations work together. This system is often used in supply chains, where organisations work together to provide products or services. This system can be used to eliminate excess stock levels by postponing customisation toward the end of the supply chain.
8	(Tan et al., 1999)	Supply chain management is the process of organising the movement of resources and materials from suppliers to customers. This includes purchasing quality materials, managing inventory, and maintaining good customer relations.
9	(Donlon, 1996)	Supply chain management is the process of organising how materials and goods are produced, transported, and sold. It includes a good supplier partnership, outsourcing cycle time compression, continuous process flow, and information sharing.

Importance of Supply Chain Management to Organization

Supply chain management relates to planning, implementing, and controlling the operations to procure raw materials and packaging materials at competitive costs, thus ensuring the organisation remains competitive in the marketplace and provides the best possible service to the customers at the optimum cost. This paper talks about how Supply chain management is an essential part of any business, and it is essential to have a good understanding of how it works in order to be successful. Supply chain man-

Strengthening Supply Chain Management Through Technology

agement has many aspects, constantly evolving as new technologies are developed. One of the serious characteristics of supply chain management is the use of technology. Technology can bring efficient procurement without compromising the quality of materials at the optimum costs from vendors and make SCM more responsive to the customer's needs. It can also be used to reduce the cost of the supply chain. The use of technology in the supply chain can be a double-edged sword. On the one hand, it can make the supply chain more efficient and responsive to the customer's needs; on the other hand, it can also make it more vulnerable to disruptions. It is essential for supply chain managers to have a good understanding of how technology works in order to be successful. While the supply chain traditionally created a link between the vendors and the organisation, the advent of ERP – the first technology introduced in all organisations- created a link between marketing, supply chain, production and finance. This ensured the elimination of bullwhip or arrested the fluctuations in demand for finished products by marketing. This technology ensures supply chain manager understands the demands and arranges the exact quantity of material from vendors for production. The technology ERP has helped the organisation better plan demand and sourcing the correct amount of materials needed for production. It eliminated excess stocking of inventories at warehouses of organisations. The first benefit of technology through ERP is reduced carrying cost of raw materials, which directly reduces the working capital requirements and thereby reduces interest costs to the organisation. The ERP also helped vendors get payments exactly on due dates as the Finance Department of the organisation has all the relevant details in time and which will enable them to release the payment on time as per the purchase order requirements. The next big change in the warehouse is the usage of RFID which ensures where the materials are kept and the exact quantity of inventory available in the warehouse. This technology enabled the supply chain manager to order the exact quantity of materials, neither less nor more, which ensured no wastage due to excessive quantities. While the sourcing group managers define strategies, technologies help them keep control of inventories through regular updation of the availability of materials and to arrange materials just in time to ensure smooth production process flow while keeping control of costs. This paper will make the readers understand the importance of technology vis a vis supply chain management and how technology usage can bring about efficiency in the supply chain and help reduce the costs of ordering materials.

Logistics as a field of study has seen an increase in researcher's interest owing to several trends such as artificial intelligence and digitisation of value chain, analytics and forward/backward integration between suppliers-manufacturers-retailers and the omnichannel approach to gain the largest possible market share in a highly competitive environment. Logistics, both forward and backward, are a vital part of the business and production operations. Customer experience is the key driver of this agile industry. Delivering the products from the manufacturer to the consumer and returning them to the warehouse has to be fast, simple and efficient, with high stress on convenience. Businesses remain competitive and garner goodwill due to internal and external challenges and quick responses (Jayaraman et al., 2001). Supply Chain Management is the process of fulfilling the dream of marketing to put the best-finished product in the marketplace and ensure that products are always available on the retail shelf. SCM ensures the smooth operation of the "Purchase to Pay "strategy of the organisation. This means SCM will not get good raw materials but will also ensure that the organisations get the payment from wholesalers before the organisations pay off the liability to the vendors.

Why Is Supply Chain Management Critical?

Supply chain management is critical to the success of any business. It manages the flow of goods and services from vendors to manufacturing to the point of consumption. It includes the management of the procurement, production, and distribution of goods and services. Supply chain management is essential because it helps businesses to optimise their operations and to improve their bottom line. It also helps businesses to manage their risks and to protect their reputation. There are many benefits of supply chain management. It can help companies to save money, improve customer service, and increase efficiency. It can also help businesses to reduce their environmental impact. Supply chain management is a complex process. It requires the coordination of many different activities. These activities include the procurement of raw materials, the production of goods, the distribution of goods, and the disposal of waste. Supply chain management is a challenging field. It requires the use of sophisticated tools and techniques. It also requires thinking strategically and making decisions in the business's best interests. The successful management of a supply chain requires the use of both technical and managerial skills. Technical skills are needed to understand the process of supply chain management. Managerial skills are required to plan, organise, control, and coordinate the supply chain's activities. Supply chain management is a dynamic field. It is constantly changing. New technologies and new methods are being developed all the time. As a result, the skills needed to manage a supply chain are also constantly evolving. The successful management of a supply chain requires the ability to adapt to change. It also requires the ability to learn new skills and apply new knowledge to the management of the supply chain.

In the FMCG industry, nearly 60% of the organisation's revenue is spent on procuring raw materials and packaging materials, which denotes the importance of SCM.

A well-oiled SCM will ensure that a lesser amount is spent on operating expenses. However, at the same, it will ensure getting the Right Quality and Right Quantity of RMs and PMs to ensure a good quality finished product to meet the satisfaction or delight of the customers.

COMPONENTS OF SUPPLY CHAIN MANAGEMENT

The supply chain should be efficient and effective so that it delivers good quality raw materials in the most cost-effective/efficient manner. No enterprise today is one brand wonder, and they have multiple brands for which 100s of raw materials and packaging materials are to be procured. A break in the supply chain due to quality, quantity, place, time or cost will affect the production, resulting in market starvation of brands.

Strengthening Supply Chain Management Through Technology

Figure 2. Component of supply chain management

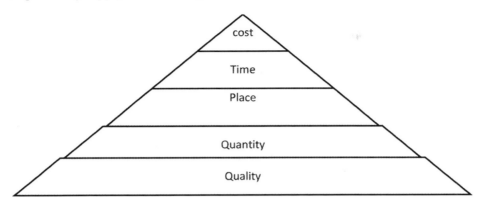

1. **Planning Strategy:** SCM will always meet marketing demand without fail on all days and throughout the year. This will ensure market always has brands and customers do not go back empty-handed, disappointed. This will ensure that the organisation's top and bottom lines are always met.
2. **Sourcing Strategy:** SCM will have to decide on quality vs. cost. Quality always takes precedence for two reasons. One, the finished product will be good, and secondly, there will be no wastage or recycling of products due to poor quality of raw materials. Sourcing also needs to think about the right quantity of materials, inventory management, credit periods, and payment terms. These all involve long strategic thinking by sourcing group managers before selecting a vendor. The association between suppliers and organisations has to be enduring rather than a hare relationship of "fly–by–night."
3. **Making of Finished Production:** The production depends on supply chain management as it has to deliver consignments of raw materials and packaging materials at the requisite place at the requisite time so that production is smooth and the organisation does not suffer any loss due to want of stocks which will have a negative impact in the market place.
4. **Delivering:** The supply chain manager has to liaise with a second-party or 3rd Party or 4th Party Logistic Providers to have a perfect delivery system to respond to the market quickly so that brands are always available.
5. **Reverse Logistics:** With the boom in E-Commerce, the supply chain fronts – both forward and reverse are being tested worldwide. Several online sites use liberal returns policies to draw a more extensive shopping base. However, this has negative references in the reverse logistic front as the numbers are exorbitantly high. Several return policies are short-term, long-term, partially enforceable, and fully enforceable, and these create a feeling of trust and perceived fairness in the minds of the consumer.
6. The supply chain manager always looks for sufficient inventories but, at the same time, looks for cost reduction. An innovative idea being practised by companies like Coco Cola and Pepsi are taking back empty bottles from the retail shelf. This way, they do not depend on bottle manufacturers who, through cartelisation, fix prices which are disproportionate to their cost of production and also supply bottles as and when they like. The reverse logistics of Coke and Pepsi ensure they have adequate stocks at all times and lesser cost as reverse transportation is lesser than the cost of new bottles. Supply Chain Managers need to innovate continuously.

THE BENEFITS OF SCM

SCM Helps Organisations to Remain Highly Competitive

Supply Chain Managers can strategically bring down the cost of RMs and PMs and source them globally. Supply chain managers can strategically procure RMs at a lesser rate during harvest and store them for future production. This will ensure lower costs even if we consider carrying costs. The SCM can go for backward integration and buy materials directly from farmers like ITC's e – Choupal. SCM can look for volume discounts by offering higher quantities to vendors so that vendors can achieve economies of scale.

Right Quality and Right Quantity

Customer retention is easier for the organisation as SCM gets the right quality materials at the right quantity at all times, which will go a long way to producing quality finished products.

Right Time

Since SCM will ensure delivery of RMs at a required time by production and marketing, the market will always have finished products of an organisation, and customers will not go disappointed for want of their favourite brand.

Challenges in Supply Chain Management

The biggest challenge in the supply chain is "bullwhip". Since marketing cannot predict the exact demand for the brands, there will always be variations. It results in changes in the requirements of RMs and PMs, leading to higher quantities of inventors and sometimes lower quantities of inventories. Obviously, vendors will be under pressure in both cases. If SCM does not place materials to meet changes in requirements by Marketing, production will suffer, and the market will not get the requisite quantities. A reduction in demand will put additional pressure on SCM, as he needs to cut down the inventory, which may not be acceptable to vendors.

Following are Global Supply Chain Challenges which need to be addressed through Technology:

Lead Times

Response to the market has to be quick as a customer look forward to faster, immediate deliveries of products as soon as they order.

The effect of Apple iPhone, Dell Computers, or Amazon is heightened expectations. Consumers cannot wait for weeks or months. It has got to be "NOW", and delivery will have to be made in a day or two. The long lead time, either at the raw material inventory level or finished goods, is challenging to balance demand and supply. The solution lies in effective planning.

HUL, India, talks about nano production, which will ensure quicker deliveries of products to the market. Amazon keeps warehouses nearer markets to reduce lead times and deliver goods faster to customers.

Long Delays

The transit time within the country or in global supply chain operations can go wrong due to high lead times, which can be a disaster in the marketplace.

Hence, it is essential to have firm completion dates both with vendors and the logistic operator. There has to be close coordination with the vendors, facility, sales depots and distributors. All stakeholders are to be in sync so that even after good planning if something goes wrong, things do not go out of hand entirely.

Cash Flow

The concept of "Purchase to Pay "suggests that organisations should recover the cost from the market by selling finished products before paying off the vendors for the raw material cost.

Organisations should also know how much it will cost to the raw materials into finished products and reach them into customers' hands. This process will include shipping, storage, manufacturing, packaging, freight forwarding, distribution, marketing, sales, and more.

The technology enables organisations to understand these costs better and helps reach the market well before they pay off vendors.

Data Management

Organisations today receive data through technologies like ERP, CRM, Business Analytics, etc., which will be overwhelming and vast data may not be either properly used or used with the wrong understanding.

In order to be successful in a highly competitive environment, businesses have to manage the global supply chain effectively and efficiently, and for that, they must have a suitable data management solution.

Figure 3. Challenges in supply chain management

Exposure to Risk

When it comes to global sourcing strategies, organisations are exposed to a high risk of currency fluctuations, political unrest, etc. Organisations will be forced to hedge funds or look at relatively stable countries or cover up such fluctuations with higher inventories, which will come with higher interest costs.

Quality Compliance/Assurance

Customers expect quality products from organisations at all times without any deviation. Customers are expecting not satisfaction but "delight" from the brands. Hence the value proposition of brands is highly demanding, and organisations will have to live up to that expectation. The supply chain should ensure that vendors give raw materials as per specification without any deviation, and there has to be clear, unambiguous communication between the organisation and suppliers.

Opportunities

In order to bring agility in supply chain operations, to bring down ordering time and lead time, to bring down fluctuations in bull-whip demand, but at the same time provide better service to customers by placing quality finished stocks in the marketplace as and when required by the customers, organisations are looking for a sound, dynamic, robust technology which will eliminate all issues in the SCM and convert challenges into opportunities.

This will lead us to a few following points, which will help us understand the importance of integrating supply chain management with technology and, more importantly, the path to establishing such an effective and efficient system.

INFORMATION TECHNOLOGIES FOR SUPPLY CHAIN MANAGEMENT AND IMPLICATIONS FOR THE ORGANISATION

As already discussed, the supply chain is a vast network, and intricate balance between suppliers, supply chains, manufacturing units, warehouses, and distributors as raw materials convert into value-added products for consumers (Chandra & Grabis, 2007).

The most crucial factor of the supply chain is its processes involving product development, procurement, physical distribution of products and measurement of its own and its suppliers (Olson, 2012). His research also led to the fact that the required products must be provided to customers as and when they require in the right quantities at the best quality, at the right location, at the right time and the optimum and competitive cost.

In order to ensure the organisation produces consistently good quality products, the supply chain aims to utilise technology connecting vendors with factories and deliver materials right first time and just in time (Shaik & Abdul-Kader, 2013).

The technology through ERP connects vendors to the facility and minimises the transaction cost as materials will be delivered by vendors just in time, and there will be no additional cost of carrying or any wastage, or damage to materials. This ensures organisation carries a substantial competitive advantage over its rivals due to reducing the transaction cost.

Nelson (2001), in his research, stressed the importance of organisations gaining sustainable benefits through a competitive edge derived from the linkage of the supply chain with information technology.

Ketchen et al. (2008) concluded that a supply chain information system is one of the critical areas which can create the best value supply chain over traditional supply chain management. Thus, developing IT systems for SCM helps speed up all activities within and outside the organisation's decision-making process and better productivity and builds competitive advantage throughout the supply chain. This is done by exploiting IT for internal and external integration of business processes.

SCM technology system encompasses warehousing, inventory management, logistics, manufacturing, vendor management and customer management (Turek, 2013).

Similarly, the Enterprise Resource Planning system forms part of the broader SCM software to unify business processes by organising, codifying and standardising business data (Norris et al., 2000). This helps all employees within the organisation access a common database and, more importantly, manage data uniformly. There will be no ambiguity in information, and that eliminates bullwhip entirely within the organisation.

The vital advantage of having information technology in the supply chain is the accuracy of data and which also helps in the elimination of data repetition. It also ensures the timely delivery of information in the entire network.

Another significant breakthrough in technology is the integration of ERP and CRM. This helps the smooth flow of information and operation, end-to-end, from the vendor to supply chain to production to distribution to end consumers. Companies can have 'extended' family members by enabling technology to link to business partners, vendors, distributors and customers. Companies can prosper only when their internal information system parallels the physical goods chain. (Norris et al. 2000, p. 6)

Yanjing (2009) in his research established that the integration of ERP and CRM should be the primary concern of organisations if they are to embark on e-business.

Shaik and Abdul-Kader (2013) suggested the adoption of inter-organizational information systems (IOS), which will link Electronic Data Interchange (EDI) networks, extranets, customer relationship management (CRM), E-Commerce and electronic markets in order to ensure timely delivery of finished goods in the marketplace and retention of customers at all times.

Whenever organisations embark on such interfaces, they must also understand the design and techniques of their partners so that both systems are compatible and synchronised (Jeyaraj & Seth, 2010).

It is also to be kept in mind whenever organisations undertake investments in IT; businesses need to maximise benefits and achieve in order to derive maximum benefit and achieve business strategies and goals (Papp, 2001). This alignment is a must and prerequisite for organisations to battle out and survive in the fierce global competition in the digital era.

Technology in supply chain management has revolutionised the way businesses operate. In the past, businesses would have to rely on manual processes and paperwork to keep track of inventory and orders. This was a time-consuming and error-prone process. With the advent of technology, businesses can now use computerised systems to track inventory and orders. This has made the supply chain management process much more efficient and accurate. Technology has also allowed businesses to automate many tasks involved in supply chain management, such as order processing and shipping. This has further increased the efficiency of the supply chain. Technology has also enabled businesses to connect easily with their suppliers and customers. This has resulted in better communication and coordination between the different parties involved in the supply chain. Overall, the technology in supply chain management has greatly improved the efficiency and accuracy of the process. It has also made it easier for businesses to connect with their suppliers and customers.

Organisations must achieve greater automation through artificial intelligence, machine learning, and efficient EFP systems to attain efficiency.

Organisations will have to be resilient and should have the ability to adapt to changes in the marketplace to remain competitive. The IT industry, which had always used brick-and-mortar models for office work, switched to a hybrid model when Covid hit the world. Adaptability is the key to success.

Similarly, SCM has to adapt new technologies for faster turnaround of inventories, reduced transportation costs, and quicker service to customers. For example, Apple Inc, though it has a manufacturing facility in China and gets chips and other hardware from India, Taipei, France, Germany, and California in the US, keeps just two days of inventories, primarily because they have efficient 3 PL Partner in DHL cargo service.

The following technologies enable supply chain operations to be super-efficient and create higher revenue for organisations through Just in Time operations and faster movement of finished goods to

Strengthening Supply Chain Management Through Technology

market and, more importantly, connecting internal and external customers to provide better service to customers in the marketplace.

Automatic Identification Technology Automatic Identification (Auto ID)

Auto ID helps to feed data into the computer, programmable logic controllers or any microprocessor-controlled device without operating a keyboard.

Auto ID is very commonly used by supply chain managers to track packages or trucks carrying goods, enabling time-bound delivery to customers.

The advantages to organisations using Auto ID are the accuracy of data, savings as costs come down and convenience of data storage.

Auto ID technologies are

- Bar Coding
- RFID

Bar Coding: This was first used in US Super Markets way back in 1952. Bar coding is a sequence of parallel lines of different thicknesses with spaces in between. These bars are items of information in the codified form and can be read with the help of scanners. The data could relate to country code, manufacturer name, product details, date of manufacture, etc. The critical function of the bar code is to keep track of inventories at retail stores.

The bar codes have multiple advantages, like identification of inventory items in the warehouse, easy to retrieve products and dispatch. The significant impact of Bar Coding on the supply chain is the speed of information, the accuracy of stocks and the reliability of data. Very importantly, inventory records are kept up-to-date, and inventories are used on a FIFO basis.

Figure 4.

The use of RFID in supply chain management is not a new concept. The technology has been used for years in other industries, such as the automotive and retail sectors. However, its use in supply chain management is still in its infancy. There are many potential benefits to using RFID in supply chain management, but some challenges also need to be addressed. One of the biggest benefits of using RFID in supply chain management is the ability to track inventory in real-time. This is a huge advantage over traditional methods, such as barcodes, which can only provide information about where an item was last scanned. With RFID, companies can always track the location of every item in their inventory. This information can be used to improve inventory management and ensure that items are always in stock. Another benefit of RFID is that it can help to reduce theft and loss. This is because RFID tags can be used to track the movement of items. If an item is stolen, the company can track and recover it. This is a huge advantage over traditional methods, such as barcodes, which can only provide information about where an item was last scanned. However, some challenges must be addressed before RFID can be fully implemented in supply chain management. One of the biggest challenges is the cost of RFID tags. They are not cheap, and the cost needs to be justified by their benefits. Another challenge is the lack of standardisation. There are many different RFID tag types, each with its own strengths and weaknesses. This makes it difficult for companies to choose the right type of tag for their needs. Despite the challenges, RFID is a promising technology that can offer many benefits to companies implementing it in their supply chain management.

Figure 5.

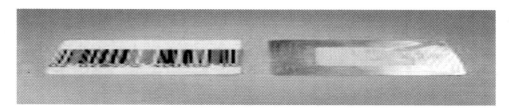

Organisations need to be smart enough to outwit the competition. Forward-thinking companies can use RFID and better and faster internet connectivity to collect data from the market on a real-time and use them to get the right quantity of materials at facilities. This information flow will ensure lesser bullwhips, if not entirely eliminate demand fluctuations.

Case Study of RFID Technology

- Procter & Gamble (P&G) Company

Initially, P&G started to use bar codes to track shipments from factory to distribution outlets but could not stop supply shortages in retail shelves.

However, with the introduction of RFID, the company started to track consignments and trucks and tracked even individual brands, thus ensuring no shortage. This enabled P&G to save US $ 400 million a year.

Strengthening Supply Chain Management Through Technology

- Ford Motor Company

Before the introduction of RFID, assembly workers used to call the warehouse to send replenishment of spare parts at the last minute and had to wait for parts to arrive, and there used to be considerable delays in the assembly of cars.

After the installation of RFID, operators in the warehouse now have instant information on the requirements of spares at the assembly line. Without asking for such spares from workers, they would send them without any production stoppage.

THE INTERNET OF THINGS (IoT)

The IoT is expected to grow in double digits in 2022 as it helps organisational functions to get connected. It also helps track the movement of goods and inventories in warehouses which will have a massive bearing on supply chain operations.

IoT helps manufacturers fix assembly lines and helps transportation companies monitor freight and fleet. This means SCM will get correct information from the operation manager on the correct requirement of inventories. Fleet management helps in timing the arrival of inventories at facilities and in the timing of sending finished stocks to wholesalers/distributors.

Liu et al. (2012), in their research, mentioned that Automobile manufacturers across the world are developing new intelligent car system that helps drivers ease of driving with wireless communication through predictive communication.

The internet, GPS, etc., will help track vehicles' location, traffic patterns, and logistics journey. All these will help to eliminate misplaced inventory or lost inventory, which will reduce the risk of transportation, leading to revenue loss to the organisation. This will ensure efficient just-in-time manufacturing as SCM knows where the materials are when it is expected to reach the facility, etc. The huge impact of internet dependency and technology on industries also has a downside or risk due to increased cyber-attack and hacking. Industries are to be well prepared for the same.

The Internet of Things (IoT) can streamline supply chain management by automating various processes and tasks. For example, IoT-enabled sensors can monitor inventory levels, track the location of assets, and detect potential issues early on. This information can then optimise the supply chain and improve efficiency. IoT can also improve communication and collaboration between different parties involved in the supply chain.

Tadejko (2015) in his research mentioned that IoT has many applications, such as a fast payment process through automatic checking out with the aid of biometrics. IoT also helps the rotation of products on retail shelves and warehouses through automatic restocking procedures.

BLOCKCHAIN

Blockchain is a shared, immutable ledger that facilitates the process of recording transactions and tracking assets in a business. This makes it well-suited for supply chain management, where tracking the provenance of goods is essential to ensuring quality control and preventing fraud. Blockchain helps to increase transparency and traceability throughout the supply chain. This would allow for better quality control and the ability to track and recall products in the event of a safety issue. In addition, blockchain could help reduce the cost of compliance with regulations and the time and effort required to manage the supply chain. While blockchain is still in its early stages, it has the potential to revolutionise supply chain management and create a more efficient, transparent and secure system. There is always mistrust or lack of confidence between SCM and vendors. However, blockchain can bring greater transparency and visibility to this process.

Blockchain potential is to facilitate track and tracing that can help SCM to document the chain of custody of goods. In doing so, SCM can prevent leakage, find out counterfeit items and pinpoint– risky suppliers. This enables two advantages to SCM, one being the efficiency to meet regulatory requirements and, more importantly, creating transparency in sourcing which gives greater confidence to vendors. At least a quarter of 'OEMs' is expected to leverage blockchain to source spare parts in 2023 by 60% and lower sourcing costs by 45%.

Many of the FMCG industries are experimenting with blockchain. Walmart is trying to use IBM Food Trust Solution to track lettuce from its suppliers.

Miraz M H & Ali M (2018), in their widely researched paper, confirm that blockchain-enabled IoT ecosystems will provide enhanced overall security to both organisations and vendors.

While many companies are trying to fix various sourcing challenges through blockchain, it is a long-drawn love affair as blockchain requires a space of a village. Also, currently, the cost is prohibitive. Firms in the industry will have to collaborate and use the common platform of blockchain to make it successful.

AI, Machine Learning, and Analytics

Baker and Smith (2019) in their research made a broad definition of AI as "computers do cognitive tasks, which are normally done by human minds, especially relating to problem-solving". They further said AI is not a single technology but consists of machine learning, natural language processing, data mining, and neural networks.

Although AI and ML are in nascent stages, these technologies have already improved warehouse operations' performance, delivery times, inventory management, and sourcing strategies. In the past, lack of data hampered analysis of customer demands, leading to the all-around problem of higher or lower inventories, production loss due to lack of inventories, and inability to meet higher demand as vendors are not ready for increased requirements.

Using algorithms and predictive methods, companies can dissect information from larger data and get insights into consumer behaviour and demand expected in the future. If such information is unavailable, organisations will have to ship huge quantities of finished inventories leading to wastage in the pipeline and stocks becoming older in the market. Also, higher finished inventories means the organisation would have to purchase large quantities of raw materials, which could have been avoided.

Also, earlier, such information was to be tabulated manually, which was highly error-prone. Using machine learning, organisations can optimise SKU data and can create production plans that are neither less nor more to meet demand, which will also optimise transport plans.

Predictive analytics companies achieve to plan correct demand levels, leading to better inventory management.

Deloitte (Pearson, 2019) identified that companies have been investing in predictive analytics in order to bring down costs (as suggested by 81% of respondents) or bring about an enlightened customer experience (60%). 32% of respondents mentioned that supply chain analytics bring high inventory visibility. In comparison, 26% said they could achieve strategic sourcing, and another 22% mentioned having real-time brand intelligence from the market.

ROBOTS AND AUTOMATION

Gharpure and Kulyukin (2008) in their research discussed the merits of robots supporting blind people for the day to day work.

Robots and automation have traditionally helped in better warehousing management, picking materials and placing materials on the shelf or loading heavy materials on the truck.

Technology in the form of artificial intelligence is significantly improving the precision with which industrial robots move while at the same time ensuring the safety of the working atmosphere.

The technology is making a significant paradigm shift with new generation cobots (collaborative robots) working alongside humans who would have otherwise cordoned off in a separate safety zone.

Researchers estimate that by 2023, 60% of global organisations will invest heavily in robots to usher in significant automation to increase productivity and close the talent gaps, if any, in human supply chain skill sets.

.Amazon, one of the very efficient operators in logistics and fulfilment, has bet big on warehouse robots with the acquisition of Kiva Systems in 2012.

Kiva robots are designed to work with human beings in warehouses. These robots bring heavy pallets to workers, who will then unpack the goods. Very importantly, workers need not walk miles of distance inside the warehouse to get work done. This has effectively increased worker productivity as machines bring the material nearer to the men.

The e-commerce giant has expanded its use of robots with cobots that help pick, sort, transport, and store packages; Amazon stores have started using robots to help pack things for shipment. The robots scan the items and then put them in a box. This helps the store ship things more quickly and efficiently (Shields, 2019). These robots can pack at four to five times the rate of the average human worker. This allows them to store more inventory and meet their Prime delivery promises.

3D PRINTING

Since consumers demand customised products, businesses today focus on 3D printing. 3D printing can be used for supply chain management in a number of ways. For example, it can be used to create prototypes of products or parts to be used in the manufacturing process. Additionally, 3D printing can be used to create customised products or parts that are not available through traditional manufacturing methods. This can improve lead times and reduce costs associated with traditional manufacturing methods.

Driverless Vehicles and Drone Delivery

With the ever-decreasing numbers of drivers or attitudes of drivers to deliver goods as per their own time frames, driverless vehicles offer excellent options for companies to utilise without human intervention.

Another significant opportunity for the companies is to reach remote and hard-to-reach territories by driverless vehicles. In India, nearly 60 crores (0.6 billion) live in rural areas, which are not easily accessible. Moreover, companies can utilise driverless vehicles to reach these areas and increase turnover and profit.

The same advantages can also be derived, maybe on a smaller scale, but can be expanded depending on

Suggestions

The role of supply chain management in business is to ensure that goods and services are delivered to customers promptly and efficiently. In order to meet customer demands, businesses need to have an effective supply chain management system in place. There are a number of elements that need to be considered when designing a supply chain management system, including: - the type of goods or services that are being delivered, the geographical location of customers, the transportation infrastructure, the resources and capabilities of the business, and the budget. An effective supply chain management system will take all of these factors into account and design a system that meets the specific needs of the business.

Technologies make company products available at all times and where there is demand. It helps organisations optimise logistics costs and directly helps reduce the carbon footprint. It helps businesses to avoid risks and tariffs relating to imports.

Made-to-order production helps reduce investments in inventories and warehousing costs and helps organisations provide better, faster customer services. A case in this regard has already been highlighted in the earlier paragraph about Zara utilising AI-driven cameras to produce apparel instantaneously to meet customer demand.

High-Stakes Makeover

While it will take a few more years for businesses to understand the advantage of technologies, businesses have clearly understood that technologies can cut down costs in supply chain operations.

Technology is a shining object, and organisations should know how far to go about investments as the return on investment is long-term and whether technology is beneficial or hamper supply chain operations. Many organisations still do not have a clear business case or road map for technology-related supply chain operations. Organisations are still evaluating the benefits of such technology and whether it will be incremental or detrimental to the business goals.

Managerial Implications and Concluding Remarks

The future of supply chain operation is to move from a linear, one-dimensional to a more holistic approach to businesses. The goal is to optimise the entire supply chain, not just individual parts. To do this, companies need to adopt new technologies and data-driven approaches.

The impact of Technology on supply chain performance happens effectively due to their marshalling of other organisational resources.

As mentioned, companies like ZARA use advanced technology to improve their supply chain processes. The ERP software helps functions to share vital information. For example, the marketing team shares information on new fashion trends with the production and supply chain so that both functions gear up to meet new demands in the market very efficiently and effectively by getting raw materials (fabric yarn, dye, etc.) just in time and produce fabric and send to the market on a timely fashion which reduces the time of producing the cloth at a competitive price and delivering the same to customers in a time-bound manner. RFID helps supply chain managers to keep tracking the raw materials to ensure there is no excess or shortage of materials since fabric manufacturers have many kinds of materials. SRM (supplier relationship management) ensures the company outperforms its competitors by offering customers an effective and efficient flow of services.

Functions within organisations work independently, and in order to link them to serve the customers better and make them delighted with the performance of the organisation, supply chain managers need to utilise RFID, GPS, Mobiles, Wireless Technology and Electronic Data Interchange. Customer delight will be known through increased demands, higher ROI, profitability, and cash flow due to their repeated purchases.

In order to embrace new technology, supply chain managers must have a keen eye on what kind of technology is suitable for their operations, as it involves a considerable cost of investment. Secondly, technologies change with the advent of AI, ML, cloud computing, ERP, etc. It is also very pertinent to note that technology may not be "fit for all" as it depends on the size of the business of the organisation and the productive utilisation of such technology. Before embarking on installing such advanced technologies, the supply chain managers need to understand the cost-benefit analysis and look into the opportunity to reduce inventory holding costs, faster reach to the market, and improve the utilisation of facilities.

Bienhaus and Haddud (2018), in their research, were of the very firm opinion that organisations do appreciate the purpose and importance of digital supply chain transformation and the benefits that derive out of such digitalisation but have a very hazy road map towards the sequencing the way of internal cooperation of functions and the way forward to link the functions within the organisation. Before embarking on digitalisation, organisations need to thoroughly look inward and understand the existing processes to sort out areas of improvement which can be accrued through digital transformation and then chart the path of their strategies and create action plans. They cannot put the cart before the house.

Before we conclude, a word of caution about data theft and cybercrimes, which regularly attacks businesses' data due to rivalry or trans-border activities. Technology can devastate businesses as competitors may gain illegally from supply chain management through phantom bids, counterfeiting, creating ghost vendors, diverting vendor payments, etc.

Munirathinam (2019), in his research paper, mentioned that more than 25% of cyber-attacks come from IoT devices. Even though Artificial Intelligence has increased the ability to process data quickly and helped in the decision-making process, and its reliability, the way data is being collected could be a security risk.

Organisations do take sufficient guard against data theft and other illegal activities through the implementation of Electronic Record Management (Bar Code, RFID, ERP (SAP, Oracle, PeopleSoft), Decision Support Systems, Electronic supply chains, etc., which will reduce e-risks and increase information technology performance in the supply chain. Governments across the globe also support businesses by creating and supporting them through National Cyber Security Policies.

In the era of information technology, it has become inevitable for organisations to share information with external customers on demand forecasts, orders, inventory levels, etc. However, companies will have to have security checks to protect such proprietary data (Ketchen et al., 2008).

Further empirical research is required to be conducted to understand the relationship between the cost of technology and the performance that is derived from such technology. Also, organisations need to look inwardly at linking all functions to derive the maximum benefit from such technology. Thirdly, technology keeps changing, and it would be wise for organisations to look at short and medium term to derive the maximum benefit out of such technologies rather than invest a high amount in bigger technologies.

REFERENCES

Adam, A. S. (2019, January 3). *An overview of Dell's supply chain strategy*. Dynamic Inventory. Retrieved September 18, 2022, from https://www.dynamicinventory.net/dell-supply-chain-strategy/

Alvarado, U. Y., & Kotzab, H. (2001). Supply Chain Management. *Industrial Marketing Management*, *30*(2), 183–198. doi:10.1016/S0019-8501(00)00142-5

Baker, T., & Smith, L. (2019). *Educ-AI-tion rebooted? Exploring the future of artificial intelligence in schools and colleges.* Retrieved from Nesta Foundation website: https://media.nesta.org.uk/documents/Future_of_AI_and_education_v5_WEB.pdf

Bentaher, C., & Rajaa, M. (2022). Supply Chain Management 4.0: A Literature Review and Research Framework. *European Journal of Business and Management Research*, *7*(1), 117–127. doi:10.24018/ejbmr.2022.7.1.1246

Bienhaus, F., & Haddud, A. (2018). Procurement 4.0: Factors influencing the digitisation of procurement and supply chains. *Business Process Management Journal*, *24*(4), 965–984. doi:10.1108/BPMJ-06-2017-0139

Chandra, C., & Grabis, J. (2007). *Supply Chain Configuration – Concepts, Solutions and Applications, Springer*. Springer Science Business Media.

Chen, I. J., & Paulraj, A. (2004). Towards a theory of supply chain management: The constructs and measurements. *Journal of Operations Management*, *22*(2), 119–150. doi:10.1016/j.jom.2003.12.007

Choon Tan, K., Lyman, S. B., & Wisner, J. D. (2002). Supply Chain Management: A strategic perspective. *International Journal of Operations & Production Management*, *22*(6), 614–631. doi:10.1108/01443570210427659

Chow, W. S., Madu, C. N., Kuei, C.-H., Lu, M. H., Lin, C., & Tseng, H. (2008). Supply Chain Management in the US and Taiwan: An empirical study. *Omega*, *36*(5), 665–679. doi:10.1016/j.omega.2006.01.001

Donlon, J. P. (1996). *Maximizing value in the supply chain*. The Free Library. Retrieved September 18, 2022, from https://www.thefreelibrary.com/Maximizingvalueinthesupplychain.-a018926696

Galaskiewicz, J. (2011). Studying supply chains from a social network perspective. *The Journal of Supply Chain Management*, *47*(1), 4–8. doi:10.1111/j.1745-493X.2010.03209.x

Gharpure, C., & Kulyukin, V. (2008, Mar.). Robot-Assisted Shopping for the Blind: Issues in Spatial Cognition and Product Selection. *International Journal of Service Robotics*.

Hippold, S. (2022, April 20). *How supply chain technology will evolve in the future*. Gartner. Retrieved September 18, 2022, from https://www.gartner.com/smarterwithgartner/gartner-predicts-the-future-of-supply-chain-technology

Jeyaraj, A., & Seth, B. (2010). Implementation of Information Systems Infrastructures for supply chain visibility. *Proceedings of the Southern Association for Information Systems Conference.*

Ketchen, D.J., Rebarick, W., Hult, G.T.M., & Meyer, D. (2008). Best value supply chains: A key competitive weapon for the 21st century. *Business Horizons, 51*, 235–243.

Lee, H. L., Padmanabhan, V., & Whang, S. (1997, April 15). The bullwhip effect in supply chains. *MIT Sloan Management Review*. Retrieved September 18, 2022, from https://sloanreview.mit.edu/article/the-bullwhip-effect-in-supply-chains

Liu, T., Yuan, R., & Chang, H. (2012). Research on the internet of things in the automotive industry. ICMeCG 2012 international conference on management of e-commerce and e-Government, 230–3. doi:10.1109/ICMeCG.2012.80

Mhugos. (2022, September 9). *Zara Clothing Company Supply Chain*. SCM Globe. Retrieved September 18, 2022, from https://www.scmglobe.com/zara-clothing-company-supply-chain/

Min, S., & Mentzer, J. T. (2004). Developing and measuring supply chain management concepts. *Journal of Business Logistics, 25*(1), 63–99. doi:10.1002/j.2158-1592.2004.tb00170.x

Miraz, M. H., & Ali, M. (2018). Blockchain Enabled Enhanced IoT Ecosystem Security. *Proceedings of the International Conference on Emerging Technologies in Computing 2018*, 38-46. https://link.springer.com/chapter/10.1007/978-3-319-95450-9_3 doi:10.1007/978-3-319-95450-9_3

Munirathinam, S. (2019). Industry 4.0: Industrial Internet of Things (IIOT). *Advances in Computers, 117*(1), 129–164.

Nelson, M. (2001). Sustainable Competitive Advantage from Information Technology: Limitations of the Value Chain. In R. Papp (Ed.), *Strategic Information Technology: Opportunities for Competitive Advantage* (pp. 40–55). Idea Group Publishing. doi:10.4018/978-1-878289-87-2.ch002

Norris, G., Hurley, J. R., Hartley, K. M., Dunleavy, J. R., & Balls, J. D. (2000). *E-business and ERP: Transforming the Enterprise*. John Wiley & Sons.

Oliveira-Dias, D., Moyano-Fuentes, J., & Maqueira-Marín, J. M. (2022). Understanding the relationships between information technology and Lean and Agile Supply Chain Strategies: A systematic literature review. *Annals of Operations Research, 312*(2), 973–1005. doi:10.100710479-022-04520-x

Olson, L. D. (2012). Supply Chain Information Technology. In S. Nahmias (Ed.), *The Supply and Operations Management Collection*. Business Expert Press.

Papp, R. (2001). *Strategic Information Technology: Opportunities for Competitive Advantage Hershey*. Idea Group Publishing. doi:10.4018/978-1-87828-987-2

Pearson, S. (2019, October 14). *Growing adoption of Supply Chain Analytics*. Deloitte United States. Retrieved September 20, 2022, from https://www2.deloitte.com/us/en/pages/operations/articles/digital-disruption-supply-chain-analytics.html

Shaik, M. N., & Abdul-Kader, W. (2013). Interorganizational Information Systems Adoption in Supply Chains: A Context-Specific Framework. *International Journal of Information Systems and Supply Chain Management, 6*(1), 24–40. doi:10.4018/jisscm.2013010102

Shields, N. (2019). *Amazon is Rolling Out New Warehouse Robots*. Business Insider. Retrieved September 20, 2022, from https://www.businessinsider.com/amazon-introduces-new-warehouse-robots-2019-5?IR=T

Shin, H., Collier, D. A., & Wilson, D. D. (2000). Supply Management Orientation and supplier/buyer performance. *Journal of Operations Management, 18*(3), 317–333. doi:10.1016/S0272-6963(99)00031-5

Sukati, I., Abdul Hamid, A. B., Tat, H. H., & Said, F. (2012). A study of Supply Chain Management Practices: AN Empirical Investigation on consumer goods industry in Malaysia. *International Journal of Business and Social Science, 2*(17), 166–176.

Tadejko, P. (2015). Application of Internet of Things in logistics-current challenges. Ekonomia i Zarzadzanie, 7(4), 54–64.

Tan, K. C., Kannan, V. R., Handfield, R. B., & Ghosh, S. (1999). Supply Chain Management: An empirical study of its impact on performance. *International Journal of Operations & Production Management, 19*(10), 1034–1052. doi:10.1108/01443579910287064

Turek, B. (2013). *Information systems in supply chain integration and management*. Retrieved from https://www.ehow.com/info_8337099_information-supply-chain-integration-management.html

Wang, Y., Han, J. H., & Beynon-Davies, P. (2019). Understanding blockchain technology for future supply chains: A Systematic Literature Review and Research Agenda. *Supply Chain Management, 24*(1), 62–84. doi:10.1108/SCM-03-2018-0148

Wieland, A., & Wallenburg, C. M. (2012). Dealing with supply chain risks. *International Journal of Physical Distribution & Logistics Management, 42*(10), 887–905. doi:10.1108/09600031211281411

Yanjing, J. (2009). Integration of ERP and CRM in an E-commerce environment. *Proceedings of the International Conference on Management and Service Science*, 1–9.

Section 2
Overview of Blockchain Technology

Chapter 3
Overview of Blockchain Technology Diffusion and Adoption:
Theoretical Analysis Based on IDT Theory

Ennajeh Leila
https://orcid.org/0000-0002-6725-9370
Gabes University, Tunisia

ABSTRACT

The main focus of the chapter is to study the diffusion of blockchain technology. Under the theoretical framework of innovation diffusion theory (IDT) analyses were conducted with the aim to localize blockchain technology in the adoption decision process and in the adoption curve. Thus, innovators and adopters of blockchain in different economic activities such as finance and banking, manufacturing, healthcare, education, and agriculture were presented. The purpose is to identify what economic sectors are reaping benefits from blockchain technology and what sectors are yet far away from its adoption. Furthermore, advantages of blockchain technology were also addressed because they are able to influence and accelerate its adoption. Insights are particularly relevant for future adopters and policy makers to enhance emergent technology adoption and reach economic benefits in the digitalization era.

INTRODUCTION

Blockchain technology is one of the most important innovations of this century. It is considered as the most relevant innovation after the Internet. It is becoming an increasingly hot topic of interest for different domains and multidisciplinary fields (Jraisat et al, 2022; Ennajeh, 2021; Attaran, 2020).

Blockchain is a distributed ledger technology that has disrupted the global economy with the use of cryptocurrencies such as Bitcoin and Ethereum. This disruptive technology has a significant impact in our daily lives in the 21st century. It has the potential to transform the current Internet from "The Internet of Information Sharing" to "The Internet of Value Exchange" (Ullah et al., 2021). It can solve

DOI: 10.4018/978-1-6684-7455-6.ch003

Overview of Blockchain Technology Diffusion and Adoption

a variety of challenges in a modern manufacturing environment. Blockchain technology is expected to revolutionize the operating modes of commerce, industry, and education, as well as to promote the rapid development of knowledge-based economy on a global scale. Blockchain is considered a key part of the 4th industrial revolution (Ullah et al., 2021; Chen et al, 2018; Javaid et al., 2021).

Blockchain is a database that stores transaction-based records, continually recording all completed transactions in a block of data. More importantly, database systems, known as chains within a network of linked peer-to-peer nodes, are usually called digital ledgers in business (Jraisat et al., 2022). Blockchain technology is used in many fields because of its distributed database nature and the prospect of audit trails (Ullah et al., 2021). Due to its immutability, transparency, and trustworthiness for all transactions executed in a Blockchain network, this innovative technology has many potential applications (Chen et al, 2018). Initially, Blockchain has been largely used for cryptocurrency and financial transactions. In the last couple of years, the upsurge in Blockchain technology has obliged scholars and specialists to scrutinize new ways to apply Blockchain technology with a wide range of domains. The dramatic increase in Blockchain technology has provided many new applications opportunities ranging from healthcare, finance and banking, governance, supply chain, energy etc (Yadav and Singh, 2019; Seyednima et al, 2019). Furthermore, other industries, including entertainment and manufacturing are adopting Blockchain technology to leverage its benefits of enhanced security as well as privacy (Attaran, 2020).

Actually, demand for Blockchain applications is rapidly growing in various industries (Javaid et al., 2021). Recent statistics published by Ruby (2023) find that the compound annual growth of Blockchain industry is about 56.3%. There are over 170 million Blockchain wallets worldwide. Many IT and digital experts suggest that Blockchain will reshape every industry in the future. This is also endorsed by renowned and reliable firms such as Gartner, PwC, Wintergreen, and IDC. They predicted that the Blockchain market would reach USD 176 billion to USD 3.1 trillion between 2025 and 2030 (Malik et al, 2021).

The evolution of Blockchain technology in term of adoption rate and applications development stimulates questions to understand its diffusion and adoption for many stakeholders: Blockchain technology providers, actual and future adopters, decision makers and researchers.

The purpose of this chapter is to analyze the diffusion of Blockchain technology among economic sectors under the theoretical framework of Rogers' Innovation Diffusion Theory (Rogers, 1995). IDT is universal to study any innovation in any time. It gives the opportunity to study innovation adoption in a holistic view that schematizes the evolution of innovation diffusion among communities overtime. Thus, an overview of Blockchain technology diffusion and adoption among economic sectors will be presented. This is interesting to trace actual and future trends of this technology for practitioners, decision makers as well as researchers.

The chapter will reproduce main topics of Innovation Diffusion Theory where the adoption decision process, adopters' categories and adoption factors are advanced. In accordance with IDT, the chapter tries to answer the following questions:

Where is Blockchain technology located in the adoption curve?
What economic sectors are reaping benefits from Blockchain Technology?
What are the main advantages of Blockchain that encourage its adoption?

To answer above questions, the chapter is organized in the three major parts: the first one introduces Blockchain technology by giving definitions, characteristics and applications derived from existing literature.

Then, the main focus of the chapter will be addressed and organized in three subsections. First, a brief presentation of innovation diffusion theory as developed by Rogers (1995) will be described. Then, the adoption decision process will be presented to identify the diffusion phase of Blockchain technology. Moreover, the purpose is to identify what economic sectors are reaping benefits from Blockchain technology and what sectors are yet far away of its adoption. Thus, different adopters of Blockchain in different economic sectors will be presented according to existing literature (finance, manufacturing, healthcare, education and agriculture). A tentative to schematize the adoption curve of Rogers adapted to Blockchain technology evolution in terms of time and adopters. Furthermore, the last part will address main advantages of Blockchain technology that are able to influence and accelerate its adoption.

The last subsection is dedicated to results discussions and managerial implication of the study generated by IDT. It highlights main insights of analysis advanced in the chapter and introduces, based on limitations, suggestions to future researches.

BLOCKCHAIN LITERATURE REVIEW

Blockchain Definition and Characteristics

Blockchain is a distributed ledger technology DLT (Jraisat et al., 2021; Attaran, 2020; Mohammed et al., 2021; Sarote and Shukla, 2021). DLT is a technological protocol that allows data to be exchanged freely by individual network participants without intermediaries or third parties being used (Mohammed el al., 2021). Blockchain has captured the imaginations and wallets of the financial services institutions (Attaran, 2020).

The most popular definition of Blockchain is that advanced by Don and Alex Tapscott (Golosova and Romanovs, 2018) which consider it as "an incorruptible digital ledger of economic transaction that can be programmed to record no just financial transactions but virtually everything of value".

In its simplest meaning, a Blockchain is a decentralized, continuously growing list of records, called 'blocks', that are linked together in the chain through a process called mining. This process turns pending transactions into a mathematical puzzle. Miners (people) solve the puzzle using computer systems and produce what is called a hash. Hash function is a sequence of letters and numbers unique to the block. It is often compared with a fingerprint as it is unique and essential for identification of a block.

Each block contains a cryptographic hash of the previous block, a timestamp, and transaction data. It also contains information from all previous blocks and transactions to create a network of linked peer-to-peer nodes, called digital ledgers in business. The digital ledger can be linked to a large, distributed, secure spreadsheet that is tied to many computers on the network. It can be viewed by anyone who accesses it to learn how the whole supply chain was implemented for putting the final finished goods in the consumer's hands. If the data inside any one of the blocks changes, it sets up a chain reaction that could freeze up the whole Blockchain. Once the Blockchain processes the information, every computer in the network locks in at the same time, creating a permanent, immutable digital record (Attaran, 2020; Sarote et Shukla, 2021; Jraisat et al, 2022).

Advantages of Blockchain are that it allows sharing data and transactions on an immutable P2P network to enhance transparency, security, and trust. Furthermore, decentralization and reliability are also the most cited advantages of this distributed ledger technology (Attaran, 2020; Ennajeh, 2021 and Golosova and Romanovs, 2018).

Blockchain is divided into three types: public, private, and consortium. The distinction is based on the access to the network which can be private or public. A public Blockchain is open to everyone with their transactions which are permanently recorded. This type is consistent with cryptocurrencies applications (Bitcoin, Ethereum). A private Blockchain allows only a group of verified entities to have insights to the network (partial centralization). Consortium Blockchain is a protocol modified to make two or more enterprises responsible for a Blockchain. It incorporates many parties where main nodes are initially and strictly selected. Blockchain solutions provided by Hyperledger Fabric is suitable to this type of Blockchain (Sarote and Shukla, 2021; Gosh et al, 2020).

Blockchain Technology Applications

The development of Blockchain applications could be divided into three stages: first, Blockchain 1.0 is the deployment of cryptocurrencies as a peer-to-peer cash payment system. Second, Blockchain 2.0 is the extensive Blockchain applications than simple cash transactions, including stocks, bonds, loans, smart property, and smart contacts. Third, Blockchain 3.0 is developing Blockchain applications beyond currency, finance, and markets, such as in the areas of government, health, science, literacy, culture, and art (Chen et al, 2018; Alshamsi et al., 2022).

Blockchain Technology for Cryptocurrencies

Blockchain is the core technology used to create the cryptocurrency, Bitcoin, through the maintenance of immutable distributed ledgers in thousands of nodes. It was proposed by an anonymous person or group that chosen the pseudonymous of Satoshi Nakamoto in 2008. Blockchain was invented as a peer to peer cash system introducing and exchanging digital currency (Nakamoto, 2008).

Blockchain technology has disrupted the global economy with the use of cryptocurrencies such as Bitcoin and Ethereum. By using cryptocurrencies, organizations can transfer funds globally without the need for any formal intermediaries such as banks. Many IT and digital experts suggest that Blockchain will reshape every industry in the future (Malik et al, 2021).

During the initial stages of its appearance, Blockchain technology was not able to draw a lot of attention. However, as Bitcoin continues to run safely and steadily over the years, the society has since become aware of the enormous potential of the underlying technology of this invention in its application to not only cryptocurrency but also in many other areas (Chen et al, 2018).

Blockchain for Supply Chain Digitalization

The most promising nonfinancial Blockchain applications include supply chain management by offering new ways of communication and asset transfer between peers without the assistance of third party intermediaries. In industrial supply chains, the distributed ledger technology supports a growing number of supply chain management use cases (Rejeb et al., 2021).

Blockchain is a technology that has gained much recognition and can enhance the manufacturing and supply chain environment. A network like a Blockchain will put more supply chain members into one network that offers full component traceability and parts traceability, allowing the process to be paid faster. This helps to increase the level of automation by codifying market provisions between Blockchain supply chain members, reducing human interference and errors (Javaid et al., 2021).

Saberi et al, (2019) show that Blockchain technology has significant implications for the trade in global supply chains. Blockchain technologies promises important future capabilities in supply chain by facilitating auditability, improving accountability, enhancing data and information transparency and improving trust in B2B relationships (Rejeb et al., 2021).

Blockchain for Industry 4.0

Industry 4.0 is a synthesis of the new production methods that allow manufacturers to achieve their target more rapidly. Industry 4.0 involves innovations with upcoming digital technologies, and Blockchain is one of them. In fact, the distributed ledger technology is considered a key part of the 4th industrial revolution (Ullah et al., 2021; Chen et al., 2018; Javaid et al., 2021).

The transition to Industry 4.0 has brought with Blockchain a range of emerging technologies. Blockchain can be incorporated to improve security, privacy, and data transparency. The promise of Blockchain helps us to adjust a modern business paradigm that is more effective, scalable and optimized, focused on the protection of Industry 4.0. Thus, Blockchain is a vital partner in industry-related growth (Javaid et al., 2021).

There are various challenges of Industry 4.0 that can be easily undertaken by Blockchain technology: storing all data digitally for the enhancement of manufacturing processes; solving data privacy issues with proper implementation; easily sharing business data and facilitating cross-organizational data exchange. Furthermore, Blockchain comprises smart factories that enable real-time interoperability. This technology can connect to single or multiple networks. Flaws in any of those pieces of equipment could leave the system vulnerable to attack (Javaid et al., 2021).

BLOCKCHAIN TECHNOLOGY DIFFUSION: INNOVATION THEORY PERSPECTIVE

In management information system field, few studies focus on the diffusion phenomenon of Blockchain technology. Major research interests are going on acceptance and adoption (Dede et al., 2021; Malik et al., 2021; Ullah et al., 2021). Studying the diffusion phenomena is interesting for any innovation. Its gives an overview about the evolution of adopters' categories involved successively in the adoption decision process. The innovation diffusion theory IDT proposed by Rogers (1995) is one of the most used models to analyze the process of communicating any innovation through a system' members. It was and still employed in more than a thousand studies mainly that deal with IT innovations at individual and organizational levels (Menzli et al., 2022).

Innovation Diffusion Theory IDT

Due to the disruptive nature of Blockchain, IDT (Rogers, 1995) is interesting to study the diffusion and adoption of this technology. According to Rogers, innovation is "an idea, practice, or object that is perceived as new by an individual or another unit of adoption". Diffusion is "the process by which an innovation is communicated through certain channels over time among the members of a social system".

IDT explains how an innovation is adopted through a system over time. IDT postulates that there are five categories of adopters: Innovators (2.5%), early adopters (13.5%), early majority (34%), late major-

Overview of Blockchain Technology Diffusion and Adoption

ity (34%) and laggards (16%). Categorization of adopters is based on the innovativeness factor which is defined as the degree to which an individual, group or organization is relatively quick in adopting new innovation compared to others in the society.

Complementarily with the adoption curve, Rogers defined the adoption decision process which is composed of five stages: knowledge, persuasion, decision, implementation and confirmation. The chapter will focus also in the evolution of the decision process in dependence with adopters of Blockchain and their behavior toward this technology.

Furthermore, IDT argues that potential users make decisions to adopt or reject an innovation based on beliefs that they form about the innovation. According to Rogers, adoption of innovation is determined by five attributes: the relative advantage (innovation is better than the idea it replaced), observability (visibility of results), triability (experimentation), complexity (degree of ease of use associated to the technology) and compatibility (with current systems and resources).

Accordingly, this section will be organized in consistence with Rogers Theory. Thus, the adoption decision process of Blockchain technology will be analyzed first. Then, adopters of Blockchain (in different economic sectors) as founded in previous studies will be presented. Finally, IDT adoption factors will be adapted to the specific case of Blockchain technology.

Blockchain Adoption Decision Process

This subsection is focusing in the adoption decision process of Blockchain technology as defined originally by Rogers (knowledge, persuasion, decision, implementation and confirmation).

Nearly every industry is exploring the use of Blockchain technology to a significant extent (Ali et al., 2020). However, Blockchain software is still in its infancy; it is being developed and refined (Attaran, 2020). According to Fedorova and Skobleva (2020), current applications of Blockchain are still in the 1.0 and 2.0 stages. Most people do not know about the term "blockchain," not to mention the potential applications of using Blockchain technology (Chen et al., 2018). Therefore, Blockchain is not known and appreciated by all parts (individuals or organizations). Nevertheless, the rapid extension of Blockchain market (Ruby, 2023) can be interpreted by quick advancement of this technology in the decision process in the near future.

Some previous theoretical analyses argued that manufacturing industry is between knowledge, persuasion and decision stage. Transportation, communications, electric, gas and sanitary services and trading industry had reached to the decision stage. Services and industries have reached to implementation stage while finance and banking have reached the confirmation stage of innovation-decision process. However, public administration is at persuasion stage (Crover and Kumar kar, 2019; Ennajeh, 2021).

Insights about the progress of the decision adoption process of Blockchain technology according to economic sectors involvement are presented in the following section (see Figure 1).

Adopters of Blockchain Technology

Blockchain technology is new and has not been adopted by all industries at the same rate. An analysis of investment contracts for Blockchain applications has shown great growth in multiple sectors. Blockchain has got application in many areas ranging from healthcare, finance and banking, governance, supply chain, energy. Furthermore, other industries, including entertainment, manufacturing are adopting Blockchain technology to leverage its benefits (Attaran, 2020; Yadav and Singh, 2019; Sarote and Shukla, 2021; Jraisat et al., 2022; Ali et al., 2020).

The main focus of this section is to identify adopters of Blockchain technology as founded in the literature. Classification is first based on economic sectors implicated in Blockchain adoption and use. Second, rapprochement with Rogers Theory summarizes categories of adopters regarding to their involvement in the adoption curve. Thus, innovators (developers or providers of Blockchain technology), early adopters, early majority, late majority and laggards will be synthesized by the end of this section.

INNOVATORS AND DEVELOPERS OF BLOCKCHAIN TECHNOLOGY

Blockchain technology was first introduced by the unknown person (or group) named Satoshi Nakamoto through his Bitcoin cryptocurrency technology. Satoshi Nakamoto described the technology of the new cash system, which he named bitcoin, as an electronic payment system based on cryptography, not on trust. The system works without intermediary (banks) and resolves the issue of "double spending". The author suggested a new technology of decentralized digital cash turnover, which consists of two elements: the distributed registry (Blockchain) and the cryptographic algorithm of bitcoin mining (Nakamoto, 2008; Fedorova and Skobleva, 2020; Sarote and Shukla, 2021).

In the second generation, smart contracts were introduced for assets and trust agreements. It was initiated by Ethereum, one of the most renowned Blockchain-based software platforms (Alshamsi et al., 2022).

As several years have passed, the system suggested by Nakamoto has become of special value for programmers; it has been promoted and enhanced (Fedorova and Skobleva, 2020). The dramatic increase in Blockchain technology has provided many new application opportunities (Seyednima et al, 2019) and many developers emergence. Hyperledger is one of the most known providers of Blockchain solutions to business in the world. Hyperledger is a collaboration of the Linux Foundation's open-source Blockchain to promote the shared creation of distributed ledgers (Mohammed el al., 2021).

Many other providers of Blockchain solutions emerged and developed. For example, in healthcare several companies have begun the development and the distribution of Blockchain technologies for this industry (Attaran, 2020). Also, many startups in developing countries are investing in Blockchain technology solutions developments (Ennajeh, 2021) even for private, permissioned and public blockchains.

Blockchain in Finance

The first application of Blockchain technology was in finance. Blockchain has been largely used for cryptocurrency and financial transactions (Attaran, 2020). Blockchain technology is a financial technology (FinTech) which is first developed as the distributed ledgers for bitcoin. For some time, Blockchain technology was overshadowed by the bitcoin phenomenon, but in current years it has started to attract attention in its own right and is becoming a core technology in the FinTech family (Ali et al., 2020)

Despite the lack of major academic studies and publications in this emerging field, Blockchain is one of the most promising advanced technologies in the overall FinTech field (Du et al., 2019). While it was first designed to serve as a distributed ledger for tracking bitcoin transactions, blockchain's potential extends beyond bitcoin. Indeed, it can change many business operations in both financial and other commercial domains (Ali et al., 2020).

While blockchain are now playing a significant role in financial innovations and is the backbone technology that is driving the Fintech revolution, the predominant usage of blockchain thus far has been in the area of payments. The main objective of any payment system is safe and smart transactions. The development of digital currencies using blockchain technology is the latest revolution in the domain of money transfer. Cryptocurrencies utilize decentralized peer-to-peer (P2P) networks, encryption techniques, cryptography and a public key infrastructure in which pairs of public and private keys are used to secure transfer of data (Ali et al., 2020).

Financial services industry, however, remains to be the strongest driver of Blockchain adoption. As reported by the World Economic Forum, 80% of banks were involved in some blockchain project in 2017 and over 90 central banks have growingly engaged in Blockchain considerations (Adamkiewicz and Jabbar, 2020).

Blockchain in Industry and Manufacturing

Smart factories, smart products, supply chains, and smart solutions are some of the quality drivers and enablers been employed to develop blockchain technology for their specific services from industrial perspectives. The productivity, quality products, utmost customer satisfaction, precised services…are the significant features of blockchain technology towards industry 4.0 applications (Javaid et al., 2021). Blockchain has many technological implementations and continually introduces innovative applications. There is a growing global interest in the use of blockchain technology in the manufacturing sector. Overall, the case studies regarding blockchain implementation in supply chains are dominated by food supply chains. Logistics, pharmaceuticals, and retail industries are the next common areas of investigation, but still far behind food supply chains. Finally, automotive, maritime, construction, and green operations are found to be the other significant areas for case studies (Dede et al., 2021).

Demand for Blockchain applications is rapidly growing in various industries; the automotive sector is more inclined to introduce Blockchain technologies (Javaid et al., 2021).

Blockchain in Healthcare

Healthcare seems one of the most promises applications of blockchain technology especially after the covid-19 crisis. Research about Blockchain in healthcare is exponentially growing. Benefits of Blockchain in healthcare are detected in two levels. First, patients' benefits like security & authorization, personalized healthcare, monitor health status and tracking health data are guaranteed. Second, for healthcare industry and organization, benefits are related to pharmaceutical supply chains, clinical trials, managing medical insurance, health information exchange (Abu-elezz et al., 2020).

Healthcare providers can use blockchain to store details about patients' records where patients and doctors can directly check those records through the network, anytime, anywhere (Attaran, 2020).

Current literature provides overview of applications that have been developed, tested, and/or deployed. However, healthcare industry is still in the beginning stages of developing infrastructure, computer programs, and strategic methods that can bring together different types of data available on a reliable, secure, and consistent basis.

Previous studies found that the research on the explorative use of blockchain in healthcare is in its infancy, but the number of proposed solutions currently is growing exponentially.

Early applications of blockchain in healthcare have shown that successful implementation requires redefining the relations of all involved players from healthcare providers to patients and the pharmaceutical industry. While the technology has not been universally adopted in the healthcare sector yet, its application will only be going to broaden in the future (Attaran, 2020).

Blockchain in Education

The number of researches of the blockchain technology in education sector is also growing at a significant pace. Quite frequently, technological developments and solutions in education field become a base and a stimulus for academic research. One can state that if several years ago researches suggested some particular fields of applying blockchain in education, nowadays there is a tendency to accumulate the entire range of university functions in blockchain projects (Fedorova and Skobleva, 2020).

The first review of application of Blockchain in education is "Blockchain in Education" of Grech and Camilleri (2017). Application of the Blockchain technology in higher education started in 2014, when the University of Nicosia, Cyprus (UNIC) commenced to apply this technology on an official basis to store and confirm its diplomas; it was also the first university that began to accept fees for studies as bitcoins.

The Massachusetts Institute of Technology (MIT) developed its blockchain-based Blockcerts in 2017; this application makes it easier to issue digital diplomas and professional certificates. In addition, Sony Global schooling and Holberton School are examples of first users of Blockchain technology for many services related to education (build a transparent evaluation framework, online learning, store degrees and shared educational information). The distributed ledger can fit any type of information with unique student ID. It includes learning behavior in class, micro academic project experience, and macro educational background, etc (Ullah et al., 2021; Fedorova and Skobleva, 2020; Chen et al., 2018).

Data can be safely stored and accessed on a Blockchain network in appropriate ways in the formal and informal learning context. So that not only information about students' achievements and academic certificates but also information about research experience, skills, online learning experience as well as individual interests are included. Blockchain can be used also as a "capacity-currency transformation bank" as said by Chen et al. (2018).

Blockchain technology in education contributes to reducing degree fraud due to the reliability and authority ensured by Blockchain applications. Data matched with users' ID and stored in Blockchain are checked, validated, and maintained by the miners from all over the world. Blockchain distributed ledger is immutable and trustworthy (Chen et al., 2018).

Nevertheless, application of the Blockchain technology in education is only at its initial stage; only a small number of educational institutions apply it actually. This technology has an outstanding potential in the sphere of higher education (Fedorova and Skobleva, 2020).

Blockchain in Agriculture

Agriculture has been a very promising for Blockchain but not much review exists in this area except one which focuses on only ten studies lacking the detail module. Blockchain based system could be savior for different agricultural stakeholder like farmers which are mainly deprived due to various reasons (Yadav and Singh, 2019).

Properties of Blockchain (decentralization, transparent, immutable, autonomy, open-source, anonymity, and consensus) help in agriculture sector applications (Sajja et al., 2021).

Overview of Blockchain Technology Diffusion and Adoption

The literature was classified under four head namely traceability, architecture and security, information systems and other applications namely food safety, sustainable agro-practices and agrofinance. Possibilities to use Blockchain in agri-business were investigated and founded that such system could bring transparency through effective monitoring of agricultural trade. Blockchain based app for payment in online food court ordering on Ethereum Platform was also developed (Yadav and Singh, 2019).

Sajja et al. (2021) added that major applications of Blockchain in agriculture are: Agricultural Insurance, Smart Farming, Traceability, Land Registration, Food Supply Chain, Security and Safety f Farms, E Commerce of Agricultural Products.

Toward the Schematization of the Adoption Curve

The purpose here is to summarize theoretical analysis above and identify adopters' categories and their localization in the adoption curve in respect with IDT.

As advanced by Ali et al, (2020), the rapid market growth of Blockchain technology (rate 37/3%) is explained by an increasing demand for this technology across all industries, from financial services, through consumer and industrial goods, transport, healthcare, and public services. As a result, Blockchain technology has spread to other sectors such as manufacturing (17.6% of the market share), distribution and services (14.6%), public sector (4.2%), and infrastructure (3.1%).

According to Tozex (2019) cited in Adamkiewicz and Jabbar (2020), the application of the IDT to Blockchain reveals that adoption was at the end of the early adopters cycle which began in 2013. Thus, Blockchain is believed to be on the verge of "early majority" phase, with mature businesses from various sectors having entered the market. Accordingly, Blockchain seems currently at the early majority phase in the adoption curve.

Above discussions demonstrate that Blockchain in education and healthcare are yet at the beginning stages of developing infrastructure. In manufacturing and industry, the automotive sector is more inclined to introduce Blockchain technologies. The public sector seems potential adopter of Blockchain because of its looking at the potential of Blockchain to serve as the official registry for citizen-owned assets. It could also facilitate voting, reduce fraud, and improve back-office functions like purchasing (Javaid et al., 2021).

As a consequence categorization of adopters can be addressed as following:

- **Innovators:** Satochi Nakamoto, developers of Blockchain Technologies, startups and open source communities (Hyperlegder).
- **Early Adopters:** Finance and banking.
- **Early Majority:** Some manufacturing and industries, energy, healthcare, education, agriculture.
- **Late Majority:** Public sector, automotive and other industries.
- **Laggards:** Not yet reached, but it concerns all remaining economic activities.

Figure 1 summarizes both the adoption decision process and adopters categories of Blockchain technology according to existing literature and in consistence with Rogers's insights. The opposite direction of decision process (from left to right) and the adopters' categories (from right to left) is justified by timing of involvement in the process. For example, the financial sector is the first economic sector involved in the adoption of Blockchain (early adopter); thus, finance is placed at the last stage of adoption decision process which is confirmation. Furthermore, innovators are not mentioned in the figure because they are providing Blockchain applications for current and potential adopters.

Figure 1. Blockchain technology adoption decision process and adopters categories according to economic sectors involvement

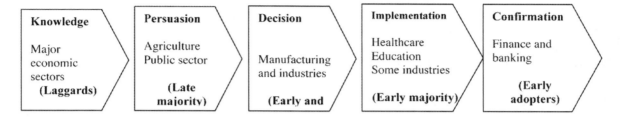

Factors Affecting Blockchain Adoption

According to IDT, there are five attributes of an innovation that affect its adoption: relative advantage, complexity, observability, trialability and compatibility.

Relative Advantage

Relative advantage is the degree to which an innovation is perceived as being better than the product or service it supersedes. IDT suggest that more an innovation has clear and unambiguous advantage more it will be adopted and implemented. Previous studies generally indicate Blockchain advantages to justify its relevance for transactions and economic exchange in all types of Blockchain. Thus, benefits are clear for current and potential adopters.

Despite particularity of each economic sector, there are common perceived advantages of Blockchain that can be summarized in the following points (Wang et al. 2016; Chen et al, 2018; Golosova and Romanovs, 2018):

- **Reliability:** the decentralized nature of a Blockchain network changes the databases of the entire transaction records from closed and centralized ledgers to open distributed ledgers. The failure of a single node does not affect the operation of the whole network. This avoids the single point of failure and ensures the high reliability of the application.
- **Trust:** Blockchain network acts as new trust bearers with decentralized ledgers. These ledgers are shared among a network of tamper-proofed nodes.
- **Security:** Blockchain network uses the one-way hash function which is a mathematical function that takes a variable-length input string and converts it into a fixed-length binary sequence (like a fingerprint). The process is hard to reverse. Furthermore, the newly generated block is strictly following the linear sequence of time.
- **Efficiency:** Blockchain technology can not only significantly reduce the cost of labor but also improve efficiency. Blockchain technology could speed the clearing and settlement of certain

Overview of Blockchain Technology Diffusion and Adoption

transactions by reducing the number of intermediaries involved, and by making the reconciliation process faster and more efficient.

Table 1. Advantages of blockchain technology for economic sectors implicated in the adoption process

Application Area (Economic Sector)	Main Advantages	References
Banking and finance	Security, efficiency, decentralization, reducing the number of intermediaries involved, process are faster and more efficient	(Ali et al., 2020; Chen et al., 2018)
Manufacturing and industries	Immutability, decentralization, transparency, reliability, trust, efficiency and traceability	(Javaid et al., 2021)
Healthcare	Immutability, decentralization, transparency and traceability. Blockchain can improve access control, interoperability, provenance, and data integrity. Flexibility, adaptable, agility, and secure infrastructure with high performance and low latency. Unified and secured view and exchange of electronic health records	(Abu-elezz et al., 2020; Attaran, 2020)
Education	Formation of a single educational environment, Creation of network communities, Exchange with technologies and scientific knowledge, Copyright protection of the network participants.	(Fedorova & Skobleva, 2020)
Agriculture	Decentralization, transparency, immutability, autonomy, anonymity.	(Sajja et al., 2021)

Other IDT Adoption Factors

Compatibility is the degree to which an innovation fits with the existing values, past experiences and needs of potential adopters. Blockchain Technology is seen as disruptive innovation by conducting new ways of doing transaction digital economy. So that, Blockchain does not feat with compatibility and this adoption factor could be considered as an obstacle to adoption.

Complexity is the degree to which an innovation is perceived as difficult to understand and use. IDT assume that if the new innovation is seeing as simple to use it will be more easily adopted.

Trialability id the degree to which an innovation may be experimented with on a limited basis. Generally, innovations require investing time, energy and resources to be implemented. Innovation that can be tried before are more readily adopted.

Observability is the degree to which the results of an innovation are visible to adopters. If positive outcomes are perceived, the innovation is more adopted.

Given the novelty of research in the adoption of Blockchain technology, there are no much studies used IDT for empirical evidence (Alshamsi et al., 2022). As a consequence, IDT adoption factors are not tested empirically and there are no much results to include.

The main factor that seems influencing the adoption decision of Blockchain is the relative advantage (Ennajeh, 2021). Other factors advanced by IDT: complexity, observability, trialability and compatibility are playing an opposite role because they complicate the task of adopting Blockchain technology given its disruptive nature.

Accordingly, as advanced by Attaran (2020) and Adamkiewicz and Jabbar (2020), cost, complexity, uncertainty and users' lack of awareness are main difficulties faced the adoption of Blockchain technology. Implementation (replacing or adapting existing systems), regulatory issues and potential security threats are the three top organizational barriers to greater investments in Blockchain.

DISCUSSIONS AND MANAGERIAL IMPLICATIONS

Initially, Blockchain is considered as novel and unique way of storing and managing data developed to solve the double-spending problem in virtual currencies. Later, the technology has consistently advanced and a Blockchain type has developed dramatically. Many different use cases were proposed like electronic voting, network security, healthcare, human resource management, internet of things (IoT), cloud computing, music, supply chain, banking and finance, industry 4.0… In fact, Blockchain is revolutionizing almost every industry. It has emerged as a disruptive technology, which has not only laid the foundation for all crypto-currencies, but also provides beneficial solutions in other fields of technologies (Malik et al, 2021; Javaid et al., 2021).

The added value of Rogers's theory is the introduction of the innovation life cycle; so that time that takes an innovation to reach the critical mass of adopters can be estimated. Most applications of IDT are limited to use adoption factors. Analysis about adoption curve, adoption stages and adopters categories have little attention and subsequently no deep analyses were made in this specific topic. In the field of IT systems, Rogers' theory presents the strengths to study the adoption process and to explain which factors influence an individual's decision to accept or reject innovation.

Theoretical analyses advanced in the chapter focuses on the localization of each economic sector involved in the adoption process and the adoption curve. In fact, localization is not easy enough because statistics differ from a study to another. Furthermore, Blockchain diffusion is rapidly growing as shown by some statistics which make it difficult to schematize the adoption curve.

Localization of Blockchain on the innovation diffusion curve should be addressed from two different angles: investment and technology as suggested by Adamkiewicz and Jabbar (2020). This idea can make different perspective on analyzing the adoption curve evolution.

Despite difficulties, studying diffusion and adoption of Blockchain technology is relevant not only to describe the current situation and predict the future but also to promote the adoption of this technology that has many advantages for economic transactions and exchanges in digital economy context.

Blockchain is not predicted to be in the mainstream until 2025 and is still an 'immature opportunity space' (Lin et al., 2017). Khazaei (2020) has argued that Blockchain is seen as a communal technology. Thus, the positive view of innovators and early adopters will increase its diffusion in society. In the same vein, Francisco and Swanson (2018) argued that Blockchain applications are social technologies by design. The increased normative pressure and a critical mass of users could lead to greater intention to use.

In another hand, benefits of Blockchain technology are relevant to know and communicate because they can accelerate the adoption of the technology and make all economic sectors in developed and developing countries reaping benefit from this innovative technology. So that decision makers can use insights about adoption factors and demonstrate advantages of the technology for potential adopters; this can accelerate the adoption rate horizontally (economic sectors) and vertically (adoption rate). The most relevant adoption factor of Blockchain is its relative advantage as demonstrated in the chapter. Other IDT adoption factors are not very explored in the literature. They are playing an opposite role in this case of technology because of its disruptive nature.

Overview of Blockchain Technology Diffusion and Adoption

Theoretical analysis above demonstrated also that diffusion of Blockchain seems rapid and penetrating all economic sectors. Financial services industry is therefore the early adopter of blockchain and remains the strongest driver of Blockchain adoption. In fact, this is not verified empirically in all countries because there is reticence toward cryptocurrency adoption in some cases.

As discussed earlier, many economic sectors are early adopters of Blockchain technology; but it is important to mention that the adoption rate in the same sector differ between countries (developing and developed). Since the divergence nature of adopters in different economic field (healthcare, education, manufacturing, finance, agriculture...), it is suggested to conduct the same type of research in specific context of developing countries or targeting specific economic sector.

CONCLUSION

Blockchain is one of more effective tools to deal with digitalization, unpredictable crisis and uncertainties. Features of the technology (transparence, reliability, trust, decentralization and immutability) give it a great potential to revolutionize economic transactions and social systems particularly in the context of industry 4.0 and supply chain digitalization.

The rapid diffusion of Blockchain technology in recent years proves its relevance for business operation, and services like education, healthcare and many other activities. The distributed ledger technology penetrates all economic sectors in different rate. Many IT and digital experts suggest that Blockchain will reshape every industry in the future (Malik et al, 2021).

Despite the relevance of previous studies in Blockchain technology, an overview of its diffusion and adoption was necessary. It seems like a holistic view that gives many lessons to actual and future use of the technology for many stakeholders.

The main concern of the chapter was identifying adopters of Blockchain technology according to Rogers' theory. As result, the financial sector is the early adopter of Blockchain technology and is, as consequence, at the confirmation stage in the adoption decision process. Manufacturing, healthcare, education, agriculture are the sectors that reaping benefits from this technology despite their localization at the beginning stages of adoption. In manufacturing and industry, the automotive sector is more inclined to introduce Blockchain technologies. Other manufacturing activities and supply chain are benefiting from the distributed ledger technology in their operation. As a consequence, those activities are between persuasion, decision and confirmation in the adoption process of Blockchain. The public sector seems potential adopter of Blockchain regarding perceived benefits that seems in favor of it future adoption. Thus, public sector is at the persuasion stage.

Special concern was oriented to Blockchain technology developers and providers like Hyperledger given the role they play in developing Blockchain solutions for business and then the expansion of Blockchain applications market.

Localization of Blockchain technology in the adoption curve was not easy enough because statistics and studies contexts are different. Despite difficulties, the application of the IDT to Blockchain reveals that we are at the beginning of "early majority" phase. This is proved by the rapid growth of Blockchain application and economic activities involvement in the adoption process.

Nevertheless, the relevance of the study seems in its role to promote the adoption of Blockchain technology among economic activities in general.

The chapter addressed also Blockchain adoption factors in respect with IDT. The goal was to communicate Blockchain benefits in order to accelerate its diffusion among economic sectors. Analyses demonstrate that the most determinant adoption factor is the relative advantage because of Blockchain technological features.

Despite the relevance of the study, there are some limitations and difficulties encountered. First, the chapter content and the nature of Blockchain technology are multidisciplinary what makes analyses difficult and maybe superficial in some cases. Since the room of research is broad because of adopters in different economic field (healthcare, education, manufacturing, finance, agriculture...), it is suggested to conduct the same type of research in specific context of developing countries or targeting specific economic sector. Future research could concentrate on each sector and apply the IDT in more restrictive manner which gives deeper analyses of localization in the adoption curve for any economic activity implicated in the adoption process.

Furthermore, the chapter focused only on enablers of Blockchain diffusion. Barriers of adoption were not treated. Thus, legal, social, technological and organizational limitations are among barriers facing investments in Blockchain that could be addressed in future researches.

REFERENCES

Abu-elezz, I., Hassan, A., Nazeemudeen, A., Househ, M., & Abd-alrazaq, A. (2020). "The benefits and threats of blockchain technology in healthcare: A scoping review", International Journal of Medical Informatics. *International Journal of Medical Informatics*, *142*, 104246. doi:10.1016/j.ijmedinf.2020.104246 PMID:32828033

Adamkiewicz, W., & Jabbar, K. (2020). *Crossing the Chasm: Blockchain as an Innovation Driver in Broader Adoption of Carbon Offsetting Solutions* [Thesis]. CBS.

Ali, O., Ally, M., Clutterbuck, & Dwivedi, Y. (2020). The state of play of blockchain technology in the financial services sector: A systematic literature review. *International Journal of Information Management*, *54*, 2020. doi:10.1016/j.ijinfomgt.2020.102199

Alshamsi, M., Al-emran, M., & Shaalana, K. (2022). Systematic review on Blockchain adoption. *Applied Sciences (Basel, Switzerland)*, *2022*(12), 4245. doi:10.3390/app12094245

Attaran, M. (2020). Blockchain technology in healthcare: Challenges and opportunities. *International Journal of Healthcare Management*. doi:10.1080/20479700.2020.1843887

Chen, G., Xu, B., Lu, M., & Chen, N.-S. (2018). Exploring blockchain technology and its potential applications for education. *Smart Learning Environments*, *5*(1), 1. doi:10.118640561-017-0050-x

Dede, S., Köseolu, M.C., & Yercan, F.H. (2021). Learning from Early Adopters of Blockchain Technology: A Systematic Review of Supply Chain Case Studies. *Technology Innovation Management Review*, *11*(6).

Ennajeh, L. (2021). Blockchain Technology Diffusion and Adoption: Tunisian Context Exploration. In Digital Economy. Emerging Technologies and Business Innovation. ICDEc 2021. Springer. doi:10.1007/978-3-030-92909-1_6

Fedorova, E. P., & Skobleva, E. I. (2020). Application of Blockchain Technology in Higher Education. *European Journal of Contemporary Education, 9*(3), 552-571. www.ejournal1.com doi:10.13187/ejced.2020.3.552

Ghosh, A., Gupta, S., Dua, A., & Kumar, N. (2020). Security of Cryptocurrencies in blockchain technology: State-of-art, challenges and future prospects. *Journal of Network and Computer Applications, 163*, 102635. Advance online publication. doi:10.1016/j.jnca.2020.102635

Golosova, J., & Romanovs, A. (2018). *The Advantages and Disadvantages of the Blockchain Technology.* Elsevier Ltd. https://creativecommons.org/licenses/by/4.0/ doi:10.1109/AIEEE.2018.8592253

Javaid, M., Haleem, A., Singh R. P., Khan, S., & Suman, R. (2021). Blockchain technology applications for Industry 4.0: A literature-based review. *Blockchain: Research and Applications.*

Jraisat, L., Jreissat, M., Upadhyay, A., & Kumar, A. (2022). Blockchain Technology: The Role of Integrated Reverse Supply Chain Networks in Sustainability. *Supply Chain Forum: An International Journal.* doi:10.1080/16258312.2022.2090853

Lin, Y.-P., Petway, J. R., Antony, J., Mukhtar, H., Lioa, S.-H., Chou, C.-F., & Ho, Y.-F. (2017). Blockchain: The Evolutionary Next Step for ICT E-Agriculture. *Environments (Basel, Switzerland), 2017*(4), 50. doi:10.3390/environments4030050

Malik, S., Chadhar, M., Vatanasakdakul, S., & Chetty, M. (2021). Factors Affecting the Organizational Adoption of Blockchain Technology: Extending the Technology–Organization–Environment (TOE) Framework in the Australian Context. *Sustainability (Basel), 2021*(13), 9404. doi:10.3390u13169404

Menzli, L. J., Smirani, L. K., Boulahia, J. A., & Hadjouni, M. (2022). Investigation of open educational resources adoption in higher education using Rogers' diffusion of innovation theory. *Heliyon Journal, 8.* www.cell.com/heliyon doi:10.1016/j.heliyon.2022.e09885

Mohammed, A. H., Abdulateef, A. A., & Abdulateef, I. A. (2021). Hyperledger, Ethereum and Blockchain Technology: A Short Overview. *Conference Paper.* 10.1109/HORA52670.2021.9461294

Nakamoto, S. (2008). *Bitcoin: A Peer-to-Peer Electronic Cash System.* bitcoin.org

Rejeb, A., Keogh, J.G., Simske, S.J., Stafford, T., & Treiblmaier, H. (2021). Potentials of Blockchain technologies for supply chain collaboration: a conceptual framework. *The International Journal of Logistics Management.* doi:10.1108/IJLM-02-2020-0098

Rogers, E. M. (1995). *Diffusion of Innovations* (4th ed.). Free Press.

Ruby, D., (2023). *Blockchain statistics: How many people use bitcoin?* demandesage.com

Sajja, G. S., Rane, K. P., Phasinam, K., Kassanuk, T., Okoronkwo, E., & Prabhu, P. (2021). Towards applicability of blockchain in agriculture sector. *Materials Today: Proceedings.* Advance online publication. doi:10.1016/j.matpr.2021.07.366

Sarote, P., & Shukla, O. J. (2021). Blockchain Technology Adoption in Healthcare Sector for Challenges Posed by COVID-19. In Recent Advances in Smart Manufacturing and Materials. Springer. doi:10.1007/978-981-16-3033-0_34

Schlund, J., Ammon, L., & German, R. (2018). ETHome: Open-source blockchain based energy community controller. *e-Energy '18, International Conference on Future Energy Systems.*

Seyednima Khezr, S., Moniruzzaman, M., Yassine, A., & Benlamri, R. (2019). Blockchain Technology in Healthcare: A Comprehensive Review and Directions for Future Research. *Applied Sciences, 9*(1736). www.mdpi.com/journal/applsci doi:10.3390/app9091736

Shi, X., Yao, S., & Luo, S. (2021). Innovative platform operations with the use of technologies in the blockchain era. *International Journal of Production Research*, 1–19. Advance online publication. doi:10.1080/00207543.2021.1953182

Ullah, N., Mugahed Al-Rahmi, W., Alzahrani, A. I., Alfarraj, O., & Alblehai, F. M. (2021). Blockchain Technology Adoption in Smart Learning Environments. *Sustainability (Basel), 2021*(13), 1801. doi:10.3390u13041801

Yadav, S. V., & Singh, A. R. (2019). A Systematic Literature Review of Blockchain Technology in Agriculture. *Proceedings of the International Conference on Industrial Engineering and Operations Management Pilsen.*

KEY TERMS AND DEFINITIONS

Adopters: Adopters are individuals or organizations that are currently or potentially users of an innovation. Rogers (1995) defined five adopters' categories regarding to the time taken to be implicated in the adoption process: innovators, early adopters, early majority, late majority, and laggards.

Adoption Curve: Adoption curve is a graphic S curve that schematizes the emplacement of adopters regarding to their adoption status' evolution on time.

Adoption Decision Process: The adoption decision process is the process of an innovation that will be finally adopted by individuals or organizations. It is composed of five stages: knowledge, persuasion, decision, implementation, and confirmation.

Blockchain Technology: Blockchain is a distributed ledger technology or simply a technological protocol that allows data to be exchanged freely by individual network participants without the intermediaries of third parties.

Economic Sectors: Economic sectors are grouping of similar economic activities that are implicated in the adoption of blockchain technology. In the present chapter, the following economic sectors where studied: finance, industry and manufacturing, healthcare, education, and agriculture.

Innovation Diffusion Theory (IDT): The innovation diffusion theory IDT proposed by Rogers (1995) is one of the most used models to analyze the process of communicating any innovation through a system' members. It focuses on the diffusion of an innovation through a social system on time. It defines five adopters' categories, five stages of the adoption decision process and five adoption factors.

Chapter 4
Blockchain and Governance Structure

Rohan Srivastava
Vellore Institute of Technology, India

Ramani Selvanambi
Vellore Institute of Technology, India

ABSTRACT

The rapid growth in the advancement of blockchain technology and its development has brought its usage in every field. Traditional legal frameworks, which depend on establishing central points of accountability and responsibility, have difficulties as a result of the characteristics of blockchain, such as decentralisation, transparency, integrity, and immutability, among others. A key challenge behind the adoption of blockchain is understanding the dynamics of blockchain governance. With the promise of an efficient network owing to the elimination of intermediaries, governance in blockchain may be understood as addition of standards and culture, laws and codes, people, and institutions that promote coordination and jointly decide a particular organisation. As a result, having a headquarters is not necessary; instead, development can rely on a globally dispersed network of programmers who create the software protocol, giving rise to the idea of a DAO (decentralized autonomous system).

INTRODUCTION TO BLOCKCHAIN

The features of blockchain, such as transparency and immutability with decentralization, to create and implement an open governance structure. As a result, organisations are being driven to innovate in all facets of their operations. (Zheng, Z et al., 2018) Therefore, having a headquarters or CEO is not required, and development may instead depend on a worldwide distributed network of programmers who build the software protocol, giving birth to the concept of a DAO (decentralized autonomous system). Dash introduced the concept of blockchain governance first.

The term "blockchain" refers to both a data structure that (Atzori, 2017; Tasca & Tessone, 2017) stores transactional information and ensures security, transparency, and decentralization as well as a chain of

DOI: 10.4018/978-1-6684-7455-6.ch004

records maintained in the form of blocks that are managed by several parties. Anyone with a computer and an internet connection may access a blockchain, which is a distributed ledger. It is very difficult to update or modify information after it has been recorded in the form of a block on a blockchain.

A digital signature that verifies the legitimacy of each transaction protects it. Once a block is formed, the data saved on the blockchain can't be changed and is anonymous, thanks to the use of encryption and digital signatures (De Filippi et al., 2018). Consensus, often known as universal agreement, is made possible by blockchain technology. Every piece of information saved on a blockchain is digitally preserved, and each network member has access to a database containing the whole history of the data. The likelihood of fraud or cybercrime is decreased in this manner. It is thus more trustworthy and safer than any other method of transaction.

To better understand blockchain technology, A broad alternative that you may typically utilize can be a bank or through a payment transfer application like PayPal, Paytm, or UPI. Let's take an example where Rahul is seeking a way to send some money to his friend Rohan who lives in a different area (Andoni Merlinda et al., 2019). An additional sum of your money is taken out as a transfer charge since this option uses third parties to handle the transaction. Additionally, in situations like these, you cannot guarantee the security of your money since there is a significant chance that a hacker may interrupt the network and take your money. The client loses out in both situations. Blockchain can help with this.

If we utilize a blockchain in such situations, the procedure is significantly simpler and more secure than utilizing a bank (a third party) for money transfers (Jairam Shiva et. al., 2021). As the tax is handled directly by you, there is no additional cost because a third party is not required. In addition, the blockchain database is decentralized and not confined to a single place, making all the data and records maintained public and decentralized. There is less risk of hacking and code corruption since the data is not kept in a single location. Decentralization, which allows parties to deal directly with one other, for example via smart contracts, reduces costs and is the core benefit of blockchain technology. On a broad scale, this basically entails the dismantling of power centers like governing bodies and their institutions, central banks, etc.

Main Contribution of This Chapter

This chapter works on the use of blockchain in governance structure and how it can be implemented so to make government and its structure more efficient and reliable. The first part elaborates about the blockchain, its working and architecture where second part talks about the implementation of blockchain in governance structure.

Main Organizations of the Chapter

The introduction section of the chapter gives a basic understanding of the blockchain, literature survey section explains the background of blockchain in governance, detailed explanation of blockchain in governance structure is explained, working of blockchain is discussed in the next section, the detailed explanation of the blockchain applications and its use cases is explained in the next section, finally the chapter concludes with the conclusion section with the future assessment.

Motivation

Blockchain is the trend of this era and can be implemented in every sector, being the future of the internet, it contains features like immutability, non-recoverability (Treleaven Philip et al., 2017) and this structure reduces the dependency on a central authority and protects sensitive citizen and government data. This technology can be implemented on the government side to improve the efficiency of the government work, projects and plans and can make decision making and development faster as everything will be decentralized. Government can use the private blockchain network for whole country to the government employees and to the public where only citizens of that nation can access that network and can transact over it. This will also make decision taking easier as people can vote and give their consensus over various policy. This will reduce public conflict and revolts on various issues as the policy will only be applied when more than 50% people will say yes.

Additionally, it can eliminate the problems with the past and provide the following benefits:

- Reduce potential of corruption and abuse.
- Enhanced trust in government with no third parties involved.
- Better implementation of government schemes.
- Faster decisions and easy voting on each agenda.
- Secure Storage of governments, citizens, and business data.
- Reduction of access cost associated with managing accountability.

LITERATURE SURVEY

The authors has discussed the application of blockchain in governance by analyzing the framework, difficulties and challenges of applying the blockchain to e-government and public services. (Henderson & Clark, 1990) They talked about the improvements in quality and quantity of government services., greater transparency of the government and more wide knowledge to the public, no middlemen so fast wok and development, cost and reliability was seen as a major problem still while implementing the idea.

This research work seeks to close the gap and explores the essential elements of blockchain-based decentralized governance, which to varied degrees undermines the traditional structures of democracy, citizenship, and State power (Narayanan & Clark, 2017). The article establishes the degree to which blockchain technology and decentralized platforms may be viewed as hyper-political instruments that can control social interactions on a massive scale and do away with traditional central authority. The research draws attention to the dangers posed by private entities holding a disproportionate amount of authority in a decentralized way.

The author contends that blockchains provide a means of enforcing agreements and achieving collaboration and coordination that is unique from both conventional contractual and relational governance as well as from other information technology solutions (Werbach et al., 2018). The authors also look at the potential of blockchains as effective governance. The interaction between blockchain governance and conventional governance methods is covered, including both substitute and complimentary effects.

The author talks about rising number of social and political criticisms of blockchain technology. The article concentrate on the alleged potential of blockchain technology to alter fundamental political institutions including money, property rights regimes, and democratic governance systems. The goal is to investigate how blockchain technology may introduce and support new forms of governance. It start by contrasting the arguments of governance put out within social contract theories with those supplied by members of the blockchain development community. Next, focusing on the concepts of sovereignty, the starting situation, decentralization, and distributive justice, we assess the degree to which the model of governance provided by blockchain technology follows important governance themes and assumptions present within social contract theories.

Mosley et al. (2022) works upon to leverage Dash's governance system to shed light on the administration of blockchain voting systems using a data mining technique to enlighten decision makers about possible advantages, vulnerabilities, and integrity factors that must be considered before any comprehensive organizational transformation. This article aims to put forward a methodical network approach to examine the accuracy of on-chain voting records in order to comprehend the flaws in decentralized voting. It anticipate that the universality of their methodology will enable analysis of any on-chain governance voting mechanism.

The authors conducted a thorough literature study using 37 main research to understand the current state of blockchain governance (Liu, et al., 2022). To address the requested research questions, the primary study data that was retrieved is then prepared. The study's findings include the following key conclusions: (1) While current studies ignore broader ethical responsibilities as the objectives of blockchain governance, governance can improve the adaptability and upgradeability of blockchain. (2) Governance is along with the development process of a blockchain platform, but ecosystem-level governance process is missing. (3) The responsibilities and capabilities of blockchain stakeholders are discussed in detail, but the decision rights, accountability, and incentive are still not.

BLOCKCHAIN IN GOVERNANCE STRUCTURE

Blockchain technology enables governments and public sector organisations get rid of ineffective centralised systems. Blockchain networks provide more secure, adaptable, and economical architectures than current systems, which are by nature unsecure and expensive leading to economic losses.

To decide on project direction, new regulations, and to make sure the protocol and ecosystem function smoothly and effectively, blockchain governance often uses mechanisms. Governance mechanism are either off-chain or on-chain (Beck Roman et al., 2018). Off-chain mechanism includes public discussions, collective proposal and need to agree upon together where in On-chain mechanism stakeholders vote with native coins to make changes directly in the blockchain.

All governance pertains to dynamic changes and change is induced and hence governance is required and here we need public blockchain.

Transition of Governance

The switch from a traditional governance paradigm to a blockchain-based governance model signifies a fundamental transformation in how we create and oversee trust in digital systems. Under a traditional governance model, decision-making and property rights are delegated through legal contracts, paperwork which can be challenging to uphold and expensive to defend in conflict. Moreover, needs verification like stamp or any authorised signature to be valid.

Blockchain and Governance Structure

Blockchain technology, on the other hand, makes it possible to create governance models that rely on managing trust through smart contracts (Calcaterra, 2018). Self-executing programmes known as "smart contracts" run on a blockchain and have the ability to autonomously enforce predefined rules and circumstances. As a result, the governance model can be implemented directly into the technology and enforced without the use of middlemen or formal agreements.

Decision-making authority can be decentralised in a governance paradigm based on blockchain, with various parties participating via consensus procedures. As all stakeholders can see the decisions being taken and the justification for them, this promotes more transparency and accountability. A judgement cannot be readily modified or overturned after it has been made thanks to the immutability of the blockchain.

Overall, switching to a blockchain-based governance model offers the chance for more effective and efficient decision-making, as well as increased openness and confidence in digital systems (Andoni Merlinda et al., 2018). Yet it also necessitates a mental adjustment and a readiness to accept new tools and methods of operation. Smart Contracts are just set of rules or conditions that are executed when certain conditions are met, they are immutable and transparent.

'Smart Contracts': A Step Towards Blockchain Governance

With smart contracts, the details of the agreement between the buyer and seller are directly encoded into lines of code. These contracts self-execute. The code and the agreements inside reside on a decentralised blockchain network, which means they are not under the jurisdiction of a single organisation or body. Nick Szabo initially proposed the idea of smart contracts in 1994, proposing the use of computer protocols to enforce contractual agreements. The Ethereum blockchain platform, which allowed for the formulation and execution of smart contracts, was created in 2014, furthering the idea's development.

Smart contracts automate the process of confirming, carrying out, and upholding a contract's terms using computer code. The code is kept on a blockchain network, which guarantees its transparency, immutability, and resistance to tampering. Every user with network access can access and use a smart contract after it has been written and put on the blockchain. Defining the rules of the contract in code, which may contain requirements like payment amounts, delivery dates, and other variables, is the first step in constructing a smart contract. The code is subsequently published on the blockchain, where the contract's participants can use a web interface or other software tools to communicate with it.

The smart contract automatically runs, and the necessary actions are carried out when the contract's conditions are satisfied. For instance, if a contract requires payment to be made only after the delivery of goods, the smart contract will immediately transfer the funds to the seller as soon as it is verified that the products have been delivered. Smart contracts have a variety of uses, including supply chain management, real estate deals, and financial transactions. Compared to conventional contracts, they provide a number of benefits, such as improved security, efficiency, and openness.

The strength of smart contracts is to automate complex transactions and store them in a secure manner. Smart contracts have a wide range of use cases:

1. **Supply Chain Management:** All the goods can be seen and all the parties can be monitored.
2. **Financial Services:** For automating financial transaction such as payment of loans, insurance claims, investment etc. can be help and monitored easily.
3. **Real State:** In providing sales and transfer of property and vehicles etc smart contract can be used for fair dealing and no after denial of parties as the when the contract is set it is immutable.

4. **Voting:** Smart contracts can be helpful in conducting elections and can help in ensuring that each vote is counted accurately and transparently. Moreover e-voting can be carried out, and can be a halt to malpractices in election.

IT Trust Management With Smart Contracts

Smart contracts can be a big part of IT trust management because they make it possible to automate trust-related tasks and reduce the need for middlemen. Establishing and sustaining trust in the context of a certain IT system or environment is the process of trust management. Automating the verification of identification and access privileges is one way that smart contracts may be utilised for trust management. For instance, a smart contract may be used to confirm a user's identity before providing them access to a certain system or resource. A contract can also guarantee that a user has the authorizations necessary to access a resource and that access is only allowed for a predetermined amount of time.

Moreover, security rules and regulatory compliance may be enforced via smart contracts. A smart contract can be used, for instance, to guarantee that data is encrypted before it is sent over a network or that specific data types are only available to authorised users. By facilitating the establishment of decentralised trust networks, smart contracts may also be utilised for IT trust management. Without a centralised authority or middleman, these networks may be utilised to build and maintain trust between parties. For instance, a smart contract may be used to allow two parties to share data in a trustworthy and safe manner without the need for a third party to vouch for the accuracy of the information.

In conclusion, smart contracts are self-executing contracts that are kept on a decentralised blockchain network and have the contents of the agreement expressed in code. They provide several benefits over conventional contracts by automating the processes of contract verification, execution, and enforcement.

Prerequisite for the Use of Governance in Blockchain

These conditions must be met before excellent governance can be implemented in blockchain systems.

Clarity of Purpose: The blockchain project's goal must be stated clearly and precisely. This aim must be consistent with the organization's objectives and should be successfully conveyed to all stakeholders.

Transparency: With the blockchain, transparency is a crucial component of effective governance. In the blockchain, all transactions and activity should be open, visible, and auditable.

Decentralization: Blockchain is built on the idea of decentralisation, and successful blockchain governance demands decentralised decision-making. No one entity or group should be able to dominate the blockchain, hence the governance structure should be created to achieve this.

Consensus Mechanism: A consensus mechanism is a procedure that makes sure that everyone using the blockchain network agrees that a transaction is legitimate. The consensus process needs to be strong and well-designed to thwart any harmful behaviour.

Community Involvement: The blockchain community ought to take a leading role in the governance procedure. The community ought to have a say in decision-making and a chance to take part in the creation of the blockchain.

Regulatory Compliance: Compliance with applicable rules and regulations is necessary for good blockchain governance. The governance structure must be planned to guarantee adherence to legal standards.

Blockchain and Governance Structure

Continuous Improvement: Effective governance necessitates ongoing development. Regular reviews of the governance structure are important to find opportunities for development and implement the necessary adjustments.

In general, a well-designed governance framework that is open, decentralised, and inclusive is necessary for successful governance in blockchain. The governance system should support ongoing improvement, encourage community involvement, and assure compliance with legal standards.

IMPACT OF BLOCKCHAIN IN THE GOVERNANCE

On the System

The following are some effects of blockchain on governance:

Transparency: By offering a decentralised, tamper-proof record of every transaction, blockchain technology allows transparency in governance. As a result, it is simpler to monitor the movement of cash and assures responsibility.

Enhanced Security: By employing cutting-edge cryptographic methods to shield data from illegal access or manipulation, blockchain technology offers a safe platform for governance. This guarantees the privacy and security of critical information.

Decentralization: Blockchain makes it possible for decision-making to be decentralised, which can assist to fight corruption and advance democracy. This enables more inclusive and egalitarian decision-making processes.

Efficiency: By decreasing paperwork and automating administrative activities, blockchain technology may dramatically increase the efficiency of governance operations. This can help governments better serve their residents by saving time and resources.

Cost Savings: By simplifying procedures and eliminating the need for middlemen, blockchain technology can assist governments in cutting expenses. Over time, this may save you a lot of money.

Digital Identity: Secure, open, and decentralised digital identification systems may be established using blockchain technology. This may lessen identity theft and increase service accessibility.

Citizen Engagement: By providing safe and transparent voting and polling, blockchain technology can let citizens participate in government. This may aid in advancing democracy and raising levels of citizen involvement in decision-making.

Overall, blockchain is expected to have a substantial impact on governance, with the potential to increase openness, security, effectiveness, and public participation. Nonetheless, rigorous preparation, teamwork, and the creation of efficient governance institutions will be required for the successful use of blockchain in governance.

On the Staff

Here are some possible effects that could be seen:

Less Administrative Burden: By automating administrative activities and removing the need for human data input, blockchain technology can lessen the administrative workload for government employees.

Efficiency Increases: By automating administrative activities and using blockchain for safe, transparent record-keeping, government procedures may become more effective, allowing personnel to do more in a shorter amount of time.

Reskilling and Mentoring: To adapt to new tools and procedures, the deployment of blockchain may necessitate retraining and upskill of government personnel.

Reduced Corruption: By fostering a more moral and accountable workplace, the adoption of blockchain for transparent and tamper-proof record-keeping can contribute to a reduction in corruption.

Enhanced Accountability: Because blockchain records are transparent and unchangeable, government employees will be held more accountable because their activities and choices will be easier to track and verify.

Collaboration: Teamwork between government departments and agencies may be improved thanks to blockchain technology, which also makes it easier to share data and resources.

New Opportunities: The use of blockchain technology may present new chances for government employees to engage on creative initiatives, learn new skills, and consider other career routes.

Overall, the long-term effects of blockchain on government employees are probably good, while there could be some immediate difficulties with retraining and adjusting to new tools and procedures. Governments may make their workplaces more effective, responsible, and creative by using the prospective advantages of blockchain technology.

Blockchain Governance Framework

The term "blockchain governance framework" refers to the system of guidelines, procedures, and controls established inside a blockchain network to maintain accountability, enforce regulations, and guide decision-making. It is made to make sure that everyone has a say in decision-making and that the blockchain network runs efficiently, safely, and transparently.

A blockchain governance framework's main components are as follows:

Decentralized Decision-Making: A crucial component of blockchain technology, decentralisation should be reflected in the governance structure. The architecture should support distributed decision-making, allowing each member to influence the network's growth and direction. To guarantee that choices are taken in the network's best interest, this may use a variety of processes, such token-based voting or community-driven proposal systems.

Consensus Mechanisms: Consensus methods are used to approve network updates and verify transactions. The network's consensus mechanism should be described in terms of how it operates, how individuals are encouraged to join, and how disputes or assaults on the network are handled.

Protocol Updates: Blockchain networks are dynamic and may require protocol updates and modifications over time. Governance frameworks should outline the steps involved in proposing, considering, and implementing modifications to the protocol. All participants should be able to access, participate in, and understand this procedure.

Token Economics: Many blockchain networks are built on tokens, and governance frameworks should outline the network's token economics, including how tokens are produced, distributed, and used.

The usage of tokens as governance tokens to give holders the ability to vote on network choices may be involved in this, as well as processes like token burning or inflation.

Accountability and Transparency: Blockchain networks are intended to be transparent, and governance systems should make sure that this is the case. This may include using open-source software, disclosing network measurements to the public, and conducting frequent audits to make sure the network is functioning as intended. Mechanisms for enforcing network regulations and policies should also be included in the framework, such as the ability to prohibit problematic actors or levy penalties for non-compliance.

Community Involvement: Blockchain networks are driven by the community, hence governance structures should encourage community involvement. This might incorporate forums, meetings, or social media platforms where users can debate network advancements and make modification suggestions. The structure should also guarantee that everyone has a say in decision-making, regardless of their involvement in the network.

Handling of Conflicts: Blockchain networks are no different from other governance systems in that disputes may occur. To ensure that everyone is treated equally and that problems are handled in a timely way, governance frameworks should specify the procedure for resolving disagreements and disputes inside the network. This might include automated conflict resolution techniques like smart contracts, arbitration, or mediation.

Ultimately, a strong blockchain governance architecture is necessary to guarantee that the network functions efficiently, safely, and openly, and that all users have a voice in making decisions. It should encourage involvement and development of the community as well as decentralisation, accountability, and openness.

CHALLENGES IN ADOPTION OF BLOCKCHAIN IN GOVERNANCE

The use of blockchain in governance systems is confronting several difficulties. These issues may be roughly divided into three groups: organisational, cultural, and technology.

Technological

1. **Scalability:** Blockchain networks, particularly those implementing Proof of Work consensus algorithms, might have trouble with high transaction volumes. This is because when more transactions are added, the network may become slower as a result of the need for a network of nodes to verify each transaction. Due to this, blockchain technology may not be as beneficial for certain applications, such as data-intensive or high-volume financial transactions.
2. **Interoperability:** Data sharing across various blockchain networks may be difficult due to the fact that they may employ different protocols. This may reduce the ability of blockchain networks to cooperate with one another or to interact with current systems.
3. **Security:** While blockchain networks are intended to be safe, there have been a number of high-profile security lapses in the past. These assaults have been caused by a variety of issues, some of which are inherent in the blockchain technology itself, while others are the result of human mistake or defects in third-party apps.

Cultural

1. **Resistance to Change:** Many individuals may be averse to change, and they may be unsure of how blockchain technology may be employed in governance systems or distrustful of it. Due to this, it may be difficult to execute changes that are required for blockchain adoption or to get support from stakeholders.
2. **Lack of Comprehension:** Since blockchain technology may be complicated, many individuals may not completely comprehend how it operates or how it could be put to use. This might make it difficult to explain the advantages of adopting blockchain technology or to create efficient governance structures that make use of it.
3. **Lack of Trust:** Blockchain networks are based on trust, and it may be difficult to establish confidence in new governance models or technologies. Since stakeholders could be wary of any new governance structure in environments where there was a history of corruption or poor management, this can be especially difficult.

Organizational

1. **Regulatory Barriers:** Blockchain technology is currently largely unregulated, and in some situations, regulatory impediments to its implementation may exist. Due to this, implementing blockchain governance systems in situations requiring regulation may be difficult.
2. **Coordinating Issues:** It can be difficult to get all stakeholders on board with a new governance structure, and blockchain networks require collaboration between various parties. This can be particularly difficult when there is a lack of trust amongst stakeholders or when there are competing stakeholder interests.
3. **Governance Issues:** Blockchain networks need to have governance mechanisms in place, but it might be difficult to create one that is just, open, and efficient. This necessitates giving considerable thought to problems like decision-making authority, accountability, and the rights of many stakeholders.

In general, cooperation between many stakeholders, including technical experts, policymakers, and community members, will be necessary to address these difficulties. In order to overcome technological issues and guarantee that blockchain networks are secure, scalable, and interoperable, it will also be necessary to conduct continual research and development. Finally, it will necessitate a dedication to creating governance institutions that are open, equitable, and successful and that reflect the needs and viewpoints of all stakeholders.

WORKING OF A BLOCKCHAIN

Figure 1 shows the full life cycle of creation of block form request of user till the addition of it in the blockchain including consensus mechanism involved and node validation. Various steps involved are transaction declaration, authentication, block creation, validation, and chaining.

Blockchain and Governance Structure

Figure 1. Working of a blockchain

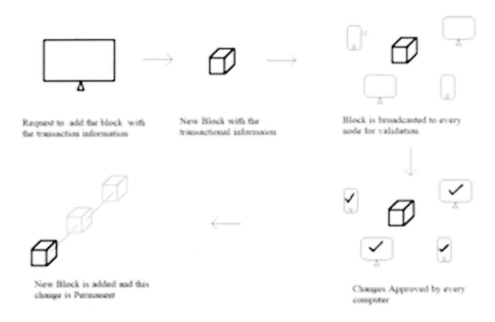

Step 1. Transaction Declaration

A user makes are quest and sends data to the blockchain before adding the data to blockchain it is first converted to the block. This block stores the payload and the header. (Gupta Sahil et. al, (2020) this payload is hashed using a hash key. Hence making it more secure as the data payload changes, hash value is changed hence any modification leads to change in hash which disturbs the chain and is rejected.

Step 2. Transaction Authentication

Now this node is validated by the users in the network before creation of the block by decryption of digital signature, the validation comes with the majority voting technique like if 51% or more users or node gets agreed then the transaction stays valid. Hence this comes with the limitation i.e., 51% attack where hackers capture more than 50% of the node seats and says valid for false transaction also.

Step 3. Block Creation

Now the block is created, with the body and the header in it. The data is stored inside the body of the block and hash value in the header. There is no cap on the amount of blocks because there are always more blocks added to chains. Every computer in the network updates its blockchain whenever a new block is added to the blockchain.

Step 4. Block Validation

The new block is now verified by miners, and they use the concept of proof of work to validate the transaction in the network and are awarded. In a proof-of-work (PoW) system, nodes (the computers that make up the blockchain network) can acquire the privilege of validating a block while also adding transactions to the ledger. Usually, the node that receives the designation of "winner" is rewarded with substantial incentives. The power to approve the block is granted to the winner.

Step 5. Block Chaining

New block is now added to the network with the hash and related to the previous hash of the block. And the now the block becomes immutable as now nothing can be changed, any change will lead to the change of hash and invalid block.

Structure of a Block

From splitting the word, blockchain we can roughly infer Block and Chain which means that a chain of blocks. Here blocks, means block of data, and Chain means the interlinking of these blocks with each other (Danilo et al., 2021). These blocks rely on a distributed ledger and contains information across different computer networks called nodes. Moreover, each node carries a copy of this ledger which contains all of the processing going upon these nodes and simultaneously verifies it on their device. Any discrepancy happened in one of the computers is matched with the ledgers in the different computers and then majority wins and that ledger is copied and the processing is continued again. As you can see in Figure 2. Block has two parts as a header and a body header gets connected to another header of the block and hence forms chain.

Figure 2. Blockchain block

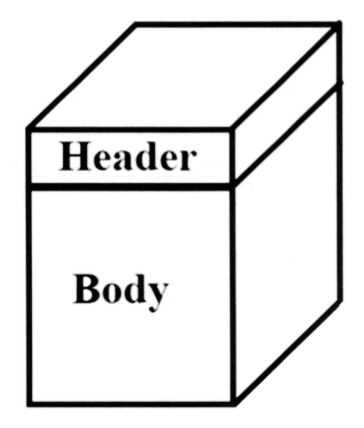

Blockchain and Governance Structure

Header

A Header contains all relevant information about the block that helps connects the current block with the previous block and verifies its authenticity before adding (Thomas et al., 2018). The fields in the block header provide a unique summary of the entire block. As shown in Figure 3 we can see header contains 5 parts mainly as hash_prev, timestamp, nonce, Merkel root, and payload. Mainly the size of header is 80 Byte and contains the metadata about the block that is the block data. But a transaction may be of 250 bytes and a block may contains more than 500 transactions also, hence to maintain the integrity and to detect a small change also we use Merkel tree and on basis of that hash root value the block gets the hash value.

Figure 3. Header of block

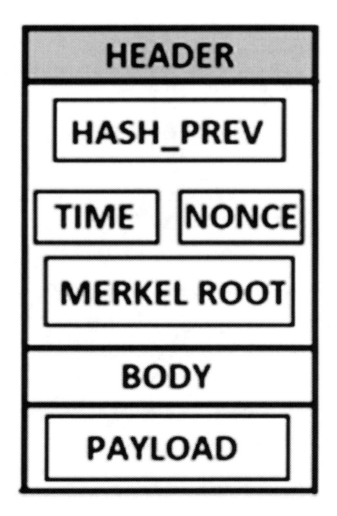

Fields Inside the Header:

PrevHash: Previous hash means hash value stored in the previous block. This helps to connect the current block to previous block and build the chain. This helps to verify the next block and hence the whole blockchain.

Timestamp: Is a time stamp that stores both the date and time of the block created and store it inside the block? It records the time when the block was created and stores it to be verified whenever needed. For example, 2018-02-24 21:27:29.

Nonce: It is an abbreviation for "number used once". It is a one-time value that is added to the hash when block is being created. It is a 32 bit number that helps in security purpose that miner use it for their hash calculation this nonce is guessed to calculate hash.

Merkel Tree: As we know each block may have multiple transactions and each transaction has its own hash, so to get a common hash, Merkel tree comes into play. It generates the common hash which is given to the block. Merkel Root consist of the common hash.

For Example:

Figure 4 shows the example in which different hash is taken form each and combined to make the final root hash (Garry, 2016). This final root hash is taken and is stored as the block hash and any change in any of the transaction changes this main hash as it is derived from these small hash only.

Figure 4. Merkel tree

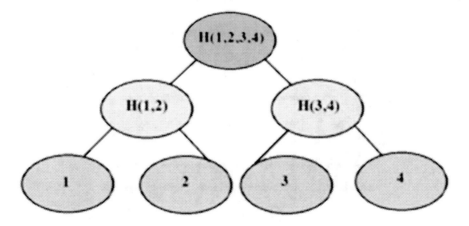

As now we know that to form chain of valid blocks we need hash value associated to each block when each block is assigned with hash then this given to previous block and is connected to next block which is shown in Figure 5.

Blockchain and Governance Structure

Figure 5. Two connected blocks

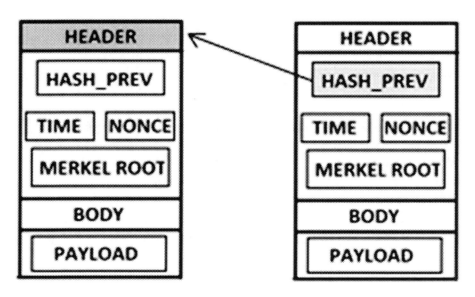

As shown in Figure 5 the chain in blockchain is created by connecting these hash values only. These hash values are fixed at the time of creation of block and cannot be changed. The change in data changes the hash value of that block and hence it does not match with the connecting block that contains the hash value of its previous block and hence chain is broken which gets disapproved by the other nodes and hence the change is rejected.

MAIN FEATURES OF BLOCKCHAIN

Let's examine the main characteristics of blockchain technology (Mosley et al., 2022):

1. **Decentralized:** It means that there is no single authority controlling the network and no one is in charge or can control the network.
2. **Peer-to-Peer Networks:** There are no middlemen hence direct transaction take place between the sender and receiver.
3. **Immutable:** Blocks once created cannot be altered and if gets changed the hash is also altered which comes into notice of the other miners and hence does not get validated.
4. **Tamper Proof:** Blockchain are tamper free means that there is less chance of attack, as there is no third-party involvement and a change in data changes the value of hash.
5. **Transparent:** Blockchain is said to be transparent as all the records or transactions or blocks are added, is visible to every node and is registered in the public ledger that anyone can see.
6. **Anonymous:** Blockchain is said to be anonymous as all the data is encrypted and secure and no one can see anything about the user who did the transaction or received it.

Blockchain Architecture

Hardware components including network connections, network computers, and data servers make up the first layer of the blockchain. Data servers house the data that is kept inside a blockchain, and computers connected to the blockchain network can exchange this data. As a result, a P2P network is developed in which each network node (or computer) independently verifies information.

The management of network-stored data takes place at the data layer, which is the second layer of this structure. Every block of information in this layer is related to the one before it. The genesis block is the sole one that is not connected to any other blocks (the first block in the network). A private key and a public key are used to protect each transaction that is written on these blocks. A public key is used to confirm who has signed for the transaction, whereas a private key is a digital signature that is only known to its owner and is used to authorise transactions. Simply said, for you to receive cryptocurrency, you must use your private key to validate the transaction and demonstrate your ownership to your blockchain wallet. If someone wants to send you cryptocurrency, they will need to know your public key.

Network layer makes it easier for nodes in the blockchain network to communicate with one another. Additionally, blocks are created and uploaded to the blockchain in this layer. This layer is also known as the propagation layer as a result. Consensus layer is responsible for all the agreements that are made within the network. This layer comes into the picture at the time when some decision is needed to be taken by most of the nodes in the network this may include block addition, generation, verifying transaction etc. this layer upholds all the rules and regulation and moreover counter actions when something goes wrong.

Application layer makes it easier to use the blockchain for many different things. This layer provides a user interface to run programs deployed by programmers and help users to interact with the network. Main functionalities are programs, scripts, API, Smart contracts and decentralised applications (DApps).

Blockchain and Governance Structure

Figure 6. Blockchain high-level architecture

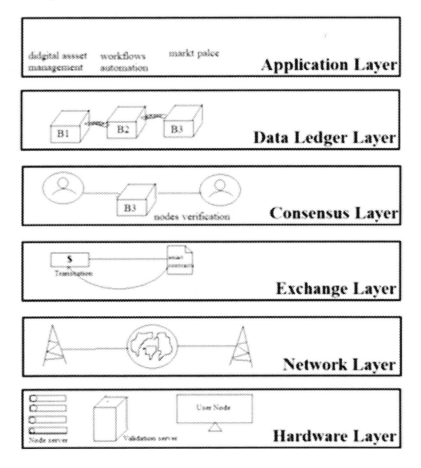

BLOCKCHAIN TYPES

Depending on the requirements of the application, different applications are using blockchain in different ways. Let's examine the many blockchain types.

1. Public Blockchain
2. Private Blockchain
3. Hybrid Blockchain
4. Consortium Blockchain

As shown in Figure 7, there are four types of blockchain. Each has different use case as per the requirements and has different restrictions. These are used in different scenarios and with different use cases. Public blockchain is also called universal blockchain is used in most popular cryptocurrency. So to be available to everyone, where, Ethereum private network is based on the private network and is totally isolated where only particular or specific people can access it.

Public Blockchain: There is no restriction in the network and also called Permission-less blockchain. Anyone having internet and computer can participate in the network and can also perform verifications of records (Artyom, 2020). Each node has equal rights. Nodes solve cryptographic equations and hence gets awards in form of cryptocurrency.

Private Blockchain: Also called as managed blockchain these are not as open as public blockchain and are permissioned, only selected nodes can participate in the network. With no equal rights to all nodes in the network. These blockchain are operated in the closed network. Rate of transaction is high, more balanced as there is controlling organization in private blockchain. For example ripple and Hyperledger.

Figure 7. Types of blockchain

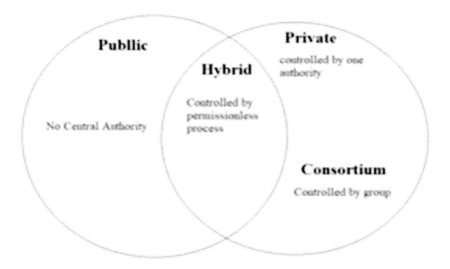

Hybrid Blockchain

It is the mixed content of private and public Blockchain. User access information via smart contracts, permission based and permissionless systems are used. For example IBM food trust developed to improve food supply chain. Its transparency depends on the owners set of rules.it is partially decentralized and hence privacy is less and there is lack of trust.

Consortium Blockchain

It is a creative approach that solves the needs of organization. In this more than one organization manages the network. Some part is public, and some is private. Hence governed by the group of organizations, not by one entity. They are more decentralized than private blockchain increase the level of security but at the same time requires the cooperation of multiple organization at one time. For example, CargoSmart developed to digitalize the shipping industry.

Components of Governance

Just like consensus between nodes is required to validate and secure the data, consensus is also required among network of stakeholders to change its law and processes. Because there is no centralized authority, hence governance mechanism relies upon making essential decision like exacting irreversible chain forks, change in token monetary policy, etc. (Zibin, 2018).

Hence in simple terms, groups or peoples who are authorised to see or apply rules that must be follow by all and updates required and must be implemented are key governance considerations for blockchain-based systems.

Blockchain helps in creating smart contracts i.e. is digital contracts. They are applicable in many fields such as IOT, HealthCare, Banks, Stocks which helps in reducing the problem of governance like errors (Human errors, typing Error, Calculation Error, etc.), Voting (Corruption or false Voting), privacy of data (Cyber-attacks or DDos attacks to steal data), Blockchain becomes very helpful here, use of Smart contracts.

Figure 8. Components of governance

As shown in Figure 8, there are three main components of governance involves participants, proposal process and design process.

Three types are:

Participants are users which join the network to conduct transaction with other network user. Some with special permission can see the transaction happening within the network also.
Proposal process determines what need to be changed, which can improve the efficiency of governance structure, this is a simple structure or a document that just suggest what can be done.
Design process involves the implementation of the suggested changes in the proposal and experimenting it over a virtual network, check its behaviour and verifies the document.

As depicted in Figure 9, four types of stakeholders in public blockchain are:

Core Operators

The group in charge of managing and maintaining the code is known as the core developers. In addition, they keep tabs on the deployment of the operational portion of the blockchain.

Node Operators

Node operator's runs the full part of the blockchain software and verifies the bugs and user friendliness of the software as a system tester and maintains a full copy of the ledger and provide storage and computation power for blockchain operations (Glaser et al., 2019). They are the helping hands of the blockchain and maintains the smooth working by providing the required resource.

Figure 9. Stakeholders in public blockchain

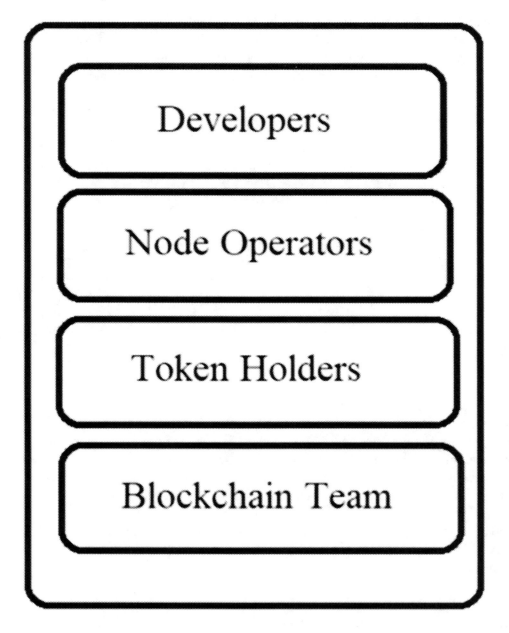

Token Holders

Token holders vote on major issues to ensure the project's development. They hold tokens for stability and decision making. They help in decision making in the blockchain and help in bringing up new updates.

Blockchain Team

Blockchain team collaborates with all other departments and helps in funding, negotiation, and communication, interaction with the ledger and other integrated system (Thomas et al., 2018).

Things that need to be governed in blockchain:

- Data definition
- Upgrades and bug fixes
- Replacing lost keys
- Inserting "correcting transactions"

BLOCKCHAIN USE CASES AND THEIR APPLICATIONS

Blockchain in Smart Cities: A smart city uses IOT, cloud computing and blockchain technology (Howell et al., 2019) making it easier to send data wirelessly and securely with the help of blockchain, moreover better e-services are there with no involvement of middle men.

Blockchain in Central Banking: Real-time fast settlements is the continuous daily process of bank .Each payments in central bank is recorded and the calculations are done at the end of the day, now blockchain comes into the picture and solve the issue by bringing faster speed in RTGS with full security and with real time updating of data and no confusion and recounting of money daily at the end.

Blockchain in Tracking Vaccinations: Recording vaccination data of public is very easy and can be accessed very quickly and with full security with no modification possible and less chance of false id.

Blockchain in Healthcare: Blockchain can make huge difference in this sector by storing the patient records, disease, hospitals referred, treatment received, etc., which will give provide the smooth treatment of the patient providing full knowledge to the doctors, this will also maintain the data integrity like reports or tests taken by the patient and their results in encrypted format.

Blockchain in Payroll Tax Collection: Tax collection is one of the major department where the corruption is at its peak and government at loss. Blockchain features like transparent nature and removal of third parties helps in computing tax and social security deductions and linking tax data with income transactions, smart contracts may accelerate the tax collecting process. Net wage and tax payments are automatically sent to the correct recipients using a blockchain-based system. Tax collection is made more efficient, quick, and secure through coordinated automation (Dylan et al., 2019).

BLOCKCHAIN GOVERNANCE ELEMENTS

Consensus

Consensus algorithm takes care of the transaction verification. Different blockchain implements different consensus algorithm. Popular ones are POW, POS and so on. POW refers to proof of work, which choose some network participants as Miners, to handle the task of verifying the new data and are rewarded with the new crypto. It is simply a software algorithm used by bitcoin to keep a check on upcoming new blocks. Miners compete and only fastest one to solve the puzzle gets the reward which helps in reducing the time to add new blocks. POW helps in overcoming the issues of double spending in bitcoin.

Example: Bitcoin, Dogecoin, Litecoin.

POS refers to proof of stake, here we get validators who checks transaction and verify the activity, votes on outcomes and maintain the records. As the word stake is used, validators stake some of their initial coins as stake and then are able to validate the transactions, in doing an improper validation or wrong validation causes penalty and hence loss of staked coins.

Incentives

This is applicable to miners that helps in smooth working of network. In simple terms, an award is given, who utilize his resource for verification and smooth working of the network. Incentives are one way of getting bitcoins without buying it as the rewards, one must need a high computational system and electricity to generate bitcoins. Incentives help miners to compete and race for solving the puzzle as soon as possible to be eligible for getting awards.

Information

No central authority is present in blockchain. Hence data is needed to be stored in the network with every nodes, every node gets a copy of the ledger and every time the node or block is added, each copy of the ledger gets updates and hence addition of new blocks takes time in verification and chaining.

Structure

In blockchain, structure changes to ensure that it fits the ever-changing dynamic nature of the network. Being a private or public or any other type, should be chosen well as per the requirements and its use. Example, for trading purpose and for transactional needs, bitcoin is best to be a public blockchain to give access to all users to participate and transact.

Integration of Blockchain in Governance

As we all know that with the help of blockchain we can do transaction more securely, fast and without intermediaries with an immutable records and anonymous nature, but all the time this not to be quantities of money but it can also be texts or certain rule-based agreements or paper work or digital signed contracts, or an agreement between two parties, government matters such as property rights, regimes, insurance contracts and even so-called "decentralized autonomous organizations" (DAOs) – organizations such as companies or government institutions that are managed by means of decentralized, blockchain-based interactions can be reorganized and managed through blockchain technologies.

By offering a decentralised and trustworthy method for organising and motivating individuals, blockchain technology has the ability to fundamentally alter how organisations are built and operated. The classic centralised and hierarchical structures of agency theory, such as the agent-principal paradox and agency costs, may be eliminated as a result. A principal engages an agent to carry out a task on their behalf under a classic agency arrangement. Yet, there could be a misalignment of interests and the possibility of agency costs if the agent has different priorities or goals than the principal. For instance, if a person knows that they will receive a fixed wage regardless of their performance, they may not be encouraged to participate.

The agent-principal problem may be solved by blockchain technology, which makes it possible to establish new decentralized organisations (DAOs). DAOs are organization that are governed by smart contracts, operate on a blockchain, and distribute decision-making authority among all of their members. This establishes a more democratic and open structure in which everyone has a voice in how the company functions. Participants in a DAO are encouraged to contribute to the organization's common objectives since their benefits are correlated with its performance. This reduces the possibility of agency costs by creating a more balanced incentive structure. A transparent and auditable approach for monitoring the behaviour of organisation participants is also provided by blockchain technology. This increases accountability and decreases the chance of fraud or crime.

In general, the emergence of blockchain-based organisations like DAOs has the potential to fundamentally alter how we perceive integrated approach and structure. Blockchain technology has the potential to mark the end of traditional centralised and hierarchical structures and create opportunities for new types of organisations that are more transparent, accountable, and productive by providing a decentralised and trustless system for coordinating and empowering participants.

BLOCKCHAIN GOVERNANCE STRATEGIES

On-Chain Governance

On-chain governance describes procedures that are carried out directly on the platform in accordance with the guidelines laid down in the blockchain's source code. (Beck Roman et. al., (2018)) Voting using the platform's governance token is one kind of on-chain governance. By directly voting on the chain, it is a decentralised type of governance that updates the blockchain. One must own the native currency of the blockchain in order to participate in its governance, which takes the form of voting on proof of stake blockchains. The quantity of coins in your possession determines how much influence you have.

Although on-chain governance has shown amazing potential in a short amount of time, it has been condemned as plutocratic since the quantity of coins you own decides how much influence you have in voting (Zibin et al., 2018). In on-chain governance, the process of participation and decision-making is directly inscribed in the supporting infrastructure. When 95% of the blocks indicate support for the upgrade, the modifications are immediately implemented. Miners employ on-chain mechanisms to support the proposed upgrades.

On-chain governance's enforcement mechanism is its main strength; if a decision is reached, it is carried out by adhering to the code's internal rules (Zwitter et al., 2020). Hard forks are avoided, and chain split hazards are reduced. This mechanism's drawback is that it automates winner-takes-all principles. Similar to majoritarian democracy, a less-developed type of democracy, the majority that wins dictates how the whole system operates. It has helped in the rise of DAO decentralized autonomous organization. DAO is a community-run platform where rules enforced are agreed upon by the user.

Consensus: Voting is done directly via the protocol of on chain governance where decisions are made directly on the distributed ledger and blockchain improvements are implemented.
Incentive: To level it up, there is a shift in control from miners to developers and subsequently to users.
Information: It is transparent and trust less as everyone can see the code and the how consensus is established, and decision are made.
Governing Structure: Completely decentralized. Example is EOS.

Off-Chain Governance

Off-chain governance includes all governance-related operations, both formal and often informal, that take place away from the platform (Fridgen et al., 2018). Online forums, conferences, and other events are examples of off-chain conversation. It alludes to the endogenous and exogenous norms and procedures of protocol-related discussions that support the functioning and advancement of blockchain systems. There is no code that ties these groups to precise actions. Holding mining power does not give equivalent share of the governance rights. Bitcoin uses BIP's and Ethereum uses EIP's. It is a more centralized because of the dependence on financial and technical knowledge to take part in network decision.

Consensus: In off chain consensus is set by the community leaders. In bitcoin, miners help in validating and putting blocks in the chain.
Incentive: In Bitcoin, miners get the rewards and the developers get ability to make changes to the network.
Information: Transparency is higher than on-chain.
Governing Structure: Typically centralized.

Moreover, the off chain is more private and secure, we can also say that it is more anonymous too.
For example, if person A sends 20 bitcoin to person B, then in On chain it will show that A -> B (20 coins) but in Off chain this does not happen it will show that something was sent from person A to person B but the actual numbers are not revealed in public and hence making it more private and more secured.

Blockchain and Governance Structure

Table 1. Key difference between on-chain and off-chain governance

	On-Chain Governance	**Off-Chain Governance**
Definition	Governance decisions are made through changes to the blockchain itself	Governance decisions are made through a separate, centralized process outside the blockchain
Decision-making process	Decisions are made through on-chain voting by token holders	Decisions are made through a centralized authority, such as a board of directors or a government agency
Speed	On-chain governance decisions can be made quickly, as there is no need for an external decision-making process	Off-chain governance decisions may take longer to make, as they often require a more complex decision-making process involving multiple stakeholders
Transparency	On-chain governance decisions are transparent, as they are recorded on the blockchain and can be audited by anyone	Off-chain governance decisions may be less transparent, as the decision-making process may be less visible to external stakeholders
Security	On-chain governance is more secure, as decisions are recorded on the blockchain and cannot be altered without consensus from the network	Off-chain governance may be less secure, as decisions may be vulnerable to attack or manipulation by external parties
Flexibility	On-chain governance can be more flexible, as changes to the blockchain can be made quickly and easily	Off-chain governance may be less flexible, as changes may require a more complex decision-making process and may be subject to regulatory constraints.

Perspective of Adoption of Blockchain in the Near Future

Soon, it's anticipated that public sector adoption of blockchain technology will increase. This is since blockchain has the ability to raise citizen trust in their government while also enhancing transparency, security, and efficiency in government operations.

In the management of public records and identities, blockchain is anticipated to have a big impact. Governments can increase the security and accuracy of citizen identity records by utilising blockchain-based identity systems, lowering the risk of fraud and identity theft. The management of public finances is another area where blockchain is expected to be used in the public sector. Blockchain can make financial transactions more transparent and efficient, lowering the risk of corruption and boosting public confidence in the government. Finally, blockchain can help offer public services like healthcare and education more effectively. Blockchain can increase the effectiveness and accessibility of public services by facilitating the secure and effective flow of data between government organisations and service providers.

However, there are obstacles to blockchain adoption in the public sector as well, including regulatory concerns, privacy difficulties, and the requirement for interoperability between various blockchain networks. Yet, as governments all over the world continue to investigate the potential advantages of blockchain technology, it is anticipated that in the near future, we will see an increase in the adoption of blockchain-based solutions in the public sector.

CONCLUSION

Blockchain is new in this market but has the potential to lead the future. Blockchain had been implemented as bitcoin and can be used wherever transaction is included but now blockchain is in new stage having limitations and challenges that must be governed and needs updates. After implementing, next area of research is defining what good governance is in blockchain. Good governance can highlight different quality properties such as degree of transparency, efficiency, and balance of power. On other hand being a new technology, blockchain has multiple challenges and problems i.e., Scalability, privacy leakage, self-mining which needs to be solved for its further implementation in various sector which can create a probable impact on whole economics. Blockchain technology has the potential to be applied to a wide range of fields, but the specific applications will depend on the needs and requirements of each industry. Blockchain technology may be used in supply chain management to monitor the flow of products and services from manufacturing to consumption with the use of IOT in background, sensors and devices like RFID for tracking. Blockchain technology may also be utilised in the healthcare industry to securely store and manage patient data. In addition to enabling quicker and more accurate diagnosis and treatments, this can assist to increase patient privacy and lower the danger of data breaches. Hence Blockchain can be used some or the other way in every field as it comes with the lots of advantages over the traditional system.

REFERENCES

Andoni, M., Robu, V., Flynn, D., Abram, S., Geach, D., Jenkins, D., McCallum, P., & Peacock, A. (2019). Blockchain technology in the energy sector: A systematic review of challenges and opportunities. *Renewable & Sustainable Energy Reviews*, *100*, 143–174. doi:10.1016/j.rser.2018.10.014

AtzoriM. (2017). Blockchain governance and the role of trust service providers: The TrustedChain® network. doi:10.2139/ssrn.2972837

Beck, R., Müller-Bloch, C., & King, J. L. (2018). Governance in the blockchain economy: A framework and research agenda. *Journal of the Association for Information Systems*, *19*(10), 1. doi:10.17705/1jais.00518

Calcaterra, C. (2018). On-chain governance of decentralized autonomous organizations: Blockchain organization using Semada. Available at SSRN 3188374.

Chaudhry, N., & Yousaf, M. M. (2018). Consensus algorithms in blockchain: comparative analysis, challenges and opportunities. In *2018 12th International Conference on Open Source Systems and Technologies (ICOSST)* (pp. 54-63). IEEE. 10.1109/ICOSST.2018.8632190

De Filippi, P., & McMullen, G. (2018). *Governance of blockchain systems: Governance of and by Distributed Infrastructure* [PhD diss.]. Blockchain Research Institute and COALA.

Eberhardt, J., & Heiss, J. (2018). Off-chaining models and approaches to off-chain computations. *Proceedings of the 2nd Workshop on Scalable and Resilient Infrastructures for Distributed Ledgers*, 7-12. 10.1145/3284764.3284766

Efanov, D., & Roschin, P. (2018). The all-pervasiveness of the blockchain technology. *Procedia Computer Science, 123*, 116–121. doi:10.1016/j.procs.2018.01.019

Francati, D., Ateniese, G., Faye, A., Milazzo, A. M., Perillo, A. M., Schiatti, L., & Giordano, G. (2021). Audita: A blockchain-based auditing framework for off-chain storage. *Proceedings of the Ninth International Workshop on Security in Blockchain and Cloud Computing*, 5-10. 10.1145/3457977.3460293

Fridgen, G., Lockl, J., Radszuwill, S., Rieger, A., Schweizer, A., & Urbach, N. (2018). A Solution in Search of a Problem: A Method for the Development of Blockchain Use Cases. AMCIS, 1(1), 1-11.

Gabison, G. (2016). Policy considerations for the blockchain technology public and private applications. *SMU Sci. & Tech. L. Rev., 19*, 327.

Glaser, F., Hawlitschek, F., & Notheisen, B. (2019). *Blockchain as a Platform. InBusiness transformation through Blockchain*. Palgrave Macmillan.

Hardwick, F. S., Akram, R. N., & Markantonakis, K. (2018). Fair and transparent blockchain based tendering framework-a step towards open governance. In *2018 17th IEEE International Conference On Trust, Security And Privacy In Computing And Communications/12th IEEE International Conference On Big Data Science And Engineering (TrustCom/BigDataSE)* (pp. 1342-1347). IEEE. 10.1109/TrustCom/BigDataSE.2018.00185

Henderson, R. M., & Clark, K. B. (1990). Architectural innovation: The reconfiguration of existing product technologies and the failure of established firms. *Administrative Science Quarterly, 35*(1), 9–30. doi:10.2307/2393549

Hepp, Sharinghousen, Ehret, Schoenhals, & Gipp. (2018). On-chain vs. off-chain storage for supply-and blockchain integration. *IT-Information Technology, 60*(5-6), 283-291.

Howell, Potgieter, & Sadowski. (2019). *Governance of blockchain and distributed ledger technology projects*. Available at SSRN 3365519.

Jairam, S., Gordijn, J., Isaac da Silva, T., Kaya, F., & Makkes, M. (2021). A decentralized fair governance model for permissionless blockchain systems. *Proceedings of the International Workshop on Value Modelling and Business Ontologies*, 4-5.

Kosmarski, A. (2020). Blockchain adoption in academia: Promises and challenges. *Journal of Open Innovation, 6*(4), 117. doi:10.3390/joitmc6040117

Liu, Y., Lu, Q., Zhu, L., Paik, H. Y., & Staples, M. (2022). A systematic literature review on blockchain governance. *Journal of Systems and Software*, 111576.

MosleyL.PhamH.GuoX.BansalY.HareE.AntonyN. (2022). Towards a systematic understanding of blockchain governance in proposal voting: A dash case study. *Blockchain: Research and Applications, 100085*.

Narayanan, A., & Clark, J. (2017). Bitcoin's academic pedigree. *Communications of the ACM, 60*(12), 36–45. doi:10.1145/3132259

Priyadarshini, I. (2019). Introduction to blockchain technology. *Cyber security in parallel and distributed computing: Concepts, techniques, applications and case studies*, 91-107.

Tasca, P., & Tessone, C. J. (2017). *Taxonomy of blockchain technologies. Principles of identification and classification.* arXiv preprint arXiv:1708.04872.

Treleaven, P., Brown, R. G., & Yang, D. (2017). Blockchain technology in finance. *Computer, 50*(9), 14–17. doi:10.1109/MC.2017.3571047

van Pelt, R., Jansen, S., Baars, D., & Overbeek, S. (2021). Defining blockchain governance: A framework for analysis and comparison. *Information Systems Management, 38*(1), 21–41. doi:10.1080/10580530.2020.1720046

Werbach, K. (2018). Trust, but verify: Why the blockchain needs the law. *Berkeley Technology Law Journal, 33*(2), 487–550.

Yaga, D., Mell, P., Roby, N., & Scarfone, K. (2019). *Blockchain technology overview.* arXiv preprint arXiv:1906.11078.

Yli-Huumo, J., Ko, D., Choi, S., Park, S., & Smolander, K. (2016). Where is current research on blockchain technology? A systematic review. *PLoS One, 11*(10), e0163477. doi:10.1371/journal.pone.0163477 PMID:27695049

Zheng, Z., Xie, S., Dai, H.-N., Chen, X., & Wang, H. (2018). Blockchain challenges and opportunities: A survey. *International Journal of Web and Grid Services, 14*(4), 352–375. doi:10.1504/IJWGS.2018.095647

Zwitter, A., & Hazenberg, J. (2020). Decentralized network governance: Blockchain technology and the future of regulation. *Frontiers in Blockchain, 3*, 12. doi:10.3389/fbloc.2020.00012

Section 3
Security and Blockchain Technology

Chapter 5
Blockchain-Based Secure Transactions

Kawsalya M.
Hindusthan College of Arts and Science, India

Senthil Kumar A. V.
Hindusthan College of Arts and Sciences, India

Akash V.
Hindusthan College of Arts and Science, India

M. Villanueva Lolit
Xavier University, Philippines

Shadi Rasheed Masadeh
Isra University, Jordan

Anamika Rawat
SAGE University, India

ABSTRACT

Traditional transactions have several issues, like physical cash, for instance, boarding fake bank notes and also building stock to use money significantly less complex. In this digital marketing world, hackers are using many ways and techniques to scam money. The three most common online transaction frauds in India are scam using QR codes, UPI frauds, remote access/screen sharing frauds. Protection and privacy are the main anticipated features in the field of online transactions, which can be fulfilled by blockchain technology. This proposal is crucial as it is the first attempt to apply blockchain technology to payment services. In the proposed system, due to high level of fraud, blockchain technology is used. Hackers attack one block and change their address, and hence, transaction is blocked and amount will also be refunded using blockchain approach hashing algorithms. The main steps of blockchain used in the proposed system are transaction data, changing blocks with a hash, and creating signature (hash) using cryptographic hash function.

DOI: 10.4018/978-1-6684-7455-6.ch005

INTRODUCTION

Nowadays financial transactions are more vulnerable to hackers or fraudulent attackers through bank cards and mobile banking apps. More alertness is needed for online transaction and there is also a compulsory need for cyber security .in this emerging digital technology world each organization has cyber threat and security issues without a good cyber security team. India ranks third place in the top ten most targeted countries by cyber attackers. The Methods of protecting data networks and business system from unauthorized accessing of data and theft with the help of various cyber security tools is cyber security. The Federal Bureau of invest how given a warning to people about the threat of technical support scams and how they criminals attack by pretending themselves as support staff from computer or software companies and trick into pc and get the access to bank accounts. The scammers are posing as a service representative of software technology tech professionals or computer repair service by phishing email or phone.

Blockchain Technology

Block chain also called as a distributed ledger, is a trustless, decentralized tamper proof and distributed traceable database management system used by multiple participants and also maintaining transaction of bitcoin ledger. It consists of a growing list of records called Blocks and these blocks are securely linked together using cryptography system. Each one of the blocks contains a hash (sigh) of the previous block, timestamp, and transaction data.

The time stamp proves that the transaction data existed when each block was created. Each block created has information about the previous block which in term form chain like linked list in data structure, with additional block linking to the one before it. Hench Block chain transaction is irreversible. Once recorded data in the block cannot be retroactively altered without change in all subsequent blocks. It is a peer-to-peer computer network. Nodes in the block chain keep replicas of the blocks containing the ordered set of modifying state of transaction and all nodes will agree with their transaction and order. Though block chain records are alterable, block chain forks are possible sometime, hence they are considered secure by design and an example of a distributed computing system. It was first developed for the process of bit coin crypto currency.

The more important platforms used in the blockchain are.

- Avalanche block chain platform: The fastest smart platform reviewed for the development of the new time to-finality platform.
- Cardanol block chain platform: The more efficient and low cost.
- Chain analysis block chain platform: Analyzed each block with transparency.
- Ethereum block chain platform: The best platform in the block chain
- Hyperledger Fabric block chain platform: Low cost and transparency.
- Hyperledger sawtooth block chain platform:
- IBM blockchain block chain platform: Used for IBM network.

Components of Blockchain Architecture

- **Node:** Each node will contain an independent copy of the entire Block chai ledger. Node is a computer in a block chain system.
- **Trasaction:** A data record verified by block chain system, and it also serves as an immutable conformation of financial transaction authenticity or its contract.
- **BLOCK:** It is a sealed data content that contain
  - A set of time stamp transactions.
  - A hash code which identifies the block.
  - A hash code from previous block of sequence.
- **Chains:** It is an ordered sequence of a block.
- **Miners:** A validating node of block before adding to the block structure.
- **Consensus:** It is a protocol which defines a set of rules and agreement that performs a block chain system.

A blockchain network will not work with a centralized server and transactions made are verified by the decentralized nodes and are stored in blocks using timestamp. And the size limit will vary from block to block. The blocks are linked in chronological order which contain cryptographic hash of previous block and structural block.

Explanation of Blockchain Architecture:

In a blockchain transaction each transaction is authenticated and authenticated by an open financial ledger or record. It is a decentralized design network of millions of networks called nodes which are distributed.

Figure 1. Centralized network

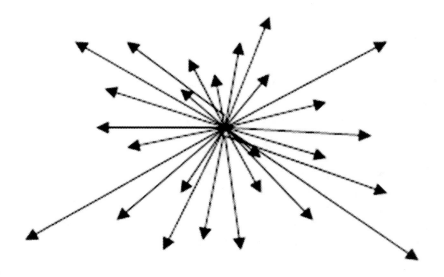

In distributed database architecture a group of nodes form a network in which each node performs the work of the administrator. It supports a growing list of blocks where records are stored and each block will maintain a timestamp and a previous block link.

Figure 2. Decentralized network

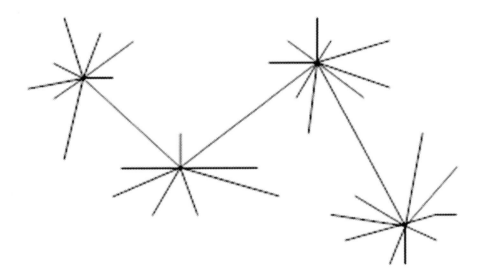

In blockchain there is no centralized node connection hence the possibility of hacking in less or not possible.

Types of Blockchain Architecture

- Public Blockchain architecture
- Private blockchain architecture
- Consortium blockchain architecture
- Hybrid blockchain architecture

Public Blockchain Architecture:

A Public blockchain algorithm will use appropriate protocol and basis of proof of work consensus algorithm. It will make transactions possible with the entire network of blockchain which allow transaction of anonymous or pseudonymous. Public blockchain is a open source and can detain new blocks to check transaction code on network. Examples of block chain architecture are Ethereum, Litecoin and Bitcoin.

Private Blockchain Architecture

For increasing the overall benefit and efficiency, Organization built their own private block architecture which will allow only a certain group of people of participant called the private blockchain architecture. It uses proof-of stake and byzantine fault tolerance consensus algorithm to achieve high reliability. Using smart contract layer a private blockchain architecture decouples the main blockchain protocol.

Consortium Blockchain Architecture

A Consortium or public-permission block chain architecture is domain any one can connect and accesses blockchain but can connect with a node only with the permission of the participant. It's built by organization for increasing the trustworthy transaction like proof-of stake and byzantine fault algorithms.

Hybrid Blockchain Architecture

Hybrid blockchain is developed by complaining about both public blockchain and private blockchain. They will contain both keys, likewise one has a public permission-less system, and another has a private permission-based system.

Key Characteristics of Blockchain Architecture

Some build in characteristics of block chain architecture is:

- **Cryptography:** Transactions are verified trustworthy because of cryptography and complex computational methods.
- **Immutability:** In blockchain system record in the blocks cannot be altered or deleted.
- **Decentralization:** In Centralized system consensus algorithm is used but in block chain system every member in the structure can assess decentralized database.
- **Transparency:** Takes enormous computing power to completely rewrite block network system.
- **Anonymity**: Anonymity of user in public block chain is preserved because Every member of block chain system create address not as User ID.
- **Provenance:** There is a possibility of tracing the origin of each network in block chain ledger.

Online Transaction

Online Transaction Is the Process of Transaction in Business conducted through internet also called as cash less transaction. Online Transaction process (OLTP) transfer money in electronic fund transfer mode and it's also secure and password protected. The three steps of online transaction are registering, placing an order, and payment.

The different types of online transactions are:

- NEFT-National Electronic fund transfer.
- RTGS-real time gross settlement.
- ECS-electronic clearing system.

- IMPS-immediate payment processing.

OLTP processing system responds immediately to user requests. An ATM (Automated Teller Machine) of a bank is a commercial transaction processing application. It reduced paperwork and faster and more accurate forecasts for government and revenue processing. In database management it is having high level of throughput and update intensive. The key goals of OLTP Applications are availability scalability, speed, concurrency, and recoverability. The elements which are crucial for the performance of OLTP are Roll back segment, cluster, discrete transaction, block size, buffer cache size, Dynamic allocation, and Transaction processing. The transaction process monitoring is used for coordinating services and like an operating system coordinates high level of granularity and spam multiple computing devices.

The key Components of Online Transaction

The key components of online transactions are:

- **Payment Process:** Manages the card transaction by transmitting information from customer's credit/debit card to bank of merchant and customer's bank. Card payment deals with the issues like card limit, validity, security, and payment process is an intermediate between the bank and the merchant.
- **Payment Gateway:** An online version of a point-of-scale device, which connects the website and the payment processor and merchant account with credit/debit card issuers. It handles the technical side of transaction and ensures customer receives the payment.
- **Merchant Account:** Specific type of bank account that enables business to accept online payment. There will not be any direct access between customer and merchant fund transfer.

Nowadays online transaction frauds and hackers are increasing which creates great impact in customers and merchant. These fraudulent transactions are detected by using block chain transaction system.

LITERATURE REVIEW

Fraud detections for online business: a perspective from blockchain technology by Yuanfeng Cai and Dan Zhu has been added to the developed system. Here the method of redesigning the reputation system by using opportunistic blockchain technology is used. The blockchain technology is very effective in preventing loan application information which is very fraudulent based information and preventing from whitewashing attack, but it will not that effective in ballot-stuffing in Sybil attack, constant attack, and camouflage attack. the whitewashing attack they are using injecting rater to identify the target entity for certain period. A content driven and user driven proactive system is also introduced in this proposed system (Yan et al., 2022).

A review on blockchain technology and blockchain projects foresting open science has been added to the developing system. Here, Leible et al. (2019) presented about the open science technology and block chain interaction with the foresting open science technology. They explained that in case of single element block technology will be void but as bulk data elements are decentralization, immutability, transparency, and cryptographic hashing are unique and avoiding the double-spending problem. Here the characteristics of block technology are compared with the need of open science infrastructure. And build a matrix which shows the important block content to provide trust worthy environment a trail of research and no censorship (Liu et al., 2022).

A systematic review of blockchain by Xu, Chen, and Kou (2019) has been added to the proposed system. They presented the issues related to commercial application of block chain are critical for both academic and social practice. For these issues they are promising several research directions. They are (a) Understanding the mechanism through which block chain influences corporate and market efficiency. (b)Potential research direction privacy protection and security issues. (c) How to regulate cryptocurrency market and how to manage digital currencies. (d) How to deeply integrate block chain technology and fintech. (e) Cross- chain technology, if each industry has its own block chain system, it's a key to achieving the internet of value. So business can considerably get benefit by using block chain technology and this methods are developed in their proposed system (Fernandez et al., 2022).

Blockchain-Based Sharing Services: What blockchain technology can contribute to smart cities by Sun, Yan, and Zhang (2016) has been added to developing system. Here they are using the triangular framework of service-oriented technology and summarize the features of the management and computing of blockchain. It mainly deals with relationships involving people and sharing services relates to the relationship involving technology. This paper proposes a three conceptual framework dimensions that is human, technology and organization, and exploring a set of factor that will make a smart city by sharing economy perspective (Yang et al., 2022).

A Blockchain Abnormal Behavior Awareness Methods: A survey article by Yan et al. (2022) has been added to the proposed system. They explained about the abnormal behavior awareness methods of the existing public blockchain and consortium blockchain and also analyses the existing data set of mainstream security. Transaction behavior awareness, contract behavior awareness and account behavior access are the 3 types of awareness behavior used in public behavior analysis. Increasing the abnormal cues and cognition on-chain behavior for accurate subsequent supervised learning method and rule based learning method for perseverance behavior techniques is used in their proposed system(LingyunLi,et al,2022).

A machine learning and blockchain based efficient fraud detection mechanism by Tehreemashfaq, Rabiya Khalid, Adamusaniyahaya, Sherazaslam, Ahmed Taher Azar, Safa Alsafari, Ibrahim A. Hameed has been implemented in the proposed system. Here the proposed system uses Data-balancing techniques, machine learning and processing techniques. For data classification machine learning, Boost, random forest techniques are used, and data are divided into training data set and a test data set to identify data as fraudulent or non-fraudulent data. Smart contract is written in which machine learning and blockchain techniques deployed and used to detect fraud transaction. Two attackers' models are proposed and blockchain model initiate transaction and machine learning will classify data as malicious and non-malware data or legitimate. For checking the nature of data for legitimacy consensus algorithm and new solutions using supervised machine learning technique to eliminate vulnerabilities in existing system is used (Xiao et al., 2022).

Fraud Detection: A Review on Blockchain by Anuska Rakshit, Shriya Kumar, Ramanathan L. has been added to the proposed system. Here they are deploying the blockchain work-History prevention technique and checking whether blockchain is immune to malicious attacks. This proposed system Analysis video fraud detection by a workable prototype of a rudimentary block chain constructed as a part of analysis, and to avoid insurance fraud by vehicle sector of blockchain design, Bitcoin fraud detection by global and outliner based multifaceted approach, counterfeit detection of documents by issuing certificate in the form of paper by organization which in turn altered by modern technology, detecting fraud and fake transaction using influence of block code (Rakshit et al., 2022).

A summary of research on blockchain in the field of intellectual property by Juyang Wang, Shenling Wang, Jungi Guo, Yanchang Du, Shochi Cheng has been used in the proposed system. Here using 4 main concepts which are blockchain and intellectual property conformation, blockchain and intellectual property transaction, blockchain and intellectual property protection and blockchain and intellectual property incentive mechanism. Comparing both the blockchain and intellectual part of transaction in academicresearch, medical and financial research and security mechanism (Tehreemashfaq et al., 2022).

Threats, attacks and defenses to federated learning: issues, taxonomy and perspectives by Pengurui Liu, Xiangrui Xu, Wei Wang has been added to the proposed system. Here the empirical attacks on federated learning by executing them with numerous attack surface and the attacks will get private information and cause system full fail. The three processing phases in the Federated learning data and beheavior auditing phase,training phase and predicting phase will survey threats, attacks, and defenses to federated learning throughout the process. Mainly risk factors are focused on training phase (Leible et al., 2019).

Abstract security patterns and the design of secure system by Edurdo B. Fernandez, Nobukazu Yoshioka, Hironori Washizaki, Joseph Yoder has been added in the developing system. In this proposed system security pattern and security solution frames are deployed. The Abstract Security Patterns (ASP) and abstract security patterns hierarchies while the relationship between ASP-Based hierarchies and security solution frame (SSFs) explained in the secure conceptual model. Deriving concrete pattern from ASPs starting with Formation of ASP, Evaluation of effectiveness. The main entity in abstract security pattern are identity, proof of identity, authentication, proof of authentication, authentication information and credential based authentication and password based authentication (Xu et al., 2019).

A flexible approach for cyber threat hunting based on kernel audit records by Fendyu Yang, Yanni Han, Ying Ding, Qian Tan, Zhen Xu has added in the proposed system. Here the cyber threat hunting technique and threat intelligence computing and ontology model and threat modal are employed in the proposed system. It defined a automated threat assessment system for the development of the system log by a threat intellectual ontology and augmented cyber defensive capability. The threat hunting technique that generate cyber key and compressed minimum dependence graph by a naval modeling approach (Juyangwang et al., 2019).

Hash based signature revisited by Lingyan Li, Xianhui, Kunpeng Wang has been added to the proposed system. Here the digital signature based on public-key cryptosystem for online transaction and RSA designed with the difficulty assumption of factoring large integer database. In Hash-based signature review they are classifying the three based public key authentication schemes and also few times and one-time signatures for limited and unlimited number of state full and stateless schemes (Verma et al., 2019).

The differential fault analysis on block cipher few by Haiyan Xiao, Lifang Wang and Jinyong Chang has been taken for the proposed system. Here the Feather Weight cipher (light weight block ciper) of 64-bit ciphertext is used in the proposed system. The encryption algorithm and key schedule algorithm are emended in the proposed algorithm. DFA key algorithms are mainly prosed to detect fraud in blocks of the correct ciphertext and master secrete key (Morgen, 2017).

Property Fraud Detection and Prevention Using Blockchain system by Varid Verma, Swati Priya, Somya Mishra, Rojalina Priyadarshini, Rachita Misra has been added in the proposed system. Here in the proposed system, they detailed explain about the Bitcoin. For studying the process of the blockchain architecture bitcoin knowledge is very used. And mainly blockchain structure in this proposed system is used to speed up transaction and decrease third party control over any transaction of digital currencies. The information stored is dependent on the types of blockchain used and a chain of blocks held for the digital signature information. The current block digital signature will detect the next block digital signature and the chain will continue likewise in the linked data structure. Fastest evolving technology that is replacing the old traditional transaction management (Jianjunsun et al., 2016).

Reinforcing the links of the blockchain by morgen peck has been added in the proposed system. Here unique features of the standard database system built in applications are used for the proposed architecture. Without single-entity phrases functionally stored data and programs on blockchain will be sate with adding new entity. the description of the idealized blockchain has the features of distributed verification-programs and data reside in different or multiple location, resilience- diversity of participants and has a full copy of running blockchain application, flexibility- participant information composition sifting, and collaboration with competitors (Cai & Zhu, 2016).

EXISTING SYSTEM

In the existing system, a normal transaction pattern system is used called Online Transactional Pattern (OLTP) is the one where the basic electronic and online payment is used out which will be done with multi feature patterns. The existing system will be used with different formulation where the data storage proposed on normal transactional mean modulations. The transaction process will be carried out on the advent on the internet where the data will be sending through a protocol change out. Mostly the online transaction will be the one with the database storage system which there will be a deletion, updating, retrieval function where a complete authentication mechanism can be done. Mostly the online transaction only focuses on the different authentication system but not the server-side efficiency. The security is only given with the online focusing on different authentication levels. The two levels of the dependent seek with bearer identity where the maintaining evident holds on another identity. Concurrent database back up taking up in the existing system where the phases of the storage will be in a huge, big data storage system is done. The maintaining up the modular functionality which will be given with separate hard and fraudulent transaction verification.

Figure 3. Shows the existing system of the online payment approach

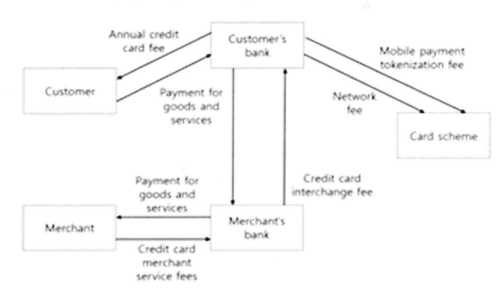

Usually in the normal bank payments system a merchant bank tokenization system is used. The tokenization makes a concentration over the multiple accesses of the card scheme and the merchant interaction system. The different way of interaction with the customer and the customer bank on merchant access is the secured thing added here in the existing approach over the goods and the services made with the bank side.

Challenges in the Existing System

- **Concurrency:** OLTP systems have the potential to have extremely huge user bases, with many users attempting to access the same data concurrently. All these users trying to read from or write to the system simultaneously must be supported by the system. A database system's concurrency controls ensure that two users who are simultaneously accessing the same data cannot alter it and that one user must wait until the other has finished processing before changing it.
- **Scale:** No matter how many users are attempting to access the system, OLTP systems must be able to scale up and down rapidly to handle the transaction volume in real time and complete transactions simultaneously.
- **Availability:** An OLTP system must be accessible and prepared to always take transactions. The failure of a transaction may result in financial loss or have legal repercussions. The system must be accessible around-the-clock since transactions can be carried out at any time and from anywhere in the world.
- **High Throughput and Quick Response Times:** OLTP systems need millisecond or even faster reaction times to fulfil rising consumer expectations and keep business users active.
- **Reliability:** OLTP systems often read and work with little, extremely selective quantities of data. It is essential that the data in the database is accurate and trustworthy at all times for the users and applications accessing that data.

- **Data Security:** Is essential because these systems handle extremely sensitive client transaction data. Any breach might cost the business a lot of money.
- **Recovery:** OLTP systems must be capable of returning to normal operation in the event of a hardware or software failure.

Disadvantages of Existing System

- Server-Side Security is not enhanced.
- Identification of authentic access is not made.
- Hackers or attackers inside the server can be noted easily.

PROPOSED SYSTEM

In the proposed system transaction of information secularly using blockchain is achieved. the more important key components of block chain used in the proposed system are distributed ledger technology which have accesses of all networks, immutable records where the block information are stored and the smart contract which is the agreement of organizations. The step-by-step method for building the blockchain design is:

Designing Blockchain solution by:

- **Case Making:** Three basic key steps are required for making cases they are opportunistic assessment, strategic assessment, readiness assessment.
- **Functional Requirement Definition:** Specific functional and performance requirements are defined in this system for blockchain ecosystem and governance. the functional data decentralization storage, application execution, represent digital and immune data of business assets.
- **Non-Functional Requirement Definition:** The nonfunctional requirements are customer satisfaction, privacy, performance, reliability, Usability, maintainability, and security.
- **Platform Selection/Platform Deep-Drive:** In this process block key will drive into the key platforms such us Hyperledger, Ethereum.
- **Solution Implementation:** In this designing process the functional and nonfunctional requirements of the blockchain are assessed and then the platform evaluation framework and vendor assessment framework are implemented.

Security Using Blockchain

Security in blockchain networks can be achieved only by the high-level infrastructure establishing. When a private blockchain is taken then the inheritance properties of the blockchain and their vulnerabilities are defined by:

- **Prevent Anyone:** It will prevent accessing sensitive information for even the root users and transaction of amount in blockchain server storage administrators.
- **Deny Illicit Attack:** Prevent the data or application from the hacking of the illicit attack.

Blockchain-Based Secure Transactions

- **Carefully Guard Encryption Keys:** Guarding the encryption keys by using misappropriated highest standard guard keys.

Transaction of Data in Blockchain

In the proposed system the transaction of block information is given after the transaction request. First the request for the transaction is given then the blocks are created for each respective block. Then the next process will be transaction of information to each and every block with the node information. Then the nodes will receive awards for the proof of work network and the new nodes will be added to the existing block then the transaction is completed. The proof of network algorithm will provide security for the transferred information.

Figure 4. Transaction of amount in blockchain server storage

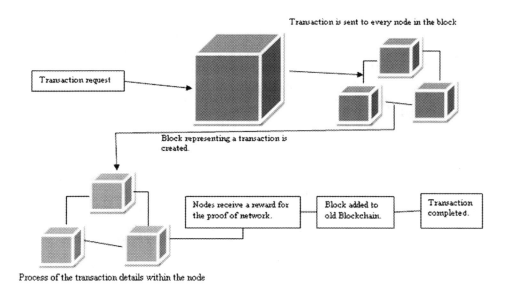

Fraud Detection in the Proposed System

The Fraud detection using the blockchain architecture has developed a specific framework for fraud detection. The five main framework layers are.

- **Central Authority in General:** For verifying documents and building the terms of the smart contract.
- **Federal Administrator:** Governing overall block process.
- **The Administrator in General:** Review and transmit the block data from one block to another.
- **Additional and Sub-Departments:** Verifying each node for leakages of information and cyber security details in depth.

- **Counterfeit Detection of the Documents:** Central Authority will develop the smart contracts for verification, the counterfeit detector detects the loopholes in these contracts and also amend the other entities for the smart contract and publish it.

The smart contract is very immutable to the other organization and security and transparency of the proposed system is increased. Generation of digital signature certificates will contain more precise information for the contract or schemes.

Preventing Fraud in Finance

The factors that complicate the online transaction mainly are time requirement, currency denomination differences, settlement issues, collateral need, third party interference and attackers.

But by using blockchain the technique of sharing information in real time, and the ledgers are updated or changed only when the organization agrees. The process with human interaction and multiple processing are the main target of the attackers hence in this the information's are prevented from fraudsters by the direction of the counter fraud management. In this time, cost, and the opportunities to commit fraud are reduced. Bank to bank financial transactions and mobile banking are prevented using the authority key management. The blockchain system is used by the Latin American stock market for reducing processing time, Errors, and fraud possible to occur.

Preventing Identity Fraud

The person's digital identification might be secured in a manner that differs from being tampered with or utilized in an unsanctioned manner. Blockchain should make this possible by figuring out facts is positioned on a permission blockchain framework and legal parties could have get admission to at least one model of the truth, and best acknowledged individuals can affirm transactions and make certain facts are valid. In Canada, Secure Key Technologies is performing on a brand-new digital identity management and attribute sharing network supported blockchain. By reducing redundant verification processes and therefore the quantity of work required to execute them, there would be fewer vulnerabilities for criminals to exploit. The network can enable individual customers to regulate what info they share, whereas organizations will expeditiously validate a customer's identity and organize new services.

Preventing Fraud in a Supply Chain

Blockchains can facilitate cutting back and even forestall fraud within the provide chain through larger transparency and improved traceability of products. It is terribly troublesome to govern the blockchain, that is an immutable record which will solely be updated and valid through agreement among network participants. The fraud relating to monetary establishments tends to induce a lot of media attention, fraud in provide chains is simply the maximum amount of Associate in Nursing issue result in supply chains which are advanced and typically involve many folks and moving parts, there are tons of holes within which fraud will be committed and go undetected. And if a product is digitized on blockchain, it can simply be derived back to its origin because of the data is on shared, distributed ledger.

Importance of Blockchain in Fraud Detection

The digitalization of technology changes business life with broad usage of preventing algorithms. The blockchain or the big digital notebook is the database which will store data, record of transaction and the record of network assets. Blockchain mainly helps in the modern and developing industrial revolution by giving the highest degree of privacy and security information. The areas where the blockchain system has a very important role are asset management, supply chain management, health care, large level of data collection and financial transactions.

Benefits of Blockchain

The benefits of blockchain technology are:

1. High security measurements which will prevent hackers and fraud.
2. Reduced the need for centralized platform and intermediary institutions anddecreased cost.
3. Block access to the company information and privacy of business data are restricted.
4. Transactions are faster than the other systems.
5. Transparency of data to track the blockchain system.

METHODOLOGY

Usually, the methodology shows a wide variety of access with the given execution pattern. The papers show a good block chain transaction which has been widely researched in all countries. This methodology of execution will be shown out over the identity pattern which is done and made.

- Entity access
- Transaction processing
- Amount Encryption
- Secure Block Chain storage
- Receivers Decryption
- Refund Initiation

Entity Access

Mostly entity access will be the first method where the concern will be given on the user and the admin side. The main attributes here will be the user and the admin. The user will be divided on the basis of the sender and the receiver where the sender is the one who sends the money, and the receiver will receive the money. The admin will completely maintain the log with a separate account management system.A simple storage system will be created with a banking server access where the UI designing with an account creation accessing has been done in the first phase generation. The maintenance of the multiple access features can be done with the banking approach which is generated with a separate part. The transaction process with a different trusted party can be accessible at any mode and the challenges can be done throughout the execution made.

Transaction Processing

The transaction processing is the main module in this system where a accurate transaction leveling can be made. As of the automated existing transactional working the proposed methodology focused on the same method where a manual selection of the account with the transaction authenticated ID, UPI ID, phone number etc where the recipients can be called with the given system. The main functional storage serves a high level of storage claim authority where the exact retrieval of the data for the sender and the user can be made. Multiple fusion of same authenticated name matching password can be distinguished with collaborative filtering methods.

Amount Encryption

Encryption is the main advantage for the security enhancement level. The normal chat-based application focused on the main encryption pattern for the amount transaction system. The amount which the transaction system can be made with a different processing step which here will be the Honey Encryption (HE) algorithm where the admin will tend to make a secured transaction level. The HE is the level where the complete data encryption system. Here the data like the amount, sender transaction details, receiver transaction details account number, CVV etc. will be completely changed to user non understandable format. The hacker/ attacker cannot be shown on the server-sideverification system which will be shown with a different methodology of extension shown. The algorithm tends to show an efficient identified transaction successfully with multi feature analysis which are shown. A dual layer of the given pattern mining can be shown with different proposed systems.

$$transaction = encrypt\ (merchant\_ID,\ receiver\_accno, payment\_amount) \tag{1}$$

The given encryption format shows an exact identification of the amount transaction with the encrypted pattern. The system can be done with a decode and encode system with 64-bit binary format which will be completely different with a ASCII value. The implementation will be shown with any symbols format for the traitor who is in the server moment.

Secure Blockchain Storage

The secure block chain storage system, which will be the main processing module of the given paper. The paper mainly focuses on a storage security system. Here the block chain-based storage system is enhanced where the Block chain consensus algorithm is used. The block chain-based storage will be a decentralized storage system where the data will be divided and forwarded with a attribute based extraction pattern which will be given. The paper focuses on the above module where the amount transaction will be encrypted with a low level of non-readable format system. High level of language modulation will be done on a attribute based division can be made. The consensus algorithm will be the one with the development based on a hash code generation system. The hash code will be done as memory storage. First a genesis block and the end block will be created, and each block initiation will be based with a memory address system. The hash address will be shown with each block connectivity where the connection of this ledger is done. The ledger will completely show on the developmental of the data sharing and the address will not be viewed out by any other.

Receiver's Decryption

The receiver will get a decryption system with an authentication mechanism. Here the dual model authentication verification on the user side will be checked out where only on the authenticated account the decryption will be made. The receiver will get the amount with a complete verification on the server side. Mainly the hashing function will be done with the multiple developmental management system. The back tracking will be made in this paper where the verification of the payment at the receiver's end is known. The payment gateway protocol tends to show out the different levels of the transaction working environment with the processing fee generation. The protocol shows here is that the Peer –to- Peer protocol where the connectivity has enhanced with the person-to-person connection. The two maintenances will be tending to give out a server's storage and claim connectivity with network. The digital process works out with a process n=n+1 connection where the multiple transaction process orders functional made with a queue generative approach. The Payment Service Provider (PSP) is the one which will be shown over the service exploded state.

Refund Initiation

In this system, the refund initiation works will be done based on the hacker/ attacker server problem made. If the hacker/ attacker tries to change the data, the hash code of the data will be changed where the connectivity will also get loss. The connectivity gets lost where the complete transactional data will be refunded to the sender side. Mainly the server-side access which will be shared with a level of access which can be completely maintained at a high level of the user side access. The transaction plotting storage will be done with a separate storage based accessing verification. Multi access verification schemes are done with the storage on the verification of the authentication mechanism which tends to give at a good level of functional systems.

ALGORITHMS AND METHOD

The block chain security algorithms are used to protect bloc chain transactions and the adaptation of block chain technology is increasing day by day. Hence the issues about security are also handled efficiently by these algorithms. The main blockchain security algorithms used are.

- Cryptography
- Peer-to-peer network protocol algorithm
- Zero-knowledge proofs
- Consensus algorithms

Cryptography Algorithms

In blockchain system new blocks and the collected data of records are added to the list continuously. Cryptography is very essential and fundamental requirement for the fraud detection and secure blockchain transaction because when the network grow and block size and no of blocks will also increasing hence it is very difficult to give that all information is free from any unwanted threats. This platform offers tailoring protocol and different techniques for avoiding any third-party interference in procuring and accessing private data. It prevents the network from third party eavesdropping the private information and the information is tracked by using cyber techniques for transmitting information. Specific code is used to cipher and decipher the data which is transmitted from one node to another. The Advanced Encryption Standard Algorithm is a Ciphertext Encryption and decryption algorithms uses different cases to code and decode transmitted data. The most efficient cryptography algorithms are.

Digital Signature

Digital signature is an Asymmetric-key cryptography algorithm, in which digital signature is required for the blockchain transaction as a private key. When a sender enters their private key for a specific-transaction, transaction data will encrypt, and the receiver must decrypt the transaction using public keys which are provided by the sender.the most popular block chain algorithm which provides high level block protection and additional layer of protection. Receiver will also transmit data along with key needed to decode the signature data.

Hashing

Block chain mainly depends on the process called hashing. All the type of data in the character string is used to classify the block in hashing, and it also provides efficient data storage apart from security. The cryptographic hashing algorithm can be more effective than the other algorithms in efficiency. HE is the most common hashing algorithm which can generate 32-byte hashing with faster and lighter hashing weight.

The key features are.

1. Hashing algorithms have always produced the same output from the same input. No matter how many times the data passes through the hashing algorithm, you can consistently use the same characters in the string to always produce the same hash. Changing the input can cause the hash in algorithm to produce a completely different output. A slight change in the case of certain characters in are cord can result in a completely different hash.

    2.Hash algorithms do not provide away to compute or infer the input from the output. It is important to note that the reis absolutely now a y to reverse the hashing process to see the original record. Finally, hashing algorithms offer unique advantages for fast blockchain security. The hashing process should be fast while avoiding in ten sieves of computing resources.
    3. The data security is done with an HE based encryption system. The implementation develops a private key and a public key called as master key for the generative approach of the encryption standards. The distinct secret key developed known as private key which will be generated with a multiple patterns decryption system. The encryption done with the master key generated pattern which on identifying the hyper plane pattern. The medical data which is going to be uploaded will be done on encryption. The data upload with the security pattern of the HE system gets changes. The algorithm generative approach will be known with the data upload. The encryption algorithm done with below set of rules and patterns:

Key Generation

```
Input: Message in, receiver's key Qs
Output: U, C, tag
Set random U£Z_p
Compute U = u • G
Compute S(x_s, y_s) = U. Q_B
Generate (k_ENRC, k_MAC) = KDF(x_s)
Encrypt C = ENC(m, k_ENC)
Generate tag = H_MAC(C, k_MAC)
```

HE Encryption

```
Input: Elliptic Curve HE, Original Message M
Output: Cipher text M_t
Begin
        Processing with starting S
        Count Region HE
        Region S_i = ∫_{=1}^{size} region  Random Regions
        Curve point R_r = HE (Si)
        End
        Generate possible regional R = ∫_{=1}^{size} random(size(Rr))
        Encryption key gives Er = Rr(R)
        Do
 Encryption
        Changed Text Mt = Encryption (Er, M)
        Binary form conversion 0 and 1
        Generate possible number Si = ∫random(100)
        If Si is odd then
                padd 0's
Else
        padd 1
End
```

By using this algorithm, the Honey Encryption encrypted amount details will be generated and then the identification of the curve will be made with the encryption of the message called data. Thus, these data will be encrypted with the generated public key and get stored.

Peer-to-Peer Network Protocol

The peer-to-peer network protocol algorithm is mainly used for large organizations and co operational projects. In bigger organizations the single centralized system must load large no of data blocks, hence the decentralized distributed peer-to-peer network will be used. The node in the block chain system will be provided with high security authentication from the third-party detection. In this algorithm the past transaction of the sender will be tracked to detect the amount of the nodes operation and each node empowers the authentication by creditability of transaction before documenting the network about their information. it will receive agreement protocol as miner from the receivers to reach the agreement on the given order and the sum of the different transactions. It also ensures the expanded data security transaction.

Zero-to-Knowledge Proof

Zero knowledge proof provides enhanced security by fully utilizing cryptographic methods possible to ensure that the prover is not required to reveal information about the transaction. The 'prover' of ZKP algorithms does not have to reveal any information, which is a key factor in their efficiency. Zero knowledge proofs is a famous example of a blockchain algorithm used for security on blockchain networks (ZKPs). Zero knowledge proof enables one party to reassure another party of the veracity of information and truly acts as a consensus decision making process. The veracity of the information and their process will be easy access to the party and protect any on related disclosures.

Consensus Algorithm

Normally blockchain have to allocate the power to the user participating in the network, and the agreement which specifies the transaction must reached by majority of the participants. Blockchain networks depend on consensus algorithms because they support the security and integrity of distributed computing systems. The most frequently chosen algorithms for blockchain security are consensus algorithms. The functionality of reaching the agreement on the specific data value will be transferred throughout the network. In the Distributed decentralized computing, consensus algorithm was used to detect whether the nodes and peers are trusted along with high security.

Evaluation of Consensus Algorithm

Table 1. The consensus algorithm execution work made

Evaluation Criteria	Algorithm Entities
Throughput	• Transaction per second • Block size • Verification time • Creation of block
Mining profit	• Rewards • Power consumption • Specification of hardware • Transaction fees
Decentralization degree	• Permission modal • Trust modal • Blockchain governance
Security issues	• Double spending • 51% Attack • Sybil Attack

Types of Consensus Algorithm

Proof of Work Consensus Algorithm

A cryptographic hash creation process in which block validates are required for taking data from block header as an input and then the input can be run through that specific block validates cryptographic hash function. Even the slight changes in the input data can also be ensured by validate by arbitrary number or nonce. The input data containing iteration will be added once through hash function. The proof of work (POW) algorithm will add data in the next consecutive block by requiring higher processing power .so they needed specialize with computer like AISC for computing any mathematical derivations.

Proof of Stake Consensus Algorithm

PoS, also known as the Proof of Stake algorithm, will replace PoW. So, it will make sense to find PoS and PoW goals that are similar. However, there are several key distinctions and features between the two consensus algorithms, particularly when it comes to validating brand new blocks on the blockchain network. To determine a node's allocation and the allocation for assessing the parties' commitment to ensuring the transaction, it essentially uses a random selection procedure. The PoS algorithm is used by the Ethereum block chain to increase scalability and reduce energy consumption. A method in the Proof of Stake algorithm permits the validation of blocks in accordance with a stake held by network users. PoS algorithms for blockchain security include staking resources in the form of tokens or digital money, as opposed to executing hash functions. It then entails choosing validates at random from among the stakeholders for each block. The computing power given to the stakeholders plays a role in choosing the validating and the interesting fact is every POS system will guarantee various implementations.

Deleted Proof of Stake Consensus Algorithm

The DPoS also called as The Deleted Proof of Stake consensus algorithm will use the voting system in which the desired validates has to be selected by the voting for the support of the new block of consensus state. The maintenance of the block and the transaction validation both will be handled by the validator of the network. The transaction fees are given to the thing validates and this algorithm is pos democratic versioned consensus algorithm. The main advantage of DPos algorithm is large data processing and faster transaction.

Proof of Elapsed Time Consensus Algorithm

The POET, also called The Proof of Elapsed Time consensus algorithm will be tailored for random leader selection challenge solving. It has the application around the network by extending the program reference modal or Software Guard Extension with the private key of blockchain. Randomized timer system is relayed on this algorithm than the old dependent mining hardware. Each node in the block must wait for a specific time to be validated and to add to the new block.

EXPERIMENTAL ANALYSIS

The experimental analysis turns with an exact and secured online transaction outcome on using block chain server accessing system. The transactional pattern with the server-side efficiency is run through the different module execution system. The main advantage of the system is that the execution of the various transactions and each customer feedbacks taken.

Storage Efficiency

First of all, on cloud storage systems the storage efficiency needs to be checked out correctly and the maintenance application need to be verified. The dominant sets of data storage and the retrieval time are completely verified with the proposed management approach system. Figure 5 shows the exact sender and recipients data retrieval.

Blockchain-Based Secure Transactions

Figure 5. Chart represents the data storage and retrieval works

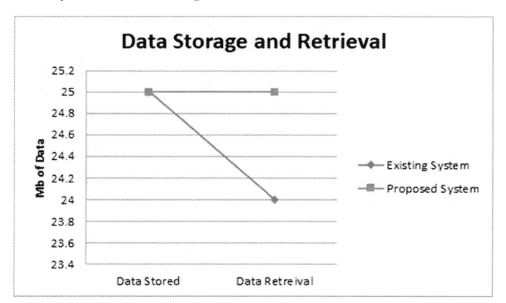

Here the existing and the proposed comparison of the data storage with retrieval get to be the same where a mild difference on getting an exact authentication. Thus, the storage efficiency is normal on their accuracy system.

Security Efficiency

Security is the main aspect of the project generated. The main thing is that the security needs to high out on the server side and the storage side. The server-side efficiency is done with the Block Chain consensus and the data side concentrated with the Honey Encryption algorithm system.

Server-Side Accuracy

The server-side accuracy is the main thing where a de-centralized storage problem is mentioned here. The normal storage server time accuracy shows with a low where easy hacking and attacking can be made where the proposed system shows a low problematic issue on the tracking of the data and changing. The change of data with hash code change makes a sudden data refundable system which the sender side problem has been overcome.

Figure 6. Server efficiency comparison chart

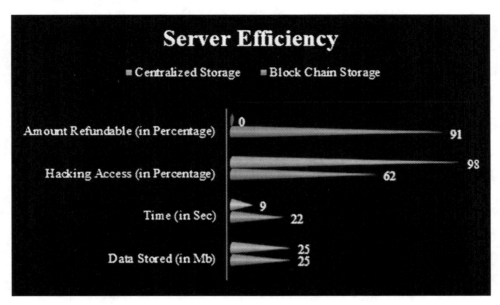

Thus, the graph depiction clearly shows the complete difference between the identification of the normal server storage and the block chain server storage. The efficiency of the block chain server storage is completely high, and the feature point is high. Thus, the maintenance over this complete extraction shows the difference of variation over the transaction plotting.

Data Side Efficiency

The data side efficiency will be done with the Honey Encryption system which will be the one component. The Honey Encryption will be stored out on the data security with the data encryption and decryption access maintenance. The normal RSA based encryption standard varies with the amount of time, execution, limitations, and security. Thus, the difference of variation is made with external scheme adoption which is made.

Table 2. Shows the highest terms of the data efficiency access

	Time (in Sec)	Security (Percentage)	Accuracy (Percentage)
RSA	25	78	91
Honey Encryption	12	89	96

The data can be set out with the high variation of the encryption standard and the below chart makes a good execution of the proposed approach with the accuracy elements.

Figure 7. Chart showing the graphical analysis of data efficiency

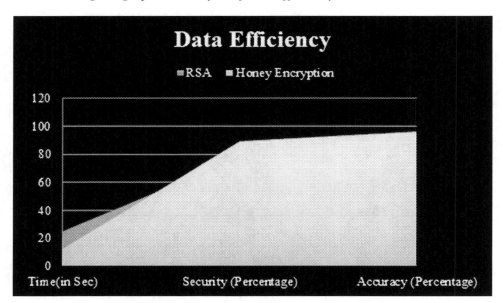

The graph clearly depicts a vulnerable under covering of the Honey Encryption algorithm with the lower time execution of the data with the higher accuracy plotting. The coverage of the normal RSA on the current usage algorithm will be on a lower execution on using the Honey Encryption Standards.

User Side Efficiency

The system is given to the user side working environment where the user side efficiency is checked out. With a normal calculative system more than 98% of the people tend to make a good decision check out on a online transaction system.

Figure 8. The customer feedback are taken with the approach

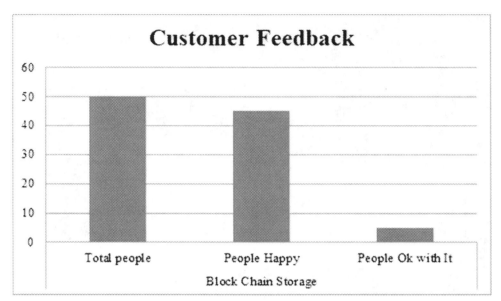

The final accuracy on combining complete data efficiency, Server efficiency, storage efficiency, security efficiency, customer feedback will be the one where the complete analysis of the best online transaction system created is stored out.

Figure 9. The accuracy of the proposed system comparison

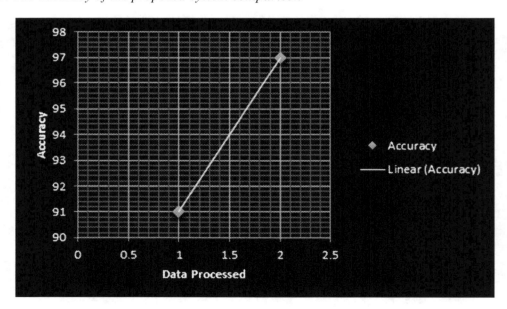

The developed system gives the best accuracy over 97% of security, data access and storage access are made. The best accuracy of the graph is tending to show with a good level of GUI finalizing system.

CONCLUSION

This chapter concludes that fraudulent transactions can be detected and prevented by using block chain algorithms. The system speed and scalability also achieved, and the smart contract process is used to prevent the accessing of information by any third party and hackers. The challenges of the old transaction management system and the blockchain management key challenge of transparency and authentications are archived in the proposed system. The proposed algorithm consensus peer to stake is implemented to detect the network attackers in every node of the block.

Blockchain has given its potential in a secure storage developmental feature system where the block chain storage makes a good and comfortable system. The storage of the transactional information in a secured server leads to a high tendency for safe user side transactional functionality. A final check out on the system shows a huge security functional processing. The conventional proof of consensus and the transactional storage algorithm gives a high security on the server side. The data security is well organized in the Honey Encryption (HE) algorithm which will be the highest accuracy on time, security and decryption access. The authentic mechanism will be the one where the recipients and the sender key are completely verified in both authentication ID. The possible attacks and the detection over the attack with the paper are completely analyzed in the experimental analysis chapter and make a preferable payment method. The main advantageous one is that the refund of the amount on the middle in the man attack where the amount refund is made which will be more secure enough on the customer side and makes a complete satisfaction. The Information Technology (IT) sharing of the technical aspect's development will be rely on security enhancement which are made with the online payment approval options. The developed block chain system makes a happy payment procedure with securing developmental options.

FUTURE ENHANCEMENT

In the future developmental system, online transactions with an authentication function with different password enhancements can be made. The time over the decryption and encryption is the main limitation of the proposed work which can be eliminated with the future works. Still good accuracy maintenance over server-side storage can be added. An authenticated message and the reply can be added with the future system. The system should also focus on the sender account transaction encryption form details with different authentication mechanisms.

REFERENCES

Cai, Y., & Zhu, D. (2016). Fraud detection for online businesses: A perspective from blockchain technology. *Financial Innovation*, 2(1), 20. doi:10.118640854-016-0039-4

Fernandez, E. B., Yoshioka, N., Washizaki, H., & Yoder, J. (2022). Abstract security patterns and the design of secure systems. *Cybersecurity*, *5*(1), 7. doi:10.118642400-022-00109-w

Leible, S., Schlager, S., Schubotz, M., & Gipp, B. (2019). A review on blockchain technology and blockchain projects fostering open science. *Frontiers in Blockchain*, 16.

Li, L., Lu, X., & Wang, K. (2022). Hash-based signature revisited. *Cybersecurity*, *5*(1), 13. doi:10.118642400-022-00117-w

Liu, P., Xu, X., & Wang, W. (2022). Threats, attacks and defenses to federated learning: Issues, taxonomy and perspectives. *Cybersecurity*, *5*(1), 4. doi:10.118642400-021-00105-6

Morgen, P. (2017). Reinforcing the links of the blockchain. *IEEE Future Directions Blockchain*.

Sun, J., Yan, J., & Zhang, K. Z. (2016). Blockchain-based sharing services: What blockchain technology can contribute to smart cities. *Financial Innovation*, *2*(1), 1–9. doi:10.118640854-016-0040-y

Verma, V., Priya, S., Mishra, S., & Priyadarshini, R. (2019). Property Fraud Detection and Prevention Using Blockchain. *International Conference on Intelligent Computing and Remote Sensing (ICICRS)*.

Xiao, H., Wang, L., & Chang, J. (2022). The differential fault analysis on block cipher FeW. *Cybersecurity*, *5*(1), 28. doi:10.118642400-022-00130-z

Xu, M., Chen, X., & Kou, G. (2019). A systematic review of blockchain. *Financial Innovation*, *5*(1), 27. doi:10.118640854-019-0147-z

Yan, C., Zhang, C., Lu, Z., Wang, Z., Liu, Y., & Liu, B. (2022). Blockchain abnormal behavior awareness methods: A survey. *Cybersecurity*, *5*(1), 5. doi:10.118642400-021-00107-4

Yang, F., Han, Y., Ding, Y., Tan, Q., & Xu, Z. (2022). A flexible approach for cyber threat hunting based on kernel audit records. *Cybersecurity*, *5*(1), 11. doi:10.118642400-022-00111-2

KEY TERMS AND DEFINITIONS

Blockchain: A system in which a record of transactions, especially those made in a cryptocurrency, is maintained across computers that are linked in a peer-to-peer network.

Crypto Currency: A digital currency in which transactions are verified and records maintained by a decentralized system using cryptography, rather than by a centralized authority.

Cryptography: Cryptography is a method of protecting information and communications through the use of codes, so that only those for whom the information is intended can read and process it.

Decentralization: The transfer of control of an activity or organization to several local offices or authorities rather than one single one.

Encryption: The process of converting information or data into a code, especially to prevent unauthorized access.

Hashing: Hashing is the process of transforming any given key or a string of characters into another value.

Transaction: A Data record verified by block chain system, and it also serves as an immutable confirmation of financial transaction authenticity or its contract.

Chapter 6
Blockchain Arbitration:
A Supply Chain Perspective

Marianna Riabova
https://orcid.org/0000-0002-4100-0977
CERAG, Université Grenoble Alpes, Grenoble, France

Paul Reaidy
CERAG, Université Grenoble Alpes, Grenoble, France

ABSTRACT

Blockchain technology offers substantial benefits to supply chains (SCs). Along with transparency and traceability and other undeniable advantages, blockchain technology enables smart contract integration. Blockchain and smart contracts are, however, not flawless and can create a new category of disputes. The recognition of these disputes by traditional legal institutions is questionable. This chapter presents the concept of blockchain arbitration that allows for smart contract and blockchain dispute settlement via a decentralized resolution platform. The chapter reveals that despite existing challenges, blockchain arbitration can enhance the resolution process in terms of flexibility, cost, and time reduction, increase trust among SC stakeholders, and boost overall SC performance.

INTRODUCTION

In recent decades, the world has become more open than before. The economic globalization process has accelerated international trade and the overall movement of products, information, and funds. Supply Chains, that are an integral part of every organization, had to adapt to the new competitive environment (Meixell & Gargeya, 2005). They have become more dynamic and complex in order to ensure the continuous transportation of goods worldwide and a high level of service that meets customer needs (Cohen & Mallik, 1997). Due to the complexity and geographical distribution, modern supply networks face critical challenges like lack of transparency, security, trust etc. (Sanders & Wagner, 2011). These difficulties motivate companies to look for the best supply chain management solutions and to integrate

DOI: 10.4018/978-1-6684-7455-6.ch006

innovative technologies. One of the revolutionary technologies that now gets a lot of attention in the Supply Chain is Blockchain (Casado-Vara et al., 2018; Dutta et al., 2020; Živković et al., 2023).

The immutable and distributed blockchain technology is expected to provide undeniable advantages to globalized supply networks like transaction transparency, transaction security and higher level of trust between SC parties (Azzi et al., 2019; Hughes et al., 2019; Saberi et al., 2019). In addition, blockchain technology allows for Smart Contracts integration. These agreements are drafted in code can automate contract conclusion and execution (Prause, 2019). This is a substantial breakthrough compared to traditional contracts that require a lot of paperwork, manual labor and working hours to be drafted and monitored, are dependent on third parties for the execution (ex. banks for money transfers) and are very vulnerable to tampering (Lim et al., 2021).

Despite these benefits, the innovative nature of blockchain technology and Smart Contracts is not flawless and can create an absolutely new category of disputes related to the adoption and usage of these novel technologies (Buchwald, 2020; Schmitz & Rule, 2019). Disputes that arise from blockchain and Smart Contract adoption are a very recent phenomenon and existing dispute resolution methods (ex. litigation, Alternative Dispute Resolution or Online Dispute Resolution) are not prepared for resolving disputes arising from Smart Contracts and decentralized blockchain transactions (Guillaume & Riva, 2022; Michaelson & Jeskie, 2021; Schmitz, 2020). This regulatory uncertainty is dangerous for Supply Chain actors as they do not know how to address the new kind of disputes swiftly and efficiently (Guillaume & Riva, 2022; Živković et al., 2023).

The main objective of this book chapter is to contribute to this research lacuna by exploring Blockchain Arbitration – an innovative dispute resolution method specifically designed for blockchain and smart contract disputes – and to highlight its potential for the Supply Chain domain. The following research questions are addressed:

1. What is Blockchain Arbitration and what are its specificities?
2. What advantages can Blockchain Arbitration bring to the SC dispute resolution?
3. What are the challenges for the adoption of Blockchain Arbitration?

This book chapter explores the motivation of Supply Chain companies for blockchain and Smart Contracts adoption and the advantages these technologies bring. It also analyses the risk that SC disputes represent and the regulatory lacuna concerning blockchain and Smart Contract disputes. The Blockchain Arbitration method as well as the most developed Blockchain Arbitration platforms are discussed, and the main advantages and challenges of Blockchain Arbitration adoption are highlighted.

BACKGROUND

Supply Chains, that consist of the series of activities and organizations that materials move through on their journey from initial suppliers to final customers (Waters, 2003), are nowadays an essential part of most companies and effective supply chain management can contribute to better firms' performance and customers' satisfaction (Zhang et al., 2021). Modern supply chains are becoming increasingly complex, dynamic and are transforming into more worldwide networks because of economic globalization (Kazancoglu et al., 2022; Tan & Sidhu, 2022; Wang et al., 2021). Globalization contributed to the high level of Supply Chains geographical dispersion and distribution (De Giovanni, 2020). Modern networks now act as a link between dozens and sometimes hundreds of suppliers, manufacturers, distributors, and customers and are becoming very vulnerable (Min, 2019).

Along with that, Supply Chain Management, that assumes efficient management of material, information, and financial flows, has become an immensely complex task and a fundamental challenge due to several main reasons (Nandi et al., 2020; Saberi et al., 2019):

SC Traceability and Transparency: Initially, traceability and transparency of the Supply Chain were primarily associated with upstream networks (identifying the origin of raw materials), but recently the downstream aspect (tracking the products up to the end customers) was also added to the scope. SC transparency and traceability make it possible for SC stakeholders, governmental organizations and consumers to have full visibility of the chain and respond quickly to unexpected disruptions (Bai et al., 2022; Chang et al., 2019). As today's supply chains are highly complex and dynamic, participants of the networks are facing visibility issues and have no reliable ways to verify the provenance of materials, final products and services (Aich et al., 2019; Mirabelli & Solina, 2020). According to a recent survey, 69% of more than 400 organizations from 64 countries do not have complete visibility into their SCs (Chang et al., 2020). This lack of visibility can be the cause of frauds and fakes in the network.

SC Security: SC implies a big number of documents that ensure transparent trade and guarantee that obligations to all parties will be fulfilled (ex. clients receive genuine products and vendors get payments for their goods). Despite their importance, these documents are not reliable - they can be easily forged by fraudsters to steal the cargo. In addition, world trade gets more dependent on Information Technologies and e-commerce platforms and digital documents. Along with these technology integrations, the number of cyberattacks and insider threats has dramatically increased, raising security risks in the Supply Chain (Aich et al., 2019; Cheung et al., 2021; Markmann et al., 2013; Marucheck et al., 2011).

Trust Among SC Stakeholders: As a consequence of transparency, visibility and security issues, there is often a lack of trust among SC partners (De Giovanni, 2020; Kshetri & Voas, 2019). Trust is one of the important elements in the SC partners' relationship as it facilitates collaborative processes, positively impacts stakeholders' satisfaction, commitment and loyalty and contributes to better performance of the whole chain (Han et al., 2021; Ferreira da Silva & Moro, 2021; Seebacher & Schüritz, 2017). Trust was recognized as a key reason for the worldwide success of Japanese auto manufacturers (Dyer & Chu, 2000) and examples of Volkswagen's plants in Brazil and Spain and Chrysler's Eurostar plant in Austria showed that trust was directly connected to the increase of Just-in-Time capabilities (Narasimhan & Nair, 2005). Lack of trust can prevent the exchange of accurate information between the parties, increase transactional costs and even hinder the process innovations in the Supply Chain (Panayides & Venus Lun, 2009; Sahay, 2003).

SC Disputes: The lack of trust among stakeholders and the complexity and dispersion of modern supply networks contributes to the increase of SC disputes. A dispute can arise at any point of the supply chain due to a variety of reasons: uncertainties in contract management, goods delivery not in full or not in time, damages of the products during transportation etc. SC disputes usually imply a lot of inconveniences, difficulties and expenses for the parties: tracking back the real cause of the dispute, finding the necessary evidence (that are reliable and trusted), preparing witnesses etc. (Chang et al., 2020). Once a dispute occurs, it is important to resolve it quickly and efficiently without deteriorating relationships and trust among SC stakeholders (Rauniyar et al., 2022).

When facing the challenges listed, Supply Chain companies are searching for the solutions that can deal with these difficulties. Technological development does not stand still and technology gains more and more importance for the Supply Chain domain and changes how globalized networks function.

Blockchain is one of the technologies that got particularly a lot of attention from practitioners and researchers that point out its potential for modern Supply Chains (Živković et al., 2023).

Blockchains are decentralized distributed ledgers first introduced by Nakamoto (2008) that register transactions in an untrustworthy environment. Blockchains represent a sort of a database that is shared, synchronized, and protected by numeric signatures and cryptographic hash functions (Hughes et al., 2019).

Blockchain can be defined by the following characteristics (Badhotiya et al., 2021; Hughes et al., 2019; Martinez et al., 2019):

- **Immutable:** As soon transactions are added to the blockchain, they cannot be changed.
- **Time Stamped:** All transactions are date and time stamped, providing a built-in audit trail for all the additions.
- **Append Only:** Data can be appended to blockchain only in the specific time order.
- **Safe:** All blockchain additions are regulated by stable algorithms that employ public key encryption, lowering the risk of data fraud.
- **Transparent and Open:** Since blockchains are distributed ledgers, all nodes in the network have access to the same master records.
- **Consensus-Driven Approach:** The data is exchanged with all participants in the network. Each participant in the distributed network keeps a copy of the ledger, which is updated and approved at the same time, preventing possible disputes.

In addition to that, blockchain allows for Smart Contracts adoption. Nick Szabo (1996) introduced Smart Contracts and defined it as a set of promises, specified in digital form, including protocols within which the parties perform on these promises. Smart Contracts can automate the contract conclusion and execution and therefore enhance the supply chain efficiency (Batwa & Norrman, 2020; Prause 2019). In addition, Smart contracts, in contrast to conventional contracts, ignore the legal model. Parties do not need to be concerned about facing the ineffectiveness of lawsuit or fighting for payment as soon as the conditions and enforcement are already predefined and set up in the computer coding per "if/then" rules (Schmitz & Rule, 2019).

Not so long ago blockchain technology and Smart Contracts were mostly associated with cryptocurrencies (like Bitcoin), but now they also receive a lot of attention from SC researchers and Supply chain specialists forecast that by 2026, most of the world's global supply networks will run on blockchain technology (Lim et al., 2021; Živković et al., 2023). The technology features make blockchain and Smart Contracts a valuable tool and a solution to modern Supply Chain challenges (Berneis et al., 2021; Kumar Singh et al., 2023):

Blockchain Enables SC Traceability and Transparency: Thanks to its distributed and decentralized nature, blockchains provide full information and transaction visibility (Batwa & Norrman, 2020; Song, Sung, & Park, 2019). Any transaction recorded on the blockchain by SC participants is visible and all the members can easily verify all the actions recorded and follow how products move: from raw material suppliers to final customers. Thanks to the immutability feature, blockchain can guarantee the reliability and authenticity of data registered by SC members (De Giovanni, 2020; Dujak & Sajter, 2019).

Blockchain Technology Can Become an Answer to SC Security Challenge: Thanks to its characteristics, blockchain can ensure transaction security and guard it at three different layers: (1) Decentralization renders data manipulation impossible, (2) the adoption of cryptographic encryption assures data security and prevents data modifications without permission and (3) the consensus approach protects the entire network by obliging all blockchain participants to follow consistent protocols (Dujak & Sajter, 2019; Lim et al., 2021). Thanks to full transaction security and visibility, companies can securely track the products along their way, be sure that the goods will be received by real clients (not thieves or fraudsters) and prevent possible cyberattacks on the SC system (Dutta et al., 2020).

Blockchain Can Add More Trust to the Supply Chain: The visibility and security of the transaction guaranteed by blockchain increases trust among the network participants (Alkhudary & Féniès, 2022; Batwa & Norrman, 2020; De Giovanni, 2020). Blockchain represents an ecosystem where parties can fully trust each other and can transact directly without any third parties. The consensus driven mechanism controls that transactions are added to the database only after all the members of the network verify, confirm, and agree on them. Such a cheap and easy way to verify and audit all the information about goods and services has the potential to eliminate the stakeholders' distrust in relation to each other, which is particularly important for SC collaboration and cooperation, partners' satisfaction and overall SC performance (Aslam et al., 2021; Seebacher & Schüritz, 2017).

Blockchain Can Eliminate SC Disputes: Blockchain technology can significantly lower the possibility of a dispute thanks to the ability to register asset provenance, legal and safety requirements transparently and in real-time (Min, 2019). Even if a dispute arises, the parties can find its source relying on blockchain data that is highly reliable, secure, authentic and is trusted by the parties. The Smart Contract built on the top of blockchain will immediately cause penalties or fines when pre-set terms are violated. This can potentially make traditional complex, costly and inflexible dispute resolution a thing from the past (Dujak & Sajter, 2019; Schmitz & Rule, 2019).

All these features make blockchain and Smart Contracts a revolutionary tool for the modern Supply Chains that can successfully deal with the most common SC challenges (Paul et al., 2021).

BLOCKCHAIN AND SMART CONTRACT DISPUTES IN THE SUPPLY CHAIN

Despite all the benefits that blockchain and Smart Contracts assume for the Supply Chain, these technologies can also cause certain difficulties for the domain. One of the recognized challenges that can represent a threat to the supply chain is the emergence of a completely new category of disputes - disputes coming from blockchain transactions and Smart Contract usage. Disputes can happen as Smart Contracts are not "smart" enough to make subjective judgements or consider elements from beyond the blockchain (Howell & Potgieter, 2019; Schmitz, 2020). What is more, the process of converting the legal terms of the contract into the smart contract's code can be subject to errors or unwanted outcome of the smart contracts can be caused by bugs/coding errors or unanticipated events, causing a variety of different disputes (Guillaume & Riva, 2022).

Supply Chain disputes are usually dangerous and destructive as they negatively influence company's profit, inventory, reputation, and goodwill and can result in clear winners and losers. The latter can be unwilling to collaborate in building Supply Chain union power (Lund & Wright, 2003). What is more, if not properly handled, Supply Chain disputes can destroy trust among partners, hinder future joint development, cooperation and collaboration and jeopardize the overall continuous operation of the whole supply chain. Consequently, Supply Chain disputes have to be addressed promptly and efficiently through well-coordinated actions (Wang et al., 2021; Wolf & Pickler, 2010).

At present, there is a regulatory gap in procedures for resolving disputes coming from the Smart Contracts and blockchain transactions on blockchain-based supply chains (Živković et al., 2023). Courts are too rigid for this kind of disputes and, therefore, cannot ensure access to justice for the parties that use blockchain and have concluded a Smart Contract. There is also no Alternative Dispute Resolution or Online Dispute Resolution procedure suitable for the resolution of these kinds of disputes, as blockchain technology and Smart Contracts are the innovations that are not yet fully researched and studied by legal institutions (Guillaume & Riva, 2022; Michaelson & Jeskie, 2021; Schmitz, 2020). This regulatory uncertainty is crucial and unacceptable for a dynamic Supply Chain sphere where disputes must be resolved as fast as possible to stay competitive. A reliable resolution method specifically designed for disputes arising in the blockchain ecosystem is therefore indispensable to maintain trust between Supply Chain partners and minimize possible undesirable dispute outcomes (like Supply Chain process disruptions, damaged partnerships, decreased profitability etc.) (Živković et al., 2023).

BLOCKCHAIN ARBITRATION AS A DISPUTE RESOLUTION METHOD

The concept of Blockchain Arbitration appeared as an answer to the existing regulatory lacuna. One of the first to announce the idea of creating such a system was the founder of Ethereum Vitalik Buterin. He stated that blockchain technology can be used to create a multi-level system with randomly selected judges operating in a decentralized judicial system (Zasemkova, 2019). As Smart Contracts cannot replace attorneys and be fully independent in case a dispute arises, the parties can secure themselves in case of a dispute and encode an arbitration clause into the smart contract (Erbguth & Morin, 2018). Building arbitration into the Smart Contracts can preserve privacy, ensure efficiency and provide expert decision-making (Schmitz, 2020). In case a dispute arises, the parties can generally just trigger the arbitration clause and send the claim to the Blockchain Arbitration platform for the settlement. Blockchain Arbitration platforms take advantage of blockchain technology and perform dispute resolution procedure mostly online in the decentralized blockchain environment. Many Blockchain Arbitration platforms operate quite independently and do not require any public authority to administer justice or enforce their decisions. In most cases the decision's execution can be fully automated thanks to the self-enforcement nature of Smart Contracts (Guillaume & Riva, 2022).

Currently, there are considerable efforts from Blockchain Arbitration startups to ensure automated dispute resolution specifically designed for Smart Contracts and blockchain transaction disputes (Michaelson & Jeskie, 2021). All the Blockchain Arbitration platforms can be divided into 2 big groups (Zasemkova, 2020):

1. Decentralized quasi-judicial systems that aim at resolving disputes with the help of crowdsourced jury voting.
2. Special Arbitration that is closer to traditional arbitration. Disputes coming from Smart Contracts and blockchain transactions are resolved by a predefined pool of arbitrators and the decision can be executed in a traditional way by applying to state courts for example or via a Smart Contract.

Decentralized Quasi-Judicial System

One of the most developed Blockchain Arbitration platforms in this first group is Kleros, which is an Ethereum-based decentralized autonomous organization that acts as a third party in resolving disputes. Every step of the arbitration procedure can be automated from the dispute initiation, evidence disclosure and to decision enforcement. Kleros provides crowdsourced arbitration based on game theory economic incentive. Once a dispute resolution procedure is triggered by the parties, Kleros starts the jurors' (arbitrators') selection procedure. Jurors are selected at random among the users registered on the platform, but the more Kleros tokens the user stakes, the higher is the chance they will be chosen as a juror for the case. After being chosen, jurors consider all the evidence presented by the parties and decide based on the options that were specified in advance by the parties in the Smart Contract (this assumes mostly binary outcomes). Instead of traditional moral sense, the fairness jurors' decisions are ensured by game theory, more precisely Schelling Point. Schelling's point characterizes a situation where all the parties tend to choose the same outcome without any mutual communication. In the dispute resolution context this means that jurors will vote fairly, since they expect other jurors to do the same. Jurors who voted in the minority lose a certain number of tokens they staked, which are transferred to jurors who voted in the majority. Once all jurors have voted, the votes are aggregated, and the joint decision is enforced via Smart Contracts. If parties are dissatisfied with jurors' decision, they can make an appeal and the claim will be reviewed again (Jevremovic, 2020; Lesaege et al., 2019; Schmitz & Rule, 2019).

Jur is another key player that also promises a fully automated fast and fair dispute resolution through a combination of crowdsourcing and game theory for simple to complex disputes (Zasemkova, 2020). Jur focuses on enterprise use cases and aims at covering a wide range of disputes through three different dispute resolution layers. The first is the Court Layer which is comparable to a standard ODR system with traditional arbitrators and can generate decisions that are legally binding. The second layer is the Open Layer that proposes a collective intelligence decision-making solution which is a lot analogous to Kleros. The last layer is Community Layer which provides a sort of a private court with certain rules that were determined by the creators. Jur platform allows for choosing jurors based on certain criteria like, for example, skills and reputation. In other respects, Jur is very similar to Kleros platform (Aouidef et al., 2021).

Special Arbitration

One of the most developed startups belonging to the second group is Mattereum, which is also designed to resolve disputes arising from Smart Contracts, operates quite differently. Mattereum aims at covering real-world physical assets by Smart Contracts and has created an "automated custodian" which serves as the registrar and legal owner of real-world assets. The parties can conclude a Ricardian contract, which allows for creating a traditional legal contract and a corresponding smart contract to facilitate legal procedures (Metzger, 2019). Mattereum has also integrated an off-chain arbitration which is performed by external independent arbitrators. If a dispute occurs the parties may resort to arbitration which is conducted by independent arbitrators. The parties may select an arbitrator among the options offered to them or if they cannot come to an agreement, the arbitrator will be appointed to them. The expenses for arbitration are part of the fee that Mattereum charges for the audit of the Smart Contracts, which is done to find errors, areas of ambiguity and other possible issues. In this regard, Mattereum provides not only post-conflict resolution services, but also works actively to prevent disputes. Arbitrators produce final legally binding decisions based on Digital Dispute Resolution Rules that were published by LawtechUK's UK Jurisdiction Taskforce in 2021 to facilitate resolution of commercial disputes involving novel technologies (LawtechUK, 2022). Summing up, Mattereum uses blockchain technology for off-chain assets that broadens the range of disputes that can be resolved this Blockchain Arbitration platform and applies conventional arbitration instead of crowdsourced jury voting (Allen et al., 2019; Rabinovich-Einy & Katsh, 2019).

Another Blockchain Arbitration platform which also offers a more traditional arbitration for Smart Contract disputes is Cryptonomica. Cryptonomica is an international arbitration authority registered in England and Wales that offers a London based arbitration with arbitrators' awards that are legally enforceable under international law almost worldwide. The main mission of this project is to use modern technologies such as cryptography, blockchain, decentralized applications, and international law with some law hacks, to build global borderless space for contracts and electronic documents interchange, where applicable law can be chosen and even created by users, but contracts are still recognizable and enforceable in legacy national legal systems (Cryptonomica, 2022). Dispute resolution process offered by Cryptonomica is very close to the traditional arbitration process and is regulated by special Arbitration Rules that were developed based on the UNCITRAL Arbitration Rules. If a dispute arises, the parties should first send their claim to registrar@international-arbitration.org.uk with the indication of "Cryptonomica". Each dispute is resolved by 1 or 3 arbitrators (according to parties' preference) that are appointed by Cryptonomica or are chosen by the disputants. Arbitration fees can be paid in the Bitcoin, Ether, the euro or the United States dollar. The arbitral tribunal generally uses videoconference for communication and all the documents are exchanged online. The arbitrators decide on each case "according to the right and good" principle (ex aequo et bono). Arbitrators' decisions are produced in writing and are final and binding on the parties (Cryptonomica, 2018; Zasemkova, 2020).

To summarize, the projects described are at different stages of development and imply different mechanisms for the selection of arbitrators, but all of them pursue one goal - offering a dispute resolution tool for Smart Contracts' and blockchain transaction disputes. The main features of these Blockchain Arbitration platforms are presented in Table 1.

Table 1. Key features of blockchain arbitration platforms

Platform Features	Decentralized Quasi-Judicial System		Special Arbitration	
	Kleros	Jur	Mattereum	Cryptonomica
Platform can solve complex non-binary cases	+ (Very limited)	+	+	+
Dispute Resolution process can be fully automated for the parties (from dispute initiation to decision enforcement)	+	+	−	−
Arbitrators are selected randomly	+	+	−	−
Platform allows for the arbitrators' selection based on their skills	−	+	+	+
Platform decisions are currently legally enforceable under international law in most countries	−	−	+	+
Platform offers an appeal opportunity for the parties that are dissatisfied with the initial resolution	+	−	−	−
"+" - Yes; "−" - No.				

Source: Authors

ADVANTAGES OF BLOCKCHAIN ARBITRATION FOR SUPPLY CHAIN DISPUTE RESOLUTION

Blockchain Arbitration can offer many advantages to the Supply Chain dispute resolution process. As Blockchain Arbitration is literally an arbitration process carried out with the help of blockchain technology on the decentralized environment, Blockchain Arbitration advantages can be categorized into 2 categories: (1) advantages coming from the nature of the arbitration process itself and (2) advantages that are specifically brought by blockchain technology integration.

Advantages Coming From the Nature of the Arbitration Process

Arbitration as a form of dispute settlement provides a neutral forum that allows parties to settle disputes in front of impartial and independent arbitrators by following transparent rules. Arbitration excludes the possibility of "home court" advantage for certain parties and eliminates the concerns regarding the corruption and expertise of domestic judicial systems. What is more, the parties can choose the arbitrators (or arbitrators will be appointed to the parties) according to their skills and experience which are most suitable for the dispute in question. This is particularly important for the conflicts arising in the supply network, where the dispute may concern highly engineered products and may require presenting highly technical and scientific information (Rathke, 2015). Another big benefit of the arbitration process is its flexibility. Parties can better monitor the expenses, the overall process and scope of arbitration (Baker et al., 2021). In addition, the arbitration process is less formal than traditional litigation which helps the parties to find a mutual resolution peacefully and maintain good relationships which is particularly important for the Supply Chain domain where collaboration is one of the key performance indicators of the network (Fawcett et al., 2012; Wolf & Pickler, 2010).

Advantages Brought by Blockchain Technology Integration in the Arbitration Process

The blockchain technology integration into arbitration can bring significant benefits to the process that are valuable for Supply Chain dispute settlement. All stages of the arbitration procedure can be ameliorated through blockchain technology.

When a dispute arises the first step is dispute initiation. If parties have integrated Smart Contracts into their operations and a dispute arises between Supply Chain stakeholders, the parties can just generally simply trigger an arbitration clause that was encoded into the contract in advance. As soon as the arbitration clause is activated, the dispute is sent to the predefined Blockchain Arbitration platform. Following the dispute initiation comes the jurors' selection. Some Blockchain Arbitration platforms offer automatic jurors' selection according to some predefined rules, which saves time, eliminates manual labor, prevents bribery attempts and minimizes the chance of corruption (Guillaume & Riva, 2022; Zasemkova, 2020).

The parties can submit their evidence as soon as jurors are chosen. If the parties integrate blockchain technology into their daily activities, all the transactions related to the parties' operations are stored as independent transactions in the decentralized distributed blockchain ecosystem (Barnett & Treleaven, 2018; Michaelson, 2020). Thanks to the new and secure blockchain technology the parties can disclose all the needed evidence promptly and can be sure that the evidence is reliable, highly accurate and was never altered, should a dispute arise (Michalko, 2022). This is valuable as authenticity and provenance is always a problem during the resolution process (Barnett & Treleaven, 2018). Consequently, all the relevant evidence in the form of transactions on the blockchain will be accessible by arbitrators via secure read access (Michaelson, 2020). This way of evidence disclosure provides an opportunity to get rid of intermediaries like lawyers helping to find necessary documents and brings confidence to SC stakeholders (Zasemkova, 2019).

The arbitration process starts when all the evidence has been submitted by the parties. As the decision-making process is performed in the decentralized blockchain environment, it is highly secure and well protected from cyberattacks. In addition, all the personal information of the parties as well as of arbitrators is kept private and confidential, making Blockchain Arbitration platforms a trusted information hub (Barnett & Treleaven, 2018; Shehata, 2018). Data confidentiality is an important aspect of arbitration, but this is especially valuable for Supply Chain dispute resolution as the process can contain sensitive information and its leakage can cause serious damage to a company's reputation (Michaelson, 2020; Michaelson & Jeskie, 2021).

As soon as a decision is taken by the arbitrators it is presented to the parties. If the Blockchain Arbitration platform implies the possibility of an appeal, the parties can file an appeal fully automatically via the platform if they are dissatisfied with the resolution. However, if the decision of the arbitrators was found reasonable by the parties, it will be enforced. Blockchain technology with Smart Contracts assumes a big innovation in terms of automatic enforcement of the decision taken by the arbitrators. This is a substantial breakthrough compared to conventional litigation and arbitration, where the parties have to fight for payments and rely on the coercive state judicial system to enforce the decision. As a result, Blockchain Arbitration can become an autonomous and self-reliant resolution tool and the blockchain integration can ensure that the decision taken by the jurors will be necessarily enforced (Guillaume & Riva, 2022).

Considering the winning points that blockchain can bring to the arbitration process like full automation of all the steps of the resolution process and elimination of unnecessary third parties, Blockchain Arbitration is more time- and cost-efficient than conventional dispute resolution (Michalko, 2022; Zasemkova, 2019). Giving companies an opportunity to resolve disputes with significantly reduced settlement expenses and time needed for the resolution can considerably increase access to justice for smaller supply chain companies, decrease cash-to cash cycle time and enhance SC profitability (Chang et al., 2019; Dylag & Smith, 2023).

The efficiency of Blockchain Arbitration platforms can also be explained by the fact that they can operate worldwide owing to blockchain technology and are usually independent from state courts (Dylag & Smith, 2023; Shehata, 2018). Moreover, Blockchain Arbitration is the solution that can bring additional flexibility to the legal system and the parties as with the development of smart contracts law processes are expected to become more agile (Fenwick & Wrbka, 2016; Živković et al., 2023). Flexibility is an integral part of supply chain dispute resolution as it positively contributes to the overall network flexibility so that supply chains can faster and easier adapt to the competitive environment and possible unforeseen circumstances and can respond better to customer needs (Seebacher & Winkler, 2015).

Last but not least, Blockchain Arbitration has the potential to increase the level of trust between the parties. Automatic jurors' selection that avoids bribery attempts and corruption, usage of trusted evidence that comes from blockchain and security and confidentiality during the resolution process enabled by blockchain add trust to the SC stakeholders' relationship. This is a major benefit for the Supply Chain that can positively impact SC responsiveness, establish long-term consumer loyalty, commitment and

Blockchain Arbitration

product acceptance and improve such KPIs as integration with partners' and partners' satisfaction (Aslam et al., 2021; Handfield & Bechtel, 2002; Ferreira da Silva & Moro, 2021; Sahay, 2003).

CHALLENGES FOR BLOCKCHAIN ARBITRATION ADOPTION

Although there are many advantages that Blockchain can bring into Supply Chain resolution, there are certain challenges that can hinder its mass adoption in the domain.

All the challenges can be categorized into 4 extensive categories: (a) Legal, (b) Technical, (c) Cultural and (d) Education challenges.

Legal Challenges

There are many challenges that are coming from the legal side of Blockchain Arbitration. The first barrier is explained by the fact that agreements to arbitrate should be in writing to be enforced internationally under the New York Convention on the Enforcement of Foreign Arbitral Awards (Michaelson, 2020). However, Smart Contracts are just software code that can be fully understood only by programmers. So, it is quite doubtful that the arbitration clause that is encoded into the Smart Contract can comply with the New York Convention on the written form of an arbitration agreement. It is almost impossible to comply with the Convention's requirements without a traditional text-based contract that will go in conjunction with a Smart Contract (Michaelson, 2020; Zasemkova, 2019).

Even if it is possible to overcome the "in writing" challenge, the decision-making process in Blockchain Arbitration is also questionable from a legal point of view. A big disadvantage of Blockchain Arbitration compared to state judicial systems is that it does not offer any predictability about the outcome of the dispute. This is because arbitrators on Blockchain Arbitration platforms generally decide on the case based on common sense and do not rely either on a specific framework of rules and norms nor on the precedent. If dispute resolution platforms based on the blockchain want to become a credible and reliable solution, they should establish a configuration that will offer a certain level of predictability, confidence, and fairness of their judgments. In addition to the uncertainty of the blockchain arbitration process, the legal community is also quite skeptical about the enforceability of blockchain arbitration decisions, which is an integral part of every justice system. Arbitration platforms built on blockchain technology like Kleros or Jur are nowadays mostly limited to assets within blockchain ecosystem and actions that can be encoded into the Smart Contract. A Supply chain dispute can, however, also involve non-crypto assets or specific actions that need to be undertaken beyond the blockchain ecosystem, so Smart Contracts cannot be fully used to automatically enforce the arbitrators' decisions. To enforce a decision in the real, non-blockchain, world the participation of state authorities can be needed. This brings up a problem of Blockchain Arbitration decisions recognition and enforcement by state authorities regarding non-crypto assets. If arbitrators' decision will not be considered fair in the legal sense and will not comply with public policies, enforcement by state authorities beyond the blockchain ecosystem will not be feasible. Finding a state authority with jurisdiction over Blockchain Arbitration is just the first obstacle. Even if a state jurisdiction recognizes the Blockchain Arbitration decision, it can find it difficult to enforce this decision if the losing party refuses to voluntarily comply. This is because of the immutability of blockchain technology that prevents any authority from changing the data contained within the decentralized ecosystem. It is very difficult to change the code of the Smart Contracts once they are programmed. Currently state authorities can only enforce their decisions on the blockchain if the parties agree on the decision and are willing to execute it (Guillaume & Riva, 2022).

However, now considerable efforts are made in the judicial system for recognition of blockchain and Smart Contracts. The US justice department, American Arbitration Association, China's Supreme Court and legal institutions of Dubai, UK and Azerbaijan have announced active research in the area of blockchain to advance the adoption of this technology within the legal domain and recognize the technology's legal validity (Dylag & Smith, 2023; Michaelson & Jeskie, 2021; Michalko, 2022). Summing up, given the current stage of Blockchain Arbitration development, there is still a fundamental need to rethink justice and existing legal procedures in order to recognize and enforce the decisions produced by this dispute resolution method worldwide (Dylag & Smith, 2023).

Technical Challenges

Currently there are significant technological challenges that can considerably complicate the blockchain dispute resolution procedures that run on blockchain platforms (Shehata, 2018). For example, some of the existing Blockchain Arbitration platforms cannot deal with all kinds of disputes and are mostly restricted to disputes where parties have just two options for the resolution. Binary outcomes are, however, not suitable for many supply chain disputes, as they usually assume a series of small decisions according to the process of reasoning and this can hardly be achieved in a binary way. However, more complex Blockchain Arbitration solutions are already on the doorstep that can execute more complex decisions. In addition, as was mentioned in the legal part, technology constraints limit the ability to enforce Blockchain Arbitration decisions. Blockchain Arbitration decisions can only be enforced with the help of the smart contract on the assets that were integrated into the blockchain ecosystem. Consequently, Blockchain Arbitration enforcement mechanisms can only be functional with crypto assets and have no power over real-world assets (Guillaume & Riva, 2022). What is more, blockchain is just starting to develop actively and technology still lacks speed and scalability. In addition, Smart Contracts contain a big number of errors in the programming language that can hinder correct execution of blockchain arbitration decisions. The novelty of blockchain technology presents a big challenge for supply chain companies as it requires a lot of research and understanding of its main characteristics and specificities. If not eliminated, these technological challenges can stop the companies from using Smart Contracts and applying to blockchain arbitration platforms for a fast resolution (Baharmand et al., 2021; Fulmer, 2019).

Cultural Challenges

The principle of legitimacy is the core of conflict settlement because it is based on trust and therefore readiness to comply with the outcomes. However, blockchain technology was designed and developed in the culture where the concept of trust and human factor are replaced by the immutability of blockchain technology and its ability to prevent disputes. Consequently, blockchain creates a safe enough ecosystem so that trust in something other than blockchain itself is not essential. When technology struggles to perform, the trust is broken, and there are no processes to re-establish it (Rabinovich-Einy & Katsh, 2019). Moreover, the blockchain community values absence of intermediaries to prevent the concentration of power and centralized oversight. This culture of decentralization is alien to the judicial system as without centralized monitoring there is a higher chance that the dispute resolution system will be abused (Erbguth & Morin, 2018). What is more, for SC companies that can have quite complex disputes with sensitive

Blockchain Arbitration

data, dispute resolution tools should have a central body that initiates their implementation, monitors their execution, and assures that they are operating efficiently and fairly. Yet, such central authority is traditionally criticized in the blockchain environment (Heiskanen, 2017).

Educational Challenges

Blockchain technology and Smart Contracts built on top of it are complex and require substantial research and efforts to understand how they function. Companies that want to implement Smart Contracts and Blockchain arbitration have to invest time, efforts and even money to adequately educate and inform their staff on functionalities of the distributed ledgers and Blockchain Arbitration platforms. The educational challenge also refers to lawyers that want to work with Blockchain Arbitration platforms and to arbitrate disputes coming from Smart Contracts and to lawyers that tend to help companies when a dispute arises. The majority of lawyers do not understand how smart contracts and blockchain function and lack knowledge about computer coding languages that are used to program a Smart Contract (Fulmer, 2019). Just like lawyers, arbitrators have little knowledge of what Smart Contracts really are and how to read them (Schmitz, 2020). To be adopted by Supply Chain companies, Blockchain Arbitration platforms should ensure the ready supply of jurors who have enough knowledge in the supply chain sphere, legal domain and technological aspect of Smart Contracts to be fully equipped to make affordable, fast and enforceable decisions (Sayanika Dey & Sneha Chatterjee, 2021). These factors establish high educational barriers for the juror selection (Evans, 2019). To promote the adoption of Blockchain Arbitration platforms for Smart Contract dispute resolution, the whole business and legal communities have to be adequately educated about blockchain as despite the growing interest in this technology, there are still numerous misconceptions on how technology functions and what benefits it can provide (Dylag & Smith, 2023).

FUTURE RESEARCH DIRECTIONS

Currently Blockchain Arbitration adoption for Supply Chain disputes is a topic that is debated in research communities in the fields of law, IT and Supply Chain management. Due to the multidisciplinary nature of Blockchain Arbitration concept, it is important to conduct extensive research in the main domains concerned:

- Scholars working in the law domain need to research and improve the decentralized justice model in terms of fairness and full transparency in the selection of jurors and decision-making process and study the ways to shorten the time and reduce the costs related to the dispute resolution within the limits of procedural fairness (Allen et al., 2019; Bathurst, 2012);
- In the IT community comprehensive research is required for better scalability and security of the decentralized environment for Blockchain Arbitration (Pal et al., 2021);
- Supply Chain Management researchers, that are concerned about the market opening, supply chain efficiency and performance (Fosso Wamba et al., 2020), need to work on the opportunities to integrate Blockchain Arbitration to achieve the goals mentioned.

The future research collaborations between these different domains becomes an absolute necessity for Blockchain Arbitration to become a full-fledged, enforceable, and widely accepted dispute resolution method.

To contribute to the interdisciplinary topic of Blockchain Arbitration adoption for the Supply Chain chapter authors plan to expand their work and conduct qualitative research aimed at identifying the business view on Supply Chain disputes, the main dispute resolution strategies the company is using, their advantages and limits and to access the impact of SC disputes on SC performance. The research will also seek to identify the SC companies' need and interest in Blockchain Arbitration as a dispute resolution method.

CONCLUSION

Blockchain technology is gaining more and more attention from SC professionals and researchers. Thanks to such technology characteristics as immutability, security, transparency etc., blockchain can successfully deal with modern SC challenges: lack of transparency, visibility and security and low level of trust between SC parties. The blockchain technology also allows for Smart Contracts integration that have the potential to automate and facilitate the whole contract process in the Supply Chain.

Despite these advantages, blockchain and Smart Contracts are not flawless. In case some of the Smart Contract terms were violated by the parties or a mistake was made in the contract coding, or some other disagreement occurred between SC parties, a dispute can arise. Supply Chain disputes are harmful for the whole network as they can destroy trust among the participants and jeopardize their relationship and collaboration. Disputes that arise from blockchain and Smart Contract usage, however, pose a particular danger to SC participants as traditional dispute resolution methods like litigation or Alternative Dispute Resolution procedures are not suitable for their settlement.

This book chapter has presented Blockchain Arbitration as a possible solution for this regulatory lacuna. Blockchain Arbitration assumes many potential benefits for the Supply Chain dispute resolution as it generally implies performing the dispute resolution procedure on a special platform fully (or partially) online on the decentralized blockchain environment with the help of selected jurors without any need for the public authority to administer justice. In addition, the process of dispute resolution (from dispute initiation to decision enforcement) is usually almost fully automated, which eliminates unnecessary third parties and manual labor. Considering these features, the innovative blockchain arbitration process is more flexible, time- and cost-efficient and less formal than conventional resolution methods. In addition, the random and automated jurors' selection and full data security provided by blockchain technology during the resolution process boost trust between SC stakeholders. All these aspects can potentially have a positive impact on SC responsiveness such SC KPIs as profitability and flexibility of the chain, cash-to-cash cycle time, customer and SC partners' satisfaction, cooperation and loyalty, and integration with SC partners. Relations with clients can also be improved as a result of increased consumer trust, loyalty, commitment and product acceptance.

Although many advantages and benefits exist for the Supply Chain dispute resolution, Blockchain Arbitration is just at the start of its development and encounters quite a big number of legal, technical, cultural and education challenges. Despite these challenges, the potential of the Blockchain Arbitration platforms for the Supply Chain can be observed already today. This dispute resolution method can bring many advantages for pharmaceutical and food supply chains that are often subject to frauds and are facing a big number of disputes (Donoghue et al., 2012; Kamilaris et al., 2019), pooled warehousing services, where numerous disputes occur due to high level of spaces and resources sharing between the participants (Makaci et al., 2017) and for logistics services (maritime and road transportations, third-party logistics), where building and maintaining trust with partners is always difficult (Pierce, 2020; Yang, 2019).

REFERENCES

Aich, S., Chakraborty, S., Sain, M., Lee, H., & Kim, H.-C. (2019). A Review on Benefits of IoT Integrated Blockchain based Supply Chain Management Implementations across Different Sectors with Case Study. In *Proceedings of the 2019 21st International Conference on Advanced Communication Technology (ICACT)* (pp. 138 - 141). 10.23919/ICACT.2019.8701910

Alkhudary, R., & Féniès, P. (2022). Blockchain and Trust in Supply Chain Management: A Conceptual Framework. *IFAC-PapersOnLine*, *55*(10), 2402–2406. doi:10.1016/j.ifacol.2022.10.068

Allen, D. W. E., Lane, A. M., & Poblet, M. (2019). The Governance of Blockchain Dispute Resolution. *SSRN*, *25*, 75–101. doi:10.2139srn.3334674

Aouidef, Y., Ast, F., & Deffains, B. (2021). *Decentralized Justice: A Comparative Analysis of Blockchain Online Dispute Resolution Projects*. Retrieved November 14, 2022, from https://www.frontiersin.org/articles/10.3389/fbloc.2021.564551/full

Aslam, J., Saleem, A., Khan, N. T., & Kim, Y. B. (2021). Factors influencing blockchain adoption in supply chain management practices: A study based on the oil industry. *Journal of Innovation & Knowledge*, *6*(2), 124–134. doi:10.1016/j.jik.2021.01.002

Azzi, R., Chamoun, R. K., & Sokhn, M. (2019). The power of a blockchain-based supply chain. *Computers & Industrial Engineering*, *135*, 582–592. doi:10.1016/j.cie.2019.06.042

Badhotiya, G. K., Sharma, V. P., Prakash, S., Kalluri, V., & Singh, R. (2021). Investigation and assessment of blockchain technology adoption in the pharmaceutical supply chain. *Materials Today: Proceedings*, *46*(20), 10776–10780. doi:10.1016/j.matpr.2021.01.673

Baharmand, H., Maghsoudi, A., & Coppi, G. (2021). Exploring the application of blockchain to humanitarian supply chains: Insights from Humanitarian Supply Blockchain pilot project. *International Journal of Operations & Production Management*, *41*(9), 1522–1543. doi:10.1108/IJOPM-12-2020-0884

Bai, C., Quayson, M., & Sarkis, J. (2022). Analysis of Blockchain's enablers for improving sustainable supply chain transparency in Africa cocoa industry. *Journal of Cleaner Production*, *358*, 131896. doi:10.1016/j.jclepro.2022.131896

Baker, M., Dowling, C. & Proudfoot, C. (2021). Supply chain disputes: Avoidance, mitigation and resolution. *International arbitration report*. Norton Rose Fulbright.

Barnett, J., & Treleaven, P. (2018). Algorithmic Dispute Resolution—The Automation of Professional Dispute Resolution Using AI and Blockchain Technologies. *The Computer Journal*, *61*(3), 399–408. doi:10.1093/comjnl/bxx103

Bathurst, T. F. (2012). The role of the courts in the changing dispute resolution landscape. *The University of New South Wales Law Journal*, *35*(3), 870–888. doi:10.3316/informit.075130696127938

Batwa, A., & Norrman, A. (2020). A Framework for Exploring Blockchain Technology in Supply Chain Management. *Operations and Supply Chain Management: An International Journal*, *13*(3), 294–306. doi:10.31387/oscm0420271

Berneis, M., Bartsch, D., & Winkler, H. (2021). Applications of Blockchain Technology in Logistics and Supply Chain Management—Insights from a Systematic Literature Review. *Logistics*, *5*(3), 43. doi:10.3390/logistics5030043

Buchwald, M. (2019). Smart Contract Dispute Resolution: The Inescapable Flaws of Blockchain-Based Arbitration. *University of Pennsylvania Law Review*, *168*, 1369–1423. https://scholarship.law.upenn.edu/penn_law_review/vol168/iss5/3

Casado-Vara, R., Prieto, J., la Prieta, F. D., & Corchado, J. M. (2018). How blockchain improves the supply chain: Case study alimentary supply chain. *Procedia Computer Science*, *134*, 393–398. doi:10.1016/j.procs.2018.07.193

Chang, S. E., Chen, Y.-C., & Wu, T.-C. (2019). Exploring blockchain technology in international trade: Business process re-engineering for letter of credit. *Industrial Management & Data Systems*, *119*(8), 1712–1733. doi:10.1108/IMDS-12-2018-0568

Chang, Y., Iakovou, E., & Shi, W. (2020). Blockchain in global supply chains and cross border trade: A critical synthesis of the state-of-the-art, challenges and opportunities. *International Journal of Production Research*, *58*(7), 2082–2099. doi:10.1080/00207543.2019.1651946

Cheung, K.-F., Bell, M. G. H., & Bhattacharjya, J. (2021). Cybersecurity in logistics and supply chain management: An overview and future research directions. *Transportation Research Part E, Logistics and Transportation Review*, *146*, 102217. doi:10.1016/j.tre.2020.102217

Cohen, M. A., & Mallik, S. (1997). Global Supply Chains: Research and Applications. *Production and Operations Management*, *6*(3), 193–210. doi:10.1111/j.1937-5956.1997.tb00426.x

Cryptonomica. (2018). *Cryptonomica Arbitration Rules*. Retrieved November 30, 2022, from https://github.com/Cryptonomica/arbitration-rules/blob/master/Arbitration_Rules/Cryptonomica/Cryptonomica-Arbitration-Rules.EN.clearsigned.md

Cryptonomica. (2022). *Cryptonomica Advanced Tools for Smart People*. Retrieved November 30, 2022, from https://www.cryptonomica.net/#!/

De Giovanni, P. (2020). Blockchain and smart contracts in supply chain management: A game theoretic model. *International Journal of Production Economics*, *228*, 107855. doi:10.1016/j.ijpe.2020.107855

Dey, S., & Chatterjee, S. (2021). Blockchain Arbitration and Smart Contracts in India. *NyaayShastra Law Review*, *2*(1), 1-14. doi:10.17613/ebks-ec42

Donoghue, D., Taylor, E., & Steffe, E. K. (2012). *Commercial disputes in the biotech and pharma sector*. Retrieved December 2, 2022, from https://www.financierworldwide.com/commercial-disputes-in-the-biotech-and-pharma-sector

Dujak, D., & Sajter, D. (2019). Blockchain Applications in Supply Chain. In A. Kawa & A. Maryniak (Eds.), *SMART Supply Network* (pp. 21–46). Springer. doi:10.1007/978-3-319-91668-2_2

Dutta, P., Choi, T.-M., Somani, S., & Butala, R. (2020). Blockchain technology in supply chain operations: Applications, challenges and research opportunities. *Transportation Research Part E, Logistics and Transportation Review*, *142*, 102067. doi:10.1016/j.tre.2020.102067 PMID:33013183

Dyer, J. H., & Chu, W. (2000). The Determinants of Trust in Supplier-Automaker Relationships in the U.S., Japan and Korea. *Journal of International Business Studies*, *31*(2), 259–285. doi:10.1057/palgrave.jibs.8490905

Dylag, M., & Smith, H. (2021). From cryptocurrencies to cryptocourts: Blockchain and the financialization of dispute resolution platforms. *Information Communication and Society*, *26*(2), 1–16. doi:10.1080/1369118X.2021.1942958

Erbguth, J., & Morin, J.-H. (2018). Towards Governance and Dispute Resolution for DLT and Smart Contracts. In *Proceedings of the 2018 IEEE 9th International Conference on Software Engineering and Service Science (ICSESS)* (pp. 46-55). 10.1109/ICSESS.2018.8663721

Evans, T. (2019). The Role of International Rules in Blockchain-Based Cross-Border Commercial Disputes. *Wayne Law Review*, *65*(1), 1–16. https://waynelawreview.org/role-of-international-rules-in-blockchain-based-cross-border-commercial-disputes/

Fawcett, S. E., Jones, S. L., & Fawcett, A. M. (2012). Supply chain trust: The catalyst for collaborative innovation. *Business Horizons*, *55*(2), 163–178. doi:10.1016/j.bushor.2011.11.004

Fenwick, M., & Wrbka, S. (2016). The Flexibility of Law and its Limits in Contemporary Business Regulation. In M. Fenwick & S. Wrbka (Eds.), *Flexibility in Modern Business Law: A Comparative Assessment* (pp. 1–12). Springer. doi:10.1007/978-4-431-55787-6_1

Ferreira da Silva, C., & Moro, S. (2021). Blockchain technology as an enabler of consumer trust: A text mining literature analysis. *Telematics and Informatics*, *60*(2), 101593. doi:10.1016/j.tele.2021.101593

Fosso Wamba, S., Queiroz, M. M., & Trinchera, L. (2020). Dynamics between blockchain adoption determinants and supply chain performance: An empirical investigation. *International Journal of Production Economics*, *229*, 107791. doi:10.1016/j.ijpe.2020.107791

Fulmer, N. (2019). Exploring the Legal Issues of Blockchain Applications. *Akron Law Review*, *52*(1), 162–191. https://ideaexchange.uakron.edu/akronlawreview/vol52/iss1/5/

Guillaume, F., & Riva, S. (2022). Blockchain Dispute Resolution for Decentralized Autonomous Organizations: The Rise of Decentralized Autonomous Justice. In A. Bonomi & M. Lehmann (Eds.), *Blockchain and Private International Law*. Brill Nijhoff. doi:10.2139srn.4042704

Han, W., Huang, Y., Hughes, M., & Zhang, M. (2021). The trade-off between trust and distrust in supply chain collaboration. *Industrial Marketing Management*, *98*, 93–104. doi:10.1016/j.indmarman.2021.08.005

Handfield, R. B., & Bechtel, C. (2002). The role of trust and relationship structure in improving supply chain responsiveness. *Industrial Marketing Management, 31*(4), 367–382. doi:10.1016/S0019-8501(01)00169-9

Heiskanen, A. (2017). The technology of trust: How the Internet of Things and blockchain could usher in a new era of construction productivity. *Construction Research and Innovation, 8*(2), 66–70. doi:10.1080/20450249.2017.1337349

Howell, B. E., & Potgieter, P. H. (2019). Governance of Smart Contracts in Blockchain Institutions. SSRN *Electronic Journal.* doi:10.2139/ssrn.3423190

Hughes, L., Dwivedi, Y. K., Misra, S. K., Rana, N. P., Raghavan, V., & Akella, V. (2019). Blockchain research, practice and policy: Applications, benefits, limitations, emerging research themes and research agenda. *International Journal of Information Management, 49*, 114–129. doi:10.1016/j.ijinfomgt.2019.02.005

Jevremovic, N. (2020). Blockchain, Smart Contracts and ADR. SSRN *Electronic Journal.* doi:10.2139/ssrn.3699422

Kamilaris, A., Fonts, A., & Prenafeta-Boldύ, F. X. (2019). The rise of blockchain technology in agriculture and food supply chains. *Trends in Food Science & Technology, 91*, 640–652. doi:10.1016/j.tifs.2019.07.034

Kazancoglu, I., Ozbiltekin-Pala, M., Kumar Mangla, S., Kazancoglu, Y., & Jabeen, F. (2022). Role of flexibility, agility and responsiveness for sustainable supply chain resilience during COVID-19. *Journal of Cleaner Production, 362*, 132431. doi:10.1016/j.jclepro.2022.132431

Kshetri, N., & Voas, J. (2019). Supply Chain Trust. *IT Professional, 21*(2), 6–10. doi:10.1109/MITP.2019.2895423

Kumar Singh, R., Mishra, R., Gupta, S., & Mukherjee, A. A. (2023). Blockchain applications for secured and resilient supply chains: A systematic literature review and future research agenda. *Computers & Industrial Engineering, 175*, 108854. doi:10.1016/j.cie.2022.108854

LawtechUK. (2022). *Digital representation and ownership of physical assets.* Retrieved December 7, 2022, from digital_representation_ownership_physical_assets.pdf

Lesaege, C., Ast, F., & George, W. (2019). *Kleros Short Paper v1.0.7.* Kleros.

Lim, M. K., Li, Y., Wang, C., & Tseng, M.-L. (2021). A literature review of blockchain technology applications in supply chains: A comprehensive analysis of themes, methodologies and industries. *Computers & Industrial Engineering, 154*, 107133. doi:10.1016/j.cie.2021.107133

Lund, J., & Wright, C. (2003). Building Union Power Through the Supply Chain Mapping Opportunities and Jurisdictional Boundaries in Grocery Distribution. *Labor Studies Journal, 27*(4), 59–75. doi:10.1353/lab.2003.0012

Makaci, M., Reaidy, P., Evrard-Samuel, K., Botta-Genoulaz, V., & Monteiro, T. (2017). Pooled warehouse management: An empirical study. *Computers & Industrial Engineering, 112*, 526–536. doi:10.1016/j.cie.2017.03.005

Markmann, C., Darkow, I.-L., & von der Gracht, H. (2013). A Delphi-based risk analysis — Identifying and assessing future challenges for supply chain security in a multi-stakeholder environment. *Technological Forecasting and Social Change*, *80*(9), 1815–1833. doi:10.1016/j.techfore.2012.10.019

Martinez, V., Zhao, M., Blujdea, C., Han, X., Neely, A. & Albores, P. (2019). Blockchain-driven customer order management. *International Journal of Operations & Production Management, 39*(6-8), 993-1022. doi:10.1108/IJOPM-01-2019-0100

Marucheck, A., Greis, N., Mena, C., & Cai, L. (2011). Product safety and security in the global supply chain: Issues, challenges and research opportunities. *Journal of Operations Management*, *29*(7-8), 707–720. doi:10.1016/j.jom.2011.06.007

Meixell, M. J., & Gargeya, V. B. (2005). Global supply chain design: A literature review and critique. *Transportation Research Part E, Logistics and Transportation Review*, *41*(6), 531–550. doi:10.1016/j.tre.2005.06.003

Metzger, J. (2019). The current landscape of blockchain-based, crowdsourced arbitration. *Macquarie Law Journal*, *19*, 81–101. doi:10.3316/informit.394273690449964

Michaelson, P. (2020). Arbitrating Disputes Involving Blockchains, Smart Contracts, and Smart Legal Contracts. *SSRN*, *74*(4), 89–133. doi:10.2139srn.3720876

Michaelson, P., & Jeskie, S. A. (2021). A Guidebook to Arbitrating Disputes Involving Blockchains and Smart Agreements. *Alternatives to the High Cost of Litigation*, *74*(4), 89–133. doi:10.1002/alt.21887

Michalko, M. (2019). Blockchain 'Witness': A New Evidence Model in Consumer Disputes. *International Journal on Consumer Law and Practice, 7*, Article 3. https://repository.nls.ac.in/ijclp/vol7/iss1/3/

Min, H. (2019). Blockchain technology for enhancing supply chain resilience. *Business Horizons*, *62*(1), 35–45. doi:10.1016/j.bushor.2018.08.012

Mirabelli, G., & Solina, V. (2020). Blockchain and agricultural supply chains traceability: Research trends and future challenges. *Procedia Manufacturing*, *42*, 414–421. doi:10.1016/j.promfg.2020.02.054

Nakamoto, S. (2008). *Bitcoin: A Peer-to-Peer Electronic Cash System*, Retrieved December 10, 2022, from https://bitcoin.org/bitcoin.pdf

Nandi, M. L., Nandi, S., Moya, H., & Kaynak, H. (2020). Blockchain technology-enabled supply chain systems and supply chain performance: A resource-based view. *Supply Chain Management*, *25*(6), 841–862. doi:10.1108/SCM-12-2019-0444

Narasimhan, R., & Nair, A. (2005). The antecedent role of quality, information sharing and supply chain proximity on strategic alliance formation and performance. *International Journal of Production Economics*, *96*(3), 301–313. doi:10.1016/j.ijpe.2003.06.004

Pal, A., Tiwari, C. K., & Haldar, N. (2021). Blockchain for business management: Applications, challenges and potentials. *The Journal of High Technology Management Research*, *32*(2), 100414. doi:10.1016/j.hitech.2021.100414

Panayides, P. M., & Venus Lun, Y. H. (2009). The impact of trust on innovativeness and supply chain performance. *International Journal of Production Economics*, *122*(1), 35–46. doi:10.1016/j.ijpe.2008.12.025

Paul, T., Mondal, S., Islam, N., & Rakshit, S. (2021). The impact of blockchain technology on the tea supply chain and its sustainable performance. *Technological Forecasting and Social Change*, *173*, 121163. doi:10.1016/j.techfore.2021.121163

Pierce, F. (2020). *Consignment theft dispute ruling has implications for logistics industry*. Retrieved December 12, 2022, from https://www.supplychaindigital.com/supply-chain-2/consignment-theft-dispute-ruling-has-implications-logistics-industry

Prause, G. (2019). Smart Contracts for Smart Supply Chains. *IFAC-PapersOnLine*, *52*(13), 2501–2506. doi:10.1016/j.ifacol.2019.11.582

Rabinovich-Einy, O., & Katsch, E. (2019). Blockchain and the Inevitability of Disputes: The Role for Online Dispute Resolution. *Journal of Dispute Resolution*, *2019*(2), 47–75. https://ssrn.com/abstract=3508461

Rathke, S. K. (2015). *Supply Chain Dispute Resolution in the US*. Retrieved November 28, 2022, from https://www.globalsupplychainlawblog.com/wp-content/uploads/sites/22/2015/07/Supply-Chain-Dispute-Resolution-in-the-US.pdf

Rauniyar, K., Wu, X., Gupta, S., Modgil, S., & Lopes de Sousa Jabbour, A. B. (2022). Risk management of supply chains in the digital transformation era: Contribution and challenges of blockchain technology. *Industrial Management & Data Systems*, *123*(1), 253–277. doi:10.1108/IMDS-04-2021-0235

Saberi, S., Kouhizadeh, M., Sarkis, J., & Shen, L. (2019). Blockchain technology and its relationships to sustainable supply chain management. *International Journal of Production Research*, *57*(7), 2117–2135. doi:10.1080/00207543.2018.1533261

Sahay, B. S. (2003). Understanding trust in supply chain relationships. *Industrial Management & Data Systems*, *103*(8), 553–563. doi:10.1108/02635570310497602

Sanders, N. R., & Wagner, S. M. (2011). Multidisciplinary and Multimethod Research for Addressing Contemporary Supply Chain Challenges. *Journal of Business Logistics*, *32*(4), 317–323. doi:10.1111/j.0000-0000.2011.01027.x

Schmitz, A., & Rule, C. (2019). Online Dispute Resolution for Smart Contracts. *Journal of Dispute Resolution*, *2019*(2), 103–125. https://papers.ssrn.com/sol3/papers.cfm?abstract_id=3647573

Schmitz, A. J. (2020). *Making Smart Contracts "Smarter" with Arbitration*. University of Missouri School of Law Legal Studies Research Paper Series, Paper No. 2020-18. https://scholarship.law.missouri.edu/facpubs/726/

Seebacher, G., & Winkler, H. (2015). A capability approach to evaluate supply chain flexibility. *International Journal of Production Economics*, *167*, 177–186. doi:10.1016/j.ijpe.2015.05.035

Seebacher, S., & Schüritz, R. (2017). Blockchain Technology as an Enabler of Service Systems: A Structured Literature Review. In W. Van der Aalst, J. Mylopoulos, S. Ram, M. Rosemann, & C. Szyperski (Eds.), *Exploring Services Science. IESS 2017. Lecture Notes in Business Information Processing* (pp. 12–23). Springer. doi:10.1007/978-3-319-56925-3_2

Shehata, I. (2018). Smart Contracts & International Arbitration. SSRN *Electronic Journal*. doi:10.2139/ssrn.3290026

Song, J. M., Sung, J., & Park, T. (2019). Applications of Blockchain to Improve Supply Chain Traceability. *Procedia Computer Science*, *162*, 119–122. doi:10.1016/j.procs.2019.11.266

Szabo, N. (1996). S*mart Contracts: Building Blocks for Digital Markets*. Retrieved December 2, 2001, from http://www.truevaluemetrics.org/DBpdfs/BlockChain/Nick-Szabo-Smart-Contracts-Building-Blocks-for-Digital-Markets-1996-14 591.pdf

Tan, W. C., & Sidhu, M. S. (2022). Review of RFID and IoT integration in supply chain management. *Operations Research Perspectives*, *9*, 100229. doi:10.1016/j.orp.2022.100229

Wang, J., Zhou, H., & Jin, X. (2021). Risk transmission in complex supply chain network with multi-drivers. *Chaos, Solitons, and Fractals*, *143*, 110259. doi:10.1016/j.chaos.2020.110259

Waters, D. (Ed.). (2003). *Logistics: An Introduction to Supply Chain Management*. Palgrave Macmillan.

Wolf, F., & Pickler, L. (2010). Supply Chain Dispute Resolution: A Delphi Study. *International Journal of Information Systems and Supply Chain Management*, *3*(3), 50–65. doi:10.4018/jisscm.2010070104

Yang, C.-S. (2019). Maritime shipping digitalization: Blockchain-based technology applications, future improvements, and intention to use. *Transportation Research Part E, Logistics and Transportation Review*, *131*, 108–117. doi:10.1016/j.tre.2019.09.020

Zasemkova, O. (2019). Dispute resolution by means of blockchain technology. *Actual Problems of Russian Law*, *4*(4), 160–167. doi:10.17803/1994-1471.2019.101.4.160-167

Zasemkova, O. (2020). Methods of Resolving Disputes Arising from Smart Contracts. *Lex Russica*, *2020*(4), 9–20. doi:10.17803/1729-5920.2020.161.4.009-020

Zhang, Y., Montenegro-Marin, C. E., & Díaz, V. G. (2021). Holistic cognitive conflict chain management framework in supply chain management. *Environmental Impact Assessment Review*, *88*, 106564. doi:10.1016/j.eiar.2021.106564

Živković, P., McCurdy, D., Zou, M., & Raymond, A. H. (2021). Mind the gap: Tech-based dispute resolutions in global supply blockchains. *Business Horizons*, *66*(1), 13–26. doi:10.1016/j.bushor.2021.10.008

ADDITIONAL READING

Ast, F. (2019). *Dispute Revolution—The Kleros Handbook of Decentralized Justice*. Kleros.

Casino, F., Dasaklis, T. K., & Patsakis, C. (2019). A systematic literature review of blockchain-based applications: Current status, classification and open issues. *Telematics and Informatics*, *36*, 55–81. doi:10.1016/j.tele.2018.11.006

Centobelli, P., Cerchione, R., Vecchio, P. D., Oropallo, E., & Secundo, G. (2022). Blockchain technology for bridging trust, traceability and transparency in circular supply chain. *Information & Management*, *59*(7), 103508. doi:10.1016/j.im.2021.103508

Chevalier, M. (2021). From Smart Contract Litigation to Blockchain Arbitration, a New Decentralized Approach Leading Towards the Blockchain Arbitral Order. *Journal of International Dispute Settlement*, *12*(4), 558–584. doi:10.1093/jnlids/idab025

Durach, C. F., Blesik, T., von Düring, M., & Bick, M. (2021). Blockchain Applications in Supply Chain Transactions. *Journal of Business Logistics*, *42*(1), 7–24. doi:10.1111/jbl.12238

Gudkov, A. (2020). Crowd Arbitration: Blockchain Dispute Resolution. *Legal Issues in the Digital Age*, *3*(3), Article 3.

Horvath, L. (2001). Collaboration: The key to value creation in supply chain management. *Supply Chain Management*, *6*(5), 205–207. doi:10.1108/EUM0000000006039

Koulu, R. (2016). Blockchains and Online Dispute Resolution: Smart Contracts as an Alternative to Enforcement. *Script-ed*, *13*(1), 40–69. doi:10.2966cript.130116.40

Kumar, A., Liu, R., & Shan, Z. (2020). Is Blockchain a Silver Bullet for Supply Chain Management? Technical Challenges and Research Opportunities. *Decision Sciences*, *51*(1), 8–37. doi:10.1111/deci.12396

KEY TERMS AND DEFINITIONS

Alternative Dispute Resolution (ADR): Dispute resolution procedures that are short versions of full-scale court proceedings or alternatives to them (ex. negotiation, mediation, conciliation, arbitration).

Blockchain: A distributed and decentralized ledger that registers transactions in an untrustworthy environment and is protected by numeric signatures and cryptographic hash functions.

Blockchain Arbitration: A blockchain-based decentralized system of dispute resolution based that was specifically designed for smart contract and blockchain disputes where the settlement process is carried online, and the arbitrators' decisions can be executed automatically with the help of a Smart Contract without any public authority intervention.

Dispute: Any kind of disagreement that can arise between Supply Chain stakeholders due to, for example, incorrect invoice of a shipment, poor contract management, not on time/in full deliveries etc.

Dispute Resolution: A process of resolving (settling) a dispute between parties.

Online Dispute Resolution (ODR): A disputes resolution mechanism that uses electronic or digital platforms and other information and communication technologies during the resolution process.

Smart Contract: A sort of digital agreement stored on a blockchain that self-executes when pre-defined conditions are met.

Supply Chain: A complete process of manufacturing and selling products that includes all the steps from the supply of raw materials to the final products' distribution and sale.

Supply Chain Management: Management of product, information and financial flows that refer to a product or service at all the stages - from the purchase of raw materials to product delivery to final customers.

Supply Chain Performance: How effective each stage of the supply chain is in reducing inefficiencies, meeting end-customer requirements and optimizing the costs and speed in the network.

Section 4
Blockchain Technology's Impact on the Supply Chain

Chapter 7
Managing Supply Chain Digitalization With Blockchain Technology

Kamalendu Pal

https://orcid.org/0000-0001-7158-6481

University of London, UK

ABSTRACT

Digitization of manufacturing supply chain operations is essential in changing management practices and enhancing business transparency-related aspects. The digitalization of supply chain business processes often exploits emerging technologies such as radio frequency identification (RFID), the internet of things (IoT), data analytics, cloud computing, and blockchain technology to reshape supply chain management. The IoT technology integrates various smart objects (or things) to form a network, share data among the connected objects, store data, and process data to support business applications. However, some of the IoT infrastructural components are a shortage of computational processing power and local data storing ability, and these components are very vulnerable to the privacy and security of collected data. This chapter presents an information system architecture consisting of IoT and blockchain technology to maintain data security and transparency and how this helps improve business operations.

INTRODUCTION

As a result of changes in the economic, environmental, and business environments, the modern manufacturing industry appears to be riskier than ever before, which created a need for improving its supply chain privacy and security. These changes are for several reasons. First, the increasing global economy produces and depends on people's free flow of goods and information. Second, disasters have increased in number and intensity during recent decades. Natural disasters such as earthquakes, floods, or pandemics (e.g., coronavirus) strike more often and have a more significant economic impact. Simultaneously, the number of human-made disasters such as industrial sabotage, wars, and terrorist attacks that affects manufacturing supply networks has increased (Colema, 2006). These factors have created significant

DOI: 10.4018/978-1-6684-7455-6.ch007

challenges for manufacturers, the country, and the global economic condition. Simply put, manufacturers must deploy continuous improvement in business processes, which improve both supply chain activities execution and security enhancement.

Besides, today's manufacturing industry (e.g., apparel, automobile) is inclined to worldwide business operations due to the socioeconomic advantage of the globalization of product design and development (Pal, 2020). For example, a typical apparel manufacturing network consists of organizations' sequence, facilities, functions, and activities to produce and develop an ultimate product or related services. The action starts with raw materials purchased from selective suppliers and products produced at one or more production facilities (Pal, 2019). Next, these products are moved to intermediate collection points (e.g., warehouses, distribution centers) to store temporarily to move to the next stage of the manufacturing network and finally delivered the products to intermediate storages or retailers or customers (Pal, 2017) (Pal, 2018).

This way, global manufacturing networks are increasingly complicated due to a growing need for inter-organizational and intra-organizational connectedness enabled by advances in modern Information technologies (e.g., RFID, Internet of Things, Blockchain, Service-Oriented Computing, Big Data Analytics) (Okorie et al., 2017) and tightly coupled business processes. Also, manufacturing business networks use information systems to monitor operational activities in nearly real time.

Digitalizing business activities attract attention from manufacturing network management, improving communication and collaboration, and enhancing trust within business partners due to real-time information sharing and better business process integration. However, the above new technologies come with different disruptions to operations and ultimate productivity. For example, some operational disruptions are malicious threats that hinder the safety of goods and services, and ultimately customers lose trust in doing business with the manufacturing companies.

As a potential solution to tackle security problems, practitioners and academics have reported attractive research with IoT and blockchain-based information systems for maintaining transparency, data integrity, privacy, and security-related issues. In a manufacturing data communication network context, the Internet of Things (IoT) system integrates different heterogeneous objects and sensors which surround manufacturing operations (Pal, 2019) and facilitates information exchange among the business stakeholders (also known as nodes in networking terms). With the rapid enlargement of the data communication network scale and the intelligent evolution of hardware technologies, typical standalone IoT-based applications may no longer satisfy the advanced need for efficiency and security in the context of the high degree of heterogeneity of hardware devices and complex data formats. Firstly, centralized architecture's burdensome connectivity and maintenance costs result in its low scalability. Secondly, centralized systems are more vulnerable to adversaries' targeted attacks under network expansion (Pal & Yasar, 2020).

Intuitively, a decentralized approach based on blockchain technology may solve the above problems in a typical centralized IoT-based information system. Mainly the above justification is for three reasons. Firstly, an autonomous decentralized information system is feasible for trusted business partners to join the network, independently improving the business task-processing ability. Secondly, multiparty coordination enhances nodes' state consistency, so that information system crashes due to being a single-point failure is avoidable. Thirdly, nodes could synchronize the whole information system state only by coping the blockchain ledger to minimize the computation-related activities and improve storage load. Besides, blockchain-based IoT architecture for manufacturing information systems attracted researchers' attention (Pal, 2020).

Despite the potential of blockchain-based technology, severe security issues have been raised in its integration with IoT to form an architecture for manufacturing business applications. This chapter presents different types of security-related problems for information system design purposes. Below, this chapter introduces first the basic idea of digitation of manufacturing business process. Next, the chapter presents the use of blockchain technology in IoT for the manufacturing industry. Then, it discusses future research directions, including data security and industrial data breach-related issues. Finally, the chapter presents the concluding remarks and future research directions.

DIGITATION OF MANUFACTURING BUSINESS PROCESS

Inherent within manufacturing is information creation, communication, and decision making (or action). While its output is a physical object, manufacturing inevitably begins with information. For example, a design is created via a drawing, design software, or scanning a physical object, creating data. These data are then communicated to machines that execute the design, bringing it forth from the digital to the physical realm. Ideally, data from the creation process (and subsequent use) is further captured, sparking ongoing cycles between the digital and physical realms. Information Technology (IT) is crucial in capturing, storing, and processing stored data. Besides, manufacturing business networks use information systems to monitor manufacturing business network activities (Pal, 2017, 2020). Technological advances in modern technologies and tightly coupled business processes enable organizational connectedness. Therefore, the essential strategic asset in manufacturing business operational information has been critical.

Figure 1. A diagrammatic representation of the manufacturing business process

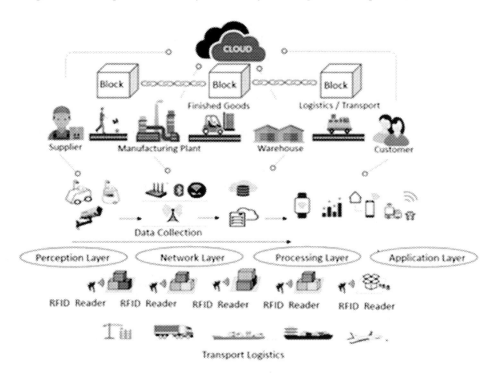

An EIS is to acquire and manages data and serves as a decision-making system within an enterprise. Therefore, the characteristics of an EIS can be analyzed in the context of decision-making purposes. Figure 1 illustrates data generation sources (e.g., RFID scanner, sensor, security camera, intelligent machine) in a manufacturing environment, divided into different layers (e.g., perception layer, network layer, processing layer, application layer). With the evolution of the manufacturing system, inputs, outputs, and system parameters can significantly change concerning time. One can find that design variables have increased exponentially with the evolution of manufacturing EIS. In addition, the information systems for modern manufacturing systems must accommodate the changes in the IT infrastructure (e.g., IoT, blockchain, SOC) and the changes and uncertainties in the system environments.

Evolution of IT Infrastructure

The primary functions of an EIS are (i) to acquire static and dynamic data from objects; (ii) to analyze data based on computer models; and (iii) to plan and control a system and optimize system performances using the processed data. The implementation of a manufacturing system paradigm relies heavily on available IT. In this sub-section, the IT infrastructure related to manufacturing is discussed. As a result, IoT has been identified as a critical technology with a significant impact on the manufacturing industry (Pal, 2021).

IoT becomes the foundation for connecting things, sensors, actuators, and other smart technologies. IoT is an extension of the Internet, and IoT technology gives immediate access to information about physical objects and leads to innovative services with high efficiency and productivity. The characteristics of IoT include (i) the pervasive sensing of objects; (ii) the hardware and software integration; and (iii) many nodes. In developing an IoT, objects must interact with each other, reacting autonomously to the changes in the manufacturing environment (e.g., temperature, pressure).

Radio Frequency Identification (RFID) technology has received massive attention from the manufacturing industry's daily operations as a critical component of the Internet of Things (IoT) world. In RFID-enabled manufacturing chain automation, an EPC (Electronic Product Code) is allocated to an individual item of interest and is attached to an RFID tag for tracking and tracing purposes. RFID tag-attached items are transported from one business activity to another or even move within the manufacturing partners. During transportation, individual partners interrogate RFID tags and add business-related contextual information into tags. In this way, involved business partners can check whether the items of interest have passed through the legitimate manufacturing network. If any inappropriateness is traced, such items may be classified as counterfeit products.

Also, wireless sensor networks (WSNs) provide enterprises with cloud computing services. WSNs are the essential infrastructure for the implementation of IoT. Various hardware and software systems are available to WSNs: (i) Internet Protocol version 6 (IPv6) makes it possible to connect an unlimited number of devices, (ii) Wi-Fi and WiMAX provide high-speed and low-cost communication, (iii) Zigbee, Bluetooth, and RFID provide the communication in low-speed and local communication, and (iv) a mobile platform offers communications for anytime, anywhere and anything.

A simple IoT architecture composed of devices (e.g., machinery and equipment), networks, cloud-based storage, and information system applications are shown in Figure 1. This architecture consists of four layers, such as perception, network, processing, and application layer. The perception layer consists of electromechanical devices like different types of sensors, RFID tag readers, security surveillance cameras, geographical positioning system (GPS) modules, and so on. These devices may be accompanied

Managing Supply Chain Digitalization With Blockchain Technology

by other industrial appliances like conveyor systems, automated guided vehicles (AGVs), and different industrial robots for a manufacturing industry context. These devices' primary function is to capture sensory data, monitor environmental conditions and manufacturing assembly areas, and transport materials (e.g., semi-finished, finished products). These collected data need transportation to the processing layer. The processing layer consists of dedicated servers and data processing software that ultimately produce management information, and operational managers can act based on the produced information. In this way, the application layer produces user-specific decision information. A few critical IoT-based information system applications in the manufacturing industry are smart factories, smart robotics, intelligent supply chains, and smart warehouse management. Besides, the importance of WSNs to industrial control systems has been discussed by researchers (Araujo et al., 2014). In the research field of WSNs, most ongoing work focuses on energy-efficient routing, aggregation, and data management algorithms; other challenges include the large-scale deployment and semantic integration of massive data (Aberer et al., 2014) and security (Gandino et al., 2014).

In industrial infrastructures, for the global manufacturing industry, dominated by physical systems, many processes address the needs of many t of data collected in real-time by many networked sensors that must be analyzed in real-time. Big data and real-time analytics applied to big data in cloud computing systems enable the implementation of these techniques to extract new information from the data. In addition, several industrial applications already use cloud computing architectures and services (Pal, 2020).

The trend toward virtualization of resources and critical aspects of real-world processes addresses the needs of many organizations for scalability and more efficient use of resource ownership. This way, cloud computing also plays a vital role in the modern manufacturing information system's automation purpose. Cloud computing is a large-scale, low-cost processing unit based on the IP connection for calculation and storage. The essential characteristics, such as on-demand self-service, are essential to support cloud computing applications for an enterprise in cost reduction, system flexibility, profit, and competitiveness.

However, a group of researchers has reported disadvantages of the centralized IoT information system architecture issues (Ali et al., 2019). A central point of failure could easily paralyze the whole data communication network. Besides, it is easy to misuse user-sensitive data in a centralized system; users have limited or no control over personal data. Centralized data can be tampered with or deleted by an intruder, and therefore the centralized system lacks guaranteed traceability and accountability.

The vast popularity of IoT-based information systems in the manufacturing industry also demands the appropriate protection of security and privacy-related issues to stop any system vulnerabilities and threats. Also, traditional security protections are not always problem-free. Hence, it is worth classifying different security problems based on objects of attack relevant to IoT-based systems. This classification of security-related attacks would help industry-specific practitioners and researchers to understand which attacks are essential to their regular business operations. The additional layer-specific security-related research is shown in Table 1, Table 2, and Table 3.

Blockchain technology is based on a distributed database management system that keeps records of all business-related transactional information that has been executed and shared among participating business partners in the network. This distributed database system is a distributed ledger technology (DLT). Individual business exchange information is stored in the distributed ledger and must be verified by most network members. All business-related transactions that have ever been made are contained in the block. Bitcoin, the decentralized peer-to-peer (P2P) digital currency, is the most famous example of blockchain technology (Nakamoto, 2008).

Table 1. Perception layer attacks

Type of Attack	Description
Tampering	Physical damage is caused to the device (e.g., RFID tag, Tag reader) or communication network (Andrea et al., 2015).
Malicious Code Injection	The attacker physically introduces a malicious code onto an IoT system by compromising its operation. For example, attackers can control the IoT system and launch attacks (Ahemd et al., 2017).
Radio Frequency Signal Interference (Jamming)	The predator sends a particular type of radiofrequency signal to hinder communication in the IoT system, and it creates a denial of service (DoS) from the information system (Ahemd et al., 2017).
Fake Node Injection:	The intruder creates an artificial node and the IoT-based system network and illegally accesses information from the network or controls data flow (Ahemd et al., 2017).
Sleep Denial Attack	The attacker aims to keep the battery-powered devices awake by sending them with inappropriate inputs, which causes battery power exhaustion, leading to nodes shutting down (Ahemd et al., 2017).
Side-Channel Attack	In this attack, the intruder gets hold of the encryption keys by applying malicious techniques on the devices of the IoT-based information system (Andrea et al., 2015), and by using these keys, the attacker can encrypt or decrypt confidential information from the IoT network.
Permanent Denial of Service (PDoS)	In this attack, the attacker permanently damages the IoT system using hardware sabotage. The attack can be launched by damaging firmware or uploading an inappropriate BIOS using malware (Foundry, 2017).

The convergence of IoT with blockchain technology will have many advantages. The blockchain's decentralization model will have the ability to handle processing a vast number of transactions between IoT devices, significantly reducing the cost associated with installing and maintaining large, centralized data centers and distributing computation and storage needs across IoT devices networks. Working with blockchain technology will eliminate the single point of failure associated with the centralized IoT architecture. The convergence of Blockchain with IoT will allow P2P messaging, file distribution, and autonomous coordination between IoT devices with no centralized computing model.

Table 2. Network layer attacks

Type of Attack	Description
Traffic Analysis Attack	Confidential data flowing to and from the devices are sniffed by the attacker, even without going close to the network to get network traffic information and attacking purposes (Andrea et al., 2015).
RFID Spoofing	The intruder first spoofs an RFID signal to access the information imprinted on the RFID tag (Ahemd et al., 2017). Using the original tag ID, the intruder can send its manipulated data, posing it as valid. In this way, the intruder can create a problem for the business operation.
RFID Unauthorized Access	An intruder can read, modify, or delete data present on RFID nodes because of the lack of proper authentication mechanisms (Andrea et al., 2015).
Routing Information Attacks	These are direct attacks where the attacker spoofs or alters routing information and makes a nuisance by creating routing loops and sending error messages (Andrea et al., 2015).
Selective Forwarding	In this attack, a malicious node may alter, drop, or selectively forward some messages to other nodes in the network (Varga et al., 2017), therefore, the information that reaches the destination is incomplete.
Sinkhole Attack	In this attack, an attacker compromises a node closer to the sink (known as the sinkhole node) and makes it look attractive to other nodes in the network, thereby luring network traffic toward it (Ahemd et al., 2017).
Wormhole Attack	In a wormhole attack, an attacker maliciously prepares a low-latency link and then tunnels packets from one point to another through this link (Varga et al., 2017).
Sybil Attack	Here, a single malicious node claims multiple identities (known as Sybil nodes) and locates itself at different places in the network (Andrea et al., 2015). It leads to colossal resource allocation unfairly. • Man in the Middle Attack (MiTM): Here, an attacker manages to eavesdrop or monitor the communication between two IoT devices and access their private data (Andrea et al., 2015).
Replay Attack	An attacker may capture a signed packet and resend the packet multiple times to the destination (Varga et al., 2017). It keeps the network busy, leading to a DoS attack.
Denial/Distributed Denial of Service (DoS/DDoS) Attacks	Unlike a DoS attack, multiple compromised nodes attack a specific target by flooding messages or connection requests to slow down or even crash the system server/network resource (Rambus).

An attacker launched software attacks taking advantage of the associated software or security vulnerabilities presented by an IoT system, as shown in Table 3. This way, malicious code can attack IoT-based infrastructure applications and create disruption (e.g., repeating the request for a new connection until the IoT system reaches the maximum level) of an existing service for global connectivity.

Table 3. Software layer attacks

Type of Attack	Description
Virus, Worms, Trojan Horses, Spyware, and Adware	Using this malicious software, an adversary can infect the system by tampering with data, stealing information, or even launching DoS (Andrea et al., 2015).
Malware	Data present in IoT devices may be affected by malware, contaminating the cloud or data centers (Varga et al., 2017).

Blockchain technology offers a mechanism to record transactions or any digital interaction designed to be secure, transparent, highly resistant to outages, auditable, and efficient. In other words, blockchain technology has introduced an effective solution to IoT-based information systems security. For example, a blockchain enables IoT devices to send inclusion data in a shared transaction repository with tamper-resistant records. In addition, it improves business partners to access and supply IoT data without central control and management, which creates a digital fusion.

BACKGROUND OF BLOCKCHAIN TECHNOLOGY

The blockchain technology infrastructure has motivated many innovative applications in manufacturing industries. This technology's ideal blockchain vision is tamper-evident, and tamper-resistant ledgers are implemented and distributed without a central repository. The central ideas guiding blockchain technology emerged in the late 1980s and early 1990s. A research paper (Lamport, 1998) was published with the background knowledge of the Paxos protocol, which provided a consensus method for reaching an agreement resulting in a computer network. The central concepts of that research were combined and applied to the electronic cash-related research project by Satoshi Nakamoto (Nakamoto, 2008), leading to modern cryptocurrency or bitcoin-based systems.

Distributed Ledger Technology (DLT)-Based Blockchain

The blockchain's initial basis is to institute trust in a P2P network, bypassing any third managing parties' needs. For example, Bitcoin started a P2P financial value exchange mechanism where no third-party (e.g., bank) is needed to provide a value-transfer transaction with anyone else on the blockchain community. Such a community-based trust is the main characteristic of system verifiability using mathematical modeling techniques for evidence. The mechanism of this trust provision permits peers of a P2P network to transact with other community members without necessarily trusting each other. This behaviour is often referred to as the trustless behaviour of a blockchain system. The trustlessness also highlights that a blockchain network partner interested in transacting with another business entity on the blockchain does not necessarily need to know the real identity.

It permits users of a public blockchain system to be anonymous. A record of peer-to-peer transactions is stored in a chain of a data structure known as blocks, the name blockchain's primary basis. Each block (or peer) of a blockchain network keeps a copy of this record. Moreover, a consensus, a digital voting mechanism to use many network peers, is also decided on the blockchain state that all network stores' nodes. Hence, blockchain is often designed as distributed ledger-based technology. An individual instance of such a DLT is stored at each node (or peer) of the blockchain network and gets updated simultaneously with no mechanism for retroactive changes in the records. In this way, blockchain transactions cannot be deleted or altered.

Intelligent Use of Hashing

Intelligent techniques are used in hashing the blocks encapsulating transaction records together, which makes such records immutable. In other words, blockchain transactions achieve validity, trust, and finality based on cryptographic proofs and underlying mathematical computation between different trading peers (or partners), known as a hashing function. Encryption algorithms are used to provide confidentiality for creating hash functions. These algorithmic solutions have the essential character that they are reversible in the sense that, with knowledge of the appropriate key, it must be possible to reconstruct the plaintext message from the cryptographic technique. This way hashing mechanism of a piece of data can be used to preserve the blockchain system's integrity. For example, Secure Hash Algorithm 256 (SHA256) is a member of the SHA2 hash functions currently used by many blockchain-based systems such as Bitcoin.

A simplified blockchain is shown in Figure 2. A block consists of four main fields (i.e., block number, previous hash (or prev), hash, and data). Block numbers (e.g., #1, #2, #3) uniquely identify a block. The Prev field contains the previous block's (i.e., the block that comes before it) hash value. It is the way the chain of blocks stays together. The first block in a blockchain, often called the genesis block, is shown by its Prev field initialized to all zeros. The fourth field is the Merkle tree root, a data structure that keeps all the block's transaction-related information. Thus, the block body records all transactions categorized into input and output.

It should be noted that there is a technical difference between a transaction chain and a blockchain. Every block in a blockchain can contain multiple transaction chains, as shown in Figure 3. Each transaction chain shows the value transferred from one network peer to another. Each transaction chain is sometimes referred to as a digital coin or, more usually, a token.

Figure 2. An immutable hashing mechanism in blockchain

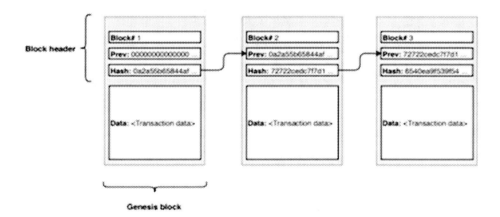

The communication among peers (or users) on blockchain uses a decentralized network in which an individual peer represents a node at which a blockchain client is installed. Once a peer performs a transaction with another peer or receives data from another user, it verifies its authenticity. Afterward, it broadcasts the validated data to all other relevant nodes for business operation purposes.

Blockchain systems need acceptance and verification by all the chain peers, and this mechanism is known as a consensus. However, there are different algorithmic solutions available to cope with the distributed nature of this problem.

Distributed Consensus

These distributed consensus algorithms help the blockchain system users say regarding the overall state of the records preserved (or stored) in the blockchain network blocks. This section briefly introduces four of these algorithms and are – (i) Proof-of-Work (PoW), (ii) Proof of Stake (PoS), (iii) Practical Byzantine Fault Tolerance (PBFT), and (iv) Delegated Proof of Stake (DPoS).

The PoW consensus algorithm is widely popularised by Bitcoin and assumes that all users vote with their "computing power" by solving consensus instances and creating the appropriate blocks. The PoS algorithm uses the existing way of achieving consensus in a distributed system. This algorithm needs the user to prove ownership of an amount of currency. It provides more efficient energy consumption in comparison to PoW. The PBFT consensus algorithm uses a state machine replication method to maintain Byzantine faults. This algorithm uses an effective authentication method based on public-key cryptography. The DPoS uses a democratic technique to validate a block and can confirm the transaction quickly.

Figure 3. Diagrammatic representation of transaction chain

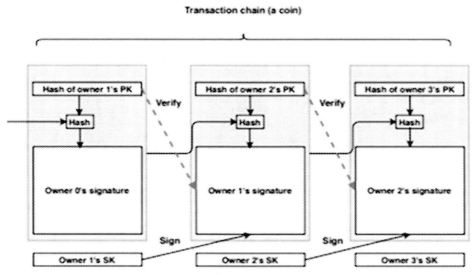

Blockchain technology is proposed for many manufacturing use cases where a business needs data immutability and P2P consensus, and transaction confidentiality. There are different types of blockchain-based architectures available as industry-specific solution platforms.

Blockchain Technology Architecture in Manufacturing Industry

Blockchain is bringing new technological innovation to business operating models in the manufacturing industry. These business models eventually lead operational managers to develop new processes, which help automate manufacturing functions effectively. This trend is not the cheapest, most effective way to use something, but it is also presumably game-changing for manufacturing industries. As a result, changes occur in the manufacturing network's nature governing a business's relationships with its business partners. In turn, these blockchain-governed business models lead to significant shifts in the competitive structure of manufacturing companies.

Managing Supply Chain Digitalization With Blockchain Technology

Many researchers argue that blockchain technology's effects on manufacturing networks typify this process and usher new business practices using appropriate information systems architecture (Pal, 2020). Before discussing the effect of blockchain technology and its security-related issues, one should note that it is not the first time the manufacturing business network has undergone a revolution. The first occurred at the turn of the nineteenth century, followed by the twentieth century, and formed the manufacturing and distribution model throughout the twenty-first century. Information systems and their architectures play a dominating role in this revolutionary business transformation process. Hence, it is instructive to consider a simple blockchain architecture.

An overview of blockchain architecture is shown in Figure 4. In simple, blockchain can be of three different types: (i) public blockchain, (ii) private blockchain, and (iii) hybrid blockchain. A blockchain is permissionless when anyone is free to be involved in the process of authentication, verification, and reaching a consensus. A blockchain is a permission one where its participants are pre-selected. A few different variables could apply to make a permissionless or permission system into some form of hybrid.

Figure 4. An overview of blockchain architecture

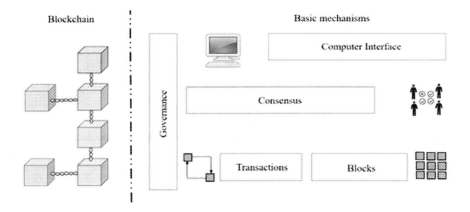

The validation occurs in the next layer of the blockchain infrastructure, consensus, where nodes must agree on which transactions must be kept and validated in the blockchain. There are different security measures used to verify transactions within a blockchain system, the most known approaches to research a consensus today are PoW, PoS, and PBFT. Having a good consensus algorithm means better efficiency, safety, and convenience; nevertheless, which consensus an organization should choose depends on the use case.

The upper layer, the computer interface, allows blockchains to offer more functionality to the system. In this part, the blockchain stores information on all the transactions that the users have made. For more advanced applications, one needs to store complex states which are dynamically changing, which means that the state shift from one to another once specific criteria are met in this system. These applications have given rise to smart contracts.

Smart contracts are the most transformative blockchain application, which could dramatically change how organizations work. For example, smart contracts can automate the transfer of assets when the negotiated conditions are met in this application; for example, when a shipment is delivered and verified, the contract will automatically enforce payments.

The governance layer (as shown in Figure 4) is human-centered in blockchain architecture. Blockchain protocols are affected by inputs from different people who integrate new methods, improve the blockchain protocols, and patch the system.

In blockchain systems, assets and monetary values are called tokens, and as stated by Nakamoto (Nakamoto, 2008), these are essential building blocks for the technology. The term tokenization means converting the rights and values of an asset into a digital token. Blockchain technology turns assets into digitally encoded tokens that can be registered, tracked, and traded with a private key (Francisco & Swanson, 2017), meaning that everything of value can be uploaded as a digital object in the blockchain system.

One of the critical aspects of blockchain technology is the decentralization of its operations. Decentralization means that each transaction in a blockchain transaction system does not need to be validated through a central trusted agency (e.g., a bank or other financial organizations). This new validation technique implies that third parties resulting in higher costs and performance bottlenecks at the central services, are no longer needed. Here, consensus algorithms are used to maintain data consistency in a distributed network. For example, for an entity to operate in a decentralized network, an organization would be issued a digital identity that it could use in all business interactions.

In blockchain-based information systems, users are anonymous, but their account identifiers are not. Also, all asset transactions are publicly visible. Since blockchain technology users are unknown, creating trust in this system architecture is essential. To build trust within a blockchain network enabled by four critical characteristics, as described below:

Ledger: One of the essential characteristics of blockchain-based operation is distributed ledger technology (DLT). It is a decentralized technology to eliminate the need for a central authority or intermediary to process, validate or authenticate transactions. Manufacturing businesses use DLT to process, validate or authenticate transactions or other types of data exchanges.
Secure: Blockchain technology produces a structure of data with inherent security qualities. It is based on principles of cryptography, decentralization, and consensus, which ensure trust in transactions. Blockchain technology ensures that the data within the network of blocks is not tampered with and that the data within the ledger is attestable.
Shared: Blockchain data is shared amongst multiple users of this network of nodes. It gives transparency across the node users in the network.
Distributed: Blockchain technology can be geographically distributed. The decentralization helps to scale the number of nodes of a blockchain network to ensure it is more resilient to predators' attacks. By increasing the number of nodes, a predator's capability to impact the blockchain network's consensus protocol is minimized.

Also, for blockchain-based system architectures that permit anyone to anonymously create accounts and participate (called *permissionless* blockchain networks), these capabilities produce a level of trust amongst collaborating business partners with no prior knowledge of one another. Blockchain technology provides decentralization with the collaborating partners across a distributed network. This decentralization means there is no single point of failure, and a single user cannot change the record of transactions.

SECURITY-RELATED RESEARCH FOR BLOCKCHAIN TECHNOLOGY

Manufacturing businesses have leveraged blockchain technology and its built-in capabilities as an essential component within the software system architecture to provide more secure and dependable computation capability. However, ill-informed or incorrect design decisions related to the choice and usage of a blockchain, and its components are probably the root cause of potential security risks to the system. For example, adversaries can exploit the envisioned design and verification limitations to compromise the system's security. The system becomes vulnerable to malicious attacks from cyberspace (Sturm et al., 2017). Some of the well-known attacks (e.g., Stuxnet, Shamoon, BlackEnergy, WannaCry, and TRITON) (Stouffer, 2020) created significant problems in recent decades.

The distributed manufacturing industry's critical issues are coordinating and controlling secure business information and its operational network. Applying cybersecurity controls in the operating environment demands the most significant attention and effort to ensure that appropriate security and risk mitigation is achieved. For example, manufacturing device spoofing and false authentication in information sharing (Kumar & Mallick, 2018) are significant problems for the industry. Besides, the heterogeneous nature of diversified equipment and the individualized service requirements make it difficult for blockchain-based P2P business operations (Leng et al., 2020).

In blockchain-based manufacturing business applications, trust and confidentiality among corporate partners play crucial roles in day-to-day operations (Ghosh & Tan, 2020). These issues also get compounded with individual products' personalization requirements across systems, which massively complicates the manufacturing and supply business activities (Mourtzis & Doukas, 2012). The other important issue is related to the manufacturing information system's data storage strategy. It is easier to keep data and other files secure on a decentralized server than on a centralized one. With data stored across many computers in multiple locations, the risk of a single-entry point is mitigated, making fewer data accessible at each end. Decentralized platforms can even avoid holding sensitive information altogether, and it makes a better choice for manufacturing information systems (Shen, 2002).

A literature survey shows that the techniques and methods of cybersecurity issues have been applied to the field of modern manufacturing information management systems, including traceability of operations (Mohamed & Al-Jaroodi, 2019), cyber-attacks on the digital thread (Sturm et al., 2017). Advanced virus on control system (e.g., Stuxnet) (12), device spoofing and false authentication in data sharing (Kumar & Mallick, 2018), interoperability among heterogenous equipment (Leng et al., 2020), confidentiality and trust between participants (Debabrata & Albert, 2020), information vulnerability and reliability across systems (Mourtzis & Doukas, 2012), and failure of critical nodes in centralized platforms (Shen, 2002).

Leveraging the advantages of integrating blockchain in IoT, academics and practitioners have investigated how to handle critical issues, such as IoT device-level security, managing enormous volumes of data, maintaining user privacy, and keeping confidentiality and trust (Pal, 2020) (Dorri et al., 2019) (Shen et al., 2019). In research work, a group of researchers (Kim et al., 2017) have proposed a blockchain-based IoT system architecture to prevent IoT devices' hacking problems. Besides, blockchain-based technologies are used to protect IoT application vulnerabilities.

Applications on the Internet of Things Devices Management

In IoT, device management relates to security solutions for the physical devices, embedded software, and residing data on the devices. The Internet of Things (IoT) comprises "Things" (or IoT devices) that have remote sensing and data collecting capabilities and can exchange data with other connected devices and applications (directly or indirectly). For example, IoT devices can collect data and process it locally or send it to centralized servers or cloud-based application back-ends for processing. A recent on-demand manufacturing model leveraging IoT technologies is called Cloud-Based Manufacturing (CBM), enabling ubiquitous, convenient, on-demand network access to a shared pool of configurable manufacturing business processes information collection and uses it service provision.

However, attackers seek to exfiltrate IoT devices' data using malicious codes in malware, especially on the open-source Android platform. Gu et al. (Gu et al., 2018) reported a malware identification system in a blockchain-based system named CB-MDEE composed of detecting consortium chains by test members and public chain users. The CB-MDEE system uses a soft-computing-based comparison technique and multiple marking functions to minimize the false-positive rate and improve malware variants' identification ability. A research group (Lee et al., 2017) uses a firmware update scheme based on blockchain technology to safeguard the IoT system's embedded devices.

Applications on the Internet of Things Access Management

Access control is a mechanism in computer security that regulates access to information systems. Access control systems face many problems, such as third-party, inefficiency, and lack of privacy. These problems can be address by blockchain, the technology that received significant attention in recent years and has much potential. Jemel and other researchers (Jemel & Serhrouchni, 2017) report several centralized access control systems problems. As a third party has access to the data, the risk of privacy leakage exists. Also, a major party controls the access, so the risk of a single point of failure also exists. This study presents an access control mechanism with a temporal dimension to solve these problems and adapts a blockchain-based solution for verifying access permissions. The attribute-based Encryption method (Sahai & Waters, 2005) also has some problems, such as privacy leakage from the private key generator (PKG) (Hur & Noh, 2011) and a single point of failure, as mentioned before. Wang and colleagues (Wang et al.,2018) introduce a framework for data sharing and access control to address this problem by implementing decentralized storage.

Blockchain can be classified as private (permission) or public (permissionless). Both classes are decentralized and provide a certain level of immunity against faulty or malicious users for blockchain technology. The significant differences between private and public blockchains lie in the consensus protocol's execution, the ledger's maintenance, and the authorization mechanism to join the distributed network.

Recently, there has been a tremendous investment from the industries and significant interest from academia to solve significant research challenges in blockchain technologies. For example, consensus protocols are the primary building blocks of blockchain-based technologies. Therefore, the threats targeting the consensus protocols become a significant research issue in the blockchain.

BLOCKCHAIN SECURITY AND PRIVACY ISSUES

Blockchain technology offers an approach to storing information, executing transactions, performing functions, and establishing trust in secure computing without centralized authority in a networked environment. Although blockchain has received growing interest in academia and industry in recent years,

Managing Supply Chain Digitalization With Blockchain Technology

blockchain's security and privacy continue to be at the center of the debate when deploying blockchain in different industrial applications.

Key Security Risk Areas of Blockchain

The main areas of security in blockchain technology are (i) Ledger, (ii) Consensus Mechanism, (iii) Networking Infrastructure, (iv) Identity Access Management, and (v) Cryptography. A diagrammatic representation is present in the risk areas in Figure 5.

Ledger: The ledger is used to register all transactions and changes in the data status. The ledger is distributed by smart design and shared between the blockchain-participating nodes. Two challenging problems (or hazards) generally threaten the applicability of the ledger technology in blockchain applications: (a) unauthorized entry into the ledger; and (b) unauthorized (or improper, or illegal) operations on recorded ledger data.

Consensus Mechanism: A consensus mechanism is a protocol (i.e., a set of rules) to ensure that all the blockchain network participants comply with the agreed rules for day-to-day operations. It ensures that the transactions originate from a legitimate source by having every participant consent to the distributed ledger's state. The public blockchain is a decentralized technology, and no centralized authority is in place to regulate the required act. Therefore, the network requires authorizations from the network participants to verify and authenticate any blockchain network activities. The whole process is done based on the network participants' consensus, making the blockchain a trustless, secure, and reliable technology for digital transactions. Distinct consensus mechanisms follow different principles, enabling network participants to comply with those rules. Several consensus mechanisms have been introduced considering the requirements of secure digital transactions. However, proof of work (PoW), proof of stake (PoS), and delegated proof of stake (DPoS) are the few consensus protocols used by the industries. In this way, the blockchain relies on the distributed consensus mechanism to establish mutual trust. However, the consensus mechanism itself has a vulnerability that attackers can exploit to control the entire blockchain. Although a few approaches, e.g., (Muhammad et al., 2018), are highlighted in blockchain-related research to deter and prevent attacks. Due to the inherent characteristics of openness, PoW-based permissionless blockchain networks may not be completely secure.

Network Infrastructure: The network infrastructure requirements for blockchain and Distributed Ledger Technology (DLT). The network infrastructure threats can detect nodes being stopped by a malicious attacker using good anticipatory mechanisms. In August 2016, nearly 120,000 Bitcoin (over US $60mn at the time) were stolen from Bitfinex (Nagaraj & Maguire, 2017). Based in Hong Kong, Bitfinex is one of the world's largest digital and cryptocurrency exchanges. The incident exploited security vulnerabilities within individual organizations. The blockchain network itself remained fully functional and operated as envisioned. The incident may have prevented a detailed end-to-end review of security using scenarios, meaning there would have been a higher chance of identifying risks upfront and mitigating them at that point.

Figure 5. Various security risk areas of blockchain

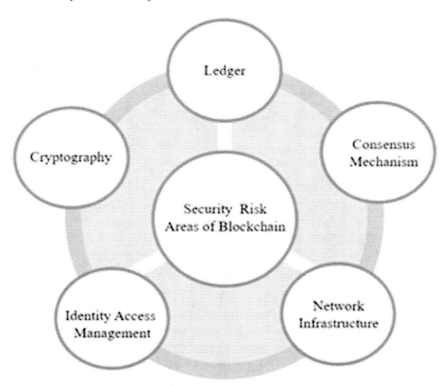

Identity Access Management: Privacy in blockchain enables the client/user to perform transactions without leaking its identification information in the network. Also, blockchain technology uses numerous techniques to achieve the highest level of privacy and authenticity for transactions. As information comes from different users within the blockchain industrial ecosystem, the infrastructure needs to ensure every user's privacy and authenticity. Blockchain-based information system often employs a combination of the public and private key to encrypt and decrypt data securely.

Cryptography: The records on a blockchain are secured through cryptography. Network participants have their private keys assigned to their transactions and act as a personal digital signatures. If a record is altered, the signature will become invalid, and the peer network will know that something has happened. However, there could be software bugs and glitches in cryptography coding. These could include developers' coding mistakes, inappropriate design, and an underlying defect in the cryptography routines. Also, trained coders can make a mistake in putting together well-known and tested cryptographic tools to not secure. As a result, hackers can take advantage of this weakness.

Safety is an essential aspect of blockchain-based transaction processes. All the data within the blockchain ecosystem needs to be secured and tamperproof. The security ensures no malicious nodes within the blockchain-based enterprise ecosystem. As mentioned earlier, the data inserted into a public ledger or inside the blockchain is distributed to individual users, and everyone maintains their local copy of the blockchain. In that local copy, that individual cannot tamper but upgrade the data and retransmit the

Managing Supply Chain Digitalization With Blockchain Technology

network's data. However, for the transaction to be validated, the other nodes should be convinced that the broadcasted information is not malicious and that system security is ensured.

THREAT MODELS FOR BLOCKCHAIN

This section explains the threat models that are considered by the blockchain protocols in IoT networks. Threat agents are mostly malicious users whose intention is to steal assets, break functionalities, or disrupt services. However, threat agents might also be inadvertent entities, such as developers of smart contacts who unintentionally create bugs and designers of blockchain applications who make mistakes in the design or ignore some issues.

Threats facilitate various attacks on assets. Threats arise from vulnerabilities at the network, smart contracts, consensus protocol deviations or violations of consensus protocol assumptions, or application-specific vulnerabilities. Countermeasures protect owners from threats. They involve various security and safety solutions and tools, incentives, reputation techniques, best practices, and so on. Threats and their agents cause risks. They may lead to a loss of monetary assets, a loss of privacy, a loss of reputation, service malfunctions, and disruptions of services and applications (i.e., availability issues).

Blockchain-based information systems owners wish to minimize the risk caused by threats that arise from threat agents. This section presents five types of attacks: *identity-based attacks*, *manipulation-based attacks*, *cryptanalytic attacks*, *reputation-based attacks*, and *service-based attacks*.

Identity-Based Attacks

The emergence of DLT based upon a blockchain data structure has given rise to new approaches to identity management, aiming to upend dominant approaches to providing and consuming digital identities. These new approaches to identity management (IdM) propose to enhance decentralization, transparency, and user control in transactions that involve identity information. In identity-based attacks, the attacker forges identity to masquerade as an authorized user to access the system and manipulate it. Again, identity-based attacks can be broadly classified into four different types, and they are (i) Key attack, (ii) Replay attack, (iii) Impersonation attack, and Sybil attack.

Key Attack: In blockchain technology, certificates, and identities are validated and protected in Hyperledger Fabric by asymmetric cryptography. How each participant stores and protects their private key is up to them. A wide range of wallets and management methods available as Hyperledger Fabric requires no cohesive management scheme. An outside attacker obtaining private key(s) could lead to any number of attacks. LNSC (Lightning Network and Smart Contract) protocol (Huang et al., 2018) provides an authentication mechanism between the electric vehicles and charging piles to deal with this attack. It uses elliptic curve encryption to calculate the hash functions, ensuring resiliency against the critical leakage attack.

Replay Attack: This attack aims to spoof two parties' identities, intercept their data packets, and relay them to their destinations without modification. To resist this attack, LNSC (Huang et al., 2018) uses the idea of elliptic curve encryption to calculate the hash functions. On the other hand, Benin (blockchain-based system for secure mutual authentication) (Lin et al., 2018) uses a fresh one-time public/private key pair.

153

Impersonation Attack: An attacker tries to masquerade as a legitimate user to perform unauthorized operations. As presented in Table 2, three methods are proposed to protect against this attack. The elliptic curve encryption idea to calculate the hash functions is proposed by the LNSC protocol (Huang et al., 2018). Wang et al. (Wang et al., 2018) propose a distributed incentive-based cooperation mechanism, which protects the user's privacy and a transaction verification method. On the other hand,

Benin (Lin et al., 2018) use the concept of attribute-based signatures (i.e., legitimate devices can produce a valid signature, and hence any impersonation attempt will be detected when its corresponding authentication operation fails.

Sybil Attack: A Sybil attack is when an attacker creates multiple accounts on a blockchain to deceive the other blockchain participants. A successful Sybil attack increases the reputation of some agents or lowers the reputation of others by initiating interactions in the network. These attacks should not be an issue on a permissioned blockchain since the members are clearly identified and wallets are not normally used. TrustChain (i.e., capable of creating trusted transactions among strangers without central control) (Otte et al., 2017) addresses this issue by creating an immutable chain.

Whitewashing: When an agent has a negative reputation, it can eliminate its identity and make a new one. There is no remedy to prevent this behaviour. However, it is suggested in (Otte et a., 2017) to give lower priorities to new identities agents when applying the allocation policy.

Service-Based Attacks: The attacker tries either to make the service unavailable or behave differently from its specifications. Under this category, we can find the following attacks:

DDoS/DoS Attack: A distributed denial-of-service (DDOS) attack is a prevalent type of network attack against a website, a communication network node, or even a membership service provider. The objective of this attack is to slow down or crash the system. The concentrated attack and subsequent shut down of the system result in a "denial of service" for legitimate users. Denial of Service (DoS) and DDoS are common security problems. DoS attacks on the connectivity of consensus nodes may result in a loss of consensus power, thus preventing consensus nodes from being rewarded. It involves sending a huge number of requests to cause the failure of the blockchain system. CoinParty (Ziegeldorf et al., 2018) proposes the idea of a decentralized mixing service. Liu et al. (Liu et al., 2018) employ a ring-based signature with the Elliptic Curve Digital Signature Algorithm (ECDSA). The resilience against DoS in BSeIn (Lin et al., 2018) is achieved by limiting the block size and using the '*multi-receivers*' encryption technique to provide confidentiality for authorized users.

FUTURE RESEARCH DIRECTIONS

The growth of IoT itself and its advancement in the industrial sector is putting a strain on the computing resources needed to maintain the level of connectivity and data collection that IoT devices require (Chan, 2017). This is where service-oriented computing comes into the picture by acting as the backbone of everything IoT offers. Cloud computing, setting up virtual servers, launching a database instance, and creating data pipelines to help run IoT solutions become easier (Chan, 2017). Moreover, data security is an essential concern in such an environment where the cloud can improve security by providing proper authentication mechanisms, firmware, and software update procedures. Besides, the major data attacks that are prevalent in the IoT world today: (i) data inconsistency, which helps an attack on data integrity, leading to data inconsistency in transit or data stored in a central database is referred to as Data Inconsistency (ii) unauthorized access control; and with unauthorized access, malicious users can gain data ownership or access sensitive data., and (iii) data breach or memory leakage refers to disclosing personal, sensitive, or confidential data in an unauthorized manner.

The data breach has severely threatened users' personal information in recent years. Researchers are highlighting different aspects of data breach-related issues. One such work (Gope & Sikdar, 2018) on preventing data breaches has proposed a lightweight privacy-preserving two-factor authentication scheme for securing communication between IoT devices. In the future, this research will review other research in IoT technology and data breach-related issues.

CONCLUSION

The current manufacturing industry operating environment has been extensively scrutinized to determine the primary needs of the enterprise information system's architecture purpose. It is encouraging that the emerging IoT infrastructure can appropriately support the information systems of next-generation manufacturing enterprises. Data collection systems are more than appropriate for gathering and sharing data among manufacturing supply chain resources anywhere and anywhere. IoT technology-based information systems bring different opportunities to advance manufacturing businesses to sustain good system performance in a distributed and globalized environment. However, the application of IoT in executive information systems is at its primitive age; more research is needed in the areas (e.g., modularization, semantic integration, standardization) of encouraging technologies for safe, effective, reliable communication and operational decision-making.

The domain of global manufacturing communication systems is well suited to a hybrid (i.e., IoT and blockchain) information system architecture approach because of its distributed nature and operating characteristics. From a smart manufacturing management perspective, blockchain-based systems' most appealing traits are autonomy, collaboration, and reactivity. Blockchain-based systems can work without the direct intervention of humans or others. This feature helps to implement an automated information system in the global manufacturing industry.

The modern manufacturing industry is a paradigm that is changing the way that factories operate on the edge of emerging IT-based applications (e.g., IoT, blockchain, big data, SOC). A driver of industrial sustainability concerns these technologies' security and safety. Blockchain technology, which has been used successfully for cryptocurrencies, contributes to this industrial sustainability by providing security, immutability, trust, and a higher degree of automation through smart contracts.

REFERENCES

Aberer, K., Hauswirth, H., & Salehi, A. (2006). *Middleware Support for the Internet of Things*. Available: www.manfredhauswirth.org/research/papers/WSN2006.pdf

Adat, V., & Gupta, B. B. (2017). A DDoS attack mitigation framework for Internet of things. *2017 International Conference on Communication and Signal Processing (ICCSP)*, 2036–2041. 10.1109/ICCSP.2017.8286761

Ahemd, M. M., Shah, M. A., & Wahid, A. (2017). IoT security: a layered approach for attacks and defenses. *2017 International Conference on Communication Technologies (ComTech)*, 104–110. 10.1109/COMTECH.2017.8065757

Airehrour, D., Gutierrez, J. A., & Ray, S. K. (2019). Sectrust-rpl: A secure trust-aware rpl routing protocol for the Internet of things. *Future Generation Computer Systems*, *93*, 860–876. doi:10.1016/j.future.2018.03.021

Al-Turjman, F., & Alturjman, S. (2018). Context-sensitive access in industrial Internet of things (IoT) healthcare applications. *IEEE Transactions on Industrial Informatics*, *14*(6), 2736–2744. doi:10.1109/TII.2018.2808190

Alaba, F. A., Othman, M., Hashem, I. A. T., & Alotaibi, F. (2017). Internet of things security: A survey. *Journal of Network and Computer Applications*, *88*, 10–28. doi:10.1016/j.jnca.2017.04.002

Alccer, V., & Cruz-Machado, V. (2019). Scanning the industry 4.0: A literature review on technologies for manufacturing systems, Engineering Science and Technology. *International Journal (Toronto, Ont.)*, *22*(3), 899–919.

Ali, M. S., Vecchio, M., Pincheira, M., Dolui, K., Antonelli, F., & Rehmani, M. H. (2019). Applications of blockchains in the Internet of things: a comprehensive survey. IEEE Commun. Surv. Tutorials.

Aman, M. N., Chua, K. C., & Sikdar, B. (2017). A lightweight mutual authentication protocol for IoT systems. *GLOBECOM 2017 - 2017 IEEE Global Communications Conference*, 1–6.

Andoni, M., Robu, V., Flynn, D., Abram, S., Geach, D., Jenkins, D., McCallum, P., & Peacock, A. (2019). Blockchain technology in the energy sector: A systematic review of challenges and opportunities. *Renewable & Sustainable Energy Reviews*, *100*, 143–174. doi:10.1016/j.rser.2018.10.014

Andrea, I., Chrysostomou, C., & Hadjichristofi, G. (2015). Internet of things: Security vulnerabilities and challenges. *2015 IEEE Symposium on Computers and Communication (ISCC)*, 180–187. 10.1109/ISCC.2015.7405513

Araujo, J., Mazo, M., Anta, A. Jr, Tabuada, P., & Johansson, K. H. (2014, February). System Architecture, Protocols, and Algorithms for Aperiodic wireless control systems. *IEEE Transactions on Industrial Informatics*, *10*(1), 175–184. doi:10.1109/TII.2013.2262281

Ashibani, Y., & Mahmoud, Q. H. (2017). An efficient and secure scheme for smart home communication using identity-based encryption. *2017 IEEE 36th International Performance Computing and Communications Conference (IPCCC)*, 1–7.

Atlam, H. F., Alenezi, A., Alassafi, M. O., & Wills, G. B. (2018). Blockchain with Internet of things: Benefits, challenges, and future directions. *International Journal of Intelligent Systems and Applications*, *10*(6), 40–48. doi:10.5815/ijisa.2018.06.05

Azzi, R., Chamoun, R. K., & Sokhn, M. (2019). The power of a blockchain-based supply chain. *Computers & Industrial Engineering*, *135*, 582–592. doi:10.1016/j.cie.2019.06.042

Boyes, H., Hallaq, B., Cunningham, J., & Watson, T. (2018). The industrial Internet of things (IoT): An analysis framework. *Computers in Industry*, *101*, 1–12. https://dzone.com/articles/. doi:10.1016/j.compind.2018.04.015

Cervantes, C., Poplade, D., Nogueira, M., & Santos, A. (2015). Detection of sinkhole attacks for supporting secure routing on 6lowpan for Internet of things. *2015 IFIP/IEEE International Symposium on Integrated Network Management (IM)*, 606–611. 10.1109/INM.2015.7140344

Cha, S., Chen, J., Su, C., & Yeh, K. (2018). A blockchain connected gateway for ble-based devices in the Internet of things. *IEEE Access : Practical Innovations, Open Solutions*, *6*, 24639–24649. doi:10.1109/ACCESS.2018.2799942

Chan, M., (2017). *Why Cloud Computing Is the Foundation of the Internet of Things*. Academic Press.

Chaudhary, R., Aujla, G. S., Garg, S., Kumar, N., & Rodrigues, J. J. P. C. (2018). Sdn-enabled multi-attribute-based secure communication for smart grid in riot environment. *IEEE Transactions on Industrial Informatics*, *14*(6), 2629–2640. doi:10.1109/TII.2018.2789442

Chen, G., & Ng, W. S. (2017). An efficient authorization framework for securing industrial Internet of things. TENCON 2017 - 2017 IEEE Region 10 Conference, 1219–1224. doi:10.1109/TENCON.2017.8228043

Chen, L., Lee, W.-K., Chang, C.-C., Choo, K.-K. R., & Zhang, N. (2019). Blockchain-based searchable encryption for electronic health record sharing. *Future Generation Computer Systems*, *95*, 420–429. doi:10.1016/j.future.2019.01.018

Choi, J., & Kim, Y. (2016). An improved lea block encryption algorithm to prevent side-channel attack in the IoT system. *2016 Asia-Pacific Signal and Information Processing Association Annual Summit and Conference (APSIPA)*, 1–4. 10.1109/APSIPA.2016.7820845

Colema, L. (2006). Frequency of man-made disasters in the 20th century. *Journal of Contingencies and Crisis Management*, *14*(1), 3–11. doi:10.1111/j.1468-5973.2006.00476.x

De, S.J., & Ruj, S., (2017). Efficient decentralized attribute-based access control for mobile clouds. *IEEE Transactions on Cloud Computing*.

DorriA.KanhereS. S.JurdakR.GauravaramP. (2019). *LSB: A Lightweight Scalable Blockchain for IoT Security and Privacy*. http://arxiv.org/ abs/1712.02969

Esfahani, A., Mantas, G., Matischek, R., Saghezchi, F. B., Rodriguez, J., Bicaku, A., Maksuti, S., Tauber, M. G., Schmittner, C., & Bastos, J. (2019). A lightweight authentication mechanism for m2m communications in industrial IoT environment. *IEEE Internet of Things Journal*, *6*(1), 288–296. doi:10.1109/JIOT.2017.2737630

Fernndez-Carams, T. M., & Fraga-Lamas, P. (2018). A review on the use of blockchain for the Internet of things. *IEEE Access : Practical Innovations, Open Solutions*, *6*, 32979–33001. doi:10.1109/ACCESS.2018.2842685

Ferran, M.A., Derdour, M., Mukherjee, M., Dahab, A., Maglaras, L., & Janicke, H., (2019). Blockchain technologies for the Internet of things: research issues and challenges. *IEEE Internet Things J*.

Forbes. (2019). *Blockchain in healthcare: How it Could Make Digital Healthcare Safer and More Innovative*. Author.

Frustaci, M., Pace, P., Aloi, G., & Fortino, G. (2018). *Evaluating critical security issues of the IoT world: present and future challenges*. IEEE Internet Things.

Gai, J., Choo, K., Qiu, K. R., & Zhu, L. (2018). Privacy-preserving content-oriented wireless communication in internet-of-things. *IEEE Internet of Things Journal*, 5(4), 3059–3067. doi:10.1109/JIOT.2018.2830340

Gandino, F., Montrucchio, B., & Rebaudengo, M. (2014). Key Management for Static Wireless Sensor Networks with Node Adding. *IEEE Transaction Industrial Informatics*.

Gibbon, J. (2018). *Introduction to Trusted Execution Environment: Arm's Trust zone*. Academic Press.

Glissa, G., Rachedi, A., & Meddeb, A. (2016). A secure routing protocol based on rpl for Internet of things. *IEEE Global Communications Conference (GLOBECOM)*, 1–7. 10.1109/GLOCOM.2016.7841543

Gomes, T., Salgado, F., Tavares, A., & Cabral, J. (2017). Cute mote, a customizable and trustable end-device for the Internet of things. *IEEE Sensors Journal*, 17(20), 6816–6824. doi:10.1109/JSEN.2017.2743460

Gope, P., & Sikdar, B. (2018). *Lightweight and privacy-preserving two-factor authentication scheme for IoT devices*. IEEE Internet Things.

Granville, K. (2018). *Facebook and Cambridge Analytica: What You Need to Know as Fallout Widens*. Academic Press.

Griggs, K. N., Osipova, O., Kohlios, C. P., Baccarini, A. N., Howson, E. A., & Hayajneh, T. (2018). Healthcare blockchain system using smart contracts for secure automated remote patient monitoring. *Journal of Medical Systems*, 42(7), 1–7. doi:10.100710916-018-0982-x PMID:29876661

Guan, Z., Si, G., Zhang, X., Wu, L., Guizani, N., Du, X., & Ma, Y. (2018). Privacy-preserving and efficient aggregation based on blockchain for power grid communications in smart communities. *IEEE Communications Magazine*, 56(7), 82–88. doi:10.1109/MCOM.2018.1700401

Guin, U., Singh, A., Alam, M., Caedo, J., & Skjellum, A. (2018). A secure low-cost edge device authentication scheme for the Internet of things. *31st International Conference on VLSI Design and 17th International Conference on Embedded Systems (VLSID)*, 85–90. 10.1109/VLSID.2018.42

Hei, X., Du, X., Wu, J., & Hu, F. (2010). Defending resource depletion attacks on implantable medical devices. *2010 IEEE Global Telecommunications Conference GLOBECOM 2010*, 1–5. 10.1109/GLOCOM.2010.5685228

Huang, J., Kong, L., Chen, G., Wu, M., Liu, X., & Zeng, P. (2019b). Towards secure industrial IoT: blockchain system with credit-based consensus mechanism. IEEE Trans. Ind.

Huang, X., Zhang, Y., Li, D., & Han, L. (2019a). An optimal scheduling algorithm for hybrid EV charging scenario using consortium blockchains. *Future Generation Computer Systems*, *91*, 555–562. doi:10.1016/j.future.2018.09.046

Huh, J.-H., & Seo, K. (2019). Blockchain-based mobile fingerprint verification and automatic log-in platform for future computing. *The Journal of Supercomputing*, *75*(6), 3123–3139. doi:10.100711227-018-2496-1

Huh, S.-K., & Kim, J.-H. (2019). The blockchain consensus algorithm for viable management of new and renewable energies. *Sustainability (Basel)*, *11*(3184), 3184. doi:10.3390u11113184

Islam, S. H., Khan, M. K., & Al-Khouri, A. M. (2015). Anonymous and provably secure certificateless multireceiver encryption without bilinear pairing. *Secure. Commun. Netw.*, *8*(13), 2214–2231. https://onlinelibrary.wiley.com/doi/abs/10.1002/sec.1165

Kang, J., Xiong, Z., Niyato, D., Ye, D., Kim, D. I., & Zhao, J. (2019a). Toward secure blockchain-enabled Internet of vehicles: Optimizing consensus management using reputation and contract theory. *IEEE Transactions on Vehicular Technology*, *68*(3), 2906–2920. doi:10.1109/TVT.2019.2894944

Kang, J., Yu, R., Huang, X., Maharjan, S., Zhang, Y., & Hossain, E. (2017). Enabling localized peer-to-peer electricity trading among plug-in hybrid electric vehicles using consortium blockchains. *IEEE Transactions on Industrial Informatics*, *13*(6), 3154–3164. doi:10.1109/TII.2017.2709784

Kang, J., Yu, R., Huang, X., Wu, M., Maharjan, S., Xie, S., & Zhang, Y. (2019b). Blockchain for secure and efficient data sharing in vehicular edge computing and networks. *IEEE Internet of Things Journal*, *6*(3), 4660–4670. doi:10.1109/JIOT.2018.2875542

Karati, A., Islam, S. H., & Karuppiah, M. (2018). Provably secure and lightweight certificateless signature scheme for IoT environments. *IEEE Transactions on Industrial Informatics*, *14*(8), 3701–3711. doi:10.1109/TII.2018.2794991

Khan, F. I., & Hameed, S. (2019). Understanding security requirements and challenges in the Internet of things (iots): A review. *Journal of Computer Networks and Communications*. doi:10.1016/j.future.2017.11.022

Khan, M.A., & Salah, K., (2018). IoT security: review, blockchain solutions, and open challenges. *Future Generation Computer Systems*, *82*, 395–411. doi:10.1016/j.future.2017.11.022

Kim, J.-H., & Huh, S.-K. (1973). A study on the improvement of smart grid security performance and blockchain smart grid perspective. *Energies*, 11.

Kim, S.-K., Kim, U.-M., & Huh, H. J. (2017). A study on improvement of blockchain application to overcome vulnerability of IoT multiplatform security. *Energies*, *12*(402).

Konigsmark, S. T. C., Chen, D., & Wong, M. D. F. (2016). Information dispersion for trojan defense through high-level synthesis. *ACM/EDAC/IEEE Design Automation Conference (DAC)*, 1–6. 10.1145/2897937.2898034

Kouicem, D. E., Bouabdallah, A., & Lakhlef, H. (2018). Internet of things security: A top-down survey. *Computer Networks*, *141*, 199–221. doi:10.1016/j.comnet.2018.03.012

Li, C., & Palanisamy, B. (2019). Privacy in Internet of things: From principles to technologies. *IEEE Internet of Things Journal*, *6*(1), 488–505. doi:10.1109/JIOT.2018.2864168

Li, R., Song, T., Mei, B., Li, H., Cheng, X., & Sun, L. (2019). Blockchain for large-scale Internet of things data storage and protection. *IEEE Transactions on Services Computing*, *12*(5), 762–771. doi:10.1109/TSC.2018.2853167

Li, X., Niu, J., Bhuiyan, M. Z. A., Wu, F., Karuppiah, M., & Kumari, S. (2018a). A robust ECC-based provable secure authentication protocol with privacy-preserving for industrial Internet of things. *IEEE Transactions on Industrial Informatics*, *14*(8), 3599–3609. doi:10.1109/TII.2017.2773666

Li, Z., Kang, J., Yu, R., Ye, D., Deng, Q., & Zhang, Y. (2018b). Consortium blockchain for secure energy trading in industrial Internet of things. *IEEE Transactions on Industrial Informatics*, *14*(8), 3690–3700.

Lin, C., He, D., Huang, X., Choo, K.-K. R., & Vasilakos, A. V. (2018). Basin: A blockchain-based secure mutual authentication with fine-grained access control system for industry 4.0. *Journal of Network and Computer Applications*, *116*, 42–52. doi:10.1016/j.jnca.2018.05.005

Ling, Z., Liu, K., Xu, Y., Jin, Y., & Fu, X. (2017). An end-to-end view of IoT security and privacy. *IEEE Global Communications Conference*, 1–7. 10.1109/GLOCOM.2017.8254011

Liu, C., Cronin, P., & Yang, C. (2016). A mutual auditing framework to protect iot against hardware trojans. *2016 21st Asia and South Pacific Design Automation Conference (ASP-DAC)*, 69–74. 10.1109/ASPDAC.2016.7427991

Liu, C. H., Lin, Q., & Wen, S. (2019b). *Blockchain-enabled data collection and sharing for industrial IoT with deep reinforcement learning*. IEEE Transaction Industrial Informatics. doi:10.1109/TII.2018.2890203

Liu, J., Zhang, C., & Fang, Y. (2018). Epic: A differential privacy framework to defend smart homes against internet traffic analysis. *IEEE Internet of Things Journal*, *5*(2), 1206–1217. doi:10.1109/JIOT.2018.2799820

Liu, Y., Guo, W., Fan, C., Chang, L., & Cheng, C. (2019a). A practical privacy-preserving data aggregation (3pda) scheme for smart grid. *IEEE Transactions on Industrial Informatics*, *15*(3), 1767–1774. doi:10.1109/TII.2018.2809672

Longo, F., Nicoletti, L., Padovano, A., d'Atri, G., & Forte, M. (2019). Blockchain-enabled supply chain: An experimental study. *Computers & Industrial Engineering*, *136*, 57–69. doi:10.1016/j.cie.2019.07.026

Lu, Y., & Li, J. (2016). A pairing-free certificate-based proxy re-encryption scheme for secure data sharing in public clouds. *Future Generation Computer Systems*, *62*, 140–147. doi:10.1016/j.future.2015.11.012

Machado, C., & Frhlich, A. A. M. (2018). IoT data integrity verification for cyber-physical systems using blockchain. *2018 IEEE 21st International Symposium on Real-Time Distributed Computing (ISORC)*, 83–90. 10.1109/ISORC.2018.00019

Makhdoom, I., Abolhasan, M., Abbas, H., & Ni, W. (2019). Blockchain's adoption in iot: The challenges, and a way forward. *Journal of Network and Computer Applications*, *125*, 251–279. doi:10.1016/j.jnca.2018.10.019

Manditereza, K., (2017). *4 Key Differences between Scada and Industrial IoT*. Academic Press.

Manzoor, A., Liyanage, M., Braeken, A., Kanhere, S. S., & Ylianttila, M. (2019). Blockchain-Based Proxy Re-encryption Scheme for Secure IoT Data Sharing. *Clinical Orthopaedics and Related Research*.

Mondal, S., Wijewardena, K. P., Karuppuswami, S., Kriti, N., Kumar, D., & Chahal, P. (2019). Blockchain inspired RFID-based information architecture for food supply chain. *IEEE Internet of Things Journal*, *6*(3), 5803–5813. doi:10.1109/JIOT.2019.2907658

Mosenia, A., & Jha, N. K. (2017). A comprehensive study of security of internet-of-things. *IEEE Transactions on Emerging Topics in Computing*, *5*(4), 586–602. doi:10.1109/TETC.2016.2606384

Naeem, H., Guo, B., & Naeem, M. R. (2018). A lightweight malware static visual analysis for IoT infrastructure. *International Conference on Artificial Intelligence and Big Data (ICAIBD)*, 240–244.

ObserveIT. (2018). *5 Examples of Insider Threat-Caused Breaches that Illustrate the Scope of the Problem*. Author.

Okorie, O., Turner, C., Charnley, F., Moreno, M., & Tiwari, A. (2017). A review of data-driven approaches for circular economy in manufacturing. *Proceedings of the 18th European Roundtable for Sustainable Consumption and Production*.

Omar, A. A., Bhuiyan, M. Z. A., Basu, A., Kiyomoto, S., & Rahman, M. S. (2019). Privacy-friendly platform for healthcare data in cloud-based on blockchain environment. *Future Generation Computer Systems*, *95*, 511–521. doi:10.1016/j.future.2018.12.044

Oztemel, E., & Gusev, S. (2018). Literature review of industry 4.0 and related technologies. *Journal of Intelligent Manufacturing*.

Pal, K. (2017). Building High Quality Big Data-Based Applications in Supply Chains. IGI Global.

Pal, K. (2018). *Ontology-Based Web Service Architecture for Retail Supply Chain Management*. The 9th International Conference on Ambient Systems, Networks and Technologies, Porto, Portugal.

Pal, K. (2019). Algorithmic Solutions for RFID Tag Anti-Collision Problem in Supply Chain Management. *Procedia Computer Science*, *151*, 929–934. doi:10.1016/j.procs.2019.04.129

Pal, K. (2020). *Information sharing for manufacturing supply chain management based on blockchain technology*. In I. Williams (Ed.), *Cross-Industry Use of Blockchain Technology and Opportunities for the Future* (pp. 1–17). IGI Global.

Pal, K. (2021). Applications of Secured Blockchain Technology in Manufacturing Industry. In Blockchain and AI Technology in the Industrial Internet of Things. IGI Global.

Pal, K., & Yasar, A. (2020). Internet of Things and blockchain technology in apparel manufacturing supply chain data management. *Procedia Computer Science*, *170*, 450–457. doi:10.1016/j.procs.2020.03.088

Park, N., & Kang, N. (2015). Mutual authentication scheme in secure Internet of things technology for comfortable lifestyle. *Sensors (Basel)*, *16*(1), 20. doi:10.339016010020 PMID:26712759

Porambage, P., Schmitt, C., Kumar, P., Gurtov, A., & Ylianttila, M. (2014). Pauthkey: A pervasive authentication protocol and key establishment scheme for wireless sensor networks in distributed IoT applications. *International Journal of Distributed Sensor Networks*, *10*(7), 357430. doi:10.1155/2014/357430

Pu, C., & Hajjar, S. (2018). Mitigating forwarding misbehaviors in rpl-based low power and lossy networks. *2018 15th IEEE Annual Consumer Communications Networking Conference (CCNC)*, 1–6. 10.1109/CCNC.2018.8319164

Rahulamathavan, Y., Phan, R. C., Rajarajan, M., Misra, S., & Kondoz, A. (2017). Privacy-preserving blockchain-based IoT ecosystem using attribute-based encryption. *IEEE International Conference on Advanced Networks and Telecommunications Systems (ANTS)*, 1–6. 10.1109/ANTS.2017.8384164

Rambus. (n.d.). *Industrial IoT: Threats and countermeasures.* https://www.rambus.com/iot/industrial-IoT/

Reyna, A., Martn, C., Chen, J., Soler, E., & Daz, M. (2018). On blockchain and its integration with iot. challenges and opportunities. *Future Generation Computer Systems*, *88*, 173–190. doi:10.1016/j.future.2018.05.046

Sfar, A. R., Natalizio, E., Challal, Y., & Chtourou, Z. (2018). A roadmap for security challenges in the Internet of things. *Digital Communications and Networks*, *4*(2), 118–137. doi:10.1016/j.dcan.2017.04.003

Shen, M., Tang, X., Zhu, L., Du, X., & Guizani, M. (2019). Privacy-preserving support vector machine training over blockchain-based encrypted IoT data in smart cities. *IEEE Internet of Things Journal*, *6*(5), 7702–7712. doi:10.1109/JIOT.2019.2901840

Shrestha, R., Bajracharya, R., Shrestha, A. P., & Nam, S. Y. (2019). A new type of blockchain for secure message exchange in vanet. *Digital Communications and Networks*.

Shukla, P. (2017). Ml-ids: A machine learning approach to detect wormhole attacks in the Internet of things. Intelligent Systems Conference (IntelliSys), 234–240. doi:10.1109/IntelliSys.2017.8324298

Sicari, S., Rizzardi, A., Miorandi, D., & Coen-Porisini, A. (2018). Reatoreacting to denial-of-service attacks in the Internet of things. *Computer Networks*, *137*, 37–48. doi:10.1016/j.comnet.2018.03.020

Singh, M., Rajan, M. A., Shivraj, V. L., & Balamuralidhar, P. (2015). Secure MQTT for the Internet of things (IoT). *5th International Conference on Communication Systems and Network Technologies*, 746–751. 10.1109/CSNT.2015.16

Song, T., Li, R., Mei, B., Yu, J., Xing, X., & Cheng, X. (2017). A privacy-preserving communication protocol for IoT applications in smart homes. *IEEE Internet of Things Journal*, *4*(6), 1844–1852. doi:10.1109/JIOT.2017.2707489

SOPHOS. (2015). *49 Busted in Europe for Man-In-The-Middle Bank Attacks.* https://nakedsecurity.sophos.com/2015/06/11/49-busted-in-europe-for-man-in-themiddle-bank-attacks/

Sreamr. (2017). *Streamr White Paper v2.0.* https://s3.amazonaws.com/streamr-public/streamr-datacoin-whitepaper-2017-07-25-v1_0.pdf

Srinivas, J., Das, A. K., Wazid, M., & Kumar, N. (2018). Anonymous lightweight chaotic map-based authenticated key agreement protocol for industrial Internet of things. *IEEE Trans. Dependable Secure Comput.*

Su, J., Vasconcellos, V.D., Prasad, S., Daniele, S., Feng, Y., & Sakurai, K. (2018). Lightweight classification of IoT malware based on image recognition. *IEEE 42nd Annual Computer Software and Applications Conference (COMPSAC), 2*, 664–669.

Team, V. (2018). *Vechain White Paper.* https://cdn.vechain.com/vechain_ico_ideas_of_ development_en.pdf

Varga, P., Plosz, S., Soos, G., & Hegedus, C. (2017). Security Threats and Issues in Automation IoT. *2017 IEEE 13th International Workshop on Factory Communication Systems (WFCS)*, 1–6. 10.1109/WFCS.2017.7991968

Waltonchain. (2021). *Waltonchain white paper v2.0.* https://www.waltonchain.org/en/ Waltonchain_White_Paper_2.0_EN.pdf

Wan, J., Li, J., Imran, M., Li, D., & e-Amin, F. (2019). A blockchain-based solution for enhancing security and privacy in smart factory. *IEEE Transaction.*

Wan, J., Tang, S., Shu, Z., Li, D., Wang, S., Imran, M., & Vasilakos, A. V. (2016). Software-defined industrial Internet of things in the context of industry 4.0. *IEEE Sensors Journal, 16*(20), 7373–7380. doi:10.1109/JSEN.2016.2565621

Wang, Q., Zhu, X., Ni, Y., Gu, L., & Zhu, H. (2019b). *Blockchain for the IoT and industrial IoT: a review.* Internet Things.

Wang, X., Zha, X., Ni, W., Liu, R. P., Guo, Y. J., Niu, X., & Zheng, K. (2019a). Survey on blockchain for Internet of things. *Computer Communications, 136*, 10–29. doi:10.1016/j.comcom.2019.01.006

Wurm, J., Hoang, K., Arias, O., Sadeghi, A., & Jin, Y. (2016). Security analysis on consumer and industrial IoT devices. *21st Asia and South Pacific Design Automation Conference (ASP-DAC)*, 519–524. 10.1109/ASPDAC.2016.7428064

Xiong, Z., Zhang, Y., Niyato, D., Wang, P., & Han, Z. (2018). When mobile blockchain meets edge computing. *IEEE Communications Magazine, 56*(8), 33–39. doi:10.1109/MCOM.2018.1701095

Xu, L. D., He, W., & Li, S. (2014). Internet of things in industries: a survey. *IEEE Trans. Ind. Inf., 10*(4), 2233–2243. doi:10.1080/00207543.2018.1444806

Xu, L.D., Xu, E.L., & Li, L. (2018). Industry 4.0: state of the art and future trends. *International Journal of Production Research, 56*(8), 2941–2962. doi:10.1080/00207543.2018.1444806

Xu, Y., Ren, J., Wang, G., Zhang, C., Yang, J., & Zhang, Y. (2019). *A blockchain-based non-repudiation network computing service scheme for industrial IoT.* IEEE Transaction Industrial Informatics.

Yan, Q., Huang, W., Luo, X., Gong, Q., & Yu, F. R. (2018). A multi-level DDoS mitigation framework for the industrial Internet of things. *IEEE Communications Magazine*, *56*(2), 30–36. doi:10.1109/MCOM.2018.1700621

Yang, W., Wang, S., Huang, X., & Mu, Y. (2019a). On the Security of an Efficient and Robust Certificateless Signature Scheme for IIoT Environments. *IEEE Access : Practical Innovations, Open Solutions*, *7*, 91074–91079. doi:10.1109/ACCESS.2019.2927597

Yang, Y., Wu, L., Yin, G., Li, L., & Zhao, H. (2017). A survey on security and privacy issues in internet-of-things. *IEEE Internet of Things Journal*, *4*(5), 1250–1258. doi:10.1109/JIOT.2017.2694844

Yang, Z., Yang, K., Lei, L., Zheng, K., & Leung, V. C. M. (2019b). Blockchain-based decentralized trust management in vehicular networks. *IEEE Internet of Things Journal*, *6*(2), 1495–1505. doi:10.1109/JIOT.2018.2836144

Yao, X., Kong, H., Liu, H., Qiu, T., & Ning, H., (2019). An attribute credential-based public-key scheme for fog computing in digital manufacturing. *IEEE Trans. Ind. Inf.*

Yin, D., Zhang, L., & Yang, K. (2018). A DDoS attack detection and mitigation with software-defined Internet of things framework. *IEEE Access : Practical Innovations, Open Solutions*, *6*, 24694–24705. doi:10.1109/ACCESS.2018.2831284

Zhang, H., Wang, J., & Ding, Y. (2019b). Blockchain-based decentralized and secure keyless signature scheme for smart grid. *Energy*, *180*, 955–967. doi:10.1016/j.energy.2019.05.127

Zhang, N., Mi, X., Feng, X., Wang, X., Tian, Y., & Qian, F. (2018). *Understanding and Mitigating the Security Risks of Voice-Controlled Third-Party Skills on Amazon Alexa and Google Home*. Academic Press.

Zhang, Y., Deng, R., Zheng, D., Li, J., Wu, P., & Cao, J. (2019a). *Efficient and Robust Certificateless Signature for Data Crowdsensing in Cloud-Assisted Industrial IoT*. IEEE Transaction Industry. doi:10.1109/TII.2019.2894108

Zheng, D., Wu, A., Zhang, Y., & Zhao, Q. (2018). Efficient and privacy-preserving medical data sharing in the Internet of things with limited computing power. *IEEE Access : Practical Innovations, Open Solutions*, *6*, 28019–28027. doi:10.1109/ACCESS.2018.2840504

Zhou, R., Zhang, X., Du, X., Wang, X., Yang, G., & Guizani, M. (2018). File-centric multi-key aggregate keyword searchable encryption for industrial Internet of things. *IEEE Transactions on Industrial Informatics*, *14*(8), 3648–3658. doi:10.1109/TII.2018.2794442

Ziegeldorf, J. H., Morchon, O. G., & Wehrle, K. (2014). Privacy in the Internet of Things: Threats and Challenges. https://arxiv.org/abs/1505.07683 doi:10.1109/TII.2018.2794442

KEY TERMS AND DEFINITIONS

Block: A block is a data structure used to communicate incremental changes to the local state of a node. It consists of a list of transactions, a reference to a previous block and a nonce.

Blockchain: In simple, a blockchain is just a data structure that can be shared by different users using computing data communication network (e.g., peer-to-peer or P2P). Blockchain is a distributed data structure comprising a chain of blocks. It can act as a global ledger that maintains records of all transactions on a blockchain network. The transactions are time-stamped and bundled into blocks where each block is identified by its *cryptographic hash.*

Cryptography: Blockchain's transactions achieve validity, trust, and finality based on cryptographic proofs and underlying mathematical computations between various trading partners.

Decentralized Computing Infrastructure: These computing infrastructures feature computing nodes that can make independent processing and computational decisions irrespective of what other peer computing nodes may decide.

Immutability: This term refers to the fact that blockchain transactions cannot be deleted or altered.

Internet of Things (IoT): The Internet of Things (IoT), also called the Internet of Everything or the Industrial Internet, is now a technology paradigm envisioned as a global network of machines and devices capable of interacting with each other. The IoT is recognized as one of the most important areas of future technology and is gaining vast attention from a wide range of industries.

Provenance: In a blockchain ledger, provenance is a way to trace the origin of every transaction such that there is no dispute about the origin and sequence of the transactions in the ledger.

Supply Chain Management: A supply chain consists of a network of *key business processes* and facilities, involving end-users and suppliers that provide products, services, and information.

Warehouse: A warehouse can also be called a storage area, and it is a commercial building where raw materials or goods are stored by suppliers, exporters, manufacturers, or wholesalers, they are constructed and equipped with tools according to special standards depending on the purpose of their use.

Chapter 8
Blockchain Supply Chain Integration Relation

Vishesh Bansal
Vellore Institute of Technology, India

Varun Murpani
Vellore Institute of Technology, India

Ramani Selvanambi
Vellore Institute of Technology, India

ABSTRACT

In this chapter, the authors aim to focus to integrate blockchain with the existing infrastructure, such that it works with the underlying core infrastructure to automate the supply chain integration as much as possible to decrease human intervention to the bare minimum level and solve the underlying problems that might occur due to the human factor in the supply chain integration. The authors will also shed light on the various regulatory issues associated with blockchain technologies. At the same time, one will also try to keep in mind that the newly proposed system can be well integrated with the existing and well-established system. The goal is to address problems that can arise from the human factor in supply chain management. The proposed system can be used in various industries requiring inventory management, the authenticity of goods, digital escrow services, etc. The authors have also discussed various regulatory issues as well as environmental concerns and procurement of raw materials associated with blockchain technologies.

INTRODUCTION

Supply Chain refers to the process of moving goods between stakeholders and parties according to the agreement about quality and timing. The affiliation of consumers, suppliers, and stakeholders in such a way that they may communicate information effortlessly and maximise their collective productivity in the production, distribution, and support of an end product is referred to as supply chain integration. This process is continuous and requires significant transparent alignment and coordination in order to

DOI: 10.4018/978-1-6684-7455-6.ch008

ensure that everyone is working toward a common, aligned goal effectively at all times, when each and every individual or party involved is aware of important events taking place at every level of the chain.

Supply Chain has undergone a dynamic change under the industrialization era, and with the advancement of technologies, it has grown to be more self-sustaining, transparent as well as integrated. With the onset of digitalization, the separate tasks have become more integrated, allowing for efficient communication and a reduction in delays between the different stages beginning from the procurement of the raw goods to shipping out the final goods. It has also eliminated the need for more storage space and helped manufacturers and businesses reduce the cost of manufacturing, delivering and marketing the product.

Blockchain is a distributed, transparent, and immutable ledger that simplifies the process of to record transactions and assets. It also shares this data with network nodes that have permission to access it. Almost anything that has some value can be tracked with the help of Blockchain. Over the years, blockchain technologies have been the backbone of many cryptocurrency assets like Bitcoin and Ethereum.

One of the current challenges faced by supply chain integration is the lack of transparency and end-to-end visibility. This can cause customer and cost related issues, which can be quite harmful to a brand name in the wrong. Another big challenge that is an issue with most supply chains is the lack of transparency. (National Research Council, (2000))Most of these issues can be fixed with Blockchain Technology. Blockchain is transforming the way supply chain functions. Not only does it help improve the traceability and transparency in supply chain management, but it can go a long way in reducing costs, reducing risks and increasing the overall efficiency. With the help of it, one can go an extra mile to ensure that the quality of the product being delivered to the end user is at least of the bare minimum quality standards promised by the company, at reasonable or pre-decided prices. Since the entire system is highly transparent in nature, with accountability and details related to the product. This information is accessible to system participants at each specific level, including suppliers, manufacturers, couriers, and end-users, which promotes confidence between them. Thus, blockchain ensures "only version of the truth" at all stages starting from serialisation, shipping, receiving to installation, such that if someone tries to attempt a fraud, they will be out of sync with the entire system, and can be easily detected as a threat actor to the supply chain.

Using blockchain, one can maintain a chronological string of blocks involving all parties in the transaction. Such details aren't recorded in a financial-ledger system. Smart contracts can be issued to automatically trigger transactions. In the case of blockchain, where there is no central authority to control the data, i.e., blockchain is decentralised, data integrity is an issue for different entities on the supply chain. Linking the blockchain with the Internet of Things and smart contracts can help solve this issue. Financial systems can be automated to process payments and transactions once feedback is received from a sensor or an automated data source or reaches a particular stage in the supply chain as well as integration with existing infrastructure.

BACKGROUND

Human Factor

If the majority of logistical procedures are taken into consideration, the human factor may be seen to have a significant impact. For instance, the majority of Customs procedures still call for human data entry into multiple Customs information systems and hardcopy paperwork. As a result, the human factor makes it more difficult to monitor the origin of items and to find accurate information about their present state in the supply chain. Having limited knowledge on the state of commodities generates many issues in world trade. Also, there is some uncertainty regarding the veracity of the information offered. Under these circumstances, applying distributed register or block-chain technology has the potential to resolve numerous accumulated conflicts. It is possible to considerably increase the effectiveness of logistical processes. With a large number of stakeholders, distributed registry technology performs a great job of assuring data transparency. The cluster system's security features foster confidence among participants in the logistics process's information flows.

Supply Chain Management (SCM)

Supply chain management is the process of managing the transfer of products and services, including the processing of raw materials into completed commodities (National Research Council, 2000). By enhancing the supply chain, companies can cut excess costs, guarantee faster deliveries, and communicate efficiently with all the parties involved. One of the aims of SCM has always been to focus on adding and integrating technology to enhance the supply chain.

The Fourth Industrial Revolution, sometimes known as "Industry 4.0," is upon us, and the integration of contemporary technology promises significant improvements in a number of industries, including manufacturing and logistics. Industry 4.0 envisage physical assets that are intelligent and networked, or smart goods and equipment that can function independently and create self-coordinating systems like smart factories or smart SCs. BCT and its effects on SCM are receiving more attention as a result of these advancements (Höllein et al., 2016).

BLOCKCHAIN

Figure 1. Chaining blocks in a blockchain

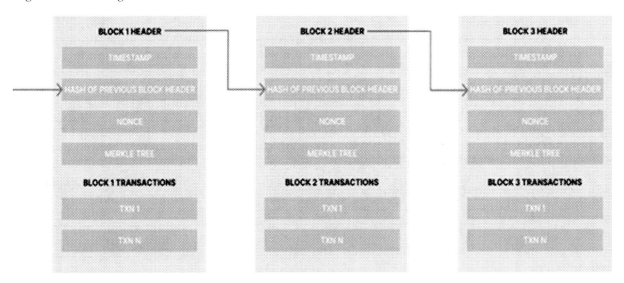

Blockchain is a distributed, irreversible, and decentralised ledger. The ledger consists of ordered records, called blocks. As shown in Figure 1, each block has a header and a body, with the header including data on the date, preceding block's hash, nonce, and merkle tree, and the content containing all transactional information. Peer-to-Peer networks control blockchain technology. Peer-to-peer (P2P) networking is a decentralised network communications model that consists of a group of devices (nodes) that collectively store and share files, with each node acting as an individual peer. Since there is no central administration or server in this network, all nodes have equal power and perform the same tasks. Table 1 shows a comparative study between traditional databases and blockchain databases. In comparison with the traditional Client-Server architecture, The P2P network is run by a decentralized network of users, where each node can function as both a server and a client, unlike traditional networks that have a dedicated server and particular clients (Yakovenko, 2018).

Table 1. Comparison of conventional databases and blockchain databases

	Conventional Database	**Blockchain Database**
Database Operations	Write-read-update-delete operations are available	Write-only option is available as it is immutable
Security of Data	Authenticated and authorised users only can access the database	All blocks are cryptographically secure
Validation of Data	Integrity is solely dependent on the owner of the database	Peer based validation that negotiate and agree on each transaction, hence power is decentralised
Data Collaboration	Database owner controls the structure and the data itself	The ecosystem follow globally agreed-upon rules
Replication of Data	Traditional concepts of database replication are applied	Each peer on the blockchain has full replica of the database,

CONSENSUS MECHANISM

Consensus mechanisms are the complete collection of rules, incentives, and ideas that allow a network of nodes to agree on the status of a blockchain. Blockchains like Solana and Ethereum employ a proof-of-stake consensus mechanism that draws its crypto economic security from a system of incentives and penalties applied to capital locked up by stakers (Goranović, 2017). Due to the extraordinarily high cost of an attack on the network, this incentive structure pushes individual stakeholders to run honest validators, penalises those who don't, and rewards those who do.

There is also a protocol that specifies how trustworthy validators are chosen to submit or validate blocks, handle transactions, and cast votes for their preferred candidate to lead the chain. There is a fork-choice mechanism that chooses the blocks that make up the "heaviest" chain when multiple blocks are in the same location near the head of the chain (Yakovenko, 2017). This is determined by the number of validators who voted for the blocks and how heavily they were weighted by the staked ether balances of the validators. Certain ideas that are crucial to consensus but are not clearly described in code include the ability for out-of-band social cooperation to provide extra security as a final line of defence against network attacks.

PROOF OF WORK (PoW)

Proof-of-Work, also abbreviated as PoW, was the first consensus technique used in Blockchain networks, where users transfer digital tokens, validate transactions, and add blocks to the chain. In this arrangement, all miners or validators are rewarded for verifying and confirming the network's transactions (Duong et al., 2020). The distributed ledger collects and organises into blocks all of the network's verified transactions. The name of this process is mining. A system known as "proof of work" protects against cyber risks such as distributed denial-of-service (DDoS) assaults, which try to consume computer resources by flooding them with a high number of bogus requests.

To find crypto coins, the miner or validator must do complicated mathematical calculations. The correctly validated transactions are subsequently recorded in the new block, creating a new block group in the blockchain, a public distributed ledger. There are two essential parts of mining: validating transactions and creating new cryptocurrency. If the miner completes the assignment first, they will be awarded with fresh cryptocurrency, which will attract further miners. In addition, the mining process increases the network computer power and computation required to produce a coin, making the mining process for the currency more complex and costly for a single miner.

PROOF OF STAKE (PoS)

Proof of Stake-based consensus techniques are used by several blockchains to achieve broad agreement (PoS). In this manner, validators voluntarily invest bitcoin funds in a Blockchain-based smart contract. The staked coin serves as collateral and is subject to destruction if the validator behaves dishonestly or recklessly. Therefore, the validator is responsible for checking that freshly formed blocks are valid before they are propagated over the network, as well as creating and propagating new blocks on occasion.

Compared to the now-deprecated proof-of-work method, proof-of-stake offers a number of advantages. Due to the fact that proof-of-work calculations do not need a significant amount of energy, a few of them have increased energy efficiency (Duong et al., 2020). Other advantages include lowered entrance barriers, fewer hardware requirements, and lowered centralization risk as proof-of-stake should increase the number of nodes safeguarding the network due to the low energy demand. Economic sanctions for misconduct make 51%-type attack tenfold more expensive for an offender relative to proof-of-work, and if a 51% attack were to manage to overcome crypto-economic safeguards, the community may resort to social recovery of an honest chain. Less bitcoin supply is needed to encourage participation.

DIRECTED ACYCLIC GRAPH (DAG)

A DAG-based system (Directed Acyclic Graph) is a type of blockchain architecture where transactions are recorded in a DAG structure instead of a linear chain. In a DAG-based system, transactions are linked together in a directed graph, where each transaction points to two or more previous transactions. This structure allows for multiple transactions to be processed concurrently, providing a more scalable and efficient solution for recording and verifying transactions. Each transaction in a DAG-based system is responsible for validating two or more previous transactions in the DAG structure. This process is called a "pay-it-forward" consensus mechanism, which strengthens the validity of transactions the more transactions are added to the DAG.

DAG-based blockchain systems can offer several advantages for supply chain integration compared to other consensus mechanisms such as PoW or PoS (Muneeb & Raza, 2021). DAG can potentially provide a more scalable and efficient solution for recording and verifying transactions, which is critical for managing the complex and large-scale supply chain networks. In a DAG-based system, transactions can be processed in parallel, which can lead to faster confirmation times and higher transaction throughput. This can be particularly useful in a supply chain context where transactions occur frequently, and the need for quick and secure data exchange is essential.

Furthermore, DAG-based systems can potentially reduce transaction fees, as it eliminates the need for miners to validate transactions and perform complex mathematical computations required in PoW and PoS mechanisms. This can be beneficial for supply chain integration, as it can help reduce costs associated with transaction processing, thereby increasing the efficiency and profitability of supply chain operations. However, it is essential to note that DAG-based systems still face challenges in achieving consensus in a networked environment. Therefore, careful consideration and testing are needed to determine whether DAG is suitable for supply chain integration and how it can be implemented to ensure the security and integrity of the supply chain data.

IOT AND BLOCKCHAIN USE CASES

Inventory Management

Inventory management is the act of keeping a record of and analysing the demand for a company's stock of products. It is the most desired quality of any manufacturing plant—to maintain the optimum amount of inventory and ensure timely delivery of the product. This can be achieved by having effective communication among all involved parties, i.e., third-party logistics, suppliers of raw materials and the consumer of the product. Using smart IoT sensors and other smart devices to track the location of the components, quantity and efficiency of machines while making them available to all the peers on the blockchain can contribute to improvements in just-in-time logistics, the reduction of storage costs and the fluidity of funds.

Drug Authenticity

According to the Centres for Disease Control and Prevention, studies show that about 9% - 41% of medicines sold in low- and middle-income countries are counterfeit. In contrast, in high-income countries such as the United States, less than 1% of medicines sold are counterfeit (Buterin, 2014). With IoT integrated blockchain, the pharmaceutical supply chain can be made transparent with the storage of the National Drug Code (NDC), expiration date and other essential details to trace the origin and ensure authenticity. So, smart sensors would be needed to help scan this data and cut down on the number of middlemen in the industry, which would make things safer and more cost efficient.

Digital Escrow

Escrow is a type of account with pre-established terms for the release of money and goods. The seller can deposit the deliverables in accordance with the agreed-upon parameters, and the buyer can put money into the escrow account under the supervision of a third party. Only after all of the predetermined requirements have been satisfied does the third party disburse the money to the seller and deliverables to the buyer. In the past, opening an escrow account required a lot of effort and money. The use of escrow accounts has, however, grown as digital economies have taken hold, including in areas like the supply chain. As shown in Figure 2, Sensor based logistics, with the help of existing Bitcoin escrows, can automate this process. This facilitates enhanced safety for the buyer and the seller, who are protected from unexpected recompense while the timely delivery of shipments is ensured.

Figure 2. Functioning of digital escrow accounts

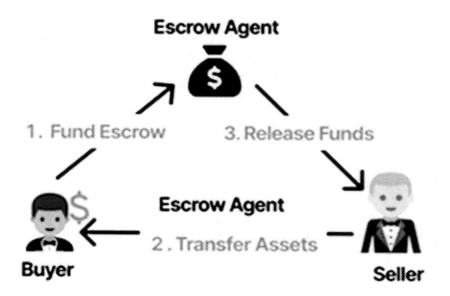

Electric Microgrid Power Supply

An electric microgrid is a small-scale electric power system that is used to supply electricity to a local area. Typically, it is a combination of distributed energy resources (DERs) such as solar panels, wind turbines, and energy storage devices, as well as conventional generators (Tsao et al., 2021). The goal of an electric microgrid is to give a certain area, like a community, campus, or industrial facility, a reliable and stable source of electricity.

Blockchain technology can potentially be used in the supply chain of electricity in an electric microgrid to improve transparency, security, and efficiency. For example, a blockchain-based platform could be used to track the production and distribution of electricity within the microgrid, as well as facilitate the trading of excess electricity between users within the microgrid. This could enable users to buy and sell electricity directly from one another, rather than relying on a centralised utility (Wang et al., 2020).

In addition, a blockchain-based platform could be used to enable real-time monitoring and control of the electric microgrid, allowing for the optimization of DERs and the integration of variable renewable energy sources. This could help to improve the reliability and stability of the microgrid, as well as reduce the cost of electricity for users (Sagan et al., 2021).

ISSUES

Regulatory Issues

A number of regulatory issues turn up with the use of Blockchain technologies, which serve as major obstacles to it being used in practice, with one or more grey areas primarily regarding matters including but not limited to accountability, jurisdiction, insufficiency of laws, lack of infrastructure and governance.

Accountability

The biggest issues are accountability, or who is supposed to be held accountable in the event that something goes wrong, as well as incidents where breaches of the law were reported. The advent of blockchain foresaw a paradigm shift in both society and business. It also promised a world without boundaries and disintermediation. It is a technology created to circumvent boundaries and space. This poses a lot of jurisdictional issues since the blockchain is not present in one single location, each node of a large blockchain system might be subject to different jurisdictions since they might span different locations across the world (Michael, 2018). Currently, most countries have their own regulations and there is no single authority that oversees blockchain governance.

Volatility

Even though Blockchain has a lot of advantages over technologies, de facto the major reason that blockchain is still not being adapted or used as a mechanism in global businesses and supply chains is its volatility. This happens due to a majority of factors (Michael, 2018). Blockchain and cryptocurrencies are a sentiment driven market that plays a major factor in the price and volatility of the cryptocurrency. In the past, a number of these incidents have taken place including Tesla's Chairman Elon Musk and the Dogecoin incident being among the most popular ones. The other major reason is limited supply for most of these cryptocurrencies, unlike traditional fiat currencies issued by Governments. For instance Bitcoin supply is limited to 21 million and Litecoin has the supply limited to 84 million, and the price for the above are determined by the laws of demand and supply. Thus, if a large organisation or consortium holds a majority holding, they can determine the price of the cryptocurrency by buying/selling them in a huge number. Not only this, but people investing in the cryptocurrency also tend to quit markets whenever they incur losses, thus leaving a lot of surplus which further tends to contribute to the volatility.

GDPR and Other International Laws

Over the past few years, there has been substantial discussion about the incompatibility between blockchain and the European Union's General Data Protection Regulation (GDPR) in policy circles, academia, and the corporate sector.

First, the GDPR is predicated on the premise such that at least one natural or legal person exists. —the data controller—relative to each individual to whom entities may apply to claim their rights under EU data protection law. They have duties under the GDPR. Blockchains, however, are distributed databases that frequently aim to accomplish decentralisation by substituting a number of diverse participants for a unitary actor. The distribution of duty and accountability is hampered by the lack of agreement on how (joint) controllership should be defined.

Second, the GDPR is predicated on the idea that data can be changed or deleted when required to satisfy legal obligations, such as those outlined in GDPR Articles 16 and 17. To ensure data integrity and increase network trust, however, blockchains make unilateral data modification intentionally difficult. Blockchains also highlight the difficulties in upholding the demands of data minimization and purpose limitation in the contemporary data economy. It is advised that interdisciplinary studies looking at how the technological architecture and governance solutions of blockchains could be modified to meet the criteria of the GDPR should be carried out since it is a grey area. Not only this, but Codes of Conduct and certification mechanisms for the same are to be supported and encouraged.

The World Bank, along with academics from MIT and other parts of the world came to realise a "new social contract for data" (Blossey et al., 2019). An analysis of the legitimacy of the use of blockchain by international organisations confirms the perceived need to move beyond the conventional models and schemes of legitimacy and governance without abandoning the core of all legitimacy models: that public power is and eventually should be accountable to the public. A new social contract for the technology will need to be built around the new concepts of publicness that blockchain has helped to bring into being. (Karacaoglu, Y, (2018)) To ensuring that no one is denied fundamental political rights or the means to survive in the digital age is the main objective of all public institutions, including international organisations.

OTHER ISSUES

Sustainability Concerns

Within the previous five years, estimates of the total power needed for Bitcoin have risen. For example, network power estimates for 2018 range from 2,500 megawatts (MW) to 7,670 MW or little under 1% of the ability of the United States to produce electricity (Sun et al., 2018). Whether Bitcoin's expansion in the future will have a significant impact on energy use and associated carbon dioxide (CO2) emissions is a matter of debate. According to SAP, mining for blockchain uses so much energy that, if it were a nation, miners would be near Austria in terms of energy usage. As much energy is used in one Bitcoin transaction as there is in 100,000 Visa transactions (De Vries, 2018). The energy crisis brought on by blockchain technology and cryptocurrencies has become so severe that cryptocurrency miners are erecting server farms in areas with cheap electricity, such as Iceland (which has abundant geothermal power), rural China (which has underutilised hydroelectric power plants), and small-town America, placing a strain on these areas' electrical infrastructure. According to the New York Times, "The Bitcoin network uses more than one-third of what residential cooling in the United States uses, and more than seven times as much electricity as Google's entire global operations."

Semiconductor Shortage

With the onset of the COVID-19 pandemic and the rise of electronic devices due to the work-from-home trend that was rising at the time, in addition to little investment in the industry. About 4–6% of Taiwan Semiconductor Manufacturing Company's (TSMC) top-node production capacity is dedicated to Bitcoin mining (Yakovenko, 2018). There was no corresponding growth in chip supply despite the fact that semiconductor demand rose by 17% between 2019 and 2021. Recent studies have shown that most chip factories are already producing at roughly 90% of their capacity, leaving little room for immediate expansion of production at semiconductor fabrication operations. As technologies that require large quantities of semiconductors, such as blockchain processing, cryptocurrency growth, 5G, and electric vehicles, gain in popularity, the demand for chips is likely to rise. The supply of some microprocessor chips is currently insufficient to meet the high demand. These days, its common practice for businesses to keep a supply of chips on hand while they work on new goods for sale (Aich et al., 2019).

Integration With Existing Systems

Integration of existing systems with a Blockchain powered solution poses a lot of issues and can serve as a real challenge for a legacy system. This is usually due to the fact the different stakeholders in the process such as manufacturers, suppliers, etc. rely on different tools such as tracking solutions, ERP Systems, inventory systems that are usually dated and very mature applications which may or may not have APIs to exist to newer blockchain systems. The architecture of the system needs to be planned after careful consideration and weightage of a lot of factors such as the APIs, containers and microservices while also considering data security and integrity.

Ecosystem and Mindset

Companies can only do business with other companies that have also integrated blockchain into their supply chain. Hence, blockchain would be useful only if it were a two way process. It will take time to change people's attitudes toward new technologies and to dismantle age-old institutions such as banks and government-signed agreements.

PROPOSED SOLUTION

After a thorough analysis of the present issues associated with the technologies involved, the authors came to realise that blockchain can have a revolutionising impact if properly integrated directly with the Supply Chain with clear vision and laws backing for the same, in addition to leveraging IoT devices for automating the processes. A private blockchain is a great way of accomplishing this. These are administered and controlled by one organisation, or a group of organisations, which has the authority to impose restrictions on who has access to and control over the blocks and to implement limited access protocols to that purpose. Additionally, there exist hybrid public-private blockchains, wherein nodes having privileged access can examine all the data on a specific blockchain but others cannot, or vice versa. Using "smart contracts" is another method for accomplishing this. Token exchanges can have smart contracts added on top of it using blockchain technology, so that trades only take place when certain criteria are satisfied (Aich et al., 2019).

Blockchain and smart contracts can automatically facilitate and uphold enforceable contracts, or perhaps partially replace them. In a private blockchain system, with clear ownership and responsibility, law enforcement authorities can work with regulators to ensure that blockchain technologies can cater to the supply chain (Dutta, 2020).

Figure 3. Process of flow of goods and financial transactions enabled via blockchain in supply chain

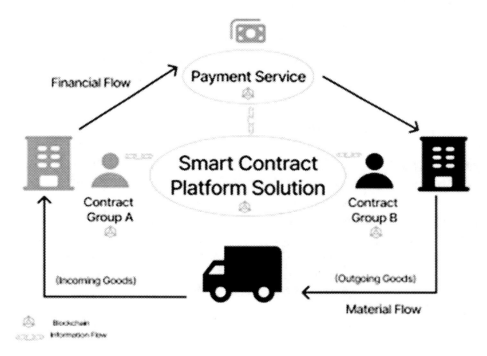

This can be done via ensuring that the details of the order at every step are determined by smart contracts, and upon fulfilment, as expected the smart contract gets fulfilled. For example, for an order placed on an e-commerce website, as soon as the order is issued, a smart contract is signed between the pickup agency and the producer. As soon as the pickup agency delivers an order to the warehouse for the next steps of packaging and distribution, the smart contract gets fulfilled and the pickup agency gets their share for the package. This can be automated via sensors which are capable of reading barcodes and QR codes, with minimal or no human intervention (Wang, 2011). This can be coupled with GPS tracking and RFID Scanners effectively to ensure tracking and accountability of goods. A good example of the workflow would include RFID Scanners detecting a truck leaving depot. This would be a good checkpoint to signify a part of the contract has been completed with some incentive for the producer. This will be followed by tracking of the vehicle using GPS tracking services to track and estimate the arrival time of the vehicle, including several factors like accidents, weather conditions to account for delays. As soon as the goods arrive at the arrival depot and scanned in, the next part of the transaction gets fulfilled. Subsequently, similar steps are followed during the later life cycle of the delivery process until the order reaches the consumer or end-user. The payment process at each and every step is facilitated and processed with the help of digital escrow accounts.

While digital escrow services still carry the risk of sending money to a stranger, there are reputed bitcoin escrow services on the rise with the growth of bitcoin-based transactions. These services can be verified on public platforms where the trust rankings can be viewed and verified. A multi-signature wallet shared by three parties that requires only two signatures to release funds can be used as an alternative to escrow services. These payment services can provide enhanced security for both the buyer and the seller in case of a breach of agreement on either end.

Not only are this, a major factor that contributes to Supply Chains globally government policies and laws, including trade agreements. Strengthening policies between countries can have a significant impact on supply chain management and integration with blockchain technology. For instance, the bilateral Agri-connect conference summit of 2019 hosted by the UK's Department for International Trade in collaboration with Uganda Export Promotion Board, is a step towards enhancing trade ties between the different countries. This kind of cooperation can facilitate the establishment of more robust and secure supply chains, which can be further improved by blockchain technology (Muneeb & Raza, 2021). By establishing a trusted network of partners, as required for blockchain integration in supply chain management, governments can ensure that their trading partners are reliable and committed to maintaining the integrity of the supply chain. This kind of collaboration can help mitigate risks such as counterfeiting, fraud, and other security threats that could compromise the supply chain. Moreover, stronger policies and regulations can create a conducive environment for blockchain technology adoption, which can offer various benefits such as faster and more cost-efficient product delivery, enhanced traceability, and streamlined financing processes. By working together, countries can establish standards and protocols that are compatible with each other, making it easier to integrate their supply chains and realize the full potential of blockchain technology. In summary, strengthening policies between countries can foster collaboration, trust, and transparency, which are essential for efficient and secure supply chains. By working together, countries can create an environment that is conducive to blockchain technology adoption, enabling them to reap the benefits of a more efficient, reliable, and secure supply chain.

CONCLUSION

In conclusion, the integration of blockchain technology into the supply chain has the potential to revolutionize traditional supply chain management practices, increasing efficiency and reducing the need for human intervention. The use of private or hybrid public-private blockchains and smart contracts can facilitate the automation of supply chain processes, including the fulfilment of orders and the enforcement of legal contracts. However, to fully experience the benefits of this technology, there are regulatory issues that need to be addressed. By working with law enforcement authorities and regulators, it is possible to establish a secure and efficient system that leverages blockchain and smart contracts to streamline the supply chain and reduce the risk of fraud and other issues. In addition, the use of digital escrow services and multi signature wallets can provide enhanced security for both buyers and sellers in the event of a breach of agreement. The authors are hopeful that if proper steps are implemented, it will lead to a revolutionary breakthrough that will increase efficiency, transparency, and trust in the supply chain.

REFERENCES

Aich, S., Chakraborty, S., Sain, M., Lee, H. I., & Kim, H. C. (2019, February). A review on benefits of IoT integrated blockchain based supply chain management implementations across different sectors with case study. In *2019 21st international conference on advanced communication technology (ICACT)* (pp. 138-141). IEEE. 10.23919/ICACT.2019.8701910

Blossey, G., Eisenhardt, J., & Hahn, G. (2019). *Blockchain technology in supply chain management: An application perspective*. Academic Press.

Buterin, V. (2014). A next-generation smart contract and decentralized application platform. *White Paper, 3*(37), 2-1.

Cao, B., Zhang, Z., Feng, D., Zhang, S., Zhang, L., Peng, M., & Li, Y. (2020). Performance analysis and comparison of PoW, PoS and DAG based blockchains. *Digital Communications and Networks, 6*(4), 480–485. doi:10.1016/j.dcan.2019.12.001

Clark, C. E., & Greenley, H. L. (2019). *Bitcoin, blockchain, and the energy sector*. Congressional Research Service.

De Vries, A. (2018). Bitcoin's growing energy problem. *Joule, 2*(5), 801–805. doi:10.1016/j.joule.2018.04.016

Dimitropoulos, G. (2022). The use of blockchain by international organizations: Effectiveness and legitimacy. *Policy and Society, 41*(3), 328–342. doi:10.1093/polsoc/puab021

Duong, T., Fan, L., Katz, J., Thai, P., & Zhou, H. S. (2020, September). 2-hop blockchain: Combining proof-of-work and proof-of-stake securely. In *Computer Security–ESORICS 2020: 25th European Symposium on Research in Computer Security, ESORICS 2020, Guildford, UK, September 14–18, 2020, Proceedings, Part II* (pp. 697-712). Cham: Springer International Publishing.

Dutta, P., Choi, T. M., Somani, S., & Butala, R. (2020). Blockchain technology in supply chain operations: Applications, challenges and research opportunities. *Transportation Research Part E: Logistics and Transportation Review, 142*, 102067.

Goranović, A., Meisel, M., Fotiadis, L., Wilker, S., Treytl, A., & Sauter, T. (2017, October). Blockchain applications in microgrids an overview of current projects and concepts. In *IECON 2017-43rd Annual Conference of the IEEE Industrial Electronics Society* (pp. 6153-6158). IEEE. 10.1109/IECON.2017.8217069

Höllein, L., Kaale, E., Mwalwisi, Y. H., Schulze, M. H., & Holzgrabe, U. (2016). Routine quality control of medicines in developing countries: Analytical challenges, regulatory infrastructures and the prevalence of counterfeit medicines in Tanzania. *Trends in Analytical Chemistry*, *76*, 60–70. doi:10.1016/j.trac.2015.11.009

Karacaoglu, Y., Mocan, S., & Halsema, R. A. (2018). The World Bank group's technology and innovation lab, from concept to development: A case study in leveraging an IT department to support digital transformation. *Innovations: Technology, Governance, Globalization*, *12*(1-2), 18–28. doi:10.1162/inov_a_00264

Karaesmen, F., Liberopoulos, G., & Dallery, Y. (2003). Production/inventory control with advance demand information. In *Stochastic Modeling and Optimization of Manufacturing Systems and Supply Chains* (pp. 243–270). Springer. doi:10.1007/978-1-4615-0373-6_10

Michael, J., Cohn, A., & Butcher, J. R. (2018). Blockchain technology. *The Journal*, *1*(7).

Muneeb, M., & Raza, Z. (2021). Tree-based blockchain architecture for supply chain. *International Journal of Blockchains and Cryptocurrencies*, *2*(2), 143–160. doi:10.1504/IJBC.2021.118113

National Research Council. (2000). *Surviving supply chain integration: Strategies for small manufacturers*. National Academies Press.

Sagan, A., Liu, Y., & Bernstein, A. (2021). Decentralized low-rank state estimation for power distribution systems. *IEEE Transactions on Smart Grid*, *12*(4), 3097–3106. doi:10.1109/TSG.2021.3058609

Sun, X., Chen, M., Zhu, Y., & Li, T. (2018, October). Research on the application of blockchain technology in energy internet. In *2018 2nd IEEE Conference on Energy Internet and Energy System Integration (EI2)* (pp. 1-6). IEEE. 10.1109/EI2.2018.8582599

Tsao, Y. C., Thanh, V. V., & Wu, Q. (2021). Sustainable microgrid design considering blockchain technology for real-time price-based demand response programs. *International Journal of Electrical Power & Energy Systems*, *125*, 106418. doi:10.1016/j.ijepes.2020.106418

Wang, M. (2011). *Multi-channel peer-to-peer streaming systems as resource allocation problems*. The University of Nebraska-Lincoln.

Wang, M., Wu, Y., Chen, B., & Evans, M. (2020). Blockchain and supply chain management: A new paradigm for supply chain integration and collaboration. *Operations and Supply Chain Management: An International Journal*, *14*(1), 111–122. doi:10.31387/oscm0440290

Yakovenko, A. (2018). *Solana: A new architecture for a high performance blockchain v0. 8.13*. Whitepaper.

Yeoh, P. (2017). Regulatory issues in blockchain technology. *Journal of Financial Regulation and Compliance*.

Chapter 9
Enhancing Supply Chain Efficiency Through Blockchain Integration

Bharathi Putta
Texas A&M University, USA

Dulal Chandra Kar
Texas A&M University, USA

ABSTRACT

Blockchain technology offers several beneficial features that make it well-suited for supply chain management (SCM). Particularly, it can improve transparency, traceability, security, efficiency, and accountability in supply chains (SC). This chapter focuses on how blockchain technology can completely transform SC processes due to its inherent features. By implementing blockchain, businesses can cut costs, improve efficiency, and ensure accountability. The chapter explains the basics of blockchain technology and its potential benefits for SCM. The various beneficial features of blockchain technology such as trust, immutability, reliability, and security are discussed and highlighted in the chapter. The chapter showcases real-world uses of blockchain technology in SCM to depict the possible benefits. Benefits and challenges of incorporating blockchain into SC processes are also discussed in the chapter. Finally, this chapter emphasizes how crucial it is for companies to identify the factors that weaken their SC and to ensure that blockchain is applied to address such issues.

INTRODUCTION

A supply chain, defined simply as a group of people, companies, and resources, is involved to effectively develop and market a product. Many businesses can reduce expenses in product development and distribution with the aid of the supply chain (Chang et al., 2020). According to (Blossey et al., 2019), a supply chain, from the starting step of raw materials to the last step of production and distribution, supervises and regulates the flow of merchandise throughout the chain. Supply chain entities include

DOI: 10.4018/978-1-6684-7455-6.ch009

raw material vendors, manufacturers, distributors, retailers, and retail customers. Supply chain managers constantly assess whether the stockpile exceeds the demands for a more streamlined supply chain as they attempt to maintain a competitive edge by reducing costs. Specifically, an efficient supply chain enables businesses to cut costs associated with order fulfillment, warehousing, distribution, shipping, and similar other activities.

The supply chain sector of the information technology industry is expanding. All areas of information technology, including cloud computing, manufacturing, and blockchain, have integrated supply chains. In industry, supply chain experts are in high demand. Many businesses may outsource the entire product development process to a third party because they lack the resources (both financial and human) to do so. To manage today's supply chains, technology is essential, and suppliers provide solutions that concentrate on important supply chain management (SCM) tasks. A corporation needs to understand vulnerabilities and improve its marketing strategy by keeping track of the supply chain. Fortunately, there are providers of business software who specialize in supply chain management, and hence, can help corporations to keep track of their supply chain.

LITERATURE REVIEW

Supply chain management is a complex process that involves multiple stakeholders, including suppliers, manufacturers, distributors, and customers. Blockchain technology has been proposed as a solution to address the challenges associated with supply chain management. A system based on blockchain is presented by (Agrawal et al., 2021), for supply chain traceability in the textile and apparel sector that can provide stakeholders a transparent and immutable platform to access up-to-date product information and can lower the danger of counterfeit goods, strengthen supplier accountability, and improve inventory management. In (Agrawal et al., 2018), an integration of digital tools to improve supply chain efficiency, visibility, and responsiveness is presented for digital supply chain management. In (Agrawal et al., 2021) and (Agrawal et al., 2018), the potential of using cutting-edge technologies like blockchain and IoT is shown to boost supply chain management's effectiveness and efficiency. The authors assert that through lowering costs, boosting efficiency, and improving customer satisfaction, the integration of these technologies can increase the effectiveness of the supply chain.

A blockchain-enabled supply chain management system that offers accountability, transparency, and traceability is presented by (Kumar et al., 2023). The method outlined in this work automates the execution of supply chain activities using smart contracts. A study by (Azzi et al., 2019) examines how a blockchain-based supply chain management system might increase supply chain security, efficiency, and transparency as a blockchain-based system would enable real-time data sharing between supply chain participants. From a transportation and blockchain standpoint, (Bekrar et al., 2021) focuses on digitalizing the closing-of-the-loop for supply chains. The solution outlined in this work makes use of a public blockchain network that enables data access and sharing for all participants. Both (Bekrar et al., 2021) and (Azzi et al., 2019) note the potential advantages of supply chain management offered by blockchain, such as increased efficiency, lower prices, and greater transparency. A thorough literature research was carried out by (Berneis et al., 2021) to examine the possible uses of blockchain in logistics and supply chain administration. Similar to this, in (Blossey et al., 2019), a study on potential blockchain applications in supply chain management is shown from an application perspective that includes the applications of blockchain technology in areas such as inventory control, freight forwarding, supply chain finance, supplier relationship management, and supply chain traceability.

In (Casado-Vara et al., 2018), the authors illustrate how blockchain technology may enhance transparency, trust, and accountability in the food supply chain through a case study of an alimentary supply chain that can increase consumer confidence, lessen food fraud, and improve the traceability of food items. A thorough literature assessment of the current state of play and possible uses of blockchain in supply chain management was carried out by (Chang et al., 2020). Six areas of blockchain applications in the supply chain were identified: supply chain traceability, supply chain financing, supply chain collaboration, supply chain risk management, supply chain sustainability, and supply chain quality management. According to (Cole et al., 2019), blockchain technology can reduce transaction costs and hazards by generating a single, tamper-proof record for all parties involved in a supply chain. Blockchain technology, according to (Durach et al., 2021), can enable automatic and transparent contract execution as well as make it easier to track and monitor payments and commodities in real-time. Blockchain technology can improve supply chain traceability by providing immutable records of transactions and raising data visibility, according to a systematic literature analysis of implementations done by (Dasaklis et al., 2022). They emphasize the significance of data standardization and the necessity of interoperability between various blockchain platforms. According to (Eljazzar et al., 2018), combining supply chain and blockchain technology can result in a decentralized supply chain network where trust is built through smart contracts. However, (Etemadi et al., 2021), did a dynamic literature analysis and indicated that scalability, interoperability, and regulatory compliance issues may arise when implementing blockchain technology in supply chain management.

With a focus on cybersecurity, (Etemadi et al., 2021), provide an ISM (Interpretive Structural Modeling) model to assess the supply chain adoption constraints for blockchain technology. A paradigm and reference implementation for the use of blockchain in operations and supply chains are put out by (Helo & Hao et a., 2019). This work gives insights into the advantages of blockchain in boosting supply chain visibility, security, and efficiency in addition to presenting a conceptual framework for blockchain-enabled supply chain management. A blockchain architecture for real-time supply chain management that focuses on project delivery is presented by (Helo & Shamsuzzoha et al., 2020). for tracking project deliveries in real-time, increasing transparency and lowering transaction costs. In their paper, (Kawaguchi et al., 2019), present a flexible blockchain architecture that can address the limitations of standard blockchain systems in terms of scalability, privacy, and interoperability.

A study on leveraging Blockchain technology to secure supply chains and logistics systems was presented by (Kumar et al., 2021). They discussed the difficulties and possibilities of implementing blockchain technology in the logistics sector. A thorough literature study on the use of Blockchain technology in supply chains was done by (Lim et al., 2021). They looked at several themes, approaches, and sectors that have used Blockchain technology. To look into the viability and effectiveness of applying blockchain in a supply chain, (Longo et al., 2019), carried out an experimental study. They suggested a Blockchain-enabled supply chain platform and performed a simulation to assess its efficacy. A Blockchain-based framework for managing logistics was proposed by (Tijan et al., 2019). They highlighted how integrating blockchain in logistics might provide advantages including lower operational costs, improved supply chain visibility, and improved productivity. Similarly, several examples of Blockchain deployments in logistics and supply chain management were presented by (Verhoeven et al., 2018). They presented the benefits and drawbacks of using Blockchain technology and underlined the significance of adopting this technology with caution. The relationship between Blockchain technology and sustainable supply chain management was addressed by (Saberi et al., 2019). They addressed the possible advantages, difficulties, and future research possibilities of integrating Blockchain into sustainable supply chain management and provided a conceptual framework for doing so. Blockchain technology for future supply chains was the subject of a thorough literature study by (Wang et al., 2019). They outlined a study agenda for future studies in this field and noted potential and problems related to the adoption of blockchain in supply chain management.

The literature also highlights the debate surrounding the implementation of blockchain technology in the supply chain. While some researchers have praised blockchain's potential to improve supply chain management, others have raised concerns about the technology's scalability, interoperability, and governance. (Gonczol et al., 2020), noted that the lack of a standardized blockchain protocol could hinder the adoption of the technology in supply chain management. Similarly, (Durach et al., 2021), highlighted the need for a comprehensive regulatory framework to address the challenges of governance and standardization.

In terms of gaps in the literature, some studies only focused on specific industries, limiting the generalizability of their findings. For instance, (Azzi et al., 2019), only focused on the pharmaceutical industry, while (Agrawal et al., 2021), only examined the textile and clothing industry. Furthermore, some studies only focused on the benefits of blockchain technology, without providing a comprehensive analysis of its challenges and limitations.

Overall, the examined literature points to the potential importance of blockchain technology for supply chain management, including improvements to traceability, security, and transparency. The adoption of blockchain technology, however, necessitates rigorous evaluation of its advantages and disadvantages as well as its compliance with current supply chain procedures and systems. To fully utilize the capabilities of blockchain technology in supply chain management, standardization, and interoperability of blockchain platforms are also crucial.

DIGITAL SUPPLY CHAIN

The supply chain management supervises the entire process, from the product's acquisition to its development, and it undertakes all operations relating to the manufacturing and shipment of the product (Blossey et al., 2019). All the operations that provide fiscal value to the client are under the purview of supply chain management. The duty for overseeing the efficiency and transparency of the operational activities required to satisfy consumer needs both within and across organizations falls within the scope of supply chain management (Blossey et al., 2019).

Exchange of information amongst the parties concerned is one of the important components of supply chain management. For a supply chain to thrive, information must be shared at all levels of the system. Sharing data throughout the digital supply chain is not limited to providers on a commercial level but can also include device information from internet of things (IOT) sensors. For the successful and timely supply of goods and services, the parties involved must be informed at every stage with information about the product, including storage, defective items, and resources. The economic advantages of open communication would result in new significance being brought to stakeholders, as well as this information aiding in decision making and the integrity of the firm. A company can make better decisions if exact information is delivered to the proper individuals at the proper time. For greater transparency, the supply chain should adapt to more electronic transfers rather than conventional transactions (Korpela et al., 2019). With transparent information available to stakeholders, they can comprehend the product's integrity, and the firm can identify potential product risks and implement mitigation strategies.

Typically, every task in a supply chain is completed manually, which is prone to errors, hence the supply chain can reduce labor-intensive expenses by allowing automated systems to input data more accurately and consistently (Korpela et al., 2019).

Elements of Supply Chain

A supply chain consists of four elements. The first is integration; it is a trustworthy source of information that is accessible to all stakeholders. It promotes open communication among all interested parties and the ability to exchange relevant data adeptly throughout a product's development. All parties involved in the process receive accurate information about product design, operation, industrial production, circulation, and warehouse management (Aslam et al., 2021). By offering a safe and transparent platform for all participants to share information and interact, blockchain facilitates open communication for supply chain management. This is accomplished by using a distributed ledger, which records all transactions and data in a decentralized manner and makes it available to all supply chain participants.

Let us use a consumer electronics company as an example, whose worldwide supply chain relies on blockchain technology to promote open communication between its manufacturers, distributors, and retailers. The business can use blockchain to build a shared database that tracks all supply chain events and transactions. This makes it possible for everyone to see and follow the development of items from the sourcing of raw materials to the delivery of finished goods. To guarantee that all participants have access to the most recent information, any modifications or updates made to the supply chain are immediately recorded on the blockchain.

Additionally, by utilizing smart contracts, the business can automate several supply chain procedures, including quality assurance inspections and shipment tracking. As a result, fewer middlemen are required, and participants may communicate more quickly and effectively. Any flaws or anomalies in the supply chain may be promptly discovered and fixed using blockchain-enabled open communication, decreasing the possibility of delays or disruptions. Blockchain can also foster trust and cooperation between partners in the supply chain by enhancing transparency and traceability, which will ultimately result in better goods and services for consumers.

The second component is operation, which is vital in the supply chain. This aids in obtaining a detailed real-time view of supply and production plans to anticipate sales and to obtain an estimate of products that failed to sell, as well as empowering stakeholders in determining how many products can be approved for the next production batch. Materials can be ordered based on demand and sales (Agrawal et al., 2018). With real-time information, the next batch of industrial production can be reduced based on product bookings. This aids stakeholders in the administration of materials, circulation, and wholesales. To balance user demands, stockpile planning and industrial production process management are critical.

The third component is purchasing. Retail prices should be set appropriately while going to compete in the market to fully make a significant amount of the products. This necessitates a thorough integration of inventory control, industrial production, and development. Because having the product at the time of demand is critical, a company must manage the supply and production for the business's efficiency. It is critical that all stakeholders have up-to-date information on the status of all their operations. Sales forecasting will assist a company in stocking the appropriate number of products (Zhang et al., 2019).

Keeping track of vendors, rival producers, and the supply cycle can assist with lowering operating costs throughout the procurement and financing process.

Distribution is the fourth step in the supply chain. A company should have detailed information about the cargo, circulation, and return of goods to optimize operating costs. To make business choices, shipment and return of goods should be updated in the real-time view of stocks. The company attempts to optimize the path of commodities to their desired location. All distribution parties will be responsible for the product from its provenance to the consumer. It manages the movement of goods from retailers to their destination. Packaging, stockpile control, and logistic operations are examples of such activities. It also includes responsibilities such as managing payments from pre-sale to purchase and ensuring that individuals have access to the product's specifications and its services.

Limitations of Digital Supply Chain

Even with all the advantages offered by supply chain technology, it has some limitations. Understanding consumer purchasing patterns can be difficult. Inconsistent stockpiles may lead to poor strategic decisions. Economic costs in the supply chain include unprecedented exchange rate movements and the need for additional funding. There is also the possibility of poor data security, fraudulent activities, security breaches, and human errors in the supply chain. A traditional supply chain lacks transparency which can result in discrepancies in data. There is a risk of suspicious purchases in the traditional supply chain (Etemadi et al., 2021).

Another potential downside in the supply chain is an absence of reliable information exchange among the parties involved. A supply chain cannot function without the participation of several individuals at multiple levels in the chain. As a result, there is an increase in supply chain risk due to presumed risk throughout every level, resulting in a disreputable supply chain. To function properly, a supply chain necessitates a significant investment in terms of financial terms and human involvement (Helo & Hao, 2019), If not properly operated, it will lead to substantial operational expenses. If credible information is not shared throughout the supply chain, it will result in disgruntled customers due to late deliveries or consumers receiving counterfeit items. The supply chain requires agreement between the parties involved, and the terms of the agreement must not be tampered with. However, tampering can happen in the traditional supply chain. Nevertheless, it is possible to overcome this by integrating smart contracts with advanced security protocols. Because smart contracts are irreversible once they are set up and deployed on the blockchain, they cannot be altered with. And, to achieve transparency and counteract counterfeiting, blockchain can be used to mitigate those risks. Blockchain is a digital decentralized ledger that, once verified and stored in the ledger, cannot be modified without being caught, even by administrators. By combining both technologies, supply chain limitations can be overcome.

BLOCKCHAIN BASICS

A distributed digital ledger of transactions known as a blockchain is kept on a network of computers. Each block in the chain contains a record of multiple transactions that have been validated by a network of computers known as nodes. It uses cryptography to secure and verify transactions. Once a block is included in the chain, it cannot be removed or changed, serving as a permanent and impenetrable record of all network transactions (Dutta et al., 2020). Transparency and immutability are made possible in a blockchain because each member of the network possesses a copy of the ledger. The ability of this distributed ledger technology to track transactions safely and openly in sectors including finance, supply chain management, and healthcare has made it popular.

A blockchain maintains a list of digital blocks of information that are linked together through a cryptographic mechanism known as hashing. In 2009, an anonymous individual with a pseudonym of Satoshi Nakamoto released the design and implementation of blockchain for a decentralized digital currency system known as Bitcoin. The bitcoin software system runs on a peer-to-peer network that maintains a single blockchain as an openly accessible, secure ledger that holds the records of all valid and verifiable transactions. On the peer-to-peer network, all or some active nodes can have the copy of the same blockchain as needed for various purposes such as for supporting security and operational needs.

Public Key Cryptography

Public key cryptography plays a significant role in ascertaining the authenticity of a digital content transmitted on a blockchain network. In public key cryptography, a pair of keys related to each other through number-theoretic properties is used. An owner needs to generate a key pair for his or her use for the purpose of encryption/decryption and for signing a message for authentication. In the pair of keys, one key is designated as private (K_s) and only known to the user and the other corresponding key is designated as public (K_v) and is available to anyone and verifiable through some certifying authority about the ownership of the key to avoid any attack that involves replacing the public key with a fake one by an adversary. This is one of the important reasons to register a public key with a trusted certifying authority. It is be noted that K_s and K_v are chosen in such a way that they maintain some number-theoretic properties so that encryption/decryption is possible while it is infeasible computationally to derive the private key component K_s given the public key component K_v. To encrypt a message m, a sender uses the receiver's public key K_v to encrypt message m to generate a ciphertext $c = E(m, K_v)$ where E is the encryption algorithm. To decrypt ciphertext c, the receiver uses his or her private key K_s to obtain the message or plaintext back $p = D(c, K_s) = D(E(m, K_v), K_s) = m$ where D is the corresponding decryption algorithm (Jakobsson & Juels, 1999).

Public algorithms are computationally slow and hence are used for encryption of short messages such as for sharing of a secret session key between a sender and a receiver or signing a message. For signing a message, the signer uses the private key, and the verifier uses the public key of the signer to verify authenticity of a message. If the public key of the supposedly signer fails to verify the signature, it is evident that the message was not signed by using the private key corresponding to the public key used to verify or the signature was tempered (Nguyen et al., 2019). Typically, a message is long; hence, to save time for encryption and to produce a short signature, first the hash value of the message, which has a fixed number of bits, is obtained, and then the hash is used for signing with the private key for authentication of the message. In a bitcoin network, ECDSA (Elliptic curve digital signature algorithm) is used as a secure signature algorithm. In the following, some details about hashing are provided for better understanding of hash functions for cryptographic uses.

Hash Function

Given a sequence of bytes, m of any arbitrary size, a cryptographic hash function H creates a fixed-sized block of data message digest or hash value $H(m)$ which is a unique sequence of bits for message m. A cryptographic hash function is a one-way function. That is, it is infeasible to find m given its hash *H(m)*. A hash function *H* must be collision resistant on message *m*. It must be infeasible to find another *m' ≠ m* such that *H(m) = H(m')*. If *H(m) = H(m')* then *m' = m* which guarantees the integrity of message *m*. When a verifier receives some digital content along with the hash of the digital message, the verifier computes the hash of the received message to see whether it matches with one received with the message. If they are equal, the verifier will accept the digital message as unmodified; otherwise, it can reject the digital message. However, there is a security flaw in this approach. If *H(m)* is sent along with message *m*, some attacker in the middle of the communication path can easily replace *m* with *m'* and then replace *H(m)* with *H(m')* after recomputing *H(m')* using the same known hash function. The receiver will not notice any modification since the hash value computed by him or her will be the same as the one sent by the attacker with the modified message (Jakobsson & Juels, 1999). One way to avoid this security flaw is to authenticate the hash value or send a digitally signed message, in which the hash of the original message is included in the digital signature. Since the attacker does not have access to the private key of the signer/sender, the attacker will not be able to use *H(m')* to produce a valid digital signature of the sender to sign the modified message *m'*. If the attacker does include any arbitrary bit string as a false signature, the authentication will fail at the receiving end and the altered message will be discarded.

For various cryptographic applications, there exist many hash algorithms such as MD5, SHA1, SHA256, and SHA512. For bitcoin implementations, SHA256 is used for hashing to generate a 256-bit hash value for a given message. It is extremely unlikely that another message *m'* will produce the same hash value for any of these algorithms. Even if *m* and *m'* differ by a single bit of information, *H(m)* will not be same as or close to *H(m')*.

Blockchain Organization

Blockchain as the name suggests data is stored in the block and as a chain the blocks are strung together one after the other. When a block needs to be added to the network the data in the block needs to be verified beforehand. That is when a hash is generated for the block. Hashing is a cryptographic method of converting any kind of data into a unique string of bits. It is infeasible to reverse a hash (Lin & Lao, 2017). A block contains the data, hash of the previous block, hash of the current block and timestamp of when the block is created. This makes it hard for the hackers to break the blockchain as the entire blockchain needs to be altered to change any of the stored data. Figure 1 shows the structure of a typical blockchain linking all blocks in the chain.

Figure 1. Structure of a blockchain

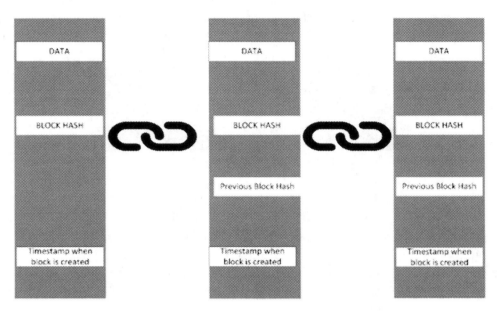

Data blocks in a blockchain are linked together using hash values or pointers. Each block contains many transactions or messages as well as a header. In addition to many other useful security and control related information in the header, the header in a block also contains the hash value of the preceding block in the chain thus establishes a link between the current block and the previous block. It is to be noted that the initial opening block in the chain does not have any meaningful entry as the hash value of the previous block. The initial block of a block chain is known as the *genesis block*. By keeping a record of the *genesis block* securely, it is possible to verify whether some adversary has tempered any succeeding blocks.

As stated earlier, a blockchain is a distributed ledger maintained on a peer-to-peer network. Any valid transaction that happens over the network is recorded in the blockchain. The following are the typical steps that happen in a blockchain network to record a transaction in the blockchain:

1. A client or user prepares a digitally signed transactional message. The signed transaction is checked for validity whether it is formed properly or not before broadcasting on the network.
2. The signed transaction is broadcast to all nodes on the blockchain network.
3. Some nodes known as miners on the peer-to-peer network compete to include the transaction in their block. It is to be noted that a miner typically collects several transactions from many other clients to create a single block.
4. A successful miner gathers proof of work on the assembled block by ensuring some properties of the items in the block such as hash values, nonce, etc. For the proof of work, the block is broadcast on the network.
5. Some consensus protocol is used by the network for the proof of the work on the block. If successful, the block will be accepted for appending in the blockchain. Thus, the blockchain is continuously growing as more and more new transactions are introduced into the network.

Enhancing Supply Chain Efficiency Through Blockchain Integration

It is to be noted that each block in the chain contains multiple messages (transactions). A miner, while creating a new block, retrieves the hash of the last block in the chain and uses the hash of the last block and the transactional messages togethers to create a hash for the newly created block. This new block, if accepted by the blockchain network, becomes the new end for the chain.

All the nodes in the blockchain should reach Consensus for a blockchain to be added. Consensus function is a mechanism in which all the nodes in the blockchain can agree to add a block to the network and verify its authenticity or ignore it. Consensus is done on a block to avoid any fork attacks and to prevent dishonest attempts or any other malicious attacks. Every message transmitted through the network should be approved by most nodes through a consensus-based agreement. Miners attempt to solve a challenging computation problem of producing a nonce, a number that meets the difficulty level required by the network. Miners compete to find a nonce that generates a hash with a value that is less than or equal to the network difficulty. The miner who discovers such a nonce, known as a golden nonce, earns the opportunity to add that block to the blockchain and collect the block reward in cryptocurrency.

Businesses are placing a greater emphasis on supply chain transparency because they want to understand how their products are designed, produced, and delivered. Identifying the source of the threat requires coordination across the company, managing supply chain risk is a relatively complicated challenge. Blockchain increases the efficiency of supply chains globally by allowing businesses to execute payments directly and free of the involvement of an external entity. It also promotes more data exchange between businesses and supports increased integration of monetary and logistical services (Park & Li, 2021). The business must establish trustworthy partnerships and open lines of communication with internal and external partners to adequately investigate the threat. Traceability and transparency are the two key characteristics of blockchain technology that the supply chain demands (Hackius & Petersen, 2017).

Even with these advantages, the blockchain has its own drawbacks. The storage of a decentralized network is a limitation. Every node has an exact copy of the data, thus storing and sending it requires a lot of processing power, and processing a chain becomes slower as time goes on. There is resilience as well, where each node in the network is required to authenticate and record every transaction. Data that has already been recorded cannot be changed easily and doing so necessitates investing funds and time to completely rework the codes in each block. Its drawback is that it is complicated to fix a miscalculation or make any appropriate modifications. To create consensus over a dispersed network and to guarantee security, blockchain depends on cryptography. In essence, this means that complicated algorithms, which in turn need a lot of computing resources, must be run to verify that a user has authorization to write to the chain. It would need an immense amount of energy to operate an ever-growing blockchain network.

Merkle Tree

A blockchain only keeps track of verified transactions, preventing illegal transactions. To check the integrity of information or data, hashing techniques are employed. It converts a string to a fixed length output. A hash is an exclusive value used to uniquely identify data for verification purposes. If the data has been altered in any way in a block, recalculating the value will produce a different block hash which will help to check the integrity of the block.

By securely storing information in hashes for subsequent validation of the blocks, the Merkle tree data structure can support the blockchain's authenticity. Because all transactions are always verified before being accepted into the chain, this mechanism prevents duplicate transactions from remaining in the chain. Merkle trees are more reliable than basic hashing at retaining and authenticating financial data, because when one needs to find a transaction identification number (*txid*) one can just use the Merkle root to find the *txid* of the block (Cryptopedia et al., 2021). An example of a Merkle tree is shown in Figure 2 (Merkle, 1980).

Figure 2. An example Merkle tree

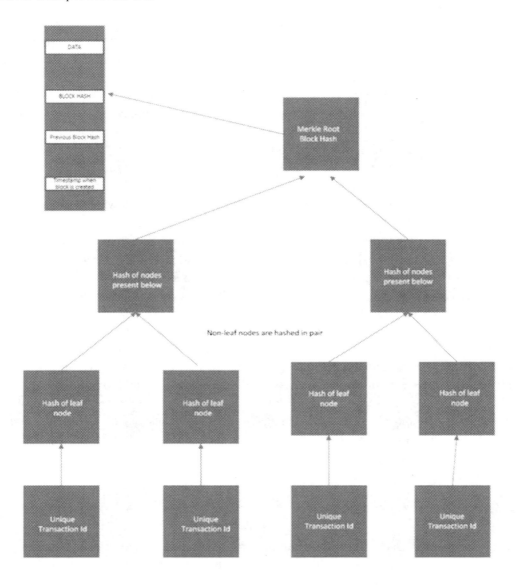

It is a one-way hash function that merges all the layers in the tree to validate the Merkle root. As shown in Figure 2, each leaf node in a Merkle tree represents a piece of data, such as a blockchain transaction, whereas non-leaf nodes indicate the hash of their offspring nodes. A cryptographic hash function, such as SHA-256, is used to the concatenation of the child nodes to get the hash of each node in the Merkle tree. The parent node's value is then determined by the hash value that was generated. Until a single

Enhancing Supply Chain Efficiency Through Blockchain Integration

hash value—known as the Merkle root—is achieved, this procedure is repeated. In blockchain, there is only one hash stored in the block, which is the block hash stored in the Merkle root. This final hash value will be recorded in the block header of the block. Merkle tree aids blockchain in making transactions unchangeable because if a data block is changed or tampered with, the hash value of that block changes, which in turn impacts the hash values of the nodes higher up the tree. By comparing the Merkle Root with a trustworthy copy of the Merkle Root, we can therefore rapidly ascertain whether any data blocks have been changed. The size of the blockchain can be decreased without sacrificing its security by storing only the Merkle root in a block as opposed to all the individual transactions. This is because any data manipulation in any of the transactions will produce a different Merkle root, which the network may identify and reject.

Proof of Work (PoW)

As a consensus algorithm, Bitcoin employs proof of work (Jakobsson & Juels, 1999) that aids the network's defense against attacks such as denial of service and double spending. Bitcoin is a decentralized network with nodes located all over the world, much like miners. As a result, miners compete to solve a computational puzzle for the block to be validated and added to the chain. When a new block is added to the chain, all miners on the network begin to work together to solve the puzzle of generating a pseudo random number. Miners compete to discover the nonce, which is a random number. When this nonce is added to the data and hashed, it should meet the required restrictions for the block to be verified.

Figure 3. Illustration of proof-of-work

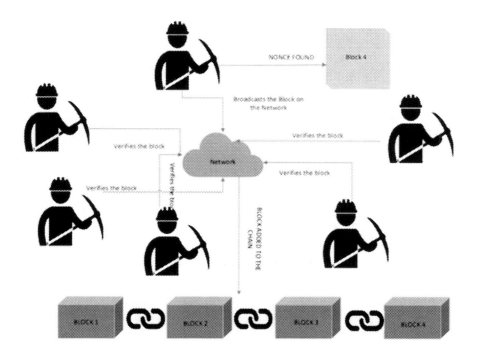

When the miner discovers the nonce, it is broadcasted to the network so that all other miners can verify whether the nonce value is legitimate and meets all the required conditions. The time it takes to verify the block and add it to the chain is less than the time it takes to solve the puzzle. The successful miner will receive a block reward for discovering the nonce. Each validated block has a block hash that represents the miner's work. This algorithm will aid the network's defense against attacks because the computational power required to carry out an attack would cost more than the reward received from the attack. Figure 3 shows an illustration of the proof-of-work on a blockchain network.

The biggest concern with proof-of-work is how much processing power is required to tackle the mathematical complexities associated in certifying blockchain operations. To handle computing power, sophisticated computers are needed, but they cost a significant amount of power to operate. For these machines to operate effectively and prevent heat buildup, as well as the associated machinery damage caused by internal overheating, they also need stronger thermal regulation or a ventilation fan. As a result, PoW-based blockchains experience scalability problems because of the expense of operating and maintaining sophisticated data centers. A variety of costs, such as quick depreciation of contemporary equipment, are borne by miners. Depending on the miner's location, mining often produces a significant amount of heat and may use a considerable amount of energy. Furthermore, during times of packet delay, the program's transactional charges double.

Proof of Stake (PoS)

Proof of stake is a consensus algorithm that can defend against attacks such as 51 percent and double spending (Nguyen et al., 2019). The validators are chosen at random based on the stake of coins they hold, rather than competing to solve a complex puzzle. Instead of solving a puzzle as in proof-of-work, a set of validators is chosen at random, and the higher the stake of coins, the higher the chances of being chosen to validate the next blocks and gain rewards. Instead of all nodes competing to solve a puzzle for a block to be accepted, only a few nodes chosen at random will work on verifying the oncoming blocks, consuming less energy.

Validators are rewarded for discovering new blocks and verifying those that have been assigned to them. The validator loses their stake if they attest for a malicious block. A validator will oversee verifying a transaction once it has been submitted to the network. As a result, the algorithm selects people at random based on their stake in the network. When the validator is selected, the block is verified and then recorded in the chain (King & Nadal, 2012). A committee oversees creating and verifying new blocks. To keep the chain safe, the committee is disbanded after a certain amount of time and reformed with random participants. Regular checkpoints are performed to protect the chain from double spending attacks. When a new block is added to the chain or the chain forks, it must search for a backup of the chain information in less than a month to verify its legitimacy. This checkpointing ensures that all nodes agree on previous transactions.

Given that the proof-of-stake mechanism depends on participants chosen to process payments, larger nodes can always trump smaller ones. The ability of the major nodes to govern the delegation selection procedure and prohibit participation from lesser nodes may cause the proof-of-stake to become less decentralized over time. When compared to proof-of-work, it is less robust. Transaction verification may be influenced by validators with substantial holdings.

Soft Fork and Hard Fork

Blockchain has been included into the supply chain for several reasons, one of which is that it is more secure. The blockchain fork will render the supply chain more secure. Therefore, through forking, a blockchain can determine its security vulnerability and subsequently fix the issue. With the aid of this technique, the supply chain will also be able to add any additional functionalities that a stakeholder could demand. When developers want to upgrade the software of an existing code, a fork in the chain occurs.

One of the following could be the reason for a fork:

1. Adding a feature – for instance, SegWit Update for block size.
2. Correcting a security flaw.
3. Reversing transaction in the block chain – for instance, the DAO hack.
4. Resolving a dispute in the cryptocurrency community.

Figure 4. Soft and hard fork

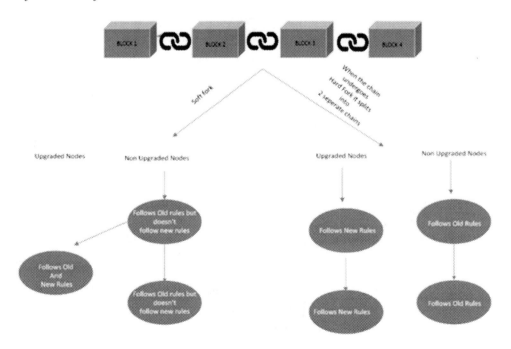

When the updated software is incompatible with the old nodes, a hard fork occurs as shown in Figure 4. A hard fork causes the block chain to split into two separate chains that are no longer backwards compatible. All nodes in the chain are required to update the agreement (Lin & Liao, 2017). Nodes that do not update will continue to operate in the old chain. Adding new code to existing code will result in a fork, with one chain following the old software and the other chain completely diverging from the old chain and following new updated agreement policies.

One example of a hard fork is the DAO hack, in which hackers stole millions of dollars and the DAO went through a hard fork to reverse the transaction and help all users get back their lost Eth, but to do so, all users had to update agreement services, resulting in a hard fork and the creation of Ethereum and Ethereum classic.

When the updated software is compatible with both the old and new nodes, this is referred to as a soft fork. Because a soft fork does not change the rules that a blockchain must follow, both new and old nodes will continue to work on the same chain. Soft forking is typically used to add functionality or implement new features (Lin & Liao, 2017). Users can gradually transition to the new agreement. The upgraded nodes can still communicate with the old nodes during a soft fork. In soft fork, a new rule is typically added without changing the existing rules, which is a much gentler process than hard fork.

The SegWit update is one such example. Segwit blocks constituted 65 percent of signature data in blocks, which was storage and time expensive, prompting developers to add a new functionality that frees up storage space by removing the signature data in the block, allowing for new transactions to be added to the chain. The goal of the Segwit update was to separate the transaction signatures from the block to save space. The Segwit update was supposed to support block sizes ranging from 1mb to 4mb. By using a soft fork, new nodes were able to accept both 4mb and 1mb blocks at the same time without violating existing rules. Soft forking allows old nodes to validate new nodes if they do not violate any existing blockchain rules.

Without dividing the blockchain in two, a soft fork can enable the supply chain to add any functions. However, the hard fork would produce two distinct blockchains: one with the updated functionalities and the other with the outdated functionalities. Therefore, any stakeholder would prefer a soft fork so that they may continue employing the same blockchain network while having access to new features. Therefore, a supply chain management may choose a soft fork even when updating the code for security fixes, which would be more dependable. A supply chain can add new features and address security vulnerabilities using the forking technique.

Tokenization

A token is an electronic version of any property or commodity in the blockchain. Blockchain tokens can be thought of as digital representations of goods and commodities that can be used to trace them throughout the supply chain. Tokenization now allows for the supply chain to be credited for moving bulk materials (Bekrar et al., 2021). Tokenizing tangible assets in the supply chain, such as technology and equipment, supplies more options in asset management. Ordering goods could be allotted as tokens in the contractual agreement. If the products in the inventory fail to sell, they can be monetized using these digital tokens. As a result, stakeholders can develop a new system where payments for returned goods can be compensated in bitcoin. Tokenization can be done at distinct levels, including the product, unit, and batch levels.

Trust

Blockchain technology facilitates confidence between participants without the need for intermediaries, such as banks or governments. This is because transactions on a blockchain are validated and recorded by a network of computers, rather than a centralized authority. Blockchain transactions are therefore incredibly safe and open (Queiroz et al., 2019). For instance, in a conventional banking system, a bank

Enhancing Supply Chain Efficiency Through Blockchain Integration

acts as a reliable middleman between two parties looking to conduct a transaction. Nevertheless, with a blockchain-based system, the network of computers confirms the transaction and maintains its authenticity. As a result, there is no longer a need for a middleman, which lowers transaction costs and speeds up the transaction process.

By giving all stakeholders a safe and transparent platform to transfer data, blockchain technology promotes trust. This lowers the risk of fraud and fosters more trust between parties by ensuring that all participants in the supply chain have access to authentic and unchangeable data. In general, the trust element of blockchain transactions helps supply chain management by giving all parties a safe and open platform to share information, work together, and raise the effectiveness of the supply chain management process. Supply chain management can make sure that things go smoothly from one end to the other by utilizing blockchain technology, leading to a more sustainable and robust supply chain.

Immutability

Once a transaction is recorded on a blockchain, it cannot be edited or removed. This is so that each computer in the network may retain a copy of the data that is stored in a distributed ledger called a blockchain. It would be virtually hard to amend or delete a transaction without the consensus of the whole network. Its immutability guarantees the accuracy and immutability of any data stored on the blockchain. This is especially helpful in sectors like finance, healthcare, and supply chain management where data integrity is essential.

The immutable record of every transaction in the supply chain is created by blockchain technology, enabling traceability. This enables everyone to track the origin of the products and confirm their ethical and sustainable sourcing (Kouhizadeh & Sarkis, 2018). A transparent and auditable record of each transaction is produced, which promotes accountability. As a result, the risk of fraud is decreased, and parties' trust is increased because everyone involved in the supply chain is held accountable for their activities. Additionally, by enabling supply chain process automation, it lessens the need for manual intervention and the possibility of errors. As a result, the supply chain management process is improved in terms of efficiency and cost.

Reliability

The continuous, interruption-free operation of blockchain technology makes it incredibly dependable. This is because, as opposed to being kept on a single server or database, data on a blockchain is kept on a decentralized network of computers. The blockchain keeps running as a result, making sure that data is still available and accurate even if some nodes on the network crash.

Blockchain technology has a highly resilient architecture that prevents downtime or interruptions. This is because the blockchain continues to run, guaranteeing that the data is accessible and accurate even if some nodes on the network fail (Queiroz et al., 2019), This lowers the possibility of delay or interruption and guarantees that the supply chain management process is always dependable and functional. It makes blockchain technology an attractive solution for applications that demand high levels of reliability and availability, such as financial transactions or supply chain management.

Also, the implementation of cryptographic methods in blockchain technology boosts its dependability. Complex cryptographic techniques are used to validate transactions on a blockchain, ensuring that the data is secure and impenetrable. The blockchain network gains an additional layer of dependability and security as a result. Overall, blockchain technology is quite dependable and suited for a variety of applications due to its decentralized architecture and cryptographic security. In contrast to conventional centralized systems, it delivers a level of reliability that is challenging to accomplish.

Security

Due to the use of cryptography to validate transactions on a blockchain, blockchain technology is very secure. This makes sure that only parties with permission can access the data on the blockchain (Queiroz et al., 2019). The blockchain's decentralized structure also makes it less vulnerable to fraud and hacking because any attempt to tamper with the data would require the agreement of the entire network. In addition, blockchain-based solutions can be developed to provide various levels of security depending on the requirements of the application. A public blockchain network, on the other hand, can be used to assure openness and accountability while a private blockchain network can be used to limit access to approved individuals.

Blockchain can assist in lowering the cost of supply chain management by eliminating the need for middlemen and automating supply chain procedures. Overall, the trust, immutability, reliability, and security provided by blockchain technology make it an appealing solution for a variety of applications, from financial transactions to supply chain management to healthcare.

BLOCKCHAIN ADOPTION IN SUPPLY CHAIN

Smart Contracts

A smart contract operates similarly to a traditional contract that the parties can exchange goods or acquire merchandise or services in accordance with the conditions of the contract. The smart contract can also be enforceable in court if it complies with the legal requirements of a contract and is electronically signed by a person or entity approved by the government. A smart contract is primarily an electronic contract. As a result, the standards and agreements will be defined in code, and the incentive or agreed-upon service will only be provided when the requirements are met (Agrawal et al., 2021). The parties involved should first debate the parameters of the contract, and once those terms are agreed upon, the contract should be written in terms of code while adhering to all those terms. Following that, the blockchain network's operators will then receive the code, which each node in the network will subsequently execute. In the final phase, when a contract requirement is met and will be checked by all network operators in the blockchain. If and only if it is verified, the transaction will be completed; however, if the verification fails, the transaction will fail.

For instance, the operation of a smart contract is comparable to that of a vending machine. If a user initiates a payment and selects a slot of the vending machine, the machine will first determine whether the funds from the initiated transaction are equal to or greater than the price of the slot before dispensing the product. A transaction will not dispense the product if the transaction is not initialized or if the funds are inadequate (Agrawal et al., 2021). Similarly, a smart contract will only initiate a payment or service if the contract's conditions are met and verified in the blockchain. As smart contracts are automated, the time required for any human interaction is kept to a minimum. Because they are automated, smart contracts also assist in removing the need for a middleman's interactivity. In this way, the stakeholders will have greater influence over the contract and have more control over it. Broker costs will be reduced by eliminating them.

Blockchain-based smart contracts are automated programs that only run when certain criteria are met. Every blockchain node has this certified system software on it. These smart contracts can be permitted or public, meaning they can be private or public depending on the goals of the proprietor, depending on the application (Blossey et al., 2019). The public blockchain is accessible to anyone with a broadband connection, while the permission blockchain can only be accessed by users who have approval from the admin via a preset regulatory process. These smart contracts can be programmed according to the needs of the supply chain and used by supply chain management for automation and accountability. To achieve transparency and integrity, the entire supply chain tracking system can be computerized and will only be carried out when the necessary parameters are met. Smart contracts can help supply chains support transparency and automation as they operate more on automated set specifications. Smart contracts are legal contracts that compel the parties involved to fulfil their treaty duties. This will increase the speed of the process and communication between stakeholders regarding decisions circulated throughout the supply chain. Many processes that require menial work will be reduced as automation is enabled. When compared to traditional human involvement, automation allows any work to be completed accurately and without inconsistencies.

Traceability

Without a digitalized ledger, it is impossible to know the status of the commodities, stock, and transactions in the supply chain. An efficient supply chain keeps track of its items and is transparent about all transactions that take place. When the supply chain needs the transparency feature to track each step in the chain, blockchain is utilized. We need to be aware of every single detail, including inventory, product status, location, etc., to recognize threats in a supply chain. Blockchain is a decentralized transaction ledger. No matter the level of proper authorization, information entered the blockchain cannot be changed once it has been verified. In the blockchain, the data is permanent. With blockchain, the supply chain may keep track of all the information on manufacturing updates in a single ledger that can be distributed across trusted partners for improved business. As all actions are time stamped, blockchain will empower the supply chain to identify potential threats by keeping track of every single facet about the integrity of the product (Pundir et al., 2019). We can address problems like pirated products, policy violations, product shortages, and inefficiency by integrating blockchain into the supply chain (Casado-Vara et al., 2018). Figure 5 demonstrates how the supply chain can use blockchain to monitor its product at every stage of the process.

Figure 5. Blockchain integration in supply chain

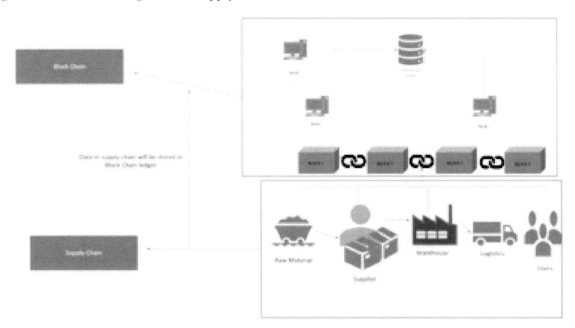

The unification of blockchain technology with the supply chain would assist management in reducing the supply of fraudulent goods and identifying the source of those fraudulent products. This evolution will also aid in the improvement of product traceability. Merchandise traceability allows stakeholders to verify the authenticity of the product by tracking its route from manufacturing process to shipment (Fosso et al., 2020). This can improve product security by increasing transparency throughout the supply chain and implementing safety measures to mitigate risk. The supply chain will be able to track shipments, supplies, and help detect fake goods due to the traceability provided by the decentralized ledger of a blockchain (Monrat et al., 2019). By doing so, the supply chain's ability to govern itself effectively will improve and pirated goods will be less prevalent. The use of blockchain traceability will make it possible to supply minute details about the transit of goods from production to shipment. It will be easier to process documents with traceability. The supply chain will be more economical, robust, and credible if it can instantly track every step of the merchandise. Additionally, the tracking will make it possible to confirm the authenticity of the supplies.

Supply chains are networks handled by corporations linked to one another through contractual agreements. The most important aspect in any supply chain network between the companies is credibility and authenticity, and the contract can only be upheld by the value of trust for any potential future commercial relationships. A blockchain, however, works without the need for trust and is distinct from a supply chain because it strives for visibility, efficiency, and authentication. Features of block chain technology can contribute to a successful supply chain (Blossey et al., 2019). Information can be efficiently transmitted throughout a network by incorporating the use of block chains. Bullwhip effects can occur in the supply chain due to communication errors. The bullwhip effect describes how minor variations in demand at the consumer level can lead to steadily radical changes at the commodity levels (Blossey et al., 2019). The block chain promotes continuous information sharing, which will boost inventory accuracy. Any quantifiable circumstance, such stock or product availability, can be tracked with the use of IOT (Internet of Things). As a result, the supply chain decision-making process is strengthened, and proactive and recurrent risk-management tactics may be employed.

Using a public database of accessible and unchangeable entries, block chain technology enables users to track assets all the way back to their original location. It holds all the information and transactions that have been logged in the blockchain since its creation. It is possible to check the validity and verification of any transaction. Information on the origin of goods, including both physical objects and associated hardware, ensures the reliability of those resources. This might make ethical sourcing required and make it possible to spot or even stop unscrupulous business activities like consumer counterfeiting. Applications may involve tracking down the owner of an object after a sale for warranty purposes. In addition to streamlining documentation, block chain technology also facilitates international trade by ensuring the validity of cargo records, such as those required for customs clearance.

REAL-WORLD BLOCKCHAIN APPLICATIONS IN SUPPLY CHAINS

Supply Chain Subsidizing

When merchandise is received in a supply chain, the cost of the asset is generated in the form of an itemized bill. This invoice will include the issuance date and the deadline by which the buyer must pay the cost of the invoice. The process of paying supply chain receipts typically takes longer because they can be paid within 30 days (about 4 and a half weeks) of receiving the goods. If there is a good working relationship, the payment due can be postponed, but the seller would not profit financially from doing so. Funding for supply chains can benefit from blockchain and smart contracts. The parties involved can use blockchain smart contracts to trigger payment as soon as the goods are delivered and accepted because all products can be tracked in real time via the blockchain ledger. Blockchain-based smart contracts can be configured to only trigger payments after certain criteria are fulfilled, such as the delivery of a product.

The whole supply chain monitoring system can be computerized to accomplish authenticity and transparency and will only be used when the required conditions are satisfied. Companies no longer use dealers, or other third parties to execute activities due to smart contracts. Businesses and shipping agents can enter into legally enforceable agreements with smart contracts that will end promptly if all predetermined conditions are not met. The incorporation of blockchain and supply chain will aid in more effective supply chain management. This will aid the supply chain in increasing automation and governance. The transactions will be more reliable with this method, and they will all be registered in the ledger. These smart contracts cut delivery times and complex and costly failures while ensuring transparency and profitability. Walmart uses cutting-edge blockchain technology to settle its invoices with its contracted transport companies.

Sweet Bridge is a London-based provider of supply chain management, shipping, and transit systems. Blockchain technology has been incorporated into this company's framework to enable equitable, efficient, flexible trade that benefits all stakeholders. Blockchain is used by this business to concentrate on its revenues and solvency (Queiroz et al., 2019). As a transportation business, it will generate an invoice following a successful shipment but will not receive payment in a timely manner, which may affect its ability to maintain fiscal stability in the market. To address this, it will use smart contracts and real-time audit ledgers to address its financial issues and receive invoices immediately after delivery rather than weeks or months later.

Logistics

In the supply chain the process of procuring goods and moving resources such as inventory from one place to another is called logistics. Most of the suppliers, distributors, providers, and customers always interact via a third-party entity rather than direct communication (Min, 2019). This communication through third parties has proven to be inefficient and the third party involved needs to be trusted with all the information, which is a security issue regarding data and information. Due to ineffective methods, unnecessary third-party service fees, thievery, and cybercrime, supply chain providers are losing out on a sizable portion of the earnings. To eliminate third parties the blockchain is required to facilitate that by using decentralized distributed ledger. With the help of this ledger all the transactions can be verified, recorded, and managed independently with involvement of any third party creating a more secure supply chain. Blockchain has made global supply chains more efficient since it empowers businesses to automate processes right away and free of a third party. Moreover, it facilitates the unification of monetary and administrative services, enhancing the integration of client information.

Cold Chain Logistics

Cold chain logistics reduces computational product loss, safeguarding the quality of product quality, and maintaining chilled and frozen products at a consistent low temperature. Cold chain traceability refers to overseeing that entire process from start to finish. The responsibility of monitoring temperature is crucial for organizations that deal with culinary goods and services since they must adhere to specified temperature or condition requirements before delivery. In general, products like seafood, poultry, and livestock need optimum temperature parameters while being transported from one site to another as a rise in temperature may cause a food's microbial growth rate to double and its storage stability to decline quickly. Temperature increases cause bacteria to proliferate quickly as well.

Blockchain traceability is attained by sharing data on a distributed, tamper-proof ledger to meet the storage and transportation requirements of the supply chain (Min, 2019). An organization would be able to monitor and manage the items from counterfeit and their quality owing to the shared blockchain technology, which allows all the information at every point to be updated in the ledger following verification in a matter of seconds. For the blockchain to track temperature, Internet of Things integration is required. Products now come with sensors that can track the temperature, humidity, and any other atmospheric statistic a business may require. Smart contracts can be used to ensure prompt rectification if any of the measurements are abnormal for the product in transit if there is any temperature rise from the data provided by sensors. Therefore, one can monitor real-time temperature metrics using blockchain, and we can regulate the temperature according to the product condition using smart contract logic. Walmart makes use of this sophisticated equipment to monitor the quality and condition of its imports. Walmart uses this strategy to track its shipment of greens and lettuce because of the successful integration of blockchain into the supply chain. Microsoft, founded in 1975, has adopted blockchain to adhere to regulations and trace its goods across the supply chain. Because of this, Microsoft can track its devices and prohibit counterfeits. Its goal is to keep track of the provenance of each item.

Enhancing Supply Chain Efficiency Through Blockchain Integration

Oracle, a 1977-founded American business, has integrated blockchain technology into its supply chain. It uses blockchain to collect information from various sources and monitor cargo from beginning to end, giving users a comprehensive understanding of material flow. The ledger will allow the business to keep track of the product's state at any time, allowing it to run more efficiently and cost-effectively. To automate the traceability function and improve transportation transactions, the American corporation Chronicled linked blockchain technology with artificial intelligence and internet of things devices. Its internet of things (IoT) sensors with blockchain support would give operations a holistic perspective and greater understanding of the environment and the shipping process. The quality of the product will be improved as a result. Additionally, this will raise overall client satisfaction with the product.

CHALLENGES AND OPPORTUNITIES

The decentralized network of block chain technology helps to mitigate a cyber-attack directed at a single point because the entire system does not go down but continues to operate independently. However, one compromised network puts the data at risk because they will have access to all the information stored on the network's ledger. As a result, it is critical to examine the impact of these risks on technology, as well as whether it can withstand breaches and keep data safe. More research into probable security breaches and solutions to limit the risk associated with block chain technology will be needed. A decentralized network's storage is also a drawback. Because every node has an identical copy of the data, storing it and transferring it takes a lot of computing power, and the time it takes to process a chain grows over time. More research is conducted on techniques for splitting up large data sets into smaller chunks. Ethereum platform, smart contracts, and bitcoin are widely used in the block chain industry, and they need to be secured as they contain digital transactions (Queiroz et al., 2019). More study can be conducted on the threats pertaining to them and review various methods in which block chain platforms can be used to develop solutions for cyber security threats. Machine learning techniques such as unsupervised learning, which is utilized for anomaly detection, can also be used to monitor network entry. These malicious traffic monitors can send out alerts to clients if there is anything unusual going on in the chain. More algorithms could be created to filter fraudulent traffic and warn users about the danger.

Even while it is vital for every individual in a supply chain to understand that after data is established on the blockchain, there is still a risk that a single error or instance of fraud may occur during the initial data entry. As a result, blockchain data is not always trustworthy and may even be deceptive. For instance, a potential attacker could record on the blockchain that a container contained a laptop even though it was packed with groceries. Technology might make it simpler to determine where in the supply chain the container with supplies was filled, but it won't stop erroneous data from eventually being added to the blockchain. It merely enables each blockchain user to attest that the data has not altered since a specific time stamp, without prohibiting flawed information from being introduced to the chain. Since the ledger cannot be changed, erroneous data recorded in the block will cause a huge commotion throughout the supply chain. The business will suffer financial loss as a result.

To increase production and improve efficiency in other areas, blockchain is emerging to be employed in a range of supply chain applications, particularly in the industrial and healthcare sectors. Among the most optimistic current technological improvements in blockchain is integration of Internet of things (Jabbar et al., 2021). Blockchain enables enterprises to accept payments directly and without the involvement of an external party, increasing the efficiency of global supply chains. Additionally, it makes it easier for fiscal and logistical solutions to be more integrated, enhancing participant data. Due to the convergence of these technologies, businesses may both retain and win over new customers while also strengthening relationships with their key partners. The supply chain in several industries, including procurement and distribution, has an immense potential owing to the Industrial Revolution 4.0 (Blossey et al., 2019). It can be used in physically connected technical components such as smart products and machines that function adaptively without human intervention and can create synchronized mechanisms, such as smart supply chains, where the entire supply chain process from production to retail is automated and managed by machineries. The acceptance of blockchain-based solutions by other market participants will be sparked by the successful projects carried out by Walmart, Amazon, and many other businesses. Research on supply chain fusion with blockchain technology is gaining greater traction (Blossey et al., 2019).

CONCLUSION

In conclusion, this book chapter has presented the basics of blockchain technology and explored the benefits and drawbacks of integrating it into a supply chain. As a distributed ledger technology, blockchain has the potential to address several issues in supply chain management, such as inventory inefficiencies, counterfeit goods, and stakeholder engagement. By integrating a blockchain network into the supply chain, businesses can manage operations more effectively and efficiently. The use of blockchain in the supply chain can aid in tracking and monitoring products, reducing counterfeit goods, and monitoring temperature-sensitive commodities. Smart contracts, supported by blockchain, can increase productivity by assisting the supply chain in various ways, such as facilitating quicker payment processing. However, there are also challenges to implementing blockchain technology in the supply chain, as well as opportunities for the technology to disrupt businesses. With growing efforts and research on blockchain, it is anticipated that many of the challenges can be overcome, and numerous opportunities will emerge to transform businesses. Overall, the potential benefits of integrating blockchain into the supply chain are significant, and companies should carefully consider the technology's potential to enhance their operations and improve their bottom line.

REFERENCES

Agrawal, P., & Narain, R. (2018). Digital supply chain management: an overview. *IOP Conf. Ser.: Mater. Sci. Eng.* 10.1088/1757-899X/455/1/012074

Agrawal, T. K., Kumar, V., Pal, R., Wang, L., & Chen, Y. (2021). Blockchain-based framework for supply chain traceability: A case example of textile and clothing industry. *Computers & Industrial Engineering*, *154*, 154. doi:10.1016/j.cie.2021.107130

Aslam, J., Saleem, A., Khan, N., & Kim, Y. (2021). Factors influencing blockchain adoption in supply chain management practices: A study based on the oil industry. *Journal of Innovation & Knowledge*, *6*(2), 124–134. Advance online publication. doi:10.1016/j.jik.2021.01.002

Azzi, R., Chamoun, R. K., & Sokhn, M. (2019). The power of a blockchain-based supply chain. *Computers & Industrial Engineering*, *135*, 582–592. doi:10.1016/j.cie.2019.06.042

Bekrar, A., Cadi, A. A. E., Todosijevic, R., & Sarkis, J. (2021). Digitalizing the closing-of-the-loop for supply chains: A transportation and blockchain perspective. *Sustainability (Basel)*, *13*(5), 2895. Advance online publication. doi:10.3390u13052895

Berneis, M., Bartsch, D., & Winkler, H. (2021). Applications of Blockchain Technology in Logistics and Supply Chain Management—Insights from a Systematic Literature Review. *Logistics*, *5*(3), 43. doi:10.3390/logistics5030043

Blossey, G., Eisenhardt, J., & Hahn, G. J. (2019). Blockchain technology in supply chain management: an application perspective. *Proceedings of the 52nd Hawaii International Conference on System Science*. 10.24251/HICSS.2019.824

Casado-Vara, R., Prieto, J., Prieta, F. D., & Corchado, J. M. (2018). How blockchain improves the supply chain: case study alimentary supply chain. *Procedia Computer Science*, *134*, 393–398. doi:10.1016/j.procs.2018.07.193

Chang, S. E., & Chen, Y. (2020). When blockchain meets supply chain: A systematic literature review on current development and potential applications. *IEEE Access : Practical Innovations, Open Solutions*, *8*, 62478–62494. doi:10.1109/ACCESS.2020.2983601

Cole, R., Stevenson, M., & Aitken, J. (2019). Blockchain technology: Implications for operations and supply chain management. *Supply Chain Management*, *24*(4), 469–483. doi:10.1108/SCM-09-2018-0309

Cryptopedia. (2021). *Merkle trees and Merkle roots help make blockchains possible*. https://www.gemini.com/cryptopedia/merkle-tree-blockchain-merkle-root

Dasaklis, T. K., Voutsinas, T. G., Tsoulfas, G. T., & Casino, F. (2022). A systematic literature review of blockchain-enabled supply chain traceability implementations. *Sustainability (Basel)*, *14*(4), 2439. doi:10.3390u14042439

Durach, C. F., Blesik, T., von Düring, M., & Bick, M. (2021). Blockchain applications in supply chain transactions. *Journal of Business Logistics*, *42*(1), 7–24. doi:10.1111/jbl.12238

Dutta, P., Choi, T.-M., Somani, S., & Butala, R. (2020). Blockchain technology in supply chain operations: Applications, challenges and research opportunities. *Transportation Research Part E, Logistics and Transportation Review*, *142*, 102067. Advance online publication. doi:10.1016/j.tre.2020.102067 PMID:33013183

Eljazzar, M. M., Amr, M. A., Kassem, S. S., & Ezzat, M. (2018). Merging supply chain and blockchain technologies. arXiv preprint, arXiv:1804.04149. doi:10.3390/info12020070

Etemadi, N., Borbon-Galvez, Y., Strozzi, F., & Etemadi, T. (2021). Supply Chain Disruption Risk Management with Blockchain: A Dynamic Literature Review. *Information (Basel)*, *12*(2), 70. doi:10.3390/info12020070

Etemadi, N., Gelder, P. V., & Strozzi, F. (2021). An ISM Modeling of Barriers for Blockchain/Distributed Ledger Technology Adoption in Supply Chains towards Cybersecurity. *Sustainability (Basel)*, *13*(9), 4672. doi:10.3390u13094672

Fosso, S., Maciel, W., & Queiroz, M. (2020). Industry 4.0 and the supply chain digitalization: A blockchain diffusion perspective. *Production Planning and Control*, *33*(2-3), 193–210. doi:10.1080/09537287.2020.1810756

Gonczol, P., Katsikouli, P., Herskind, L., & Dragoni, N. (2020). Blockchain implementations and use cases for supply chains-a survey. *IEEE Access : Practical Innovations, Open Solutions*, *8*, 11856–11871. doi:10.1109/ACCESS.2020.2964880

HackiusN.PetersenM. (2017). Blockchain in logistics and supply chain: trick or treat? *Digitization in Supply Chain Management and Logistics*. DOI: doi:10.15480/882.1444

Helo, P., & Hao, Y. (2019). Blockchains in operations and supply chains: A model and reference implementation. *Computers & Industrial Engineering*, *136*, 242–251. doi:10.1016/j.cie.2019.07.023

Helo, P., & Shamsuzzoha, A. (2020). Real-time supply chain—A blockchain architecture for project deliveries. *Robotics and Computer-integrated Manufacturing*, *63*, 101909. doi:10.1016/j.rcim.2019.101909

Jabbar, S., Lloyd, H., Hammoudeh, M., Adebisi, B., & Raza, U. (2021). Blockchain-enabled supply chain: Analysis, challenges, and future directions. *Multimedia Systems*, *27*(4), 787–806. doi:10.100700530-020-00687-0

Jakobsson, M., & Juels, A. (1999). Proofs of work and bread pudding protocols. In *Secure Information Networks: Communications and Multimedia Security*. Kluwer Academic Publishers. . doi:10.1007/978-0-387-35568-9_1

Kawaguchi, N. (2019). Application of blockchain to supply chain: Flexible blockchain technology. *Procedia Computer Science*, *164*, 143–148. doi:10.1016/j.procs.2019.12.166

King, S., & Nadal, S. (2012). *PPCoin: Peer-to-Peer Crypto-Currency with Proof-of-Stake*. Self-published Paper.

Korpela, K., Hallikas, J., & Dahlberg, T. (2019). Digital supply chain transformation toward blockchain integration. *Hawaii International Conference on System Sciences (HICSS)*. 10.24251/HICSS.2017.506

Kouhizadeh, M., & Sarkis, J. (2018). Blockchain practices, potentials, and perspectives in greening supply chains. *Sustainability (Basel)*, *10*(10), 3652. doi:10.3390u10103652

Kumar, A., Abhishek, K., Ghalib, M. R., Nerurkar, P., Bhirud, S., Alnumay, W., & Ghosh, U. (2021). Securing logistics system and supply chain using Blockchain. *Applied Stochastic Models in Business and Industry*, *37*(3), 413–428. doi:10.1002/asmb.2592

Kumar, A. S., & Anusha, M. (2023). Blockchain Enabled Supply Chain Management. *SN Computer Science*, *4*(2), 179. doi:10.100742979-022-01621-z PMID:36711045

Lim, M. K., Li, Y., Wang, C., & Tseng, M. L. (2021). A literature review of blockchain technology applications in supply chains: A comprehensive analysis of themes, methodologies and industries. *Computers & Industrial Engineering*, *154*, 107133. doi:10.1016/j.cie.2021.107133

Lin, I., & Liao, T. (2017). A Survey of Blockchain Security Issues and Challenges. *International Journal of Network Security*, *19*, 653–659.

Longo, F., Nicoletti, L., Padovano, A., d'Atri, G., & Forte, M. (2019). Blockchain-enabled supply chain: An experimental study. *Computers & Industrial Engineering*, *136*, 57–69. doi:10.1016/j.cie.2019.07.026

Merkle, R. C. (1980). Protocols for public key cryptosystems. *IEEE Symposium on Research in Security and Privacy*.

Min, H. (2019). Blockchain technology for enhancing supply chain resilience. *Business Horizons*, *62*(1), 35–45. doi:10.1016/j.bushor.2018.08.012

Monrat, A., Schelén, O., & Andersson, K. (2019). A survey of blockchain from the perspectives of applications, challenges, and opportunities. *IEEE Access : Practical Innovations, Open Solutions*, *7*, 117134–117151. doi:10.1109/ACCESS.2019.2936094

Nguyen, C. T., Hoang, D. T., Nguyen, D. N., Niyato, D., Nguyen, H. T., & Dutkiewicz, E. (2019). Proof-of-stake consensus mechanisms for future blockchain networks: Fundamentals, applications and opportunities. *IEEE Access : Practical Innovations, Open Solutions*, *7*, 85727–85745. doi:10.1109/ACCESS.2019.2925010

Park, A., & Li, H. (2021). The effect of blockchain technology on supply chain sustainability performances. *Sustainability (Basel)*, *13*(4), 1726. Advance online publication. doi:10.3390u13041726

Pundir, A. K., Jagannath, J. D., Chakraborty, M., & Ganpathy, L. (2019). Technology integration for improved performance: a case study in digitization of supply chain with integration of Internet of Things and blockchain technology. *IEEE 9th Annual Computing and Communication Workshop and Conference (CCWC)*, 170-176. 10.1109/CCWC.2019.8666484

Queiroz, M., Telles, R., & Bonilla, S. (2019). Blockchain and supply chain management integration: A systematic review of the literature. *Supply Chain Management*, *25*(2), 241–254. Advance online publication. doi:10.1108/SCM-03-2018-0143

Saberi, S., Kouhizadeh, M., Sarkis, J., & Shen, L. (2019). Blockchain technology and its relationships to sustainable supply chain management. *International Journal of Production Research*, *57*(7), 2117–2135. doi:10.1080/00207543.2018.1533261

Tijan, E., Aksentijević, S., Ivanić, K., & Jardas, M. (2019). Blockchain technology implementation in logistics. *Sustainability (Basel)*, *11*(4), 1185. doi:10.3390u11041185

Verhoeven, P., Sinn, F., & Herden, T. T. (2018). Examples from blockchain implementations in logistics and supply chain management: Exploring the mindful use of a new technology. *Logistics*, *2*(3), 20. doi:10.3390/logistics2030020

Wang, Y., Han, J. H., & Beynon-Davies, P. (2019). Understanding blockchain technology for future supply chains: A systematic literature review and research agenda. *Supply Chain Management*, *24*(1), 62–84. doi:10.1108/SCM-03-2018-0148

Zhang, H., Nakamura, T., & Sakurai, K. (2019). Security and trust issues on digital supply chain. *IEEE Intl Conf on Dependable, Autonomic and Secure Computing*, 338-343. . doi:10.1109/DASC/PiCom/CBDCom/CyberSciTech.2019.00069

Section 5
Blockchain Technology and Supply Chain Sustainability

Chapter 10
Impact of Distributed Ledger Technology on Supply Chain Sustainability

Mariana de la Roche
IOTA Foundation, Germany & INATBA, Germany

Laura Kajtazi
IOTA Foundation, Germany & INATBA, Germany

Åsa Dahlborn
IOTA Foundation, Germany & INATBA, Germany

Louis Helmer
IOTA Foundation, Germany & INATBA, Germany

ABSTRACT

This chapter describes the challenges and vulnerabilities of current supply chain management and presents the benefits of implementing blockchain and DLT technology in the supply chain processes. For a more precise understanding, the chapter presents a summary of the characteristics of blockchain technology and an overview of the energy consumption of different blockchain protocols to demystify the negative criticism of blockchain technologies in terms of energy consumption. The purpose of analyzing the characteristics and energy requirements is to present the potential of DLTs to positively impact supply chains and make the blockchain industry more sustainable. After describing the sector's challenges and the technology's characteristics, the chapter presents case studies in which DLT has been successfully integrated into the supply chain of various products and goods. The chapter concludes by highlighting the necessary conditions to promote the adoption of DLT technology globally.

DOI: 10.4018/978-1-6684-7455-6.ch010

INTRODUCTION

The Need for Better Data Collection for Sustainability and the Circular Economy

During the last few years, supply chains and their limitations have been dragged into the spotlight. The COVID-19 pandemic brought unprecedented challenges to supply chains worldwide and across all sectors (Sharma et al., 2020). Disruptions caused by lockdowns, restriction of movement and uncertainty about the future caused drastic changes in both supply and demand for different products. Supply chains barely had a chance to recover from this turmoil before being hit by new challenges arising from the economic and political world situation. Rising energy prices and other consequences of the conflict in Ukraine revealed further points of failure in supply chains worldwide, mostly perceived in the form of food shortages (Jagtap et al, 2022). Other obstacles in the economic and business environment such as Brexit provide more examples of the volatile political landscape that supply chains need to navigate. Alongside these political and economic threats, the clock is ticking faster for another crucial challenge that supply chains need to address: the environmental impact of their activities. The climate crisis is one of the most critical challenges of our time and sustainable supply chains are key to facing this challenge.

The climate crisis cannot be tackled without restructuring the way in which most supply chains currently work. According to Oberle et al. (2019), over 50% of greenhouse gas emissions and 90% of biodiversity loss and water stress (all major contributors to climate change) come from resource extraction and processing of materials, fuels, and food. These operations are an intrinsic part of global business supply chains. To make supply chains more sustainable, it is essential to measure and, where possible, adjust the environmental impact of raw material extraction, goods production and disposal, and provision of services.

Blockchain enables the collection, analysis, and reporting of supply chain data in a secure, transparent, and immutable way. By digitalizing the total life cycles of products and supply chains, from the extraction of raw materials to the refurbishment or recycling of the product, blockchain solutions support companies to track and optimize the real impact they generate in society and enable the inclusion of factors that are often overlooked when calculating generated impact, such as the carbon footprint of production and transportation, or the consumption of water and energy. This data facilitates a more sustainable manufacture of products and can moreover be used by manufacturers and those involved in the supply chain to understand where in the supply chain and product life cycle there is potential to incorporate more sustainable practices, which areas and processes are impacting the environment the most, and where action needs to be taken to mitigate that impact.

Action taken on a continental level indicates that the urgency to adopt innovative technology solutions is widely accepted. The European Union has allocated major investment in developing clean technologies that promote circularity and support the achievement of Agenda 2030[1] and the United Nations Sustainable Development Goals[2] (SDGs). The EU Innovation Fund intends to support innovative clean-tech projects with grants amounting to around €10 billion over 2020-2030, which will help bring breakthrough technologies for European decarbonization and climate neutrality to the market (Clerens, 2022). Additionally, the EU's key funding programme for research and innovation, Horizon Europe, has allocated a budget of EUR 95.5 billion to tackle climate change and contribute to the fulfillment of the SDGs (European Commission, 2022a).

Countless blockchain organizations seek a more sustainable future, for example by developing sustainable solutions based on blockchain through partnerships with businesses, industrial entities and institutions. Technology achieves its biggest impact and scale when it is interoperable and applicable across borders and jurisdictions. Blockchain offers a fully trusted, immutable, and interoperable data system that can speed up automation and innovation across a supply chain, enabling new adaptive business models to move faster towards the circular economy.

In this chapter, we will explore the potential of blockchain in supply chain use cases. We will review the unique characteristics of this technology and how it can enhance sustainability and the circular economy. Moreover, we will briefly refer to the evolution of blockchain to become greener, energy efficient, and scalable. Finally, we will review supply chain use cases in different regions.

BACKGROUND

The Potential Impact of Blockchain on the Sustainability of Supply Chains

Climate change is one of the most pressing challenges facing our world. According to Shaw et al. (2012), the majority of an organization's environmental impact lies in the supply chain, either upstream (suppliers, manufacturing) or downstream (consumers, product use). Looking into the challenges within the supply chain and identifying how these can be addressed so that sustainable supply chains can be enabled is key to an effective response by businesses to climate change. Before looking at challenges faced by supply chains, it is important to recapitulate how sustainability is defined in the context of supply chain management.

Sustainability can be defined as the Triple Bottom Line concept, which balances environmental, social and economic dimensions in supply chain management (Seuring et al., 2008). Within the triple bottom line, the environmental dimension focuses on an organization's activities that contribute to its environmental impact (such as energy consumption and waste management). The social dimension centers on the organization's undertaking of beneficial and fair business practices for workers, human capital, and the community (for example, fair wages or providing health care coverage) (Elkington, 1997). Lastly, the economic dimension focuses on the organization's practices in promoting economic prosperity (for example generating profit or long-term viability).

Figure 1. Triple bottom line

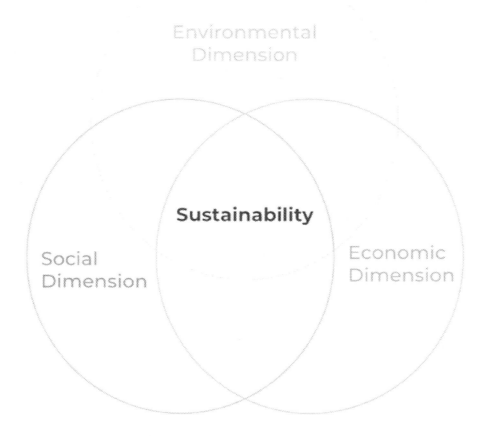

Today's supply chains are complex and consist of multiple, geographically disconnected entities that compete to supply consumers (Lambert & Enz, 2017). Not surprisingly, supply chain members often have difficulty accessing information from other supply chain partners due to the absence of a secured information-sharing infrastructure, a situation further compounded by the fact that information is dispersed among multiple actors. This makes the accurate tracking of product movement a challenge. Also, the participation of various stakeholders can raise the possibility that one of the stakeholders may act unethically.

These factors can create a lack of transparency in supply chains. For example, information about the conditions under which a product was manufactured and how much waste was generated in its production may be inaccurate. This lack of transparency makes it difficult for businesses to make decisions about removing products or processes based on their energy consumption (Varriale et al., 2020) or for consumers to decide whether to buy a product or not. A lack of transparency can also lead to the rework and recall of products which consumes more resources, increasing both costs and waste (Saberi et al., 2018).

Blockchain opens up opportunities to overcome these challenges and helps supply chains become more sustainable. In view of the rapidly progressing climate change, there is a growing effort in academia that looks specifically at the impact of blockchain in the environmental context of supply chains, which will be the focus of this chapter (Kouhizadeh & Sarkis, 2018; Saber et al., 2018; Varriale et al., 2020; Khaqqi et al., 2018; Khan et al., 2022; Friedman & Ormiston, 2022; Elhidaoui et al., 2022).

Blockchain Characteristics That Promote Sustainable Supply Chains

Commonly-mentioned beneficial aspects of blockchain found in the literature are data transparency, security, efficiency and decentralization. Furthermore, the potential of technologies like smart contracts, digital identities, and tokenization for creating more environmentally considerate supply chains have also gained a large volume of attention.

In the following paragraphs, these characteristics of blockchain will be looked at more closely. The readers will observe that some of these characteristics may overlap and be complemented by the others.

Decentralization

Decentralization is a crucial characteristic of distributed ledger technology. There is no central database or authority to manage the records of transactions (Kouhizadeh & Sarkis, 2018). Removing the need for a central controller that collectively maintains records reduces the risk of hacks, corruption, or system crashes (Kouhizadeh & Sarkis, 2018). A decentralized system architecture platform for applications involving multiple parties with little need to trust each other can be especially useful to fragmented and intransparent supply chains (Saberi et al., 2018). Paradoxically, the fact that there is no central authority that must be trusted makes trust one of the main consequences of decentralization (Nofer et al., 2017). A decentralized database enables users to interact directly through a peer-to-peer network rather than going through a central point of control. All users within the network have the same copy of the ledger, and each update in the ledger needs consensus across the network's users. This is achieved through a decentralized consensus using different algorithms, such as Proof of Work and Proof of Stake, to confirm the validity of a recorded transaction. Commonly, decentralized consensus entails voting or validation by a majority of the network's users to guarantee the reliability of transactions. (Mougayar & Buterin, 2016).

Data Security

In blockchains, value is reflected in transactions recorded in a shared ledger. The value is secured by providing a verifiable, time-stamped record of transactions (English, Auer & Domingue, 2016). Thereby, each transaction has a timestamp and a hash value that has a unique cryptographic structure that prevents any tampering and altering of the information in the ledger (Nofer et al., 2017). So no one can change a transaction after it is entered into the shared ledger.

The high level of tamper resistance minimizes the risk of unauthorized changes to already recorded data, which in turn provides more security and reliability in product and supply chain information, such as carbon footprint (Dos Santos, Torrisi & Pantoni, 2021). This in turn can improve the ability to measure trustable environmental data in general.

The security and reliability of supply chain data are also enhanced by the decentralized architecture of distributed ledger technology. In a decentralized network, the reliability of information is checked by the network's users according to the network's consensus rules. This feature limits data misuse and manipulation of the network. Having a decentralized rather than a centralized database further mitigates the single point of failure, a well-known security risk in centralized databases (Ølnes et al., 2017).

Data Transparency

In a distributed ledger network, all authorized users keep an identical copy of the ledger, which contains the list of transactions executed so far and which is updated each time a transaction is approved (Kouhizadeh & Sarkis, 2018). All network users are able to view the full history of the transactions (Friedman & Ormiston, 2022). This increases transparency, which in turn provides a key prerequisite for tracing and tracking factors such as the origin and flow of products and processes, the involved participants, and information on transportation and carbon emissions. Thus, supply chain partners from upstream to end customers can follow and audit the supply chain's history of records (Kouhizadeh & Sarkis, 2018).

As an example with blockchain technology, tracing the product footprint of companies becomes easier and can help decide the amount of carbon tax that should be charged to a company. If a product is more expensive due to its large carbon footprint, it can give customers more clarity in their decision-making when they are looking for a product that is more environmentally friendly (Saberi et al. 2018).

Also, as indicated in the previous section, because records on a blockchain are time-stamped and secure, data manipulation and fraud are detectable and traceable on the ledger. This also promotes transparency and trust among supply chain partners. The collection of trustworthy data can help prevent greenwashing and enhance consumers' decision-making (Dos Santos, Torrisi & Pantoni, 2021).

Efficiency

Sharing data digitally through blockchain avoids paper-intensive processes, which makes the process more efficient, especially in terms of the environmental impact. Increased efficiency can also be achieved through the accurate tracking and tracing of products. For example, inferior products can be tracked and prevented from being exchanged, which reduces the need for product recall, helps reduce financial loss and ozone depletion caused by greenhouse emissions, and promotes a more effective use of resources (Saberi et al., 2018).

Another area where blockchain creates efficiency is in emission trading schemes (ETS) (Khaqqi et al., 2018). Fraudulent actions such as greenwashing or double counting (i.e., two or more offset participants claiming emission reduction from the same project) can be minimized by the transparency and reliability of blockchain, which in turn improves the reputation of participants in the supply chain (Khaqqi et al., 2018). In a reputation-based system, the economic benefits of a positive reputation encourage participants to solve the inefficiency of ETS and develop long-term solutions for emission reduction (Khaqqi et al., 2018).

Blockchain technology could also help in building a more efficient recycling system by incentivizing people through financial reward in the form of a token in exchange for storing recyclable materials such as plastic bottles or paper (Saberi et al., 2018).

Smart Contracts and Digital Identities

Another beneficial characteristic of blockchain is the possibility of creating smart contracts, which are programmed rules stored in the blockchain.

Time-intensive contract procedures are no longer needed. Smart contracts support the automated execution of transactions based on programmed rules, where parties can give their consent by executing secure digital signatures within the blockchain. Whenever the contract receives a message from a user in the network or another contract, it updates the ledgers only if the message complies with the contractual terms (Peters and Panayi, 2016). As such, smart contracts can improve performance and do not necessarily require in-person contract negotiations among supply chain partners. Programmed rules for tracking and controlling sustainable terms and regulatory policy autonomously in supply chains can enforce or govern appropriate corrections (Saberi et al. 2018).

As we have already learned, blockchain can help through tracking and tracing promote transparency amongst participants. Smart contracts are a powerful tool to ensure information symmetry and thus transparency amongst participants. Through smart contracts, a transaction is made only when every participant agrees on it, bringing symmetry information among upstream and downstream partners and, therefore, avoiding possible corruption or errors (Park & Li, 2021).

Besides smart contracts there is the possibility of creating blockchain based decentralized digital Identities for an asset. With this a (decentralized) digital product passport (DPP) can be built for a supply chain product. The DPP can provide a single source of truth throughout the lifecycle of a product through its immutable record enabled by the blockchain technology (IOTA Foundation, 2022).

Reflecting on the benefits of blockchain technology reveals the possibility of creating new models in the supply chain with improved sustainability. One model that has gained increased attention and has been referred to repeatedly in this chapter is the circular economy, which will be presented in the next section.

Blockchain for the Circular Economy

In contrast to sustainability, which broadly relates to people, the planet, and the economy, the circular economy focuses on resource cycles and environmental performance. Contrary to a linear economy, in which materials are used and made into products to be eventually disposed of as waste, the circular economy aims at minimizing waste and reducing resource consumption through recycling, reuse, remanufacturing and reclamation within a closed system (De Angelis, Howard, and Miemczyk, 2018).

As explained by the Ellen MacArthur Foundation and McKinsey Center for Business and Environment (2015), the circular economy system model differentiates between two main cycles through which products and materials can be kept in circulation:

1. Biological cycles focused on returning biodegradable materials to the earth through processes such as composting and anaerobic digestion.
2. Technical cycles, whose main goal is to keep products and materials in circulation as long as possible by reusing, repairing, remanufacturing, and recycling products.

The idea is to preserve the value of the raw materials and components even if the value of the product itself is lost in the recycling process.

Regardless of whether natural or technical cycles are analyzed, the aim of the circular economy is to preserve the highest value of products and materials during their life cycle to generate economic growth and development while considering the environmental impact (Ellen MacArthur Foundation, McKinsey Center for Business and Environment, 2015). Including the benefits and costs to society beyond the customer and encompassing economic, environmental, and social considerations, the concept of value in circular economies is broader than in linear economies. More specifically, circular economies consider four types of value:

1. Sourcing value: the traditional consideration of value in linear economies and refers to direct financial gains.
2. Environmental value, generated by reducing the environmental footprint by consuming fewer resources and producing sustainable products.
3. Consumer value, generated to increase in consumer satisfaction and therefore the demand for more sustainable products.
4. Information value, acquired to learn more about customers, the life cycle of products and the supply chain.

Casado-Vara et al. (2018) have shown that past supply chains follow a take- make-dispose procedure that represents a linear economy. But in their case study about an alimentary supply chain, Casado-Vara et al. describe how blockchain can promote the circular economy by mapping the complete life cycle of food and products, showing where food and goods come from, how they are processed and distributed, and under which environmental conditions they are produced. The blockchain-based DPP mentioned in the previous section represents an ideal example with respect to this.

Therefore, to ensure that a circular solution is sustainable, it is necessary to have reliable and trustworthy data that helps in the decision-making process and the selection of alternatives when implementing circular applications and projects. Especially in technical cycles or the circular economy, data is fundamental to help producers understand which areas of the supply chain and life cycle of products and services can potentially integrate new and more sustainable practices. Moreover, data about the different parties involved can generate and promote collaboration to truly enhance circularity and sustainability among industries and sectors.

With the use of blockchain, product data can be tracked and traced from the product's origin to its sale and subsequent recycling. With characteristics such as providing transparency and data security, blockchain gives consumers confidence about factors such as the origin of the products, whether they are recycled, or whether they are used for the first time, which can be taken into consideration when making sustainability-oriented decisions. This in turn encourages the system to be self-sufficient.

Impact of Distributed Ledger Technology on Supply Chain Sustainability

OVERVIEW OF BLOCKCHAIN PROTOCOLS: PROMOTING MORE SUSTAINABLE TECHNOLOGIES USED TO DEVELOP SUPPLY CHAIN SOLUTIONS

Energy Consumption of Blockchains

As mentioned above, blockchain technology can assist supply chain solutions to become more sustainable by, for example, improving measurements and data collection of the environmental impact of supply chain operations. However, for blockchain to contribute to a net improvement in sustainability efforts, it is important that using blockchain protocols does not itself become an environmental concern. Examples include potentially high carbon emissions if the utilized blockchain has a high energy consumption profile. The potential environmental concern of energy-intensive blockchain technologies has gained public attention. One example is the growing criticism of the energy consumed by proof of work (PoW)-based blockchain projects, including the Bitcoin network.

Research from Alex de Vries (2022a) estimates that the Bitcoin network currently consumes around 135.64 TWh annually. In comparison, the energy consumption of the country of Sweden is an estimated 135.6 TWh annually (de Vries, 2022a). The statistics of Bitcoin's consumption are understandably concerning for the use of blockchain technology in supply chain solutions. However, it is important to note that not all blockchains have high energy consumption. Blockchain protocols that utilize alternative consensus mechanisms, such as proof of stake (PoS), have shown that the benefits of using blockchain technology can be achieved without immense energy requirements.

The popular blockchain network Ethereum has recently shown that adopting an alternative protocol design by moving from PoW to PoS can bring significant reductions in overall energy consumption. On September 15, 2022, Ethereum successfully migrated to a PoS blockchain. When comparing the estimated annual energy consumption values of the Ethereum blockchain from September 14 to September 16, one can observe a reduction in energy consumption of 99.98% (de Vries, 2022b). The graph below created by de Vries (2022b) highlights this improvement.

Figure 2. Ethereum energy consumption index
Source: de Vries (2022b)

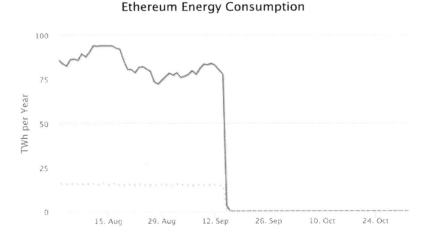

However, even though Ethereum has switched to a less energy-intensive protocol design compared to PoW, it remains in the higher range of energy consumption compared to other PoS protocols. With an annual energy consumption of 13,253,770 kWh estimated on the 16th of September 2022 (de Vries, 2022b), Ethereum shows the highest consumption among other measured PoS blockchains. This should highlight that even among blockchains with similar architecture, variation between consumption exists. Table 1 shows the data collected by Gallersdörfer, Klaaßen, and Stoll on the energy consumption of different PoS blockchains (2022).

Table 1. Overview of energy consumption of PoS blockchains

Overview of CCRI Results	Nodes [# Total]	Transactions [Tx/Year]	Total Electricity Consumption [kWh/Year]	Electricity per Node [kWh/Year]	E per Transaction for the Whole Network [Wh/Tx]	Total Carbon Emissions [tCO2e/Year]
Algorand	1,190	190,000,000	512,671	430.82	2.698	243.52
Avalanche	1,084	93,900,000	489,311	451.39	4.760	232.42
Cardano	3,002	11,900,000	598,755	199.45	51.590	284.41
Polkadot	297	4,000,000	70,237	236.49	17.420	33.36
Solana	1,015	11,800,000,000	1,967,930	1,938.85	0.166	934.77
Tezos	375	2,500,000	113,249	250.99	41.450	53.79

Source: Gallersdörfer et al. (2022)

Variations in the energy consumption between different PoS blockchains exist because, as the table suggests, the overall energy consumption of a blockchain is dependent on the number of participating network nodes and the number of transactions processed. Nodes contribute to overall energy consumption because, to run a node, a hardware device has to be powered to host that node. Transactions contribute to energy consumption because their processing requires nodes to update the ledger state and synchronize it with other network nodes (these are all computing activities that require a node to expend electricity). Besides the number of nodes and transactions, the hardware requirement for running a node on a blockchain is a major contributor to energy consumption. For example, the hardware requirements for running a Solana validator node recommend running a node on hardware with 128 GB of working memory (RAM), while Tezos enables nodes to be run on small Raspberry Pi computers (Gallersdörfer et al., 2022). Since the hardware requirements for running a node differs vastly between the PoS blockchains listed above, variations in overall energy consumption can be expected.

As the previous data suggests, moving from one generation of protocol design to another can bring significant improvements to the overall energy consumption of a blockchain. Despite PoS bringing significant improvements, there are protocol designs that aim to further improve blockchain efficiency. The IOTA Foundation is developing such a next-generation blockchain, called the IOTA protocol. It is part of a family of alternative blockchain technology based on a Directed Acyclic Graph (DAG) architecture. Examples of other blockchains that utilize a DAG design include projects such as Nano, Fantom, and AlephZero. With this novel architecture, projects such as IOTA address the energy consumption inefficiency of traditional blockchains by, for example, removing PoW as the main access control mechanism.

Impact of Distributed Ledger Technology on Supply Chain Sustainability

Along with other improvements, the need for network nodes to have large amounts of computing power is reduced. This allows alternative blockchain protocols to be run on IoT devices like Raspberry Pis, which consume low energy.

In May 2022, the IOTA Foundation published a report on the energy consumption of an IOTA test network (GoShimmer version) to highlight the possibility for blockchains to be highly energy efficient. An IOTA network of 450 network nodes, while constantly processing 50 messages[3] per second, would consume an estimated 18,923.25 kWh annually (Helmer & Penzkofer, 2022). At the time of calculation, this energy consumption value represents around 43.30% of the annual energy consumed per capita in Germany and 0.000009% of the currently estimated annual energy consumption of the Bitcoin network (Helmer & Penzkofer, 2022). For further comparison, the same IOTA network would only require 0.14% of the annual energy consumption of Ethereum after its move to PoS.

Figure 3. Prototype IOTA network consumption compared to average German per capita energy consumption
Source: Helmer and Penzkofer (2022)

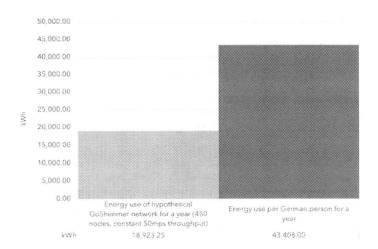

To conclude this section, PoW-based systems require the most amount of energy compared to all other types of blockchain. Switching to a PoS consensus mechanism can significantly improve the overall energy consumption of a protocol. New generations of blockchain technology, such as the IOTA protocol, show further improvements when compared to PoS systems.

The figures shown above confirm that, contrary to popular belief, blockchains can indeed be energy efficient and contribute to a net improvement in sustainability efforts when, for example, utilized in the data collection of the environmental impact of supply chain operations. However, It is therefore important that an appropriate blockchain technology with low energy consumption is selected for use in supply chain solutions to not negate the benefits created in the first place.

Hardware of Blockchains and Electronic Waste

While the high energy consumption of some PoW blockchain solutions has gained major public attention, it is not the only sustainability problem in the PoW consensus mechanism. A major issue that is often overlooked is the large amount of electrical waste produced by mining facilities. Researchers de Vries and Stoll estimate that, as of May 2021, the Bitcoin network adds 30.7 metric kilotons of e-waste annually (2021). This figure can be compared to the annual electrical waste produced by the Netherlands. E-waste is an important sustainability concern, as discarding it without proper recycling can cause toxic chemicals and heavy metals to reach into soil, air and water, causing heavy environmental pollution that damages public health. Forti et. al. (2020) estimate that only 17.4% of e-waste produced in 2019 globally was collected and recycled. With a low percentage of recycling and a high, steady production of e-waste by PoW systems, another sustainability problem arises.

The reason for the large-scale production of e-waste is that Bitcoin mining facilities need to have up-to-date mining hardware to stay profitable. This relationship is described by the Mining Profitability Threshold, which is an inequality defined by the Cambridge Center for Alternative Finance (2019). It describes that, as long as there is a continuous supply of increasingly efficient mining hardware, the profitability threshold will continuously decrease. This will result in all mining facilities having to eventually upgrade their hardware to the latest Application-Specific Integrated Circuit (ASIC) Miners[4] if they want to stay profitable. Less efficient hardware will be discarded if it falls below the threshold, regardless of its age. This means that mining companies and facilities can only achieve a competitive advantage if their hardware is more efficient than their competitors. These pressures force a short life cycle onto the hardware used for mining cryptocurrencies based on PoW systems.

Switching to alternative consensus mechanisms such as the IOTA 2.0 Consensus or PoS would help create less e-waste. By removing PoW as the main access control algorithm and making other improvements, the IOTA protocol enables the technology to be used in small, low-powered devices. Below is a table of the hardware requirements of PoS systems aggregated from the "Energy Efficiency and Carbon Footprint of PoS Blockchain Protocols" report (Gallersdörfer et al., 2022) in comparison with IOTA.

Table 2. Recommended hardware requirements of notable blockchain systems

Name	Avalanche	Algorand	Cardano	IOTA	Polkadot	Solana	Tezos
CPU	> 2 GHz	4 / 16 cores	2x2Ghz	4 cores	i7-7700k	12X2.8GHz	2 cores
RAM	6 GB	4-8 / 24 GB	8 GB	8 GB	64 GB	128 GB	8 GB
Storage size	200 GB	100/500 GB	30 GB	128 GB	80-160 GB	2 TB	100 GB
Storage type	n/a	SSD	n/a	SSD	NVMe	NVMe	SSD
Can be run on Raspberry Pi	No	Yes	No	Yes	No	No	Yes
Can be run on a MiniPC	Yes	Yes	Yes	Yes	Yes	No	Yes
Requires IPv4	n/a	n/a	Yes	n/a	n/a	Yes	n/a

Source: Gallersdörfer et al. (2022)

The table underlines that most of the blockchain systems listed above can be run on small single board computers (Raspberry Pis, for example) or small workstation computers. These devices only require a low amount of energy (ranging from 2-4W) and can be run at home and plugged into a standard outlet. For comparison, Bitcoin nodes are usually run on dedicated hardware, such as the Bitmain Antminer ASICs, which themselves are run in large data centers, which have liquid cooling and other overhead infrastructure. These require significant amounts of energy. When comparing the hardware requirements and composition of different networks, the correlation between hardware needed and energy consumption profiles becomes apparent.

The reason why IOTA and other PoS systems have a low threshold for hardware requirements is that it is no longer necessary for validators to compete with computing efficiency. In PoS, a validator is randomly selected to validate a transaction or block based on the amount of tokens they have. This means that a validator in a PoS system does not need to continuously buy more efficient hardware to achieve a profit. Their profitability is only determined by the amount of tokens they stake to the protocol and how many tokens the rest of the validators stake. The IOTA protocol, on the other hand, was designed so that every network participant is also a validator. There is no staking or mining where validators are randomly selected and rewarded. Thus, the absence of validator competition eliminates the need to have more efficient hardware than other network participants. This enables a low computational demand on IOTA nodes, and thus low hardware requirements.

Market for Crypto Assets Regulation (MiCAR)

Energy efficiency solutions acquired major relevance given the current global landscape and the need for sustainable energy alternatives. Furthermore, the new Market for Crypto Assets Regulation (MiCAR) established the obligation for all crypto assets issuers to produce a whitepaper with relevant information about their crypto assets project and its underlying technology, marketing strategies, plan for offering and trade and information about the adverse environmental impact of the consensus mechanism used (Directive 2019/1937/EU, Art. 4). In addition, the indicators will also cover the use of renewable energies and natural resources, waste production and greenhouse gas emissions. (Directive 2019/1937/EU, Art. 5). The standard and indicators for environmental impact will be produced by the European Securities and Markets Authority -(ESMA) during the 12 months following the effective date of MiCAR.

REAL-WORLD APPLICATIONS AND USE CASES

Use cases clearly show the benefits of incorporating blockchain technology into the current supply chain process and how this technology can create more sustainable operations.

Despite being a fairly new technology that still faces challenges with regards to standardization, regulations, etc., there is no lack of use cases demonstrating the advantages offered by the unique characteristics of blockchain in different real-world scenarios. As mentioned above, inherent blockchain features such as transparency, traceability, and immutability, are key to an efficient supply chain. There is no limit to the sectors that can benefit from incorporating blockchain to manage their supply chain processes. Supply chain management is not specific to any sector, and neither is the use of blockchain. Although many might associate blockchain with the financial sector due to the hype around cryptocurrencies during the last few years, its use cases stretch way beyond that.

As the world struggles with the challenges facing supply chains, there has been an increased focus on the use of blockchain in tackling sustainability issues. DIN, the German national organization for standardization, recently published a document on reference architecture for blockchain applications to create transparency in supply chains (DIN Group, 2022). The document presents the case of IotaOrigin, an initiative working on the traceability of conflict-free commodities and goods through blockchain, as an example of the standardization of blockchain applications that bring transparency to supply chains. IotaOrigin uses the previously mentioned IOTA network to bring digitization and transparency to the mining industry and promote ethical sourcing of materials (IotaOrigin UG, 2022).

Another project built on IOTA's blockchain technology to improve supply chain processes is the Trade Logistics Information Pipeline (TLIP). TLIP was initiated as a cooperation between the IOTA Foundation and TradeMark East Africa, an aid-for-trade organization working on improving trade conditions in East Africa to grow prosperity in the region. The core idea of TLIP is to "create paperless trade through a trusted infrastructure that enables secure and efficient cross-border collaboration between multiple parties" (TradeMark East Africa & IOTA Foundation, 2022). To understand the value of this, it is important to have an understanding of the context of data sharing in international trade and current challenges. In big parts of the world, today's trade processes still rely to a great extent on paper and manual processes. This does not mean that the worldwide trend for digitalization has bypassed government agencies involved in international trade processes and that they keep handling analog documents for all processes. However, it should be noted that *internal* processes and sharing of data *between* actors involved in cross-border processes are two different matters; while many government agencies are in the process of digitizing internal processes if they have not already done so, key trade documents still tend to be shared manually since external sharing of digital data involves several risks. First of all, digital documents shared externally can easily be forged. Second, they are vulnerable to the disclosure of sensitive information. Distributing and maintaining access rights to prevent confidential information from falling into the hands of unauthorized actors is a difficult task. Moreover, in addition to these risks is the question of how different agencies in today's siloed international trade can be sure that the information shared with them is the same one shared with other actors.

Manual and analog processes intended to avoid the risks rooted in the fundamental trust problem of international trade in turn lead to slow, costly, and error-prone cross-border processes. TLIP uses IOTA's blockchain technology to enable a trust infrastructure that addresses these problems. Through digital identities running on IOTA, it is possible for all actors involved in cross-border processes to create verifiable digital identities and issue secure, private, and instantly verifiable digital credentials. This allows agencies to request, receive and verify information and confirm its validity as soon as it is shared with them without even having to contact the issuer. With TLIP, inefficient and days-long verification processes dependent on emails and phone calls are replaced with an instant credential verifier mechanism. Moreover, blockchains enable the information owner to define which actors should have access to what information. Thanks to access rights based on digital identity, selected data can be shared without disclosing any unwanted information. Accordingly, blockchains offer an excellent advantage for supply chain projects where collaboration and trust between actors such as traders, governments, logistics companies, and end-consumers, are key.

Another important advantage that a solution such as TLIP brings to the global trade supply chain is improved visibility and traceability of goods in transit. Traceability is key in the supply chain – an incomplete overview of where goods are at certain times causes safety and compliance risks, logistical challenges, and a lot of extra work in terms of following up with other parties involved in the supply chain. And not only does flawed traceability result in inefficient, slow, and costly supply chain processes: it can have disastrous and even lethal consequences for some products. Perishables such as dairy products, seafood, and poultry are very vulnerable to delays and other deviations in the supply chain that can affect the quality of the goods. The blockchain technology powering TLIP enables original documents and events including important data such as location, temperature, and storage details to be reported in real-time and made available to authorized actors. This provides a clear overview of the current status and allows everyone to fetch the original data rather than relying on data sent around between different, siloed systems. Moreover, anchoring information on the blockchain prevents it from being tampered with, which ensures that users can trust its authenticity.

This infrastructure is currently being put into practice with actors involved in international trade in Kenya, Uganda, the EU, and the UK. It provides an excellent example of how silos in the global trade supply chain can be broken down to improve efficiency as well as cut costs and delays. By improving the flow of trade information, TLIP has excellent potential to increase the competitiveness of East African goods on the international market and thus create jobs and improve livelihoods in the region.

European Blockchain Infrastructure Services - Digital Product Passport: In April 2022, the European Commission announced its intention to make Digital Product Passports mandatory for selected product categories (such as electric vehicle batteries or apparel) as soon as 2024. This initiative is part of the Ecodesign for Sustainable Products Regulation of 30 March 2022 (European Commission, 2022b). It aims to establish a digital platform to enhance the sustainability of products in the European market. As a part of the EBSI project, software and services provider Digimarc and the IOTA Foundation tested the implementation of a Digital Product Passport blueprint with electric vehicle batteries, tracking products through the value chain systemic and making product recall more efficient, offering new opportunities for the recycling of products and finally achieve deep insights on the life cycle of the products (Digimarc, 2022).

Well Adapted Coffee Supply (WACS): As mentioned at the beginning of this chapter, blockchain is well suited to accurately measure the environmental impact throughout the supply chain. Showcasing the ecological footprint of products has become a popular concept; however, it is important to keep in mind that organizations have many different incentives for showing that their products and activities have a minimal ecological impact. Often, these incentives are not driven by the objective of having a minimal ecological footprint but rather to sell their products, appeal to a certain customer segment, comply with regulations and obtain funding and certificates. Without a mechanism that enables transparent tracing of supply chain processes, it is difficult to know whether the impact showcased is in fact being generated. The immutability inherent to blockchain tackles this issue, as the data registered to the ledger is tamper-proof. While this of course does not solve the problem that data entered into the ledger can still be flawed, it brings accountability to anyone providing this information, as it cannot be tampered with. Moreover, many initiatives go one step further in tackling this problem by connecting the blockchain to sensors that automatically register data on the ledger. One such initiative is Well Adapted Coffee Supply (WACS). Developed by Adaptation Ledger Ltd., WACS is an Adaptation Ledger Specific Application (ALSA) in the Adapt IT™ suite of climate adaptation tools . WACS can be integrated with other supply chain applications with different functionalities, which provides several opportunities such as using tokenized Vulnerability Reduction Credits (VRCs™) to reward projects that demonstrate climate-resilient farming practices. The main functionality of WACS is to integrate data inputs from sources such as remote sensors to create a transparent and immutable record of the VRCs generated by farm plots via adaptation efforts, which is possible thanks to the immutable characteristics of blockchain. The result is guaranteed sustainability and reduced vulnerability of the whole food supply chain through leading climate adaptation practices. It should also be noted that this concept is not limited to rewarding projects for sustainable farming practices. The same principle can be applied to reward projects for other practices such as fair working conditions (Adaptation Ledger Ltd, 2022).

SCALA (Scaling up Climate Ambition on Land Use and Agriculture): Another project demonstrating how supply chains can reap the benefits of blockchain is the SCALA program (Scaling up Climate Ambition on Land Use and Agriculture). This initiative is driven by the United Nations Development Programme, Food, and Agriculture Organization and International Climate Initiative. It targets the urgency of coping with climate change in the agriculture and land use sectors. The program supports twelve countries in Africa, Asia, and Latin America to build capacity in identifying and carrying out necessary climate actions on land use and agriculture, which helps the countries achieve their national development contribution (NDC) goals and targets and strengthens their climate resilience. Key data elements of climate-resilient practices are identified and registered on a blockchain in order to promote them and help policymakers, food producers, and audit agencies make use of them. The actions included in this initiative are crop management, water resource management, soil and land management, livestock management, fishery management, warning system development, research and technology development, food availability enhancement, and capacity development (Food and Agriculture Organization of the United Nations, 2022).

Despite the great potential for blockchain to impact sustainability as shown by these use cases, there remain several roadblocks to widespread adoption. As blockchain is still an innovative technology with an alternative philosophy, converting to such a new system requires changing the organizational culture and could lead to resistance and hesitation from individuals and organizations (Jharkharia and Shankar, 2005). As such, pushing the adoption of new technology like blockchain requires top management to have a long-term commitment to support the adoption of sustainability values. Besides that, to enable a blockchain network to interact meaningfully with other networks, interoperability is of importance. Developing or building on interoperable blockchains is key to interconnecting the systems of different stakeholders and promoting efficiency.

Other factors to be considered when driving adoption is the willingness of government and regulators to direct and support blockchain adoption to improve sustainability, an active community and well-documented and easy-to-orientate instructions for applying blockchain.

CONCLUSION

This chapter aimed to demonstrate the potential of blockchain for creating more sustainable supply chains. Blockchain contributes its specific characteristics, such as decentralization, data security, transparency, and efficiency, to increase the trusted data in supply chains and promote the creation of sustainable supply chains.

The chapter gave insights into how blockchain can promote the circular economy by being used to map the complete life cycle of food and products, showing the origin of food and goods, how they are processed and distributed, and under what environmental conditions they are produced.

However, to reach a net improvement in blockchain-based sustainability efforts, it is important that the use of blockchain protocols does not itself become an environmental concern. Therefore the energy consumption of different blockchain generations is presented in this chapter. Against this background, this chapter demonstrated that PoW-based systems such as the first.generation Bitcoin blockchain requires the most amount of energy compared to other blockchains. Switching to a PoS consensus mechanism can significantly improve the overall energy consumption of a protocol. New generations of blockchain technologies, such as the IOTA protocol, show further improvements when compared to PoS systems. This sets a favorable prerequisite that blockchain can be energy efficient and contribute to a net positive improvement in sustainability efforts.

To further increase the understanding of blockchain technology and its potential role in sustainable supply chains, the chapter presented several use cases, namely IotaOrigin, Well Adapted Coffee Supply (WACS), Trade Logistics Information Pipeline (TLIP), SCALA program (Scaling up Climate Ambition on Land Use and Agriculture), and the European Blockchain Infrastructure Services (EBSI) Digital Product Passport.

As blockchain is an innovative technology there remain challenges to be addressed for widespread adoption. Converting to a new technology sometimes requires changing the organizational culture and could lead to resistance and hesitation from individuals and organizations. Therefore the long-term commitment of top management to drive and lead blockchain adoption for increasing sustainability is important. Besides that, to enable a blockchain network to interact meaningfully with other networks, interoperability is another key point to acknowledge.

Furthermore, it is worth mentioning that unclear laws and regulations can hinder blockchain adoption, as organizations fear the unknown consequences of future regulation. Therefore the willingness of government and regulators to direct and support blockchain adoption to improve sustainability is of great importance to ensure that organizations and individuals feel encouraged to build on blockchain.

An additional aspect of driving adoption is the community of a blockchain ecosystem. An active community can contribute to increased adoption through valuable feedback and can create a space for empowering individuals to build innovative applications on top of a blockchain. Lastly, as with any other technology, having well-documented and easy-to-orientate instructions for applying blockchain increases transparency and can ease adoption.

All in all, blockchain shows great potential for creating sustainable supply chains. However, it is an innovative area awaiting mass adoption to make widespread impact. By encouraging interoperability and standardization that drives adoption, the impact on greener supply chains can be amplified.

REFERENCES

Adaptation Ledger Ltd. (2020). *Well Adapted Coffee Supply (WACS) an Adaptation Ledger Specific Application (ALSA) in the Adapt ITTM suite of climate adaptation tools.* https://www.adaptationledger.com/_files/ugd/621230_b41137a6a0524fd986184150308e22ad.pdf

Cambridge Center for Alternative Finance. (2019, July 2). *Cambridge Bitcoin Electricity Consumption Index - Methodology*. Retrieved on November 10, 2022 from https://ccaf.io/cbeci/index

Casado-Vara, R., Prieto, J., De la Prieta, F., & Corchado, J. M. (2018). How blockchain improves the supply chain: Case study alimentary supply chain. *Procedia Computer Science*, *134*, 393–398. doi:10.1016/j.procs.2018.07.193

Clerens. (2022). *Discover the Innovation Fund, one of the world's largest funding programmes, with €10 Billion funding*. https://www.euinnovationfund.eu/

de Angelis, R., Howard, M., & Miemczyk, J. (2018). Supply chain management and the circular economy: Towards the circular supply chain. *Production Planning and Control*, 29(6), 425–437. doi:10.1080/09537287.2018.1449244

de Vries, A. (2022a, April 21). *Bitcoin Energy Consumption Index*. Digiconomist. Retrieved November 3, 2022, from https://digiconomist.net/bitcoin-energy-consumption

de Vries, A. (2022b, September 25). *Ethereum Energy Consumption Index*. Digiconomist. https://digiconomist.net/ethereum-energy-consumption

de Vries, A., & Stoll, C. (2021). Bitcoin's growing e-waste problem. *Resources, Conservation and Recycling*, 175, 105901. doi:10.1016/j.resconrec.2021.105901

Digimarc. (2022). *A Blueprint for a Decentralized EU Digital Product Passport Model*. YouTube. https://www.youtube.com/watch?v=NfJ4yiyAriw

DIN Group. (2022). *DIN SPEC 32790:2022-11, Referenzarchitektur für Blockchain-Applikationen zur Schaffung von Transparenz in Supply-Chains*. BEUTH publishing DIN. doi:10.31030/3385071

DIN Group. (2022). *DIN SPEC 32790:2022-11, Referenzarchitektur für Blockchain-Applikationen zur Schaffung von Transparenz in Supply-Chains*. BEUTH publishing DIN. doi:10.31030/3385071

Directive 2019/1937/EU. (n.d.). *Markets in Crypto-assets*. European Parliament and Council. https://eur-lex.europa.eu/legal-content/EN/TXT/?uri=CELEX%3A52020PC0593&qid=1668704840208

Dos Santos, R. B., Torrisi, N. M., & Pantoni, R. P. (2021). Third party certification of agri-food supply chain using smart contracts and blockchain tokens. *Sensors (Basel)*, 21(16), 5307. doi:10.339021165307 PMID:34450749

Elhidaoui, S., Benhida, K., El Fezazi, S., Kota, S., & Lamalem, A. (2022). Critical Success Factors of Blockchain adoption in Green Supply Chain Management: Contribution through an Interpretive Structural Model. *Production & Manufacturing Research*, 10(1), 1–23. doi:10.1080/21693277.2021.1990155

English, M. A., Auer, S., & Domingue, J. B. (2015). *Block Chain Technologies & The Semantic Web: A Framework for Symbiotic Development*. http://cscubs.cs.uni-bonn.de/2016/proceedings/paper-10.pdf

European Commission. (2022a). Horizon Europe. *Research-and-innovation*. ec.europa.eu. https://research-and-innovation.ec.europa.eu/funding/funding-opportunities/funding-programmes-and-open-calls/horizon-europe_en

European Commission. (2022b). *Ecodesign for sustainable products*. ec.europa.eu. https://ec.europa.eu/info/energy-climate-change-environment/standards-tools-and-labels/products-labelling-rules-and-requirements/sustainable-products/ecodesign-sustainable-products_en

Food and Agriculture Organization of the United Nations. (2022). *Scaling up Climate Ambition on Land Use and Agriculture (SCALA)*. fao.org. https://www.fao.org/in-action/scala/en

Forti, V., Balde, C. P., Kuehr, R., & Bel, G. (2020). *The Global E-waste Monitor 2020: Quantities, flows and the circular economy potential*. United Nations University/United Nations Institute for Training and Research, International Telecommunication Union, and International Solid Waste Association. https://collections.unu.edu/view/UNU:7737#viewMetadata

Friedman, N., & Ormiston, J. (2022). Blockchain as a sustainability-oriented innovation?: Opportunities for and resistance to Blockchain technology as a driver of sustainability in global food supply chains. *Technological Forecasting and Social Change*, *175*, 121403. doi:10.1016/j.techfore.2021.121403

Gallersdörfer, U., Klaaßen, L., & Stoll, C. (2022). *Energy Efficiency and Carbon Footprint of PoS Blockchain Protocols*, CCRI GmbH. Retrieved from https://www.carbon-ratings.com/

Helmer, L., & Penzkofer, A. (2022, May 25). *Report on the energy consumption of the IOTA 2.0 prototype network (GoShimmer 0.8.3) under different testing scenarios*. IOTA Foundation. /arXiv.2210.1396 doi:<ALIGNMENT.qj></ALIGNMENT>10.48550

IOTA Foundation. (2022). *Digital Product Passport: Anchoring Product Data on the Tangle for a Green Circular Economy*. https://blog.iota.org/digital-product-passport/

IotaOrigin UG. (2022). *IotaOrigin*. iotaorigin.de. https://www.iotaorigin.de/de.html

Jagtap, S., Trollman, H., Trollman, F., Garcia-Garcia, G., Parra-López, C., Duong, L., Martindale, W., Munekata, P. E. S., Lorenzo, J. M., Hdaifeh, A., Hassoun, A., Salonitis, K., & Afy-Shararah, M. (2022). The Russia-Ukraine Conflict: Its Implications for the Global Food Supply Chains. *Foods*, *11*(14), 2098. doi:10.3390/foods11142098 PMID:35885340

Jharkharia, S., & Shankar, R. (2005). IT-enablement of supply chains: Understanding the barriers. *Journal of Enterprise Information Management*, *18*(1), 11–27. doi:10.1108/17410390510571466

Khan, S. A., Mubarik, M. S., Kusi-Sarpong, S., Gupta, H., Zaman, S. I., & Mubarik, M. (2022). Blockchain technologies as enablers of supply chain mapping for sustainable supply chains. *Business Strategy and the Environment*, *31*(8), 3742–3756. Advance online publication. doi:10.1002/bse.3029

Khaqqi, K. N., Sikorski, J. J., Hadinoto, K., & Kraft, M. (2018). Incorporating seller/buyer reputation-based system in blockchain-enabled emission trading application. *Applied Energy*, *209*, 8–19. doi:10.1016/j.apenergy.2017.10.070

Kouhizadeh, M., & Sarkis, J. (2018). Blockchain practices, potentials, and perspectives in greening supply chains. *Sustainability (Basel)*, *10*(10), 3652. doi:10.3390u10103652

Lambert, D. M., & Enz, M. G. (2017). Issues in Supply Chain Management: Progress and potential. *Industrial Marketing Management*, *62*, 1–16. doi:10.1016/j.indmarman.2016.12.002

MacArthur Foundation. (2015). *Growth within: A circular economy vision for a competitive Europe*. https://ellenmacarthurfoundation.org/growth-within-a-circular-economy-vision-for-a-competitive-europe

Mougayar, W., & Buterin, V. (2016). *The Business Blockchain: Promise, Practice, and Application of the Next Internet Technology* (1st ed.). Wiley. https://www.wiley.com/en-ca/The+Business+Blockchain%3A+Promise%2C+Practice%2C+and+Application+of+the+Next+Internet+Technology-p-9781119300311

Nofer, M., Gomber, P., Hinz, O., & Schiereck, D. (2017). Blockchain. *Business & Information Systems Engineering, 59*(3), 183–187. doi:10.100712599-017-0467-3

Oberle, B., Bringezu, S., Hatfield-Dodds, S., Hellweg, S., Schandl, H., Clement, J., Cabernard, L., Che, N., Chen, D., Droz-Georget, H., Ekins, P., Fischer-Kowalski, M., Flörke, M., Frank, S., Froemelt, A., Geschke, A., Haupt, M., Havlik, P., Hüfner, R., . . . Zhu, B. (2019). *Global Resources Outlook 2019*. United Nations Environment Programme. https://www.resourcepanel.org/reports/global-resources-outlook

Ølnes, S., Ubacht, J., & Janssen, M. (2017). Blockchain in government: Benefits and implications of distributed ledger technology for information sharing. *Government Information Quarterly, 34*(3), 355–364. doi:10.1016/j.giq.2017.09.007

Park, A., & Li, H. (2021). The Effect of Blockchain Technology on Supply Chain Sustainability Performances. *Sustainability (Basel), 13*(4), 1726. doi:10.3390u13041726

Peters, G. W., & Panayi, E. (2016). Understanding modern banking ledgers through blockchain technologies: Future of transaction processing and smart contracts on the internet of money. In *Banking beyond banks and money* (pp. 239–278). Springer., doi:10.1007/978-3-319-42448-4_13

Saberi, S., Kouhizadeh, M., Sarkis, J., & Shen, L. (2018). Blockchain technology and its relationships to sustainable supply chain management. *International Journal of Production Research, 57*(7), 2117–2135. doi:10.1080/00207543.2018.1533261

Seuring, S., Sarkis, J., Müller, M., & Rao, P. (2008). Sustainability and supply chain management – An introduction to the special issue. *Journal of Cleaner Production, 16*(15), 1545–1551. doi:10.1016/j.jclepro.2008.02.002

Sharma, M., Luthra, S., Joshi, S., & Kumar, A. (2020). Developing a framework for enhancing survivability of sustainable supply chains during and post-COVID-19 pandemic. *International Journal of Logistics Research and Applications, 25*(4–5), 433–453. 3 doi:10.1080/13675567.2020.181021

Shaw, K., Shankar, R., Yadav, S. S., & Thakur, L. S. (2012). Supplier selection using fuzzy AHP and fuzzy multi-objective linear programming for developing low carbon supply chain. *Expert Systems with Applications, 39*(9), 8182–8192. doi:10.1016/j.eswa.2012.01.149

TradeMark East Africa & IOTA Foundation. (2022). *Trade and Logistics Information Pipeline*. https://www.tlip.io/

Van de Velde, J., Scott, A., Sartorius, K., Dalton, I., Shepherd, B., Allchin, C., Dougherty, M., Ryan, P., & Rennick, E. (2016). *Blockchain in Capital Markets - The Prize and the Journey*. Oliver Wyman and Euroclear. https://www.oliverwyman.de/our-expertise/insights/2016/feb/blockchain-in-capital-markets.html

Varriale, V., Cammarano, A., Michelino, F., & Caputo, M. (2020). The Unknown Potential of Blockchain for Sustainable Supply Chains. *Sustainability (Basel)*, *12*(22), 9400. doi:10.3390u12229400

ENDNOTES

1. To review the SDG Agenda see the following link: https://sdgs.un.org/2030agenda
2. To review the SDG Goals see the following link: https://sdgs.un.org/goals
3. Messages are data transactions without direct monetary value.
4. Specialized hardware designed solely for bitcoin mining.

Chapter 11
Blockchain-Enabled Internet of Things Application in Supply Chain Operations Sustainability Management

Kamalendu Pal
University of London, UK

ABSTRACT

In recent decades, sustainability and green supply chain management have played essential roles in business operations. This chapter examines how the textile and apparel supply chains can comply with the United Nations Sustainable Development Goals. In particular, verifying the source of raw materials and maintaining visibility of merchandise products and related services while moving through the value-chain network is challenging. The internet of things (IoT) application can help textile and apparel supply chain operation managers observe, monitor, and track products and relevant business processes within their respective value chain networks. However, the IoT infrastructural components have a shortage of computational processing power and local saving capability, and these components are vulnerable to the privacy and security of collected data. This chapter presents blockchain technology with IoT-based infrastructural elements and service-oriented computing architecture as a solution for information processing for apparel supply chain management.

INTRODUCTION

The image of a modern textile and apparel supply chain has become inseparably associated with its care for ecological aspects and sustainable development. The United Nations' new sustainable development goals for 2030 have come into force since 2016, which initiated seventeen sustainable development goals (SDGs, 2023). The SDGs will demonstrate the new objectives of economic, social, and environmental developments, such as ending poverty, economic growth, and environmental protection are the few important ones. SDGs call for everyone worldwide to contribute to the goals, including governments,

DOI: 10.4018/978-1-6684-7455-6.ch011

companies, civil organizations, and the public. For example, the textile and apparel industries require labour-intensive manufacturing, an extended value chain, and relatively high environmental pollution (Choi et al., 2019), attracting researchers and practitioners' significant attention to find solutions for industry-specific sustainability-related issues.

In this way, supply chain sustainability is a central theme of most business organizations. The main objective of sustainable supply chains is to create and maintain long-term economic, social, and environmental value for all stakeholders involved in delivering products and services to specific markets. Consequently, all businesses today appreciate the value of supply chain management (SCM) and sound operational practices, and the advantages of digitization of its business processes have become a popular topic in both sustainable commercial operations and academic research purposes (Pal, 2019). Research has shown that sustainability has become necessary for businesses considering social and environmental issues in their strategies. It is also essential that businesses and their supply chains accelerate the shift from focus to sustainability and use technologies to digitalize business processes (Pal, 2019). In addition, business organizations are already making significant investments in digital supply chains because they recognize that digitalization will give them five big prizes: integration, transparency, productivity, sustainability, and, ultimately, the opportunity to transform their supply chain operating model.

Moreover, sustainability is essential for accessing global markets and accomplishing high profits (Pal, 2021). For example, while sustainable shipment management was considered a cost in the past, now, thanks to modern technologies (e.g., IoT, radio frequency identification, blockchain, and cloud computing), it is possible to guarantee sustainable logistics. Indeed, using these emerging technologies, improving carbon emissions-related issues and saving resources is possible. One of the most critical requirements for sustainable supply chain management demands the transparency of information and appropriate communication mechanisms between the supply chain business stakeholders. In order to earn these goals, it is essential to have adequate information and communication technology (ICT) standards that ensure the reliability of information systems architectures and foolproof security of operational data.

As to emerging technologies, the Internet of Things (IoT) and radio frequency identification (RFID) technology are heavily used in supply chain operations. These technologies can shake up an industry or enable a business model that creates an entirely new way of operations management, even though these technologies may be unfavorable to the users at the early stage (Pal, 2021). Besides, disruptive technologies dominate different industries with new, exciting features that are differentiated from existing technologies (Pal, 2019). Business models based on disruptive technologies are typically more efficient, productive, and convenient than those established on the incumbent technology (Pal, 2021). For example, the IoT has radically changed warehouse and inventory management by tightly coupling distribution centers, transportation, and customer relationship management (CRM) systems. As a result, IoT could reduce operational costs and provide more customized, responsive, and innovative customer service.

The recent emergence of the digitation of supply chain business processes is attracting massive attention from academics and practitioners. However, evaluating and adopting modern technologies in supply chain operations are strategically complex. Strategic thinkers are putting forward a cautious reminder that digital supply chain transformation projects are not all about doing everything at once. Instead, commercial industries need to consider the scale of the opportunities across the supply chain and the risks involved, prioritize those technology interventions that impact most on supply chain regular operations, and deliver outcomes that best support corporate strategic goals.

Moreover, the data exchanges between autonomous networks over untrusted channels are also significant. Blockchain technology opens new dimensions towards the data exchange mechanism, intelligent resource management, user access control, audibility, and chronology in stored transactions to ensure data security, privacy, and stakeholder trust. Besides, academics and practitioners are concentrating their research activities on two particular areas: (i) supply chain management-related sustainability issues and (ii) deploying emerging technologies to improve the supply chain business-partners collaboration. In doing so, they are ensuring broader business operations transparency and traceability of resources along the supply chain networks by exchanging operational data.

Modern technologies emerging under industry 4.0 create new business and financial opportunities for supply chain management. For example, in emerging technologies, researchers reported blockchain as a disruptive technology that guarantees greater transparency and traceability in the exchange of data (Pal & Yasar, 2020). Besides, blockchain technology enables supply chain managers to enhance and track goods and other resources in real-time from their origins through the overall operational business processes network. In this way, blockchain technology enables the supply chain stakeholders to know who is performing which actions by defining and evidencing the time and location of the actions. One of the essential advantages of blockchain technology is providing viable solutions for identity management (Liu et al., 2020), and It also provides greater spatial and temporal flexibility. In this way, blockchain technology is bringing operations, production, and sales closer together, and it promises significant changes by rethinking, redesigning, and reshaping the operational management of the supply chain.

Indeed, one of the most investigated topics is the use of blockchain for product tracking and tracing, and the evidence is available in the research literature (Bai & Sarkis, 2020) (Tang & Veelenturf, 2019). Specifically, the research literature has analyzed detection systems such as RFID, GPS technology, and IoT infrastructures (Bouzembrak et al., 2019) (Chanchaichujit et al., 2020) (Lam & Ip, 2019) (Ketzenberg et al., 2015) (Wognum et al., 2011). These systems have brought forward new ways of monitoring products and business processes, from the origin to the end consumer, regarding price, date, location, and quality assurance certificates. However, they suffer from many drawbacks related to security issues, standardization, interoperability, and distribution among the players on a large scale (Zhang & Kitsos, 2016) (Matharu et al., 2014). Blockchain technology can fill these inefficiencies by allowing goods management without intermediaries or trusted parties (Chang et al., 2020) (Min, 2019). The effectiveness of supply chain transactional performances can be improved by crediting to the distinctive features of blockchain. Indeed, to achieve adequate traceability, the visibility of the business process needs to have a unified, assured, and tamper-proof shared ledger that is globally accessible by all the stakeholders (Lezoche et al., 2020) (Kamble et al., 2020). Furthermore, optimizing the entire supply chain can take place through smart contracts to verify and permit actions by physical devices that collect information from the operational areas, enhancing the security of the IoT systems architectures (Pournader et al., 2020). Smart contracts help the system automation for particular actions based on the constant detection by the sensors along the supply chain operations, such as automatic financial payment after receipt of the required product (Habib et al., 2020) or appropriate management of anomalies along the shipment (Hasan et al., 2019).

Therefore, this chapter aims to test further insights for increasing the literature on improving sustainability issues using modern technologies. The rest of the chapter is structured as follows. Section 2 presents the overview of the modern technologies allowing goods tracking within supply chains. Section 3 highlights the discussions focusing on sustainability issues and managerial implications. Finally, Section 4 concludes the chapter with concluding remarks, limitations, and insights for future research.

BACKGROUND AND RELATED RESEARCH

This section presents an overview of sustainable development, the applications of sustainability in the context of SCM, and a review of recent research on the sustainability issues of Industry 4.0 and the impact of evolving technologies on supply chains.

Sustainable Development

The central concept of sustainability focuses on economic viability and the industry's role in implementing sustainable solutions for economic advantage. Academics and practitioners often consider the sustainable solution as a way to mitigate the limitations of linear production and consumption models for increasing resource use efficiency. At the same time, some of the researchers are debating on the conceptual view of *circular economics* (CE) and sustainability. The CE introduces better balances of sustainability's economic, environmental, and social aspects. Countries such as China promote CE as a cleaner production strategy that endorses efficient use of resources. At the same time, other regions, such as the European Union, Japan, and the USA, also consider it a waste management strategy (Ghisellini et al., 2016).

Economic system circularity was introduced with the law of thermodynamics as its fundamental principle (Pearce & Turner, 1990). Initially, this was conceptualized to describe matter and energy degradation to maintain the sustainability of the earth's natural resources. In these initial CE descriptions, the environment has three main functions: supply resources, provide a life support system, and offer a sink for emissions and waste. Unlike other economic functions with direct pricing, sometimes no direct price or market for environmental goods exists (what is the price of air and water quality?). However, recent Life Cycle Assessment (LCA) methods have tried to monetize environmental prices, indicating the loss of economic welfare as a result of environmental emissions (De Bruyn et al., 2018) (Weidema, 2015). In addition, environmental policies and consumer and producer responsibilities have been employed to mitigate the high consumption of resources (Ghisellini et al., 2016).

CE provides many advantages to industrial applications: (i) elongating an asset's usage cycle, (ii) improving asset utilization through sharing, (iii) asset reusing, recycling, and remanufacturing, (iv) regenerating and preserving natural resources by returning biological elements to their original ecosystem and avoid nutrients leakage from one system to another. In order to implement these advantages and value drivers, a framework named ReSOLVE - Regenerate, Share, Optimize, Loop, Virtualize, and Exchange has been introduced by the Ellen MacArthur Foundation (Ellen MacArthur Foundation, 2015).

However, CE and its basic conceptual principles are not without criticism (Prendeville et al., 2018): (i) First is the definition of CE. Practitioners are often unclear regarding the fundamental principles of CE. Some consider it a macro-level activity, while others consider it a micro-level intervention. (ii) Second, some principles may not necessarily benefit the environment. For example, infinite recycling of materials and energy will not be without efficiency loss; reuse of old technologies may result in higher energy consumption or sharing economy initiatives that may not be as environmentally viable as promoted. (iii) Third, very few businesses adopt CE-related strategies. Also, CE models often give more authority to businesses than consumers and social communities.

While CE can help companies realize business outcomes of implementing sustainable operations, the implementation scope and scale of CE efforts are currently limited. As new technologies emerge, novel business models can orient organizations towards enhancing sustainability outcomes through CE principles.

Industry 4.0

The term Industry 4.0 presents a promise of a new industrial revolution, which integrates advanced manufacturing methods with the Internet of Things to create interconnected manufacturing systems that communicate, analyze, and use the information to drive further intelligent action back in the physical world. Industry 4.0 originated from the German word Industrie 4.0, a set of connected cyber-physical objects capable of using Big Data analytics within the manufacturing and production domains (Vogel-Heuser & Hess, 2016). Industry 4.0 is part of the Industrial Internet of Things (IIoT) (Lom et al., 2016), and different characteristics have been assigned to Industry 4.0 to equip not only manufacturing systems with advanced data acquisition technologies but also value generation and service innovation (Kagermann, 2015).

In recent decades, Germany has developed a four-step strategic plan for transforming industries of the information age to industry 4.0: (i) building a network of CPSs, (ii) researching the 'smart factory' and 'intelligent production' concepts, (iii) integrating the elements of value chains on three levels of horizontal integration, vertical integration, and end-to-end integration, and finally (iv) achieving eight planning objectives. The proper planning objectives include standardization, efficient management, a reliable industrial infrastructure, safety and security, organization and work design, workforce training, creating a regulatory framework, and improving the efficiency of resources (Zhou et al., 2015).

Figure 1. A digital supply chain applications scenario

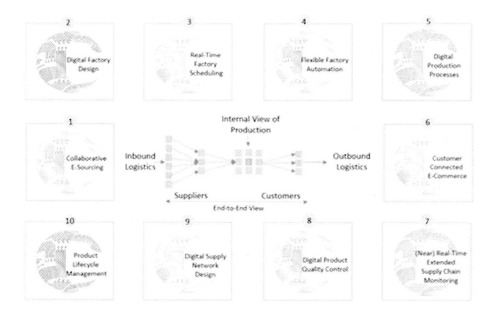

Given that Industry 4.0 is such a broad topic, blockchain technology is evaluated to show its potential as one of the most recent elements. However, the importance of blockchain resides in its ability to enhance information integration across supply chains and between various business stakeholders, one of the main agendas of industry 4.0.

With so many potential opportunities to digitalize various aspects of the supply chain, business organizations must take a structural approach to strategic decision-making. In order to help the supply chain strategic decision-makers, this chapter presents a series of digitalization business scenarios covering inbound, internal, outbound, and end-to-end perspectives, as shown diagrammatically in Figure 1.

By breaking down the supply chain into a series of digital scenarios, the chapter has presented a framework for robust decision-making based on a clear understanding of what outcomes business corporations seek. In addition, this section highlighted maturity models for each scenario to help businesses think about which areas they want to focus on, assess their level of achievement to date, and prioritize their efforts. Besides, the framework starts by defining the practical application of digital technologies at the appropriate stage in the value chain. Finally, before assessing current and required capabilities in terms of technology and skills, the business benefits and challenges finish with assessing achievability.

Collaborative Electronic Sourcing

Recent global events have presented new dimension of supply chain visibility into business and operations. In the face of disruption, organizations could not forecast demand, predict supply, and meet delivery schedules. As a result, organizations of all sizes need to speed up their transformation initiatives to increase flexibility, agility, and visibility for a more resilient supply chain. Digitizing supply chains through modern integration, automation, and secure and connected ecosystems makes it easy to manage information flows and uncover insights to ensure continued operations, even in the face of significant disruptions. The dominating options are electronic data interchange (EDI) and automated call-off are established forms of digital sourcing; businesses are trying to extend this to manage tiers beyond direct suppliers and to provide the option of initiative-taking warning systems.

Further, business organizations try to create deeper strategic engagement with supplier communities. In addition, business organizations need seamless connectivity among themself, by which automated replenishment from the supplier network (multiple tiers) with real-time business operation monitoring and predictive disruption analysis capabilities. At the same time, businesses must score how significant they consider the opportunities and advantages this operation practice could bring and the challenges and uncertainties. The proceeding step is to take the initiative to evaluate how mature the current enabling technologies are now and over the coming years and how well-developed their organizational skills, know-how, and attitudes are. By repeating this process for the other nine scenarios outlined below, businesses can develop concrete strategic business cases where they must concentrate their corporate resources to attain strategic goals.

Digital Factory Design

The digital economy represents the pervasive use of IT (hardware, software, applications, and data communication technologies) in different areas of the economy, including internal operations of organizations (business, government, and non-profit); transactions between organizations; and transactions between individuals, acting both as consumers and citizens, and organizations. Digital 3D modelling systems for factory design are becoming increasingly sophisticated. This process, coupled with the advent of flexible manufacturing systems and data connectivity, these advances stimulate a new paradigm in factory layout design, process, and material flows. As well as looking different, tomorrow's digital factory will significantly impact takt time, buffers, skills, and staffing. It should also be easily reconfigurable in response to change conditions.

Real-Time Factory Scheduling

How manufacturers run factories, as well as how they design them, will change dramatically, and this requires s form of digital business process re-engineering. The prize could significantly increase productivity, improve delivery performance, respond to change, and have fewer missed sales. However, making full use of the sensor-enabled, smart device, real-time opportunity with seamlessly joined-up ERP, MES, and cloud systems is not easy. Instead, it needs careful navigation to maximize business benefits and avoid costs and complexity.

Flexible Factory Automation

Ever-cheaper technology, collaborative robotics, and machine learning mean manufacturers are entering a new era of factory automation. The business benefits include lower variable costs, increased customization, labour saving, quality assurance, closer-to-make location, and improved health and safety. One crucial aspect is introducing equipment modularity and standards into the overall vision, supporting the necessary economies, and enabling flexible reconfiguration.

Digital Production Processes

The shift towards replacing 'subtractive' manufacturing processes (such as machining) with 'additive' processes (such as laser sintering and digital printing) has obvious benefits in cost, with even more significant opportunities in enabling new product designs and enhanced customization. In addition, these new techniques could bring about the disruptive reconfiguration of complete supply chains and industry sectors.

Customer Connected E-Commerce

At a minimum, companies should aim to extend e-commerce to optimize web-based order management, including personalized configuration, omnichannel access, and last-mile delivery. The latter is becoming a critical competitive differentiator, particularly in retail consumer goods, where 'last-mile' costs often outstripped the total cost of manufacturing and primary distribution. As a result, companies are now looking beyond stereotypical business operations and will use completely new business models based on customer-connected supply chains – constantly monitoring product usage and experience and tailoring the offering to suit.

Extended Supply Chain Monitoring

It involves the entire network, using data science, predictive analytics, real-time risk management, and dynamic resource optimization – enabled by distributed sensors and track-and-trace to create visualization optimize information systems integration, predict disruptions, and support dynamic decision-making.

Digital Product Quality

The vision for Total Quality Management (TQM) in the digital context involves end-to-end transparency, real-time root cause analytics, and initiative-taking resolution driven by customer connectivity. The challenge is to connect a series of 'traceability islands' back from customers, across internal operation networks, right through to suppliers. The potential benefits are considerable, from faster problem resolution, problem prevention, customer satisfaction, performance, compliance verification, and avoided warranties.

Digital Supply Network Design

It presents the opportunity at the total supply network level. This involves digital network design, modelling, and visualization tools that support a deeper understanding of fundamental dynamics and drivers covering the cost, responses, risk, resource access, and innovation. The tools also support rapid experimentation regarding possible future network options leading to breakthrough scenarios and faster transformation. This can lead to new network design principles and step changes in supply collaboration, site location, capacity, inventory, and customer response.

Product Lifecycle Management

There is a growing need to integrate product-based data systems with supply chain-based systems, aligned with a single vision for product lifecycle management (PLM) and value capture. These next-generation PLM systems can provide accurate, up-to-date product information accessible throughout the value chain and product lifecycle. This enables enhanced cross-function and cross-organizational involvement in the design, collaborative innovation, design for manufacture, procurement, platform-based design philosophies, quicker time-to-market, and improved portfolio management.

IoT for the Supply Chain Management

The vision behind the IoT is to create real-time connection and data communication with people or any business process along supply chain operation, anytime, anywhere, using any network. It facilitates overcoming the limitations of legacy systems and ways of data communication and processing. In this way, IoT systems embedded with industrial operations often consist of software, electronic components, actuators, sensors, detectors, and wireless connectivity that enable them to collect data from these objects can be defined as the "IoT". An IoT system has the following essential characteristics:

- IoT is a ubiquitous technology advancement that enables supply chain business-related objects to be connected to the internet via wired or wireless networks to communicate.

- Several wireless sensor networks are available for IoT devices, including near-field communication (NFC), Zigbee, radio frequency identification (RFID), Bluetooth, and Wi-Fi.
- The sensors can be connected to various technologies, including long-term evolution (LTE), general packet radio service (GPRS), and global system for mobile communication (GSMC).
- The efficiency of an IoT system is largely determined by three main components, each of which is vital to its day-to-day operation: (i) perception layer, (ii) network and middleware (Edge, Fog, and Cloud) layer, and (iii) application layer.

Nevertheless, cloud computing offers virtually unlimited storage and system capabilities to address many IoT-related challenges. Consequently, the phrase "cloud of things" (CoT) is used to allude to the fusion of IoT and cloud computing. The CoT is a paradigm for increasing productivity and improving system performance that is widely used by most industries and manufacturers. Several researchers discussed in their research (Pal, 2023) the use of the cloud to analyze vast amounts of data (i.e., Big Data) when data storage and processing are required.

With the advent of the IoT, vast amounts of data are generated in real-time, which poses a significant concern for traditional cloud computing network topologies (Fang & Ma, 2020). A traditional cloud infrastructure condenses all processing, storage, and networking into a limited set of data centers, and the distance between remote devices and remote data centers is relatively wide (Wang et al., 2010). Edge computing could address this challenge since it provides access to computing resources closer to IoT edge devices and may lead to a new ecosystem for IoT innovation (Jiang et al., 2020). In this way, architectural issues on IoT systems in automating supply chain operations play a significant role, and there are diverse types of layered architecture for supply chain industrial applications (Pal & Yasar, 2020).

IoT Systems Architecture

The layered architecture is designed to meet the requirements of various industries (e.g., manufacturing, retail), enterprises, societies, institutions, and governments. The functionalities of the various layers are (Pal, 2023): (i) edge layer: This is the hardware layer and consists of sensor networks, embedded systems, RFID tags, and readers or several types of sensors in different forms. Many of these hardware elements provide identification and information storage, information collection, information processing, communication, control, and actuation, (ii) access gateway layer: It takes care of message routing, publishing, and subscribing and performs cross-platform communication if required, (iii) the middleware layer interfaces the access gateway layer and the application layer. It is responsible for functions and takes care of issues like data filtering, data aggregation, semantic analysis, access control, and information discovery, such as EPC (Electronic Product Code) information service and ONS (Object Naming Service), and (iv) application layer that is responsible for delivering various applications to different users in IoT. Figure 2 represents a simplified IoT technology-based architecture for SCM.

About the technologies of IoT, (Jiang et al., 2020) presents the technology areas enabling the IoT: (i) identification technology: The purpose of identification is to map a unique identifier or UID (globally unique or unique within a particular scope) to an entity to make it retrievable and identifiable without ambiguity, (ii) IoT architecture challenges: Scalability, modularity, extensibility, and interoperability among heterogenous things and their environments are the essential design requirements for IoT, (iii) communication technology, (iv) network technology: The IoT deployment requires the development of suitable network technology for implementing the vision of IoT to reach out to objects in the physical world and to bring them into the internet, (v) software and algorithms, and (vi) hardware technology which includes intelligent devices with enhanced inter-device communication.

Figure 2. A layered IoT architecture for supply chain operation

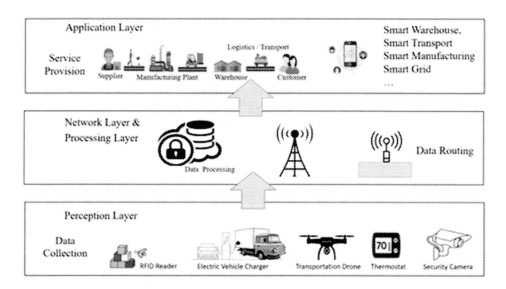

The other essential technologies necessary for the IoT-based sensing environment are: (i) data and signal processing technology, (ii) discovering and search engine technology, (iii) relationship network management technology in managing networks that contain a vast number of heterogeneous things, and (iii) power and energy storage technology, (iv) security and privacy technologies to maintain two significant issues in IoT system, and (iv) standardization which should be designed to support a wide range of applications and address standard requirements from a wide range of industrial SCM systems.

Review of Recent Literature

In this way, information technology enables effective supply chain management; and information sharing capability. This section presents a brief review of IoT technology and its uses in SCM's different application areas: (i) procurement process, (ii) make process, (iii) delivery process, (iv) return process, and (v) industry-specific deployment.

Table 1. Applications of IoT technology for supply chain operations

Procurement Process: The request for materials and services by companies is the sourcing process. Planning source activities strategically across the supply chain is a sign of success. Yuvaraj and Sangeetha (Yuvaraj & Sangeetha, 2016) highlighted how to monitor goods anytime and anywhere by integrating RFID tags with GPS technology to track indoor and outdoor products in a supply chain environment. The impact of IoT on supplier selection was studied by Yu and colleagues (Ng & Wakenshaw, 2017). Also, several advantages of IoT regarding the sourcing process have been identified. For example, in analyzing the impact of the cost of sensors and notifications on the purchase cost of a unit, researchers (Decker et al., 2008) developed a simple linear cost model.
Make Process: The operational areas that IoT applications can enhance and relevant to the supply chain make process involves factory visibility as in (Wang et al., 2016), management of innovative production networks as by (Veza & Gjeldum, 2015), intelligent design and production control as by (Zawadzki & Zywickl, 2016) systematic design of the virtual factory as by (Choi et al., 2015), smart factory in the petrochemical industry (Li, 2016), opportunities for sustainable manufacturing in industry 4.0 (Stock & Seliger, 2016).
Delivery Process: The delivery function is one of the most significant logistics tasks. Logistics includes planning, storing, and controlling goods and services flows (Ballou, 2007). The delivery process in the supply chain concerns the warehouse, inventory, order management, and transportation. The main impact of IoT on the supply chain delivery process includes: (i) Warehousing function: the IoT enables timesaving of joint ordering via smart RFID tags (Angeles, 2005). IoT also achieves collaborative warehousing via using smart things and multi-agent systems. It also increases the safety and security of the supply chain (Liukkonen & Tsai, 2016). (ii) In order and inventory management: the IoT enables sharing of information and inventory accuracy (Bowman et al., 2009) using RFID tags. [iii] In transportation function: the IoT achieves accurate and timely delivery using sensors and networks (Fang et al., 2013). It also saves smartphone scanning and recording time (Li et al., 2014).
Return Process: A closed-loop supply chain model to meet the demand of sales collection centers using new and remanufactured products presented by researchers (Paksovy et al., 2016). The e-reverse logistic framework was designed by Xing et al (Xing et al., 2012). Fang and other searchers proposed an integrated three-stage model for optimizing procurement, pricing, product recovery, and strategy of return acquisition (Fang et al., 2016).
Industry-Specific Deployment: IoT technology is also deployed in various supply chain applications. For example, a group of researchers used IoT for a pharmaceutical supply chain (Yan & Huang, 2009), and it has also been used for the construction industry (Shin et al., 2011), the petrochemical industry (Li, 2016), retail industry, and food supply chains (Verdouw et al., 2016).

The IoT technology can potentially *'connect the unconnected,'* It introduces a new concept that aims to enhance the forms of communication the individual supply chain business partners need today. In this way, it addresses many supplies chain operational challenges, including the enhanced business need to improve supply chain information transparency and introduce the integrity of production data and the identity of products. At the same time, IoT applications generate vast volumes of data along the supply chain operations, and often this data resides in silos, which are generally underutilized and present to extract real-time business insights information. These data silos can be considered trapped or hidden sources of potential business insights and value, which can be made available after appropriate processing steps. For example, appropriate processing steps can provide facilities with the shift from mass to customized products for specific customers. Finally, the research community highlights the requirements to establish interoperable data exchange standards among production business partners (Pal, 2021).

The other essential characteristics of these data silos are distributed in nature, and the service-oriented computing (SOC) paradigm presents an attractive solution for providing business services. These services are self-contained application systems used over industry-specific middleware architecture, capable of describing, publishing, locating, and orchestrating over dedicated data communication networks. These architectures are often used in large-scale data center environments. These architectures are often used in large-scale data center environments. However, data centers' consolidation and centralization produce a significant problem due to the increased distance between customers and relevant services for business. Besides, this arrangement creates different outcomes in high variability in latency and bandwidth-related issues. To address this issue, decentralized SOC architectures, namely cloudlets, have emerged, particularly regarding resource-intensive and interactive applications. Cloudlets are small-scale data centers near user applications and can mitigate low latency and high bandwidth guarantees.

Despite the potential, as mentioned earlier, IoT technology is also facing many challenges: (i) device reliability and durability, (ii) security and privacy issues, (iii) scalability and latency, and (iv) standardization. Device reliability and durability often relate to industrial operations (e.g., manufacturing, transportation, and retail business). These issues include remote access control, reliability, connectivity, and reliable services provision. The other significant challenge is security and privacy issues. It includes authentication and access control in industrial control systems security, data protection, privacy preservation under data protection regulations, and the protection and security of human, industrial assets, and critical infrastructures. Unfortunately, conventional security and privacy approaches are not extremely helpful to IoT-based industrial supply chain applications due to their dynamic topology and distributed nature. In addition, the present Internet architecture, with its server-based infrastructure, might be unsuitable for managing numerous devices and substantial amounts of data because individual servers may pose a single point of failure for cyber-attacks and physical damage.

Moreover, centralized information systems may pose a fragility for IoT deployments in the supply chain for traceability purposes. A centralized data hosting and control approach can lead to several business risks and operational issues related to data integrity, security, and privacy. For example, cloud-based solutions for monitoring IoT data may be subject to manipulation and privacy legislation issues that arise when exporting substantial amounts of confidential and susceptible information to external services in other jurisdictions (Kshetri, 2017) (Cam-Winget et al., 2016). Additionally, these solutions may cause opacity and increase information asymmetry between supply chain exchange partners. Blockchain technology can help to alleviate several of these problems.

Blockchain Technology

Blockchain is a new type of database. In this database, the data is saved in a block linked to other blocks in a chain creating the blockchain. This way, a blockchain is distributed data structure, a distributed ledger, in which the data is shared on a peer-to-peer network. The network members and nodes communicate and validate the data following a predefined protocol without a central authority. Distributed ledgers can be either decentralized, giving equal rights to all users, or centralized, providing specific users with special rights. In addition, blockchain is, by nature, a distributed ledger since each network node has a copy of the ledger. Depending on the right of the users, blockchain can be designed as a centralized or decentralized ledger. If blockchain is designed to share decision-making among multiple users, it is decentralized; if one central entity is the primary decision-maker, it is centralized.

Blockchain technology was popularized with the 'Bitcoin' cryptocurrency peer-to-peer network. Blockchains are created using cryptography in which each block – transaction, file of data – has a cryptographic hash and is linked to a previous block. Once a block is verified by a certain percentage of the network nodes, it is added to previous blocks and forms a blockchain, also known as a public ledger of transactions (Casado-Vara et al., 2018).

Blockchain technology alters how administrative control is digitally regulated and maintained. In blockchains, data are converted to digital codes, stored in shared databases, have higher transparency, and limited risk of deletion and revision – immutability. Blockchain potential lies with every agreement, payment, and transactional activity having a digital record. These records may be validated and shared among individuals, machines, algorithms, and organizations. Intermediaries such as brokers, bankers, and lawyers are needed less often (Lansiti & Lakhani, 2017). Intermediaries function as intermediaries and oversee the accuracy and verification of transactions in different industries. With blockchain, trust is shifted from human and traditional agents for verifying transactions to computer codes.

Figure 3. A diagrammatic representation of a blockchain

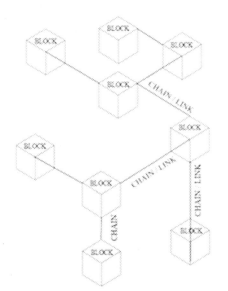
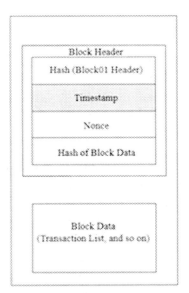

Blockchain technology appears in the commercial world with enormous promise. Bitcoin was an audacious idea: until cryptocurrencies came along, no one could transmit value at a distance without the permission and support of a third party. In this way, it is a simple but revolutionary idea of instant value transfer. For example, in the Bitcoin market, an individual has complete control over their Bitcoin balance. Unlike a bank balance, an individual's Bitcoin balance cannot be manipulated or viewed digitally. If the individual has the proper passcode, they can authorize entry on the blockchain ledger and transfer it to another individual's address (Athey et al., 2016). Among blockchain technology advantages are transparency, less risk of fraud, instantaneous transactions, privacy and security, financial data assurance, and no exchange costs (Sharma et al., 2017) (Crosby et al., 2016). In addition, blockchain technology can provide the following capabilities, which may be dependent on the platform needed to be used (Barton, 2018): (i) *Shared ledger*: a data structure that is distributed locally and shared between different participants; (ii) *Permissioning*: secure and authenticated transactions that ensure privacy and transparency of data; (iii) *Smart contract*: business terms are embedded in a database and are implemented with transactions; and (iv) *Consensus*: transactions are endorsed by relevant users that ensure the immutability and traceability of data.

Most existing blockchain researchers concentrate on Bitcoin and cryptocurrency-related industrial applications (Yli-Huumo et al., 2016). However, the technology can be employed in different industrial applications. Although blockchain is in its relative infancy, some consider it a general-purpose technology (GPT) with several key features of GPTs (Kane, 2017). GPTs such as the steam engine, electricity, and the internet result in innovation and productivity gains among multiple industries, leading to economic growth for years (Catalini & Gans, 2016), and this outcome is part of the blockchain promise; whether it comes to fruition is an open question.

Blockchain technology has attracted wide attention due to cryptocurrencies (e.g., bitcoin) (Nakamoto, 2008). Technically, a blockchain is managed by a network of nodes, and every node executes and records the transactions. A simple blockchain diagram is shown in Figure 3.

Industry users of the blockchain-based information system network use mining nodes to create new blocks, verified by algorithmic software for their information, and ultimately add them to a distributed P2P network. Blockchain technology uses the consensus algorithm to add a new block to the network and follow the steps below:

1. Blockchain network user uses the cryptographic-based private key to sign a transaction and advertises the book to their peers.
2. Blockchain network peers validate the received transaction and advertise it over the blockchain network.
3. Involved users generally verify the transaction to meet a consensus algorithmic digital agreement.
4. The miner nodes add the valid transaction into a time-stamped block and broadcast it again into the blockchain network.
5. Next, verifying the advertised block and matching its hash with the previous block, the block in consideration adds to the blockchain network.

This way, consensus algorithms are one of blockchain technology's most essential and revolutionary aspects. For example, consensus algorithms use rules and verification methods to validate data that lets the blockchain network, including devices, agree about adding data to the blockchain network (Bashir, 2017).

One of the benefits of blockchain-based technology is to validate the block's trustfulness in a decentralized, trustless business operating environment without the necessity of the trusted third-party authority. In a blockchain-based P2P network environment, reaching a *consensus* on a newly generated block is challenging as the consensus may favour malicious nodes. This challenge can be mitigated by using dedicated *consensus* algorithms. Typical consensus algorithms are – proof of work (PoW), proof of stake (PoS), and practical byzantine fault tolerance (PBFT) (Bach et al., 2018).

In this way, blockchain can be defined as a decentralized, encrypted database distributed across a peer-to-peer network without a central authority to control and secure it. A consensus mechanism protects and validates the information stored in the Blockchain. Consensus algorithms refer to the different mechanisms used to reach an agreement and ensure security in a distributed system. This kind of system faces a fundamental problem similar to the Byzantine Generals Problem, which relies on achieving consensus in the presence of several faulty and malicious participants. As it is based on a decentralized and distributed network, Blockchain also needs such algorithms to handle data and reach consensus. There are several types of consensus algorithms used in a real-world implementation. The most common algorithms are Proof of Work, the first consensus algorithm implemented by the first Blockchain (Bitcoin), Proof of Stake, and Delegated Proof of Stake.

Blockchain technology can significantly transform many activities and operations in the supply chain that require increased attention from academics and practitioners (Pal, 2022). Numerous studies have reported significant advantages of blockchain technology in logistics and supply chain management (Kamble et al., 2019). These benefits include improvement in cybersecurity and protection (Kshetri,

2017), transparency and accountability (Kshetri, 2018) (Zou et al., 2018), traceability and fraud prevention (Biswas et al., 2018), and researchers highlight many other operational management issues. Blockchain technology can redefine, redesign, and remodel the characteristics of the relationships between all the players in the supply chain (Queiroz & Fosso Wamba, 2019).

Blockchain technology in SCM makes operation management safer, more transparent, traceable, and efficient (Aste et al., 2017; Kshetri, 2018). Furthermore, blockchain technology can increase the cooperation between the members of SCM (Aste et al., 2017), with indirect positive effects on cost and efficiency in the supply chain. Blockchain technology can also enhance customers' trust, thanks to the traceability of goods throughout their journey across the supply chain (Biswas et al., 2017), and supports the prevention of product fraud and fakes across the supply chains (Chen, 2018), which has a positive impact in terms of cost reduction and efficiency.

BLOCKCHAIN-BASED IoT APPLICATION

This section presents some of the crucial challenges and the related application solutions of deploying blockchain technology, which designs for devices with permanent storage capability and computing capability on the minimal resources of IoT hardware. Some significant integration challenges can be found in the previous research (Reyna et al., 2018).

Blockchain and IoT Integration Challenges

Scalability: The blockchain size widens with an increasing number of connected devices because it needs to store and validate all the transactional information. This is a significant integration disadvantage as IoT networks are expected to contain many nodes that can generate big data in real time.

Security: The increasing number of security-related attacks on IoT networks and their ultimate impacts make securing IoT devices with blockchain technology essential. This integration characteristic may create a severe problem when IoT-based applications do not operate appropriately, and corrupted data arrives and remains in the blockchain. As a result, IoT devices need to be tested before their integration with blockchain because of the undetectable nature of this problem (Roman et al., 2013). Unfortunately, they are often hacked since their constraints limit the firmware updates, stopping them from actuating possible bugs or security breaches. Besides, updating devices one by one is challenging, as required in global IoT deployments in the production industry. Hence, run-time up-grading and reconfiguration mechanisms are needed in IoT devices to keep running over time (Reyna et al., 2018).

Anonymity and Data Privacy: Privacy is an essential concern in IoT applications. Massive amounts of privacy-sensitive data can be generated, processed, and transferred between device applications. Blockchain technology presents an ideal solution to address identity management in IoT to protect the person's identity when sending personal data that protects user data privacy instead of identities. User anonymity can be revealed by examining the address of the transaction advertised to every participant (He et al., 2018). The IoT devices secured data storage, and authorization of access is a significant challenge since accomplishing it requires integrating cryptographic security solutions into the device, considering limited resources.

Resource Utilization and Consensus: Trusted authority in centralized architectures make sure consensus integrity, while in the decentralized environment, nodes of the blockchain network need to reach consensus by voting, which is a resource-intensive process. IoT devices are attributed to relatively low computing capabilities, power consumption, and wireless bandwidth. For example, blockchains that utilize PoW as a consensus mechanism need vast computational power and utilities a considerable amount of energy for the mining process. Computationally complex consensus algorithms do not apply to IoT scenarios, and limited resources should be allocated to find a possible agreement. However, PoS is more likely to be used in IoT, but none of these issues has yet been deployed in IoT as a commercial adoption (Atlam et al., 2018) (Danzi et al., 2018).

A distributed and decentralized blockchain architecture can reduce the overall cost of the IoT system compared to centralized architectures. However, a decentralized blockchain architecture suffers from a new type of resource-wasting, which challenges its integration with IoT. Resource requirements depend on the blockchain network consensus algorithm. Typically, solutions to this problem are to delegate these tasks to an unconstrained device or another gateway device capable of catering to the functionality. Otherwise, off-chain solutions are also useable in this situation, and off-chain moves information outside the blockchain to minimize the high latency in the blockchain could provide the functionality (Reyna et al., 2018).

Smart Contracts: Devices can use smart contract techniques with addresses or guide them as application reactions to listening events. They provide a dependable and secure IoT feature, which records and manages their interactions. Working with smart contracts requires using oracles that consist of specific entities that provide real-world data in a trusted manner. Smart contracts should consider the heterogeneity and limitations presented in the IoT. Also, actuation mechanisms directly from smart contracts would help faster reactions with the IoT (Reyna et al., 2018).

IoT designers should select a solution based on their restrictions and requirements, the diversity of solutions for blockchain integration with IoT, and the diverse types of IoT devices and their applications. The following section presents the proposed IoT, blockchain, and SOC technologies architecture.

PROPOSED ENTERPRISE ARCHITECTURE

This section explains how service-oriented computing (SOC) technology will improve efficiencies, provide new business opportunities, address regulatory requirements, and improve transparency and visibility of global production activities. Figure 4 represents the proposed enterprise architecture, which consists of multilayered IoT, blockchain, and service-oriented computing. The IoT systems allow for capturing real-time production business process data from the plant-level operational environment. The enterprise architecture for distributed production (e.g., apparel) supply network used for the current research is shown in Figure 5. The architecture mainly consists of three layers: (i) IoT-based service, (ii) blockchain-based data control, and (iii) data storage and processing part.

IoT-Based Service Layer

The IoT technology development created many opportunities, such as interconnected and interoperable data collection and exchange devices. The data obtained from IoT devices can make production more convenient through numerous types of decision-making at all levels and areas of production business activities.

Blockchain-Based Data Controlling

The blockchain-based controlling part can potentially improve the IoT technology used in the production industry. The production industry is part of a complex and information-intensive supply chain comprising a set of globally connected and distributed organizations, including other critical infrastructures supporting world trade, such as transport and international border management.

Figure 4. Enterprise information system architecture for production (e.g., apparel) business

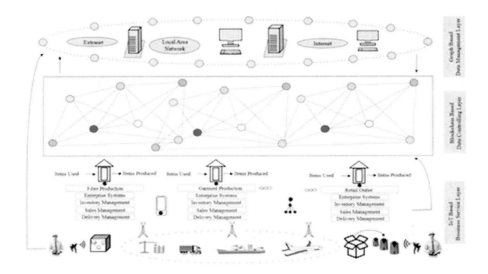

Production and its supply chain management are regarded as a domain where blockchains are good fits for distinct reasons. During the product's lifecycle, as it flows down the value chain network (from production to consumption), the data produced in each step can be present as a transaction, making a permanent history of the item of interest (i.e., product). Among other things, blockchain technology can effectively contribute to (i) recording every single asset (from product to containers) as it flows through the production chain nodes, (ii) tracking orders, receipts, invoices, payments, and any other official documents, and (iii) track digital assets (e.g., certifications, warranties, licenses, copyrights) in a unified way and parcels with physical assets, and others. Moreover, through its decentralized nature, the blockchain can effectively share information regarding the production step, delivery, and maintenance schemes of products between suppliers and vendors, bringing new collaboration opportunities in complex assembly lines.

The challenges in transportation modeling parameters, such as delays in delivery, loss of documentation, unknown source of products, and errors, can be minimized and even avoided by blockchain implementation. Integrating the production supply chain with blockchain benefits are enhanced environmental audit-related issues, minimized errors and delays, reduced transport costs, faster issue identification, increased trust (consumer and partner trust), and improved product transport and inventory management.

Data Management Layer

Industries use different blockchain platforms, and different data models are used on the platforms (e.g., Ethereum (Ethereum, 2021) adopted a key-value data model, while a few of them, like R3 Corda (Corda, 2021), use a relational data model). This characteristic emphasizes that no single blockchain platform is suitable for diverse types of data used in a wide range of product supply chain applications. For example, geolocation data recorded from supply chain transport vehicles may not be efficiently queried using a key-value store. Also, even though blockchain platforms such as Hyperledger Fabric (Hyperledger, 2021) use a pluggable storage model, service users must decide at development time which storage to use (e.g., either Level DB (Kim, 2016), or key-value store using CouchDB (CoucDB, 2021) (document store). Thus, special techniques are required for supporting multiple types of data stores such as key-value, document, SQL, and spatial data stores simultaneously in the same blockchain system. In the proposed architecture, a generic graph database model has been used.

FUTURE RESEARCH DIRECTIONS

Blockchain technology with the Internet of Things applications is getting importance in production industry automation. Besides, data privacy issues remain a fundamental challenge for regulatory bodies. The European General Data Protection Regulation (GDPR) lays the foundation for users to control their data and information about any devices involved in collecting and processing this data. The main objective is to provide individual entities must have the authoritative power and control over their data assets and to be able to transfer their data without any unmitigated risk. Blockchains give the advantages of distributed ledgers that can securely manage digital transactions, where data centralization is unnecessary. In the future, this research will take the initiative of how blockchain technology can be used to develop an audit trail of data generated in IoT devices, providing GDPR rules to be verified on such a trail. This mechanism will help translate such rules into smart contracts to protect personal data transparently and automatically.

CONCLUSION

Supply chains are extraordinarily complex organisms, and no business organization has yet succeeded in building one that is truly digital. Indeed, many regular operations are automated using modern information and communication technologies; but many of the applications required are not yet widely used. However, the trend of business process automation using modern evolving technology will change radically over the coming years, with different industries implementing distributed supply chains at varying speeds. Enterprises that get there first will gain a difficult-to-challenge advantage in the race to Industry 5.0 and can set, or at least influence, technical standards for their particular industry. The advantage will come by no means to stop for significant efficiencies. The main objective will be the different business models and revenue streams the digital supply chain will open up.

This chapter presents a hybrid enterprise information systems architecture of IoT applications and a blockchain-based distributed ledger to support transaction services within a multi-party global production business network. The IoT is an intelligent global network of connected objects, which through unique address schemes, can help to collaborate with other business partners to achieve common objectives. The data obtained from the IoT applications along production business processes can make operational decision-making much more accessible. However, standalone IoT application systems face *security* and *privacy*-related problems. Finally, the chapter presents a research proposal outlining how blockchain technology can impact the IoT system's essential aspects of GDPR-related issues and thus provide the foundation for future research challenges.

REFERENCES

Angeles, R. (2005). RFID technologies: Supply-chain applications and implementation issues. *Information Systems Management*, 22(1), 51–65. doi:10.1201/1078/44912.22.1.20051201/85739.7

Athey, S., Parashkevov, I., Sarukkai, V., & Xia, J. (2016). *Bitcoin pricing, adoption, and usage: Theory and evidence*. Academic Press.

Atlam, H. F., Alenezi, A., Alassafi, M. O., & Wills, G. (2018). Blockchain with Internet of Things: Benefits, challenges, and future directions. *International Journal of Intelligent Systems and Applications*, 10(6), 40–48. doi:10.5815/ijisa.2018.06.05

Bai, C., & Sarkis, J. (2020). A supply chain transparency and sustainability technology appraisal model for blockchain technology. *International Journal of Production Research*, 2020(58), 2142–2162. doi:10.1080/00207543.2019.1708989

Ballou, R. H. (2007). *Business Logistics/supply Chain Management* (5th ed.). Pearson Education India.

Bouzembrak, Y., Klüche, M., Gavai, A., & Marvin, H. J. P. (2019). Internet of Things in food safety: Literature review and a bibliometric analysis. *Trends in Food Science & Technology*, 2019(94), 54–64. doi:10.1016/j.tifs.2019.11.002

Bowman, P., Ng, J., Harrison, M., Lopez, S., & Illic, A. (2009). *Sensor based condition monitoring, Building Radio frequency IDentification for the Global Environment*. Euro RFID project.

Casado-Vara, R., Prieto, J., De la Prieta, F., & Corchado, J. M. (2018). How Blockchain improves the supply chain: Case study alimentary supply chain. *Procedia Computer Science*, 134, 393–398. doi:10.1016/j.procs.2018.07.193

Catalini, C., & Gans, J. S. (2016). *Some simple Economics of the Blockchain*. National Bureau of Economic Research. doi:10.3386/w22952

Chanchaichujit, J., Balasubramanian, S. & Charmaine, N.S.M. (2020). A systematic literature review on the benefit-drivers of RFID implementation in supply chains and its impact on organizational competitive advantage. *Cogent Bus. Manag.*

Chang, Y., Iakovou, E., & Shi, W. (2020). Blockchain in global supply chains and cross border trade: A critical synthesis of the state-of-the-art, challenges and opportunities. *International Journal of Production Research*, 58(7), 2082–2099. doi:10.1080/00207543.2019.1651946

Choi, S., Kim, B. H., & Noh, S. D. (2015). A diagnosis and evaluation method for strategic planning and systematic design of a virtual factory in smart manufacturing systems. *International Journal of Precision Engineering and Manufacturing*, 16(6), 1107–1115. doi:10.100712541-015-0143-9

Choi, T. M., Cai, Y. J., & Shen, B. (2019). Sustainable Fashion Supply Chain Management: A System of Systems Analysis. *IEEE Transactions on Engineering Management*, 66(4), 730–745. doi:10.1109/TEM.2018.2857831

Corda. (2021). https://www.corda.net

CouchDB. (2021). https://www.couchdb.apache.org

Crosby, M., Pattanayak, P., Verma, S., & Kalyanaraman, V. (2016). Blockchain technology: Beyond Bitcoin. *Appl. Innov.*, 2, 6–10.

Danzi, P., Kalor, A. E., Stefanovic, C., & Popovski, P. (2018). Analysis of the communication traffic for blockchain synchronization of IoT devices. In *2018 IEEE International Conference on Communications (ICC)*. IEEE. 10.1109/ICC.2018.8422485

De Bruyn, S., Ahdour, S., Bijleveld, M., de Graaff, L., Schep, E., Schroten, A., & Vergeer, R. (2018). Environmental Prices Handbook 2017: Methods and Numbers for Valuation of Environmental Impacts. CE Delft.

Decker, C., Berchtold, M. L., Chaves, W. F., Beigl, M., Roehr, D., & Riedel, T. (2008). Cost benefit model for smart items in the supply chain. In The Internet of Things. Springer. doi:10.1007/978-3-540-78731-0_10

Ellen MacArthur Foundation, (2016). *Intelligent assets: unlocking the circular economy potential*. Author.

Ethereum. (2021). https://www.ethereum.org

Fang, C., Liu, X., Pardalos, P. M., & Pei, J. (2016). Optimization for a three-stage production system in the Internet of Things: Procurement, production and product recovery, and acquisition. *International Journal of Advanced Manufacturing Technology*, 83(5-8), 689–710. doi:10.100700170-015-7593-1

Fang, J., & Ma, A. (2020). IoT application modules placement and dynamic task processing in edge-cloud computing. *IEEE Internet of Things Journal*, 8(6), 12771–12781.

Fang, J., Qu, T., Li, Z. G., Xu, G., & Huang, G. Q. (2013). Agent-based gateway operating system for RFID-enabled ubiquitous manufacturing enterprise. *Robotics and Computer-integrated Manufacturing*, 29(4), 222–231. doi:10.1016/j.rcim.2013.01.001

Ghisellini, P., Cialani, C., & Ulgiati, S. (2016). A review on circular economy: The expected transition to a balanced interplay of environmental and economic systems. *Journal of Cleaner Production*, *114*, 11–32. doi:10.1016/j.jclepro.2015.09.007

Gubbi, J., Buyya, R., Marusic, S., & Palaniswami, M. (2013). Internet of Things (IoT): A vision, architectural elements, and future directions. *Future Generation Computer Systems*, *29*(7), 1645–1660. doi:10.1016/j.future.2013.01.010

Habib, M. A., Sardar, M. B., Jabbar, S., Faisal, C. M. N., Mahmood, N., & Ahmad, M. (2020). Blockchain-based Supply Chain for the Automation of Transaction Process: Case Study based Validation. *Proceedings of the 2020 International Conference on Engineering and Emerging Technologies, ICEET 2020*. 10.1109/ICEET48479.2020.9048213

Hasan, H., AlHadhrami, E., AlDhaheri, A., Salah, K., & Jayaraman, R. (2019). Smart contract-based approach for efficient shipment management. *Computers & Industrial Engineering*, *136*, 2019. doi:10.1016/j.cie.2019.07.022

He, Q., Guan, N., Lv, M., & Yi, W. (2018). On the consensus mechanisms of blockchain/dlt for internet of things. In *2018 IEEE 13th International Symposium on Industrial Embedded Systems (SIES)*. IEEE. 10.1109/SIES.2018.8442076

Jiang, J., Li, Z., Tian, Y., & Al-Nabhan, N. (2020). A review of techniques and methods for IoT applications in collaborative cloud-fog environment. *Security and Communication Networks*, *2020*, 1–15. doi:10.1155/2020/8849181

Kagermann, H. (2015). Change through digitization—Value creation in the age of Industry 4.0. In *Management of Permanent Change*. Springer.

Kamble, S., Gunasekaran, A., & Arha, H. (2019). Understanding the Blockchain technology adoption in supply chains-Indian Context. *International Journal of Production Research*, *57*(7), 2009–2033. doi:10.1080/00207543.2018.1518610

Kamble, S. S., Gunasekaran, A., & Gawankar, S. A. (2020). Achieving sustainable performance in a data-driven agriculture supply chain:A review for research and applications. *International Journal of Production Economics*, *2020*(219), 179–194. doi:10.1016/j.ijpe.2019.05.022

Kane, E. (2017). *Is Blockchain a General Purpose Technology?* Academic Press.

Ketzenberg, M., Bloemhof, J., & Gaukler, G. (2015). Managing perishables with time and temperature history. *Production and Operations Management*, *2015*(24), 54–70. doi:10.1111/poms.12209

Kshetri, N. (2018). Blockchain's roles in meeting key supply chain management objectives. *International Journal of Information Management*, *39*(April), 80–89. doi:10.1016/j.ijinfomgt.2017.12.005

Lam, C. Y., & Ip, W. H. (2019). An Integrated Logistics Routing and Scheduling Network Model with RFID-GPS Data for Supply Chain Management. *Wireless Personal Communications*, *2019*(105), 803–817. doi:10.100711277-019-06122-6

Lansiti, M., & Lakhani, K. (2017). The truth about Blockchain. *Harvard Business Review*.

Lasi, H., Fettke, P., Kemper, H.-G., Feld, T., & Hoffmann, M. (2014). Industry 4.0. *Business & Information Systems Engineering*, *6*(4), 239–242. doi:10.100712599-014-0334-4

Lezoche, M., Panetto, H., Kacprzyk, J., Hernandez, J. E., & Alemany Díaz, M. M. E. (2020). Agri-food 4.0: A survey of the Supply Chains and Technologies for the Future Agriculture. *Computers in Industry*, *2020*(117), 103187. doi:10.1016/j.compind.2020.103187

Li, B., Yang, C., & Huang, S. (2014). Study on supply chain disruption management under service level dependent demand. *Journal of Networking*, *9*(6), 1432–1439. doi:10.4304/jnw.9.6.1432-1439

Li, D. (2016). Perspective for smart factory in petrochemical industry. *Computers & Chemical Engineering*, *91*, 136–148. doi:10.1016/j.compchemeng.2016.03.006

Liukkonen, M., & Tsai, T. N. (2016). Toward decentralized intelligence in manufacturing: Recent trends in automatic identification of things. *International Journal of Advanced Manufacturing Technology*, *87*(9-12), 2509–2531. doi:10.100700170-016-8628-y

Lom, M., Pribyl, O., & Svitek, M. (2016). Industry 4.0 as a Part of Smart Cities. In *Smart Cities Symposium Prague (SCSP)*. IEEE. 10.1109/SCSP.2016.7501015

Matharu, G. S., Upadhyay, P., & Chaudhary, L. (2014). The Internet of Things: Challenges & security issues. *Proceedings of the 2014 International Conference on Emerging Technologies, ICET 2014*. 10.1109/ICET.2014.7021016

Min, H. (2019). Blockchain technology for enhancing supply chain resilience. *Business Horizons*, *2019*(62), 35–45. doi:10.1016/j.bushor.2018.08.012

Nakamoto, S. (2008). *Bitcoin: A peer-to-peer electronic cash system*. Academic Press.

Narayanan, A. (2015). *'Private Blockchain' is just a confusing name for a shared database*. Available:https://freedom-to-tinker.com/2015/09/18/private-blockchainis-just-a-confusing-name-for-a-shared-database/

Ng, I. C., & Wakenshaw, S. Y. (2017). The Internet-of-Things: Review and research directions. *International Journal of Research in Marketing*, *34*(1), 3–21. doi:10.1016/j.ijresmar.2016.11.003

Paksoy, T., Karaoğlan, I., Gökçen, H., Pardalos, P. M., & Torğul, B. (2016). Experimental research on closed loop supply chain management with internet of things. *Journal of Economics Bibliograph.*, *15*(3), 1–20.

Pal, K. (2017). Supply Chain Coordination Based on Web Services. In H. K. Chan, N. Subramanian, & M. D. Abdulrahman (Eds.), *Supply Chain Management in the Big Data Era* (pp. 137–171). IGI Global Publication. doi:10.4018/978-1-5225-0956-1.ch009

Pal, K. (2017). Supply Chain Coordination Based on Web Services. In Supply Chain Management in the Big Data Era. IGI Global.

Pal, K. (2018). A Big Data Framework for Decision Making in Supply Chain. In Predictive Intelligence Using Big Data and the Internet of Things. IGI Global.

Pal, K. (2019). Algorithmic Solutions for RFID Tag Anti-Collision Problem in Supply Chain Management. *Procedia Computer Science*, 929-934.

Pal, K. (2019). Quality Assurance Issues for Big Data Applications in Supply Chain Management. In Predictive Intelligence Using Big Data and the Internet of Things. IGI Global.

Pal, K. (2020). Internet of Things and Blockchain Technology in Apparel Supply Chain Management. In H. Patel & G. S. Thakur (Eds.), *Blockchain Applications in IoT Security*. IGI Global Publication.

Pal, K. (2021a). Applications of Secured Blockchain Technology in Manufacturing Industry. In Blockchain and AI Technology in the Industrial Internet of Things. IGI Global.

Pal, K. (2021b). Privacy, Security and Policies: A Review of Problems and Solutions with Blockchain-Based Internet of Things Applications in Manufacturing Industry. *Procedia Computer Science*, *191*, 176–183. doi:10.1016/j.procs.2021.07.022

Pal, K. (2021c). Privacy, Security and Policies: A Review of Problems and Solutions with Blockchain-Based Internet of Things Applications in Manufacturing Industry. *Procedia Computer Science*, *191*, 176–183. doi:10.1016/j.procs.2021.07.022

Pal, K. (2023). Security Issues and Solutions for Resource-Constrained IoT Applications Using Lightweight Cryptography. In Cybersecurity Issues, Challenges, and Solutions in the Business World. IGI Global.

Pal, K., & Yasar, A. U. H. (2020). Internet of Things and Blockchain Technology in Apparel Manufacturing Supply Chain Data Management. *Procedia Computer Science*, *170*, 450–457. doi:10.1016/j.procs.2020.03.088

Pearce, D. W., & Turner, R. K. (1990). *Economics of Natural Resources and the Environment*. JHU Press.

Pournader, M., Shi, Y., Seuring, S., & Koh, S. C. L. (2020). Blockchain applications in supply chains, transport, and logistics: A systematic review of the literature. *International Journal of Production Research*, *2020*(58), 2063–2081. doi:10.1080/00207543.2019.1650976

Prendeville, S., Cherim, E., & Bocken, N. (2017). Circular cities: Mapping six cities in transition. *Environmental Innovation and Societal Transitions*.

Reyna, A., Martin, C., Chen, J., Soler, E., & Diaz, M. (2018). On blockchain and its integration with IoT, Challenges and opportunities. *Future Generation Computer Systems*, *28*, 173–190. doi:10.1016/j.future.2018.05.046

SDG. (2023). https://www.un.org/sustainabledevelopment/sustainable-development-goals

Sharma, P. K., Moon, S. Y., & Park, J. H. (2017). Block-VN: A distributed Blockchain based vehicular network architecture in smart city. *Journal of Information Processing Systems*, *13*(1), 84.

Shin, T. H., Chin, S., Yoon, S. W., & Kwon, S. W. (2011). A service-oriented integrated information framework for RFID/WSN-based intelligent construction supply chain management. *Automation in Construction*, *20*(6), 706–715. doi:10.1016/j.autcon.2010.12.002

Stock, T., & Seliger, G. (2016). Opportunities of sustainable manufacturing in industry 4.0. *Procedia CIRP*, *40*, 536–541. doi:10.1016/j.procir.2016.01.129

Tan, J., & Koo, S. (2014). A survey of technologies in internet of things, in IEEE. *Computers & Society*, 269–274.

Tang, C. S., & Veelenturf, L. P. (2019). The strategic role of logistics in the industry 4.0 era. Transp. Res. Part E Logist. *Transport Reviews*, *2019*(129), 1–11.

Verdouw, C. N., Wolfert, J., Beulens, A., & Rialland, A. (2016). Virtualization of food supply chains with the internet of things. *Journal of Food Engineering*, *176*, 128–136. doi:10.1016/j.jfoodeng.2015.11.009

Veza, I., Mladineo, M., & Gjeldum, N. (2015). Managing innovative production network of smart factories. *IFAC-PapersOnLine*, *48*(3), 555–560. doi:10.1016/j.ifacol.2015.06.139

Vogel-Heuser, B., & Hess, D. (2016). Guest editorial Industry 4.0–prerequisites and visions. *IEEE Transactions on Automation Science and Engineering*, *13*(2), 411–413. doi:10.1109/TASE.2016.2523639

Wang, L., Laszewski, G. V., Young, K. M., & Tao, J. (2010). Cloud Computing: A Perspective Study. *New Generation Computing*, *28*(2), 137–146. doi:10.100700354-008-0081-5

Wang, T., Zhang, Y., & Zang, D. (2016). Real-time visibility and traceability framework for discrete manufacturing shopfloor. *Proceedings of the 22nd International Conference on Industrial Engineering and Engineering Management*, 763–772. 10.2991/978-94-6239-180-2_72

Weidema, B. P. (2015). Comparing three life cycle impact assessment methods from an endpoint perspective. *Journal of Industrial Ecology*, *19*(1), 20–26. doi:10.1111/jiec.12162

Wognum, P. M., Bremmers, H., Trienekens, J. H., Van Der Vorst, J. G. A. J., & Bloemhof, J. M. (2011). Systems for sustainability and transparency of food supply chains—Current status and challenges. *Advanced Engineering Informatics*, *2011*(25), 65–76. doi:10.1016/j.aei.2010.06.001

Xing, B., Gao, W. J., Battle, K., Nelwamondo, F. V., & Marwala, T. (2012). e-RL: the Internet of things supported reverse logistics for remanufacture-to-order. *International Conference in Swarm Intelligence: Advances in Swarm Intelligence*, 519–526.

Yan, B., & Huang, G. (2009). Supply chain information transmission based on RFID and internet of things in Computing. *Communication, Control, and Management, ISECS International Colloquium on*, 166–169.

Yli-Huumo, J., Ko, D., Choi, S., Park, S., & Smolander, K. (2016). Where is current research on Blockchain technology? A systematic review. *PLoS One*, *11*(10), 1–27. doi:10.1371/journal.pone.0163477 PMID:27695049

Yuvaraj, S., & Sangeetha, M. (2016). Smart supply chain management using internet of things (IoT) and low power wireless communication systems. *Wireless Communication, Signal Processing and Networking, International Conference*, 555-558.

Zawadzki, P., & Zywicki, K. (2016). Smart product design and production control for effective mass customization in the industry 4.0 concept. *Management of Production Engineering Review*, 7(3), 105–112. doi:10.1515/mper-2016-0030

Zhang, Y., & Kitsos, P. (2016). *Security in RFID and Sensor Networks* (1st ed.). Auerbach Publications.

Zhou, K., Liu, T., & Zhou, L. (2015). Industry 4.0: towards future industrial opportunities and challenges. In *2015 12th International Conference on Fuzzy Systems and Knowledge Discovery (FSKD)*. IEEE.

KEY TERMS AND DEFINITIONS

Block: A block is a data structure used to communicate incremental changes to the local state of a node. It consists of a list of transactions, a reference to a previous block and a nonce.

Blockchain: In simple, a blockchain is just a data structure that can be shared by different users using computing data communication network (e.g., peer-to-peer or P2P). Blockchain is a distributed data structure comprising a chain of blocks. It can act as a global ledger that maintains records of all transactions on a blockchain network. The transactions are time-stamped and bundled into blocks where each block is identified by its *cryptographic hash*.

Cryptography: Blockchain's transactions achieve validity, trust, and finality based on cryptographic proofs and underlying mathematical computations between various trading partners.

Decentralized Computing Infrastructure: These computing infrastructures feature computing nodes that can make independent processing and computational decisions irrespective of what other peer computing nodes may decide.

Immutability: This term refers to the fact that blockchain transactions cannot be deleted or altered.

Internet of Things (IoT): The Internet of Things (IoT), also called the Internet of Everything or the Industrial Internet, is now a technology paradigm envisioned as a global network of machines and devices capable of interacting with each other. The IoT is recognized as one of the most critical areas of future technology and is gaining vast attention from a wide range of industries.

Provenance: In a blockchain ledger, provenance is a way to trace the origin of every transaction such that there is no dispute about the origin and sequence of the transactions in the ledger.

Supply Chain Management: A supply chain consists of a network of *key business processes* and facilities, involving end-users and suppliers that provide products, services, and information. In this chain management, improving the efficiency of the overall chain is an influential factor; and it needs at least four important strategic issues to be considered: supply chain network design, capacity planning, risk assessment and management, and performances monitoring and measurement.

Warehouse: A warehouse can also be called a storage area, and it is a commercial building where raw materials or goods are stored by suppliers, exporters, manufacturers, or wholesalers, they are constructed and equipped with tools according to special standards depending on the purpose of their use.

Section 6
Blockchain Technology's Application in the Supply Chain

Chapter 12
Moderating Role of Supplier Coordination Level in Relation to Data-Driven Supply Chain and Supply Chain Coordination Capability

Karahan Kara
Artvin Coruh University, Turkey

Galip Cihan Yalçın
Kırıkkale University, Turkey

Abdullah Önden
Yalova University, Turkey

ABSTRACT

Big data and big data analytics have contributed to the collection of large amounts of data. This has led to the transformation to data-driven supply chain (DDSC) structures. The supply chain coordination capability (SCCC) has also been strengthened in DDSC. In this study, the effect of DDSC on SCCC and the moderator effect of supplier coordination (SCO) have been investigated. The research was carried out in the manufacturing firms. Three hundred eighty-three pieces of data were obtained between August and December 2021 by the simple random sampling method. Two hypotheses were developed. Simple regression analysis was used to test the first hypothesis, and moderator effect analysis was performed with the SPSS process to test the second hypothesis. It has been determined that the DDSC has a significant effect on the SCCC. In addition, SCO has a moderating effect, and when there is a high SCO, the DDSC has a greater effect on the SCCC.

DOI: 10.4018/978-1-6684-7455-6.ch012

INTRODUCTION

In today's world, where the transition from Industry 4.0 to Industry 5.0 is experienced, the level of commitment to information technologies and the level of benefiting from information technologies is increasing. "Big data (BD)" and smart systems that came with Industry 4.0 have taken their place in all industrial activities and have enabled the transition to big data-based applications (Shin et al., 2018). BD has enabled the collection and storage of large amounts of data. "Big data analytics (BDA)", on the other hand, enabled BD analyzes (Tsai et al., 2015). The competitive advantage gained by performing real-time data analysis with BDA has played a triggering role in the transformation of organizations into data-based structures (Sundarakani et al., 2021). This change has also taken place in supply chains. Supply chain integration is also increasing in supply chains where the use of information technologies is increasing (Khanuja and Jain, 2021). Thus, the gap between companies and organizations in the supply chain is closed, contributing to the formation of sustainable supply chain structures (Bag et al., 2020). BD and BDA usage approaches in the supply chain have developed the data-driven supply chain (DDSC) structure (Yu et al., 2018).

DDSC provides various advantages at different nodes of the supply chain (Biswas and Sen, 2017). Li and Liu (2019) demonstrated the benefits of BD and BDA in the design and development of the supply chain, purchasing, manufacturing, logistics, customer service, marketing, and sales stages, and developed a DDSC management model based on these benefits. Thekkoote (2021) states that DDSC has developed supply chain applications especially in terms of information sharing, integration, and coordination, and has increased customer satisfaction to the highest level. Supply chain coordination (SCC) has been discussed in the literature from four different perspectives (Kanda and Deshmukh, 2008). The first perspective is fully collaborative working within the supply chain (Larsen, 2003). The second perspective is partial collaborative work within the supply chain (Simatupang and Sridharan, 2002). The third perspective is coordination based on a win-win policy (McClellan, 2003). The fourth perspective is coordination against the difficulties encountered in the supply chain (Xu and Beamon, 2006).

Information technologies play an active role in the rise of SCC (Bi et al., 2011). In addition, the DDSC structure, which is mainly used in supply chain management of information technologies, plays an active role in raising SCC. Supply chain coordination capability (SCCC) is needed to ensure coordination within the supply chain, especially in the Resource-based view (RBV) approach. This capability is used to establish an effective coordination structure within the supply chain. In addition, the existing supplier coordination (SCO) between suppliers also indicate the existence of SCCC. At this point, it is expected that there is a significantly relationship among DDSC, SCCC and SCO. This expectation creates two basic research questions. The research questions that inspired this study are as follows:

- **Research Question 1:** Does DDSC have a significant positive effect on SCCC?
- **Research Question 2:** Does SCO have a moderating role in the relation of DDSC and SCCC?

This paper is designed as seven parts. In the second part, the concepts discussed in the research and the theoretical background are mentioned. In the third part, the related literature is given, and the models and hypotheses of the research are presented. In the fourth part, the methodology of the research is included, and the sample area of the research and the scales used in the research are explained. In the fifth part, the findings of the research are explained. In the sixth part, the results based on the findings are explained. In the seventh, the implications of the research are presented, and suggestions are developed.

THEORETICAL BACKGROUND AND CONCEPTUAL FRAMEWORK

Data-Driven Supply Chain

Today, due to the rapid change in customer/supplier demands and needs, supply chain professionals expect instant data to be collected, analyzed, and made available instead of analysis based on past data (Yu et al., 2019). Changing and revolutionizing the understanding of competition in commercial transactions, BD plays an active role in meeting the expectations of supply chain professionals today (Sundarakani et al., 2021). In the literature, BD is discussed in five basic features: "Volume, veracity, velocity, variety, and value (5Vs)" (Lycett, 2013; Anuradha, 2015). At the same time, BD provides four main benefits: cost reduction, better understanding of customer needs, improved process efficiency, and better identification of risks (Sommanawat et al., 2019). With these features and benefits, BD technologies are used in different industries and fields, and transform companies into data-based organizational structures (Kamble et al., 2020). BDA, in which analyzes are made using BD technologies, is the set of techniques used in the process of collecting, preparing, processing, and transforming data into useful values (Jeble et al., 2018). BDA provides competitive advantage by making the data collected with large amount, different quality, and different acquisition times with various analysis techniques (Mondal and Samaddar, 2021). In supply chain management, BDA ensures the optimization of the supply chain by collecting information and using it in decision-making processes (Fernández-Caramés et al., 2019). Kamble and Gunasekaran (2020) point out that supply chains should be transformed into a big data driven supply chain structure for BDA applications to become applicable. Thus, BD transfer can take place (Wamba et al., 2017). In addition, by obtaining real-time customer data, demand forecasts can be made more accurately, and cargoes can be moved on time by obtaining real-time decisions about changes in orders (Gawankar et al., 2020). Based on the use of information technologies, DDSC also provides benefits in the successful management and development of the collaborative relationship between supply chain members (Wu et al., 2006).

Biswas and Sen (2017) emphasized the importance of BD in the supply chain and pointed out the existence of the general structure of DDSC. The feature that distinguishes this structure from other supply chain structures is that the data of suppliers, manufacturers, warehouses, distributors, and customers are made accessible to all stakeholders simultaneously by using cloud technology. Thus, with the help of DDSC, it is possible to manage and operate the knowledge-based supply chain and gain competitive advantage (Waller and Fawcett, 2013). Kamboj and Rana (2021) stated that there should be an integration of traditional supply chain structures and BD technologies (Blockchain, cloud technology, etc.) to create the DDSC structure. This integration offers great opportunities to the supply chain in many areas such as value creation, customer loyalty and customer satisfaction. The benefits of DDSC have made it increasingly important in logistics and supply chain literature (Govindan et al., 2018).

Common BDA technologies should be used for efficient data transfer of all stakeholders involved in the DDSC supply chain. Another aspect of increasing the overall success of effective data transfer is the recognition of BD as one of the key assets of the supply chain (Yu et al., 2019). Thus, BD used for data transfer is accepted as one of the main sources of the supply chain and its effective use is theoretically based on RBV (Dubey et al., 2019). The RBV theory points out that companies tend to their resources and provide competitive advantage by using resources effectively. In this respect, BD is the main source for the DDSC structure. To create competitive advantage, it is necessary to turn to the BD source and reveal the tacit knowledge (Sanders, 2014).

Supply Chain Coordination Capability

Supply chain coordination (SCC) is the mutual benefit-based joint action of all actors involved in the supply chain to achieve the supply chain objectives to supply chain integration (Simatupang et al., 2002). SCC helps to redesign resources to improve supply chain performance by raising it from the intra-firm coordination level to the supply chain level (Lee, 2000). SCC contributes to the product development processes of manufacturing companies and contributes to the creation of more qualified products (Mostaghel et al., 2019). At the same time, SCC plays an active role in increasing supply chain performance (Kanda and Deshmukh, 2007).

Kanda and Deshmukh (2006) suggest the establishment of the SCC mechanism and the development of "Supply chain contracts, Information sharing, Information technology, Collaborative decision-making, Frequent meetings with supply chain members, Technical assistantship" within this mechanism. In addition, Kanda and Deshmukh (2008) explain that the concept of SCC is handled from different perspectives in the literature and classify these perspectives as follows: "Resource sharing, Risk and reward sharing, Holistic view of coordination, Workflow and resource dependency, Mutuality, Joint promotional activities, forecasting, Joint decision making, Benefit sharing". SCC activities can occur between different relationships within the supply chain. These are (i) product and distribution coordination, (ii) purchasing and production coordination, (iii) production and inventory coordination, (iv) distribution and inventory coordination (Arshinder et al., 2011).

If SCC is accepted as a basic mechanism, three basic services are expected from this mechanism. These are (i) optimizing the supply chain, (ii) improving the supply chain, (iii) generating viable solutions throughout the supply chain system (Vosooghidizaji et al., 2020). In addition, this mechanism is expected to take an active role in both forward logistics and reverse logistics processes (Su et al., 2019). This mechanism also should operate by considering the legal regulations enacted by governments (Zhang and Yousaf, 2020). A successfully established SCC mechanism is critical for both companies and supply chains (Huo et al., 2015). Therefore, successful SCC mechanism is expected to increase supplier-customer coordination (Li et al., 2018).

There are two main benefits that SCCC provides to supply chain members. The first is to provide information about supply chain activities by providing information flow. The second is the participation of all member companies in the supply chain decision-making processes (Patnayakuni et al., 2006). Teece (2007) expresses the coordination capabilities of firms among dynamic capabilities. At this point, it can be said that SCCC, which expresses the capabilities of coordination activities in the supply chain, is among the dynamic capabilities (Gao and Tian, 2014). Cao and Jiang (2020) cite SCCC as one of the sub-dimensions of supply chain dynamic capabilities. Asamoah et al. (2021), on the other hand, explains that SCCC is among the intra-organizational and inter-organizational capabilities within the scope of supply chain management. In this case, SCCC is basically among the capabilities of the firm and affects all supply chain members (Wu et al., 2018). At the same time, due to the "Bullwhip effect", SCCCs owned by all supply chain member companies also affect SCCCs of other companies (Holweg et al., 2005). For this reason, companies in the same supply chain must act in a synchronized manner.

Supplier Coordination Relationship

Firms need to coordinate with their suppliers to avoid disruptions in production processes, to complete production successfully, and to prepare the final products until the final delivery time. In the literature, coordination is discussed as vertical and horizontal. Coordination between firms refers to horizontal coordination, and supplier coordination refers to vertical coordination (Fan et al., 2018). Buvik and John (2000) state that if firms are insufficient to adapt to rapidly changing environmental conditions, vertical coordination increase transactions difficulties. The level of supplier coordination relationship is important for achieving common goals and successful supply chain integration (Simatupang et al., 2002). High supplier coordination has a positive effect on supplier relations and supplier collaborations. Jayaram et al. (2011) explain that supplier coordination relationship increases firm performance in terms of flexibility and quality.

Vanichchinchai (2021) points out that supplier relations have a total of 2 sub-dimensions. These are "supplier coordination", which means joint information flow and joint action with suppliers, and "supplier collaboration", which means cooperation with suppliers. Mettler and Rohner (2009) state that supplier relationship management is based on two basic approaches, "management-oriented" and "technology focused", and supplier coordination is included in the management-oriented approach. At this point, it can be mentioned that supplier coordination can be achieved with successful management outputs. In addition, the coordination phase in management processes observes, manages, and takes control of changes and complexities.

The buyer-supplier relationship applies strategies to act in joint collaborations to increase their current business volumes and market shares. The scope of these strategies also includes strengthening the supplier coordination relationship (Jap, 1999). When the SCO relationship level is high, the speed of information exchange between firms and suppliers is high. Thus, information about order and demand changes can be shared simultaneously between both suppliers and manufacturers. This situation affects the general coordination level of the supply chain by reflecting on other phases of the supply chain. A low SCO relationship is expected to have a negative impact on SCCC. In this study, the supplier coordination relationship is handled at three levels as low, medium and high, and it is explained how the relationships between DDSC and SCCC are formed at each level.

RELATED LITERATURE AND HYPOTHESES DEVELOPMENT

In the DDCC literature, it is emphasized that supply chain structures are based on information technologies. In the SCC literature, on the other hand, it is seen that the concept of coordination is handled with different approaches. Kumar and Singh (2017) classified the coordination agendas in the literature. Within these classes, there are two groups based on knowledge and coordination of knowledge, namely "Information sharing with all members" and "Data integration among internal functions through networking". It can be clearly stated that the most suitable supply chain structure for both groups is the DDSC structure. When the concept of SCC is handled with an RBV-based approach, SCCC is mentioned by highlighting its supply chain capabilities. In this study, a literature review of studies dealing with the relationships between DDSC and SCCC was conducted.

Some of the studies discussed in the literature are as follows. Yu et al. (2018) examined the effect of DDSC on supply chain capabilities in their research in the Chinese manufacturing industry. According to the research, the DDSC has a positive and significant effect on the SCCC of the firms. Govindan et al. (2018), who classify the studies in the fields of supply chain and logistics management of big data analysis, emphasized that there has been an increase in academic studies since 2012. Yu et al (2020) found that the supply chain based on upstream and downstream data, in a sample of 296 e-commerce companies operating internationally, has a statistically significant effect on supplier-customer integration. In 193 sample working in different manufacturing areas, Asamoah et al. (2021) found that companies' inter-organizational information sharing systems in DDSC structures have a significant effect on their supply chain capabilities (supply chain information exchange, supply chain integration, supply chain coordination, supply chain responsiveness). Wu et al. (2006) determined that the supply chain integration, coordination, and responsive capabilities of the firms play an active role in maximizing the benefit from supply chain information technologies. Lee et al. (2014) explained that the coordination and responsiveness capabilities of the firms increase the visibility in the supply chain and increase the supply chain performance. Kamboj and Rana (2021) have shown among practical implications that coordination and responsiveness practices play an active role in increasing performance in DDSC. In a study conducted in the sample area of 19 milk producers, Bin Dost et al. (2016) explained that SCCC has a mediating effect in the relationship between knowledge-based management practices and supply chain performance.

In general, according to studies examining the relationships between DDSC and SCCC in the literature, it is expected that there is a significant relationship between DDSC and SCCC. At this point, the first hypothesis is formed to determine the effect of DDSC on SCCC to contribute to the literature and find answers to research questions. To test whether the supplier coordination relationship level has a mediator effect in the relationship between DDSC and SCCC, our second hypothesis is formed. The research models for testing the two hypotheses of this research are as seen in Figure 1. The research hypotheses are as follows:

H1: DDSC has a significant effect on SCCC.
H2: SCO has a moderating effect in the relationship between DDSC and SCCC

Figure 1. Research models

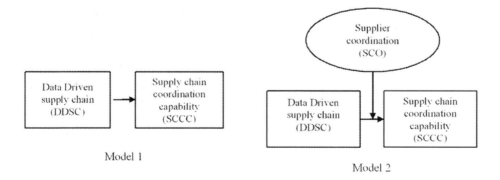

METHODOLOGY

Scales of Variables

To determine the DDSC, SCCC and SCO levels of manufacturing firms operating in Trabzon Arsin Organized Industrial Zone in Turkey, validity and reliability tested scales in the literature are used. DDSC scale has been developed by Yu et al. (2018). The scale consists of single dimension and 4 items. Yu et al.

stated that the reliability and validity levels of the scale has been appropriate (Cronbach's Alpha=0.887; AVE=0.666; CR=0.889). The SCCC scale has been developed by Wu et al (2006) as a sub-dimension of the supply chain capabilities scale. In the study by Yu et al (2018), SCCC scale has been applied. The SCCC scale consists of a single dimension and a total of 5 items. Yu et al. (2018) stated that the reliability and validity levels of the scale are high (Cronbach's Alpha=0.944; AVE=0.774; CR=0.945). The SCO scale is included in the literature as a sub-dimension of the supply chain relations scale. The SCO scale has been obtained from the supply chain relations scale developed by Lee et al (2007) and used in the literature by Vanichchinchai (2019) and Vanichchinchai (2021). The SCO scale consists of a single dimension and a total of 5 items. Vanichchinchai (2021) has determined that the reliability and validity levels of the scale were high (Cronbach's Alpha=0.863; AVE=0.560; CR=0.864). The scales of the variable were first translated into Turkish, and the appropriateness of the translation was determined by experts in the field. Scale items were arranged in a 7-point likert scale ("1" strongly disagree, "7" strongly agree.). In addition, questions about demographic variables were asked to the participants in the questionnaire form. Demographic characteristics of the participants are presented in the sampling section.

Sampling

Trabzon Arsin Organized Industrial Zone was chosen as the sample area. Manufacturing companies in the industrial zone are: Wood, Wood Products and Cork Products Manufacturing (5 firms), Basic Metal Industry (6 firms), Machinery and Equipment Manufacturing Not Classified Elsewhere (5 firms), Manufacturing of Leather and Related Products (2 firms), Manufacturing of Other Non-Metallic Mineral Products (4 firms), Fabricated Metal Products (2 firms), Manufacturing of Food Products (21 firms), Manufacturing of Clothing Items (1 firm), Paper and Paper Products Manufacturing (2 firms), Manufacturing of Rubber and Plastic Products (7 firms), Production of Printing and Reproduction of Recorded Media (5 firms), Manufacturing of Chemicals and Chemical Products (5 firms), Furniture Manufacturing (3 firms), Motor Land Vehicle, Trailer(Trailer and Semi-Trailer Manufacturing (3 firms) and Other (7 firms) (TOSBOL, 2022). In addition, this organized industrial zone employs approximately 5 thousand people. In the selection of the sample area, the participants were determined by choosing a random sample within the organized industry. Yu et al (2018) explained that not only CEOs, but also operations managers, suppliers and experts who are involved in supply processes can be considered as participants in choosing participants about the DDSC. At this point, while determining the participants in the research, senior and middle level managers who are involved in the supply processes of the firms and specialists who take part in the supply chain processes (warehouse manager, stock control specialist, vehicle driver, handling equipment users, intra-production logistics personnel, etc.) were preferred. Questionnaire application was carried out between August and December 2021 through face-to-face and electronic questionnaire application. Demographic findings of the participants are presented in Table 1.

Table 1. Frequency of the sample

Gender	No	%	Industrial Area	No	%
Woman	64	16.71	Wood, Wood Products and Cork Products Manufacturing	16	4.18
Man	319	83.29	Base Metal Industry	22	5.74
Total	383	100	Machinery and Equipment Manufacturing Not Elsewhere Classified	17	4.44
Age	**No**	**%**	Manufacturing of Leather and Related Products	12	3.13
18-30	89	23.24	Manufacturing of Other Non-Metallic Mineral Products	27	7.05
31-40	141	36,81	Fabricated Metal Products	21	5.48
41-50	108	28,20	Manufacturing of Food Products	83	21.67
50 +	45	11,75	Manufacturing of Clothing	22	5.74
Total	383	100	Paper and Paper Products Manufacturing	32	8.36
Tenure	**No**	**%**	Manufacturing of Rubber and Plastic Products	28	7.31
0-5	97	25,33	Printing and Reproduction Manufacturing of Recorded Media	23	6.01
5-10	117	30,55	Manufacturing of Chemicals and Chemical Products	9	2.35
10-20	121	31,59	Furniture Manufacturing	13	3.39
20 +	48	12,53	Motor Land Vehicle, Trailer (Trailer and Semi-Trailer) Manufacturing	16	4.18
Total	383	100	Other	42	10.97
			Total	383	100

FINDINGS

Reliability and Validity of the Scales

To determine the relationship among DDSC, SCCC and SCO variables, scales dealing with these variables are used in the literature. In the Questionnaire design section, the reliability and validity information of the scales are included. In this study, as explained in the Sampling section, the sample area consists of businesses operating in Trabzon-Arsin Industrial Zone. "The Kolmogorov and Smirnov normality test" was conducted to determine whether our data set based on the data obtained from the sample area has a normal distribution. As can be seen in Table 2, Asymp. Sig. values are significant. Therefore, it is considered that it does not show a normal distribution. However, when the skewness and kurtosis values were examined, it was determined that the values were between 1.5 and +1.5. Tabachnick and Fidell (2013) explain that if the kurtosis and skewness values are between 1.5 and +1.5, the data set of the variables has a normal distribution. At this point, it has been determined that our data set has a normal distribution.

Table 2. One-Sample Kolmogorov-Smirnov normality test, skewness and kurtosis values

Scales	N	Mean	SD	Kolmogorov-Smirnov Z	Asymp. Sig.	Skewness	Kurtosis
DDSCM	383	5.18	1.25	2.306	0.000	- 0.657	- 0.198
SCCC	383	4.94	1.13	1.553	0.016	- 0.253	- 0.736
SCO	383	5.10	1.07	2.007	0.001	- 0.400	- 0.468

The factor loads of the expressions used in the scales of the variables are determined by exploratory factor analysis (EFA). The proficiency level for factor analysis of the sample area is determined by Kaiser Meyer Olkin (KMO) and Bartlett's Test of Sphericity. For the sample area to be at a sufficient level, the KMO test value must be greater than 0.60 and Bartlett's Test of Sphericity must be less than 0.01 (Tabachnick and Fidell, 2013). As seen in Table 3, the KMO values of the variables are greater than 0.60 ($KMO_{DDSCM}=0.837$, $KMO_{SCCC}=0.820$, $KMO_{SCO}=0.865$), and Bartlett's Test of Sphericity test significance values are less than 0.01 (sig. = 0.000). These findings explain that our sample area is sufficient.

Table 3. KMO and Bartlett's test of sphericity tests

		DDSCM	SCCC	SCO
Kaiser-Meyer-Olkin Measure of Sampling Adequacy.		0.837	0.820	0.865
Bartlett's Test of Sphericity	Approx. Chi-Square	849.017	992.173	868.517
	df	6	10	10
	Sig.	0.000	0.000	0.000

EFA analysis is performed to determine the factor loads of the scale items. The reason for the EFA analysis is that the original scale items are applied in a different language and in a different sample area. This study was translated into Turkish and applied. In social science studies, factor loads of each item in EFA analysis results should be greater than 0.32 (Büyüköztürk et al., 2017). As seen in Table 4, all factor loads of scale items are higher than 0.60. This situation explains that the scale items have sufficient factor level. In addition, the total explanation variance percentages of the scales are above 60%.

AVE and CR values are calculated to determine the convergent and divergent validity of the scales. For the scales to be valid, the AVE value should be greater than 0.5 and the CR values should be greater than the AVE value (Yaşlıoğlu, 2017; Yildirim et al., 2022). As seen in Table 4, all the AVE values of the scales are greater than 0.5. At the same time, the CR value of each scale is greater than the AVE value. In addition, the reliability analysis results of the scales are presented in Table 4. The Cronbach's Alpha value of the DDSC scale is 0.889, the Cronbach's Alpha value of the SCCC scale is 0.872, and the Cronbach's Alpha value of the SCO scale is 0.871. These values explain that the scales are at a high level of reliability.

Table 4. Exploratory factor analysis findings

Items	Factor Loads	Eigenvalues / Total Variance Percentage	AVE / CR	Cronbach's Alpha
DDSCM2- "Aggregate customer data and make them widely available to improve service level, capture cross-and up-selling opportunities, and enable design-to-value."	0.883	3.003 / % 75.07	0.751 / 0.923	0.889
DDSCM3- "Implement advanced demand forecasting and supply planning across suppliers."	0.877			
DDSCM1- "Build consistent interoperable, cross-functional department databases to enable concurrent engineering, rapid experimentation and simulation, and co-creation."	0.859			
DDSCM4- "Implement lean manufacturing and model production virtually (such as digital factory) to create process transparency, develop dashboards, and visualize bottlenecks."	0.847			
SCCC4- "Our company has reduced coordination costs more than our competitors."	0.868	3.336 / % 66.76	0.667 / 0.908	0.872
SCCC5- "Our company can conduct the coordination activities at less cost than our competitors."	0.856			
SCCC1- "Our company is more efficient in coordination activities with our partners than are our competitors with theirs."	0.814			
SCCC3- "Our company spends less time coordinating transactions with our partners than our competitors with theirs."	0.800			
SCCC2- "Our company conducts transaction follow-up activities more efficiently with our partners than do our competitors with theirs."	0.739			
SCO2- "Our company and suppliers coordinate and exchange information at operational level."	0.831	3.304 / % 66.07	0.660 / 0.906	0.871
SCO5- "Our company and suppliers jointly forecast customer demand as well as plan production and sales."	0.826			
SCO4- "Our company and suppliers jointly resolve upfront problems or contingencies, effectively."	0.815			
SCO3- "Our company and suppliers urgently inform each other when contingencies occur."	0.803			
SCO1- "Our company and suppliers exchange important business information at strategic level."	0.788			

Test of the Research Hypothesis

Correlation analysis is performed in the SPSS package program to explain the interrelationships among the variables included in the research. The correlation relationships obtained as a result of the correlation analysis are as seen in Table 5. The highest correlation is seen between DDSC and the SCO ($r(383)=0.784$, $p<0.01$). The correlation between the DDSC and the SCCC variables is high ($r(383)=0.775$, $p<0.01$). Likewise, the relationship between supply chain coordination ability and supplier coordination is at a high level ($r(383)=0.744$, $p<0.01$). The high correlation relationship between the variables indicates that the hypotheses determined in the research are formed correctly.

Table 5. Correlation relations of variables

Variables	Mean	S.D.	DDSCM	SCCC	SCO
DDSCM	5.18	5.18	1		
SCCC	4.94	4.94	0.775*	1	
SCO	5.10	5.10	0.784*	0.744*	1
Notes: * p < 0.01					

Simple regression analysis was performed with the help of SPSS package program to test the first research question and the first hypothesis formed in this direction. In the regression model, DDSC is determined as the independent variable, and SCCC is determined as the dependent variable. The findings of the simple regression analysis model are explained in Table 6. As a result of the analysis, it is determined that the DDSC has a significant effect on the SCCC ($\beta = 0.702$, p <0.01). This finding proves that *the first hypothesis is supported.*

Table 6. Simple regression analysis findings

Model		Unstandardized Coefficients		Standardized Coefficients	t	Sig.
		B	Std. Error	Beta		
1	(Constant)	1.310	.156		8.394	.000
	DDSC	.702	.029	.775	23.950	.000
Note: Dependent variable is SCCC						

The second research question of the study is to determine whether SCO has a moderating effect on the relationship between DDSC and SCCC. In this context, the second hypothesis of the research is formed. SPSS process is used to test the moderator effect. To test the moderator effect model, Model-1 structure is applied in the SPSS process program. In the moderator model, DDSC is determined as the independent variable (X), SCCC as the dependent variable (Y), and SCO as the moderator variable (W). To determine the moderator factor, it must be calculated by multiplying the dependent and independent variables and the interaction value (X.W) must be found (Baron and Kenny, 1986). In addition, it is aimed to determine whether there are differences in the relations between the DDSC and the SCCC according to the level of SCO with the moderator model analysis. Outputs of the moderator model are as seen in Table 7.

The significance level of the variables included in the model for the moderating relationship is expected to be at an acceptable level. At the same time, LLCI and ULCI values, which explain the lower and upper security levels, are expected to be different from 0 (Hayes, 2013). As seen in Table 7, the significance level of all variables and interactional effect status is sufficient (p<0.005). It is also seen that LLCI and ULCI values are different from "0". These findings explain that the moderator model is significant ($\beta = 0.0701$, p <0.05). According to the model summary, the percentage of DDSC and SCO variables explaining the SCCC variable (R^2) is approximately 65%.

Moderating Role of Supplier Coordination Level

The SCO, which is the moderator variable, is divided into three categories and determined as low, medium, and high supplier coordination. The effect of DDSC on SCCC at low SCO level is 0.5244 (p<0.01). The effect of DDSC on SCCC at medium SCO level is 0.6030 (p<0.01). The effect of DDSC on SCCC at high SCO level is 0.6680'tür (p<0.01). According to the findings, it is clearly seen that the effect of DDSC on SCCC increases as the SCO level increases. In Figure 2, the relationship between DDSC and SCCC is presented graphically according to SCO levels.

Table 7. Moderator model analysis findings

Variables	Coeff	S.E.	t	p	LLCI	ULCI
Constant	4.8872	0.0433	112.8062	0.0000	4.8021	4.9724
DDSC *(X)*	0.5961	0.0573	10.3963	0.0000	0.4834	0.7089
SCC *(W)*	0.4099	0.0554	7.3918	0.0000	0.3008	0.5189
Int_1 *(X.W)*	0.0701	0.0339	2.0644	0.0397	0.0033	0.1368
Low SCO	0.5244	0.0586	8.9461	0.0000	0.4089	0.6393
Medium SCO	0.6030	0.0583	10.3390	0.0000	0.4884	0.7177
High SCO	0.6688	0.0749	8.9304	0.0000	0.5215	0.8160
Model Summary	R	R^2	F		P	
	0.8080	0.6528	237.5577		0.0000	

Figure 2. Graphical representation of moderator effect

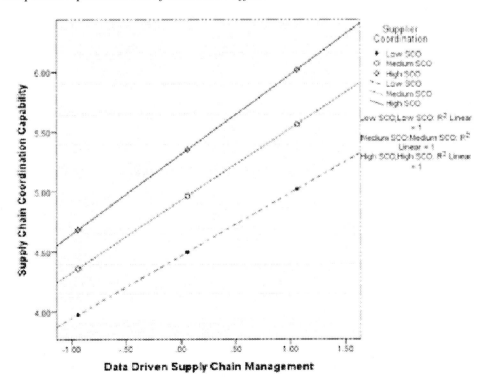

CONCLUSION AND DISCUSSION

This study has two main purposes. The first is to determine whether DDSC has a significant effect on SCCC. The second is to determine whether SCO has a moderator effect on the relationship between DDSC and SCCC. For the first purpose, a simple regression analysis was performed based on the data collected from the sample area. As in the analysis findings, it is concluded that DDSC has a positive and significant effect on SCCC. Thus, the expectations that exist in the formation of research hypotheses are met. Yu et al (2018) found that DDSC practices positively affect all SCC, including coordination. This research is in parallel with the result we obtained. At this point, it indicates that DDSC is the appropriate supply chain structure for SCCC upgrade. It is known that SCC, one of the knowledge-based capabilities among supply chain capabilities, increases supply chain integration and improves overall supply chain performance (Asamoah et al., 2021). The BD-based nature of DDSC reveals the importance of data. Thus, DDSC can be shown as an ideal supply chain for the development of knowledge-based capabilities. In the research conducted in the clustered manufacturing industry, it has been determined that the data-based work of the firms serving in various manufacturing areas is at a high level. In addition, it has been evaluated that manufacturing companies need high coordination in supply chain activities before, during and after production, and this can be achieved with DDSC.

Considering the relationship levels of manufacturing companies with their suppliers, it has been observed that manufacturing companies with low relationship levels have a lower relationship between DDSC and SCCC. At the high level of supplier coordination, it has been determined that firms perform DDSC applications more, SCCC is more developed, and the relationship between DDSC and SCCC is higher. At this point, it can be clearly said that there is a significant relationship between the supply chain structure of a firm and its coordination ability, and this relationship differs according to the level of coordination relationship with the suppliers. The simultaneous exchange of data with suppliers is beneficial in planning and revising production plans. It also contributes to the prevention of disruptions in production lines by improving material supply operations. Finally, with the arrival of Industry 5.0, it is clearly seen that the commitment to BD and BDA will increase more, thus DDSC structures will gain more importance, supply chain capabilities will be further developed, and supplier coordination relations will also improve.

IMPLICATION AND LIMITATION

Developing information technologies, especially in the development of information-based supply chain capabilities, will lead to DDSC structures, which will increase supply chain integration and successful resource planning can be achieved with simultaneous information flow among all supply chain members. In this case, supply chain professionals are recommended to prepare the appropriate infrastructure for DDSC management. This study points out that it is imperative to utilize BD in the manufacturing industry to respond promptly to customer demands. In addition, this study explains the need to collect data on current customers and prospective customers and make the data meaningful with BDA techniques. At this point, it should not be forgotten that the level of supplier coordination plays an active role. For this reason, it is recommended to supply chain managers working in the manufacturing industry to increase the information technology use capabilities of supply chain members and to create high supplier coordination within the supply chain. Supply chain managers are required to develop joint databases with customers and suppliers, to perform production data analysis and to provide simultaneous data flow between departments in order to improve their production capabilities. Supply chain managers are also required to develop joint databases with customers and suppliers, to perform production data analysis and to provide simultaneous data flow between departments to improve their manufacturing capabilities. Thus, it will be easier for production companies to take place in the market under tight competition conditions. The increasing importance of DDSC in the last period motivates academicians to conduct academic studies on this subject. Therefore, there is a need for academic studies examining the relationships between DDSC and other supply chain capabilities, and it is suggested that academics should focus on working in this direction.

The sample area constraint of this research is manufacturing firms. If academic studies are carried out in different industrial areas, it will contribute to the literature. The fact that the research was conducted under pandemic conditions constitutes the time constraint of the study. Therefore, reconsidering the study to determine what differences can be achieved after the pandemic will contribute to the literature. This study was handled in the form of a survey application. The questionnaires were collected based on the subjective evaluations of the employees. Therefore, subjective evaluations are among the research limitations. The methodological limitation of this study is the research method based on relationship analysis. It is suggested to explain the relationship among DDSC, SCCC and SCO with different methodology applications.

REFERENCES

Anuradha, J. (2015). A brief introduction on Big Data 5Vs characteristics and Hadoop technology. *Procedia Computer Science*, *48*, 319–324. doi:10.1016/j.procs.2015.04.188

Arshinder, K., Kanda, A., & Deshmukh, S. G. (2011). A review on supply chain coordination: coordination mechanisms, managing uncertainty and research directions. *Supply chain coordination under uncertainty*, 39-82. doi:10.1007/978-3-642-19257-9_3

Asamoah, D., Agyei-Owusu, B., Andoh-Baidoo, F. K., & Ayaburi, E. (2021). Inter-organizational systems use and supply chain performance: Mediating role of supply chain management capabilities. *International Journal of Information Management*, *58*, 102195. doi:10.1016/j.ijinfomgt.2020.102195

Bag, S., Wood, L. C., Xu, L., Dhamija, P., & Kayikci, Y. (2020). Big data analytics as an operational excellence approach to enhance sustainable supply chain performance. *Resources, Conservation and Recycling*, *153*, 104559. doi:10.1016/j.resconrec.2019.104559

Baron, R. M., & Kenny, D. A. (1986). The moderator–mediator variable distinction in social psychological research: Conceptual, strategic, and statistical considerations. *Journal of Personality and Social Psychology*, *51*(6), 1173–1182. doi:10.1037/0022-3514.51.6.1173 PMID:3806354

Bi, R., Kam, B., & Smyrnios, K. X. (2011). IT Resources, Supply Chain Coordination Competency And Firm Performance: An Empirical Study. *PACIS 2011 Proceedings*, 27. https://aisel.aisnet.org/pacis2011/27

Bin Dost, M. K., & Rehman, C. A. (2016). Significance of knowledge management practices effecting supply chain performance. *Pakistan Journal of Commerce and Social Sciences*, *10*(3), 659–686. https://www.econstor.eu/handle/10419/188273

Biswas, S., & Sen, J. (2017). A Proposed Architecture for Big Data Driven Supply Chain Analytics. *The IUP Journal of Supply Chain Management, 13*(3), 7-33. https://doi.org//arXiv.1705.04958 doi:10.48550

Buvik, A., & John, G. (2000). When does vertical coordination improve industrial purchasing relationships? *Journal of Marketing, 64*(4), 52–64. doi:10.1509/jmkg.64.4.52.18075

Büyüköztürk, Ş., Çakmak, E. K., Akgün, Ö. E., Karadeniz, Ş., & Demirel, F. (2017). *Bilimsel araştırma yöntemleri*. Pegem Atıf İndeksi. doi:10.14527/9789944919289

Cao, Y., & Jiang, H. (2020, April). Dimension construction and test of dynamic capability of enterprise supply chain. In *2020 International Conference on E-Commerce and Internet Technology (ECIT)* (pp. 310-314). IEEE. 10.1109/ECIT50008.2020.00078

Dubey, R., Gunasekaran, A., Childe, S. J., Blome, C., & Papadopoulos, T. (2019). Big data and predictive analytics and manufacturing performance: Integrating institutional theory, resource-based view and big data culture. *British Journal of Management, 30*(2), 341–361. doi:10.1111/1467-8551.12355

Fan, J., Kwasnica, A. M., & Thomas, D. J. (2018). Paying for teamwork: Supplier coordination with endogenously selected groups. *Production and Operations Management, 27*(6), 1089–1101. doi:10.1111/poms.12856

Fernández-Caramés, T. M., Blanco-Novoa, O., Froiz-Míguez, I., & Fraga-Lamas, P. (2019). Towards an autonomous industry 4.0 warehouse: A UAV and blockchain-based system for inventory and traceability applications in big data-driven supply chain management. *Sensors (Basel), 19*(10), 2394. doi:10.339019102394 PMID:31130644

Gao, T., & Tian, Y. (2014). Mechanism of supply chain coordination cased on dynamic capability framework-the mediating role of manufacturing capabilities. *Journal of Industrial Engineering and Management, 7*(5), 1250–1267. doi:10.3926/jiem.1266

Gawankar, S. A., Gunasekaran, A., & Kamble, S. (2020). A study on investments in the big data-driven supply chain, performance measures and organisational performance in Indian retail 4.0 context. *International Journal of Production Research, 58*(5), 1574–1593. doi:10.1080/00207543.2019.1668070

Govindan, K., Cheng, T. E., Mishra, N., & Shukla, N. (2018). Big data analytics and application for logistics and supply chain management. *Transportation Research Part E, Logistics and Transportation Review, 114*, 343–349. doi:10.1016/j.tre.2018.03.011

Hayes, A. F. (2013). *Introduction to mediation, moderation, and conditional process analysis: Methodology in the Social Sciences*. Kindle Edition.

Holweg, M., Disney, S., Holmström, J., & Småros, J. (2005). Supply chain collaboration: Making sense of the strategy continuum. *European Management Journal, 23*(2), 170–181. doi:10.1016/j.emj.2005.02.008

Huo, B., Zhang, C., & Zhao, X. (2015). The effect of IT and relationship commitment on supply chain coordination: A contingency and configuration approach. *Information & Management, 52*(6), 728–740. doi:10.1016/j.im.2015.06.007

Jap, S. D. (1999). Pie-expansion efforts: Collaboration processes in buyer–supplier relationships. *JMR, Journal of Marketing Research, 36*(4), 461–475. doi:10.1177/002224379903600405

Jayaram, J., Xu, K., & Nicolae, M. (2011). The direct and contingency effects of supplier coordination and customer coordination on quality and flexibility performance. *International Journal of Production Research*, *49*(1), 59–85. doi:10.1080/00207543.2010.508935

Jeble, S., Dubey, R., Childe, S., Papadopoulos, T., Roubaud, D., & Prakash, A. (2018). Impact of big data and predictive analytics capability on supply chain sustainability. *International Journal of Logistics Management*, *29*(2), 513–538. doi:10.1108/IJLM-05-2017-0134

Kamble, S. S., & Gunasekaran, A. (2020). Big data-driven supply chain performance measurement system: A review and framework for implementation. *International Journal of Production Research*, *58*(1), 65–86. doi:10.1080/00207543.2019.1630770

Kamble, S. S., Gunasekaran, A., & Gawankar, S. A. (2020). Achieving sustainable performance in a data-driven agriculture supply chain: A review for research and applications. *International Journal of Production Economics*, *219*, 179–194. doi:10.1016/j.ijpe.2019.05.022

Kamboj, S., & Rana, S. (2021). Big data-driven supply chain and performance: a resource-based view. *The TQM Journal*. doi:10.1108/TQM-02-2021-0036

Kanda, A., & Deshmukh, S. G. (2006). A coordination-based perspective on the procurement process in the supply chain. *International Journal of Value Chain Management*, *1*(2), 117–138. doi:10.1504/IJVCM.2006.011181

Kanda, A., & Deshmukh, S. G. (2007). Supply chain coordination issues: An SAP-LAP framework. *Asia Pacific Journal of Marketing and Logistics*, *19*(3), 240–264. doi:10.1108/13555850710772923

Kanda, A., & Deshmukh, S. G. (2008). Supply chain coordination: Perspectives, empirical studies and research directions. *International Journal of Production Economics*, *115*(2), 316–335. doi:10.1016/j.ijpe.2008.05.011

Khanuja, A., & Jain, R.K. (2021). The conceptual framework on integrated flexibility: an evolution to data-driven supply chain management. *The TQM Journal*. doi:10.1108/TQM-03-2020-0045

Kumar, R., & Kumar Singh, R. (2017). Coordination and responsiveness issues in SME supply chains: A review. *Benchmarking*, *24*(3), 635–650. doi:10.1108/BIJ-03-2016-0041

Larsen, T. S., Thernoe, C., & Andresen, C. (2003). Supply chain collaboration: Theoretical perspective and empirical evidence. *International Journal of Physical Distribution & Logistics Management*, *33*(6), 531–549. doi:10.1108/09600030310492788

Lee, C. W., Kwon, I. W. G., & Severance, D. (2007). Relationship between supply chain performance and degree of linkage among supplier, internal integration, and customer. *Supply Chain Management*, *12*(6), 444–452. doi:10.1108/13598540710826371

Lee, H., Kim, M. S., & Kim, K. K. (2014). Interorganizational information systems visibility and supply chain performance. *International Journal of Information Management*, *34*(2), 285–295. doi:10.1016/j.ijinfomgt.2013.10.003

Lee, H. L. (2000). Creating value through supply chain integration. *Supply Chain Management Review*, *4*(4), 30-36.

Li, Q., & Liu, A. (2019). Big data driven supply chain management. *Procedia CIRP*, *81*, 1089–1094. doi:10.1016/j.procir.2019.03.258

Li, S., Zhao, X., & Huo, B. (2018). Supply chain coordination and innovativeness: A social contagion and learning perspective. *International Journal of Production Economics*, *205*, 47–61. doi:10.1016/j.ijpe.2018.07.033

Lycett, M. (2013). 'Datafication': Making sense of (big) data in a complex world. *European Journal of Information Systems*, *22*(4), 381–386. doi:10.1057/ejis.2013.10

McClellan, M. (2003). Collaborative manufacturing: A strategy built on trust and cooperation. *Instrumentation & Control Systems*, *76*(12), 27–31.

Mettler, T., & Rohner, P. (2009). Supplier relationship management: A case study in the context of health care. *Journal of Theoretical and Applied Electronic Commerce Research*, *4*(3), 58–71. doi:10.4067/S0718-18762009000300006

Mondal, S., & Samaddar, K. (2021). Reinforcing the significance of human factor in achieving quality performance in data-driven supply chain management. *The TQM Journal*. doi:10.1108/TQM-12-2020-0303

Mostaghel, R., Oghazi, P., Patel, P. C., Parida, V., & Hultman, M. (2019). Marketing and supply chain coordination and intelligence quality: A product innovation performance perspective. *Journal of Business Research*, *101*, 597–606. doi:10.1016/j.jbusres.2019.02.058

Patnayakuni, R., Rai, A., & Seth, N. (2006). Relational antecedents of information flow integration for supply chain coordination. *Journal of Management Information Systems*, *23*(1), 13–49. doi:10.2753/MIS0742-1222230101

Sanders, N. R. (2014). *Big Data Driven Supply Chain Management: A Framework for Implementing Analytics and Turning Information Into Intelligence*. Pearson Education.

Shin, W. S., Dahlgaard, J. J., Dahlgaard-Park, S. M., & Kim, M. G. (2018). A Quality Scorecard for the era of Industry 4.0. *Total Quality Management & Business Excellence*, *29*(9-10), 959–976. doi:10.1080/14783363.2018.1486536

Simatupang, T. M., Wright, A. C., & Sridharan, R. (2002). The knowledge of coordination for supply chain integration. *Business Process Management Journal*, *8*(3), 289–308. doi:10.1108/14637150210428989

Sommanawat, K., Vipaporn, T., & Joemsittiprasert, W. (2019). Can Big Data Benefits Bridge Between Data Driven Supply Chain Orientation and Financial Performance? Evidence from Manufacturing Sector of Thailand. *International Journal of Supply Chain Management*, *8*(5), 597.

Su, J., Li, C., Zeng, Q., Yang, J., & Zhang, J. (2019). A green closed-loop supply chain coordination mechanism based on third-party recycling. *Sustainability (Basel)*, *11*(19), 5335. doi:10.3390u11195335

Sundarakani, B., Ajaykumar, A., & Gunasekaran, A. (2021). Big data driven supply chain design and applications for blockchain: An action research using case study approach. *Omega*, *102*, 102452. doi:10.1016/j.omega.2021.102452

Tabachnick, B., & Fidell, L. (2013). *Using multivariate statistics* (6th ed.). Pearson.

Teece, D. J. (2007). Explicating dynamic capabilities: The nature and microfoundations of (sustainable) enterprise performance. *Strategic Management Journal*, *28*(13), 1319–1350. doi:10.1002mj.640

Thekkoote, R. (2021). Understanding big data-driven supply chain and performance measures for customer satisfaction. *Benchmarking: An International Journal*. doi:10.1108/BIJ-01-2021-0034

TOSBOL. (2022). *Trabzon-Arsin Organize Sanayi Bölgesi Yönetim Kurulu Başkanlığı*. Retrieved from https://www.tosbol.org.tr/

Tsai, C. W., Lai, C. F., Chao, H. C., & Vasilakos, A. V. (2015). Big data analytics: A survey. *Journal of Big Data*, *2*(1), 1–32. doi:10.118640537-015-0030-3 PMID:26191487

Vanichchinchai, A. (2019). The effect of lean manufacturing on a supply chain relationship and performance. *Sustainability (Basel)*, *11*(20), 5751. doi:10.3390u11205751

Vanichchinchai, A. (2021). The linkages among supplier relationship, customer relationship and supply performance. *Journal of Business and Industrial Marketing*, *36*(8), 1520–1533. doi:10.1108/JBIM-01-2020-0033

Vosooghidizaji, M., Taghipour, A., & Canel-Depitre, B. (2020). Supply chain coordination under information asymmetry: A review. *International Journal of Production Research*, *58*(6), 1805–1834. doi:10.1080/00207543.2019.1685702

Waller, M. A., & Fawcett, S. E. (2013). Data science, predictive analytics, and big data: A revolution that will transform supply chain design and management. *Journal of Business Logistics*, *34*(2), 77–84. doi:10.1111/jbl.12010

Wamba, S. F., Gunasekaran, A., Akter, S., Ren, S. J. F., Dubey, R., & Childe, S. J. (2017). Big data analytics and firm performance: Effects of dynamic capabilities. *Journal of Business Research*, *70*, 356–365. doi:10.1016/j.jbusres.2016.08.009

Wu, F., Yeniyurt, S., Kim, D., & Cavusgil, S. T. (2006). The impact of information technology on supply chain capabilities and firm performance: A resource-based view. *Industrial Marketing Management*, *35*(4), 493–504. doi:10.1016/j.indmarman.2005.05.003

Wu, H., Han, X., Yang, Q., & Pu, X. (2018). Production and coordination decisions in a closed-loop supply chain with remanufacturing cost disruptions when retailers compete. *Journal of Intelligent Manufacturing*, *29*(1), 227–235. doi:10.100710845-015-1103-z

Xu, L., & Beamon, B. M. (2006). Supply chain coordination and cooperation mechanisms: An attribute-based approach. *The Journal of Supply Chain Management*, *42*(1), 4–12. doi:10.1111/j.1745-493X.2006.04201002.x

Yaşlıoğlu, M. M. (2017). Sosyal bilimlerde faktör analizi ve geçerlilik: Keşfedici ve doğrulayıcı faktör analizlerinin kullanılması. *İstanbul Üniversitesi İşletme Fakültesi Dergisi*, *46*, 74-85.

Yildirim, U., Toygar, A., & Çolakoğlu, C. (2022). Compensation effect of wages on decent work: A study on seafarers attitudes. *Marine Policy*, *143*, 105155. doi:10.1016/j.marpol.2022.105155

Yu, W., Chavez, R., Jacobs, M. A., & Feng, M. (2018). Data-driven supply chain capabilities and performance: A resource-based view. *Transportation Research Part E, Logistics and Transportation Review, 114*, 371–385. doi:10.1016/j.tre.2017.04.002

Yu, W., Jacobs, M. A., Chavez, R., & Feng, M. (2019). Data-driven supply chain orientation and financial performance: The moderating effect of innovation-focused complementary assets. *British Journal of Management, 30*(2), 299–314. doi:10.1111/1467-8551.12328

Yu, Y., Huo, B., & Zhang, Z. J. (2020). Impact of information technology on supply chain integration and company performance: Evidence from cross-border e-commerce companies in China. *Journal of Enterprise Information Management, 34*(1), 460–489. doi:10.1108/JEIM-03-2020-0101

Zhang, X., & Yousaf, H. A. U. (2020). Green supply chain coordination considering government intervention, green investment, and customer green preferences in the petroleum industry. *Journal of Cleaner Production, 246*, 118984. doi:10.1016/j.jclepro.2019.118984

Chapter 13
A New Panacea for Supply Chains?
Experience Feedback From Blockchain Technology Adopters

Ulpan Tokkozhina
ISCTE, University Institute of Lisbon, Portugal

Ana Lúcia Martins
ISCTE, University Institute of Lisbon, Portugal

João C. Ferreira
ISCTE, University Institute of Lisbon, Portugal

ABSTRACT

Blockchain technology (BCT) is being actively discussed for application in business contexts to digitalize supply chains (SCs). The current nascent level of BCT adoption in businesses creates resistance for further scalability in the industry. This study explores real pilot cases and experiences of BCT pioneers from various continents and industries, revealing the intentions behind the adoption, feasible improvements, and challenges that need to be further addressed. Findings reveal the business incentives of decentralizing trust constituent and efficiency improvements of data sharing. However, the challenges remain in scaling the adoption to a broader level and guaranteeing the accurate input of data.

INTRODUCTION

Shift towards digitalization of business practices can be witnessed in nearly every industry nowadays. Fast paced global trade reveals the current supply chains (SCs) complications, such as lack of reliable data, shortage of raw materials, transportation difficulties, increased lead times and orders delays. Today consumers are setting importance not only to the availability of a product, but also to its quality, where provenance of a product can impact on the consumption decision (Hay et al., 2021). In order to meet the

DOI: 10.4018/978-1-6684-7455-6.ch013

expectations and needs of their consumers, SC participants need to be mutually motivated and open to collaborate to reach a common objective. Here, another angle of supply chain management (SCM) resistance arises: parties are seeking for a higher dedication and openness to designate mutual dependency, as the trust level between parties impacts on their willingness to collaborate with each other (Han et al., 2021).

Various innovative technological solutions are arising for businesses, one of the most promising technologies today is blockchain technology (BCT). Blockchain can be characterized as a "digital, decentralized and distributed ledger in which transactions are logged and added in chronological order with the goal of creating permanent and tamper-proof records" (Treiblmaier, 2018, p.547). When applied to a business context, BCT is disrupting the current processes with its native immutable nature – information and transactions throughout the SC processes cannot be altered or removed later due to the architecture of technology, that links the blocks together (Sunny et al., 2020). Like that, BCT is claimed to bring product provenance (Montecchi et al., 2019), ensure transparency and traceability (Centobelli et al., 2021), enable trust with end-consumer, by allowing end-consumers to check the product origins (Shahid et al., 2020), as well as promote mutual trust between SC parties by protecting shared data (Al-Rakhami & Al-Mashari, 2021).

Extant literature reveals academic interest in disruptive technology solutions for global SCs. Currently there are various studies with literature systematization of BCT use in SCs (Queiroz et al., 2019; Pournader et al., 2020; Wan et al., 2020; Reddy et al., 2021). Theoretical discussions of BCT applications and their potential results for specific industries, such as oil (Vishnubhotla et al. 2020), pharmaceutical products (Bamakan et al., 2021; Musamih et al., 2021), food (Kamilaris et al., 2019; Menon and Jain, 2021), luxury goods (Choi, 2019; Berneis & Winkler, 2021) and other industries. The nascent stage of BCT adoption makes it challenging for academic research to find real use-cases for exploration and adoption results discussion. Thus, the gap remains to bring the real application results and experiences of BCT adoption pioneers to academic literature.

The purpose of this study is to explore the benefits, challenges and real experiences from BCT adoption in SCM, based on feedback collected from early industry pioneers. Thus, the goal of this study is to reveal the potential of the BCT adoption to enhance SC operations and create a base for decision-making process for suitability assessment of the BCT as a solution to a specific SC case.

To address the purpose of this study, qualitative research was conducted and the BCT adoption to SC activities was investigated through semi-structured interviews with representatives of pioneering companies. Semi-structured approach allowed gaining real opinions of the BCT adoption experience in SC practices. In the next sections the findings from the real industry pilots and applications of BCT will be revealed to shed light on intentions for the technology adoption, feasible improvements and remaining challenges in the context of SCM.

The remaining of the paper is structured as following: Section 2 reviews the current academic literature in the field of BCT applications to SCM; Section 3 explains the methodology and the procedures of the data collection; Section 4 reveals the major findings; Section 5 discusses the findings and provides paths for future research.

LITERATURE REVIEW

Blockchain was first introduced by Nakamoto et al. (2008) as a platform for Bitcoin cryptocurrency. Blockchain belongs to the category of a Distributed Ledger Technologies (DLT), and it operates as an immutable database, that keeps and records every transaction that is being instantly shared across a network of participants (Tian, 2017). This technology is built on the concepts of disintermediation and decentralization of data, which means that update, record and collection of data can be performed by every network participant, making it visible to the rest of the network (Monteiro, 2018). Through its decentralized nature, BCT is enabling transparency across the SC, in this way providing products' provenance reliance and decreases counterfeit possibilities through ensuring the confidence of products' origins (Montecchi et al., 2019). Blockchain networks can be broadly divided into two opposite types – public (permissionless) and private (permissioned). Permissionless blockchain allows any player to be freely involved in the process of reaching consensus (Pal, 2021), therefore it is open to anyone who wants to join the chain without particular identity and it mostly uses the proof-of-work consensus to run the network (Verma et al., 2021). Whereas nowadays, private or permissioned blockchains are considered to be more beneficial for most of SC applications, as there is normally a limited number of participating nodes (Rejeb et al., 2019).

Another important technological novelty of BCT are smart contracts. IBM defines smart contracts as "programs stored on a blockchain that run when predetermined conditions are met, they typically are used to automate the execution of an agreement so that all participants can be immediately certain of the outcome, without any intermediary's involvement or time loss" (ibm.com). Chang et al. (2019) claim that the unique characteristics of smart contracts, together with the inherited features of BCT would allow the improvement of the automation and synchronization of business processes. Like this, smart contracts allow faster transactions within the SC network, creating automation and peer-to-peer trust (Köhler et al., 2021), running transactions without any trusted third-party or intermediary (Wu et al., 2022).

Blockchain Contributions in Supply Chain Management Context and Current Applications

The BCT contribution in SCs digitalization is often enhanced by the application of other novel technologies, such as Internet of Things (IoT) applications for SC traceability processes improvement; RFID sensors, wireless technologies for monitoring throughout networks and other technologies (Dasaklis et al., 2022). BCT-based solutions are able to provide an instant, real-time, immutable ledger of transactions, including information sharing and financial transactions between various business entities, enabling thus a more organized, coordinated and efficient network of SCM through a single truthful ledger access across the network (Sangari & Mashatan, 2022). In the context of small and medium-sized manufacturing enterprises, Jiang et al. (2022) highlighted that BCT is able to introduce the three main contributions: (1) authenticity and information sharing improvement, (2) reduction of labor costs and managerial risks and (3) potential solution to a traditional trust-lacking model.

Practical aspects of BCT implementation in a SCM context is crucial to understand, considering that this study is focused on the feedback of early adopters, thus it is important to review the practical side of the novel technology application as reflected in the current academic literature. According to Vu et al. (2022), one of the most critical aspects of BCT adoption is understanding of its implementation at the organizational level. Issues such as ERP performance in the context of BCT integration (Morawiek et al., 2022), data ownership and control (Kayikci et al., 2022), public key infrastructure deployment and establishment (Viriyasitavat et al., 2022), connectability to the data for smart contracts off-chain, also called as an "oracle problem" (Pasdar et al., 2023) and many other issues still exist in the context of practical BCT integration with SC practices. According to Tanha et al. (2022), an inaccurate and unprepared launch of new technology implementation in a business context may lead to high costs, credit losses, as well as a general resource and time waste. Thus, the implementation of a disruptive technology needs to be carefully prepared and justified.

BCT use was explored for many different fields in the context of SCM in academic literature. The food and beverage industry is one of the commonly explored, as here BCT can provide safety assurance of products to consumers, such as agri-food products (Zhao et al., 2019), marine conservations (Howson, 2020), perishable commodities (Kayikci et al., 2021), wine SCs (Tokkozhina et al., 2021), drinkable yoghurts (Hay et al., 2021) and other. Apart from being proposed for food SCs implementation, BCT has potential to be used in drugs distribution (Haq & Esuka, 2018), oil and gas industry (Ajao et al., 2019), e-commerce applications (Liu & Li, 2020), automobile SCs (Ada et al., 2021), textile and clothing (Agrawal et al., 2021) and many more fields.

Challenges Remaining in the Blockchain Implementation for Supply Chains

Despite of attractiveness of BCT-based solutions, there are still some challenges existing for its full integration to SC operations. Various institutional, regulatory and technical issues need to be addressed before BCT-based solutions can reach upon maturity stage (Kamble et al., 2020). Some constraints, that were detected in previous studies include challenges like high cost of the technology and its technical support (Zhao et al., 2019), organizational readiness for change, lack of technical expertise, and consequently scalability threats (Malik et al., 2018) may show up during the technology adoption process. Comprehensive management procedures for BCT-based networks, when used by multi-actor SCs are still lacking (Sternberg et al., 2020), and generally a lot of current BCT pilots have difficulties in growing forward from the pioneering stage, as organizational changes are required for this technology to reach scalability and become ubiquitously adopted in businesses (Behnke & Janssen, 2020).

From the technological side, there are also some challenges that remain unsolved. Cybersecurity is one of the challenges associated with BCT adoption, because the depth of cybersecurity considering specifics for a particular industry sector remains highly unexplored (Mahmood et al., 2022). Moreover, smart contracts also highlight some challenges related with its successful deployment, according to Lin et al. (2022) the auditability and verifiability of smart contracts needs to be further addressed and developed. Erol et al. (2022) explained technology adopters in different levels of adoption, starting from 'innovators', which are the first to try the innovation, moving towards 'early adopters', that are considered opinion leaders, then 'early majority, 'late majority', and finally 'laggards', the ultimate stage that proves the innovation to be self-sustaining. When talking about BCT adoption in the SCM context, the level of adoption is more justifiable to be categorized between the 'innovators' and 'early adopters' stages, as the real-life experiences are still in minority from the perspective of business context. It once again highlights the importance of analyzing the real adoption cases to gain the feedback of managers regarding their experience with BCT as a solution to SC challenges.

METHODOLOGY

This is a qualitative study, where data was collected via semi-structured interviews with representatives of various industries that are currently adopting BCT in their SCs. Participants were searched through LinkedIn platform based with required element of working in an organization being involved in the pilot of BCT in SC activities. Data was collected between May 2021 and January 2022. Potential participants were contacted and asked about the interest of participating in study, those who were interested received a list of topics to be covered during the interview session. The search of participants was not limited by a specific country or industry; thus, the sample includes representatives of various sectors – food, health and beauty, logistics, from across the world. The total of 8 individuals, representing 8 different organizations and from different supply chains, who are currently involved in organizational BCT adoption to SC activities were interviewed. Figure 1 shows the location of focal companies, whose representatives were interviewed for this study, and Table 1 categorizes the industry, final product of the given SC and the BCT adoption stage of the interviewees.

Table 1. Details about interviewees' industry and blockchain adoption stage

Interviewee	Industry	Final Product Category	Country of the Focal Company	Blockchain Adoption Stage
Interviewee 1	Food	Perishable food products	Portugal	Early pilot stage
Interviewee 2	Food	Non-perishable beverage	USA	Several years
Interviewee 3	Health and beauty	Health-sensitive non-perishable product for women	South Africa	Early pilot stage
Interviewee 4	Logistics	Transportation for various products categories	Mexico	Early pilot stage
Interviewee 5	Logistics	Transportation for various products categories	Denmark	Several years
Interviewee 6	Food	Perishable food products	Portugal	Early pilot stage
Interviewee 7	Logistics	Cold chain transportation for perishable products	Portugal	Early pilot stage
Interviewee 8	Food	Perishable food products	Portugal	Early pilot stage

The format of interviews was an online session that had an average duration of 40 minutes per interview. The interviews were conducted individually (1:1) according to the availability of the interviewee. Interviewer was asking questions according to the semi-structured interview guide, that was built in advance and divided into four broad sections (overall goals of BCT adoption/visible benefits of adoption/technology limitations/and main challenges at the current adoption level). Each participant was asked for a possibility to record the interview for transcription purposes, and later each interview was transcribed verbatim. Prior to interview conductions, research topics and exemplary questions were reviewed by academicians for language clarity and ethical accuracy in order to follow academic integrity purposes. All preparation material and interviews were fully in English. The transcribed interviews were coded and analysed using qualitative content analysis software MAXQDA Analytics Pro 2022.

Figure 1. Geographical location of interviewees' focal companies

FINDINGS

Due to semi-structured nature of the interviews conducted, it was possible to make interviewees "speak up" about a broad spectrum of adoption experience. Firstly, participants were asked to share their opinions on what in their views are the main challenges, that SCs are facing nowadays. It was interesting to see those opinions of various SC players were repeating themselves based on their SC position. Like this, players, that are closer to the downstream levels of SC, mainly retailers, were referring to the challenge of inability to quickly obtain information about a specific batch of products, which can be crucial to the health issues of final consumers. As the SC position moves more upstream, a different challenge is being revealed. Both suppliers, and logistics providers referred to the challenge of gaining trust across the SC. As per Interviewee 1: "It is always hard to find an entity that everyone will trust to keep records straight about what are the transactions and what are the contract conditions".

As can be seen from Table 1, the majority of interviewed participants are currently at a pilot stage of the BCT adoption, as the technology is still at the nascent stages in terms of business applications. Nevertheless, they can already see tendency towards SC improvements with the adoption. The impact of BCT adoption on transparency enhancement and traceability enabling, is one of the most valuable improvements that adopters can see in their SC cases. Like this, Interviewee 2, from the side of a supplier argues: *"With blockchain you are getting to the* next level of traceability – before my traceability ended when I sold the product, and then they [distributors] would print their label with a new serial number. Now I am getting the continuity in the process where the label is being reused in the SC.". Traceability is, generally one of the most iconic features that is being discussed under the context of BCT. Some of the pilots of BCT adoption to SCs start as a tool for gaining traceability, such as the network, where Interviewee 1 operates: "…we have seen participants eager to have the technology, that will allow giving value to products with traceability assurance". Moreover, the transparency of sourcing and procurement activities are important not only for upper tiers of SC, but as per Interviewee 3, it is an important aspect for final customers: "…sustainability of sourcing the raw material and product compliance can be shown in a simplified way, being transparent [to final recipient of the product]".

Together with a possibility to trace products backwards, BCT brings another important feature – the improvement of the efficiency of the data sharing and access. Interviewee 4 refers to the importance of BCT-based efficiency in their SC network: "We sell different kinds of products and it is very difficult to manage all those operations…the main reason of adoption is to be more efficient". Increased trust factor is another angle of adoption that is being discussed in literature. Our findings revealed the real value of trust in BCT adoption to SC operations. In this context, Interviewee 5 highlights: "I do not think that blockchain itself came as a solution for a technical problem, I think it came as a solution to a mental psychological problem - trust part among parties". Apart from bringing more trust among suppliers and retailers, BCT can also solve trust issues with final consumer, as information availability on the digital ledger "…is also going to enhance consumer experience and expectations" (Interviewee 3).

However, the inherited features of BCT, sometimes instead of bringing improvements, may highlight the vulnerabilities of the current SC issues. As BCT is, essentially, a technology that allows a novel way of sharing and keeping the data, the challenge is to ensure a quality and correct data input initially. Interviewee 6 refers to the challenge in terms of data: "If you fail to record information correctly, you will have garbage going in [to the ledger] and getting out of it". Interviewee 3 is involved in a SC that distributes a health-sensitive product, thus evaluating everything also from the perspective of a final product recipient: "…when you say this is traceable, do I actually trace X (product name is confidential), or it is just a low-quality data out there?". Interviewee 7 is dealing with the transportation of perishable goods, and considers accurate information capturing as one of the most important factors for the BCT-based SCs, already planning to take an action to increase quality: "…we will have to put some more trainings to our operations to know what is the impact of the non-correct information input".

Other challenges detected are related to the infant stage of BCT application in business processes. Since BCT requires a network of participants to operate in its full potential, scalability is one of the fundamental challenges in this sense, as per Interviewee 5: "…if half of participants use BCT network, the other half is not – you disrupt the process, because you cannot really have an end-to-end process using this technology… so until you reach a scale where you have the vast majority of the players using the platform, it makes the process to a certain extent more complicated". Therefore, the challenge remains of establishing and forming the network of participants itself, which sometimes creates resistances, as "…not all players would be eager to use the technology, that is the possibility, because digital literacy is different around players", says Interviewee 1.

Moreover, the technological change needs to mainly address the needs of participants and bring value to the product, which again needs an evaluation from the side of customers for a particular product – does BCT mean something to them? An answer to this question can sometimes be tricky due to a lower awareness about BCT. Interviewee 3 explains: "For [BCT] adoption to happen we need to 'decrypt' blockchain language and relate it to ordinary people". The value of BCT application to the product is crucial for some pilots, as for instance in case of food SC, where Interviewee 8 operates: "…our project is directed by the trust to the product", explaining that enabling full traceability of locomotion of the product from the origins until the final consumer is the main goal. Interviewee 1 further supports: "[BCT awareness] is very important for participants within the network, but also important to the general public - what blockchain is and is not in terms of how they can use it and how they can trust it".

DISCUSSION AND CONCLUSION

Findings revealed real experiences of SC players that are participating in disruptive technology adoption to their operations. As any innovative solution, at early stages of adoption there is a possibility to see the potential improvements the solution can bring, as well as challenges that still require attention.

The first important finding disclosed different views on the main goals of adoption depending on their SC position. Like this, our study showed that upstream players (suppliers and logistics providers) are generally pursuing the BCT adoption to improve trust relationships across the chain. Mani and Gunasakeran (2021) found that value co-creation activities and ethical performance of upstream SC are important for keeping a strong reputation of focal companies. Our findings suggest that upstream SC elements are seeking for additional trust-enabling mechanisms and technologies to strengthen relationships across the SC. Thus, it is assumed that for value co-creation activities to take place, there should be a higher level of trust and comfortable environment for upper tiers of SC, as they are located far from the final customer and might not have a strong visibility of market behavior.

On the contrary, our findings revealed that downstream SC players are seeking for BCT-based solutions mainly to be able to speed up a search for a specific batch/set of products to ensure safety measures of the product for final customers. Shiralkar et al. (2021) claim that disruptive information-sharing technologies eliminate the possibility of integrity violation in SCs. It is important to highlight the fact that BCT is in fact able to share information faster in a decentralized way, where every player can see the same data as others. However, the challenge remains to ensure the accuracy and correctness of the data. Despite the fact that BCT allows a speedy data access, if the data was not shared accurately, it can pose even a higher threat to safety assurances of final customers. This was also one of the findings of our study, the early industry adopters see the data input quality as a crucial point of improvement, when talking about BCT adoption. Wang et al. (2020) believe that a BCT-based SC will be powered with a secured, untampered data, which will solve traditionally incomplete and inaccurate data sharing, that usually got lost while travelling across the SC. However, there is a need to highlight the importance that real-life industry adopters bring to the table – if data is shared in a BCT ledger, and there is an incorrect input, then the problems it may cause are even more complicated than in traditional SC settings. Due to the immutability feature of BCT, data is tamper-proof and is very difficult to be changed, as information being kept in blocks, including the previous block of data. Therefore, to change even a minor detail would mean a lot of effort and time-consuming processes.

Going back to the advantageous sides of the findings, BCT-based networks are found to be an appropriate solution for efficiency increasing of operations, especially those involved in trade of multiple products and stock keeping units (SKUs). Latif et al. (2021) proposed a design of a BCT architecture with the possibilities of entering multiple SKUs depending on the product properties and information, with Urdu and Hindi languages supported by SKUs. To further develop this topic, it would be interesting if future studies and real-life applications to keep in mind international SCs and overseas trades, thus focusing on solutions for SKUs entries that would be appropriate for all entities involved.

One of the most discussed features that highlight innovation of BCT-based solutions for businesses are transparency and traceability assurances. Our findings also prove the importance of the above-mentioned features to industry adopters. Study participants see traceability and transparency features as a game changer for different SC tiers. Final consumers would be able to enjoy the traceable information of the product, but also the innovation touches the upstream suppliers, who would finally be able to keep an eye on the product that was already distributed to the next SC player – a feature that was not possible before.

Extant literature suggests that BCT-enabled transparency of information will bring competitive advantage, as well as being able to impact on sustainability goals achievement (Bai & Sarkis, 2020). However, this is crossing with one of the challenges that was revealed through our conducted interviews – technology unawareness and scalability difficulties for a broader adoption. Kayikci et al. (2021) admit that as any novel technology, BCT adoption has a threat of facing with barriers, such as resistance of organizations to apply changes in current operations. It is suggested that such resistances should be addressed through an active awareness raise, which may include some extra activities as workshops, trainings and seminars for industry representatives. Thus, for BCT-based transparency to bring competitive advantage, challenges as scalability and lower levels of technology awareness need to be handled across the whole SC. Extant research as well supports this position, arguing that BCT adoption is only conditional for those cases, where traceability awareness of final consumers is already addressed (Fan et al., 2020).

Lastly, our study revealed the hopes that industry adopters put on BCT-enabled trust across the SC. Our study participants highlighted trust from different perspectives – the enhanced trust among SC entities, as well as the achievement of final customers' trust towards the product itself. Howson (2020) stressed that BCT-based solution will only prove itself as a powerful trust-enabling tool in those cases, where various stakeholders are involved and are standing for a share of benefits. Further studies found different effects of BCT-enabled trust depending on the cultural background, like this, BCT diffusion in India shows effect of trust at early stages of adoption only, whereas in US it is visible throughout both intention stage and the adoption itself (Wamba & Querioz, 2022). What was noticed in this study is that participants from different cultural backgrounds were mentioning trust as a powerful feature of BCT-based networks, one that is able to bring end-to-end trust amplification across SCs.

Critical success factors and barriers of BCT-based SCs were already examined in extant literature (Yadav & Singh, 2020; Kouhizadeh et al., 2021), thus our study contributes the academic research with evidence from the industry early adopters, involved in BCT adoption. This study shed light on the main BCT-enabled benefits that were already visible to early adopters, as well as remaining challenges, which provides practical contribution for those organizations that consider BCT pilots – here they can find scientifically analyzed experiences of pioneers. The main limitation of this study is related to the fact that due to early stage of piloting and adoption of BCT, it was challenging to conduct broad research with many participants. Thus, the number of study participants and the countries of focal companies are limited. Therefore, for future studies it is suggested to expand the research to a larger number of representatives of BCT pilots across the globe to get more generalizable results. It would also be interesting in future research to apply a different data collection method, e.g. a focus group with the representatives of various businesses to generate a discussion, as well as applying a quantitative research for a deeper analysis of BCT adoption process in SCM. Authors hope that this study will serve as an impulse for future explorations of nascent technology implementation to business practices.

ACKNOWLEDGMENT

This work was supported by EEA Grants Blue Growth Programme (Call #5), Project PT-INNOVATION-0069 – Fish2Fork. We express our gratitude to the reviewers of the study, who provided important feedback for further improvement of the chapter.

REFERENCES

Ada, N., Ethirajan, M., & Kumar, A., Kek, V., Nadeem, S. P., Kazancoglu, Y., & Kandasamy, J. (2021). Blockchain technology for enhancing traceability and efficiency in automobile supply chain—A case study. *Sustainability*, *13*(24), 13667. doi:10.3390u132413667

Agrawal, T. K., Kumar, V., Pal, R., Wang, L., & Chen, Y. (2021). Blockchain-based framework for supply chain traceability: A case example of textile and clothing industry. *Computers & Industrial Engineering*, *154*, 107130. doi:10.1016/j.cie.2021.107130

Ajao, L. A., Agajo, J., Adedokun, E. A., & Karngong, L. (2019). Crypto hash algorithm-based blockchain technology for managing decentralized ledger database in oil and gas industry. *J*, *2*(3), 300-325.

Al-Rakhami, M. S., & Al-Mashari, M. (2021). A blockchain-based trust model for the internet of things supply chain management. *Sensors (Basel)*, *21*(5), 1759. doi:10.339021051759 PMID:33806319

Bai, C., & Sarkis, J. (2020). A supply chain transparency and sustainability technology appraisal model for blockchain technology. *International Journal of Production Research*, *58*(7), 2142–2162. doi:10.1080/00207543.2019.1708989

Bamakan, S. M. H., Moghaddam, S. G., & Manshadi, S. D. (2021). Blockchain-enabled pharmaceutical cold chain: Applications, key challenges, and future trends. *Journal of Cleaner Production*, *302*, 127021. doi:10.1016/j.jclepro.2021.127021

Behnke, K., & Janssen, M. F. W. H. A. (2020). Boundary conditions for traceability in food supply chains using blockchain technology. *International Journal of Information Management*, *52*, 101969. doi:10.1016/j.ijinfomgt.2019.05.025

Berneis, M., & Winkler, H. (2021). Value proposition assessment of blockchain technology for luxury, food, and healthcare supply chains. *Logistics*, *5*(4), 85. doi:10.3390/logistics5040085

Chang, S. E., Chen, Y. C., & Lu, M. F. (2019). Supply chain re-engineering using blockchain technology: A case of smart contract based tracking process. *Technological Forecasting and Social Change*, *144*, 1–11. doi:10.1016/j.techfore.2019.03.015

Choi, T. M. (2019). Blockchain-technology-supported platforms for diamond authentication and certification in luxury supply chains. *Transportation Research Part E, Logistics and Transportation Review*, *128*, 17–29. doi:10.1016/j.tre.2019.05.011

Dasaklis, T. K., Voutsinas, T. G., Tsoulfas, G. T., & Casino, F. (2022). A systematic literature review of blockchain-enabled supply chain traceability implementations. *Sustainability (Basel)*, *14*(4), 2439. doi:10.3390u14042439

Erol, I., Neuhofer, I. O., Dogru, T., Oztel, A., Searcy, C., & Yorulmaz, A. C. (2022). Improving sustainability in the tourism industry through blockchain technology: Challenges and opportunities. *Tourism Management*, *93*, 104628. doi:10.1016/j.tourman.2022.104628

Fan, Z. P., Wu, X. Y., & Cao, B. B. (2020). Considering the traceability awareness of consumers: Should the supply chain adopt the blockchain technology? *Annals of Operations Research*, •••, 1–24. PMID:32836619

Han, W., Huang, Y., Hughes, M., & Zhang, M. (2021). The trade-off between trust and distrust in supply chain collaboration. *Industrial Marketing Management*, *98*, 93–104. doi:10.1016/j.indmarman.2021.08.005

Haq, I., & Esuka, O. M. (2018). Blockchain technology in pharmaceutical industry to prevent counterfeit drugs. *International Journal of Computer Applications*, *180*(25), 8–12. doi:10.5120/ijca2018916579

Hay, C., de Matos, A. D., Low, J., Feng, J., Lu, D., Day, L., & Hort, J. (2021). Comparing cross-cultural differences in perception of drinkable yoghurt by Chinese and New Zealand European consumers. *International Dairy Journal*, *113*, 104901. doi:10.1016/j.idairyj.2020.104901

Howson, P. (2020). Building trust and equity in marine conservation and fisheries supply chain management with blockchain. *Marine Policy*, *115*, 103873. doi:10.1016/j.marpol.2020.103873

Jiang, R., Kang, Y., Liu, Y., Liang, Z., Duan, Y., Sun, Y., & Liu, J. (2022). A trust transitivity model of small and medium-sized manufacturing enterprises under blockchain-based supply chain finance. *International Journal of Production Economics*, *247*, 108469. doi:10.1016/j.ijpe.2022.108469

Kamble, S. S., Gunasekaran, A., & Sharma, R. (2020). Modeling the blockchain enabled traceability in agriculture supply chain. *International Journal of Information Management*, *52*, 101967. doi:10.1016/j.ijinfomgt.2019.05.023

Kamilaris, A., Fonts, A., & Prenafeta-Boldú, F. X. (2019). The rise of blockchain technology in agriculture and food supply chains. *Trends in Food Science & Technology*, *91*, 640–652. doi:10.1016/j.tifs.2019.07.034

Kayikci, Y., Gozacan-Chase, N., Rejeb, A., & Mathiyazhagan, K. (2022). Critical success factors for implementing blockchain-based circular supply chain. *Business Strategy and the Environment*, *31*(7), 3595–3615. doi:10.1002/bse.3110

Kayikci, Y., Usar, D. D., & Aylak, B. L. (2021). Using blockchain technology to drive operational excellence in perishable food supply chains during outbreaks. *International Journal of Logistics Management*.

Köhler, S., Pizzol, M., & Sarkis, J. (2021). Unfinished paths—From Blockchain to sustainability in supply chains. *Frontiers in Blockchain*, *4*, 720347. doi:10.3389/fbloc.2021.720347

Kouhizadeh, M., Saberi, S., & Sarkis, J. (2021). Blockchain technology and the sustainable supply chain: Theoretically exploring adoption barriers. *International Journal of Production Economics*, *231*, 107831. doi:10.1016/j.ijpe.2020.107831

Lin, S. Y., Zhang, L., Li, J., Ji, L. L., & Sun, Y. (2022). A survey of application research based on blockchain smart contract. *Wireless Networks*, *28*(2), 635–690. doi:10.100711276-021-02874-x

Liu, Z., & Li, Z. (2020). A blockchain-based framework of cross-border e-commerce supply chain. *International Journal of Information Management*, *52*, 102059. doi:10.1016/j.ijinfomgt.2019.102059

Mahmood, S., Chadhar, M., & Firmin, S. (2022). Cybersecurity challenges in blockchain technology: A scoping review. *Human Behavior and Emerging Technologies*, *2022*, 2022. doi:10.1155/2022/7384000

Malik, S., Kanhere, S. S., & Jurdak, R. (2018, November). Productchain: Scalable blockchain framework to support provenance in supply chains. In *2018 IEEE 17th International Symposium on Network Computing and Applications (NCA)* (pp. 1-10). IEEE.

Mani, V., & Gunasekaran, A. (2021). Upstream complex power relationships and firm's reputation in global value chains. *International Journal of Production Economics*, *237*, 108142. doi:10.1016/j.ijpe.2021.108142

Menon, S., & Jain, K. (2021). Blockchain Technology for Transparency in Agri-Food Supply Chain: Use Cases, Limitations, and Future Directions. *IEEE Transactions on Engineering Management*.

Montecchi, M., Plangger, K., & Etter, M. (2019). It's real, trust me! Establishing supply chain provenance using blockchain. *Business Horizons*, *62*(3), 283–293. doi:10.1016/j.bushor.2019.01.008

Monteiro, M. (2018). *Blockchain: tecnologia da bitcoin está a chegar a múltiplas indústrias*. MaisTic.

Morawiec, P., & Sołtysik-Piorunkiewicz, A. (2022). Cloud computing, Big Data, and blockchain technology adoption in ERP implementation methodology. *Sustainability (Basel)*, *14*(7), 3714. doi:10.3390u14073714

Musamih, A., Jayaraman, R., Salah, K., Hasan, H. R., Yaqoob, I., & Al-Hammadi, Y. (2021). Blockchain-based solution for distribution and delivery of COVID-19 vaccines. *IEEE Access : Practical Innovations, Open Solutions*, *9*, 71372–71387. doi:10.1109/ACCESS.2021.3079197 PMID:34812393

Nakamoto, S. (2008). Bitcoin: A peer-to-peer electronic cash system. *Decentralized Business Review*, 21260.

Pal, K. (2021). Applications of secured blockchain technology in the manufacturing industry. In *Blockchain and AI Technology in the Industrial Internet of Things* (pp. 144–162). IGI Global. doi:10.4018/978-1-7998-6694-7.ch010

Pasdar, A., Lee, Y. C., & Dong, Z. (2023). Connect api with blockchain: A survey on blockchain oracle implementation. *ACM Computing Surveys*, *55*(10), 1–39. doi:10.1145/3567582

Pournader, M., Shi, Y., Seuring, S., & Koh, S. L. (2020). Blockchain applications in supply chains, transport and logistics: A systematic review of the literature. *International Journal of Production Research*, *58*(7), 2063–2081. doi:10.1080/00207543.2019.1650976

Queiroz, M. M., Telles, R., & Bonilla, S. H. (2019). Blockchain and supply chain management integration: A systematic review of the literature. *Supply Chain Management*, *25*(2), 241–254. doi:10.1108/SCM-03-2018-0143

Reddy, K. R. K., Gunasekaran, A., Kalpana, P., Sreedharan, V. R., & Kumar, S. A. (2021). Developing a blockchain framework for the automotive supply chain: A systematic review. *Computers & Industrial Engineering*, *157*, 107334. doi:10.1016/j.cie.2021.107334

Rejeb, A., Keogh, J. G., & Treiblmaier, H. (2019). Leveraging the internet of things and blockchain technology in supply chain management. *Future Internet*, *11*(7), 161. doi:10.3390/fi11070161

Sangari, M. S., & Mashatan, A. (2022). A data-driven, comparative review of the academic literature and news media on blockchain-enabled supply chain management: Trends, gaps, and research needs. *Computers in Industry*, *143*, 103769. doi:10.1016/j.compind.2022.103769

Shahid, A., Almogren, A., Javaid, N., Al-Zahrani, F. A., Zuair, M., & Alam, M. (2020). Blockchain-based agri-food supply chain: A complete solution. *IEEE Access : Practical Innovations, Open Solutions*, *8*, 69230–69243. doi:10.1109/ACCESS.2020.2986257

Shiralkar, K., Bongale, A., Kumar, S., Kotecha, K., & Prakash, C. (2021). Assessment of the benefits of information and communication technologies (ICT) adoption on downstream supply chain performance of the retail industry. *Logistics*, *5*(4), 80. doi:10.3390/logistics5040080

Sternberg, H. S., Hofmann, E., & Roeck, D. (2021). The struggle is real: Insights from a supply chain blockchain case. *Journal of Business Logistics*, *42*(1), 71–87. doi:10.1111/jbl.12240

Sunny, J., Undralla, N., & Pillai, V. M. (2020). Supply chain transparency through blockchain-based traceability: An overview with demonstration. *Computers & Industrial Engineering*, *150*, 106895. doi:10.1016/j.cie.2020.106895

Tanha, F. E., Hasani, A., Hakak, S., & Gadekallu, T. R. (2022). Blockchain-based cyber physical systems: Comprehensive model for challenge assessment. *Computers & Electrical Engineering*, *103*, 108347. doi:10.1016/j.compeleceng.2022.108347

Tian, F. (2017, June). A supply chain traceability system for food safety based on HACCP, blockchain & Internet of things. In *2017 International conference on service systems and service management* (pp. 1-6). IEEE.

Tokkozhina, U., Ferreira, J. C., & Martins, A. L. (2021, November). Wine Traceability and Counterfeit Reduction: Blockchain-Based Application for a Wine Supply Chain. In *International Conference on Intelligent Transport Systems* (pp. 59-70). Springer.

Treiblmaier, H. (2018). The impact of the blockchain on the supply chain: A theory-based research framework and a call for action. *Supply Chain Management*, *23*(6), 545–559. doi:10.1108/SCM-01-2018-0029

Verma, N., Jain, S., & Doriya, R. (2021, February). Review on consensus protocols for blockchain. In *2021 international conference on computing, communication, and intelligent systems (ICCCIS)* (pp. 281-286). IEEE. doi:10.1109/ICCCIS51004.2021.9397089

Viriyasitavat, W., Xu, L. D., Sapsomboon, A., Dhiman, G., & Hoonsopon, D. (2022). Building trust of Blockchain-based Internet-of-Thing services using public key infrastructure. *Enterprise Information Systems*, *16*(12), 2037162. doi:10.1080/17517575.2022.2037162

Vishnubhotla, A. K., Pati, R. K., & Padhi, S. S. (2020). Can Projects on Blockchain Reduce Risks in Supply Chain Management?: An Oil Company Case Study. *IIM Kozhikode Society & Management Review*, *9*(2), 189–201. doi:10.1177/2277975220913370

Vu, N., Ghadge, A., & Bourlakis, M. (2022). Evidence-driven model for implementing Blockchain in food supply chains. *International Journal of Logistics Research and Applications*, 1-21.

Wamba, S. F., & Queiroz, M. M. (2022). Industry 4.0 and the supply chain digitalisation: A blockchain diffusion perspective. *Production Planning and Control*, *33*(2-3), 193–210. doi:10.1080/09537287.2020.1810756

Wan, P. K., Huang, L., & Holtskog, H. (2020). Blockchain-enabled information sharing within a supply chain: A systematic literature review. *IEEE Access : Practical Innovations, Open Solutions*, *8*, 49645–49656. doi:10.1109/ACCESS.2020.2980142

Wang, Y., Chen, C. H., & Zghari-Sales, A. (2021). Designing a blockchain enabled supply chain. *International Journal of Production Research*, *59*(5), 1450–1475. doi:10.1080/00207543.2020.1824086

Wu, C., Xiong, J., Xiong, H., Zhao, Y., & Yi, W. (2022). A review on recent progress of smart contract in blockchain. *IEEE Access : Practical Innovations, Open Solutions*, *10*, 50839–50863. doi:10.1109/ACCESS.2022.3174052

Yadav, S., & Singh, S. P. (2020). Blockchain critical success factors for sustainable supply chain. *Resources, Conservation and Recycling*, *152*, 104505. doi:10.1016/j.resconrec.2019.104505

Zhao, G., Liu, S., Lopez, C., Lu, H., Elgueta, S., Chen, H., & Boshkoska, B. M. (2019). Blockchain technology in agri-food value chain management: A synthesis of applications, challenges and future research directions. *Computers in Industry*, *109*, 83–99. doi:10.1016/j.compind.2019.04.002

Chapter 14
Socio-Technical Systems Engineering Perspectives Towards a South African Halaal Blockchain System

Tahmid Al-Mumit Quazi
University of KwaZulu-Natal, South Africa

Sulaiman Saleem Patel
Durban University of Technology, South Africa

ABSTRACT

Blockchain is an emerging technology and part of the fourth industrial revolution. Its ability to improve transparency and traceability has found many supply chain applications, including the Halaal supply chain (defining a Halaal blockchain system). The religious roots of the Halaal status makes the Halaal blockchain system inherently socio-technical. This chapter first conceptualises the Halaal blockchain system using a socio-technical systems framework, and then analyses the system in the South African context. The analysis discusses the interconnected relationships between people, culture, goals, infrastructure, technology, and processes within the external environment of stakeholders, regulatory frameworks, and financial/economic circumstances. Challenges towards implementing a Halaal blockchain system in South Africa are discussed along with potential impacts for the communities. The study concludes by identifying open research areas that require further investigation to realise a Halaal blockchain system implementation in South Africa.

INTRODUCTION

Our increasingly inter-connected world has made technology an integral part of human life. Conceptualising technological systems without paying due attention to the social dimension of how these systems will be utilised is risky and may lead to unsustainable designs (Baxter & Sommerville, 2011). This

DOI: 10.4018/978-1-6684-7455-6.ch014

motivates for conceptualising modern and future systems in a socio-technical manner that considers the complex interactions between humans, machines and broader society (Baxter & Sommerville, 2011; Sony & Naik, 2020). Hence, it is important to study systems that are part of the fourth industrial revolution (4IR) using a socio-technical approach.

An emerging technology in the context of the 4IR is blockchain technology. Blockchain is a distributed ledger technology that has been proposed for supply chains in multiple industries, due to its ability to improve transparency and traceability (Ali et al., 2021; Dutta et al., 2020). Use-cases for this technology have been proposed towards achieving the United Nations Sustainable Development Goals (Medaglia & Damsgaard, 2020; The United Nations General Assembly, 2015), particularly in agricultural supply chain contexts that help monitor sustainable farming practices and promote food security (Sylvester, 2019; Tripoli & Schmidhuber, 2020).

The proposed adoption of blockchain technology for monitoring agricultural supply chains has an interesting implication for Muslim communities. The religion of Islam states that followers may only consume foods which are *Halaal* (alternatively spelt as *Halal*), a term which loosely translates to "permissible by Shariah (Islamic) Law" and mostly find application in food products derived from animals (Azam & Abdullah, 2020; Disastraa et al., 2020; Khan & Haleem, 2016; Tayob, 2016). It has also been noted that there has been an increasing interest in *Halaal* foods by the non-Muslim community, who recognise *Halaal* status as a symbol of food safety, quality and lifestyle choice (Mathew et al., 2014; Rejeb et al., 2021). The conditions of *Halaal* cover all the business operations throughout the value chain, including packaging, marketing, manufacturing, logistics, maintenance of premises, slaughtering and animal treatment when farming (Azam & Abdullah, 2020; Tayob, 2016, 2020). The *Halaal* supply chain system consists of a complex network of agricultural supply chain role-players and *Halaal* accreditation bodies. Within the agricultural supply chain, role-players include farmers, producers, distributors, wholesalers, retailers and consumers (Chandra et al., 2019). The accreditation bodies are responsible for auditing that the supply chain role-players are adhering to the conditions for *Halaal* certification. This encompasses the monitoring of processes at different points of the supply chain, verifying that activities are conducted according to prescribed religious standards and authorising the use of a *Halaal* logo on packaging to label and communicate the *Halaal* status of the product to consumers (Tayob, 2016). People, religion and culture form the roots of this complex system due to the religious nature of *Halaal*. Moreover, the scale of the *Halaal* meat industry requires the use of technology and infrastructure to support business operations and the accreditation process. Hence, the *Halaal* supply chain has both social and technical elements and is hence conducive towards being studied using socio-technical system constructs. Globally, there have been numerous reports of fraud and malpractice by businesses claiming that their products are *Halaal* (Fuseini et al., 2017; Rafudeen, 2013; Ruslan et al., 2018). Consequently, trust in the *Halaal* accreditation process has been impaired and integrity of the accreditation process has been questioned (Kamisah et al., 2018). This has led to the contemporary research into the application of blockchain technology for *Halaal* supply chains, which is termed a *Halaal* blockchain system. This nomenclature is graphically illustrated in Figure 1.

In this chapter, the authors argue that the halaal blockchain system should be conceptualised and studied by applying socio-technical systems theory, rather than in purely technology-driven manner. The authors adopt the socio-technical system model proposed by davis et al. (2014) to analyse the halaal blockchain system. The social element of the analysis is highly contextual to the community being considered. For this study, the authors focus on the south african market for the following reasons: (i) up to 60% of all products at supermarkets in south africa are halaal certified, despite muslims constituting less than 2% of the national population (bux et al., 2022; central intelligence agency, 2021; tayob, 2020); (ii) south africa has the third-highest gross domestic product (gdp) in africa (statista, 2021); and (iii) south africa's economic reconstruction and recovery plan (errp) for rebuilding the nation's economy in the aftermath of the covid-19 pandemic prioritises job creation and greener economies (the government of south africa, 2020), which the halaal blockchain system can contribute towards.

In performing the analysis, the authors had the following research objectives:

RO1: Review the existing literature on *Halaal* blockchain systems.
RO2: Conceptualise the *Halaal* blockchain system using a socio-technical systems framework.
RO3: Analyse the *Halaal* blockchain system in the South African context, using a socio-technical systems framework.
RO4: Identify open research areas related to the *Halaal* blockchain system, based on socio-technical systems engineering and the South African context.

LITERATURE REVIEW

The literature review presented in this chapter is discussed in two subsections. The first subsection broadly reviews the reported benefits of adopting blockchain technology in the agri-food sector, and its feasibility. This gives important context to the background of this chapter. Within the context of the agri-food sector, assurance of *Halaal* status is of importance for Muslim communities. The second subsection of the literature review focuses on the more specific topic of *Halaal* blockchain systems.

Blockchain in the Agri-Food Sector

Blockchain technology has arisen as a key enabler of transparency and trust in a variety of sectors, notably the agri-food sector. Xiong et al. (2020) provide examples of several businesses that have established partnerships with technology companies, such as IBM, towards adopting blockchain for their supply chain activities. Notable among these early-adopters are multi-national companies Walmart, Alibaba, JD.com, Dole, Nestle and Golden Food (Xiong et al., 2020). This is indicative that corporations and conglomerates are recognizing the value provided by blockchain technology and investing in its adoption. Some of the benefits of blockchain technology for enterprises include ensuring that the quality and standard of inbound products is maintained, and creating an environment in which unethical and unsustainable practices are reported transparently. This, in turn, creates sectors where fraud and malpractice is more easily identified, punitive measures against perpetrators can be instated and businesses and individuals are held accountable for their practices (Xiong et al., 2020).

In addition to enterprises, the value of blockchain technology is realized by other stakeholders in the agri-food. Consumers are provided with authentic assurance around the safety, sustainability and quality of the food they consume, due to the transparency inherent to blockchain systems. Producers associated with consistently high-quality products benefit from improved reputation and credibility among consumers, as the blockchain provides a transparent link between all producer and products (Shahid et al., 2020; Xiong et al., 2020).

Literature has shown that blockchain in the agri-food sector is realizable and implementable. Recently, Shahid et al. (2020) presented an end-to-end blockchain system design that was benchmarked against other recent systems, such as those reported by Tsang et al. (2019), Behnke and Janssen (2020) and Hao et al. (2018). The design achieves the intended features of traceability, accountability, credibility and verification of authenticity, as well as user-oriented enhancements related to automating payments and delivery tracking.

Halaal Blockchain Systems

The literature review in this section summarises many of the findings from the recent systematic review by Katuk (2019), and augments this with other studies. Katuk (2019) studied the application of blockchain for *Halaal* product assurance and focused on understanding how blockchain technology works in the context of *Halaal* product assurance and what initiatives have been taken to implement such systems. This study also reviewed the state-of-the-art research in implementing blockchain systems for *Halaal* product assurance and suggested future directs of research.

In reviewing the conceptualisation and structure of blockchain systems when applied to the problem of *Halaal* product assurance, Katuk (2019) overviewed both the structure of blockchain systems, as well as the evolving maturity of blockchain technology from its initial application in supporting digital currencies, to the emerging uses of blockchain in daily life to create a digital society. Katuk (2019) also illustrated the *Halaal* product supply chain from supplier to consumer; and furthermore presented how the supply chain elements could be captured in implementing a *Halaal* blockchain system based on the work by Chandra et al. (2019). Other similar conceptual diagrams were presented by Bux et al. (2022), Ali et al. (2021), Surjandari et al. (2021) and Vanany et al. (2020).

Katuk (2019) further reviewed implementations of *Halaal* blockchain systems and categorised the initiatives into three classes. The first class of initiatives were seminars for *Halaal* industry stakeholders to share knowledge and discuss the potential impacts/challenges of blockchain technology on the sector. Katuk also made mention of initiatives in place to provide greater awareness to the public on the application of blockchain for *Halaal* product assurance. In particular, the online portals Asia Blockchain Review (https://www.asiablockchainreview.com/) and Salaam Gateway (https://www.salaamgateway.com/) were identified. The second class of initiatives referred to digital solutions offered by technology service providers. Katuk (2019) identified seven blockchain solutions that were in development at the time of their research being conducted, in countries such as Malaysia, Singapore, India, the United Arab Emirates, the United Kingdom and the Kingdom of Bahrain[1]. More recently, Sidarto and Hamka (2021) presented a case-study on the Sreeya Sewu implementation of a *Halaal* blockchain system for poultry in Indonesia. The final class of initiatives identified by Katuk (2019) were strategic partnerships between businesses and digital solution providers. Katuk provided an overview of seven partnerships that were established in countries such as Malaysia, the United Kingdom, Slovenia, Hong Kong, and the United Arab Emirates.

There have been many recent articles that have considered the design of *Halaal* blockchain systems and attempted to formulate theoretical and/or conceptual frameworks to guide their design and implementation.

Rejeb (2018) developed a conceptual framework based on applying the Hazard Analysis and Critical Control Points approach to *Halaal* food production, and utilising both blockchain and Internet of Things (IoT) technology. More recently, Tan et al. (2020) studied three implementations of *Halaal* blockchain systems and developed a conceptual framework for future system implementations. The Tan framework leverages IoT technology for data capture and a combination of consortium blockchain networks and smart contracts to ensure food traceability throughout the supply chain. Another conceptual framework was proposed by Abidin and Perdana (2020), which provides a more detailed view on the precise items to be tracked at each point of the supply chain. The data points described by this framework cover those related directly to the *Halaal* products, as well as related environmental variables such as the temperature and humidity during storage. The Abidin framework also acknowledges the role of sensors and monitoring systems in accurately acquiring the data points to be stored on the blockchain ledger.

A common theme in the frameworks discussed above is the role of IoT devices and sensor networks in capturing data for a *Halaal* blockchain system. Rejeb et al. (2021) explored this in more detail and conducted a systematic review of literature on the integration of IoT in the *Halaal* food supply chain. The study discussed five tangible benefits of integrating IoT technology to the supply chain, namely:

1. Traceability of products,
2. Improvement of supply chain efficiencies,
3. Facilitation of livestock management,
4. Authentication of foods' *Halaal* status, and
5. Monitoring of *Halaal* certifications.

Rejeb et al. (2021) also identified challenges that are faced in the adoption of IoT technology for *Halaal* food supply chains. These challenges relate to technical limitations of existing IoT technologies, user acceptance and technology adoption, as well as cost and regulatory barriers.

On a more technical level, there have been other articles that have documented and studied *Halaal* blockchain implementations. The study by Vanany et al. (2020) looked at the blockchain architecture for a *Halaal* blockchain system in Indonesia. The architecture and associated framework were designed based on feedback from interviews with stakeholders from businesses and *Halaal* certification authorities in Indonesia. The architecture designed by Vanany et al. (2020) was based on a permissioned blockchain, the Hyperledger fabric platform and smart contracts to execute agreements between different role players in the supply chain. Similarly, Surjandari et al. (2021) presented a permissioned blockchain network using the Hyperledger fabric platform with three channels and the Raft consensus algorithm. The study concludes through simulation that the blockchain system not only facilitates secure transactions, but also offers effective transaction and data transfer rates. Chandra et al. (2019) discuss the application, architecture and technological components of a consortium blockchain for the *Halaal* food supply chain. Their work presented an experimental study to examine how ownership of a *Halaal* product may be tracked on the blockchain from a distributor to the customer. However, this approach is limited as it does not consider the complete farm-to-consumer supply chain. In a related work, Sidarto and Hamka (2021) present a case study of a blockchain-based traceability system that has been implemented and rolled-out in the Indonesian poultry industry. The case study concluded that the implementation achieved the desired level of transaction immutability and transparency.

Other literature analyses blockchain for *Halaal* certification from a more socially-oriented perspective, which considered the environmental, social and economic sustainability of *Halaal* foods (Bux et al., 2022). In their systematic review, Bux et al. (2022) unpack the state of the *Halaal* certification process globally and draw parallels between *Halaal* certification and other food safety certifications. The review further discusses the heterogeneity of certification processes between different *Halaal* accreditation bodies at a global level. The study also outlines an interesting difference between Muslim-majority and Muslim-minority countries: countries with a greater density of Muslims in their population tend to have fewer *Halaal* accreditation bodies, and as a result, more standardisation in the certification processes (Bux et al., 2022). This is echoed by Hew et al. (2020), whose study emphasises the role of policymakers in promoting participation in blockchain programs through mechanisms such as tax incentives. Bux et al. (2022) further discussed the role of blockchain technology in enhancing trust in the certification process and enhancing consumer loyalty. Interestingly, the study highlighted the opportunities that a blockchain-based *Halaal* certification process provides for small-medium enterprises. This is an important consideration for understanding the impact of a *Halaal* blockchain system in the context of developing economies. In a related study, Ali et al. (2021) developed a framework for adopting blockchain technology for small-medium enterprises that focuses on the challenges and opportunities arising from adopting this technology. The Ali framework provides a means for businesses to evaluate the feasibility and financial rationale behind adopting a *Halaal* blockchain system, based on considering the following five dimensions (Ali et al., 2021):

1. Complexity and capabilities,
2. Costs and competitive advantages,
3. Change management and external pressure,
4. *Halaal* sustainable production, and
5. Regulatory culpability.

Another related study developed a multi-objective mathematical model for the *Halaal* meat supply chain that maximises return on investment and the integrity of the system, while simultaneously minimising total investment costs (Mohammed et al., 2017). This model may be adapted and applied to evaluate the feasibility of introducing any technology to the *Halaal* supply chain.

Other conclusions from the review by Bux et al. (2022) include that blockchain technology has the potential to monitor the use of chemical inputs and fertilisers by farmers and food manufacturers, hereby exposing the environmental impacts of the supply chain to consumers. This contributes to greater environmental and social sustainability by creating a more environmentally-conscious and informed society.

The primary aim of many of the works reviewed in this section has been to present the *Halaal* blockchain system from a conceptual or technical point of view. The few that considered the social aspects of the system discussed the social challenges to its technical design and adoption. Thus, even the sociological studies motivated for the implementation of the *Halaal* blockchain and discussed its feasibility. The limitation of these research efforts is that none of studies reviewed consider the conceptualization, design and deployment of the *Halaal* blockchain system in a holistic manner. As there are both social and technological elements to the *Halaal* blockchain system, conceptualisation of it is conducive to using a socio-technical framework. As discussed by Davis et al. (2014), the founders of socio-technical systems thinking have argued that designing a change in one part of a complex inter-dependent system should be in a holistic manner. If designers do not consider how the change may affect, or require other changes to, other aspects of the system; the effectiveness, and sustainability in the system development can be compromised. The socio-technical system concept advocates the consideration of both technical and social factors when change is sought in an organization or a complex socio-technical system (Davis et al., 2014). Prior to this way of thinking, technological interventions were often designed without considering the behaviours and opinions of the technology users. The norm was to first develop a technological solution, and then convince users to adopt it without fully understanding their perspectives and requirements. On the other hand, using the socio-technical systems framework, system designers also re-designed job descriptions and work processes, alongside the technology. This led to improved user-experience for employees and better effectiveness of the complete, holistic system (Davis et al., 2014).

The aim of this chapter is to argue that the complex *Halaal* blockchain system should be considered using a socio-technical system framework in its conceptualisation, and socio-technical system engineering, as described by Baxter and Sommerville (2011), in its design and deployment. A similar study was undertaken by Sony and Naik (2020), who used a socio-technical perspective to propose a holistic methodology to design system architectures for 4IR technology in the context of Industry 4.0.

METHODOLOGY

Choice of Socio-Technical Systems Analytical Framework

In conceptualising and analysing socio-technical systems, it is important to consider a holistic approach that accounts for technical and social elements in tandem (Sony & Naik, 2020). A leading model for analysing socio-technical systems was proposed by Davis et al. (2014), which describes the interconnected relationships and dependencies between people, processes, culture, technology, goals and infrastructure; embedded within the external environment. The Davis model, illustrated in Figure 2, considers the external environment to comprise of various sets of stakeholders, regulatory frameworks and the financial and economic circumstances. The Davis model was designed to be more generic than other socio-technical frameworks – such as the Human Factors Analysis and Classification System (Wiegmann & Shappell, 2017), Accimap (Rasmussen, 1997) and Systems Theoretic Accident Modelling and Process model (Leveson, 2004) – and it is hence more appropriate for the study of complex interdependent systems such as the *Halaal* blockchain (Davis et al., 2014; Sony & Naik, 2020).

The analysis is guided by the work of Appelbaum (1997), whose work provides a set of questions for identifying and understanding the interactions between different components of the socio-technical system.

Data Sources

The analysis presented in this chapter considers data from the following sources:

- Academic literature,
- Commercial white papers and reports,
- Journalism articles from reputable South African news agencies, and
- Government reports and policy documents.

Data Analysis

When analysing the data, the authors make use of the document analysis methodology. Benefits of this methodology include: lack of obtrusiveness when considering social communities, stability and non-reactivity when considering social communities, exactness and efficiency (Bowen, 2009). Some of the potential flaws in the document analysis methodology arise when documents are not retrieved or cannot be accessed, when documents contain insufficient detail and in cases where an incomplete selection of documents results in biased selectivity (Bowen, 2009).

For this study, the researchers have scrutinised the documents that were analysed, and have established that the quality of documents available are sufficient for meaningful results to be obtained.

The *Halaal* blockchain system was decomposed and conceptualised from the perspective of each of the six core system components of the Davis socio-technical system framework, depicted in Figure 2. Appropriate documents to describe the South African social context and relevant technology for the *Halaal* blockchain system were identified from the data sources. Discussions were held between the researchers to identify limitations and common themes. The researchers also reflected on their own lived experiences as members of the South African Muslim community; and questioned their inherent biases to ensure that the research presented was objective and fair in its reporting. A further advantage of the document analysis methodology in this study is that it ensures that researchers were not reliant on tacit knowledge or biased perspectives, and that the credibility of the research is maintained.

ANALYSIS AND DISCUSSION

Goals

The main goal of the *Halaal* supply chain is to provide assurance to consumers that correct processes have been followed throughout the supply chain for all products labelled as *Halaal*. Without the use of blockchain technology, this done through *Halaal* accreditation bodies conducting audits of facilities along the supply chain and certifying their status as *Halaal*. The products made available to a consumer are identified as *Halaal* through a logo on their packaging, which indicates that the cumulative supply chain processes meet the requirements for *Halaal* certification.

However, as discussed in the introduction, globally there have been numerous cases of fraud and malpractice which undermines the above process. A famous example in South Africa includes the Orion meat scandal (Rafudeen, 2013).

To prevent fraud and malpractice the *Halaal* accreditation process, it is important to improve transparency and traceability in the supply chain. This would improve the ability of the system to meet its goal of providing assurance to consumers. Studies of *Halaal* blockchain systems that have been implemented have concluded that the blockchain technology was able to successfully improve transparency and traceability (Sidarto & Hamka, 2021).

People and Culture

The people element of the *Halaal* blockchain system is potentially the most diverse component. "People" encompasses the individual workers, managers and leaders at each of the facilities along the supply chain; as well as the members of the *Halaal* accreditation bodies. "Culture", from a socio-technical perspective, refers to the customs, ideologies and social behaviours of these groups of people (Davis et al., 2014). As such, the analysis presented discusses the "people" and "culture" components of the Davis socio-technical systems framework concurrently.

Appelbaum (1997) has highlighted the importance of understanding the attitudes of the various groups of people within a system, and the effect of their respective attitudes on their behaviours. Tayob (2020) indicated that as much as 60% of products at South African supermarkets are certified as *Halaal*. This indicates that businesses are aware of the financial benefits of *Halaal* certification associated with

Socio-Technical Systems Engineering Perspectives

making goods available to the local Muslim consumers. However, the evidence of fraud in the South African *Halaal* supply chain indicates that there are groups who have negligent, careless or deceitful attitudes towards *Halaal* certification (Rafudeen, 2013).

The *Halaal* blockchain system was conceived using electronic monitoring devices and IoT technology to capture data points and store them on the blockchain. This creates a higher degree of transparency in supply chain activities, which makes organizations and individuals along the supply chain more accountable.

Another dimension that is critical to consider is the attitude of people towards the technology that underpins the *Halaal* blockchain system. As discussed by Rejeb et al. (2021), there are significant knowledge barriers that inhibit the uptake of new technologies by *Halaal* consumers with low digital literacy. In South Africa, the general community (including the Muslim community) does not have a high level of digital literacy (Chetty et al., 2018; Hanekom, 2020; Krönke, 2020). However, in their study of 34 African countries, Krönke (2020) showed that the digital literacy of South Africans (52%) is much higher than the average digital literacy of the African countries surveyed (31%). The results also showed that, on average, there are greater levels of digital literacy among the youth. Further to this, Krönke (2020) showed that formal education and financial standing were also associated with higher levels of digital literacy among respondents. In addition, building digital literacy and technological skills in South Africa is a priority at government level, as indicated in the Implementation Programme for the National Digital and Future Skills Strategy of South Africa (Abrahams & Burke, 2022). Hence, it is foreseen that the digital literacy of the general South African population will rise in coming years, but the authors have not identified any specific education initiatives on blockchain technologies to directly improve the attitudes of people towards a *Halaal* blockchain system. These education interventions are particularly important for Muslim communities, as there has been ongoing debate on whether cryptocurrencies (the most well-known application of blockchain technology) are *Halaal* or not (Asif, 2018). As a result, people from the Muslim community who do not understand the difference between blockchain technology and its application to cryptocurrencies may have false perceptions and biases towards blockchain technology, affecting their attitudes towards its application in the context of the *Halaal* supply chain. This aligns to studies that described the complexities involved in preparing role-players in the *Halaal* supply chain to participate in a *Halaal* blockchain project (Hew et al., 2020). The issue of education also affects consumers, as it impacts their ability to derive benefit from the blockchain technology.

A second element of understanding the people and cultural components of a socio-technical system is to identify the sources of conflict between groups of people (Appelbaum, 1997). Historically, surety of the *Halaal* status of food products was built upon inter-personal trust within Muslim communities (Tayob, 2020). That there are over 300 *Halaal* certification bodies across the globe (Chandra et al., 2019). Although there are commonalities, the standards used by each body are not consistent. This is due to differences in ideologies, legal interpretations, cultures, and aims and objectives of the certification process for the community. In the South African context, there are many certifying organizations, such as the South African National *Halaal* Authority (SANHA), the Muslim Judicial Council (MJC), the *Halaal* Foundation of South Africa and the National Independent *Halal* Trust (NIHT), who compete for the lucrative local market (Bux et al., 2022; Tayob, 2020). Tayob (2020) has highlighted that different accreditation bodies – in particular, SANHA and the MJC – have different ideological viewpoints and religious standards as to what constitutes acceptable practices to warrant *Halaal* certification. The differences in these opinions, as well as how these options align to the opinions and ideological beliefs of consumers, is a frequent source of debate and conflict in the South African Muslim community (Tayob,

2016, 2020). The transparency provided by the *Halaal* blockchain system gives consumers higher visibility of the supply chain activities, the certifying processes adopted and the certifying authorities who have audited the processes. While this does not alleviate the issue of different ideological standards among accreditation bodies, it provides the consumers with knowledge and empowers their ability to make informed decisions based on their personal beliefs.

Another aspect of how the *Halaal* blockchain system affects people is its potential to create job opportunities. One of the priority interventions described by the South African ERRP is Presidential Employment Stimulus (The Government of South Africa, 2020). This intervention addresses job lost due to the Covid-19 pandemic. The ERRP plans to create and support 800 000 new jobs in South Africa. The design, deployment and operation of the *Halaal* blockchain system would create job opportunities contributing to achieving this target.

Processes/Procedures

The processes and procedures in a socio-technical system should facilitate the system meeting its goals (Appelbaum, 1997). Sony and Naik (2020) describe the processes involved in digitising a 4IR system using socio-technical systems thinking in terms of vertical integration and horizontal integration. In the context of the *Halaal* blockchain system, vertical integration refers to how individual facilities (e.g. farms, abbatoirs, distribution centres, etc.) digitise their operations. Horizontal integration refers to how there is digitisation along the supply chain and data logging between facilities.

IoT technology is perceived as the main intervention to achieve vertical integration at each facility. The extent to which IoT technology needs to be adopted will differ between facilities along the supply chain, depending on the data points that need to be logged and evaluated for that facility. Hence, the specific IoT devices, sensors and technology stack will vary between facilities. Vertical integration through adopting IoT creates transparency around the operations at the facility, which assists the *Halaal* accreditation process. The procedures at each facility that must be followed for a product to be considered *Halaal* are defined primarily by Shariah Law, and secondarily by the ideologies of *Halaal* accreditation body that audits the processes. Vertical integration of the technology also requires that people at each facility to be sufficiently educated in the operation of the technology, and re-designing of their job descriptions and internal procedures to align with the new technologies.

Blockchain technology is the main technological intervention to achieve horizontal integration. A common blockchain platform needs to record and store data blocks from all facilities along the supply chain. The data blocks need to also cater for differences in tagging/identification/labelling structures and mechanisms between facilities. For example, an animal may come to an abattoir with an RFID tag to identify it, but the meat product that leaves the abattoir is packaged with a serial bar-code that is used for the rest of the supply chain. The common blockchain platform allows the *Halaal* blockchain system to improve product traceability.

Infrastructure and Technology

Two of the components of the Davis socio-technical systems framework are "technology" and "infrastructure". In this analysis, the authors consider the technology of the *Halaal* blockchain system and the infrastructure that it is built upon concurrently. The infrastructure, in this case, refers to state-provided or state-regulated resources that enable the system. Examples of such resources include: electricity

Socio-Technical Systems Engineering Perspectives

supply from the national power grid, road and rail networks for transportation services, and network connectivity and Internet access.

The technology component of the *Halaal* blockchain system, adapted from the frameworks reviewed (Abidin & Perdana, 2020; Chandra et al., 2019; Rejeb et al., 2021; Tan et al., 2020), can be summarised as:

- The IoT devices and sensor networks that will monitor the supply chain operations, capture data and record transactions that will be stored on the blockchain network.
- The communication network that will interconnect nodes in IoT networks. This will also facilitate connectivity for the blockchain network, allowing the blockchain system to access data from the nodes.
- The blockchain platform that creates, verifies and authenticates data blocks, and distributes them across the blockchain network. Data blocks are created from the transactional data that originated from the IoT devices. These blocks are distributed across the network. Verification and authentication is done using consensus algorithms at each blockchain server on the network to ensure that only valid blocks are stored on the blockchain. This creates an immutable record that is stored on each server, ensuring data integrity and transparency.
- The end-user applications to access data stored on the blockchain ledger. Different groups stakeholders would interact with this data according to their needs.

Appelbaum (1997) has also alluded to the need for technology to be developed with due consideration for user-experience. The objective of a technological intervention is to reduce human effort while improving accuracy and/or efficiency. Reduction in human effort is ideally achieved by simplifying of processes and procedures, or ensuring that any re-designed processes do not burden end-users. If achieved, the reduction in human effort positively impacts the attitude of people that use the technological system.

Load-Shedding

One of the most apparent infrastructural challenges for technological developments in South Africa is the unreliability of its electricity supply. Most electricity in South Africa is produced by the sole parastatal entity, Eskom, which has struggled to consistently meet the energy demand of the nation during times of high demand (Eskom, n.d.). Since 2007, Eskom has often resorted to implementing a system of rolling, localised power outages – referred to locally as "load-shedding" – to manage the strain on the national grid and prevent a complete national blackout (Eskom, n.d.; Maune, 2019). Although energy security is a priority intervention in the South African ERRP (The Government of South Africa, 2020), load-shedding is expected to remain an intermittent part of South African life for years to come (Khoza, 2021), as Eskom struggles to address challenges such as:

- The urgent need to perform regular plant maintenance and address existing maintenance deficits and backlogs (Paton, 2021).
- Ongoing and historic issues arising from maladministration, corruption, poor governance and debt (Blom, 2017; Bowman, 2020; Lawrence, 2020).
- Mounting pressure for some of the older coal-fuelled plants to be shut down and upgraded due to their high pollution output (de Wet, 2021; Myllyvitra, 2021).

The implications of load-shedding on economic activities in South Africa have been well-documented by the likes of du Venage (2020), Goldberg (2015) and Laher et al. (2019), among others. The *Halaal* blockchain system is fundamentally a technological solution, and so the effects of load-shedding on the system must be considered during its design and implementation. Some of the effects of load-shedding on the *Halaal* blockchain system include:

- The need for secondary power sources, such as battery backups, for the sensors and IoT devices to prevent downtime. Furthermore, the power-surges that occur after load-shedding may damage more sensitive devices, and protection against this should be considered at the design phase.
- Power consumption of all hardware devices deployed at scale should not over-burden the already strained national power grid. Alternate renewable energy sources and power-efficiency of hardware devices must be carefully considered.
- Disruption to external dependencies, such as telecommunication infrastructure, may result in connectivity downtime and link outages. The extent to which hardware devices are able to continue operating with only local, on-board resources should be considered, as well as the self-healing capabilities of the network itself.
- Load-shedding affects traffic control lights, leading to traffic congestion. This impacts the distribution and logistics elements of the supply chain.
- A disrupted electricity supply results in the attitude of people towards more technology-driven systems being impacted negative, as manual (non-technological) processes are not impacted by load-shedding.

In 2020, the South African ERRP indicated the South African Government's intention to stabilise their electricity supply, improve infrastructure and combat load-shedding by the end of 2022 (The Government of South Africa, 2020). However, between September and October 2022, South Africa experienced consecutive days of load-shedding for the longest period in its history (Staff Writer, 2022). As such, it is expected that load-shedding will remain a long-term challenge for South Africa, and an important factor to consider in the design of future technological systems.

Communication Infrastructure and Connectivity

Another important consideration for the system development is the communications infrastructure to support the IoT systems and blockchain network. This infrastructure has two key roles:

- To connect IoT devices and sensors that capture data to be stored on the Halaal blockchain ledger.
- To provide the connectivity for the blockchain network. This may include internet access for designs that consider a cloud-based (Blockchain-as-a-Service (BaaS)) architecture.

South Africa spans across a large geographical area and the communications infrastructure available varies from the major cities to the rural areas. Land dedicated to agriculture may also suffer from poor access to telecommunications infrastructure, which affects which areas can be integrated into the *Halaal* blockchain system. Leading South African telecommunication service providers MTN and Vodacom have recognised the growth of IoT in the country and have developed supporting infrastructure to support these devices (The MTN Group, 2015; Vodacom, n.d.). Many of the solutions proposed for providing

Socio-Technical Systems Engineering Perspectives

connectivity to remote geographic areas has included the use of long-range 2G+ technology towards Narrow-Band IoT (NB-IoT) networks. The NB-IoT offerings from service providers represent a feasible solution for developing IoT systems, resolving the cost barrier that historically inhibited internet access in South Africa (Electronic Communications Network, n.d.). Robinson (2020) evaluated the performance of the communication infrastructure supporting NB-IoT, and noted the variability in the services offered by different providers. Patel and Quazi (2022) also discussed the need for enabling internet penetration to remote and rural areas, and emergence of terrestrial satellite networks to achieve this. As such, the communication interface for the IoT devices within the *Halaal* blockchain network must adapt to the available access networks.

As mentioned in the discussion of load-shedding, network downtime for any reason affects the ability of IoT devices to communicate with each other and the larger blockchain network. This impacts their ability to store data on the blockchain ledger, leading to transactions (that represent procedures along the supply chain) not being recorded timeously.

In addition, the national commitment to investing in infrastructure described by the South African ERRP includes the telecommunication infrastructure that supports the *Halaal* blockchain network (The Government of South Africa, 2020). The auctioning of radio spectrum, conducted in March 2022, was one such initiative towards developing this infrastructure (South African Government News Agency, 2022).

Embedded Devices and IoT Networks

The complexities of designing embedded devices and IoT systems for agricultural supply chains is represents a standalone open research area (Kumari et al., 2015). In their systematic review of the field, Rejeb et al. (2021) explore the specific nuances of IoT systems for *Halaal* supply chains. This is a key technology for the *Halaal* blockchain system. Insights from the review show that research in this area is sparse, but that the field has been gaining attention, as evidenced by the timeline of publications contributing to the review – 77.0% of the reviewed publications between 2008 and 2020 were published in the last six years of the review period (Rejeb et al., 2021). As with the *Halaal* blockchain, IoT research for *Halaal* supply chains has been mostly conducted in Malaysia, which contributed to 60.8% of the publications (Rejeb et al., 2021). It was also noted that the dominant technology explored for *Halaal* supply chains was radio-frequency identification (RFID) tagging, as it is a cost-effective technology to enable efficient, real-time data capture to track and trace food products through the supply chain. Challenges with RFID tagging were also noted, including security risks due to tag counterfeiting and hacking (Khosravi et al., 2018; Rejeb et al., 2021).

An apparent gap in the research is that sensor networks and IoT systems for *Halaal* contexts may require additional functionality beyond what is needed for a generic agricultural supply chain. These systems would aid in continuously monitoring that the correct religious practices and control standards are maintained throughout the supply chain. For example, the IoT devices may need to determine whether the correct prayers are read when slaughtering an animal, or to verify that no cross-contamination between *Halaal* and non-*Halaal* products occur during storage and transportation. This fundamentally impacts how data related to the different processes and procedures in the *Halaal* supply chain is captured.

The External Environment

Per the Davis model illustrated in Figure 2, the external environment of a socio-technical system considers multiple groups of stakeholders, regulatory frameworks and the financial/economic context. The authors have identified the following impacts that a successful implementation of the *Halaal* blockchain may have for South Africa:

Food Retailers and Dining Establishments

As indicated in the introduction, South Africa is country with a large demand for *Halaal* products and a Muslim population with high spending power. This points to a sizable market for *Halaal* products, which is supplemented by the growing portion of non-Muslim consumers who purchase *Halaal* products for non-religious reasons (cleanliness, hygiene, food quality, etc.) (Mathew et al., 2014). Further to this, a technologically-driven approach to *Halaal* certification will improve access to *Halaal* products for large, chain-retailers that typically do not participate in the traditional, community-based model of *Halaal* trade (Tayob, 2020). This benefits Muslim communities by making *Halaal* foods more accessible, while simultaneously providing businesses with access to new consumer markets and improving competitiveness in the *Halaal* foods industry.

The adoption of a *Halaal* blockchain system also holds interesting implications for dining establishments. The current model of certification in South Africa involves individual dining establishments applying for *Halaal* certification at a monetary cost (The Muslim Judicial Council Halaal Trust, n.d.), which creates a financial burden on smaller businesses. As discussed by Bux et al. (2022), the *Halaal* blockchain system is expected to alleviate this financial burden and create business opportunities for small-medium enterprises.

Fraud Prevention

There have been many historic instances where food goods were fraudulently represented as *Halaal* without undergoing proper accreditation by a *Halaal* certification body (Fuseini et al., 2017; Ruslan et al., 2018). Ab Talib and Mohd Johan (2012) report on this, among other challenges, in a study of challenges during the traditional *Halaal* packaging process. The transparency and traceability afforded by a blockchain-based certificate will mitigate these fraudulent crimes.

International Trade

The immutable nature of blockchain technology creates transparency across international borders. By adopting a *Halaal* blockchain system, South Africa will be able to provide potential customers with evidence of the extent to which locally-farmed meat products are compliant with international *Halaal* requirements and standards. This will enable South Africa to advertise its *Halaal* products to other nations, and address the declining trends in meat export reported by the South African government (Department of Agriculture, Land Reform and Rural Development (DALRRD), 2020). This aligns to the South African ERRP priority intervention of strategic localisation, industrialisation and export promotion (The Government of South Africa, 2020).

International Tourism

Tourism contributed 2.9% of the South Afican GDP in 2016, at which point it was a greater contributor to the economy than agriculture (Statistics South Africa, 2018). The 2021 and 2022 editions of the Global Muslim Travel Index (Mastercard-Crescentrating, 2021, 2022) indicate that internationally, Muslim tourism that grew over 48% between 2013 and 2019 prior to the Covid-19 pandemic and forecasts that travel will recover to 80% of 2019 volumes by 2023. The 2022 report indicates that South Africa is positioned joint-sixth in the world amongst countries that do not belong to the Organisation of Islamic Cooperation (OIC), and 34th overall. South Africa is also indexed as the best Muslim tourism destination in Southern and Middle Africa.

This Global Muslim Travel Index ranking is derived from a score that emphasises the importance of access to *Halaal* food, stating that this the "key service" that Muslim travellers look for when choosing a destination. Currently, South Africa scores 60/100 for *Halaal* dining per the 2022 report, while countries in the Top 20 score [3] 80 for this metric (Mastercard-Crescentrating, 2022). A blockchain-based *Halaal* assurance that meets global standards will hence improve international trust in *Halaal* dining in South Africa; and contribute positively to the South African Muslim Tourism sector. Tourism recovery and growth is another of the priority interventions mentioned in the South African ERRP (The Government of South Africa, 2020).

Green Economy

As discussed in the introduction, there is ongoing research into the use of blockchain technology for sustainable agricultural practices. The *Halaal* blockchain systems synergises with potential agricultural blockchain systems and may be developed as an extension or complementary technology. This is in agreement with the findings of Bux et al. (2022).

OPEN RESEARCH AREAS BASED ON SOCIO-TECHNICAL SYSTEMS ENGINEERING

Baxter and Sommerville (2011) have identified sensitisation and constructive engagement as two key processes of socio-technical systems engineering. The following recommendations and open research areas have been conceived using this theoretical framework:

- Development of strategies for increasing digital literacy and building social capital related to blockchain technology. This will include the development of technical training and knowledge management strategies to support a *Halaal* blockchain system. This directly relates to the "sensitisation" process described by Baxter and Sommerville (2011).
- Investigating the level of trust in the *Halaal* accreditation/certification industry (holistically, or with respect to individual accreditation bodies). This could then be compared to a similar study after the implementation of a *Halaal* blockchain system to quantify the impact of the technological intervention. This study relates to how well the *Halaal* blockchain system meets the goals of the *Halaal* supply chain.

- Developing the business case for developing and deploying a *Halaal* blockchain system. This would involve investigating the direct and indirect costs, qualifying the risks to adoption and associated controls to be implemented, and ultimately determining the potential return-on-investment. The multi-objective financial model developed by Mohammed et al. (2017) can be adapted for this study.

In addition, the authors have identified the following technical open research areas. Throughout the design, development and deployment processes, constructive engagement should be undertaken with stakeholders from across the supply chain (Baxter & Sommerville, 2011).

- Design of IoT systems, sensor networks and algorithms for the *Halaal* supply chain. The nuances of *Halaal* certification need to be considered for these devices. For example, bespoke devices/algorithms may be designed to detect that the appropriate religious practices are carried out during the slaughtering process. The relevant supporting infrastructure (such as available communication networks and electricity supply) available in South Africa should be considered in the designs.
- Thoroughly compare the technical features and limitations of blockchain platforms to determine the most suitable option for the *Halaal* blockchain system in South Africa. This may be inspired by existing blockchain systems for supply-chain applications. The breadth of blockchain platform configuration parameters should be considered and optimised. The economic limitations of the South African context should be considered.

LIMITATIONS OF WORK

Socio-technical analyses are contextual in nature. This study was conducted in the South African context, and as such, some of the analyses cannot be readily extrapolated to other contexts. However, the methodology applied in conducting the study can be adapted and applied for other contexts. Future research can consider performing similar contextualized studies in other settings.

CONCLUSION

In this chapter, the authors adopted the Davis socio-technical systems framework to analyse the *Halaal* blockchain system. The core components of the system (goals, people, culture, processes/procedures, technology and infrastructure) and the interconnected relationships between them were investigated. The study was conducted in the South African context. The analysis found that there are a range of challenges in South Africa which must be overcome to successfully implement a *Halaal* blockchain system, such as insufficient digital literacy in communities. Other factors that would impact a *Halaal* blockchain implementation include unreliable electricity supply, poor network coverage in rural areas and differing ideologies among *Halaal* accreditation bodies. However, despite these challenges, benefits have been identified for a range of stakeholders, including businesses, government agencies and communities. These benefits are derived from the increased accountability, credibility, transparency, traceability and auditability of *Halaal* status enabled by the blockchain system. The study concludes by

REFERENCES

Ab Talib, M. S., & Mohd Johan, M. (2012). Issues in halal packaging: A conceptual paper. *International Business Management*, 5(2), 94–98.

Abidin, N. Z., & Perdana, F. F. P. (2020). A Proposed Conceptual Framework for Blockchain Technology in Halal Food Product Verification. *Journal of Halal Industry and Services*, 3(Special Issue), 1–8. doi:10.36877/jhis.a0000079

Abrahams, L., & Burke, M. (2022). *Implementation Programme for the National Digital and Future Skills Strategy of South Africa, 2021–2025*. Retrieved from https://www.gov.za/sites/default/files/gcis_document/202203/digital-and-future-skillsimplementation-programmefinal.pdf

Ali, M. H., Chung, L., Kumar, A., Zailani, S., & Tan, K. H. (2021). A sustainable Blockchain framework for the halal food supply chain: Lessons from Malaysia. *Technological Forecasting and Social Change*, 170, 120870. doi:10.1016/j.techfore.2021.120870

Appelbaum, S. H. (1997). Socio-technical systems theory: An intervention strategy for organizational development. *Management Decision*, 35(6), 452–463. doi:10.1108/00251749710173823

Asif, S. (2018). The halal and haram aspect of cryptocurrencies in Islam. *Journal of Islamic Banking and Finance*, 35(2), 91–101.

Azam, M. S. E., & Abdullah, M. A. (2020). Global Halal Industry: Realities and Opportunities. *International Journal of Islamic Business Ethics*, 5(1), 47. Advance online publication. doi:10.30659/ijibe.5.1.47-59

Baxter, G., & Sommerville, I. (2011). Socio-technical systems: From design methods to systems engineering. *Interacting with Computers*, 23(1), 4–17. doi:10.1016/j.intcom.2010.07.003

Behnke, K., & Janssen, M. F. W. H. A. (2020). Boundary conditions for traceability in food supply chains using blockchain technology. *International Journal of Information Management*, 52, 101969. doi:10.1016/j.ijinfomgt.2019.05.025

Blom, T. (2017). *Unplugging corruption at Eskom*. https://static.pmg.org.za/171018OUTA_report.pdf

Bowen, G. A. (2009). Document Analysis as a Qualitative Research Method. *Qualitative Research Journal*, 9(2), 27–40. doi:10.3316/QRJ0902027

Bowman, A. (2020). Parastatals and economic transformation in South Africa: The political economy of the Eskom crisis. *African Affairs*, 119(476), 395–431. doi:10.1093/afraf/adaa013

Bux, C., Varese, E., Amicarelli, V., & Lombardi, M. (2022). Halal Food Sustainability between Certification and Blockchain: A Review. *Sustainability (Basel)*, 14(4), 2152. https://www.mdpi.com/2071-1050/14/4/2152. doi:10.3390u14042152

Central Intelligence Agency. (2021). *The World Factbook: South Africa*. Retrieved 29 Nov. 2021 from https://www.cia.gov/the-world-factbook/countries/south-africa/#people-and-society

Chandra, G. R., Liaqat, I. A., & Sharma, B. (2019). *Blockchain Redefining: The Halal Food Sector. 2019 Amity International Conference on Artificial Intelligence (AICAI)*, Dubai, UAE. 10.1109/AICAI.2019.8701321

Chetty, K., Qigui, L., Gcora, N., Josie, J., Wenwei, L., & Fang, C. (2018). Bridging the digital divide: measuring digital literacy. *Economics, 12*(1).

Davis, M. C., Challenger, R., Jayewardene, D. N., & Clegg, C. W. (2014). Advancing socio-technical systems thinking: A call for bravery. *Applied Ergonomics, 45*(2), 171–180. doi:10.1016/j.apergo.2013.02.009 PMID:23664481

de Wet, P. (2021). Eskom says it is now legally obliged to shut down one-third of its generating capacity. *Business Insider South Africa*. https://www.businessinsider.co.za/eskom-says-pollution-decision-will-cost-it-16000mw-of-capacity-if-implemented-2021-12

Department of Agriculture, Land Reform and Rural Development (DALRRD). (2020). *A profile of the South African beef market value chain*. https://www.dalrrd.gov.za/doaDev/sideMenu/Marketing/Annual\%20Publications/Beef\%20Market\%20Value\%20Chain\%20Profile\%202020.pdf

Disastraa, G. M., Suryawardanib, B., Sastikac, W., & Hanifa, F. H. (2020). Religiosity, Halal Awareness, and Muslim Consumers' Purchase Intention in Non-Food Halal Products. *International Journal of Innovation, Creativity and Change*, 813-828.

du Venage, G. (2020). South Africa comes to standstill with Eskom's load shedding. *Engineering and Mining Journal, 221*(1), 18–18.

Dutta, P., Choi, T.-M., Somani, S., & Butala, R. (2020). Blockchain technology in supply chain operations: Applications, challenges and research opportunities. *Transportation Research Part E, Logistics and Transportation Review, 142*, 102067. doi:10.1016/j.tre.2020.102067 PMID:33013183

Electronic Communications Network. (n.d.). *Telecommunications in South Africa*. Retrieved 2 March from https://www.ecn.co.za/telecommunications/

Eskom. (n.d.). *What is load shedding?* Retrieved 17 Feb. from https://loadshedding.eskom.co.za/LoadShedding/Description

Fuseini, A., Wotton, S. B., Knowles, T. G., & Hadley, P. J. (2017). Halal Meat Fraud and Safety Issues in the UK: A Review in the Context of the European Union. *Food Ethics, 1*(2), 127–142. doi:10.100741055-017-0009-1

Goldberg, A. (2015). *The economic impact of load shedding: The case of South African retailers*. University of Pretoria.

Hanekom, P. (2020). Covid-19 exposes South Africa's digital literacy divide. *The Mail & Guardian*. https://mg.co.za/opinion/2020-09-08-covid-19-exposes-south-africas-digital-literacy-divide/

Hao, J., Sun, Y. L., & Luo, H. (2018). *A Safe and Efficient Storage Scheme Based on BlockChain and IPFS for Agricultural Products Tracking*. Academic Press.

Hew, J.-J., Wong, L.-W., Tan, G. W.-H., Ooi, K.-B., & Lin, B. (2020). The blockchain-based Halal traceability systems: A hype or reality? *Supply Chain Management*, 25(6), 863–879. doi:10.1108/SCM-01-2020-0044

Kamisah, S., Mokhtar, A., & Hafsah, A. (2018). Halal practices integrity and halal supply chain trust in Malaysian halal food supply chain. *International Food Research Journal*, 25, S57–S62.

Katuk, N. (2019). The application of blockchain for halal product assurance: A systematic review of the current developments and future directions. *International Journal of Advanced Trends in Computer Science and Engineering*, 8(5), 1893–1902. doi:10.30534/ijatcse/2019/13852019

Khan, M. I., & Haleem, A. (2016). Understanding "Halal" and "Halal Certification & Accreditation System"- A Brief Review. *Saudi Journal of Business and Management Studies*, 1(1), 32–42. doi:10.36348jbms.2020.v05i01.005

Khosravi, M., Ali, N. I., Karbasi, M., Brohi, I. A., Shaikh, I. A., & Shah, A. (2018). Comparison between NFC/RFID and bar code systems for Halal tags identification: Paired sample T-test evaluation. *International Journal of Advanced Computer Science and Applications*, 9(4). Advance online publication. doi:10.14569/IJACSA.2018.090435

Khoza, A. (2021). Load-shedding is here to stay, Cyril Ramaphosa tells parliament. *TimesLIVE*. https://www.timeslive.co.za/politics/2021-11-25-load-shedding-is-here-to-stay-cyril-ramaphosa-tells-parliament/

Krönke, M. (2020). *Africa's digital divide and the promise of e-learning* [Policy Paper]. Academic Press.

Kumari, L., Narsaiah, K., Grewal, M., & Anurag, R. (2015). Application of RFID in agri-food sector. *Trends in Food Science & Technology*, 43(2), 144–161. doi:10.1016/j.tifs.2015.02.005

Laher, A., Van Aardt, B., Craythorne, A., Van Welie, M., Malinga, D., & Madi, S. (2019). 'Getting out of the dark': Implications of load shedding on healthcare in South Africa and strategies to enhance preparedness. *South African Medical Journal*, 109(12), 899–901. doi:10.7196/SAMJ.2019.v109i12.14322 PMID:31865948

Lawrence, A. (2020). Eskom and the Dual Character of the South African State. In *South Africa's Energy Transition* (pp. 59–83). Springer. doi:10.1007/978-3-030-18903-7_3

Leveson, N. (2004). A new accident model for engineering safer systems. *Safety Science*, 42(4), 237–270. doi:10.1016/S0925-7535(03)00047-X

Mastercard-Crescentrating. (2021). *Global Muslim Travel Index 2021*. https://www.crescentrating.com/halal-muslim-travel-market-reports.html

Mastercard-Crescentrating. (2022). *Global Muslim Travel Index 2022*. https://www.crescentrating.com/halal-muslim-travel-market-reports.html

Mathew, V. N., Abdullah, A. M. R. A., & Ismail, S. N. M. (2014). Acceptance on Halal Food among Non-Muslim Consumers. *Procedia: Social and Behavioral Sciences, 121*, 262–271. doi:10.1016/j.sbspro.2014.01.1127

Maune, B. (2019). *Load shedding: Timeline of Eskom's battle to keep the lights on.* Retrieved 17 Feb. from https://www.thesouthafrican.com/news/eskom-load-shedding-timeline-since-2007/

Medaglia, R., & Damsgaard, J. (2020). Blockchain and the United Nations Sustainable Development Goals: Towards an Agenda for IS Research. *24th Pacific Asia Conference on Information Systems: Information Systems (IS) for the Future, PACIS 2020.* doi:10.1080/10942912.2016.1203933

Mohammed, A., Wang, Q., & Li, X. (2017). A study in integrity of an RFID-monitoring HMSC. *International Journal of Food Properties, 20*(5), 1145–1158. doi:10.1080/10942912.2016.1203933

Myllyvitra, L. (2021). *Eskom is now the world's most polluting power company.* https://energyandcleanair.org/wp/wp-content/uploads/2021/10/Eskom-is-now-the-worlds-most-polluting-power-company.pdf

Patel, S. S., & Quazi, T. (2022). A multiple-input, multiple-output broadcasting system with space, time, polarization, and labeling diversity. *Transactions on Emerging Telecommunications Technologies*, e4663. https://doi.org/https://doi.org/10.1002/ett.4663

Paton, C. (2021). Eskom: Massive maintenance delays on the back of worst load shedding year ever. *News24.* https://www.news24.com/fin24/Economy/eskom-massive-maintenance-delays-on-the-back-of-worst-load-shedding-year-ever-20220127

Rafudeen, A. (2013). The Orion Cold Storage Saga: Debating 'Halaal' in South Africa. *Alternation Journal, 11*, 134-162. https://journals.ukzn.ac.za/index.php/soa/article/view/406

Rasmussen, J. (1997). Risk management in a dynamic society: A modelling problem. *Safety Science, 27*(2), 183–213. doi:10.1016/S0925-7535(97)00052-0

Rejeb, A. (2018). Halal Meat Supply Chain Traceability based on HACCP, Blockchain and Internet of Things. *Acta Technica Jaurinensis, 11*(4), 218–247. doi:10.14513/actatechjaur.v11.n4.467

Rejeb, A., Rejeb, K., Zailani, S., Treiblmaier, H., & Hand, K. J. (2021). Integrating the Internet of Things in the halal food supply chain: A systematic literature review and research agenda. *Internet of Things, 13*, 100361. https://doi.org/https://doi.org/10.1016/j.iot.2021.100361

Robinson, D. (2020). *NB-IoT (LTE Cat-NB1/narrow-band IoT) performance evaluation of variability in multiple LTE vendors, UE devices and MNOs.* Stellenbosch University.

Ruslan, A. A. A., Kamarulzaman, N. H., & Sanny, M. (2018). Muslim consumers' awareness and perception of Halal food fraud. *International Food Research Journal, 25*, S87–S96.

Shahid, A., Almogren, A., Javaid, N., Al-Zahrani, F. A., Zuair, M., & Alam, M. (2020). Blockchain-Based Agri-Food Supply Chain: A Complete Solution. *IEEE Access : Practical Innovations, Open Solutions, 8*, 69230–69243. doi:10.1109/ACCESS.2020.2986257

Sidarto, L. P., & Hamka, A. (2021). Improving Halal Traceability Process in the Poultry Industry Utilizing Blockchain Technology: Use Case in Indonesia. *Frontiers in Blockchain, 4*(27), 612898. Advance online publication. doi:10.3389/fbloc.2021.612898

Sony, M., & Naik, S. (2020). Industry 4.0 integration with socio-technical systems theory: A systematic review and proposed theoretical model. *Technology in Society, 61*, 101248. Advance online publication. doi:10.1016/j.techsoc.2020.101248

South African Government News Agency. (2022). *Radio spectrum auction a catalyst for digital development*. Retrieved 23 March from https://www.sanews.gov.za/south-africa/radio-spectrum-auction-catalyst-digital-development

Staff Writer. (2022). New data reveals ugly truth about load shedding in South Africa. *BusinessTech*. https://businesstech.co.za/news/energy/632229/new-data-reveals-the-ugly-truth-about-load-shedding-in-south-africa/

Statista. (2021). *African countries with the highest Gross Domestic Product (GDP) in 2021*. Retrieved 29 November from https://www.statista.com/statistics/1120999/gdp-of-african-countries-by-country/

Statistics South Africa. (2018). *How important is tourism to the South African economy?* Department: Statistics South Africa. Retrieved 6 March from http://www.statssa.gov.za/?p=11030

Surjandari, I., Yusuf, H., Laoh, E., & Maulida, R. (2021). Designing a Permissioned Blockchain Network for the Halal Industry using Hyperledger Fabric with multiple channels and the raft consensus mechanism. *Journal of Big Data, 8*(1), 10. Advance online publication. doi:10.118640537-020-00405-7

Sylvester, G. (2019). *E-agriculture in action: blockchain for agriculture. Opportunities and challenges*. Academic Press.

Tan, A., Gligor, D., & Ngah, A. (2020). Applying Blockchain for Halal food traceability. *International Journal of Logistics Research and Applications*, 1-18. doi:10.1080/13675567.2020.1825653

Tayob, S. (2016). 'O You who Believe, Eat of the Tayyibāt (pure and wholesome food) that We Have Provided You'—Producing Risk, Expertise and Certified Halal Consumption in South Africa. *Journal of Religion in Africa. Religion en Afrique, 46*(1), 67–91. doi:10.1163/15700666-12340064

Tayob, S. (2020). Trading Halal: Halal Certification and Intra-Muslim Trade in South Africa. *Sociology of Islam, 8*(3-4), 322–342. doi:10.1163/22131418-08030003

The Government of South Africa. (2020). *Building a new economy: Highlights of the reconstruction and recovery plan* [Economic Recovery Action Plan]. https://www.gov.za/sites/default/files/gcis_document/202010/building-new-economy-highlights-reconstruction-and-recovery-plan.pdf

The MTN Group. (2015). *MTN Business unveiles Internet of Things (IoT) platform* https://www.mtnbusiness.co.za/en/Pages/Press-detail.aspx?queryString=mtnbusinesslaunchesfirsttrulypanafricaninternetofthingsplatform

The Muslim Judicial Council Halaal Trust. (n.d.). *MJC Halaal Trust: Certification Process Flowchart*. Retrieved 12 January from https://mjchalaaltrust.co.za/halal-certification-process/

The United Nations General Assembly. (2015). *Transforming Our World: The 2030 Agenda for Sustainable Development*. Author.

Tripoli, M., & Schmidhuber, J. (2020). *Emerging opportunities for the application of blockchain in the agri-food industry*. https://policycommons.net/artifacts/1422549/emerging-opportunities-for-the-application-of-blockchain-in-the-agri-food-in dustry/

Tsang, Y. P., Choy, K. L., Wu, C. H., Ho, G. T. S., & Lam, H. Y. (2019). Blockchain-Driven IoT for Food Traceability With an Integrated Consensus Mechanism. *IEEE Access : Practical Innovations, Open Solutions*, 7, 129000–129017. doi:10.1109/ACCESS.2019.2940227

Vanany, I., Rakhmawati, N. A., Sukoso, S., & Soon, J. M. (2020, 17-18 Nov. 2020). Indonesian Halal Food Integrity: Blockchain Platform. *2020 International Conference on Computer Engineering, Network, and Intelligent Multimedia (CENIM)*.

Vodacom. (n.d.). *The Internet of Things (IoT) is transforming assets into intelligent devices*. Retrieved 2 March 2022 from https://www.vodacom.com/internet-of-things.php

Wiegmann, D. A., & Shappell, S. A. (2017). *A human error approach to aviation accident analysis: The human factors analysis and classification system*. Routledge. doi:10.4324/9781315263878

Xiong, H., Dalhaus, T., Wang, P., & Huang, J. (2020). Blockchain Technology for Agriculture: Applications and Rationale [Mini Review]. *Frontiers in Blockchain*, 3, 7. Advance online publication. doi:10.3389/fbloc.2020.00007

KEY TERMS AND DEFINITIONS

Blockchain: A fourth-industrial revolution technology that logs data immutably on a distributed ledger. This technology is lauded for its ability to provide security, traceability and transparency of all transactions logged on the ledger.

Halaal: The notion of *Halaal* originates from the religion of Islam and loosely translates to 'permissible by Islamic law'. In this chapter, *Halaal* is referred to in the context of meat for human consumption.

Halaal Accreditation: The monitoring and assurance that meat is produced in a manner consistent with the religious requirements for *Halaal* status.

Halaal Blockchain System: A system that adopts blockchain technology to enhance transparency and traceability of the *Halaal* supply chain.

Halaal Supply Chain: The *Halaal* supply chain encompasses both the agricultural supply chain involved in producing meat for human consumption, and the *Halaal* accreditation processes that take place across the supply chain.

Internet of Things (IoT): The Internet of Things is a fourth-industrial revolution technology that refers to mass-deployed, large-scale networks of embedded systems that communicate over the Internet. Typically, IoT systems have a backbone of cloud technology.

Socio-Technical Systems Thinking: Socio-technical systems thinking relies on considering technology and society holistically, such that due consideration is paid to how technology must be shaped by social influences, as well as the impacts of technology on society.

ENDNOTE

[1] The article also mentions, incorrectly, that a blockchain solution (PO Certify) was implemented in South Africa. However, the article referenced by Katuk (2019) was of a conceptual nature and this solution was never actually implemented in the South African market.

Chapter 15
Time Stamp and Immutability as Key Factors for the Application of Blockchain in the Cultural Sector

Laura Clemente
Sapienza University of Rome, Italy

Francesco Bifulco
University of Naples Federico II, Italy

ABSTRACT

In recent years, blockchain, a new and potentially disruptive technology, has come to the fore. Despite its widespread use in several fields, it is in the cultural sector that it can offer numerous advantages. The implementation of a blockchain system could make the traditional art market less opaque by recording data on an encrypted and immutable register, and its use could also improve the circulation of works of art, encourage their collection, and promote a new form of ownership. This chapter highlights the features of blockchain that make it suitable for the management and enhancement of cultural heritage, considering the different fields of application as well as the way in which it can be integrated to support the sale and management of cultural assets and to develop new business models for cultural and creative firms.

INTRODUCTION

The intense technological advancement over the last two decades has led to major innovations in several areas including computer security (cryptography) and decentralized data management (Morabito, 2017). This has resulted in a new and potentially disruptive technology, referred to as Blockchain, coming to the fore.

It is a tool capable of bringing numerous benefits to the economic system, despite the unknowns being numerous. Among the various fields of application, it is in the cultural sector that Blockchain can

DOI: 10.4018/978-1-6684-7455-6.ch015

offer the most satisfying benefits, although it generates quite a few perplexities and imposes a renewal of established practices and models on a sector traditionally reluctant to change and innovate.

Creative and cultural industries are vital sources of innovation and nowadays digital technologies play a central role in supporting culture-led development strategies (Bosone et al., 2021) and several scholars recognized the importance of digital technologies such as Blockchain on the mechanisms at the core of value creation (Sashi, 2021).

The implementation of a Blockchain system could make the traditional art market less opaque by recording data on an encrypted and immutable register, and could improve the circulation of works of art, encourage their collection, and promote a new form of ownership. Emerging platforms where consumers trade fractional ownership of artwork that is tokenized on Blockchain is an innovative business model utilizing the characteristics of this technology in the art market (Kim, 2020).

Within this scenario, specific attention has been paid to the emerging phenomenon of non-fungible tokens (NFTs), on which the spotlights of cultural, academic, institutional, and business realities are projected. NFTs seem to offer Blockchain an opportunity for expansion, moving from a specialised audience to a broader one.

This technology might contribute to the definition of new rules and offer different mechanisms to institutionalize markets (Russo-Spena *et al.*, 2022).

Thus, the use of Blockchain technology in the cultural scenario has the potential to revitalize a sector severely hit by the economic crisis following the Covid-19 pandemic, but the efforts that cultural industries must put forth to adopt it are not understated, together with the significant up-skilling and re-skilling costs that firms must bear.

Drawing on these considerations, this chapter aim to offer an overview of the uses of Blockchain technology in the field of cultural heritage and to assess the ways in which it can support the creation of a new ecosystem for the management of cultural and creative industries thanks to its intrinsic characteristics of immutability, traceability, and transparency that are essential features for ensuring the fairness and transparency of transactions taking place in the art industry.

Specifically, the analysis carried out in this contribution aims to fulfil the following research objectives:

- Review the existing literature related to the application fields of blockchain in the cultural and creative sector.
- Identify and analyze concrete use cases of blockchain technology in cultural and creative enterprises and verify if they align with the evidence emerged from the literature review.
- Clarify what are the key features of blockchain technology that contribute to generating value for the business of these cultural companies.

THEORETICAL BACKGROUND

Recent literature highlights growing attention on the dialogue between innovative technologies and the cultural and creative sector. In addition, the term "Blockchain" is increasingly used in studies concerning cultural heritage.

The authors consider it appropriate to systematize the literature review into three key concepts: Innovation in the cultural and creative industry; Blockchain Technology and Blockchain application in the cultural and creative industry.

Innovation in the Cultural and Creative Industry

Although there are many definitions of cultural and creative industries, UNCTAD (2022) summarises their main aspects and defines them as cycles of creating, producing, and distributing goods and services, linked to the culture, that use creativity and intellectual capital as primary inputs. They comprise a set of knowledge-based activities that produce tangible goods and intangible intellectual or artistic services with creative content, economic value, and market objectives.

It should not be overlooked however, that cultural industries are deeply affected by changes in society, people and technology. For this reason, in recent years they have come to a turning point: the COVID pandemic and the presence of a target group of customers increasingly used to technology have led to an acceleration of the digital transformation process which was already partly underway and which has affected the entire art market to an uneven extent (Calluso & D'Angelo, 2022).

The introduction of innovative tools is changing the way individuals experience cultural and artistic assets, as well as the way cultural and creative companies are structuring their business strategies (Coppola et al., 2021).

The digital revolution has reached new horizons and above all are the creation and marketing of non-fungible tokens (NFTs) that allow any unique goods to be mapped in a digital environment (Borri et al., 2022). These tokens appeared in numerous sectors, but the art market is one of the first in which they are applied, given the need to provide proof of authenticity and ownership for artists and buyers (Rehman et al., 2021).

NFTs play a key role in the production of crypto art: a recent artistic movement, which also includes generative art, involving the creation of entirely digital works of art, created through the use of new technologies such as artificial intelligence (AI). Crypto art relies on distributed ledger technologies, allowing the hyperportability of the object and the rejection of conventional markets and institutions (Franceschet et al., 2021). As a result of this, it can pave the way for a democratization of the arts sector and represent, in the light of the splitting and of property rights in NFTs, a shifting paradigm of ownership (Belk et al., 2022) and a new form of art acquisition that ensures faster transactions and can take place without intermediaries.

Innovative technologies have therefore become rightfully part of the art sector and have the potential to create new values for customers and managers (Ozer et al., 2022).

It must also be considered that the complexity of the administrative and legal aspects of handling cultural goods, both in physical and digital form, has opened the door to various forms of scams and fraud. As Malik and his colleagues point out (2022), the problem of trust does not only affect creators but also customers since the journey that a work of art takes can be long, making it difficult for the end consumer to verify its authenticity.

For the foregoing reasons, the potential and margins for growth that reside in the encounter between the cultural sector and digital transformation remain evident (Holcombe, 2022): the cultural and creative sector presents itself as an elective field of application for the development of new investments in technologies that can protect cultural heritage, ensure the authenticity of the goods, and support the financial sustainability of cultural institutions (Cosimato et al., 2022).

Blockchain Technology

The Blockchain is part of the Distributed Ledger Technologies family (Fosso Wamba et al., 2020) and is considered its best-known example. It is defined as a distributed ledger database structured as a chain of blocks, storing transactions that are related in chronological order and whose integrity is ensured by a system of algorithms and cryptographic rules (Del Vacchio & Bifulco, 2022). A network of computers (i.e., nodes) verify all the operations before they are approved, and each participant maintains a replica of the shared ledger. This means that data are not under the control of a single central authority and modification is only possible if an agreement is reached through consensus mechanisms.

Although the origins of Blockchain date back to research carried out by Haber and Stornetta in 1991, the turning point of this technology only came in 2008, when Satoshi Nakamoto (a pseudonym used by an individual or a group of peoples) published *Bitcoin: A Peer-to-Peer Electronic Cash System*. The paper aims to propose a solution to the double spending problem *using a distributed peer-to-peer timestamping server to generate computational proof of the chronological order of transactions* (Nakamoto, 2008). The architecture of Blockchain fully meets this purpose, decreasing security risks associated with the execution of commercial transactions; it also guarantees authenticity and increases trust, robustness, and traceability against fraud (Perboli et al., 2018).

Several scholars (Angelis & da Silva, 2019; Queiroz et al., 2021) have identified key features driving the specific value creation carried out by the Blockchain.

- **Decentralization:** The Blockchain is an architecturally decentralized system in which data is stored in a shared ledger accessible by all network users. No single party has control over the entire database, providing greater transparency to the network and allowing trust between its members (Friedman & Ormiston, 2022). It provides also new and efficient solutions for peer-to-peer transactions of all kinds, thereby reducing the role and importance of intermediaries and platforms that today guarantee the security of such transactions (Mele *et al.*, 2022).
- **Immutability:** The moment data enters the Blockchain system, it can never be altered or falsified, thanks to the timestamping method, which makes transactions encrypted and incorruptible (Collins & Lindkvist, 2022).
- **Tamper-proof:** the data, digitally signed and broadcasted by the participants, are grouped into the blocks in chronological order and timestamped (Calvaresi et al., 2018). A hash function is applied to the content and forms a unique block identifier, which is stored in the subsequent block. Due to the properties of the hash function, it can be easily verified if the stored information was modified by comparing the hash of the block with the identifier of the subsequent one.
- **Traceability:** Blockchain-based networks are designed to be long-lasting and to store large amounts of information. This provides the traceability of historical data along the chain.

Thanks to these factors, Blockchain can provide faster and less expensive transactions than those completed in traditional settings. It also enables firms to automate processes that were previously manual, allowing human resources to focus on other, value generating activities (Morkunas et al., 2019) and guarantees high levels of security for all users.

Although the benefits that can be derived from Blockchain are numerous, there are several barriers and challenges to be faced, that may hinder the implementation of the system. From a technological point of view, these include the high energy consumption, which occurs mainly in cases where the consensus mechanism used is proof of work (Sedlmeir *et al.*, 2020), and the lack of standardization, that slows down cooperation and data sharing by participants of different blockchains (Prewett et al., 2020).

From a managerial point of view, it is necessary to consider that the integration process of Blockchain requires a significant financial outlay due to the initial implementation costs and the staff up-skilling and re-skilling costs. Moreover, organizations that adopt this technology in their business processes face the challenge of change management to integrate the new system with legacy ones (Toufaily et al., 2021). Lastly, attention is drawn to the fact that the technological progress of Blockchain has outpaced the development of a related regulatory framework and, from a legislative perspective, there is still much work to be done before the major regulatory hurdles to Blockchain adoption are cleared (Prewett et al., 2020; Schatsky et al., 2018).

Nevertheless, from a consumer-centric perspective, Blockchain technology has the potential to substantially transform consumer relationships by enhancing data and information transparency and improving privacy (Rejeb et al., 2020).

In this context, it seems clear that despite its widespread use in the financial field, this technology can be applied to many business functions and the attention of scholars and practitioners moved to its implementation in other domains, such as Internet of Things (IoT) (Reyna et al., 2018), supply chain (Perboli et al., 2018), media (Chen et al., 2020), and tourism (Rashideh, 2020).

Implementation of Blockchain in Cultural and Creative Industry

Among other fields of application, the role of Blockchain technology in the cultural and creative sector has aroused the attention of several scholars whose contributes help to identify four main use cases, presented below: authenticity and provenance; tokenization and sale of digital artworks; copyright and digital scarcity; traceability and monitoring.

Authenticity and Provenance

The value of a cultural asset lies in its uniqueness and non-reproducibility; indeed, the attribution of an artefact to a specific author is a fundamental element since, in addition to determining its originality, it significantly affects its artistic and economic valuation. Blockchain can undoubtedly increase the level of transparency and trust in buying and selling, guaranteeing the provenance and authenticity of works (Angelova, 2019). According to Anagnostakis (2019), the implementation of Blockchain in cultural sector will provide an invaluable and immutable record of cultural heritage documents, safeguarding the validity of the data and facilitating the resolution of ownership issues for future generations.

The registration process on the platform becomes even more important when the artist is living as it allows the artist to trace the chain of sales after the first one and to exercise their resale right (Van Haaften-Schick & Whitaker, 2022). One of the main innovations brought about by Blockchain technology is that it enables creators to prove ownership and enforce contracts programmatically, without having to rely on legal systems or intermediary platforms, which is a major change to the market structure in functional terms (Malik et al., 2022).

Tokenization and Sale of Digital Artworks

Tokenization is defined as the process by which rights to an asset are converted into a token, i.e. a set of digital information, issued on a blockchain platform in order to be exchanged between network users (Whitaker et al., 2021). Its fields of application are continuously expanding, but it is possible to trace the use of tokens mainly to the crypto art sector and fractional ownership of cultural assets. In the first case cryptocurrency-related tokens are non-fungible tokens (NFTs), cryptographic codes designed to uniquely represent a work. Once placed on the Blockchain, they provide a certificate of ownership that can be sold or traded like other cryptocurrencies (Jung, 2022). Unlike the fungible tokens, however, it must be emphasized that the characteristic of *nonfungibility* makes this type of token non-interchangeable precisely because of their uniqueness, which depends on individual characteristics such as origin, size, and number of clones produced. Despite this practice stimulating collectors' participation in the NFT market, it also incentivizes customers to focus not only on the artistic value of a NFT's content but also on its popularity or virality, increasing the risk of the creation of a speculative bubble.

The Blockchain also allows fractional or shared ownership of individual artworks; it means that multiple owners have a right to benefit financially from increases in the value of the artwork if it is resold (Belk et al., 2022). Art goods can no longer be considered the exclusive prerogative of collectors but constitute an asset that investment funds are looking at with increasing interest (Fairfield, 2022). With this in mind, it is not surprising that the virtual fractioning of a work is enjoying some success, as it allows even small investors to buy a share and market if they need liquidity. According to Bufano (2021), this trend is spreading rapidly and prefigures an innovative, extensive and widespread way of enjoying cultural heritage, paving the way for a democratization of the sector. Through the acquisition of diversified tokens, users can have the opportunity to create a vast artistic portfolio that would otherwise be the prerogative of a limited number of collectors.

Copyright and Digital Scarcity

Blockchain technology seems to be the right tool to reintroduce the concepts of scarcity and originality in freely reproducible digital works of art (Del Vacchio & Bifulco, 2022). As stated by Ch'ng (2018) it is the solution for identifying and validating the first original artworks, as well as the further creation of subsequent copies, all recorded as transactions in the blockchain. By creating a tamper-proof means of registration, the entire creation chain of the artistic and cultural asset, from the first conception to the start of production, is verifiably archived (Schönhals et al., 2018) and the copyright protection is ensured. In particular, Blockchain can make a valuable contribution to digital rights management issues. Blockchain platforms could provide a user with unrestricted use of a digital asset, while ensuring that it cannot be copied, thanks to the use of a smart contract encrypted with information on the digital good's rights and permissions (Tresise et al., 2018).

Traceability and Monitoring

Although the certification of authenticity and the tokenization of artistic assets are considered the main forms of application of Blockchain in the cultural and creative sector (Del Vacchio & Bifulco, 2022; Whitaker, 2019), there are several studies foreshadowing the use of this technology to monitor artistic heritage with advantages in terms of cost reduction and faster information exchange. As stated by Mucchi et al. (2022), Blockchain has the potential to be implemented to support important internal management processes, such as loans and exchanges of cultural objects of various cultural institutions such as museums and art galleries. The preciousness of artworks makes it essential to keep track of each move and of the time interval of the loan. The adoption of a blockchain-based tracking system streamlines the process, allowing all data to be recorded on the distributed ledger and shared with every user in the network. In addition, Blockchain technology can protect the copyright (Savelyev, 2018) and manage the intellectual property of artworks, as well as their digital documentation, which is very often under risk of loss or cancellation (Huang & Dai, 2019).

The decentralized, tamper-proof, and time-stamping characteristics of Blockchain technology can solve problems of traceability and verification in the process of entry and exit of cultural relics (Liang et al., 2020) and address the issue of information asymmetry.

METHODOLOGY

The analysis of the literature revealed a promising link between Blockchain technology and cultural heritage, highlighting different areas of application. In order to support the theoretical evidences and to explore the ways in which cultural start-ups exploit the opportunities offered by Blockchain, an empirical investigation was carried out adopting a qualitative approach (Dubois & Gadde, 2002).

Researchers chose to limit the field of investigation to five firms that have culture as their core business or have a creative-driven component within them. The Creative Trident approach devised by Higgs, Cunningham, and Bakhshi (2008) was followed, which enables an estimation of the share of employment and cultural wealth produced by activities not directly related to the cultural and creative perimeter. Considering the purpose of the research, the firms were analyzed using secondary sources such as interviews, website content, social media pages, and sector reports (Creswell & Creswell, 2017).

The five selected cases are AerariumChain, Art Blocks, Limna, Pixura, and Reasoned Art. These realities pertain to a homogeneous scenario but present a diverse range of background identities; they have been chosen in order to highlight the different applications of Blockchain technology in the projects and activities of similar cultural enterprises. In making the choice, the authors followed Magnani's (2017) definition of cultural enterprises, which can be listed in four groups:

- **First Group:** Enterprises engaged in the creation of goods with artistic/creative content.
- **Second Group:** Entities operating in the art market and capable of producing a product that could be considered a cultural asset in the future.
- **Third Group:** Enterprises involved in the process of creation and distribution of assets with artistic and cultural content.
- **Fourth Group:** Entities directly involved in the preservation, valorization, and management of cultural heritage and activities.

Each cultural firm fall within one of these definitions, and from a comparative analysis (Yin, 2018) it is possible to derive a description of their activities and the role of Blockchain in the definition and implementation of their projects.

Key Factors for the Application of Blockchain

FINDINGS

The purpose of this study is to explore the dynamics triggered by the implementation of Blockchain technology in the cultural and creative sector, in which new technological and digital trajectories are increasingly being tested. The search for new value propositions for consumers and the creation of both economic and environmental sustainability represent the main challenges for operators in the art world for whom the combination of art and innovation is becoming increasingly inseparable.

The recent explosion of the NFT art market has sanctioned the entry of Blockchain into the creative industry and at the same time given it an opportunity to expand from specialised users, as in the case of the financial markets, to a wider audience. According to the statistics of the Hiscox Online Art Trade Report, transactions of NFTs carried out in 2021 on Blockchain-based platforms have reached a value of around 11 billion dollars and around 40% of traditional art players have stated that they are interested in incorporating this technology into their business in the short term.

Through Blockchain, it is not only possible to create and transfer tokens, but also to certify the authenticity and provenance of assets. As highlighted above, and in line with what happens for the agri-food sector, Blockchain can enable higher levels of security on the right of ownership of an asset, acting as a guarantee of authenticity from the origin of the creative product to the distribution to the consumer (Del Vacchio & Bifulco, 2022).

Nowadays, there is an increasing consolidation of the digital presence in the art world, although the adoption of new technologies involves high levels of risk due to the lack of specific supranational reference legislation and the high up-skilling and re-skilling costs that companies would have to bear.

The analysis carried out by the authors of this contribution identified several companies that are successfully pursuing projects in the field of Blockchain and developing innovative products and services for the international market.

The five analyzed companies pertain to the art and cultural heritage sector and carry out several Blockchain-based activities including the valorization of physical and virtual cultural assets, the creation of NFTs for the fractioning of artwork ownership, and the sale of tokens to collectors and investors. Blockchain plays an indispensable role in the creation and registration process of crypto art although there is a significant risk of hyperinflation of digital artifacts, a factor that can lead to a considerable reduction in their market value (Franceschet et al., 2021).

A phenomenon of particular relevance concerns the increase in the number of projects that see the integration of Blockchain technology and metaverse, an immersive environment that can be a useful tool for creative industries in the entertainment sector, in order to reach, thanks to the absence of geographical limits, markets that would otherwise be inaccessible (Bushell, 2022).

The aforementioned players make different uses of Blockchain system in order to meet their business needs but, in particular, it is highlighted that most of them use this technology for tokenization of different assets: intellectual property and other assets can be digitally represented which are converted into NFTs as permanent and transferable records of ownership.

Following the research purpose of delving into the application of Blockchain in the arts sector in a deeper way, the results of five emblematic case studies are reported. Furthermore, the acquired information leads to the emergence of the characteristics and tendencies common to all the industries, which will be discussed in the implications section.

The first of the surveyed companies to have grasped the potential of Blockchain technology applied to the cultural field is Pixura, an organization founded in 2017 with the aim of fostering the creation and exchange of NFTs. It is the developer of SuperRare, one of the best-known marketplaces for the creation and sale of digital artworks. The peer-to-peer platform uses the Ethereum Blockchain on which artists can register, trade, and sell tokens associated with virtual assets under the guarantee that the information entered will not be modified. Indeed, Blockchain technology ensures the authenticity of the artworks, which can be purchased by collectors in a secure and transparent way, while the smart-contract system allows each artist to exercise their resale rights and receive royalties for each sale after the first one. The Etherehum Blockchain uses proof of stake (PoS) as a consensus mechanism, which is a viable alternative to proof of work (PoW), implemented by the well-known Bitcoin platform, in terms of efficiency and effectiveness and saves energy consumption (Li et al., 2020).

The German company Limna is among the first cultural companies to implement artificial intelligence with the support of Blockchain technology. The company, established in 2020, has developed the eponymous app which, based on a decentralized system, acts as an art advisor, enabling its users to buy fine art on the primary market according to their financial availability and by analysing a vast database containing more than 700,000 artists. Limna's mission is to make the traditional art market less obscure, meeting the needs of a new target group of collectors and at the same time guaranteeing the truthfulness and unchangeability of the information. The Blockchain's immutability feature and tamper-proof mechanism are therefore of paramount importance, as through them the veracity of the information is ensured and the provenance of the artworks is guaranteed.

Art Blocks was founded in USA in 2021 and the core of its business is the idea of using Blockchain technology to generate unique works of art. On the platform it is possible to interact directly with the algorithm by purchasing works of generative art created instantaneously: once the sale is completed, the collector receives an NFT randomly created by the algorithm designed by the artist. This makes each result different, and the combinations are almost infinite. To date, Art Blocks has a total sales volume of over $1 billion and is one of the most successful generative art NFT projects. In 2022, Art Blocks announced a collaboration with Pace Gallery with the aim of assisting NFT publication of generative art by both Pace artists and "native" crypto artists. The partnership has the merit of introducing the advantages of Blockchain among the big players in the traditional art market, who were worried about the risks of a possible bubble effect.

A further example of the trend to combine generative art, Blockchain, and NFT, is Monuverse, the project of the Italian start-up Reasoned Art, an enterprise involved in the process of creating and distributing goods with artistic and cultural content. Monuverse aims to build a metaverse in which all the well-known artistic monuments can be hosted. The first one chosen to inaugurate the project is the Arco della Pace in Milan on which were displayed works of generative art created by the Ouchhh collective. Reasoned Art has subsequently carried out the digitization of the monument and its inclusion in a virtual environment, after recording it on a Blockchain platform, which guarantees the authenticity and traceability of the created NFTs. The Monuverse project provides a concrete example of the use of Blockchain to tokenize physical cultural assets, enables a dialogue between territory and new technologies and helps to understand how technological innovations can be considered a valuable tool for the enhancement of national cultural heritage. The tokenization of the Arco della Pace in Milan with the annexed work of art led, in agreement with the Superintendence of Cultural Heritage of Milan, to the sale of approximately 10,000 NFT. Part of the proceeds of the sale will be used for the conservation of the work. A similar case was analyzed by Whitaker (2019) and concerns the tokenization of Andy Warhol's *14 Small Electric Chairs* and the subsequent sale of NFTs by the company Maecenas. Both allow fractional or shared ownership of individual works of art, but the intention of the Monuverse project is

Key Factors for the Application of Blockchain

to create a physical installation in a monument to build a community and to achieve a gamification of cultural content that can lead to a more interactive and engaging educational model.

Reasoned Art uses Polygon Blockchain, which, with the proof of stake as a consensus mechanism, manages to significantly reduce energy consumption without affecting performance.

The start-up also draws on the external contribution of two law firms for the elaboration of specific smart contracts for each artist represented, thus contributing to the development of a space to investigate legal issues with the aim of exploring how the law can better support collaborations between art and technology.

AerariumChain is an Italian start-up belonging to the fourth of the categories identified by Magnani (2017). Its services include the use of the most advanced technologies, including artificial intelligence, to monitor the conservation status of works of art. Through an initial 3D scan, a digital fingerprint of the work is created, its unique virtual image, and, thanks to subsequent scans, artificial intelligence can detect any changes and enable the activation of timely restoration actions. All steps are noted in Blockchain and allow the generation of NFTs through which museums and different cultural institutions can generate new value (www.aerariumchain.com). Blockchain technology makes it possible to keep track of the condition of cultural assets, to record data on the type, timing and cost of any restoration work and to share this information with a network of institutions and partners, as stated by Mucchi et al. (2022).

Table 1. Use of blockchain in the subjects

Name	Foundation Year	Main Activity	Type of Cultural Enterprises (Magnani, 2017)	Blockchain Application
AerariumChain	2018	Offer technological solutions for the digitization, preservation, and monitoring of artworks.	Enterprise directly involved in the preservation, valorization, and management of cultural heritage and activities.	Traceability and monitoring
Art Blocks	2021	Create a platform for the production and sale of generative art.	Enterprise operating in the art market and capable of producing a product that could be considered a cultural asset in the future.	Tokenization
Limna	2020	Develop an app using AI that helps users find artwork to buy according to their financial availability.	Enterprise involved in the process of creation and distribution of assets with artistic and cultural content.	Right Management and Autenticity
Pixura	2017	Create the first marketplace for the exchange of NFTs.	Enterprise involved in the process of creation and distribution of assets with artistic and cultural content.	Tokenization and Autenticity
Reasoned Art	2021	Carry out digitalization of important monuments and their inclusion in virtual environments.	Enterprise engaged in the creation of goods with artistic/creative content.	Tokenization and Fractional Ownership

Source: Author's elaboration

As demonstrated by the individual analysis of the selected organizations, this research fits into an emerging perspective, investigating the role that Blockchain assumes in the implementation of their activities and the impact that it can generate in the traditional art market. All companies have structured their value proposal on innovative projects which combine different technologies and aim to involve large sections of customers. Tokenization seems to be the process for which Blockchain is most involved, due to the fact that NFTs are the collector's items that gained the greatest attention from the public in 2021 and attract new bidders and potential buyers, especially millennials (Deloitte Art Finance Report, 2022). This trend is driven by the generational change of customers interested in expressing themselves through the use of modern technologies and in digital environments. Lastly, Blockchain, as has been noted, contributes to the resolution of issues related to the certification of the authenticity and provenance of works of art; in fact, the companies analyzed use it to preserve the validity of data, aspect that have in common with industries operating in other fields, such as the supply chain.

IMPLICATIONS

From a theoretical point of view, this work contributes to the debate on the use of Blockchain in the cultural and creative sector that has emerged in recent years.

It must be underlined that many of the previous studies that have discussed the adoption of Blockchain by cultural heritage organizations focused most their attention on how it guarantees authenticity and provenance, but the literature lacks discussion of the way in which this technology can be integrated to support the sale and the management of cultural assets together with other tools, such as machine learning and AI technology. Furthermore, the contributions that analyze the managerial changes within companies that have implemented Blockchain, and the impact on their cost structure, are extremely lacking.

As O'Dwyer (2020) suggests, Blockchain is able to create new financing and fractional equity models together with the tokenization and monetization of data. With reference to value creation in its economic perspective, it can be considered a key technology that can bring numerous benefits to cultural and creative industries in terms of cost reduction due to the elimination of intermediaries in transactions and increased revenues generated by the sale of tokenized digital assets.

From a managerial point of view, according to Del Vacchio and Bifulco (2022), Blockchain leads to new business opportunities, but also challenges to be faced. Managers should try to improve the efficiency and effectiveness of using this technology to provide new cultural services and to reach new target groups of customers and collectors.

The analysis of the five case studies carried out in the present contribution highlight that the technology allows challenges to be overcome, such as organizational issues related to the right management, copyright protection, and keeping artists safe from the possibility of circulating counterfeits. A further advantage is the possibility of innovating and automating all transactions involving the sale of works by smart contracts that make the purchasing process extremely fast, allowing artists to receive their fees automatically and simplify royalty management.

It is noticeable that the selected cultural realities have adopted some common managerial practices, such as the use of tokenization of physical and digital assets, in order to obtain a new and more accessible form of investment, and the storage of information concerning the artworks on the distributed ledger, which guarantees to the buyers their authenticity and accuracy thanks to the time-stamping method, which proves to be one of the key elements for a Blockchain adoption in the cultural sector.

The analysis also shows that this technology is mainly implemented by start-ups or small, digital-oriented companies particularly accustomed to adopting innovative technologies such as Blockchain, with a renewed focus on sustainability. However, it may be noted that even big players in the cultural

Key Factors for the Application of Blockchain

and creative sector are approaching Blockchain, often through collaborations with the smaller organisations just mentioned.

Cultural managers and professionals will be challenged to rethink their strategies for incorporating Blockchain into the set of business tools that they have at their disposal, as well as considering the subsequent implications in terms of costs, up-skilling, and market settling.

Furthermore, analysing the context in which these cultural enterprises operate, it is possible to note that not all countries have specific legislation for new digital technologies and there are several potential critical issues: some features of Blockchain, such as the unchangeability of data, may conflict with the General Data Protection Regulation (GDPR), which establishes the right to modify and delete information. It is therefore crucial for cultural firms to operate in accordance with privacy regulations and, at the same time, to contribute to the development of a new legal framework with the help of specialized law firms.

FINAL REMARKS AND FUTURE RESEARCH DIRECTIONS

Although the Blockchain phenomenon enjoys great media attention and is frequently in the headlines of the mainstream media, its use in the cultural and creative sector is still in its early stages and new solutions will emerge continuously over the coming years (Mucchi et al., 2022).

By providing systems for the secure creation and trade of digital assets, transparent data storage, and faster and cheaper transactions, Blockchain seems to offer promise for a lean and sustainable artist-centric ecosystem (Patrickson, 2021).

The present contribution seeks to provide an outline of the uses of Blockchain in the cultural sector and to give an overview of the good practices implemented by start-ups and small digital-oriented companies active in the sector, in order to provide exemplary cases that can serve as a benchmark for future studies.

However, Blockchain has some limitations. This technological innovation has been used by the cultural industry for too short a period to be able to define precise protocols of use and success. One line of future research is to explore and analyse more empirical cases to better understand the direction the art market will take and the role Blockchain will play within it.

The researchers recommend extending the analysis to major players on the international art scene in order to find similarities and differences between the strategies pursued by the companies presented in this chapter.

From a managerial point of view, it is also crucial to develop guidelines for cultural professionals and to analyse the changes that Blockchain implementation requires within different organisations. In particular, focus should be placed on the strategies that can be pursued to educate employees in the development of this technology and in the formation of multidisciplinary teams.

REFERENCES

Anagnostakis, A. (2019). Towards a blockchain architecture for cultural heritage tokens. In *Transdisciplinary Multispectral Modeling and Cooperation for the Preservation of Cultural Heritage: First International Conference, TMM_CH 2018, Athens, Greece, October 10–13, 2018, Revised Selected Papers, Part I* (pp. 541-551). Springer International Publishing. 10.1007/978-3-030-12957-6_38

Angelis, J., & da Silva, E. R. (2019). Blockchain adoption: A value driver perspective. *Business Horizons*, *2019*(62), 307–314. doi:10.1016/j.bushor.2018.12.001

Angelova, M. (2019). Application of Blockchain Technology in the Cultural and Creative Industries. In *2019 II International Conference on High Technology for Sustainable Development (HiTech)* (pp. 1-4). IEEE. 10.1109/HiTech48507.2019.9128267

Belk, R., Humayun, M., & Brouard, M. (2022). Money, possessions, and ownership in the Metaverse: NFTs, cryptocurrencies, Web3 and Wild Markets. *Journal of Business Research*, *153*, 198–205. doi:10.1016/j.jbusres.2022.08.031

BorriN.LiuY.TsyvinskiA. (2022). The economics of non-fungible tokens. *Available at* SSRN.

Bosone, M., Nocca, F., & Fusco Girard, L. (2021). The Circular City Implementation: Cultural Heritage and Digital Technology. In *International Conference on Human-Computer Interaction* (pp. 40-62). Springer. 10.1007/978-3-030-77411-0_4

Bufano, E. (2021). Blockchain e mercato delle opere di interesse artistico: Piattaforme, nuovi beni e vecchie regole. *Aedon*, (2), 100–110.

BushellC. (2022). *The Impact of Metaverse on Branding and Marketing*. doi:10.2139/ssrn.4144628

Calluso, C., & D'Angelo, V. (2022). The impact of Digitalization on Organizational Change Catalysts in Museums. In *Handbook of Research on Museum Management in the Digital Era* (pp. 20–36). IGI Global. doi:10.4018/978-1-7998-9656-2.ch002

Calvaresi, D., Dubovitskaya, A., Calbimonte, J. P., Taveter, K., & Schumacher, M. (2018, June). Multi-agent systems and Blockchain: Results from a systematic literature review. In *International conference on practical applications of agents and multi-agent systems* (pp. 110-126). Springer. 10.1007/978-3-319-94580-4_9

Ch'ng, E. (2018). The First Original Copy and the Role of Blockchain in the Reproduction of Cultural Heritage. *Presence (Cambridge, Mass.)*, *27*(1), 151–162. doi:10.1162/pres_a_00313

Collins, D., & Lindkvist, C. (2022, November). Block by block: Potential and challenges of the blockchain in the context of facilities management. *IOP Conference Series. Earth and Environmental Science*, *1101*(6), 062003. doi:10.1088/1755-1315/1101/6/062003

Coppola, M., Bifulco, F., Russo Spena, T., & Tregua, M. (2021). Value Propositions in Digital Transformation. In *Digital Transformation in the Cultural Heritage Sector* (pp. 69–92). Springer. doi:10.1007/978-3-030-63376-9_4

Cosimato, S., Vona, R., Iandolo, F., & Loia, F. (2022). Digital Platforms for the Sustainability of Cultural Heritage: A Focus on Clickproject.eu. In Handbook of Research on Museum Management in the Digital Era (pp. 121-136). IGI Global.

Creswell, J. W., & Creswell, J. D. (2017). *Research design: Qualitative, quantitative, and mixed methods approaches*. Sage publications.

Del Vacchio, E., & Bifulco, F. (2022). Blockchain in Cultural Heritage: Insights from Literature Review. *Sustainability (Basel)*, *14*(4), 2324. doi:10.3390u14042324

Dubois, A., & Gadde, L. E. (2002). Systematic combining: An abductive approach to case research. *Journal of Business Research*, *55*(7), 553–560. doi:10.1016/S0148-2963(00)00195-8

Fairfield, J. A. (2022). Tokenized: The law of non-fungible tokens and unique digital property. *Industrial Law Journal*, *97*, 1261.

Fosso Wamba, S., Kala Kamdjoug, J. R., Epie Bawack, R., & Keogh, J. G. (2020). Bitcoin, Blockchain and Fintech: A systematic review and case studies in the supply chain. *Production Planning and Control*, *31*(2-3), 115–142. doi:10.1080/09537287.2019.1631460

Franceschet, M., Colavizza, G., Finucane, B., Ostachowski, M. L., Scalet, S., Perkins, J., ... Hernández, S. (2021). Crypto art: A decentralized view. *Leonardo*, *54*(4), 402–405. doi:10.1162/leon_a_02003

Friedman, N., & Ormiston, J. (2022). Blockchain as a sustainability-oriented innovation?: Opportunities for and resistance to Blockchain technology as a driver of sustainability in global food supply chains. *Technological Forecasting and Social Change*, *175*, 121403. doi:10.1016/j.techfore.2021.121403

Higgs, P., Cunningham, S., & Bakhshi, H. (2008). *Beyond the creative industries: Mapping the creative economy in the United Kingdom*. Academic Press.

Huang, W., & Dai, F. (2019). Research on digital protection of intangible cultural heritage based on Blockchain technology. *Information Management and Computer Science*, *2*(2), 14–18. doi:10.26480/imcs.02.2019.14.18

Jung, Y. (2022). Current use cases, benefits and challenges of NFTs in the museum sector: Toward common pool model of NFT sharing for educational purposes. *Museum Management and Curatorship*, 1–17. doi:10.1080/09647775.2022.2132995

Kim, S. (2020). *Fractional ownership, democratization and bubble formation-the impact of Blockchain enabled asset tokenization*. Academic Press.

Li, A., Wei, X., & He, Z. (2020). Robust proof of stake: A new consensus protocol for sustainable blockchain systems. *Sustainability (Basel)*, *12*(7), 2824. doi:10.3390u12072824

Liang, W., Fan, Y., Li, K. C., Zhang, D., & Gaudiot, J. L. (2020). Secure data storage and recovery in industrial Blockchain network environments. *IEEE Transactions on Industrial Informatics*, *16*(10), 6543–6552. doi:10.1109/TII.2020.2966069

Magnani, G. (2017). *Le aziende culturali: Modelli manageriali*. G Giappichelli Editore.

Malik, N., Wei, M. Y., Appel, G., & Luo, L. (2022). Blockchain Technology for Creative Industry: Current State and Research Opportunities. *International Journal of Research in Marketing*.

Mele, C., Spena, T. R., & Kaartemo, V. (2022). Smart technologies in service provision and experience. In *The Palgrave Handbook of Service Management* (pp. 887–906). Palgrave Macmillan. doi:10.1007/978-3-030-91828-6_42

Morabito, V. (2017). *Business innovation through Blockchain*. Springer International Publishing.

Morkunas, V. J., Paschen, J., & Boon, E. (2019). How Blockchain technologies impact your business model. *Business Horizons, 62*(3), 295–306. doi:10.1016/j.bushor.2019.01.009

Mucchi, L., Milanesi, M., & Becagli, C. (2022). Blockchain technologies for museum management. The case of the loan of cultural objects. *Current Issues in Tourism, 25*(18), 1–15. doi:10.1080/13683500.2022.2050358

Nakamoto, S. (2008). Bitcoin: A peer-to-peer electronic cash system. *Decentralized Business Review*, 21260.

O'Dwyer, R. (2020). Limited edition: Producing artificial scarcity for digital art on the Blockchain and its implications for the cultural industries. *Convergence (London), 26*(4), 874–894. doi:10.1177/1354856518795097

Ozer, K., Sahin, M. A., & Cetin, G. (2022). Integrating Big Data to Smart Destination Heritage Management. In *Handbook of Research on Digital Communications, Internet of Things, and the Future of Cultural Tourism* (pp. 411–429). IGI Global. doi:10.4018/978-1-7998-8528-3.ch022

Patrickson, B. (2021). What do Blockchain technologies imply for digital creative industries? *Creativity and Innovation Management, 30*(3), 585–595. doi:10.1111/caim.12456

Perboli, G., Musso, S., & Rosano, M. (2018). Blockchain in logistics and supply chain: A lean approach for designing real-world use cases. *IEEE Access: Practical Innovations, Open Solutions, 6*, 62018–62028. doi:10.1109/ACCESS.2018.2875782

Prewett, K. W., Prescott, G. L., & Phillips, K. (2020). Blockchain adoption is inevitable—Barriers and risks remain. *Journal of Corporate Accounting & Finance, 31*(2), 21–28. doi:10.1002/jcaf.22415

Queiroz, M. M., Fosso Wamba, S., De Bourmont, M., & Telles, R. (2021). Blockchain adoption in operations and supply chain management: Empirical evidence from an emerging economy. *International Journal of Production Research, 59*(20), 6087–6103. doi:10.1080/00207543.2020.1803511

Rashideh, W. (2020). Blockchain technology framework: Current and future perspectives for the tourism industry. *Tourism Management, 80*, 104125. doi:10.1016/j.tourman.2020.104125

Rehman, W., Zainab, H., Imran, J., & Bawany, N. Z. (2021, December). NFTs: Applications and challenges. In *2021 22nd International Arab Conference on Information Technology (ACIT)* (pp. 1-7). IEEE.

Rejeb, A., Keogh, J. G., & Treiblmaier, H. (2020). How Blockchain technology can benefit marketing: Six pending research areas. *Frontiers in Blockchain, 3*.

Russo-Spena, T., Mele, C., & Pels, J. (2022). Resourcing, sensemaking and legitimizing: blockchain technology-enhanced market practices. *Journal of Business & Industrial Marketing*.

Sashi, C. M. (2021). Digital communication, value co-creation and customer engagement in business networks: A conceptual matrix and propositions. *European Journal of Marketing, 55*(6), 1643–1663. doi:10.1108/EJM-01-2020-0023

Savelyev, A. (2018). Copyright in the Blockchain era: Promises and challenges. *Computer Law & Security Report, 34*(3), 550–561. doi:10.1016/j.clsr.2017.11.008

Schatsky, D., Arora, A., & Dongre, A. (2018). *Blockchain and the five vectors of progress.* Recuperado de https://www2.deloitte.com/us/en/insights/focus/signals-for-strategists/value-of-blockchain-applications-interoperability.html

Schönhals, A., Hepp, T., & Gipp, B. (2018, June). Design thinking using the blockchain: enable traceability of intellectual property in problem-solving processes for open innovation. In *Proceedings of the 1st Workshop on Cryptocurrencies and Blockchains for Distributed Systems* (pp. 105-110). 10.1145/3211933.3211952

Sedlmeir, J., Buhl, H. U., Fridgen, G., & Keller, R. (2020). The energy consumption of blockchain technology: Beyond myth. *Business & Information Systems Engineering*, 62(6), 599–608. doi:10.100712599-020-00656-x

Toufaily, E., Zalan, T., & Dhaou, S. B. (2021). A framework of blockchain technology adoption: An investigation of challenges and expected value. *Information & Management*, 58(3), 103444. doi:10.1016/j.im.2021.103444

Tresise, A., Goldenfein, J., & Hunter, D. (2018). *What blockchain can and can't do for copyright.* Academic Press.

Van Haaften-Schick, L., & Whitaker, A. (2022). From the artist's contract to the blockchain ledger: New forms of artists' funding using equity and resale royalties. *Journal of Cultural Economics*, 46(2), 287–315. doi:10.100710824-022-09445-8

Whitaker, A. (2019). Art and blockchain: A primer, history, and taxonomy of blockchain use cases in the arts. *Artivate*, 8(2), 21–46. doi:10.1353/artv.2019.0008

Whitaker, A., Bracegirdle, A., de Menil, S., Gitlitz, M. A., & Saltos, L. (2021). Art, antiquities, and Blockchain: New approaches to the restitution of cultural heritage. *International Journal of Cultural Policy*, 27(3), 312–329. doi:10.1080/10286632.2020.1765163

Yin, R. K. (2018). Case study research and applications. *Sage (Atlanta, Ga.).*

KEY TERMS AND DEFINITIONS

Blockchain: A data structure that consists of growing lists of records, called "blocks", securely linked together using cryptography. Each block contains a unique cryptographic code that does not allow the data it contains to be altered or modified.

Crypto Art: Art movement involving digital artworks linked to the blockchain through non-fungible tokens.

Distributed Ledger Technology: Systems in which all participants in a network have the same copy of a database that can be read and modified independently by individuals.

Fractional Ownership: A form of collaborative consumption where the overall cost of an asset is split among a group of owners or users.

Generative Art: Type of art that is created almost entirely with the use of an autonomous system that determines the characteristics of a work of art otherwise dependent on the artist's decisions.

Non-Fungible Token: A special type of token, representing the deed and certificate of authenticity, written on a blockchain, of a unique asset (digital or physical). Non-fungible tokens are therefore not mutually interchangeable.

Tokenization: Process enabling the digitalization of a physical object through the conversion of its rights into a token and its registration on a blockchain.

Chapter 16
Deployment of Blockchain Technologies in Africa:
Challenges and Conditions of Success for the Performance of the Supply Chains of Cameroonian Firms

Martial Tangui Kadji Ngassam
University of Douala, Cameroon

Jean Babei
University of Douala, Cameroon

Serge Guy Biloa
University of Douala, Cameroon

ABSTRACT

The problem of this chapter is to understand how technological developments, in particular blockchain applications, affect the performance of the supply chains of companies based in Cameroon. This work will allow us to analyze the conditions for the success of the deployment of the supply chain in Cameroon in a dynamic of improving its performance. The empirical research carried out consisted in carrying out 18 semi-structured interviews lasting an average of 60 minutes with actors in the supply chain sector in Cameroon. The researchers adopted a qualitative type methodology based on a thematic content analysis. The results obtained are of two kinds: on the one hand, the results related to the challenges and conditions of success of the blockchain; and on the other hand, the results related to the contribution of the blockchain to the performance of the supply chains in Cameroon.

DOI: 10.4018/978-1-6684-7455-6.ch016

INTRODUCTION

Nowadays, faced with the globalization of markets, growing demands in terms of responsiveness and concern for the quality of services, all companies are faced with many challenges such as: competition, changing expectations and needs customers, the growth and globalization of markets. Which significantly influence performance in general and that of logistics companies in particular. Thus, Christopher, 1999, Simonot, 2012, indicate that the logistics sector must adapt to turbulent markets, changing quickly and unpredictably. Providers must respond to new demands such as niche markets, growing innovation in products and processes, shorter product life cycles, tailor-made services and complete and complex solutions, combining products and services. The results of a search based on the review of the systemic literature, show that only 27 articles relating to the integration of blockchain into the SCM have been identified over a period of almost 11 years (Lesueur-Cazé et al., 2022). This work offers an analysis of the place of the block chain on specific segments such as transport, electric power industry, safety improvement, traditional SCM. Currently, the blockchain is of crucial importance for the performance of the supply chain management, because of the advantages it offers and the extent of the areas where its deployment is possible (Chekrouni.A et al., 2022).

In Africa, according to the magazine Cemac-Eco finance, the blockchain is not a really popularized concept. The relevance of the said concept was debated during the 4th edition of Digital African. Tour 2019 in Burkina Faso. For many participants, the blockchain is an innovation that can help secure data. This security guarantees transparency, which is what administrations need. Several African countries are already experimenting with this technology in several areas. Ngueti Armand Gaëtan, president of the Government Blockchain Association cited several such as Tanzania in the fight against fictitious employees, with a saving of 195 million dollars; South Africa with the central reserve which is experimenting with electronic money; Rwanda to switch state files to the blockchain; the youth card in Cameroon; Nigeria with a pilot project to optimize customs revenue.

The Capgemini Research Institute report of October 18, 2018 in Paris entitled "Does blockchain hold the key to a new age of supply chain transparency and trust? allows us to understand how companies and countries are preparing for the arrival of the Block Chain. They indicate that the use of this technology in the supply chain should be democratized by 2025. Today, only 3% of organizations that already use blockchain are using it on a large scale, 10% have a pilot program and 87% are still in the experimental phases of this technology. In Europe, the United Kingdom (22%) and France (17%) currently lead the way in pilot or large-scale Block Chain deployments, while in terms of investments, the United States (18%) come first. The study also shows that investments in blockchain are mainly motivated by reducing costs (89%), optimizing traceability (81%) and improving transparency (79%). In addition, the Block Chain makes it possible to route information more securely, quickly and transparently. However, the progression of service and investment in the sector is quite disparate on the continent. English-speaking African countries are thus more advanced than French-speaking African countries such as Cameroon. It is therefore interesting for African countries lagging behind in the adoption of this technique to seize the opportunities it offers in areas such as the supply chain. Thus, the objectives of this paper is to contribute to the literature related to this subject which is still in an embryonic state. It should be a start in order to seek to understand how this emerging technology could be implemented in supply chain management in Cameroon.

This objective leads to the following question: how can the block chain contribute to the performance of supply chains in Cameroon? To achieve this, we have chosen a qualitative study based on 18 semi-structured interviews conducted with supply chain actors in Cameroon. The text is structured in four parts. We successively present the context of the research; the theoretical framework which revolves around the concepts of teleworking and the meaning of work; the qualitative methodological approach; results and discussion.

BACKGROUND

Supply Chain Management Facing Digital Challenges.

Presentation of the Supply Chain Concept

Kiefer and Novack (1999) define the supply chain as an integrated set of organizations that manage information, products and cash flow from a point of origin to a point of consumption with the objective of maximizing consumer satisfaction while reducing the costs of the organizations involved. Technically, the structure of a supply chain is similar to the classic structure of an industrial company, with suppliers, customers, technical means, and a set of interdependent activities participating together in the creation, distribution and sale of goods and services (Kiefer & Novack, 1999). The objectives of a supply chain naturally go beyond the egocentric objectives of the classic company, but do not revoke them. Because in addition to promising the improvement of the internal indicators of companies, new "transversal" indicators are highlighted by this concept of supply chain (Mounir & Naji, 2021) such as: collaboration and cooperation, logistics added value, management of supplier relations, integration, logistics maturity, etc., and which contribute to the evaluation of the overall performance of the chain. Supply chain management thus appears as a means of developing a competitive advantage based on cost control, differentiation and integrated coordination of processes from the initial supplier to the end customer. It aims to create more value both for the customer and for the companies (Cooper et al., 1997; Mentzer et al., 2001).

Today, it is difficult to achieve a certain level of performance by focusing solely on the optimization of internal processes. It is therefore imperative for managers to integrate a global vision to improve the performance of the entire supply chain. A supply chain is said to be efficient if and only if the company is able to satisfy the customer by ensuring the delivery of good quality products/services, in the required quantity, at the right time and place where the need exists and in consuming fewer resources.

To achieve this, synchronization of information is essential between the different players and it is also essential to master all the operational functions that exist between the different players in the supply chain, from supply to delivery, including production, routing, storage and packaging (Veny & Colin 2018).

The Digitization of the Supply Chain

Digitalization is defined as a technological innovation that consists of transforming traditional processes, transactions or operations using digital technologies such as e-commerce, blockchain, ERP, and robotics. The emergence of technological innovations has also affected the supply chain, which has turned into a digital supply chain (Büyüközkan & Göçer, 2018). Scientific research in this area is very active and many researchers have explored the phenomenon. The state of the art highlights several definitions. For (Kinnett, 2015) the Digital Supply Chain is: "an intelligent, value-driven network that leverages new technological and analytical approaches to create new forms of revenue and business value, through a centralized platform that captures and maximizes the use of real-time information from various sources". (Büyüközkan Feyzioğlu & Gocer, 2018) define the Digital Supply Chain as a set of interconnected activities that occur between suppliers and customers, and which are processed through new technologies. They go on to say that the digital supply chain is seen as an intelligent, customer-centric, system-embedded, globally-connected, data-driven mechanism that leverages new technologies to deliver products and more accessible and affordable valuable services. Finally, these authors indicate that a digital supply chain (DSC) is an intelligent, value-driven chain, an efficient process that generates new forms of commercial revenue for firms through the exploitation of both new approaches with new technological and analytical methods. The digitization of the supply chain has advantages in terms of its sustainability as well as its performance (Bennouri et al., 2020). For Kayikci (2018), the integration of digitalization has made it possible to ensure better cooperation and connectivity between the actors of the supply chain as well as the traceability of products, using smart technologies. These new technologies have transformed the digital landscape: increased speed, quality and connectivity of communication tools and multimedia content. Many sectors have taken advantage of these innovations (industry 4.0, e-commerce, telecommunications, etc.) to develop. But this growth of digital equipment and services, often perceived as dematerialized, has also been associated with a significant increase in pressures on the environment and natural resources.

Introduction to the Blockchain Concept

Blockchain Definition

Although the concept of blockchain is very recent, several authors have brought different definitions to the concept. For Ghiro et al. (2021), use of the term blockchain is documented for disparate projects, from cryptocurrencies to applications for the Internet of Things (IoT), and many others. The concept of blockchain therefore appears vague, because it is difficult to believe that the same technology can empower applications that have extremely different requirements and present dissimilar performance and security. This position paper elaborates on distributed systems theory to advance a clear definition of blockchain that allows us to clarify its role in the IoT. This definition inextricably ties together three elements that together give blockchain those unique characteristics that set it apart from other distributed ledger technologies: immutability, transparency, and anonymity. Note, however, that immutability comes at the expense of remarkable resource consumption, transparency does not require confidentiality, and anonymity prevents the identification and registration of users. This stands in stark contrast to the requirements of most IoT applications which consist of resource constrained devices, whose data must be kept confidential and the users clearly known.

For Viriyasitavat and Hoonsopon (2019), "Blockchain is a technology that enables immutability and data integrity, in which a record of transactions performed in the system is kept across multiple distributed nodes that are linked in a peer-to-peer network." The Blockchain thus refers to a digital ledger (register) (Swan, 2015) in which transaction data is recorded and shared in a private network in which the use of the data collected is not completely free, but subject to conditions of verification and control by a private or public entity, network users may not reveal their identities (remain anonymous) (Wüst & Gervais, 2017) however transactions are authorized from several members. Data is stored in blocks in chronological order without any modification (Al-Saqaf & Seidler, 2017).

According to Marin-Dagannaud (2017), blockchain is a technology for sharing a database in a decentralized way, i.e., between actors who do not necessarily trust each other and without a central control entity. It makes possible the creation of a new type of software platform, decentralized platforms. For Dhiba and Alaoui (2020), Blockchain technology is a digital register for storing and transmitting information. This register can contain a variety of data, information and transactions. It is an organized block of elements, a decentralized network, and it has no control center. Indeed the information is stored in large computers and not in servers in the form of a distributed database. In this kind of database, actors share, distribute and exchange data among themselves without going through a central control system. Ultimately, "blockchain" technology can be defined as a new type of "distributed" database, allowing information to circulate within a decentralized network (Nelson da Conceição, 2020).

Feature of Blockchain Technology

The Blockchain guarantees immediate and general transparency, and since the transactions added to the chain are timestamped and cannot be easily tampered with, Blockchain technology allows products and transactions to be easily traced (Chekrouni et al., 2022). Blockchain technology tends, through its shared and transparent nature, to restore the confidence of individuals where it may have been shaken. The blockchain consists of 3 key elements:

- **Blocks:** Blocks are defined as groupings of transactions. More or less important depending on the amount of data they contain, they are distinguished from each other by an identifier, a unique code called "hash".
- **The Nodes:** These are the computers connected to the blockchain. Each of them hosts a copy of the database. This copy is downloaded automatically when connecting to the network and contains all the exchanges between users.
- **Minors:** The latter are responsible for checking whether the new blocks created correspond to security standards. They have an absolutely essential role within the blockchain, since they guarantee the authenticity of the blocks, and therefore of the entire chain.

Blockchain data meets 3 main characteristics. They remain:

- **Chronological:** Transactions are integrated one after the other over time;
- **Immutable:** Information cannot be deleted. Once the transaction is certified, it is indelibly recorded in the history;
- **Tamper-Proof:** It is impossible to modify a transaction after it has been integrated into the blockchain. In case of error, a second transaction canceling the first must appear. Both will then be visible.

The Appropriation of the Blockchain Within Companies: The Contribution of the Theory of Structuring

Blockchain technology brings, as we have seen, to companies a promise of process optimization. To achieve positive results in the context of the deployment of the blockchain and to derive competitive advantages from it, it is necessary to take an interest in the uses made of it (Orlikowski, 2000). It is important for organizations wishing to adopt blockchain technology to pay attention to uses. Because it is this use management that will contribute to the best performance of innovative technologies (Chaabouni, & Ben Yahia, 2013). In addition, the competitive advantage that blockchain technology can bring will come from the way it is used and how it is contextualized (Jones & Karsten, 2008). Emphasis must therefore be placed on supporting uses during the ICT deployment phase. An understanding of these issues of use of technologies is offered by the theory of structuring. Proposed by Giddens (1987), this theory invites us to study social practices through the recursive relationships between actors and social structures (Jones and Karsten, 2008). Structures are characterized by three main properties (see Figure 1). The structural property of the uses of technologies allows actors to give meaning to their actions and to the relationship; the aspect of domination is manifested by the elaboration of rules of behavior and the control of the resources of the action; finally the property of legitimization which highlights the respect of the rules (Ibid, 2008).

Figure 1. Modalities of interaction between structures and actors
Source: Giddens (1987)

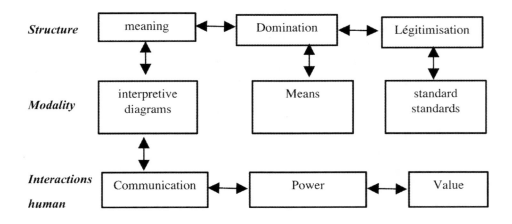

The interaction between structures and actors takes place through communication, power and values dimensions. These characteristic elements of human behavior make it possible to see how in the context of the uses of IT such as the blockchain, social structures are produced or reproduced (see Figure 2). To make it an element that contributes to performance, users of new technologies tend to transpose the rules and standards of use to similar situations (Orlikowski & Yates, 1994)

Figure 2. Mechanisms of production and reproduction of social or technical structures via uses
Source: De Vaujany (2000)

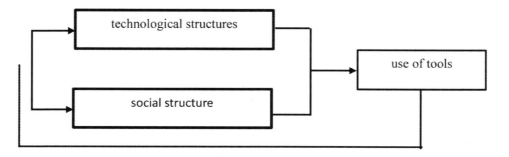

Relationship Between Blockchain and Supply Chain

Most of the malfunctions of the supply chain are related to the additional costs of the partitioning of services within the organization, the lack of cooperation between customers and suppliers and the lack of performance of the information system. It is to these new challenges that SCM management (supply chain management) must respond. In general, the supply chain never works very well in practice. Its poor functioning can cause producers or distributors to run the risk of losing huge sales. Today's supply chain suffers from inefficiencies and struggles when trying to integrate all the parties involved (products and materials, as well as money and data). Most of these problems can be solved through the use of Blockchain technology which offers new methods of recording, transmitting and sharing data.

Nowadays the blockchain intervenes in the supply chain in several sectors:

Luxury (diamonds, bags, etc.), pharmaceutical industry (recording each step in the manufacturing and distribution chain of a medicine), real estate and building (maintenance issues), heavy industries (spare parts); agri-food (ensure transparency and traceability in the food supply chain in order to reduce losses and waste and guarantee food safety). Current supply chains face problems in ensuring full product traceability, as well as a lack of flexibility and speed. This generates many external costs. Blockchain technology opens the way to much more reliable product tracking, without an individual or entity being able to modify or delete the information.

In addition, it allows actors to detect in real time where and when the fault/fraud was committed. According to recent studies carried out in different regions of the world on the relationship of the implementation of the blockchain in other fields of activity, health, education etc. For Terzi & al (2019), this technology has shown that it can bring a lot to the supply chain. Associated with the IOT, it contributes effectively to the traceability of products exposed to falsification such as agri-food products, the blockchain guarantees the quality and origin of the products (Xu et al., 2019). In addition to verifying the traceability of the product, the blockchain allows all actors access to data in a fast, transparent and inexpensive way. Because of its advantages, blockchain is in demand in other areas outside of finance. In France, for example, the blockchain has already found a place in the energy sector, in insurance, in health, but also in the supply chain and the agri-food sector.

RESEARCH DESIGN

In this section, we will present the data collection method and then describe our sampling technique and finally our data processing. In order to answer our research question, we opted for an exploratory qualitative approach. This choice is justified on the one hand by our desire to understand the different representations that the actors have about our research theme. On the other hand, this choice seemed obvious to us because of the complexity of our subject and its exploratory nature in the Cameroonian context.

Sample Selection

Using our interview guide, the researchers conducted 18 semi-structured interviews lasting an average of 60 minutes with supply chain actors in Cameroon (purchasing manager, logistics manager, delivery services manager, supply department manager string).The researchers selected the interviewees according to the snowball method and also according to the opportunities that presented themselves to us. From the seventeenth interview, the researchers realized that the information provided was already known; we had therefore reached the theoretical saturation point (Thietart et al., 2003). One of the co-authors of this research, a supply chain consultant to companies based in Cameroon, was able to observe the practices of companies that have initiated discussions on the adoption of block chain technologies as part of their supply chain activities. The authors) were able to adopt a posture of non-participating observer, concealing our status as a researcher on the question of the role of the block chain on the performance of supply chains while keeping a certain distance to limit the risks of contamination of the actors observed. This posture allowed us to complete our primary data, to reconstruct the chronology of events experienced by the actors interviewed (Leonard-Barton, 1990) and to concretize our desire to triangulate data (see Table 1).

Table 1. The different data collected

Types of Data Collected	Descriptions
Semi-structured interviews (18 interviews lasting an average of 60 minutes)	- Verbatims from transcriptions Semi-directive interview guide
Non-participant observations	- - Taking notes during meetings attended by our supply chain consultant co-author (Total: 9 pages) - Note taking during conferences and workshops organized by Cameroonian actors in the supply chain (Total: 10 pages)
Secondary data	Documentation (Total: 120 pages)
80% private players and 20% public players. 15% of our interviewees are women and the rest are men.	- Purchasing Manager, - Logistics manager, - Responsible for delivery services, - Supply chain department manager

Data Processing

Once the transcripts of our interviews were completed, The authors) added secondary data to the data processing using the thematic content analysis method. This analysis then allowed us, on the basis of structured processing, to make judgments on the sender of the speech, on the content of the message and finally on the audience of the message (Hlady-Rispal, 2002). To do this, all of our data was coded for thematic analysis. This coding was partly confirmed by a double coding process carried out by another researcher. This helped us reduce bias and maintain a degree of rigor as recommended by Cole & al (2011). Once our coding was done, we chose the QSR NVivo 12 content processing software. At the end of our analysis phase, links between the different themes and sub-themes were made in order to make connections to the context and content of the verbatims (see Table 2).

Table 2. Typology of codes used for the thematic analysis (by us)

Code Level 1	Code Level 2
Origin of the technology adoption project in supply chain activities	Willingness to adapt to technological developments
	Responding to consumer expectations
	Response to competitor practices
Barriers to the adoption of blockchain technology	Resistance to change by company employees
	Inadequate technological infrastructure
	Insufficient training and support opportunities
	Cost of investment required
Role of blockchain on supply chain performance	Supply chain management
	Security of "almost" infallible operations
	Secure payment
	No defined rules. Freedom of capture mode for everyone
	Compliance with commitments
Role of the State	Connecting actors
	Provision of adequate technological environments
	Voluntary public policy and sometimes based on injunction
	Adoption of innovation-friendly legislation
	Investment in technological infrastructures

RESULTS

In this section the authors) will present our results. We will start with the challenges and conditions for the success of the block chain in Africa (VI.1) and then the contribution of the block chain to the performance of supply chains in Africa (VI.2).

Deployment of Blockchain Technology in Africa: Challenges and Conditions for Success

Our research emphasizes the need for supply chain actors in Africa, and particularly in Cameroon, to take stock of the challenges and challenges brought about by the Block Chain deployment project. This requires ensuring the availability of human and material resources. More concretely, it is:

- Breaking down prejudices and raising awareness: adapting to the cultural specificities of Sub-Saharan African countries

Indeed, one of the peculiarities of sub-Saharan Africa and Cameroon is the climate of mistrust and risk aversion of the populations. There is a great reluctance to change. In addition, for most local players, the Block Chain mainly boils down to cryptocurrency. However, the latter enjoys a very bad reputation in the Cameroonian environment, as stated by one of our interviewees: "the block chain in Cameroon died before it was born. Unfortunately the precursors were crooks. Today it is complicated to raise awareness on the subject of the Block Chain. People always associate it with cryptocurrency scams." There have indeed been several scam scandals in Cameroon caused by cryptocurrency players. In addition, the arrest in the USA this year 2023 of one of the big players in cryptocurrency is not reassuring. We must therefore raise awareness. But evolve and change mentalities. Explain and understand the challenges of the Block Chain which beyond cryptocurrency and a technological tool likely to increase the performance of the supply chain of SMEs based in Cameroon. An SME employee that the authors) interviewed insists on the importance of awareness and the role of public decision-makers: "to speak of the same of the block chain in Cameroon and Africa is a bit exaggerated. The State should even already have a more objective and understanding view of the Block Chain. If the state understands this, it would then have to introduce it into the education system as an innovative technology because the blockchain has so many advantages, particularly in terms of security".

- Develop skills and contribute to the emergence of "real experts"

As the researchers) have seen, the popularization of the Block Chain within SMEs based in Cameroon must go upstream through skills training. One of our actors interviewed goes in this direction: "education is important here because it is an environment in which we meet a lot of scammers. If there is formal education to allow the population to know how the Block Chain works, then many young people should not engage blindly. This ignorance pushes young people to embark on the blockchain without skills, then get scammed, to then make negative evidence; saying the Block Chain is for bandits, thieves"

- Ownership of technological infrastructures (Cloud, data center, etc.)

Our study shows that for a deployment of block chain technologies it is essential to ensure the possession of energy and digital infrastructures (access to high-speed internet, data center, etc.). One of our interviewees must therefore explain investing in these infrastructures: "to really take advantage of Block Chain technology, it is necessary that in the medium and long term that African countries such as Cameroon are powerful investors in equipment likely to 'host block chain solutions'.

- A proactive public policy that is sometimes based on injunction

In Africa and Cameroon, part of the experience has shown that the diffusion of technological innovations has been accelerated by a commitment from the State. Our study shows that like the Covid-19 period and the requirement made by the State to companies to set up technological devices in order to respect the barrier measures; the State must, in the case of the Block Chain, make an injunction by encouraging public companies to take an interest in the blockchain. This will generate public orders in terms of support for the deployment of block chain technologies. This ecosystem, which will be born under the impetus of the State, will serve as an example for local SMEs. One of our interviews cites an example of action by the Cameroonian State likely to promote the development of Block Chain technology: "the current decentralization process in Cameroon is a good opportunity for the State to use Block Chain technology to intensify the process of digitizing administrative procedures and securing the dematerialization project for civil status services".

The action of the Cameroonian State can also consist in the establishment of a legislative and security environment adapted to the developments imposed by Block Chain technology.

Contribution of the Blockchain to the Performance of Supply Chains in Cameroon

One of the objectives of this work was to understand how the Block Chain can contribute to the performance of the Supply Chain of organizations based in Cameroon. Our empirical study highlights the contribution of the Block Chain for the performance of the Supply Chain on aspects such as the securing of financial and administrative transactions related to the supply chain, the speed of transactions, the optimization of traceability actions.

- Supply chain management

Our study shows that in the Cameroonian context, one of the major contributions of the block chain to the supply chain of local organizations is at the level of supply chain management. Indeed, with the multitude of intermediaries, the stakes of the supply chain constitute an aid for the optimal management of their supply chains. Indeed, for countries like Cameroon with almost no direct supply chain (non-stop) whether by rail, sea or air, delivery times are a decisive issue. Our research shows that in this context the Block Chain thanks to the coordination between partners and the facilitation of transactions improves the supply chain by allowing faster delivery and optimal traceability of products. Indeed, the verifiable and inviolable nature of the transactions offered by the blockchain; and the potential it offers for transaction automation to increase transaction speed and partner satisfaction. One of our interviews affirms on this subject: "This system can make it possible to create a certain interoperability between the various systems of traceability of logistic flows and thus to provide reliable and fast information. Because we have too many intermediaries"

With blockchain, however, every step is recorded on the blockchain and information about every interaction between two parties is visible to all.

- An "almost" infallible security system for operations

The researchers) know that supply chain operations most often involve several intermediaries. Each of these intermediaries has an internal transaction management system (ERP), however, it is complicated to have the ERPs of all the partners communicate together. This would have made it possible to detect errors and make decisions more easily. Our study shows that companies based in Cameroon are not up to date with the latest innovations in ERP, it is difficult for them to be able to communicate and exchange information with other supply chain partners. The Block Chain in the context of our study can be an answer to this problem. Indeed, each operation in the blockchain receives a unique identifier which acts as an electronic signature. One of our interviewees insists on this advantage offered by the block chain: "thanks to the block chain, all the known parties in the supply chain can consult the transactions while protecting them from malicious actors. ". In addition, the audit of transactions facilitated thanks to the Block Chain. Because it allows a chronological backup. Unlike ERPs, all partners will be able to access the encrypted information available in the blockchain. An IS manager interviewed agrees with this in his remarks: "We must regularly carry out audits. Our company with the thousands of monthly logistics transactions and the multitude of intermediaries has difficulty in detecting the sources of errors. Block Chain technology, through its secure transaction backup capacity, will allow us to carry out audits, which are inviolable, complete and reliable. »

- Secure payment

Our study shows that the Block Chain can facilitate financial transactions in supply chain activities and thus improve its performance. Payment, payment confirmation and payment security are generally elements involved in the evaluation of supply chain performance. In Cameroon, local organizations faced with the multitude of intermediaries, each with a banking system and a particular currency, regularly face problems related to the payment of operations. One of our interviews explains a situation experienced: "international financial transactions are not fast and sometimes have ceilings or maximum payment amounts. The block chain through cryptocurrency can in this context make it possible to solve the problems of reliability and speed of payment of international logistics transactions."

DISCUSSIONS

Our research is part of the continuity of the research work started having attempted to understand the contribution of the block chain to the performance of the supply chain. The researchers have analyzed in depth the characteristics and contours of the block chain in Cameroon, its deployment in Africa and finally its contribution to the performance of the supply chain. Our results highlight the fact that Africa needs technological innovations to skip a generation and catch up, the Block Chain therefore presents itself as an effective solution to this situation. Although it is currently difficult to comment on the long-term effects of the use of blockchain, our study shows that the paradigm shift that this technology induces will impact many areas. Africa is an exceptional field of exploration.

Blockchain adoption continues to grow rapidly in Africa. Even if the continent does not yet occupy the first places in the mobilization of resources, investments for the benefit of companies in the sector are accelerating. This result is in line with the work of Verny (2018) As our research shows, companies based in Cameroon have adopted blockchain in various different sectors of activity. Unlike other African countries, Cameroon does not yet have multiple concrete use cases for blockchain. In a context marked by a low rate of banking, a strong dynamic of innovation and mobile services in full explosion, the blockchain represents a real opportunity for the Cameroonian supply chains. However, we should not close our eyes to the limits of this technology. And in particular the need to adapt it to local realities. To be deployed and operate optimally, this tool must fall within a defined legal framework. This is in line with the work of authors who have dealt with the theory of structuring (Giddens, 1987). Our work highlights the need for companies wishing to adopt the Blockchain with a view to increasing performance to put in place an effective usage management system (Chaabouni, & Ben Yahia, 2013). To achieve this, our study, joining the work of Jones & Karsten (2008), recommends supporting the actors in their construction of meaning and in the interactions that they will have to have with each other in the phases of deployment and use of the blockchain in their supply chain activities.

Our work joins those of Cai (2020) and Hug (2017), about the fact that the implementation of a Block Chain in the supply chain has several advantages of particular importance. Indeed, all supply chain tasks will be able to benefit from the advantages of Block Chain either in terms of security or product traceability throughout its production process until delivery to the end customer, avoiding all bad practices and primarily counterfeiting. The Block Chain thus makes it possible to improve the transparency of operations and thus strengthen confidence in exchanges, which is in line with the work of Skema & Diallo (2022). Our study highlights the perception by actors of the Cameroonian supply chain that the blockchain offers a guarantee of transparency based on a peer-to-peer verification system, thus ensuring the integrity of the data entered, preventing at best the hacking as demonstrated by Ming & al (2021). The large flows of goods, services and data involved in an international sales operation generate tensions between sellers and buyers or suppliers and customers in Cameroon. These conflicts are mainly due to the lack of trust generated by the lack of transparency of the information transmitted during the various transactions (Singh, 2020)

In fact, the blockchain therefore makes it possible to improve operational performance within the Cameroonian supply chain (Verny, 2018) by accelerating the flow of information and financial flows, which participate in the optimization of the management of physical flows.

CONCLUSION

The purpose of our chapter is to present in a global way the state of the digitalization of the supply chain in Cameroon by seeking to highlight the relationship between the blockchain and the supply chain, these challenges, these conditions of success etc. To do so, the researchers reviewed the literature in order to present the concepts of supply chain, supply chain digitization, blockchain and the deployment of blockchain technologies in the supply chain in general and in companies based in Cameroon in particular. It also aims at the integration of blockchain in the supply chain, making a significant contribution to the literature, practitioners and policy makers interested in gaining an in-depth understanding of this cutting-edge technology. The blockchain can impact "product flows" in particular by providing finer traceability enabled by hashing algorithms, flawless transparency, secure and tamper-proof information eliminating the risk of fraud. It can also impact "service flows" by allowing data accreditation which, in the long term, will give rise to new recommendation systems and finally, it can have a significant impact on "information flows".

However, the literature on blockchain technology in the field of supply chain is still in its infancy. This chapter provides insight relevant to researchers and practitioners interested in advancing the integration of blockchain into the supply chain. The results of our research relate in particular to the following two points: the deployment of block chain technology in Africa: challenges and conditions for success on the one hand and on the other hand the contribution of the block chain to the performance of supply chains in Cameroon Moreover, our chapter showed that the main theoretical results of the study of the approaches used in the documents were conceptual. This means that there are possibilities for researchers to use other research tools. Research (econometrics and statistics) and the need to develop empirical studies. Thus, researchers have many possibilities for future studies related to blockchain and supply chain.

REFERENCES

Al-Saqaf, S. (2017). Blockchain technology for social impact: opportunities and challenges ahead. *Journal of Cyber Policy*. doi:10.1080/23738871.2017.1400084

Baudie, V., & Chang, A. (2022). The impacts of blockchain on innovation management: Sectoral experiments. *Journal of Innovation Economics & Management, 37*, 1-8.

Bennouri, (2020). Study of the impact of digital technological innovations on the sustainable performance of a supply chain: case of the halio-industrial sector. *13th International Conference on Modeling, Optimization And Simulation (MOSIM2020)*.

Blockchain Partner. (2017). *Supply chain, traceability & blockchain*. Blockchain Partner Publications.

Buterin, V. (2015). *On Public and Private Blockchains*. Ethereum Blog, Crypto Renaissance Salon.

Büyüközkan, G, (2018). *Digital Supply Chain: Literature review and a proposed framework for future research*. Elsevier.

CaiD.QianY.NanN. (2023). *Blockchain for Timely Transfer of Intellectual Property*. NBER Working Paper No. w30913. doi:10.2139/ssrn.4349546

Chaabouni, A., & Ben Yahia, I. (2013). Application de la théorie de la structuration aux systèmes ERP: Importance de la gestion des connaissances. *Recherches en Sciences de Gestion, 96*(96), 91–109. doi:10.3917/resg.096.0091

Charif, A., & Lemtaoui, M. (2022). The impact of the use of Blockchain on the performance of the supply chain. *International Review of Management Sciences, 5*(1), 22–39.

Chekrouni, A. (2022). The potential impact of Blockchain on supply chain management: What applications and what perspectives? *French Review of Economics and Management, 3*(8), 161–185.

Cooper, M. C., Lambert, D. M., & Pagh, J. D. (1997). Supply Chain Management: More Than a New Name for Logistics. *International Journal of Logistics Management, 8*(1), 1–14. doi:10.1108/09574099710805556

De Vaujany, F.-X. (2000). Use of information technologies and creation of value for the organization: proposal of a structuring analysis grid based on the key factors of success. *IXth international conference on strategic management (AIMS)*, 1-16.

Dhiba, H., & Alaoui, M. (2020). Blockchain and logistics risk management: What contribution? *International Review of the Researcher*, *1*(3), 393–413.

El Bakkouri, A. (2021). Literature Review of the "Logistics Performance" Concept: A Synthesis Essay. *European Scientific Journal*, *17*(23), 210. doi:10.19044/esj.2021.v17n23p210

Ghiro, L., Restuccia, F., D'Oro, S., Basagni, S., Melodia, T., Maccari, L., & Lo-Cigno, R. (2021). What is a Blockchain? A Definition to Clarify the Role of the Blockchain in the Internet of Things. https://doi.org//arXiv.2102.03750 doi:10.48550

Giddens, A. (1987). *The Constitution of society - Elements of the theory of structuring*. PUF.

Jones, M. R., & Karsten, H. (2008). (2008(. « Giddens's structuration theory and information systems research. *Management Information Systems Quarterly*, *32*(1), 127–157. doi:10.2307/25148831

Kennett-Herbert, J. (2020). *Conceptualising trust as a data-driven attribute in a study of supply chain relationships* [Master's thesis]. Queensland University of Technology.

Kiefer, A. W., & Novack, R. A. (1999). An empirical analysis of warehouse measurement systems in the context of supply chain implementation. *Transportation Journal*, *38*(3), 18–27.

Lasmoles O. & Diallo. (2022). Impacts of blockchains on international maritime. *Journal of Innovation Economics & Management*, 91 – 116.

Leonard-Barton. (1990). A Dual Methodology for Case Studies: Synergistic Use of a Longitudinal Single Site with Replicated Multiple Sites. *Organization Science*, *1*(3).

Lesueur-Cazé, M., Bironneau, B., Gulliver, L., &, Morvan, T. (2022). Reflections on the uses of blockchain for logistics and Supply Chain Management: a prospective approach. *French Review of Industrial Management*, 60-82.

Marin-Dagannaud, G.(2017). The functioning of the blockchain. *Annales des Mines - Industrial Realities*, *3*, 42-45.

Mentzer, J., DeWitt, W., Keebler, J., Min, S., Nix, N., Smith, C., & Zachria, Z. (2001). Defining supply chain management. *Journal of Business Logistics*, *22*(2), 1–26. doi:10.1002/j.2158-1592.2001.tb00001.x

Mounir, Y., & Naji, M. (2021). *De la mesure de performance des chaines logistiques*. Academic Press.

Olivier, L., Skema, O-L., Mamadou, T., & Diallo, M-T. (2022). Impacts of Blockchains on International Maritime Trade. *Journal of Innovation Economics & Management*, *1*(31), 91-116.

Orlikowski, W. (2000). Using Technology and Constituting Structures: A Practice Lens for Studying Technology in Organizations. *Organization Science*, *11*(4), 149–160. doi:10.1287/orsc.11.4.404.14600

Orlikowski, W. J., & Yates, J. (1994). Genre Repertoire: The Structuring of Communicative Practices in Organizations. *Administrative Science Quarterly*, *39*(4), 541–574. doi:10.2307/2393771

Print, D. (2015). *Supply Chain Performance and Evaluation Models*. ISTE.

Ripsal. (2002). *The case method, application to management research*. De Boeck University Edition.

Simonnot, B. (2012). Access to online information: Engines, devices and mediations. Hermès Lavoisier.

Soppé, F. (2005). Containerized maritime transport and globalization. *Annals of Geography, 2*(642), 187 – 200.

Swan. (2015). Blockchain-Based Equity and STOs: Towards a Liquid Market for SME Financing? *Theoretical Economics Letters, 9*(5).

Terzi, S., Terresan, S., Schneiderbauer, S., Critto, A., Zebisch, M., & Marcomini, A. (2019). Multi-risk assessment in mountain regions: A review of modelling approaches for climate change adaptation. *Journal of Environmental Management, 232*, 759–771. doi:10.1016/j.jenvman.2018.11.100 PMID:30529418

Thiétart, R.A.(1999). *Méthodes de Recherche en Management.* Dunod edition.

Verny, J. (2018). The blockchain at the service of improving the competitiveness of companies and the attractiveness of territories. Application to the pharmaceutical sector of the Seine Valley. Annals of Geography, 723-724.

Viriyasitavat, H., & Hoonsopon, D. (2019). Blockchain Characteristics and Consensus in Modern Business Processes. *Journal of Industrial Information Integration, 13*, 32–39. doi:10.1016/j.jii.2018.07.004

Wüst, K., & Gervais, A. (2017). Do you need blockchain? *Conference: 2018 Crypto Valley Conference on Blockchain Technology (CVCBT).*

Xu, C., McDowell, N. G., Fisher, R. A., Wei, L., Sevanto, S., Christoffersen, B. O., Weng, E., & Middleton, R. S. (2019). Increasing impacts of extreme droughts on vegetation productivity under climate change. *Nature Climate Change, 9*(12), 948–953. doi:10.103841558-019-0630-6

APPENDIX

Maintenance Protocol

The information collected during this survey is strictly confidential under the terms of Law No. 91/023 of December 16, 1991, relating to censuses and surveys.

The structure of this guide is built around the following themes:

TOPIC 0: introduce yourself, your activities in logistics and data management

TOPIC 1: KNOWLEDGE OF THEORETICAL CONCEPTS

For you, what is the supply chain?

What is performance
What is Blockchain?

TOPIC 2: DEPLOYMENT OF THE BLOCK CHAIN WITHIN THE CAMEROONIAN SUPPLY CHAIN

Deployment methodology
Brakes and motivations
accompaniement
Role of the State

TOPIC 3: SUPPLY CHAIN PERFORMANCE

How to assess supply chain performance?.
What are the difficulties in evaluating the blockchain in the Cameroonian context?..
What is the place of technological tools in the performance of the supply chain

TOPIC 4: THE BLOCKCHAIN AT THE SERVICE OF THE SUPPLY CHAIN

What are the difficulties of implementing block chain technologies in Cameroon
How the block chain can contribute to the performance of the supply chain in Cameroon

THEME 5: EVALUATION OF THE CONTRIBUTION OF BLOCHAIN TO THE PERFORMANCE OF SUPPLY CHAINS

How to assess the contribution of blockchain to supply chain performance
The exploitation of the answers will be made for a purely academic purpose and in the strictest anonymity.

Definition of Concept

Digitalization is a technological innovation that consists of using new digital tools in a company's organisational process

The supply chain is a set of actors forming a network so the goal is to ensure the routeing of a product from the most remote supplier to the final consumer.

The digital supply chain is an intelligent organisation connected on a global scale and based on the exploitation of new technologies via platforms aimed at creating value.

The blockchain is a new computer system based on cryptographic technology, it ensures reliable and secure information sharing.

Performance can be defined as the level reached on a measurement scale.

Technology is the set of techniques or tools used for the manufacture or realisation of a good or service in a specific field.

Deployment is the action of implementing, implementing a concept, technology, etc.

Section 7
Cryptocurrencies, Market, and Blockchain Technology

Chapter 17
The Dynamics of the Relationship Between Price and Volume of Cryptocurrencies:
A Wavelet Coherence Analysis

Najeh Chaâbane
University of Gafsa, Tunisia

Anas Elmalki
University of Gafsa, Tunisia

ABSTRACT

In this study, the authors investigate the volume as the pricing driver of the top three cryptocurrencies (Bitcoin, Ethereum, and Binance) based on a wavelet analysis from January 1, 2019 to December 31, 2021. The dynamics of the relationship between price and volume in the cryptocurrency market could have valuable market implications for stakeholders and investors and contribute to making optimal investment decisions via portfolio diversification strategies. The results reveal that the relationship between price and volume is positive in the medium and long term and that price is the leading volume for both Bitcoin and Binance markets. The findings suggest that the COVID-19 pandemic significantly affected the cryptocurrency price and volume series links. Indeed, these results contribute to the emerging and growing literature on cryptocurrencies in the time of COVID-19, which has received limited attention during the pandemic compared to the classical asset financial classes.

INTRODUCTION

Cryptocurrency with its range depth has become popular in the past few years and the volume of its transactions are continuously increasing. Sanitary crisis COVID-19 with its different waves has accelerated the integration of the digital dimension in economies in general and in particular the financial sphere, now evolving in great uncertainty and favoring fintech development.

DOI: 10.4018/978-1-6684-7455-6.ch017

The Relationship Between Price and Volume

During COVID-19 time, Bitcoin price levels have not seemed to decline but rather, have increased in 2020 and 2021. The recent advent and increasing attention given to cryptocurrencies have given rise to a continuous demand for understanding the various aspects of cryptocurrencies from an empirical and theoretical financial point of view. Cryptocurrency is presented as a type of digital financial asset that uses blockchain technology and serves peer-to-peer financial transactions. The features that distinguish cryptocurrencies are: that they are traded in many independent markets and are circulating currency controlled by a software algorithm rather than any classic way of control (company, central administration, or government) (Ciaian et al., 2016). From a practical point of view, it's believed that it necessitates a considerable volume exchange to move prices significantly (Najand and Yung, 1991). This relationship has been studied extensively for different asset classes, over different time intervals, and using different frequencies. In the financial literature, the price-volume relationship usually implies either relationship between volume and the magnitude of return, or a relationship between volume and return level. It has been established by previous studies that volume is positively related to the magnitude of return. However, it's controversial in the context of cryptocurrency and the nature of its relationship between return and volume as it is still under study as most of it is undertaken in spot markets as there are restrictions on short selling in spot markets. The continuous fluctuations in volume and price attract attention to the nature of the relationship that drives several dimensions around cryptocurrencies such as price, volume, and volatility risk.

This chapter adds to the literature in several ways. Despite the significant amount of literature dedicated to the study role of traded volume in predicting movement in stock returns and volatility (Gebka and Wohar, 2013), the question remain unclearly answered when it comes to the Bitcoin market: to what extend the traded volume can have a predictability power for returns and volatility?

It contributes to the existing literature by using wavelet analysis to investigate the dynamic relationships between price and volume in cryptocurrency markets. We chose wavelet analysis because it is a powerful and robust methodology for studying the co-movements of non-stationary financial time series. In particular, this chapter employs wavelet coherence, which provides time-varying correlations between price and volume for various investment horizons, as opposed to co-integration and VAR, which are limited to one or two holding periods. Wavelet coherence has the advantage of exposing associations between cause and effect over time and frequency by providing regions that show the direction and degree of dependence of prices and trading volumes. Our research results provide investors and portfolio managers with additional information about the relationships between the prices and trading volumes of the most commonly traded cryptocurrencies. At the time of writing this chapter, we retained the market cap cryptocurrencies as choice criteria to determine the top three cryptocurrencies of our empirical study; Bitcoin (over 1 trillion Dollars), Ethereum (540 billion Dollars), and Binance (100 billion Dollars). Bitcoin (BTC), Ethereum (ETH,) and Binance (BNB) are considered a new asset class, with a not clear predicted evolution. Several undiscovered territories and unsolved financial issues to be investigated about cryptocurrency and in this chapter; we try to explore two of these characteristics: Price and volume.

The remainder of the chapter is organized as follows. Section 2 presents the literature review. Section 3 provides the research methodology used; Section 4 describes the data; Section 5 presents and discusses our empirical results. Our conclusions and research implications are revealed in section 6.

LITERATURE REVIEW

With reference to the financial literature, the "price-volume" concept means a bidirectional senses that involves either a linkage between volume and the magnitude of return, or a linkage between volume and return. To develop a better understanding of how market information is communicated and subsequently incorporated into asset values, it is fundamental to do study on the relationship between volume and returns. Forecasting asset returns and volatility becomes more useful as a result. To better understand market booms and crashes, it is especially important to look at the return-volume relationship during stressful times (Marsh and Wagner, 2000).

The findings of several studies of the relationship between price and volume, are still controversial, although The volume-return relationship has been profoundly studied for the stock market (Karpoff, 1987; Li et al., 2016; Todorova and Souek, 2014); the bond market (Balduzzi et al., 2001); the commodity market (Chiarella et al., 2016); the interest rate and currency futures market (Puri and Philippatos, 2008); and the real estate market (Tsai, 2014); but it has not yet been sufficiently studied With the growing pace of Bitcoins as a new financial asset with its high speculative aspect (Kristoufek, 2014). From a practical angle, understanding the volume-return paradigm is crucial for illuminating potential implications of predicting possibilities of returns (Chen et al., 2001) as practitioners frequently have the opinion that it necessitates a substantial amount of volume to make a big difference in prices. (Najand and Yung, 1991). As cited by Weinstein (1988):" Never trust a breakout that isn't accompanied by a significant increase in volume". The study of the price and volume relationship allows for a better understanding of the trending price changing levels and its dynamics to be able to intervene in trading in markets and ForeX. The relationship between price and volume started long ago before cryptocurrencies' emergence. Ying (1966) concluded that a high increase in volume is related to high price decreases or increases in an asymmetric relationship between the absolute value of a daily price change and daily volume. Other similar conclusions have been found by several authors, such as Crouch (1970a), Crouch (1970b), Westerfield (1977), Tauchen and Pitts (1983), and Harris and Gurel (1986). Price and volume positive relationship has been found by many authors such as by Morgan (1976), Epps and Epps (1976), Cornell (1981), Bessembinder and Seguin (1993), Brailsford (1996), Llorente et al. (2002), Statman et al. (2006), Glaser and Weber (2009), Caporale and Plastun (2019) and Radikoko et al. (2015). On the other hand, other authors' results converged on a negative relationship between price and volume, such as Smirlock and Starks (1985), Wood et al. (1985), Moosa and Korczak (1999), Moosa (2003), Kocagil and Shachmurove (1998). The fundamental link between price (stock returns) and volume (trading volume) has been an interesting field of study applied to several asset categories from many different points of view in the literature (e.g., Clark, 1973 ; Crouch, 1970b; Rogalski, 1978; Tauchen and Pitts, 1983; Westerfield, 1977). Jain and Joh (1988) found a strong contemporaneous relation between trading volume and returns by using hourly common stock trading volume and return on NYSE. Moreover, the trading volume-returns relation is higher for positive returns than for negative returns (Bouri et al., 2017). Balcilar et al. (2017) studied the change in Bitcoin volatility price concerning the instant breaks in Bitcoin price that took place in 2013. They concluded that Bitcoin's positive return in the period of the study affected volatility more than in times of negative return. Katsiampa (2017) studied the volatility forecast for Bitcoin: Making a comparison of GARCH models and exploration of GARCH-type models to determine Bitcoin price volatility. As a result of the analysis in terms of compliance with the data, it was concluded that the suitable model is ARCGARCH. Baur et al. (2018) asked the question about Bitcoin and if it is a medium of exchange or a speculative asset? Analysis of Bitcoin data traded in their accounts shows that Bitcoin is not an alternative currency and exchange tool, it has shown that it is mostly used as a speculative investment tool. Bouoiyour et al. (2014) analyzed the price dynamic formation of Bitcoin from a new perspective with the Empirical Mode Decomposition (EMD) technique and concluded that speculative movements can guide the price of Bitcoin. Bouoiyour et al. (2016) investigated the possible prediction of the volatility of Bitcoin using the daily closing prices between 2010 and 2015, and as a result of the study, they concluded that asymmetric information is affected by negative shocks rather than positive shocks. Dyhrberg (2016) investigated whether Bitcoin obeys the rule and guiding of the financial asset classes. In the study, they used the Asymmetric GARCH model, and they found several prominent features in investments against gold and dollars in the first model established as a result of the study. They also concluded that the Asymmetric GARCH method would be a good tool for risk-loving investors against possible shocks in the market. Katsiampa (2017) tried the ARCH models that gave the best results in estimating the volatility of Bitcoin in his study and found that the AR-GARCH model was the model that gave the best results as a result of the study. Balcilar et al. (2017) studied the possible causality relationship between Bitcoin trading volume, return, and volatility. They concluded that outside of bear and bull market regimes, the trading volume could predict the returns. The results of Bouri et al. (2018) indicate negative and positive returns on the studiedcryptocurrenciess (Bitcoin, Ripple, Ethereum, Litcoin, NEM, DASH, and Stellar) caused by trading volume Granger. Volume was a Granger cause of return volatility for the three cryptocurrencies (Litecoin, NEM, and Dash) when the volatility was low. El Alaoui et al. (2019) concluded that there is a change in the prices of Bitcoin and these changes have mutually a nonlinear interaction with the trading volume.

METHODOLOGY

Wavelet Analysis

The wavelet transform can be used to analyze time series that contain non-stationary power at many different frequencies (Daubechies, 1990). Assume that one has a time series, X_n with equal time spacing Δt and n=0,..., N-1. Also assume that one has a wavelet function, $\Psi_0(\eta)$, that depends on a non-dimensional 'time' parameter η. To be admissible as a wavelet, this function must have zero mean and be localized in both time and frequency space (Farge, 1992). An example is the Morlet wavelet, consisting of a plane wave modulated by a Gaussian:

$$\Psi_0(\eta) = \pi^{-1/4} e^{i\omega_0 \eta} e^{-\eta^2/2} \tag{1}$$

where $\omega 0$ is the non-dimensional frequency, here taken to be 6 in line with most economic applications and to satisfy the admissibility condition (Farge, 1992).

In wavelet approaches, there are two types of analysis: the continuous wavelet transform (CWT) and discrete wavelet transform (DWT) (DWT). However, the CWT is preferable to the DWT because it provides an easy way to select wavelets based on data length, and it can easily reveal patterns that carry hidden information due to its redundancy (Aguiar-Conraria and Soares, 2011).

The continuous wavelet transform of a discrete sequence x_n is defined as the convolution of x_n with a scaled and translated version of $\Psi_0(\eta)$:

$$W_n(s) = \sum_{n'=0}^{N-1} x_{n'} \Psi^* \left[\frac{(n'-n)\Delta t}{s} \right] \qquad (2)$$

where the (*) indicates the complex conjugate. By varying the wavelet scale s and translating along with the localized time index n, one can construct a picture showing both the amplitude of any features versus the scale and how this amplitude varies with time.

Wavelet Coherence

Given two-time series X and Y, with wavelet transforms $W_n^X(s)$ and $W_n^Y(s)$, one can define the cross-wavelet spectrum as

$$W_n^{XY}(s) = W_n^X(s) W_n^{Y*}(s) \qquad (3)$$

Where $W_n^{Y*}(s)$ is the complex conjugate of $W_n^Y(s)$. The cross-wavelet spectrum is complex, and hence one can define the cross-wavelet power as $|W_n^{XY}(s)|$. Following Torrence and Webster (1999), the wavelet squared coherency is defined as the absolute value squared of the smoothed cross-wavelet spectrum, normalized by the smoothed wavelet power spectra,

$$R_n^2(s) = \frac{\left| s^{-1} W_n^{XY}(s) \right|^2}{\left\langle s^{-1} \left| W_n^X(s) \right|^2 s^{-1} \left| W_n^Y(s) \right|^2 \right\rangle} \qquad (4)$$

Where $\langle . \rangle$ indicates smoothing in both time and scale.

Note that in the numerator, both the real and imaginary parts of the cross-wavelet spectrum are smoothed separately before taking the absolute value, while in the denominator it is the wavelet power spectra (after squaring) that are smoothed. The factor s^{-1} is used to convert to an energy density.

The wavelet-squared coherence $R_n^2(s)$ is restricted to positive values within the range of 0 to 1 ($0 \leq R_n^2(s) \leq 1$) therefore, a difference between negative and positive co-movements in two-time series cannot be made. To deal with this issue, Torrence and Compo (1998) suggest using the phase difference, which is used to detect the direction of co-movement (i.e. positive or negative co-movements between variables X and Y). Indeed, a phase difference is defined as the whole cycle of a time series as a function of frequency, providing information on coherence between the two-time series.

The wavelet-coherency phase difference is given by:

$$\phi_n(s) = \left(\frac{\Im\{s^{-1} W_n^{XY}(s)\}}{\Re\{s^{-1} W_n^{XY}(s)\}} \right) \qquad (5)$$

The Relationship Between Price and Volume

The smoothed real ($\mathfrak{R}$) and imaginary ($\mathfrak{I}$) parts should have already been calculated in equation (4). Both $R_n^2(s)$ and $\phi n_{(}s)$ are functions of the time index n and the scale s.

The result of a cross-wavelet coherence analysis is generally a figure, which has five major parts: black arrows ($\leftarrow, \rightarrow, \uparrow, \downarrow, \searrow, \nearrow, \swarrow, \nwarrow$), warm and cold colors, black contours, two axes, and the cone. The coherence phase uses arrows, to show the relationship between two-time series; (1) when the black arrows point to the right $\rightarrow$ (left $\leftarrow$) the series show in-phase (out-of-phase) relationship, and the correlation coefficient is positive (negative), (2) when the arrows point down $\downarrow$ (up $\uparrow$) the second (first) variable leads the first (second) variable by a 90° angle, (3) the phase difference of zero means both time series are moving together at a given time-frequency. The black curves in the plots show the regions with coherence significance at a 5% level, and the solid white bell-shaped line in wavelet coherence plots is the cone of influence (the region of the wavelet spectrum in which edge effects become important).

DATA AND DESCRIPTIVE STATISTICS

From Bitcoin and Ethereum to Dogecoin and Tether, there are thousands of different cryptocurrencies. In this study, we chose to deal with the top three cryptocurrencies based on their market capitalization. At the time of writing this chapter, we retained the market cap cryptocurrencies as choice criteria to determine the top three cryptocurrencies of our empirical study; Bitcoin (over 1 trillion Dollars), Ethereum (540 billion Dollars), and Binance (100 billion Dollars). Therefore, the data used in this research consist of the daily price and trading volume of Bitcoin (BTC), Ethereum (ETH), and Binance coin (BNB), covering the sample period from January 1, 2019, to December 31, 2021. The sample studied period covers: the appearance of COVID-19, confinement, the several successive waves, and the vaccination plan. Using daily data in this sample period allows us to capture the dynamics of the relationship between price and volume within COVID-19 pandemic periods. We computed price and trading volume returns as follows:

$$P_t = \log\left(\frac{Price_t}{Price_{t-1}}\right) \times 100 \quad V_t = \log\left(\frac{Volume_t}{Volume_{t-1}}\right) \times 100$$

We start our empirical analysis with Figures 1, 2, and 3, which show, respectively, the evolution of both prices and trading volume of BTC, ETH, and BNB. They indicate that both prices and trading volumes for the three cryptocurrencies are sensitive to certain shocks, may have a positive time trend, and shows a clear non-stationarity.

Figure 1. BTC prices and trading volume evolutions

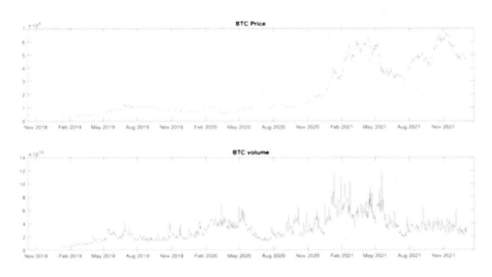

Figure 2. ETH prices and trading volume evolutions

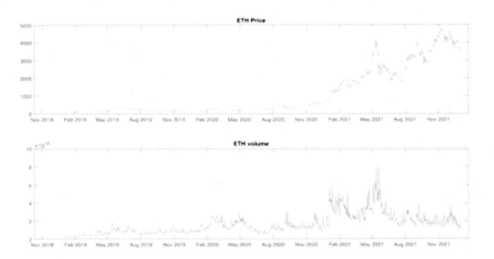

Figure 3. BNB prices and trading

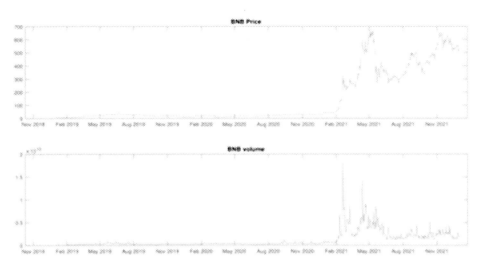

Table 1. Descriptive statistics

	Mean	Median	Std.	Min	Max	Skewness	Kurtosis
BTC P_t	0.22977	0.1741	3.9231	−46.473	17.182	−1.4343	22.871
V_t	0.15856	−0.6347	19.689	−102.14	89.458	0.21475	5.0987
ETH P_t	0.2999	0.2581	5.034	−55.073	23.07	−1.4592	19.069
V_t	0.1336	−0.4638	19.895	−78.255	82.842	0.4141	4.4922
BNB P_t	0.4072	0.2161	5.7086	−54.308	52.922	−0.1957	21.312
V_t	0.3848	−1.3164	24.04	−91.286	107.93	0.4782	4.8847

Table 1 reports the descriptive statistics of prices and trading volume returns of BTC, ETH, and BNB. Daily mean prices of BTC and ETH are analogous in magnitude. The standard deviations and minimum and maximum values show that BNB price return has the highest volatility among the other series. The average daily trading volume of BTC and ETH exhibited the same patterns with almost the same volatility. However, the mean and the standard deviation of BNB are nearly twice as high as the other series. The skewness was positive for all trading volume returns series, whereas the skewness of all price returns was negative. To that effect, the kurtosis statistic specifies that the distribution of both prices and trading volume returns for the studied series had flat tails.

EMPIRICAL RESULTS AND DISCUSSION

In this chapter, we used the continuous wavelet method to decompose the data into eight levels (2^n, $n =$ 1, 2 ...) covering different periods, namely short, medium and long-term horizons.

The horizontal axis represents the time component, which covers study periods from 2019 to the end of 2021, corresponding to 100 and 1000 (i.e. April 2019, July 2019, October 2019, February 2020, May 2020, August 2020, December 2020, March 2021, June 2021 and September 2021). Whereas, the vertical axis represents the frequency bands, which are based on daily units ranging from 4 to 256-day scales. We further divide these levels into three periods, such as the 2 to 16-day scales, which are associated with the short term, 16 to 64-day scales which are linked with medium-term dynamics, and 64 to 256-day scales, which relate to the long term.

We report the results of the continuous wavelet transform (CWT) in Figure 4, indicating that cryptocurrency prices and trading volume exhibit significant volatility at the 5% significance level. The CWT is often used for feature extraction purposes, to examine whether regions in time-frequency space with large common power have a consistent phase relationship and therefore are suggestive of causality between the time series. In Figure 4 blue and yellow regions represent low and high-intensity levels. Regions in blue show weak variation i.e. the co-movements between prices and trading volumes to external shocks are low. Whereas, regions in yellow indicate strong variation i.e. high-intensity movements between the series. The 5% significant level is presented by the black contour. Additionally, the solid curved line represents the cone of influence (COI); the region of the wavelet spectrum in which edge effects become important. The size of the COI at each scale also gives a measure of the decorrelation time for a single spike in the time series.

Table 2. The results of the wavelet power spectrum for price and volume returns

Days (Scale)	BTC	ETH	BNB
Price returns 2-16 (Short term)	July 2019-September 2019 March 2020 December 2020-June 2021	July 2019 March 2020 August 2020 January 2021 April 2021	March 200 January 2021-June 2021
16-64 (Medium term)	May 2019 - September 2019 March 2020 December 2020-June 2021	April 2019-July 2019 December 2020-June2021	February 2020 August 2020 December 2020-June 2021
64-256 (Long term)	December 2019-July 2020 August 2020-March 2021	October 2019-July 2020 March 2021-August 2021	December 2019-March 2020 July 2020-June 2021
Volume returns 2-16 (Short term)	July 2019 January 2021 September 2021	August 2020-March 2021 August 2021-September 2021	April 2019 September 2019 August 2020 January 2021 March 2021 June 2021 September 2021
16-64 (Medium term)	October 2020		January 2021-March 2021
64-256 (Long term)			

The Relationship Between Price and Volume

Figure 4. The continuous wavelet power spectrum of prices and trading volume returns of BTC, ETH, and BNB. The vertical axis is the frequency component while the horizontal axis is the time component; the thick black contour represents a significant region at the 5% level; the curved black line is the cone of influence.

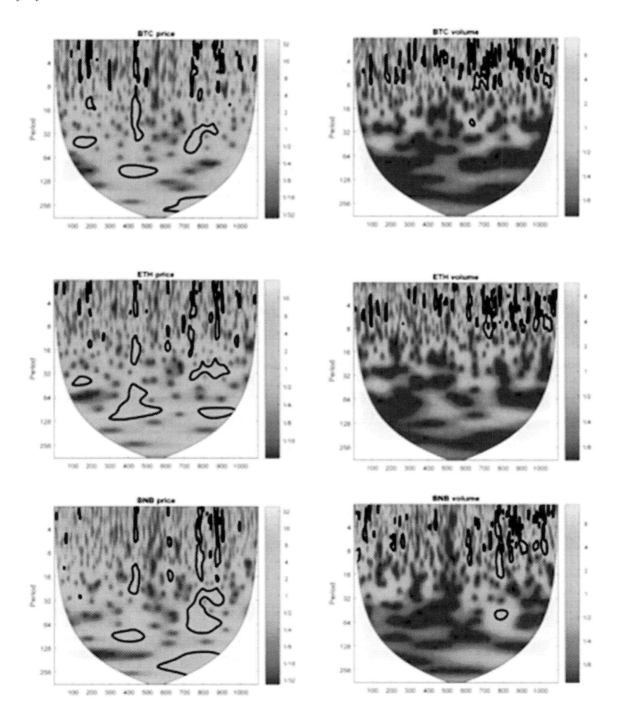

According to Figure 4 and Table 2, the price returns of the cryptocurrencies under consideration (BTC, ETH, and BNB) show an evolution of variance, implying high (low) volatility at high (low) frequency bands from 2019 to 2021. For BTC, price returns indicate significant high variation at 2-16 days between July 2019 and September 2019, March 2020 (The World Health Organization declares COVID-19 a pandemic) and from December 2020 to June 2021 (COVID-19 vaccination program); 16-64 days from May 2019 to September 2019, in March 2020 and from December 2020 to June 2021, and 64-256 days scales from December 2019 to July 2020 and from August 2020 to March 2021. Price returns for ETH indicate significant variances at different periods (July 2019, March 2020, August 2020, January 2021, and April 2021) in the 2-16 day scales, in the 16-64 day scales between April 2019 and July 2019 then from December 2020 to June 2021, and 64-256 day scales from October 2019 to July 2020 and from March 2021 to August 2021. Price returns for BNB demonstrate significant variation and structural changes over the short term in March 2020 and between January 2021 and June 2021; strong volatility in the medium term on February 2020, August 2020, and from December 2020 to June 2021; long term over the periods: December 2019-March 2020 and July 2020-June 2021.

By contrast, trading volume returns show less volatility in the medium and long term; blue is scattered across the majority of the area. Yellow areas for the short term indicate strong variation. Nevertheless, volume returns displayed high variation in 2-16 day scales in July 2019, January 2021, and September 2021 for BTC and over the periods August 2020- March 2021 and August 2021-September 2021 for ETH, and respectively in April 2019, September 2019, August 2020, January 2021, March 2021, June 2021 and September 2021 for BNB. We notice that BTC and BNB showed strong volatility in the medium-term (16-64 days) respectively in October 2020 for BTC and over the period January 2021-March 2021 for BNB.

For the studied BTC, ETH, and BNB series, the plotting pair of wavelet coherence reveals that price and trading volume returns show significant comovement over time and frequency domains. However, from Figures 5, 6, and 7 we notice that the coherence between price and volume returns increases at lower frequency bands (16-64 days and 64-256 days) and they persist from about January 2019 to December 2021.

According to Figure 5, we find co-movement between BTC price and volume returns, which suggests a strong relationship. The figure presents three significant regions with a high level of coherence in (1) 8-16 day scales corresponding to the period February 2019-Juin 2019, (2) 16-64 day scales from February 2019 to October 2019, and from October 2020 to January 2021, (3) 64-128 day scales in the period September 2019-May 2020. For the Bitcoin market, the arrows point rightward and upward suggesting an in-phase relationship (positive correlation) between price and volume returns whether the price is leading volume returns.

The Relationship Between Price and Volume

Figure 5. Wavelet coherence in prices and trading volume returns for BTC. The vertical axis is the frequency component while the horizontal axis is the time component; the thick black contour represents a significant region at the 5% level; the curved black line is the cone of influence.

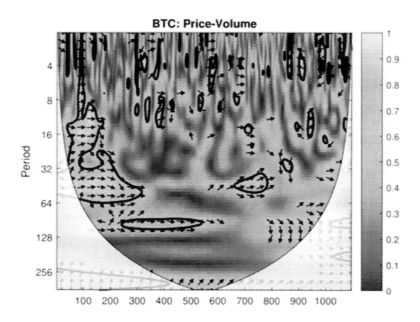

Figure 6. Wavelet coherence in prices and trading volume returns for ETH. The vertical axis is the frequency component while the horizontal axis is the time component; the thick black contour represents a significant region at the 5% level; the curved black line is the cone of influence.

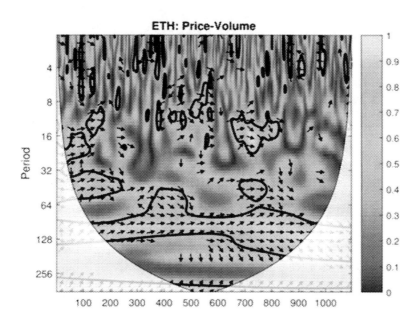

The highest level of coherence between ETH price and volume returns was recorded at scales ranging from 64 to 128-day scales from May 2019 to August 2021. Figure 6 shows also a strong coherence in the short-term scale from April 2019 to July 2019 as well as from December 2020 to March 2021. The positive causality relationship between price and volume returns is confirmed by the right-directed arrows that dominated all significant regions.

In the BNB market and according to 7, significant interdependence exists at all scales (short, medium, and long term) over 2019-2021; (a) In the short term at 2-16 day scales from February 2019 to April 2019, in February 2020 and from October 2020 to March 2021,(b) in the medium term at 16-64 day scales in two time periods March 2019-May 2019 and August 2020-April 2021 and (c) in the long term at 64-256 day scales from May 2019 to June 2021. Notably, BNB prices are strongly correlated with volume returns and persist throughout the sample period. Black arrows point rightward and most of them upward in all significant regions indicating a positive association and that price lead to volume returns.

Figure 7. Wavelet coherence in prices and trading volume returns for BNB. The vertical axis is the frequency component while the horizontal axis is the time component; the thick black contour represents a significant region at the 5% level; the curved black line is the cone of influence.

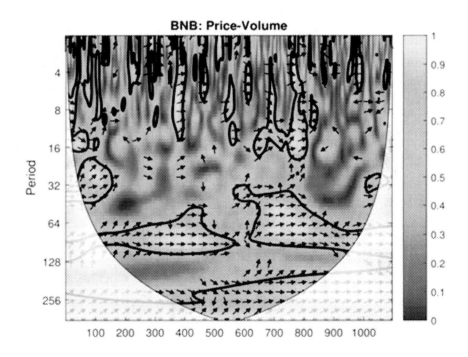

CONCLUSION AND IMPLICATIONS

Research on the nature of linkage between volume and returns is of great essential if one wants to gain a better understanding of how market information is disseminated and then absorbed into asset pricing. This reflect the usefulness to forecast asset returns and volatility and making fundamental the examination of the return-volume relationship during challenging periods in order to better comprehend market dynamics.

Despite the significant amount of literature dedicated to the study role of traded volume in predicting movement in stock returns and volatility (Gebka and Wohar, 2013, for a detailed literature review), the question remain unclearly answered when it comes to the Bitcoin market: to what extend the traded volume can have a predictability power for returns and volatility?

Cryptocurrencies' price dynamics and levels are still a controversial topic as these new financial asset classes with highly risk and speculative aspects increased inattention and became widely treated. In this chapter, we've focused on one of the price formation drivers which is the traded volume. Concerning the continuous wavelet transform approach, we investigated the possible price level significance volatility linkage with its treated volumes. The CWT is often used for feature extraction purposes, examining whether regions in time-frequency space with large common power have a consistent phase relationship and therefore are suggestive of causality between the time series. The results suggest that the price levels of the top three studied cryptocurrencies (BTC, ETH, and BNB) reflect significant and positive associated indications during the whole studied period, especially in COVID-19 times. And this is in line with Urquhart (2017) who found that Bitcoin's price and its volume have a positive relationship. These findings are well in hand with standard economic theory, and specifically, the information-based models that consider prices as a source of information that investors can use for their trading decisions (see Goodhart and O'Hara, 1997 and De Jong and Rindi, 2009, for a detailed review). Specifically, investors looking for an additional increase in cryptocurrencies prices, hesitate to trade when prices decrease, which causes a further decrease in trade volume. If an asset price falls, investors may suggest that the price will further deteriorate and refrain from buying this security. Such behavior contradicts the Walrasian paradigm of market equilibrium, according to which demand grows (falls) when price decreases (increases). The information-based models are rooted in the rational expectations theory. As cryptocurrencies are distinguished with speculative high-risk investment aspects, their price evolves as it reassures investors with the evolutions in traded volumes. Informed traders make conjectures on their rational behavior, and they do behave rationally in the sense that all their actions are focused on maximizing their wealth (or some utility function in the case of risk-averse agents). Then the cryptocurrency market in information-based models reaches an equilibrium state that satisfies participants' expectations. The interconnections between the trade volume and the prices of the studied cryptocurrencies are visible. From these findings, we can observe that both markets tend to move together very tightly in terms of both price and volume. As the cryptocurrency market is relatively a new market and very few studies have been conducted on its characteristics. Our results suggest that there is a positive and significant (both economically and statistically) relationship between volume and the absolute value of the return. This gives support to Copeland's (1976) sequential arrival of information theory. Moreover, we find evidence that volume also has a positive and significant relationship with volatility (measured by the standard deviation of returns), which lends support to Epps's (1975) mixture of distributions hypothesis. Our results concerning the relationship between volume and return per se however, are not in line with previously documented results in the literature. The traded volume as a dynamic price driver helps to analyze the price mechanism in the cryptocurrency market. The empirical findings can be of relevant practical implication for investors and portfolio managers in designing their trading strategy and decisions diversification gains as cryptocurrency markets is of important depth range that offers investors the advantages of choice, and this in lines with studies proposing that even small allocations in Bitcoin can help to increase the return of the portfolio (e.g., Platanakis and Urquhart, 2020) and offer diversification benefits (Damianov and Elsayed, 2020).

REFERENCES

Balcilar, M., Bouri, E., Gupta, R., & Roubaud, D. (2017). Can volume predict Bitcoin returns and volatility? A quantiles-based approach. *Economic Modelling*, *64*, 74–81. doi:10.1016/j.econmod.2017.03.019

Baur, D. G., Hong, K., & Lee, A. D. (2018). Bitcoin: Medium of exchange or speculative assets? *Journal of International Financial Markets, Institutions and Money*, *54*, 177–189. doi:10.1016/j.intfin.2017.12.004

Bessembinder, H., & Seguin, P. J. (1993). Price volatility, trading volume, and market depth: Evidence from futures markets. *Journal of Financial and Quantitative Analysis*, *28*(1), 21–39. doi:10.2307/2331149

Bouoiyour, J., & Selmi, R. (2016). Bitcoin: A beginning of a new phase. *Economic Bulletin*, *36*, 1430–1440.

Bouoiyour, J., Selmi, R., & Tiwari, A. (2014). *Is bitcoin business income or speculative bubble? Unconditional vs. conditional frequency domain analysis*. Academic Press.

Bouri, E., Das, M., Gupta, R., & Roubaud, D. (2018). Spillovers between bitcoin and other assets during bear and bull markets. *Applied Economics*, *50*(55), 5935–5949. doi:10.1080/00036846.2018.1488075

Bouri, E., Gupta, R., Tiwari, A. K., & Roubaud, D. (2017). Does bitcoin hedge global uncertainty? evidence from wavelet-based quantile-in-quantile regressions. *Finance Research Letters*, *23*, 87–95. doi:10.1016/j.frl.2017.02.009

Brailsford, T. J. (1996). The empirical relationship between trading volume, returns and volatility. *Accounting and Finance*, *36*(1), 89–111. doi:10.1111/j.1467-629X.1996.tb00300.x

Caporale, G. M., & Plastun, A. (2019). The day of the week effect in the cryptocurrency market. *Finance Research Letters*, *31*, 31. doi:10.1016/j.frl.2018.11.012

Ciaian, P., Rajcaniova, M., & Kancs, A. (2016). The economics of bitcoin price formation. *Applied Economics*, *48*(19), 1799–1815. doi:10.1080/00036846.2015.1109038

Clark, P. K. (1973). A subordinated stochastic process model with finite variance for speculative prices. *Econometrica*, *41*(1), 135–155. doi:10.2307/1913889

Copeland, T. E. (1976). A model of asset trading under the assumption of sequential information arrival. *The Journal of Finance*, *31*(4), 1149–1168. doi:10.2307/2326280

Cornell, B. (1981). The relationship between volume and price variability in futures markets. *The Journal of Futures Markets*, *1*, 303.

Crouch, R. L. (1970a). A nonlinear test of the random-walk hypothesis. *The American Economic Review*, *60*, 199–202.

Crouch, R. L. (1970b). The volume of transactions and price changes on the new york stock exchange. *Financial Analysts Journal*, *26*(4), 104–109. doi:10.2469/faj.v26.n4.104

Damianov, D. S., & Elsayed, A. H. (2020). Does bitcoin add value to global industry portfolios? *Economics Letters*, *191*, 108935. doi:10.1016/j.econlet.2019.108935

Daubechies, I. (1990). The wavelet transform, time-frequency localization and signal analysis. *IEEE Transactions on Information Theory*, *36*(5), 961–1005. doi:10.1109/18.57199

De Jong, F., & Rindi, B. (2009). *The microstructure of financial markets*. Cambridge University Press. doi:10.1017/CBO9780511818547

Dyhrberg, A. H. (2016). Bitcoin, gold and the dollar–a garch volatility analysis. *Finance Research Letters*, *16*, 85–92. doi:10.1016/j.frl.2015.10.008

El Alaoui, M., Bouri, E., & Roubaud, D. (2019). Bitcoin price–volume: A multifractal cross-correlation approach. *Finance Research Letters*, 31.

Epps, T. W. (1975). Security price changes and transaction volumes: Theory and evidence. *The American Economic Review*, *65*, 586–597.

Epps, T. W., & Epps, M. L. (1976). The stochastic dependence of security price changes and transaction volumes: Implications for the mixture-of-distributions hypothesis. *Econometrica*, *44*(2), 305–321. doi:10.2307/1912726

Farge, M. (1992). Wavelet transforms and their applications to turbulence. *Annual Review of Fluid Mechanics*, *24*(1), 395–458. doi:10.1146/annurev.fl.24.010192.002143

Gebka, B., & Wohar, M. E. (2013). Causality between trading volume and returns: Evidence from quantile regressions. *International Review of Economics & Finance*, *27*, 144–159. doi:10.1016/j.iref.2012.09.009

Glaser, M., & Weber, M. (2009). Which past returns affect trading volume? *Journal of Financial Markets*, *12*(1), 1–31. doi:10.1016/j.finmar.2008.03.001

Goodhart, C. A., & O'Hara, M. (1997). High frequency data in financial markets: Issues and applications. *Journal of Empirical Finance*, *4*(2-3), 73–114. doi:10.1016/S0927-5398(97)00003-0

Harris, L., & Gurel, E. (1986). Price and volume effects associated with changes in the s&p 500 list: New evidence for the existence of price pressures. *The Journal of Finance*, *41*(4), 815–829. doi:10.1111/j.1540-6261.1986.tb04550.x

Jain, P. C., & Joh, G. H. (1988). The dependence between hourly prices and trading volume. *Journal of Financial and Quantitative Analysis*, *23*(3), 269–283. doi:10.2307/2331067

Katsiampa, P. (2017). Volatility estimation for bitcoin: A comparison of garch models. *Economics Letters*, *158*, 3–6. doi:10.1016/j.econlet.2017.06.023

Kocagil, A.E., Shachmurove, Y. (1998). Return-volume dynamics in futures markets. *The Journal of Futures Markets*, *18*, 399.

Llorente, G., Michaely, R., Saar, G., & Wang, J. (2002). Dynamic volume return relation of individual stocks. *Review of Financial Studies*, *15*(4), 1005–1047. doi:10.1093/rfs/15.4.1005

Marsh, T. A., & Wagner, N. (2003). Return-Volume Dependence and Extremes in International Equity Markets. SSRN *Electronic Journal*. doi:10.2139/ssrn.424926

Moosa, I., & Korczak, M. (1999). Is the price-volume relationship symmetric in the futures markets? *Journal of Financial Studies*, 7, 1.

Moosa, I. A. (2003). *International financial operations*. Arbitrage, Hedging, Speculation. doi:10.1057/9781403946034

Morgan, I. G. (1976). Stock prices and heteroscedasticity. *The Journal of Business*, 49(4), 496–508. doi:10.1086/295881

Najand, M., & Yung, K. (1991). A garch examination of the relationship between volume and price variability in futures markets. *Journal of Futures Markets*, 11(5), 613–621. doi:10.1002/fut.3990110509

Platanakis, E., & Urquhart, A. (2020). Should investors include bitcoin in their portfolios? a portfolio theory approach. *The British Accounting Review*, 52(4), 100837. doi:10.1016/j.bar.2019.100837

Radikoko, I., & Ndjadingwe, E. (2015). Investigating the effects of dividends pay-out on stock prices and traded equity volumes of bse listed firms. *International Journal of Innovation and Economic Development*, 1(4), 24–37. doi:10.18775/ijied.1849-7551-7020.2015.14.2002

Rogalski, R. J. (1978). The dependence of prices and volume. *The Review of Economics and Statistics*, 60(2), 268–274. doi:10.2307/1924980

Smirlock, M., & Starks, L. (1985). A further examination of stock price changes and transaction volume. *Journal of Financial Research*, 8(3), 217–226. doi:10.1111/j.1475-6803.1985.tb00404.x

Soares, M. J., & Aguiar-Conraria, L. (2006). *The continuous wavelet transform: A primer*. Academic Press.

Statman, M., Thorley, S., & Vorkink, K. (2006). Investor overconfidence and trading volume. *Review of Financial Studies*, 19(4), 1531–1565. doi:10.1093/rfs/hhj032

Tauchen, G. E., & Pitts, M. (1983). The price variability-volume relationship on speculative markets. *Econometrica*, 51(2), 485–505. doi:10.2307/1912002

Torrence, C., & Compo, G. P. (1998). A practical guide to wavelet analysis. *Bulletin of the American Meteorological Society*, 79(1), 61–78. doi:10.1175/1520-0477(1998)079<0061:APGTWA>2.0.CO;2

Torrence, C., & Webster, P. J. (1999). Interdecadal changes in the enso–monsoon system. *Journal of Climate*, 12(8), 2679–2690. doi:10.1175/1520-0442(1999)012<2679:ICITEM>2.0.CO;2

Urquhart, A. (2017). Price clustering in bitcoin. *Economics Letters*, 159, 145–148. doi:10.1016/j.econlet.2017.07.035

Weinstein, S. (1988). *Secrets for profiting in bull and bear markets*. Irwin.

Westerfield, R. (1977). The distribution of common stock price changes: An application of transactions time and subordinated stochastic models. *Journal of Financial and Quantitative Analysis*, 12(5), 743–765. doi:10.2307/2330254

Wood, R. A., McInish, T. H., & Ord, J. K. (1985). An investigation of transactions data for nyse stocks. *The Journal of Finance*, *40*(3), 723–739. doi:10.1111/j.1540-6261.1985.tb04996.x

Ying, C. C. (1966). Stock market prices and volumes of sales. *Econometrica*, *34*(3), 676–685. doi:10.2307/1909776

Chapter 18
A Survey on Blockchain and Cryptocurrency-Based Systems

Atharva Deshmukh
Terna Engineering College, Navi Mumbai, India

Hariket Sukesh Kumar Sheth
Vellore Institute of Technology, Chennai, India

Pratap Dnyandeo Pawar
Vellore Institute of Technology, Bhopal, India

Amit Kumar Tyagi
Vellore Institute of Technology, Chennai, India

ABSTRACT

Projects, facilities, services, and gadgets are attracting more people as life speeds up. Blockchain and cryptocurrency systems are trending worldwide. Blockchain interests everyone with technology. They make an interesting transaction medium because they have no single powerful source. Cryptocurrencies are vital financial software platforms. Mining is crucial to its decentralised information ledger dataset. Mining adds transaction data to the chain, a decentralised ledger that lets users securely agree on actions. In 2008, Santoshi Nakamoto tried to use blockchain as a restricted ledger for bitcoin, the most successful cryptocurrency. It's unlike the internet. This chapter will discuss blockchain security, cryptocurrency fraud, cyberattacks, etc. This chapter identifies cryptocurrency blockchain threats and proposes solutions. This chapter reviews and analyses top-cited articles to reach a conclusion. In this chapter, strengths and threats of cryptocurrency and their emergence in the internet-connected financial payments in the futuristic economic world will be discussed.

DOI: 10.4018/978-1-6684-7455-6.ch018

A Survey on Blockchain and Cryptocurrency-Based Systems

INTRODUCTION

Blockchain technology is attracting the attention of people and government organisations across the world. It has the ability to significantly modify how citizen records are maintained, enabling improved information management and quicker data exchange, much like a shared ledger that is absolutely safe and available as more than simply many clones continuously altered in real time. Above all, that innovation, by allowing certification of specific acts or conformity to formal standards without such engagement of a centrally controlled admin or an external independent party (Belchior et al., 2021), foretells the Government's and government workers' inevitable exit from the area. Cryptocurrencies like Bitcoin, that are non-fiat, unregulated online payment systems work outside of the traditional finance industry, are also having an impact on the shifting landscape. Despite the reality that Bitcoin was designed as a payment system and a form of asset storage, it is unlikely that banking system currencies would be replaced given the volatility of Bitcoin's market price. The rigidity of the proof-of-work-based, fixed Bitcoin supply schedule is what causes the instability. The blockchain, on which Bitcoin's fundamental protocol is based, symbolises a development capable of transforming investment instruments and arousing existing financial, public, and safety regulations and policies, despite the fact that Bitcoin has drawn a lot of attention for its position in illicit behaviour such as financing terrorism, money laundering, the trafficking of firearms, tax avoidance, and digital ransomware (Deshmukh et al., 2022).

The rise of misunderstanding about the use of technology, the benefits and challenges it presents, has coincided with the new wave of blockchain and cryptocurrency systems. There is a lot of speculation regarding which coin or system will succeed. Due to its varied functions that are applicable worldwide, this has an impact not only on the business sector, but also on the rest of the globe. These modern technologies pose a threat to well-established business structures, eliciting a great deal of criticism, concern, and a sense of being in unfamiliar territory (Hewa, Hu, Liyanage et al, 2021). Enthusiasts also have a tendency to exaggerate this information, focusing on short-term goals and situations in order to inflate the value of the blockchain and cryptocurrency systems. Overestimating short-term rewards while underestimating long-term benefits is a common problem. They fail to consider market demand, existing frictions, and the societal consequences. Border control, government identity, insurance, shipping, real estate, advertising, waste management, energy, tourism, and a variety of other challenges can all be solved using blockchain technology. It is made up of numerous algorithms that are kept in the ledger and are used to detect faults. This even identifies the block in which the problem occurred. Several nations, namely Estonia, has experimented with blockchain in a range of fields and therefore have discovered positive outcomes that have aided its development (Zuo, 2021). Other important feature is anytime an issue arises, it leaves behind a footprint, that decreases the work required to locate the block where the problem happened. As a result of this aspect, the process becomes decentralised. Cryptocurrencies based on blockchains are becoming a new form of money in the last few years. Instead of depending on centralized authorities like the bank to manage money, cryptocurrencies depend on mathematical design and complex cryptographic protocols. Since most cryptocurrencies are fully decentralized, no individual or organization can keep track of or prevent the transfer of funds. Cryptocurrencies grew from just being an idea and model to being a worldwide prodigy with millions of individuals and organizations investing in them (Alharbi & Hussain, 2021).

Bitcoin, the first cryptocurrency, became popular because it was being controlled by a decentralized network and can avoid double-spending. Currently, Bitcoin is the leading cryptocurrency having 51% (as of June 2021) of total market share among 5000 altcoins. Blockchain is like a linked list as it doesn't keep data in a huge continuous ledger, but splits the data into nodes known as blocks. Each block contains several elements which contain the block header and its transactions (Gimenez-Aguilar, 2021). The transactions in a block account for almost all of the data, while the block header contains a timestamp, hash of the previous block, Merkle root hash, and other such essential metadata. What makes blockchain different from a linked list is that in a blockchain the hash of the previous block, also known as a reference, is cryptographically enciphered hence tamper-evident, and new data can only be added in the form of new blocks which will be linked with previous blocks of data (Liu, Zhang, Chai et al, 2021). The main technology behind Cryptocurrency is Blockchain, a shared and immutable ledger. The key elements of blockchain include hashing for security and immutability, peer-to-peer (P2P) networks for transaction verification, data structures for storing and managing the transactions, smart contracts for corporate bond transfers, consensus protocols for decentralization and avoiding double-spending issues (Dorsala et al., 2021). and incentive mechanisms for secure transactions. But cryptocurrencies still being in their early stages, create a lack of trust among many stakeholders.

The most common misbelief about cryptocurrencies is that are anonymous. Most cryptocurrencies are pseudonymous, which means that the real identities of people are represented by addresses, so the two can be connected through data analysis. But some cryptocurrencies follow certain approaches for making it difficult to trace the transactions and link addresses on the blockchain to real-world identities or follow more advanced concepts, which allows transactions to be completely private even on public blockchains (Peng et al., 2021).

Figure 1. Applications of blockchain technology in various sectors

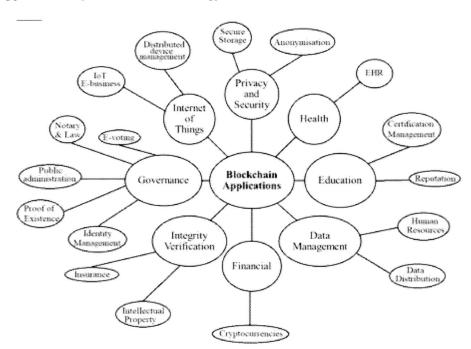

Figure 1 depicts the applications of blockchain technology in various sectors. Blockchain technology is one of the many recent revolutions in the tech sector. It is considered to be the new way of living in the near future. With its applications in most walks of life, it is seen as a revolution to the old methods. The history of blockchain technology goes way back in 1991. It was first defined by two researchers, namely, Stuart Haber and W. Scott Stornetta who desired to make a system where blocks of information could be stored along with their timestamp which could not be manipulated. But it was nearly after two decades that this technology gained popularity. Blockchain technology found its first use in cryptocurrency in 2009. This was the year when blockchain technology was seen to have its first real-life application. In 2009, the cryptocurrency, 'Bitcoin', was invented which proved to be a revelation (Bhushan et al., 2021). After that, many more cryptocurrencies were introduced and is believed that it may be the next method for money related transactions. In IoT it is used in security purposes, trusted exchanges, etc. While in healthcare blockchain technology finds its use in security and data sharing solution. In public services it is used in e-voting, propriety registration, and so on. In finance, blockchain technology is seen to have its use in running digital currencies i.e., the cryptocurrency. Bitcoin, Ethereum (Bornholdt & Sneppen, 2014).

As an organization of this work, this article discusses security and how to address it by implementing blockchain technology. The majority of blockchain security applications are seen in critical information systems, such as financial databases. In this paper, we have discussed about Merits and Demerits of using Blockchain in section 2. In the next section 3, we discuss about the implementation of Blockchain in different sectors like education, healthcare, etc. Then in section 4, we discuss about cryptocurrency systems. We also discuss Consensus Algorithms in blockchain technology in section 5. Then in next section 6, we discuss about different crypto assets in detail. In section 7, we also discuss about threats to Cryptocurrency and Blockchain. Section 8 includes few countermeasures for these mitigated threats. This paper covers the explanation of link between blockchain and cryptocurrency in section 9. Section 10 explains future work for future researchers. In the last, section 11 concludes this work in brief.

MERITS AND DEMERITS OF USING BLOCKCHAIN

Let's take a look at some of the Merits and Demerits of blockchain technology in today's applications.

Advantages of Using Blockchain

Cryptocurrencies, the digital currency or the virtual currency, demand is being increasing over a decade without the effect of inflation is the best advantage for the investors to bring their money into the world of digital currency without having the fear of inflation due to National government rules and regulations and international disputes. This design of cryptocurrencies to have a limited number of coins for a particular cryptocurrency has fulfilled to remain strong for any international crises or inflation of country currencies. Investors in stock market also need to change their investments form one stock to (Cocco et al., 2017) another or one market to another based upon the decisions of government bodies which are can't be predicted by a common man as better as big investors. One example which says that the cryptocurrencies stayed strong is the situation when whole world is under pandemic due to COVID-19, Cryptocurrencies didn't comprise to affect its value even there is a decrease in the investments in the stock market or an increase in the value of ornaments like gold due to heavy investments in the commodities. It is due to the advantage of digital currency by not restricting itself to some Government bodies or having abundant coins for a particular Cryptocurrency so that the value can be decreased as wanted (Becker, 2013). Due to these advantages and much more investments in of the Cryptocurrencies with high returns can bring a lot of attention of other small and big investors to invest and thus by increasing the value by increasing the demand of Cryptocurrencies

Protection From Payment Fraud

The best way used by the fraudsters in this digital system is by paying the same coin to two different people by giving two different transaction recipients and this cause of fraud online transaction can easily be found in today's banking system. When it comes to digital currency, the system used here to note the transactions is block Chain technology where a block is to be implemented in the chain of blocks where the details of transaction is noted which is accessible to many users without revealing the confidential information of both buyer as well as seller and not encouraging any fraudster to make double payments for the same coin (Hofman, 2014). Block Chain technology is considered as one of the highest security technologies available and Bitcoin (one of the Cryptocurrency) is the first to use this technology after it was outlined. However, other studies claim that if fraudsters have a significant stake in the proof of work hash power, they can take over the block chain's security mechanism. Hash power is a term used to describe the capacity to manage computing power. A typical burn-through force of 10 minutes includes the hash power. By retaining a higher percentage of the interest in the verification of labour, fraudsters can double spending on a comparable square by silently setting up the block chain branches in advance before alerting the chain organisation. Theoretically, big scale extortion should be possible if fraudsters can control a certain level of hash power. The Bit coin's factorial arbitrary walk calculation states that a fraudster may spend twice as much if they have control of 51% of the processing power. In this analysis, it was found that the hash strength, rather than the potential for many fake identities, is all that triple transaction verification depends on. By validating alternate tactics rather than depending solely on hash power, this has made sure that the problem of fraudsters being able to control a bigger amount of the hash rate is undermined. The assumption is that controlling the majority's personality is far harder than controlling the majority's hash power. Using digital currency to make payments is more easy and secure than doing it with credit cards.

Cryptographic money has a lot of reduced handling charges with the secured exchange it provides (Hileman, 2016), despite the fact that it is still understudied. The validation of customers and dealers is an important part of moving digital money. Fraudsters will be unable to create a new trade or postpone any discount exchange due to the verification between the two players. In contrast to MasterCard, this manufacturing has existed and will continue to exist as a result of its component. The cardholder, trader, vendor bank, Visa organisation, giving bank, and specialised co-op are all involved in the Visa exchange innovation. The conversation is more complicated than it appears in any single exchange. Before an exchange can be completed, it must first go through this load of components. In any of these steps, fraudsters and opportunities for supplying false information might arise. Despite the fact that specific precautions have been made to reduce MasterCard fraud, the architecture is less robust when compared to block chain. The framework used by charge card innovation is still not as secure as the encryption used by digital currency innovation (Doshi & Commerce, n.d.). The intricacy just exists in the hub and numerical riddle that will be addressed by the mining system. Other than that, the block chain innovation gives helpful capacities to all clients. It is probably not going to go before to tumultuous framework predicated on irreversibility and flexibility. The archives of advanced archives on the web and ID are very much safeguarded inside the block chain framework for the present and the not-so-distant future.

Potential for High Returns

Cryptocurrencies are being a unique asset for the investors due to its features and ability to provide more returns to its investors. Bitcoin, being the first digital currency facilitated about 1000-10000 percentage of profit to its investors from what they have invested during its early days of introduction. Due to extra feature of Bitcoin generation becoming halve of its usual generation when more transactions occur and limited amount of Bitcoin i.e., 21 million coins and also the belief of people that it would be the future currency, people began to invest in it to gain the high returns in the future (Bentov et al., 2014). The utilization of cryptographic money is basically similar to the utilization of fiat cash or by utilizing Mastercard's in buying genuine products from retailers. Aside from that, Bitcoin can be utilized for more extensive purposes.

Fast and Inexpensive

Sending any amount of money only takes a few seconds. Regardless of the total or the goal. The cost is either negligible or non-existent when done in bitcoins. Any nation in the world may send bitcoins abroad. Bitcoin has no geographical limitations, much like the Internet and email (Vranken, 2017). This makes Bitcoin the only genuinely worldwide money, together with the guarantee that its customers' freedoms are safeguarded. The main advantage that participants in the exchange market in bitcoin receive is the capacity to pay in instalments. They are unrestricted in their ability to send bitcoin transactions at any time and from any location (Shi, 2016).

Disadvantages of Using Blockchain

Here are few disadvantages of blockchain (during implementation in real word applications):

Volatility and High Risk of Loss

Bitcoin costs are amazingly unstable, increasing and falling at a quick rate. Theorists need to benefit from it, however real financial backers consider it to be too hazardous, so nobody puts resources into Bitcoins. One of the main disadvantages of putting resources into Bitcoin is the absence of administrative oversight (Böhme et al., 2015). Digital currency laws and charges vary from one country to another and are frequently equivocal or quarrelsome. An absence of guidelines, sadly, can prompt misrepresentation and scams. If a hard drive fails or an infection contaminates data, and the wallets document is compromised, bitcoins are practically "gone." No method exists to get it back. These coins will continue to be stuck in the scheme forever. A wealthy Bitcoin financial supporter may go quickly and irreparably bankrupt as a result of this. Coins from the financial supporter will likewise always be stranded (Bouri et al., 2017).

New System and Investor Protection

Even though it is said to have high security for the information about buyer and seller but as it is a new system which was brought recently without certified by anyone, it should also think in the way of misuse. The Bitcoin system might have bugs that still can't seem to be found. Since this is a generally new plan, in case Bitcoins were broadly executed and a bug was found, it may bring about colossal abundance for the exploiter to the detriment of the Bitcoin economy (Dos Santos, 2017). There is no overseeing body responsible for bitcoin's usefulness.

Black Market Activity

The fast development in digital currencies and the secrecy that they give clients has made impressive administrative difficulties, remembering the utilization of digital currencies for unlawful exchange (medications, hacks and burglaries, illicit porn, even homicide for-recruit), potential to support launder cash, psychological oppression, and keep away from capital controls (Van Alstyne, 2014). There is almost no doubt that cryptographic forms of money, like as bitcoin, have aided the establishment of 'darknet' online commercial hubs where illegal labour and items are transacted by providing a sophisticated and secretive payment system. The recent FBI seizure of more than $4 million in bitcoin from one such business hub, dubbed "Silk Street," provides some insight into the scope of the problem.

History of Blockchain

Figure 2 describes the history of blockchain technology in cryptocurrency over the years. Stuart Haber and W Scott Stornetta first presented it in 1991. By 1998, computer scientist Nick Szabo was working on 'Bit Gold,' a decentralised digital money. A team led by Satoshi Nakamoto published a white paper in 2008 proposing a blockchain paradigm, then in 2009, the famous 'Bitcoin' cryptocurrency was introduced by Satoshi Nakamoto and team. In 2014, another cryptocurrency, Ethereum came into the picture. It introduced computer programs which represented financial instruments such as bonds which were known as smart contracts (Khatwani, 2018).

Figure 2. History of blockchain

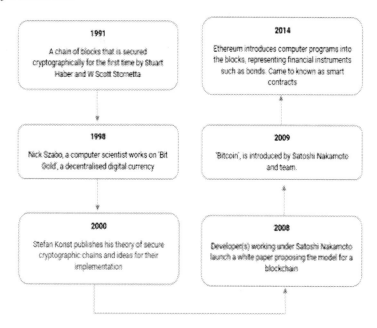

Mechanism

Blockchain is a chain containing blocks of immutable data. Each block is connected two the previous block through cryptography. It contains information of the previous block such as timestamp, transaction data and proof-of-work signature. There are certain steps to add a block into the chain. Firstly, a transaction has to be made in the network. Next, the details regarding the transaction must be approved by the participant who is referred to as 'Miner' in this case. The data is then placed in the block when the miner has confirmed the transaction. Finally, the block is added to the ledger using cryptographic procedures that include the prior block's timestamp. Once the block is added into the network, it is made public. Figure 3 represents the same set of procedure as mentioned above (Fauzi et al., 2020).

Types of Major Cryptocurrencies

Below are some of the major blockchains.

Figure 3. Creation of blocks in blockchain

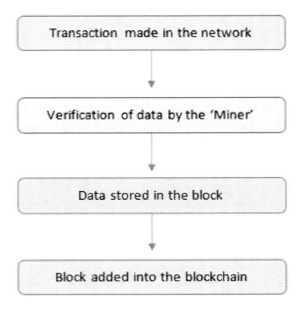

Bitcoin

Bitcoin is a decentralized cryptocurrency. It was introduced in 2009 by Santoshi Nakamoto. It is not managed by a bank or a single administrator. It operates on a peer-to-peer (P2P) network, which eliminates the need for third-party intervention in the transaction. The transactions are verified through network nodes and are stored in the form of blocks in a chain called the blockchain. Bitcoin has also been criticised for its use of bitcoins in illegal transactions. Also, the large amount of electricity used to mine a Bitcoin is one of the reasons for Bitcoin coming under scrutiny around the world (DeVries, 2016).

Ethereum

Ethereum is a decentralized, open-source, and disseminated registering stage that empowers the production of brilliant agreements and decentralized applications, otherwise called Dapps. Keen agreements are PC conventions that work with, confirm, or implement the arrangement and execution of some kind of understanding. For example, a brilliant agreement could be utilized to address a lawful agreement imitating the rationale of legally binding provisions or a monetary agreement determining liabilities of the partners and mechanized progressions of significant worth (Salcedo & Gupta, 2021).

Structure of Blockchain

The Blockchain is a collection of blocks that are back-linked together and include events that may be recorded as flat files or kept in conventional databases. Each block in the chain refers to the one before it, and the blocks are connected back-to-back. The first block ever created serves as the basis of the Blockchain, which is commonly represented as a series of layers of transactions (Wang et al., 2021).

A Survey on Blockchain and Cryptocurrency-Based Systems

The blockchain is the primary invention that underlies Bitcoin, which is recognised as first decentralised crypto-electronic money. The initial request for payment made in Bitcoin by its future owner initiates the transaction. Every time Bitcoin is supported, a computer hashed sign is used to transmit funds. Each coin has a unique location that serves as its identifier, and every transaction on the Blockchain is essentially an exchange of bitcoin, starting with one place before moving on to the next (Alofi, 2021).

A Blockchain trade takes place between two parties, and it begins if one of the complex parties informs the other about the rules governing the transaction. The citizen Blockchain record will be updated with the current status of the organization's most recent blocks after the exchange has been reviewed and approved, along with all of the organization's customers (Dibaei, 2021). Through the use of a public distributed journal and crypto algorithm components that guarantee accepted purchases won't be removed after confirmation, this decentralised structure, along with the cryptography employed, guarantees that the almost no declared payment could be changed or wiped away. It also contributes to the development of trust among parties. A most recent square, known to as one of the "parents," is referenced in each square. There is a header for each square that contains the family's hash information. Users may link each square to its parent using the hash sequence, creating a chain that goes all the way back to the first square that was produced, also known as the "beginning square." A square may have several kids although it only uses a single parent (Frikha et al., 2021). Each child can be traced all the way back to the very same square and has the same preceding block hash as its parent.

Properties of Blockchain

Blockchain is a new way to store data that offers a number of appealing properties as follows.

P2P Transmission

Each block in a blockchain is called as a 'node'. Nodes are interconnected to each other through cryptographic means. Miners can share or transmit data among nodes (Fu et al., 2021; Khan, Loukil, Ghedira-Guegan et al, 2021; Sanka et al., 2021).

Timestamped Blocks

Blocks are stored as nodes. They are stored along with the time when they have been created.

Immutable Records

Data is stored in the blocks or nodes. The data stored in a node remains completely safe as once the data is entered in the node, the data is immutable i.e., cannot be altered or modified. This is because each node or block contains hashed value of the information from the previous block and a timestamp.

Validation

On the creation of a block or node, the information needs to be verified by other participants or blocks in a blockchain. This is called mining.

Computational Logic

Blockchains include computational logic. Users can introduce algorithms and procedures known as smart contracts. These smart contracts can be executed automatically while transmitting the data.

Encrypted Data Transmission

Data of a 'Miner' is stored securely in a block or node through data encryption. The data is encrypted by the sender's 'Public key' and decrypted by the receiver's 'Private Key'.

Shared Database

Blockchain technology is implemented using shared databases which are distributed all over the network. Participants or 'Miners' in a network are required to agree on the true state of the database. There is no single party controller.

Disintermediation

Blockchain is implemented over a wide range of networks. The network uses a mechanism called as proof-of-work consensus. Proof of work (PoW) depicts a framework that requires a not-immaterial however doable measure of exertion to dissuade paltry or noxious employments of processing power, for example, sending spam messages or dispatching disavowal of administration assaults. This does not require any third-party involvement. Therefore, the dependence on any third-party gets completely removed (Bouraga, 2021). As the popularity and usage of the Internet are increasing day-by-day and on the other hand, Cryptocurrency (also called virtual currency) is increasing its popularity and drawing a lot of attention from the public, investors, businessmen and entrepreneurs. As it is becoming more popular with the advantage of not having any trade regularity, people began to invest their savings in cryptocurrencies for high returns. Bitcoin is the first digital currency/virtual currency, which came into existence without having the middleman like banks where personal data is to be revealed for any transaction to be made or done either from the buyer or seller side, thus making others to know the part of assets owned by an individual (Ahmad et al., 2021). As many of the cryptocurrencies are using blockchain technology which among the most advanced surveillance equipment with sophisticated technology that is most efficient for online transactions by preventing fraudsters from using the same money for many people, preserving users' sensitive information, and removing intermediate bodies. The value of the cryptocurrencies is usually due to the limited number of coins for a particular cryptocurrency and demand by the investors. In the case of Bitcoin, the anonymous group created some advanced mathematical and computer engineering puzzles or problems which need to be solved to use the non-useable bitcoins and this process of solving and creating the newer bitcoins is said be to mining, which is usually done with a high server and some advanced software.

So, the difficulty of the puzzles goes on increasing as the non-useable bitcoins goes on decreasing, thus creating the demand in the market which usually raises the value of the currency (Yue et al., 2021). From Figure 1, it can be observed clearly that the demand and interest in investing money in cryptocurrencies are drastically increasing from the day of its origin. Cryptocurrencies are widely experiencing fast user acceptance across the world and it will be an important subject to be learned by everyone as it

A Survey on Blockchain and Cryptocurrency-Based Systems

can transform the whole system of exchanging money. Being in the world of the internet which brings the world to such a small place with fast transferring of information, Cryptocurrencies will definitely show their rise than present as one end of the world can easily influence the other parts of the world.

Note that in Figure 4 the x-axis depicts the time period, while the y-axis depicts the quantity in millions. Hence, in summary, Blockchain is a new and effective way to store information, execute transactions, etc. But, the security and privacy of blockchains are always at the centre of the debate when using blockchain-based cryptocurrency. There is a misbelief that cryptocurrencies are an anonymous means of payment. The blockchain is a public, fully transparent ledger, so anybody can browse the data of a blockchain using a block explorer and see which addresses transferred how much amount of money and at what time. Blockchain Technology is one of the latest revolutions around the globe which is expected to have a great impact and lead to significant changes in everything, especially in the ways of business. It is a new technology of storing data which prevents the data to be stolen, tinkered with or hacked. It is a technology where data is stored as a chain of blocks and allows users to communicate with each other through a secure gateway. Although it ensures a secure gateway, as a new technology it has some threats too. This research paper would be a review of many cited papers that talk about the threats to the usage of blockchain technology in cryptocurrency.

Cryptocurrency developed and emerged as one of the financial tools about thirteen years back. As there are no barriers like exchange rates when transferred from country to country, they are going to

Figure 4. Blockchain wallet users worldwide from 2011 to 2021

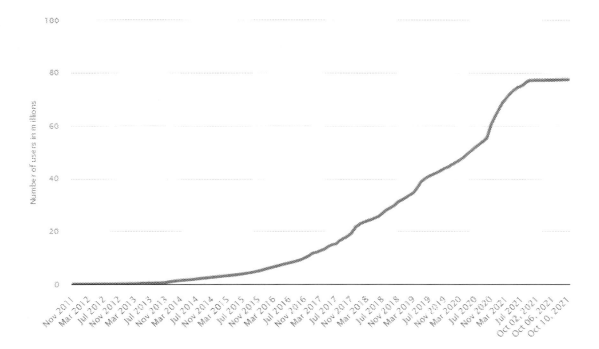

become the leading payment gateway. Bitcoin is the first and most popular cryptocurrency which was

375

introduced by the mysterious and pseudonymous Satoshi Nakamoto has shown its emergence as the digital currency which could replace the long-lasting financial payment systems. Though it can't change the traditional exchange of money, can emerge as the best payment gateway where a global transaction occurs. As cryptocurrency is a decentralized digital currency which is not physical like paper money and due to the increase in technology which is easily accessible to each and every person to promote digital payments with no exchange rates can easily emerge as a leading gateway. Though it is good to know the advantages of cryptocurrency, it is also having some disadvantages of investing and using cryptocurrency.

IMPLEMENTATION OF BLOCKCHAIN IN DIFFERENT SYSTEMS

Now we discuss different uses and implementations of the blockchain technology systems in various industries (Dwivedi et al., 2021; Hakak, 2021; Mezquita, 2021):

Educational Sector: Blockchain is a technology that can assist students with their academics. Challenges reduced by blockchain are as follows:

1. It has the potential to arise in the formation of an environment that is based on open-source software. This can provide a way for a student to store all of the data needed during his or her course of study, as well as provide an air of validity for carrying fewer books.
2. It can also establish an environment in which students' personal databases can be modified and then stored. The blockchain gives institutions access to data, and the data that is altered is a lot more exact, so any changes don't have to be as time-consuming.
3. The issue that the schools/universities face is the increasing number of incidences of fraud and unauthorised diplomas supplied to pupils. The main goal of blockchain technology is to get to a point where every block is a proven block so that any fraud can be detected.
4. One significant feature of such a technology in the educational context would be that it assigns every student a distinct id, that aids students in syncing up their findings and may easily settle possible project misunderstandings among students. The ability to see the grades in real time can be a huge benefit.

Agricultural Sector: Blockchain has an impact on the convenience of agricultural products for farm kinds of materials, farmers, loans, farmer financing, as well as many other things. Blockchain technology is based on four considerations:

1. **Consensus:** It conveys information about the dispersed trust, which may be gleaned from how farmers trust the government to protect their fundamental rights.
2. **Safety:** This discusses the part of the product export and import, as well as the safety of the farmer's data.
3. **Provenance:** This refers to the process of tracing an event's origins. In the event that a farmer-to-farmer transaction occurs. Some intermediaries may use fictitious data to defraud farmers for financial gain. Farmers benefit from blockchain because it helps them build trust.
4. **Trust:** The trust factor increases as there is no single supreme force to rule or use unfair methods to dominate.

Healthcare Sector Blockchain: There are many different business models used in the healthcare sector. Several organisations are presently developing the Proof of State (PoS) perspective for a wide range of stakeholders (Berdik, 2021). Blockchain technology is thus, in some ways, harmful. The most discussed technology of the decade is blockchain. In addition to numerous contractual obligations for health-care technologies, there is a significant chance that blockchain technology will be employed in the digitalization of pharmaceutical chains. There are 3 methods that blockchain can help change healthcare:

1. An electrical chip which can be used to help with the adoption of blockchain in each and every area of health care appears to be one possible use case for the technology. a) Records saved on the chip: Lists of all patients might be built using electro records at any given moment. Due to the fact that they are updated after each hospital visit by a patient, health files can be cumbersome.
2. **Records Kept on a Chip:** One plausible use for blockchain technology is to create a chip that may be used to help all areas achieve healthcare reform. Databases containing data on all individuals at any given time may be created using electro records. Due to the fact that they are updated after each hospital visit by a patient, health files can be cumbersome.
3. **Supply Chains:** The pharma sector adheres to the highest requirements for stability, security, and safety. For instance, supply chain management might be openly scrutinised, reducing human error and delays while simultaneously controlling prices and labour. Even a waste in missions is tracked at all times, and some logistical solutions are followed. While physical items are being transported and being recorded permanently on the blockchain, a solution may be presented to the nodes and it might be a workable choice.
4. **Genetic Industry:** In a billion-dollar business, companies like Enc and Nebula genomics employ blockchain to reliably and securely transfer genomic data. This company makes extensive use of blockchain due to the security it provides and the fact that data is delivered to users without the use of a middleman. They have excellent marketing, and they must safeguard that marketing in order to protect their market (Hewa, Ylianttila, & Liyanage, 2021). There are numerous use cases that can be generated pertaining to the health-care business.
    a. A situation in which the patient has the last say - Every patient has access to their medical information, but they are not allowed to change them. They do, however, have the option of limiting access to certain hospitals.
    b. Such innovation must be in a tabulated form, which means all information should be preserved in tables, charts, or other statistical forms.
    c. It can provide a variety of options for employers - This can be advantageous in situations when employers are needed.

Such innovation has the capacity to produce a disruptive environment if it does not match the user's demands. Consider the instance of a patient who has an immediate need to obtain information in order to offer it for any other purpose. However, because this technology prevents the patient from receiving each of the data from the hospital, the patient may feel burdened and his or her requirements may not be met.

Security and Privacy Concerns

Cryptocurrencies face some serious security concerns and risks, due to which it faces dramatic price drops many times. These concerns can be destructive to any cryptocurrency. Some of such concerns are briefly described below.

Double Spending

Double-spending is a process in which the same single unit of a cryptocurrency can be spent more than once. It occurs when a cryptocurrency is stolen by altering or damaging the blockchain network. The transaction could be erased or a copy of the transaction would be sent by the hacker to make it look authorized. Most commonly, the hacker will send numerous packets to the network for reversing a transaction, which will make it looks like it never happened (Latif, 2021).

Vulnerable Wallets

A wallet should protect our money and privacy, but cryptocurrency wallets are very vulnerable to hacking attacks and theft. Using malware, the wallet can be prevented from communicating with the PC, hence breaching the security. This affects the privacy of its users, and their transactions can now easily be redirected to different accounts.

Cyber-Attacks

A disastrous cyber-attack on not only blockchain but also cryptocurrency exchanges is one of the major concerns of its users. There have been major attacks on exchanges before, which resulted in the loss of people's money as well as the downfall of cryptocurrency value. In 2014, the Mt. Gox heist took place, in which the hackers went away with 850,000 (Bodziony et al., 2021) bitcoins which is equivalent to USD 47.03 billion as of October 2021. Distributed Denial of Service (DDoS) attacks is also a threat to cryptocurrency exchanges. There have been many such heists, which is why people don't trust the security of blockchain-based cryptocurrency.

Sybil Attack

In a Sybil Attack, numerous fake identities are created and controlled by a single entity to manipulate a peer-to-peer network Various fake nodes gather around a node so that it can't connect to the other nodes on the network, which then prevents the user from sending or receiving information to the blockchain.

Selfish Mining

Due to the proof-of-work consensus mechanism, certain cryptocurrencies can be threatened by the selfish mining of the major mining pools. Crypto mining is the process in which transactions of cryptocurrency are verified and confirmed, with miners earning cryptocurrencies in return for their computational effort (Huang et al., 2021). For selfish mining, greedy miners and hide their generated blocks from the main blockchain, and later reveal them to earn more revenue. With this combined with the Sybil attack, miners can invalidate transactions on the network with their power.

Percent Attacks

A 51 percent attack is an attack by a group of miners controlling the majority of the blockchain's computing power. The attackers can reverse transactions that were completed resulting in double-spending or can prevent new transactions from getting confirmed. In 2018, hackers pulled off more than $18 million worth of Bitcoin Gold through a 51 percent Attack (Walsh et al., 2021).

Security and Privacy Requirements

In blockchains, the usage of private keys and public keys is a critical part of privacy. To safeguard transactions between users, blockchain systems employ asymmetric cryptography. Each user has both a public key and private key in these systems. These keys are cryptographically connected random numbers strings.

Integrity of Data

Blockchains must be designed for data integrity otherwise, the data will be vulnerable or completely non-functional. The blockchain should be used to collect and manage precise, authentic, and timely data, so it is useful to the users.

Tamper-Resistant Data

The data in a blockchain should be able to resist any type of damage. The data which is stored on the blocks of the blockchain cannot be modified anyhow.

Preventing Double-Spending

Double spending means when a particular unit of currency is spent more than once. For transactions performed with a decentralized blockchain-based cryptocurrency, the blockchain should have strong security measures to prevent the double-spending of a coin.

Anonymous User Identities

If the user data is shared with various financial institutions, then the user's identity may get disclosed. Also, in a transaction, the two users might be unwilling to disclose their real identities to each other (Dabbagh, 2021). So, the blockchain must have strong security and privacy methods to make user identity anonymous or at the very least pseudonymous.

Transaction Unlikability

If all the transactions of a user could be linked then, the user's identity and other information can be deduced. So, the blockchain should have security measures to provide unlikability of transactions.

Transaction Confidentiality

The blockchain must have security measures such that the user's data couldn't be accessed or disclosed without his or her permission, even under unexpected failures (Kumar & Sharma, 2021).

DDoS Attack Resistant

A Distributed Denial of Service (DDoS) attack is a malicious attempt to flood the internet traffic of a network or server and to take advantage of its security vulnerabilities. A heavy DDoS attack could be used to knock off a blockchain network, so the blockchain should have security measures to prevent or tackle it.

51% Attack Resistant

Malicious miners can conspire and launch various security and privacy attacks like illegal transfer of cryptocurrency or reversing transactions. So, the blockchain should have security measures to prevent or tackle it.

Privacy and Security Techniques

There are various techniques a blockchain system uses or can use to achieve or enhance its privacy and security.

Change Addresses

A cryptocurrency transaction needs at least one input and output. The existing funds used for sending a transaction are called input, and when the funds are received it's called output. When a user gives an input fund more than the transaction cost, the remaining funds (or the change) are sent back to the user as a change but to a newly generated Change Address. But if the input fund is exactly equal to the transaction cost, then a change address is not needed. Most of the wallets generate change addresses automatically creating a transaction. Change address makes it difficult to track the user's transaction history, hence improving privacy.

Coin Mixing

In Coin Mixing, several input coins, in a mixing pool, are combined and then sent to their receivers' addresses. This makes tracking the transactions more difficult. Coin mixers are software companies serving as a middleman between parties looking to send and receive cryptocurrencies. If a user wants a transaction to be untraceable, he will send a particular number of coins to the coin mixer, who will then combine it with many other transactions of the same currency, and then redistributing it to the receiving addresses (Gomathi et al., 2021). A fee is charged for the mixing services by coin mixers. Coin mixing increases the level of privacy than regular transactions, but addresses can be linked by observing the amounts of coins in a mixing pool, and many mixing services are centralized.

Ring Signatures

A ring signature is a digital signature that can be created by any member of a group, and each member has their own keys. So, it is not possible to determine which group member created the signature. To sign a message, a member of the group has to use his secret key as well as the public keys of others in the group. The public keys of the group are used to validate that person signing the message is a member of the group, but it is not possible to figure out who signed the message from the group (Jang & Han, 2022). Ring Signatures are great for private transactions, but if the secret key of a person is compromised, any of his signed messages can be modified.

Homomorphic Encryption

Homomorphic encryption allows users to perform computations on encrypted data, so decrypting the data is not needed. The decrypted form of the computed results will be the same as the result of the same operations performed on the unencrypted data. Homomorphic encryption is used to ensure that the data stored on the blockchain is encrypted. The homomorphic encryption technique is used to preserve privacy and to allow access to the encrypted data over public blockchain for validation. But homomorphic encryption requires a special client-server application to work functionally (Guggenberger, 2021).

Zero-Knowledge Proofs (zk-Proofs)

Zero-knowledge proof lets someone prove the truth regarding something to the verifier without revealing any additional information. In blockchain-based cryptocurrency, the Zero-Knowledge Proofs are used for private transactions. The sender will have to create a proof, without revealing any of the actual transaction data, that the transaction will be considered valid by a verifying node. This allows the identities of both the parties and the amount to be private (Sookhak et al., 2021). Zero-Knowledge Proofs does not require any complicated encryption methods, increases the privacy of users, strengthens the security of information but a tremendous amount of computing power is needed, and if the user forgets their information, all the data is associated with it will be lost.

CRYPTOCURRENCY SYSTEMS

Investors, speculators, the general public, and regulators are all still fascinated by cryptocurrencies. Concerns about legal and regulatory evasion, significant price swings, and claims that the cryptocurrency market is a fad with no underlying value have all sparked recent public conversations regarding cryptocurrencies. These worries have sparked calls for stricter laws, if not outright bans. The use of cryptocurrencies (ICOs) to finance start-up projects, the categorization of cryptocurrencies as payment, commodities markets, or something entirely different, the advancement of credit contracts and cryptocurrency derivatives, and the issuance of cryptocurrency transactions by the fed reserve utilising cryptocurrency innovations are some of the other issues. These debates frequently produce more power as compared to light. There is still a lack of well-established scientific understanding concerning cryptocurrency markets and their influence on economies, businesses, and individuals. The goal of this unique study in the Journal of Industry and Commercial Economy (El Sobky et al., n.d.) is to help close that gap. The special issue's collection of articles presents six multiple viewpoints on cryptocurrencies, authored through both conventional and behavioural viewpoints and covering both financial and larger problems of cryptocurrencies' link to socio-economic growth and sustainability.

The legitimacy of every cryptocurrency's coin is confirmed through a blockchain. A cryptocurrency is a constantly changing group of linked, encrypted documents, or "blocks." Each block typically includes transaction information, a timestamp, and a hashed reference to the block before it. Blockchains are resistant to data alteration by design. The description calls for "an accessible, decentralised network that may reliably and persistently store transactions." Managing a bitcoin as a distributed ledger is often done through a peer network that uses a system for verifying new blocks. The network majority's participation is required since it is impossible to modify the data in any one block without also changing the data in all subsequent blocks. A computer that is connected to a public blockchain is referred to as a node in the cryptocurrency realm. The node assists to the network of the relevant cryptocurrency by relaying transactions, validating transactions, and storing an identical copy of the ledger. Each network computer (node), when it comes to transaction rehashing, has an identical copy of the ledger of the cryptocurrency it supports. When a transaction happens, the node that made it employs cryptography to simulcast transaction details to other nodes all through the network, guaranteeing that the activity (and all other transactions) is known.

Node owners include volunteers, those maintained by the entity or group responsible for developing the bitcoin blockchain network technology, and those persuaded to host a node in exchange for financial gain (Tran et al., 2021). Because the bitcoins in a wallet is linked to one and more unique keys instead of to specific people, Bitcoin is more anonymous than cash (or "addresses"). Owners of bitcoin are therefore anonymous, despite the fact that all transactions are recorded on the blockchain. In spite of this, exchanges regularly find themselves required by law to collect personal information from their users.

The mortgage lender is required by law to reimburse the owner of the asset if their management system has a weakness, including a security breach that causes theft or loss or refuses to carried out a transfer instruction. In the case of cryptocurrencies, the supporting software is responsible for conducting transactions as well as verifying ownership. There is no requirement to employ a "trusted third party." This system, meanwhile, necessitates the existence of a complete history record of prior cryptocurrency transfers that dates each coin holding back to its inception. A "blockchain," a mechanism for connecting records ("blocks"), is the foundation of this historical record. Each new structure in the "chain" of digital data contains details about previous blocks. Consensus is reached all through the whole bitcoin network to accept a new block, ensuring that each user sees the same transaction history.

CONSENSUS ALGORITHMS

Blockchain, being a distributed decentralized network with no central authority present to validate and verify the transactions, is considered to be secure only because of the consensus protocols, a core part of Blockchain networks. A consensus mechanism refers to methods used to achieve agreement, trust, and security across a decentralized blockchain network. These consensus protocols help all the nodes in the network to verify the transactions.

Proof of Work (PoW)

In 2008 Satoshi Nakamoto applied the Proof of Work algorithm in the Bitcoin whitepaper. Proof of Work algorithm is a technique used by many cryptocurrencies. Once all the nodes are brought in an agreement, the transactions will get validated and the new block will be forged on the blockchain.

In the Proof of Work consensus algorithm, miners solve a complex computational problem to create and add new blocks in the blockchain. The verification and organization of transactions in a block, and introducing the newly mined block to the blockchain network needs much less time and energy than solving the 'complex computational problems', required to add the new block in the blockchain. When a miner successfully solves the 'complex computational problem', the nodes broadcast the block to the blockchain, and the miner receives some of the cryptocurrency as a reward. Although proof of work is an efficient mechanism, it has some disadvantages, like it increases the chance of 51% attacks, finding the correct solution to the 'complex computational problems' is very time-consuming, and money and electricity consumption is too high (Nerurkar et al., 2021).

Byzantine Fault Tolerance in Practice (pBFT)

The practical Byzantine Fault Tolerance mechanism's goal is to improve features of Byzantine Fault Tolerance on a blockchain. BFT (Byzantine Fault Tolerance) is a method that allows a network to achieve an agreement despite the existence of hostile or malfunctioning nodes. The goal of a BFT technique is to reduce the impact of malfunctioning nodes by using collaborative decision-making. There are two forms of defective node failures: fail-stop and arbitrarily defined failure. The node fails and ceases functioning in the fail-stop failing, whereas the node fails to appear a result or delivers an inaccurate result in the random node failure (Ahmad, 2021). One node in a practical Byzantine Fault Tolerant enabled blockchain is set as the primary node and others as secondary nodes. A practical Byzantine Fault Tolerant system functions if the number of malicious or faulty nodes are lesser than or equal to one-third (or 34%) of all the nodes in the system. Although the practical Byzantine Fault Tolerant mechanisms are energy and time-efficient, there are a few limitations to it as it is open to Sybil attack, and it does not scale well.

Proof of Stake (PoS)

In 2012 the Proof of Stake was first used for a cryptocurrency named Peercoin. The Proof of Stake mechanism states that the mining power is directly dependent on the number of coins staked. Proof of Stake is one of the most common alternatives to Proof of Work. Proof of Stake mechanism requires users to stake their coins to become a validator in the network rather than buying expensive hardware or wasting resources to mine. Validators are randomly chosen to propose new blocks, and validate proposed blocks when they are not chosen. Validators get rewarded for doing so but validating malicious blocks will result in losing stakes.

Although being energy and money efficient, the Proof of Stake has some disadvantages such as, a staked coin can't be sold until the staking period is over, the staking reward much is lesser than the mining reward, the users holding a large number of coins can have a huge influence on the mechanism, and this mechanism is still in its early stage and the privacy and security of Proof of Stake are not proven to be even as good as that of Proof of Work (Gupta et al., 2021).

Proof of Burn (PoB)

Proof of Burn, first proposed by Iain Stewart in 2012 is an algorithm in which a miner uses a virtual rig to burn (permanently erase) their coins. The more coins they burn the better virtual mining rig they get. So, Proof of burn is Proof of Work without the high energy consumption. For burning the coins, they are sent to a verifiably spendable address. Miners are allowed to burn the coins as specified and get rewarded with tokens of that particular cryptocurrency (Kahyaoğlu & Aksoy, 2021). The Proof of Burn mechanism uses the burning of cryptocurrency coins periodically to increase the mining power. The value of burnt coins reduces with every newly mined block, to keep miners regularly engaged. The Proof of Burn mechanism is more sustainable as the power consumptions are very low, the expensive mining hardware isn't needed, which can make the miners stay dedicated to it for long. But the verification process is slow, and its efficiency and security are yet to be confirmed on larger scales.

Proof of Capacity (PoC)

The Proof of Capacity algorithm enables mining by using the hard drive space. In Proof of Capacity, a list of possible solutions is stored on the hard drive of the mining device. The number of possible solution values increases if the available space in the hard drive is more, which increases the more chances of getting the correct solution, hence increasing the chances to win the mining reward. The Proof of Capacity mechanism has two steps: plotting, and mining. In plotting, through repeated hashing of data, all the possible nonce values are listed and stored in the hard drive. In mining, a miner calculates a scoop number. For each nonce in the hard drive, the process is repeated to calculate its deadline. Then the miner chooses the one with the minimum deadline. A deadline is the amount of time that has to be passed after the creation of a block, for a miner to create a new block. A miner can create a block and gets the block reward if no one else has created a block within that time (Johar, 2021). Proof of Capacity uses just a hard drive, it is more efficient than Proof of Work and Proof of Stake mechanisms, and expensive hardware is not needed. But Proof of Capacity is still new and not adopted by many, and hackers can take advantage of it using malware.

CRYPTO ASSETS: AN INTRODUCTION

Cryptocurrencies are a subset of a larger class of financial instruments called as "digital currencies," which allow peer-to-peer supply and distribution transfers without requiring third parties to validate transactions. What sets bitcoin apart from several other digital assets? Whether they should be given with the sole intention of relocating or if they'd been given for other purposes will determine this. The discrepancies observed in regulatory modifications studies within the broad category of cryptocurrency transactions, differentiating two additional sub-categories of digital currencies, are in addition to cryptocurrencies (Shankar, 2021):

1. **Cryptocurrencies:** An asset built on the blockchain that may be exchanged or transferred between network users and is used as payment, but has no other capabilities.
2. **Crypto Securities:** a network asset with the possibility for further payments in the future, such a share of profits.

3. A bitcoin asset that can be exchanged for or utilised to get accessibility to pre-defined goods or services is known as a cryptocurrency utility asset.
4. A significant turning point in the development of cryptocurrencies and other crypto assets was the emergence of bitcoin exchanges, where anybody can establish an account and exchange virtual currencies against each other and versus fiat money.

Publications using the terms 'Cryptocurrencies' and 'Bitcoin' in the title, abstract, or keywords that are listed in the Scopus database. The graph depicts the number of articles in the Scopus database that had the terms "cryptocurrency" or "Bitcoin" in the title, abstract, or keywords as of August 10, 2019. The category Economics, Econometrics, and Finance is represented by the subsample ECON (Kshetri et al., 2021), whereas Business, Management, and Accounting is represented by the subsample BUS. Both an investment and a type of payment may be made using cryptocurrencies. Glaser et al. demonstrate that the main reason for buying cryptocurrencies is high risk investing, at least in the context of Bitcoin. Brokers are enabling a larger variety of investors to participate in speculative investments by making financial instruments like ETNs (Exchange Traded Notes) and CFDs (Derivative Products) that replicate Bitcoin's price performance available. In light of this, it becomes sense to consider cryptocurrencies as capital intermediates.

Some Interesting Statistics

One way for understanding the differences and similarities between cryptocurrencies and much more standard finance assets is to estimate associations recognized for traditional assets (Pal et al., 2021). They discover that while the amount of Bitcoin trades has no impact on the return, it has a positive impact on return volatility. These statistics support the idea that bitcoin markets and traditional financial assets are regulated by analogous features, despite the fact that their main focus is on market attention.

On-Point Accuracy of the Chain

The whole blockchain is managed by a set of computers instead of humans which leads to a very minimal fraction of error. Transactions in the blockchain are supervised by a network of computers which almost negates the possibility of human error. Even if there are computational errors, the errors are copied in only one of the blockchains and the rest remain as it is. If that error was to spread in the rest of the blockchains, it would need at least 51% of the error to creep up in all of the blockchains which is nearly impossible for large blockchains such as Bitcoin blockchain.

Cost Reductions

Since the involvement of banks and personal firms is not there in transactions related to blockchain, the third-party costs get saved while making transactions in a blockchain.

Decentralization

One of the most important advantages of blockchain technology is that it is decentralized. It means that the data in a blockchain is not stored in one chain or database rather the chain of data is copied into many more chains and shared across various networks. This means that if data gets hampered in any one of the chains, the whole database does not get corrupted. This gives blockchains protection against potential hackers as even if they alter data in a block, it won't get reflected in other chains and therefore the chance of hacking the data remains very low.

Efficient Transactions

Since blockchains are not controlled by banks or firms, they run 24 hours a day, 7 days a week and 365 days a year. Banks usually work for 5 days or 6 days a week which may lead to inefficient transactions sometime. Therefore, blockchains provide a very efficient gateway for transactions.

Transparency

This means that the code that is written to run the blockchains can be easily viewed by users and therefore the whole process of transactions remains transparent to them. Monitoring bodies can thus ensure the safety of transactions. Also, blockchains accept suggestions from people on how to improve the working of cryptocurrencies and blockchains (AlMendah, 2021).

THREATS TO CRYPTOCURRENCY AND BLOCKCHAIN

Blockchain is another breakthrough, and attacks are emerging that most clients are unaware of. Many attacks till now have targeted the Bitcoin Blockchain, which is the first Blockchain application to involve money and, if compromised, might result in monetary gain. The Blockchain framework exclusively perceives the lengthiest chain as authentic. Accordingly, it is near unthinkable for an assailant to come out with a fake exchange since it has not just needed to make a square by settling a numerical issue, yet additionally needs to contend numerically with the genuine hubs to make all succeeding squares with the goal for it to cause different hubs in the organization to acknowledge its exchange as the authentic one. Since all exchanges in the organization are cryptographically associated, this assignment goes to be extremely intense and essentially unthinkable (Steinmetz et al., 2021).

Quantum Computing

The Blockchain technology is based on the notion that due to computer limitations, it is theoretically not possible for an individual to edit or mess with it. Nevertheless, given quantum computing's growth and the potentially immense computational power it offers, the secret may become simple enough to break in a reasonable period of time. It would be disastrous for the Blockchain system as a whole, rendering it useless.

Anomality Attack

Blockchain—specifically, the Bitcoin Blockchain—is widely regarded as an anonymous platform where customers may receive and send money without having to reveal their identities. Bitcoin addresses are associated with an alias rather than a specific person. Notwithstanding, this nom de plume be connected to individuals utilizing different means, and when that happens, the assailant will actually want to discover all exchanges connected to the individual from the very first moment. A facilitated wallet, as well as online services which can track what IPs a customer visits, might be an easy means of revealing the client's persona. Client information is stored in providers, and wallets data bases can be handed to the government when requested and the necessary administrative process is completed.

A Distributed Denial of Service (DDoS) Attack

DDoS assaults are the same old thing, but with the increment of the utilization of data innovation in all parts of life, late assaults are becoming serious, muddled, and incessant. This makes them a standard issue to organizations too as to customers. The assortment of gadgets distantly controllable by applications is growing extraordinarily and the quantity of IoT gadgets is relied upon to rapidly surpass 20billion connected gadgets before the finish of 2020. A large portion of the associated gadgets are ill suited and not outfitted with wellbeing and safety efforts to stay away from vindictive just as ill-advised use (reference); They could be recorded in this way and used to guide DDoS attacks. Apart from DDoS attacks against Bitcoin cash trading exchanges, Blockchain IoT devices are the most persistent target.

Scams With Bitcoin

Bitcoin has attracted a growing number of people who are looking for a quick and easy way to get cash. Since Bitcoin is another innovation, trick methods are arising and are not completely perceived, which assists programmer with marking benefit of the excited and ineffectively educated clients.

Scams in Mining Scams

Almost every mining company that sells equipment or provides cloud services ends up being a fraud. Customers are generally promised cloud mining services or equipment, but nothing is delivered. These con artists offered to supply mining gear or cloud mining services, took victims' money, and never delivered on their claims.

Scams Involving Wallets

These are phony administrations masquerading as online Bitcoin wallets. Deceitful wallet administrations function in the identical way as genuine wallet administrations do, with the exception that they seize the victim's Bitcoin when it arrives at a certain edge. The most popular tactics were identified as Easy Coin, Onion Wallet, and Bitcoinwallet.in (Nguyen et al., 2021).

COUNTERMEASURES FOR THREATS TO BLOCKCHAIN

Blockchain systems do have threats during the implementation process or after the implementation process as mentioned above. Here are few countermeasures for threats to Blockchain.

Refrain From Spending Double

The exchange rate discrepancy and mining security procedures in Bitcoin offer an indisputable layer of safety against double spending (Anand & Vijayalakshmi, 2021). It is achieved by following a straightforward rule that permits the majority of unspent proceeds from earlier exchanges to be contributed to a successive return, and that the proposition for interactions is determined by one's chronological order in the blockchain, which is preserved using reliable cryptography techniques. This boils down to timestamping and calculating circulating agreements. The most effective but simple technique to avoid double spending is to wait for a distinct number of confirmations before delivering labour and goods to the payee. Specifically, when the number of affirmations increases, the likelihood of a successful twofold go through decreases.

Securing Wallets

The term "cold wallet" was used to describe a manual procedure for wallet insurance. A cold wallet is another record that stores the client's wealth of an amount. This method employs two PCs (the second PC must be disconnected from the Internet), and another private key is generated using Bitcoin wallet programming. The abundant money is sent from this new wallet using a client's private key (Shinde, 2021). Creators in guarantee that if the PC isn't associated with the Internet, the programmers won't become acquainted with the keys, thus the wallet security can be accomplished.

Defence Against Distributed Denial of Service (DDoS) Attacks

To mitigate DDoS attacks, a Proof of Activity (PoA) Protocol was created, which is effective against a DDoS attack that might be launched by sending a large number of bogus blocks across the organisation. Each square header in PoA is assigned a sepulchre value, which is stored by the client that records the primary exchange. These clients are referred to as "partners" in the company, and they are expected, to be honest. If there are significant partners involved with the square, any further hoarding of trades is done. The capacity of sepulchre esteem is arbitrary, and more exchanges are stored if the chain has more stake customers connected to it. If the chain is longer, the level of trust among various companions rises, and more excavators are drawn to the network. Because all of the organization's hubs are managed by partners, an opponent will no longer be able to place a malicious square or exchange.

Another option for preventing DDoS attacks is to monitor network traffic on a regular basis with tools like Tor or any other client-defined web administration. Using AI approaches like SVM and bunching, we can figure out which parts of the company are sick. As a result, that portion can be kept out of the organisation until it is rectified. Other possible DDoS defence approaches include: I arranging the organisation so that vengeful packages and requests from unnecessary ports are avoided, and (ii) implementing an outsider DoS insurance scheme that carefully filters the organise and recognises variations in the example (Wang & Nixon, 2021).

A Survey on Blockchain and Cryptocurrency-Based Systems

BLOCKCHAIN AND CRYPTOCURRENCY LINK

One event in the cryptocurrency industry is use of Bitcoin's basic source code to create alternative cryptocurrencies, or alt-coins, having characteristics that diverge slightly from those of Bitcoin. Though some of these "forks" have indeed been shady attempts to profit from speculating, others are obviously intended to fix problems that the designers see with Bitcoin and usually incorporate criticisms of the Bitcoin paradigm. Others use less exacting mining techniques or have made an effort to deliberately create a unique culture around their currency, like Dogecoin (Khan, Jung, & Hashmani, 2021), that has a hilarious non-competitive culture. Despite these modifications, cryptocurrencies are now frequently associated with the values of the free market. They have been specifically linked to the extreme individualism of conservative libertarianism. The components of cryptocurrency, but at the other hand, may enable non-hierarchical identity and peer-to-peer collaboration inside a communitarian network structure, which appeals to people to a more left-wing libertarian leaning. Therefore, there are emerging initiatives to develop digital currencies that could be used as a means of exchange for explicitly cooperative and collaborative enterprises that function outside of the logic of conventional market processes. Modern technology (Blockchain) Although there are several ideological arguments around cryptocurrencies, the majority of interested parties consider the fundamental idea of a decentralised ledger kept by a community of nodes to be crucial. The use of a blockchain ledger for reasons other than logging financial transactions has prompted interest in blockchain 2.0 efforts as a result of this.

A blockchain may be compared to a database that is accumulated over the years by a network of users who all use the same programme and are subject to the restrictions and regulations set out by the foundation programme. A blockchain is built up of data fragments that are progressively "chained" together, as the name suggests. It resembles a spreadsheet that expands as additional columns are added to the blockchain over time. A blockchain record is created and maintained as long as the software is in use. As a consequence, unlike a central database dominated by a single organization, it continues to function even if certain participants leave. It creates a permanent record that is impossible for any one party to change. The structure of the resulting blockchain also changes whenever the code of the underlying software used by participants is altered, enabling the creation of blockchain database that hold a lot of information, including title deeds, contracts, shares, vote totals, and even character ratings. All three firms are developing systems that will enable individuals and microbusinesses to use blockchain technology: Ethereum (Bhutta et al., 2021), Related party, and Blockstream25. For instance, Provenance is a start-up that uses Ethereum technology to provide a high transparency record of information from the global supply chain of businesses.

The front of the scene is experiment with smart contracts, which are little packets containing code—or screenplays may be kept on a blockchain and also that users may interact with to do basic tasks. This smart-contract is designed to use data from meteorological organisations and then, after a predetermined period of time, unlock bitcoins from escrow and send them to a farmer in need of rain protection. This blockchain-based weather derivatives contract was created. Simple building-block contracts can be used to form larger multi or multi-function organisations that some people refer to as "decentralised autonomous organisations" (DAOs). Even if strong multi-stage algorithms are controlled by a distributed network of computers rather than a single top management, such DAOs are challenging to comprehend and seem to many people to belong in the realm of science fiction.

FUTURE SCOPE

It is verifiable that the rise of digital money will assume a huge part on the planet's financial texture. Because digital money has not yet reached maturity in terms of time, further research into its innovation, potential, and risk should be considered to ensure that the possibilities are not merely a coincidence. The security convention ought to be better, if not the same than the ordinary brought together financial framework in ensuring the client's financial resources (Kaur et al., 2021). Client security necessitates a significant contribution from stakeholders in this new business, thus the blockchain innovation's certainty and confidence will allow it to become the norm for clients while conducting daily transactions over the internet. In evidence of stake strategy, an individual necessity to approve the coins that they own and the sum had. The individual requirements to make an exchange of their coins that they ship off their record as an award with the data of predefined rate (Al-Asmari et al., 2021). The evidence of stake looks like a pool like plan that give the same opportunity for all diggers. Furthermore, a cross-breed method that includes combined verification of labour and confirmation of stake has been presented, with a portion of the verification of work being compensated to all dynamic hubs and the stake determining the ticket gained to all wagers. In PoA, the movement term alludes to dynamic clients that keep up with the full internet-based hub furthermore, the one that ought to be compensated. Oppositely, in evidence of stake, disconnected clients can in any case gather the coins over the long run what's more, this can prompt twofold expenditure of a similar square. PoA provides much improved security for dealing with future threats to cryptographic money. It has more additional space, and the arrangement correspondence allows for less penalty. Furthermore, PoA has minimal exchange costs, consumes less energy, and the organization's geography may be made to work. In this way, PoA elective serve as a superior stage for digital money because of its capacity to fight of twofold spending and in particular the expense in procuring the digital money contrasted with confirmation of work (De Campos, 2021). The market has been plunged with some new digital currencies that had effectively made it into the market and there are many actually holding back to be delivered. There have been many arising monetary standards that are testing and contending Bitcoin in term of its cost and market capitalization. The model does recreation on the market where the monetary forms are exchanged. With the approval of the record holders, any monetary types can be traded among themselves. It was also discovered that Bitcoin may be swapped for other money, suggesting that the highly justified Bitcoin may be substituted through other exciting coins with superior features in the future. As a result, considering factors like as security, return on investment, and cheap mining costs can help determine which one of the new and emerging sophisticated coins will supersede Bitcoin in the near future. One of them is to improve the outcome of the work confirmation by reusing it. By remunerating other clients from the established handled issue, an all-around given customer can reuse this outcome as an asset in handling any numerical riddle. Another concept is to convert the electrical energy produced through the mining technology into warm energy (Liu, Jiang, Liu et al, 2021). This is recognised in cold-climate countries, where the substantially high heat energy liberated by solving the numerical puzzle may be used to heat private homes and other family duties that require heat energy.

Moreover this, Digital money looks to have passed the stage where new innovations are met with scepticism. Even engine vehicles were surprised by this phenomenon. Bitcoin has started to establish a specialised marketplace for itself, which may either help bring virtual currencies closer to the mainstream or be its main weakness. Virtual payment methods are still in its infancy, so it's hard to predict if they'll ever become a really popular presence in international business. The Financial world is creating new features and fixing existing issues in an effort to establish the money as a standard. Different forms of virtual currency have evolved, each with a little different appeal from Bitcoin but seemingly equal importance. It's feasible that crypto money may have a significant impact, and Bitcoin will be essential to the survival of such monetary standards. The growth of bitcoin exchanges across Europe and Latin America suggests that the currency has real legitimacy. When it came to Bitcoin as well as other digital forms of payment, there are a tonne of other factors to consider. The financial ramifications of Bitcoin's effect on traditional fiat cash execution as well as the ramifications for nations that are starting to adopt government cryptographic types of money should be carefully examined. Although this needs much more financial and marketing study to ascertain, digital money's ability to carry out minute exchanges may allow it to cover a financial vacuum that based one's monetary types are unable to fill. These are modified instalments that occur when a certain event occurs. Predetermined instalment contracts are often accomplished by an organization's whole bookkeeping branch, making this an incredibly exciting subject of extra improvement. Finally, electronic currency is a product of using encryption to create a computerised asset.

CONCLUSION

The conclusion this paper comes to is that blockchain and cryptocurrency systems are the most versatile and in demand technology in the world right now. They are useful in so many various industries and for various purposes as it as pros and benefits which the normal facilities cannot offer. But even with this, there are some disadvantages as there are with a new technology. It is still in the developing phase and will only help more and more as it improves. Educational, Agricultural and Health industries all use blockchain system for better transaction related services. The demerits are that there is no single head so everybody has power and it might be difficult to manage someday. Their fundamental principle is based on blockchain and that is what helps the system to work efficiently. The security and anonymity of blockchains have generated a great deal of attention as a result of several large institutions and organisations investing in blockchain-based cryptocurrencies. The trust that users have in the privacy and security of blockchain-based cryptocurrencies may be increased or built up by having a thorough understanding of the security and privacy features and methods of blockchain. The future growth of blockchain-based cryptocurrencies is thought to depend on adopting and developing the techniques stated above, such as consensus algorithms, mixing, etc. Above that, the users can and should use strong passwords, two-factor authentication, VPN, encrypted emails, etc. to protect their privacy. Blockchain is incredibly praised and supported for its decentralised architecture and distributed nature. However, a few studies on the blockchain region unit are protected by Bitcoin. However, blockchain is being used in a variety of sectors well outside of Bitcoin. With its main characteristics of decentralisation, persistency, secrecy, and auditability, the blockchain has demonstrated its promise for modernising outdated commerce. For upcoming scholars, this study thoroughly examines the depth of a comprehensive evaluation of blockchain technology.

Conflict of Intertest

The authors have declared that they do not have any conflict of interest regarding publication of this work.

REFERENCES

Ahmad, R. W. (2021). Blockchain for aerospace and defense: Opportunities and open research challenges. *Computers & Industrial Engineering, 151*, 106982. doi:10.1016/j.cie.2020.106982

Ahmad, R. W., Salah, K., Jayaraman, R., Yaqoob, I., Ellahham, S., & Omar, M. (2021). The role of blockchain technology in telehealth and telemedicine. *International Journal of Medical Informatics, 148*, 104399. doi:10.1016/j.ijmedinf.2021.104399 PMID:33540131

Al-Asmari, A. M., Aloufi, R. I., & Alotaibi, Y. (2021). A Review of Concepts, Advantages and Pitfalls of Healthcare Applications in Blockchain Technology. *International Journal of Computer Science & Network Security, 21*(5), 199–210.

Alharbi, M., & Hussain, F. K. (2021). Blockchain-Based Identity Management for Personal Data: A Survey. In *International Conference on Broadband and Wireless Computing, Communication and Applications*. Springer.

AlMendah, O. M. (2021). A Survey of Blockchain and E-governance applications: Security and Privacy issues. *Turkish Journal of Computer and Mathematics Education, 12*(10), 3117–3125.

Alofi, A. (2021). *Selecting Miners within Blockchain-based Systems Using Evolutionary Algorithms for Energy Optimisation*. 10.1145/3449726.3459558

Anand, M. V., & Vijayalakshmi, S. (2021). A Survey on Blockchain Adaptability in IoT Environments. In *2021 International Conference on Advance Computing and Innovative Technologies in Engineering (ICACITE)*. IEEE.

Becker, J. (2013). Can we afford integrity by proof-of-work? Scenarios inspired by the Bitcoin currency. In *The economics of information security and privacy* (pp. 135–156). Springer. doi:10.1007/978-3-642-39498-0_7

Belchior, R., Vasconcelos, A., Guerreiro, S., & Correia, M. (2021). A survey on blockchain interoperability: Past, present, and future trends. *ACM Computing Surveys, 54*(8), 1–41. doi:10.1145/3471140

Bentov, I., Lee, C., Mizrahi, A., & Rosenfeld, M. (2014). Proof of activity: Extending bitcoin's proof of work via proof of stake [extended abstract]. *Performance Evaluation Review, 42*(3), 34–37. doi:10.1145/2695533.2695545

Berdik, D. (2021). A survey on blockchain for information systems management and security. *Information Processing & Management, 58*(1).

Bhushan, B., Sinha, P., Sagayam, K. M., & J, A. (2021). Untangling blockchain technology: A survey on state of the art, security threats, privacy services, applications and future research directions. *Computers & Electrical Engineering, 90*, 106897. doi:10.1016/j.compeleceng.2020.106897

Bhutta, M. N. M., Khwaja, A. A., Nadeem, A., Ahmad, H. F., Khan, M. K., Hanif, M. A., Song, H., Alshamari, M., & Cao, Y. (2021). A Survey on Blockchain Technology: Evolution, Architecture and Security. *IEEE Access : Practical Innovations, Open Solutions, 9*, 61048–61073. doi:10.1109/ACCESS.2021.3072849

Bodziony, N., Jemioło, P., Kluza, K., & Ogiela, M. R. (2021). Blockchain-Based Address Alias System. *Journal of Theoretical and Applied Electronic Commerce Research*, *16*(5), 1280–1296. doi:10.3390/jtaer16050072

Böhme, R., Christin, N., Edelman, B., & Moore, T. (2015). Bitcoin: Economics, technology, and governance. *The Journal of Economic Perspectives*, *29*(2), 213–238. doi:10.1257/jep.29.2.213

Bornholdt, S., & Sneppen, K. (2014). Do Bitcoins make the world go round? On the dynamics of competing crypto-currencies. arXiv preprint arXiv:1403.6378. doi:10.1016/j.eswa.2020.114384

Bouraga, S. (2021). A taxonomy of blockchain consensus protocols: A survey and classification framework. *Expert Systems with Applications*, *168*, 114384. doi:10.1016/j.eswa.2020.114384

Bouri, E., Gupta, R., Tiwari, A. K., & Roubaud, D. (2017). Does Bitcoin hedge global uncertainty? Evidence from wavelet-based quantile-in-quantile regressions. *Finance Research Letters*, *23*, 87–95. doi:10.1016/j.frl.2017.02.009

Cocco, L., Concas, G., & Marchesi, M. (2017). Using an artificial financial market for studying a cryptocurrency market. *Journal of Economic Interaction and Coordination*, *12*(2), 345–365. doi:10.100711403-015-0168-2

Dabbagh, M. (2021). A survey of empirical performance evaluation of permissioned blockchain platforms: Challenges and opportunities. *Computers & Security, 100*.

De Campos, M. G. S. (2021). Towards a Blockchain-Based Multi-UAV Surveillance System. *Frontiers in Robotics and AI*, 8. PMID:34212007

Deshmukh, A., Sreenath, N., Tyagi, A. K., & Eswara Abhichandan, U. V. (2022). Blockchain Enabled Cyber Security: A Comprehensive Survey. *2022 International Conference on Computer Communication and Informatics (ICCCI)*, 1-6. 10.1109/ICCCI54379.2022.9740843

DeVries, P. D. (2016). An analysis of cryptocurrency, bitcoin, and the future. *International Journal of Business Management and Commerce*, *1*(2), 1–9.

Dibaei, M. (2021). Investigating the prospect of leveraging blockchain and machine learning to secure vehicular networks: A survey. *IEEE Transactions on Intelligent Transportation Systems*.

Dorsala, M. R., Sastry, V. N., & Chapram, S. (2021). Blockchain-based solutions for cloud computing: A survey. *Journal of Network and Computer Applications*, *196*, 103246. doi:10.1016/j.jnca.2021.103246

Dos Santos, R. P. (2017). On the philosophy of Bitcoin/Blockchain technology: Is it a chaotic, complex system? *Metaphilosophy*, *48*(5), 620–633. doi:10.1111/meta.12266

Doshi & Commerce. (n.d.). *A Study of Opinions on Future of Crypto Currency in India*. Academic Press.

Dwivedi, S. K., Roy, P., Karda, C., Agrawal, S., & Amin, R. (2021). Blockchain-based internet of things and industrial IoT: A comprehensive survey. *Security and Communication Networks*, *2021*, 2021. doi:10.1155/2021/7142048

El Sobky, Gomaa, & Hassan. (n.d.). *A Survey of Blockchain from the Viewpoints of Applications, Challenges and Chances*. Academic Press.

Fauzi, M. A., Paiman, N., & Othman, Z. (2020). Bitcoin and cryptocurrency: Challenges, opportunities and future works. *The Journal of Asian Finance, Economics, and Business*, *7*(8), 695–704. doi:10.13106/jafeb.2020.vol7.no8.695

Frikha, T., Chaari, A., Chaabane, F., Cheikhrouhou, O., & Zaguia, A. (2021). Healthcare and fitness data management using the iot-based blockchain platform. *Journal of Healthcare Engineering*, *2021*, 2021. doi:10.1155/2021/9978863 PMID:34336176

Fu, X., Wang, H., & Shi, P. (2021). A survey of Blockchain consensus algorithms: Mechanism, design and applications. *Science China. Information Sciences*, *64*(2), 1–15. doi:10.100711432-019-2790-1

Gimenez-Aguilar, M. (2021). Achieving cybersecurity in blockchain-based systems: A survey. *Future Generation Computer Systems*.

Gomathi, S., Soni, M., Dhiman, G., Govindaraj, R., & Kumar, P. (2021). A survey on applications and security issues of blockchain technology in business sectors. *Materials Today: Proceedings*. Advance online publication. doi:10.1016/j.matpr.2021.02.088

Guggenberger, T. (2021). A structured overview of attacks on blockchain systems. *Proceedings of the Pacific Asia Conference on Information Systems (PACIS)*.

Gupta, Kumari, & Tanwar. (2021). A taxonomy of blockchain envisioned edge-as-a-connected autonomous vehicles. *Transactions on Emerging Telecommunications Technologies, 32*(6).

Hakak, S. (2021). Recent advances in blockchain technology: A survey on applications and challenges. *International Journal of Ad Hoc and Ubiquitous Computing, 38*(1-3), 82-100.

Hewa, T., Ylianttila, M., & Liyanage, M. (2021). Survey on blockchain based smart contracts: Applications, opportunities and challenges. *Journal of Network and Computer Applications*, *177*, 102857. doi:10.1016/j.jnca.2020.102857

Hewa, T. M., Hu, Y., Liyanage, M., Kanhare, S. S., & Ylianttila, M. (2021). Survey on blockchain based smart contracts: Technical aspects and future research. *IEEE Access : Practical Innovations, Open Solutions*, *9*, 87643–87662. doi:10.1109/ACCESS.2021.3068178

Hileman, G. (2016). *State of Bitcoin and Blockchain 2016: Blockchain Hits Critical Mass*. Retrieved from Coindesk Website: http://www.coindesk.com/state-of-bitcoin-blockchain-2016

Hofman, A. (2014). *The Dawn of the National Currency–An Exploration of Country-Based Cryptocurrencies*. Retrieved from Bitcoin Magazine Website: https://bitcoinmagazine.com/articles/dawnnational-currency-exploration-country-based-cryptocurrencies-1394146138

Huang, H., Kong, W., Zhou, S., Zheng, Z., & Guo, S. (2021). A survey of state-of-the-art on blockchains: Theories, modelings, and tools. *ACM Computing Surveys*, *54*(2), 1–42. doi:10.1145/3441692

Jang, H., & Han, S. H. (2022). User experience framework for understanding user experience in blockchain services. *International Journal of Human-Computer Studies*, *158*, 102733. doi:10.1016/j.ijhcs.2021.102733

Johar, S. (2021). Research and applied perspective to blockchain technology: A comprehensive survey. *Applied Sciences, 11*(14).

Kahyaoğlu & Aksoy. (2021). Survey on blockchain based accounting and finance algorithms using bibliometric approach. *21st Century Approaches to Management and Accounting Research.*

Kaur, S., Chaturvedi, S., Sharma, A., & Kar, J. (2021). A Research Survey on Applications of Consensus Protocols in Blockchain. *Security and Communication Networks, 2021*, 2021. doi:10.1155/2021/6693731

Khan, Jung, & Hashmani. (2021). Systematic Literature Review of Challenges in Blockchain Scalability. *Applied Sciences, 11*(20).

Khan, S. N., Loukil, F., Ghedira-Guegan, C., Benkhelifa, E., & Bani-Hani, A. (2021). Blockchain smart contracts: Applications, challenges, and future trends. *Peer-to-Peer Networking and Applications, 14*(5), 1–25. doi:10.100712083-021-01127-0 PMID:33897937

Khatwani, S. (2018). *Explaining Hash Rate or Hash Power In Cryptocurrencies.* CoinSutra. https://coinsutra. com/hash-rate-or-hash-power/

KshetriN.BhusalC. S.ChapagainD. (2021). BCT-AA: A survey of Blockchain Technology-based Applications in context with Agribusiness. doi:10.2139/ssrn.3834004

Kumar & Sharma. (2021). Leveraging blockchain for ensuring trust in IoT: A survey. *Journal of King Saud University-Computer and Information Sciences.*

Latif, S. (2021). Blockchain technology for the industrial Internet of Things: A comprehensive survey on security challenges, architectures, applications, and future research directions. *Transactions on Emerging Telecommunications Technologies, 32*(11).

Liu, C., Zhang, X., Chai, K. K., Loo, J., & Chen, Y. (2021). A survey on blockchain-enabled smart grids: Advances, applications and challenges. *IET Smart Cities, 3*(2), 56–78. doi:10.1049mc2.12010

Liu, X. F., Jiang, X.-J., Liu, S.-H., & Tse, C. K. (2021). Knowledge discovery in cryptocurrency transactions: A survey. *IEEE Access : Practical Innovations, Open Solutions, 9*, 37229–37254. doi:10.1109/ACCESS.2021.3062652

Mezquita, Y. (2021). Cryptocurrencies and Price Prediction: A Survey. In *International Congress on Blockchain and Applications.* Springer.

Nerurkar, P., Patel, D., Busnel, Y., Ludinard, R., Kumari, S., & Khan, M. K. (2021). Dissecting bitcoin blockchain: Empirical analysis of bitcoin network (2009–2020). *Journal of Network and Computer Applications, 177*, 102940. doi:10.1016/j.jnca.2020.102940

Nguyen, T., Katila, R., & Gia, T. N. (2021). A Novel Internet-of-Drones and Blockchain-based System Architecture for Search and Rescue. In *2021 IEEE 18th International Conference on Mobile Ad Hoc and Smart Systems (MASS).* IEEE. 10.1109/MASS52906.2021.00044

Pal, O., Alam, B., Thakur, V., & Singh, S. (2021). Key management for blockchain technology. *ICT Express, 7*(1), 76–80. doi:10.1016/j.icte.2019.08.002

Peng, L., Feng, W., Yan, Z., Li, Y., Zhou, X., & Shimizu, S. (2021). Privacy preservation in permissionless blockchain: A survey. *Digital Communications and Networks, 7*(3), 295–307. doi:10.1016/j.dcan.2020.05.008

Salcedo, E., & Gupta, M. (2021). The effects of individual-level espoused national cultural values on the willingness to use Bitcoin-like blockchain currencies. *International Journal of Information Management, 60*, 102388. doi:10.1016/j.ijinfomgt.2021.102388

Sanka, A. I., Irfan, M., Huang, I., & Cheung, R. C. C. (2021). A survey of breakthrough in blockchain technology: Adoptions, applications, challenges and future research. *Computer Communications, 169*, 179–201. doi:10.1016/j.comcom.2020.12.028

Shankar, C. G. (2021). A survey on blockchain applications. *Information Technology in Industry, 9*(3), 635–639.

Shi, N. (2016). A new proof-of-work mechanism for bitcoin. *Financial Innovation, 2*(1), 31. doi:10.118640854-016-0045-6

Shinde, R. (2021). Blockchain for securing ai applications and open innovations. *Journal of Open Innovation: Technology, Market, and Complexity, 7*(3).

Sookhak, M., Jabbarpour, M. R., Safa, N. S., & Yu, F. R. (2021). Blockchain and smart contract for access control in healthcare: A survey, issues and challenges, and open issues. *Journal of Network and Computer Applications, 178*, 102950. doi:10.1016/j.jnca.2020.102950

Steinmetz, F., von Meduna, M., Ante, L., & Fiedler, I. (2021). Ownership, uses and perceptions of cryptocurrency: Results from a population survey. *Technological Forecasting and Social Change, 173*, 121073. doi:10.1016/j.techfore.2021.121073

Tran, Q. N., Turnbull, B. P., Wu, H.-T., de Silva, A. J. S., Kormusheva, K., & Hu, J. (2021). A Survey on Privacy-Preserving Blockchain Systems (PPBS) and a Novel PPBS-Based Framework for Smart Agriculture. *IEEE Open Journal of the Computer Society, 2*, 72–84. doi:10.1109/OJCS.2021.3053032

Van Alstyne, M. (2014). Why Bitcoin has value. *Communications of the ACM, 57*(5), 30–32. doi:10.1145/2594288

Vranken, H. (2017). Sustainability of bitcoin and blockchains. *Current Opinion in Environmental Sustainability, 28*, 1–9. doi:10.1016/j.cosust.2017.04.011

Walsh, C., O'Reilly, P., Gleasure, R., McAvoy, J., & O'Leary, K. (2021). Understanding manager resistance to blockchain systems. *European Management Journal, 39*(3), 353–365. doi:10.1016/j.emj.2020.10.001

Wang & Nixon. (2021). Intertrust: Towards an efficient blockchain interoperability architecture with trusted services. *Cryptology ePrint Archive*.

Wang, Z., Jin, H., Dai, W., Choo, K.-K. R., & Zou, D. (2021). Ethereum smart contract security research: Survey and future research opportunities. *Frontiers of Computer Science, 15*(2), 1–18. doi:10.100711704-020-9284-9

Werner, F., Basalla, M., Schneider, J., Hays, D., & Vom Brocke, J. (2021). Blockchain adoption from an interorganizational systems perspective–a mixed-methods approach. *Information Systems Management, 38*(2), 135–150. doi:10.1080/10580530.2020.1767830

Yue, K., Zhang, Y., Chen, Y., Li, Y., Zhao, L., Rong, C., & Chen, L. (2021). A Survey of Decentralizing Applications via Blockchain: The 5G and Beyond Perspective. *IEEE Communications Surveys and Tutorials*, *23*(4), 2191–2217. doi:10.1109/COMST.2021.3115797

Zuo, Y. (2021). Making smart manufacturing smarter–a survey on blockchain technology in Industry 4.0. *Enterprise Information Systems*, *15*(10), 1323–1353. doi:10.1080/17517575.2020.1856425

Section 8
Perspectives on AI Technologies and Blockchain

Chapter 19
Implementation of Internet of Things With Blockchain Using Machine Learning Algorithm:
Enhancement of Security With Blockchain

Hariprasath Manoharan
Department of Electronics and Communication Engineering, Panimalar Engineering College, Chennai, India

Abirami Manoharan
Department of Electrical and Electronics Engineering, Government College of Engineering, Srirangam, India

Shitharth Selvarajan
https://orcid.org/0000-0002-4931-724X
Department of Computer Science, Kebri Dehar University, Kebri Dehar, Ethiopia

K. Venkatachalam
Department of Electronics and Communication Engineering, Audisankara College of Engineering and Technology, Gudur, India

ABSTRACT

In recent days, all networks are connected by internet and all people around the world are able to control things in their remote locations. Even though these technologies have been used only by selected people, it is definite in the future that all people will use this technology and they will move towards building smart cities, homes, and industries. However, when advanced technologies are created, people always worry about security when they move towards smart environment. If the internet is connected to their home then much valuable information in their home can also be sent through smart devices. Therefore, for this IoT-based technology, a blockchain-based method can be introduced where more security for data transfer process can be provided. Also, these technologies have to work efficiently by integrating a new artificial intelligence-based machine learning algorithm. Therefore, for this, a deep learning model will be integrated, thus providing effective data transfer from transmitter to receiver.

DOI: 10.4018/978-1-6684-7455-6.ch019

INTRODUCTION TO BLOCK CHAIN TECHNOLOGY

The major reason for introducing this block chain technology is that in all Internet of Things (IoT) process which includes smart home, transportation, agriculture, medical health care etc. more data needs to be shared between transmitter and receiver where, the processed data should be more secured (i.e) the information should reach only to an authorized user. Therefore, this block chain technology is introduced for storing all information where the stored information is very difficult to steal (Chatterjee and Chatterjee, 2018). Even third party hackers cannot be able to take the information or in other words they cannot cheat the system of block chain technology. To be precise, block chain can be defined as a digital record where all information will be duplicated and all duplicated data will be sent across all networks. Therefore, if duplicated data is sent to different users then, a state of confusion will arise but the original data will be sent to authorized users and it will be stored in a more secured way. Even if any hacker tries to steal the data then, they can able to copy only false data and since the data is duplicated again and again (creation of blocks) it becomes very difficult for hackers to break the duplication blocks.

Importance of Security in Data Processing

In most of the IoT applications the communication channel which is involved in the process of data transfer must be highly secured as it is considered as major backbone for internet connectivity. Whenever a user is transmitting a data then highly secured authentication keys must be added as it can be easily tracked by other external users. Since most of the IoT data is transmitted to cloud systems where individual keys are provided it is essential to demand immediate section that is related to real time issues. Most of the cyber-attacks that is present in the data processing system must be solved by separating the data into individual clusters where data can be processed in separate groups. If the data is processed as a group then active security measure can be added to each user this increasing the security which can be established in a closed network region. Further if the data is present in IoT network then it is considered as open thereby a traditional network parameter must be added before processing an open data. But if the data is protected with network security devices then additional parameters are not needed in the data processing system therefore as a result data can be updated with continuous sharing process.

Types of Security

For a system to process the data in a more secured way three types of data security is highly important thereby adding authorization to input data. The process of data transfer includes the following types.

- Security based on connected network
- Embedded IoT security
- Firmware assessment

Security Based on Connected Network

In this type of security it is the responsibility of each user to secure the connected device from other unauthorized usages. In case if a user is connecting some new devices then a strong encryption password must be provided before adding other users. In a similar way the activity track information of all added users must be ensured thereby preventing data loss in the channel path. If the authorized user finds any data loss then continuous track of data from own devices must be checked and a management plan must be added to prevent future tampering of data. Whenever network security is added then all types of intrusions and external breaches can be prevented where high confidentiality is provided for entire data segment. The levels of network security can be divided into the following three patterns such as physical, procedural and organizational network security.

Embedded IoT Security

Most of the embedded IoT security operations are carried out for protecting the entire component that is present in connected data networks. The data that is present in entire operating component includes hardware and software with connected operating system where network instigated attacks are prevented from the network. In addition the embedded IoT security prevents all malicious attack from the application representations by processing all files in a consistent way. During the above mentioned process a separate log for each file is created and all cache files are removed from the network in order to prevent all malicious attack. Furthermore an embedded IoT security provides more features for software critical and mission created networks thereby fully connected secured network is established with intelligent computing devices.

Firmware Assessment

Firmware is added to all IoT devices in order to prevent unauthorized usage in the network as external attackers mostly targets the installed firmware at hardware component. Whenever an external user attacks the firmware then complete control of data is taken by external users where data vulnerability can never be reduced. Since firmware is defined as software that is present between true software and hardware networks an embedded firmware is needed for controlling various activities that are present in device hardware representations. Firmware can be directly programmed at reading storage space and it can be erased after adding complete security features. Once the firmware is added in the processing unit then it cannot be changed as complex process is evolved throughout the network. Based on technology based firmware three types of firmware assessment can be made as follows,

- Low level firmware
- High level firmware
- Subsystem firmware

Main Functionalities

Figure 1 shows the seven main functions performed by block chain technology which consists of current version of operation, merkle tree process, calculation of time for transaction, estimating the threshold limit with a four byte field and 256 byte parent block. The functions performed by each block are as follows,

Figure 1. Essential utilities of block chain technology

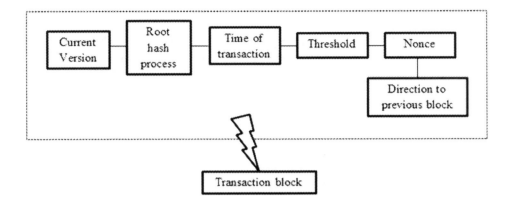

Current Version

In this phase a set of rules will be defined which is used for authorizing all necessary block set.

Merkle Tree Process

This process is used for introducing duplicate values which provides confusion in all transactions in all blocks.

Time of Transaction

All blocks will transact in certain time period and time of their transaction will be stored for future use.

Threshold

This block is used for storing target threshold values for all valid blocks.

Directions to Previous Block

A 256 byte code will be used for providing directions to all necessary stored block whenever needed.

Steps of Transaction

The steps of working model in block chain technology have been upgraded from the operation of bit coin process. In bit coin process third party users are never trusted therefore, as a result the perception of digital signature is introduced. However in bit coin two step procedure is introduced where, in first step the operator should correctly know whether the transmitter is having full privileges to pass the bit coin. In second stage the same operator should know whether the transmitter is having money in their account for transaction. This process in followed in all online transactions but no prior order of transaction is

Implementation of Internet of Things With Blockchain

followed. This, block chain technologies have been introduced for reducing double expenses. In block chain technology data will be secured using four different steps as follows. In first stage, at transmitter side all details of receiver will be stored for sending data only to that user. In second stage all previously observed values are stored in cloud and decision will be taken based on previous situations. In third stage present value which is determined as optimal value will only be sent to the receiver.

In final stage the values will be notified to network operators and if needed all controls will be provided to operators also. So during these four stages only authorized user will be having permission to operate where all transactions can be automatically minimized without any presence of third party (Tasatanattakool and Techapanupreeda,2018).

For example if IoT based technology is installed in home with Pi cameras then, the owner of house can able to see entire operation of house at his own remote location. During this process there if there is any data theft (i.e.,) if a third party is stealing data then there is a possibility that important thing in home can be filched. Therefore, to avoid this type of data theft block chain technology have been introduced and transmitter can ensure that their data is not liberated. Since, this process takes place in an online environment the use if this block chain technology is much important and if any misbelief occurs then, a duplicate value can be sent to third party and at final stage original data can be recovered only by authorized user. Further, this block chain technology can be extended to large scale system where, more data needs to be stored.

Figure 2. Transaction stages for block chain technology

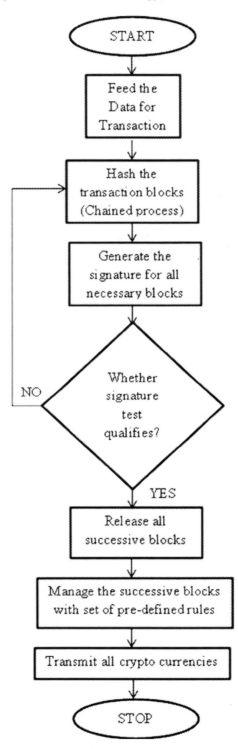

Terms in Blockchain Technology

To understand the operation of block chain technology it is important to have complete knowledge on procedural terms that are employed during transaction. Therefore, the following terms are defined clearly for different version of block chain technology.

Distributed

This term refers to a decentralized network where, all data will be stored for future use.

Translucent

Translucent in Block chain technology refers to all Transparent transactions where, everyone one in the node will be able to see all records of transaction.

Miner and Consent

Miner refers to the controller who is involved in verifying the current transaction and consent refers to the type of verification that is used by the controller.

Clefts

If block chain technology is used with different versions then, entire node will be disturbed and the delinquent that occurs in the node is termed as clefts.

Applications of Blockchain Technology

The block chain technology can be applied in various applications including trading, smart conventions, business, e-commerce, bank clearance etc. Block chain with IoT technology provides more advantage for all fields in real time particularly for health care systems. Nowadays all health care centers are maintaining the record of patients in a secured way and if any user requests it then by checking the needs of customer the data will be sent in a secured way using block chain technology and corresponding payments will be received using a bit coin. In addition, another method which is termed as request and bill processing can also be followed. During this process the user will first request the center for details. Then, once the user requests it then corresponding registration procedures will be followed. If the user request is correct then, payments have to be made to the corresponding official and in return a bill will be generated. Finally, corresponding bills can be shown at health center and requested information can be obtained. Thus, for preventing illegal activities the reports will be sent to the user where, all the records cannot be sold nor it can be copied. In significance to the all applications of block chain technology which includes health care, real estate, financial sectors etc. there should also be relevancy when a common individual is trying to access the block chain technology as follows,

Limpidity of Network

In case if ledgers are distributed among the network then high amount of transparency should be provided for all individuals. Therefore if high amount of transparency is provided then all enduring transactions will not have any inconsistency inside the operating network.

Economical Procedure

If any financial transactions are processing in the network and in case if they are more expensive then, the process should be immediately converted to low cost model by availing all financial services in the network.

Involvement in the Network

In case of trading a high secured platform should be provided where no third party involvement should be existing in entire network. The purpose of introducing block chain technology in such networks is to make all corresponding traders to bid directly in the network thus avoiding collision in the network.

Novelty

The proposed block chain technique with high security features is introduced to solve the gap that is present in existing methods where external data transfer is processed with low firmware features and even the processing unit is not separated into clusters. Therefore the projected system is focused on implementing block chain technique with importance to data security features where each data is separated into individual blocks and real time experimentation is carried out to check the security features of transmitted data. Moreover in testing phase each block of data is demonstrated with decentralized IoT data where machine learning algorithm is combined. Further both advantages and drawbacks of all types of machine learning algorithm is explained and the process of security is examined using back propagation algorithm as more advantages are observed. As compared to existing models the performance estimate is demonstrated with four main parametric factors where outcomes prove to provide high security factor.

Contributions

The major objectives of the proposed method on block chain is based on solving the security issues that are present in IoT applications where data processing unit can be secured during data transfer stage. The contributions can be separated as follows,

- To explicate the advantage of block chain technique with its supporting types in order to transfer the data into individual clusters.
- To demonstrate real time experimentation for bloc chain technique that is integrated with machine learning algorithm.
- To explain the needs of security and its types for transferring the data without any errors.

SIGNIFICANCE OF MACHINE LEARNING ALGORITHM

One of the major areas of artificial intelligence is termed as machine learning technique where, all explications will always be provided in digital form. Machine learning usually operates with the help of a computer program for performing allocated tasks. So if a machine is operating in a continuous manner (for many years) then, more knowledge will be gained by that machine and it will act to the instruction accordingly. Once the machine have been converted to make intelligent decisions then, all further measurements taken from intelligent device will have more efficiency than the one which is obtained at earlier instance. For achieving much higher efficiency input data should be fed properly by the user and if false input data is provided then, more errors will be detected at output which in turn reduces the efficiency of intelligent devices. This type of intelligent devices should be used for all medical applications for inspecting more number of patients related to their health. Apart from medical applications, machine learning can also be applied to various fields as given below,

- Transportation
- Pattern recognition
- Data mining
- Agriculture and
- For all online cares and maintenance

Different application for this machine learning in in aforementioned areas gains importance because of its function in digital field which provides much simple solution in communication process when data is transmitted from transmitter to receiver. For intelligent IoT process, a machine learning algorithm with more important decisions can be integrated. The main purpose of integrating this algorithm is that efficiency of data processing will be increased at much higher extent.

Figure 3. Flow chart of integrating IoT with blockchain technology and machine learning algorithm

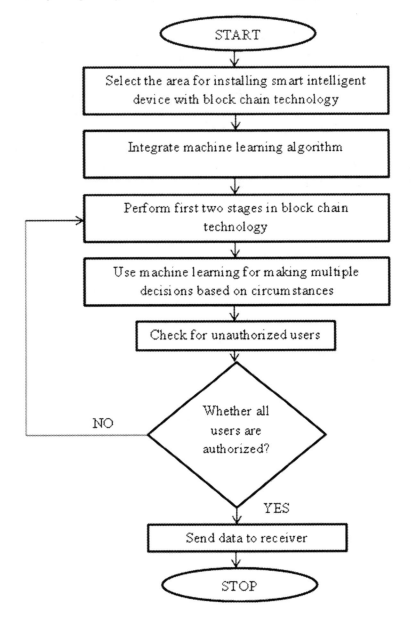

There are 11 different types of machine learning algorithm with their own benefits and detriments where, the proposed IoT with block chain technology is integrated for providing multiple solutions in digital form. Since IoT is used for monitoring all necessary utensils at continuous time period the loop will be iterated until precise values are obtained. Thus, for making multiple decisions an appropriate type of machine learning algorithm should be implemented. The flow chart of the proposed machine leaning based IoT with block chain technology is given in Figure 3. It can be seen form Figure 3 that intelligent devices should be installed with necessary security solutions. If smart intelligent devices are installed without any security measures then all values that are measured daily will be spread to third party server or other populates. For example if heart rate of patient is monitored then, the information should always be sent to particular user or surgeon. But in case if same data has been sent to some other people then there is a chance of distorted data that is sent from transmitter to receiver. Even this aforementioned real time example shows that how an individual will be affected if there is any small problem during data transfer process. Thus, data from transmitter side needs to be aggregated properly and even it can also be done with the help of secured online monitoring system. But, the artificial intelligence technique is the key way for integrating secured solutions in IoT networks and its applications. Applying machine learning technique makes the user to communicate among intelligent devices and this technology will reduce the manpower and makes all people to operate their devices at remote locations. In absence of this technique most of the people cannot control their applications remotely and if this machine learning process is implemented then each individual can feel their operation in real time which provides greater advantage. In addition, machine learning technique can be applied under three different learning processes like supervised, unsupervised and reinforcement learning which will differ by type of training data set that is provided at input side. Figure 4 explicit different types of learning in machine learning algorithm based on training data set.

Categories of Machine Learning Problem

Supervised Learning

In this type of learning raw data will be fed as input at first stage. In second stage raw data will be combined with training data set where, necessary inputs will be fed to the machine. During this stage to prevent wrong prediction of data a supervisor will be introduced thus preventing erroneous value prophecy. Once the supervisor suggests the implementation plan then, expected output will be designed according to input training data set. Once the design process is completed then, corresponding algorithm will be implemented based on parametric evaluation. At final stage correct output is attained for each input training data set. Thus, this process is capable of providing solutions to all problems in an easy way.

Figure 4. Types of learning: (a) supervised, (b) unsupervised, (c) reinforcement

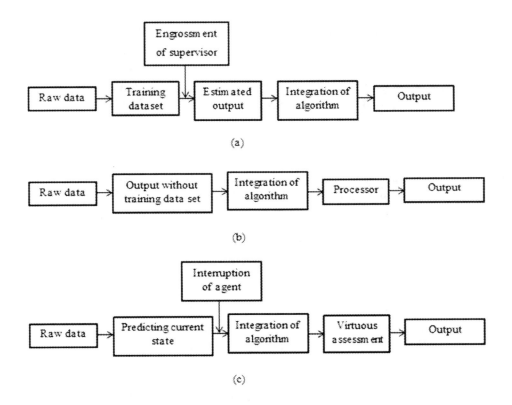

Moreover, the problems in supervised learning are divided into two types which are based in classification and regression. The main difference between these two processes is that the values in classification process are discrete whereas for regression continuous values are obtained. It is much better to decide solutions by comparing the recently obtained output with existing ones. If comparison is made in a better way then, exact results will be obtained at each stage thus preventing the misperception under different circumstances.

Unsupervised Learning

In this type of learning raw data which is fed as input at first stage will not be combined with any training data set. In addition, there is no need of controller in mid-way because perfect data set is not provided at any stage in the process of unsupervised learning. Since there is no supervisor, instructions cannot be given directly and even output cannot be designed as per requirements. Unsupervised learning can also be defined as automatic progression mechanism and it can able to solve the problems of complex data sets. In this type of learning only real time analysis is performed and only exact output will be achieved. The output will be found at final stage after integrating corresponding fast performing processor with high memory capacity. Here also the problems are classified into two types namely clustering and association.

Reinforcement Learning

This type of learning differs from other two types where, once raw data is fed at first stage then immediately output will be predicted. Also, in reinforcement learning there will be interruption from different agents. Thus, if agents are interrupted during this process then, machine learning algorithm will respond to all environments by considering different states all around current situation. The agents which are interrupting during this learning process will be driven by artificial intelligence technique at both start (transmitter) and end (receiver) states. Here, the solutions will be decided only based on trial and error basis (i.e.) more number of solutions will be obtained and it is up to the receiver to decide best solution at all points. Moreover, no predefined data will be sent to transmitter for comparing the solutions. All predicted real time values will change once the environment is altered. If the process results in attaining best solution a reward will be given and in case if the process results in failure then, no reward will be allocated. Table 1 shows the dissimilarity between three learning techniques that are used for implementing machine learning process.

Table 1. Types of learning in machine learning

Types	Supervised Learning	Unsupervised Learning	Reinforcement Learning
Description	Training data is used at input with overseer	Training data is not provided at input and no overseer is involved	Interaction with outdoor environment with communication from agents
Types	Classification and Regression	Clustering and Association	Based on Rewards
Input data	Labeled	Unlabeled	No input data
Process	Requires external controller	No controller is needed	No controller is needed
Line of attack	Training data with labels are mapped	Recognizes pattern with unlabeled data	Trial and error basis

Apart from aforementioned three types an additional type of learning is also involved in machine learning which is termed as semi-supervised learning. During this type of learning a small difference will be observed where, small expanse of labeled data will be joined with large amount of unlabeled data for decision making. This type of learning process uses the combination of both supervised and unsupervised learning with labeled and unlabeled data set.

Types of Machine Learning Algorithms

After selecting the correct learning process in the next step a best type of machine learning algorithm should be selected. Fundamentally, machine learning is divided into the following types,

1. Gradient descent algorithm (GSA)
2. Regression analysis
    - Linear regression
    - Multivariate regression
    - Logistic regression

3. Decision tree mechanism
4. Support vector machine
5. Learning based on
    - Bayesian
    - Naïve Bayes
6. K type methods
    - K nearest neighbor
    - K means clustering and
7. Back propagation method

To attain complete knowledge on machine learning the aforementioned categories should be conversed for identifying its function on different applications. If correct type is chosen then, all parametric values will be evaluated appropriately and a precise value can be obtained. It is not easy to switch different types of machine learning in case of failure in estimating parametric values. When raw data is provided as input and depending on parametric changes appropriate type of machine learning should be chosen. Each machine learning algorithm will vary by their learning characteristics. For supervised learning regression analysis, support vector machine, Bayesian algorithms and decision trees will be preferred. Similarly for unsupervised learning K type methods with clustering will be chosen.

Gradient Descent Algorithm

Figure 5. Estimating cost function

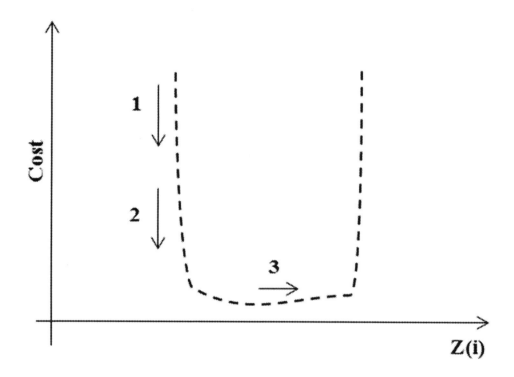

This algorithm is mainly used for finding the co-efficient where, cost function can be minimized. The algorithm starts by finding the partial derivative which is called gradient function as shown in Figure 5. From Figure 5 it can be seen that more number of iterations are performed and during each state negative derivatives are taken. Therefore, due to the presence of negative derivatives co-efficient values are reduced thus during each iteration step size is reduced (Kennedy et al., 2019). If step size is reduced then, local optimum solution will be achieved and once the solution is achieved then iteration will be stopped. At final stage (i.e) after ending the iteration it can be observed that value of cost function is reduced. The procedure of gradient descent algorithm can be understood by taking initial random variable as 0. Therefore, for evaluating cost function the following equation will be considered,

$$C_i = f(0) \qquad (1)$$

Once the coefficient function is determined then, slope at a given point can be found by calculating the co-efficient values to achieve low cost at next iteration. Since, this type of algorithm is involved with supervised learning a learning rate will be updated during each iteration. The iterations will also be repeated until the value of zero is achieved again. Therefore, the delta value can be found as,

$$\delta = D(Ci_j) \qquad (2)$$

Gradient descent algorithm is divided into three types based on observing errors in training data set as (i) stochastic gradient descent, (ii) batch gradient descent and (iii) mini-batch gradient descent. In all three types of gradient descent algorithm errors will be observed during each training data set but parameters will be updated at each training instance in stochastic gradient. However in batch gradient descent parameters will be updated only after all training data are executed. Whereas mini-batch gradient is a combination of both stochastic and batch gradient process. In most cases batch gradient will be preferred because computational efficiency of this process is much lesser when compared with other two types.

Linear Regression

In this type of algorithm values are predicted for continuous variables where, a relationship can be established between forecasting and variables. Unlike gradient descent here the output will be determined based on input training data thus linear regression can be considered as a type of supervised learning. In linear regression the predicted output will form a conventional hyper plane as shown in Figure 6. This is possible only when the relationship between both dependent and independent variables are linear (Rong and Bao-Wen, 2018). From Figure 6 it can be seen that a relationship between two variables X and Y are observed at continuous time periods.

For example, X represents the average number of students and Y represents the marks scored by those students. In this case it can be seen that if average number of students are 20 then, marks scored by those students will be 3000. Similarly the value rises when more number of students is present. In this example average marks of students (Y) will be computed only based on average number of students (X) thus a linear hyper plane is obtained. This algorithm will be mostly used when more number of data is analyzed and aggregated. But this algorithm cannot be applied in all real time scenarios because of its characteristics in addressing the output variables. In addition, if problems are more complex then there is less possibility in achieving a good solution.

Figure 6. Dependent vs. independent variables

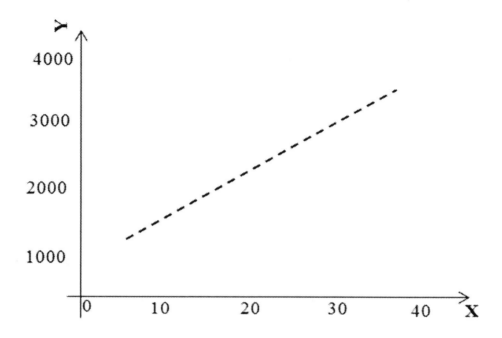

The hypothesis function of Figure 6 can be given as,

$$Y = \alpha 1 + \alpha 2 X \qquad (3)$$

Where, X and Y represents the input and labeled data; $\alpha 1$ and $\alpha 2$ are intercepts and co-efficient of X.

Once the co-efficient is updated then, precise value will be determined which in turn reduces the error between predicted and true values. Thus cost function for linear regression can be determined as,

$$C_i = min \frac{1}{n} \sum_{i=1}^{n} \left(Predicted\ value - true\ value \right)^2 \qquad (4)$$

From above equation it can be observed that cost function of linear regression can be defined as root mean square error between predicted and true values of output variable (Y). Furthermore, this type of machine learning algorithm always assumes that noise is not present at any state during whole process but all iterated linear values will be fitted inside only with correlated data. Even linear regression will try to rescale all predicted values once the input training data set is changed. Thus linear regression can be considered as having Gaussian distribution when analyzing the values in real time.

Multivariate Regression

Multivariate regression is almost similar to linear regression where, in real life situation one variable reliant on different factors. So, it is not possible to solve complex problems with one to one relationship. Therefore, in multivariate regression many to many relationships have been introduced (Zhang 2017).

Figure 7. Multiple dependent vs. independent variables

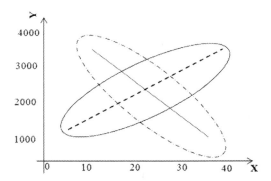

As mentioned in linear regression collision will occur even if anyone variables are present at input. But in case of multivariate regression more variables are present which causes multiple collisions between dependent and independent variables. In addition, even the efficiency of multivariate regression is similar to linear regression even if multiple variables are present.. Figure 7 represents the relationship between multiple dependent and independent variables where, in multivariate regression prior knowledge about both variable sets is required. If prior knowledge is acquired then complex problems can be solved. But one disadvantage in multivariate regression is that since the model depends on statistics the sampling size should be much higher which creates more complexity and results in bad significant analysis.

Logistic Regression

In this type of regression algorithm real world digital problems are controlled appropriately with the help of binary variables (0 and 1) (Agrawal et al., 2022). Here, the target variables will be predicted rather than continuous variable that is present in linear regression. Figure 8 portrays logistic regression with zero scaling of input types.

Figure 8. Logistic regression with zero scaling

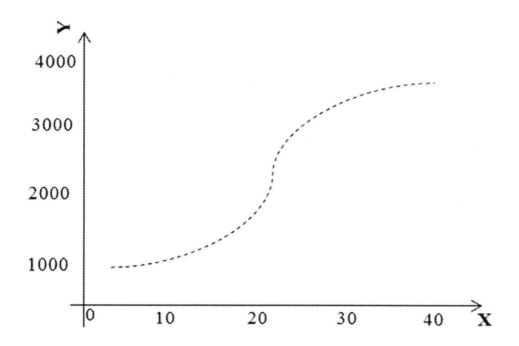

The hypothesis function of Figure 8 can be given as,

$$Y = \frac{1}{1 + e^{-(\alpha_1 + \alpha_2 X)}} \tag{5}$$

Logistic regression is used to solve all business problems because the output is a binary variable and where, grouping of target can be achieved clearly. Also, the noise provided by logistic regression is much lesser when compared to other two regression techniques. Unlike other two regressions technique which is affected by collision, logistic regression produces no collision thus reducing the computational time with high efficiency and simple implementation process.

Decision Tree

Decision tree is one type of supervised learning which is used to solve both classification and regression problems. In decision tree algorithm all necessary data will be detached correctly for making appropriate decisions. Thus, data can be aggregated properly from transmitter to receiver. The tree contains two separate paths where, one is reserved for data aggregation and other is for making decisions (Mienye, Suna and Wang, 2019). Therefore, the first path which is called leaf is used for aggregating the data and the next one which is termed as node is used for decision making. One extra benefit that is added in decision tree algorithm when compared with other algorithms that are discussed earlier is that misplaced values can be added in each features of tree with correct feasible values. Figure 9 shows the process of splitting decision tree algorithm from main node.

Figure 9. Process of decision tree algorithm

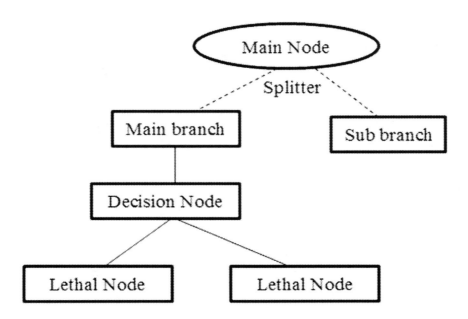

From Figure 9 it can be observed that tree is spitted many branches where, sub branch is used for backup process. The main branch will have a decision node where, simple decision rules will be incorporated for providing good solutions. Since, the tree have been spitted into different nodes it is possible to achieve only local optimum solutions whereas, global optimum solutions cannot be achieved. Also, this algorithm stores all values for future use where, training data will be directly fed as input in first step. Some important terms that are used for recognizing decision tree algorithm are main node (roots), splitter, decision node, lethal node, lopping, sub branch and parent or child nodes. Decision tree will depend only on the aforementioned terminologies using collaborative joint mechanism.

Support Vector Machine

Support vector machine is also a type of supervised learning where, the main function is to find the hyper plane within the boundary points in m dimensional space (Peng 2022). Here, distance between each data points should be maximized so that the data that are dropping on both sides can be exchanged to different classes. Also, it is important to note that the feature of support vector machine is limited up to 3. In case if the feature exceeds three then it is not possible to define exact dimensionality of hyper plane. Additionally in this type of algorithm complex problems can be solved using kernel functions. Figure 10 shows the hyper plane that exists between two boundaries.

Figure 10. Distribution of small margin in hyper plane

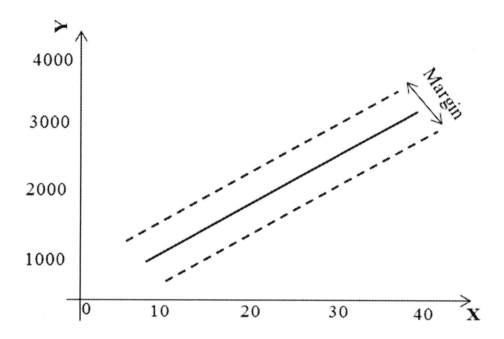

From Figure 10 it can be seen that a small margin exists between hyper plane for avoiding the problem of over fitting. In support vector machine high dimensional data can be can be scaled up to certain extent. But the performance of support vector machine is lesser when compared to linear regression because of high training time and linear regression is capable of providing solutions using hyper plane without boundaries. The cost function of support vector machine can be denoted using the following equation,

$$C_i = \begin{cases} 0 & \text{if } y_i * f(x_i) \geq 1 \\ (1-y_i)*f(x_i) & else \end{cases} \tag{6}$$

The total cost will be zero only when both predicted and actual value is identical to each other. Otherwise, a parameter for balancing the loss will be added for calculating the cost function.

Bayesian Learning

All aforementioned algorithms are based on both classification and regression but Bayesian algorithm is based on learning which defines the relationship between data and model. There are two main terms used in Bayesian learning as past and subsequent convictions (i.e) this model works by selecting the probability distribution that are existing previously and these distributions will be updated at each stage thus providing evidence for new observations as shown in Figure 11.

Figure 11. Bayesian learning hypothesis

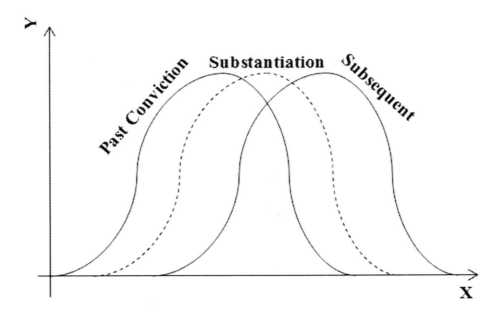

From Figure 11 it can be seen that Bayesian learning is capable of handling even incomplete data set by using past and subsequent convictions thus preventing over fitting of data (Sambasivan, Das and Sahu, 2020). The inconsistencies in Bayesian learning will be removed automatically and there is no need to perform manual operation. The probabilistic model of Bayesian learning can be given as,

$$P(\delta|Z) = P(Z|\delta) * \frac{P(\delta)}{P(Z)} \tag{7}$$

The above equation indicates that probability of given input data can be calculated by multiplying the observed data in the given input with the hypothesis that is accurate. Then, the attained values will be divided by data that is irrespective of hypothesis.

Naïve Bayes

In this learning algorithm the input variable will be independent to each other and not even single information will be known about other variables (Zhang and Gao, 2011). This type of mechanism is called conditional probability where, a probability table approach will be followed for updating the training data. Unlike other methods the training data will be much lesser with linear scaling of data points. Moreover, this method can able to handle both continuous and discrete data with association of multiple classes. The likelihood of naïve Bayes can be given as,

$$P(\delta_1 \ldots \delta_n | Z) = \prod_{i=1}^{n} P(\delta_i | Z) \tag{8}$$

Figure 12. Naïve Bayes with three classifiers

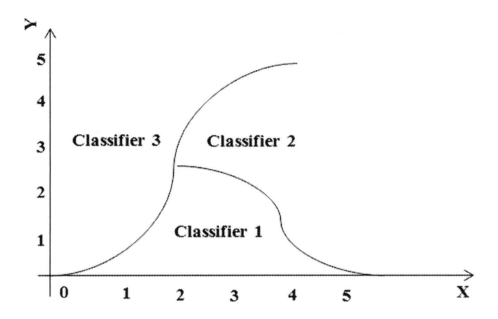

From Figure 12, it can be seen that three classifiers are present where, they are independent with each other thus following Bayes theorem of conditional probability.

K Nearest Neighbor

This algorithm comes under classification type where more data set will be used for estimation. Each data set will be having separate data points which are available in different set of classes. Further, this algorithm will organize all sample points which are considered as classification problem thus it is termed as non-parametric estimation. The main application of K nearest neighbor is that it can be used for pattern recognition techniques where, all classifications will be based on measurement of distance (Saadatfar et al., 2020). Thus, distance function can be modeled as,

$$d_i = \sum_{i=1}^{n} \sqrt{(n_i - m_i)^2} \tag{9}$$

The above equation is similar to Euclidian function where, two points will be classified and their distance will be calculated and the resultant solution which is closest will be chosen as optimal solution. The cost of implementing this algorithm is much lesser when compared to other machine learning algorithms and this method will be suitable for multi modal functionalities.

Figure 13. K nearest neighbor for two cases

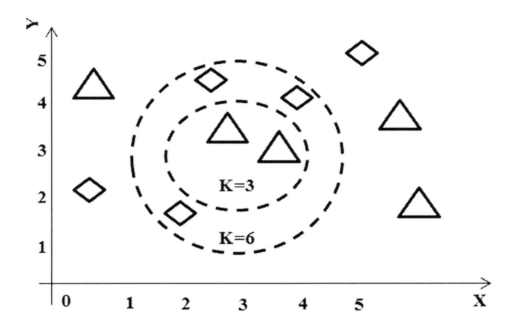

But, this type of simple classification mechanism will not keep a record of all training data it will just classify the problems and calculate the distance thus resulting in inaccurate values when dimensionality space is much higher. Figure 13 shows the class example of K nearest neighbor for two cases. From Figure 13 it can be seen that two K values are chosen (K=3 and K=6) where, the closest neighbors are lying within each boundary value. The neighbors that exist outside the boundary value will not be considered and thus by keeping the neighbors between two cases the distance will be calculated.

K Means Clustering

During data processing all data from transmitter to receiver have to be grouped in entire network. This is possible with the help of K means clustering algorithm which comes under the type of unsupervised learning. Since this type of algorithm does not use any input training data it is necessary to group all data at output that contains similar values (Olukanmi, Nelwamondo, and Marwala, 2019). In case if the values are not grouped then it becomes very difficult for transferring large amount of data. Figure 14 shows grouping of two different classes which contains same values. All these values will be transmitted using a single network at single point thus reducing the complexity of transmission process. In real time application this algorithm is suitable for merging documents and image segmentation. The distance equation for calculating this algorithm is similar to K nearest algorithm but with a small minor difference where, two different points will be considered.

Figure 14. Grouping two different classes using K clustering algorithm

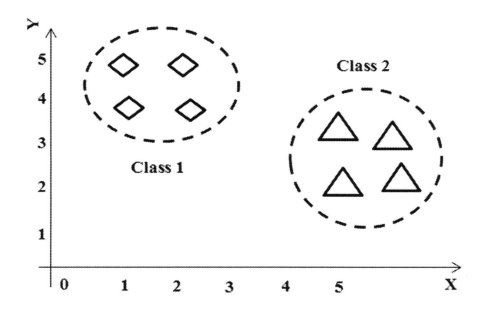

Hence, the distance between two different points in K means clustering can be calculated as,

$$d_i = \sum_{i,j=1}^{n} \sqrt{(n_i - m_j)^2} \tag{10}$$

Back Propagation Algorithm

This algorithm is a special case and it is used for deep learning analysis in neural networks. However, it can be used in combination with stochastic gradient descent which is applied in different industrial domains. Since the concept of stochastic gradient is followed, error value that is achieved during this process is much reduced. Also, this algorithm can be applied only when there is no set of rules and always a good solution will be obtained but it is very difficult to predict how the solution have been calculated (Xu et al., 2022). Moreover, the algorithm involves the operation of many hidden layers as shown in Figure 15 which in turn affects the efficiency of the process. Each and every unit that is involved in the process will try to improve the efficiency but at the same time due to continuous change of units it is much difficult to achieve good performance. In all cases the units cannot communicate with each other to know their states.

Even the weights will be changed at each stage which causes a problem in achieving local optimum solutions. The error function for back propagation algorithm can be given as,

$$E_i = \frac{1}{2}\sum_{i=1}^{n}(y_i - target) \qquad (11)$$

Figure 15. Two layer topology for back propagation algorithm

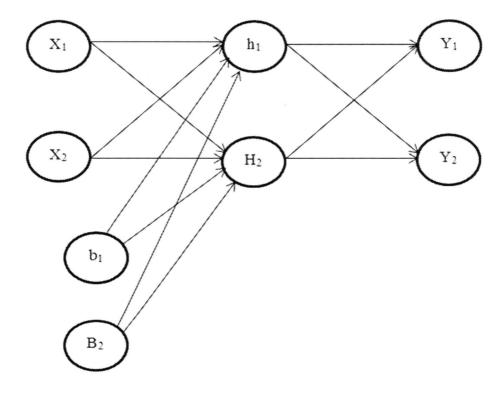

Performance Estimate

It is much important to analyze the performance of IoT when it is applied in various fields with block chain technology. Also any one type of machine learning algorithm should be able to perform much better when it is integrated with IoT devices. Therefore, for examining the applications of IoT devices major parametric evaluation have been carried out with online monitoring and the monitored results are plotted using MATLAB. Since the method focuses on attaining more number of values for a particular parametric inspection back propagation algorithm is used. The major advantage of employing this method is that target can be indicated in a correct way much better than other algorithms. Also, IoT based models will sense the values to a particular distance and after some distance new intelligent devices needs to be installed. Therefore, different output will be present at end and all can be combined at final stage with no prior knowledge of the networks. Since, no data is stored transaction in preceding stages will be carried out in a secured way. The simulated results with different stage of analysis are as follows and it should be noted that the analyzed values are collective to all applications and is carried out by connecting Raspberry pi 2 module.

Interpretation Time

The first stage of analysis have been started with examination on sensor reading time (i.e) the time taken for a sensor to transfer all data to the target with security. During this stage maximum number of allocated sensors is considered as 100 and minimum, average and maximum data transfer time is observed. This stage of analysis cannot be compared with other methods because type of intelligent devices will differ for monitoring the time period. However, it can be observed from simulation result which is shown in Figure 16 that if machine learning algorithm is employed then sensor reading time will be much lesser. For example if the number of sensors is 60 then, time taken for transacting more number of data is 1.9 seconds (minimum). Whereas, if the same process continues at next stage then, time taken for sensor reading will be 2.8 seconds (maximum). The aforementioned reading time is calculated when 500 devices are connected. This basic evaluation is much important because the outputs are not decided at previous stage using target inputs.

Figure 16. Interpretation by connected sensors

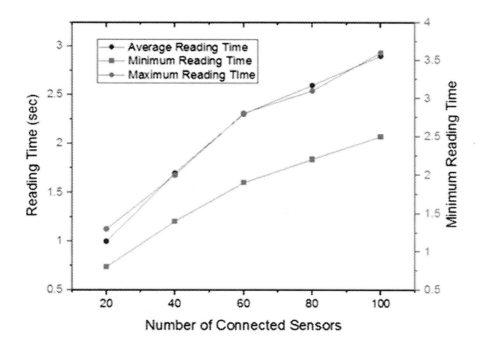

Overhead Time

Since machine learning performs fast operation for sending the data to specified target it is essential to estimate amount of memory that is needed for transaction. Therefore, using same combination of blocks which is equal to 100 IoT with block chain operation is performed. It is interesting to realize that machine learning algorithm uses very less memory space when compared other mechanism (Hang and

Kim, 2019). Figure 17 depicts the overhead time with increase in number of blocks. It can be seen that when number of blocks is equal to 80 then overhead time for machine learning algorithm will be 0.7 second whereas, for other mechanism (Hang 2019) the overhead time is much higher which is equal to 1 second. This indirect computational time will be much reduced with less number of sensors and it should always be ensured that overhead time is close to zero. Thus in machine learning algorithm the overhead time is close to zero and almost 34% of retention time is reduced.

Figure 17. Calculation of overhead time for different blocks

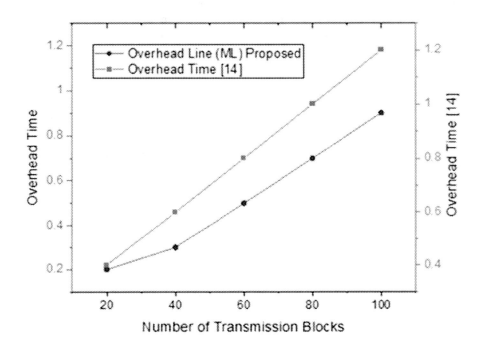

Transmission Power

For effective online monitoring it is necessary to use a power transmission line. Thus, transmission power for data from transmitter to receiver is deliberated in performance analysis. Here, the number of nodes are chosen to be 2,4,8 and 16 where, all nodes are extracted for complete utilization.. The reason behind selecting Raspberry Pi module is that it provides best optimal values with more memory space and it will keep the estimated average power much close to idle power. Figure 18 shows the transmission power of installed nodes and it can be observed that for all nodes back propagation algorithm uses only less power for transmission. For example if the number of nodes is 8 then the transmitter power for machine learning algorithm is 1576mW whereas, other methods (Kreku et al., 2017) utilizes 1612mW for transmitting data. It can also be observed that a replica between mining nodes (2 to 16) and average power exists (i.e) due to analogous execution of machine learning program (back propagation algorithm) if number of nodes increases then transmission power decreases. The aforementioned situation happens

Implementation of Internet of Things With Blockchain

even due to appearance of new blocks if it is more than 10 thus making the execution time to be much lesser.

Figure 18. Transmission power of nodes

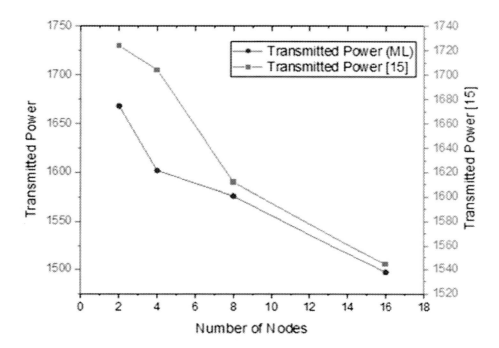

Depletion of Energy

It is always necessary that transmission energy for intelligent sensing devices which enables block chain technology should be maximized. Energy once wasted cannot be retrieved back thus energy will be allocated to users only based on request. For IoT devices with block chain technology energy will be allocated based on block release factors. If number of blocks are higher and if number of registered devices and users are higher in a particular block then more energy will be allocated to that particular block. In turn even if number of blocks are higher with less number of users then wastage of energy will be reduced by supplying sufficient amount of energy. This form of energy supply requires an online monitoring system so that supply of energy to nodes can be either increased or decreased as per request with instantaneous arrangements. Figure 19 shows the simulation plot of allocated energy to nodes that varies from 2 to 16. It can be observed that only sufficient amount of energy is required for transactions when IoT is integrated with machine learning algorithm. Even for 16 nodes energy allocated to users will be 67.4kJ whereas, for same number of nodes other methods (Kreku et al., 2017) have allocated 58.3kJ which is not sufficient for transactions. For 16 nodes with high power the energy supplied should also be higher but in (Kreku et al., 2017) high power is supplied with less energy. Thus, machine learning algorithm overcomes the drawback of IoT devices with block chain technology and it provides effective energy process.

Figure 19. Energy consumption of nodes

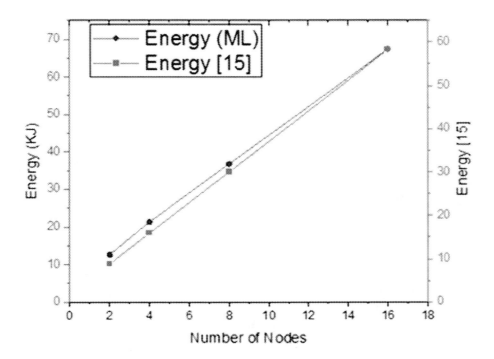

CONCLUSION

The role of machine learning technique with block chain technology in IoT devices is having huge impact around the world. The society is expecting more changes and all are moving towards a smart electronic world. But due to lack of security concerns many people are apprehensive about IoT devices when they are even connected with machine learning techniques. Thus this chapter has given clear information about the advantage of block chain technology and machine learning algorithms for connecting IoT devices. This information is also applied and tested using intelligent sensing devices with high volume of nodes. The investigation also proves that block chain technology provides more security for transfer of data when it is integrated with IoT devices. Moreover, machine learning techniques acts as a supporter for making the transmission process stronger. Therefore, all people can use this technique for different applications and they can control their surroundings using remote procedures.

REFERENCES

Agrawal, K., Aggarwal, M., Tanwar, S., Sharma, G., Bokoro, P. N., & Sharma, R. (2022). An Extensive Blockchain Based Applications Survey: Tools, Frameworks, Opportunities, Challenges and Solutions. *IEEE Access : Practical Innovations, Open Solutions*, *10*(November), 116858–116906. doi:10.1109/ACCESS.2022.3219160

Chatterjee, R., & Chatterjee, R. (2018). An Overview of the Emerging Technology: Blockchain. *Proceedings - 2017 International Conference on Computational Intelligence and Networks, CINE 2017*, 126–127. 10.1109/CINE.2017.33

Hang, L., & Kim, D. H. (2019). Design and implementation of an integrated iot blockchain platform for sensing data integrity. *Sensors (Basel)*, *19*(10), 2228. Advance online publication. doi:10.339019102228 PMID:31091799

Kennedy, R. K. L., Khoshgoftaar, T. M., Villanustre, F., & Humphrey, T. (2019). A parallel and distributed stochastic gradient descent implementation using commodity clusters. *Journal of Big Data*, *6*(1), 1–23. doi:10.118640537-019-0179-2

Kreku, J., Vallivaara, V., Halunen, K., & Suomalainen, J. (2017). Evaluating the efficiency of blockchains in IoT with simulations. *IoTBDS 2017 - Proceedings of the 2nd International Conference on Internet of Things, Big Data and Security*, 216–223. https://doi.org/10.5220/0006240502160223

Mienye, I. D., Sun, Y., & Wang, Z. (2019). Prediction performance of improved decision tree-based algorithms: A review. *Procedia Manufacturing*, *35*, 698–703. doi:10.1016/j.promfg.2019.06.011

Olukanmi, P., Nelwamondo, F., & Marwala, T. (2019). Rethinking k-means clustering in the age of massive datasets: A constant-time approach. *Neural Computing & Applications*, *0*, 19–27. doi:10.100700521-019-04673-0

Peng, C., Liu, Z., Wen, F., Lee, J. Y., & Cui, F. (2022). Research on Blockchain Technology and Media Industry Applications in the Context of Big Data. *Wireless Communications and Mobile Computing*, *2022*, 1–8. Advance online publication. doi:10.1155/2022/3038436

Rong, S., & Bao-Wen, Z. (2018). The research of regression model in machine learning field. *MATEC Web of Conferences*, *176*, 8–11. 10.1051/matecconf/201817601033

Saadatfar, H., Khosravi, S., Joloudari, J. H., Mosavi, A., & Shamshirband, S. (2020). A new k-nearest neighbors classifier for big data based on efficient data pruning. *Mathematics*, *8*(2), 1–12. doi:10.3390/math8020286

Sambasivan, R., Das, S., & Sahu, S. K. (2020). A Bayesian perspective of statistical machine learning for big data. *Computational Statistics*, *35*(3), 893–930. Advance online publication. doi:10.100700180-020-00970-8

Tasatanattakool, P., & Techapanupreeda, C. (2018). Blockchain: Challenges and applications. *International Conference on Information Networking*, 473–475. 10.1109/ICOIN.2018.8343163

Xu, W., Hu, D., Lang, K. R., & Zhao, J. L. (2022). Blockchain and digital finance. *Financial Innovation*, *8*(1), 97. Advance online publication. doi:10.118640854-022-00420-y PMID:36465063

Zhang, J. (2017). Multivariate analysis and machine learning in cerebral palsy research. *Frontiers in Neurology*, *8*, 1–13. doi:10.3389/fneur.2017.00715 PMID:29312134

Zhang, W., & Gao, F. (2011). An improvement to naive bayes for text classification. *Procedia Engineering*, *15*, 2160–2164. doi:10.1016/j.proeng.2011.08.404

Chapter 20
Blockchain-Based Decentralized Documentation System

Sriram C. R.
Vellore Institute of Technology, India

Prasanna Moorthy A. P.
Vellore Institute of Technology, India

Santhi Krishnan
Independent Researcher, India

T. Chellatamilan
Vellore Institute of Technology, India

M. Anbarasi
Vellore Institute of Technology, India

ABSTRACT

Property enrolment is a salient process. There are several escape clauses and issues. The existing system endures the fabrication of land documents which results in a loss of revenue to the government. So, developing a decentralized online registration using blockchain (BC) makes it comfortable for citizens to transfer property, prevents the touting of the same property to various buyers, and also helps the government to monitor and keep track of property movement to prevent money laundering on real estate. The process of automation eliminates the need for more humans to employ and also reduces the need for storage building which is required for storing physical documents. In this chapter, interplanetary file system (IPFS) is used for connecting all computing devices or nodes with the same system files and storing large files effectively. The land is successfully transferred between users after the successful completion of payment. Moreover, the proposed hybrid system does not require nodes to solve complex puzzles and thus reduces the use of high computational energy.

DOI: 10.4018/978-1-6684-7455-6.ch020

INTRODUCTION

Blockchain is a decentralized, distributed, tamper proof and immutable ledger which can be used to track transactions, making it secure and transparent. Several blockchain systems may materialize to be similar but they vary a lot in consensus mechanism, it represents how a blockchain persuades requirements and operates. Several blockchain systems may materialize to be similar but they vary a lot in consensus mechanism, it represents how a blockchain persuades requirement and operates (Dahlberg, Pulls, & Peeters, 2016). The imposition of any specific approach using a blockchain system assures the quality and authenticity of the information being used. Several techniques such as hashing, merkle tree, public key and private key cryptography are combined to maintain authenticity in blockchain, Conventional implementation of encryption technique guarantees information protection (Nakamoto, 2009; Sendhil Kumar et al., 2020; Patel, 2014). The idea of blockchain has become a technological revolution and is creating a major impact not only in digital payment but also in every possible sector, from agriculture to gaming industries. Crowdfunding blockchain projects have made it easy for investors to make an open source investment, there are several crypto projects developed in ongoing industries infusing the concept of play and to earn attracting gamers towards the metaverse. The idea of NFT, selling valuable artworks to interested Byers, Usually there would be only one single copy of a unique and famous artwork which could be sold in an auction but the blockchain has made it possible for multiple users to have copyrights over unique artworks, the value of the artwork keeps rising depending on its demand. The supply chain in collaboration with blockchain can lead to better and safe.

Distribution of product from the manufacturer to the end user, when a product has to reach a customer or user from the manufacturer it has to follow a supply chain route. Let's suppose a Product is manufactured and follows the supply chain route of reaching the nearest transporter for making it reach the wholesale dealer, then from the retail dealer and finally to the customer. Along the path all the arched sets are marked as logs and are created as blocks and made into chains making them immutable, thus creating robustness and authenticity in the shipment of the products. Bitcoin is one of the famous and earliest projects being implemented on blockchain lead to the evolution of cryptocurrencies, which allow exchanges and trades to happen in no time. When a customer deposits money in the bank, the bank uses the customer's money without his knowledge for lending or investment purpose, but cryptocurrencies are only accessed by the user and are not being accessed by someone without the user's knowledge until the user provides his private key. Blockchain provides support in various industries but at the time there are a few cons, cryptocurrencies are virtual currencies that work under the principle of blockchain, there is no governing body for regulation, and quite a few cryptocurrency owners are using it for payment of unlawful substance.

Blockchain works by forming a chain of blocks that are connected in series where each block contains specific information about the transaction. Every block is represented by a unique identification number and manual tampering with the block is not possible. Once payment for a transaction is completed it is then verified and added to the chain, if an intruder wants to change information in the blockchain he needs to change the entire chain, which requires a large amount of computational energy which is merely impossible and thus made to the documentation system tamper proof (Yadav et al., 2021). Blockchain creates trust between anonymous users, allowing them to trade information and exchange values without a need for an intermediary agent. The System must be delivering efficient, secure transactions and must be scaled to make it available to everyone. Research is still going on and millions of blockchain developers are working to convert this software model into real life applications so that exchange can become effortless and there would be no need to rely on third party vendors.

The present land registration system has a vast number of flaws and the involvement of human interpretation leads to unethical practices causing fraudulence and complications in the system. The registration fee collected in form of bonds is too high, so adapting to digitalization can reduce registration bond fees to transaction fees and the current system does provide features for government to have live and accessible monitoring of transactions sometimes leading to tax evasion. Details of assets and land related documents are disintegrated, found in a septic government near the asset area, since the offices are not harmonized it becomes difficult to access the Details when required immediately. Deploying a decentralized application to manage the land transaction for the Indian government using Blockchain technology makes it comfortable for citizens to transfer property, prevents touting of the same property to various buyers, also helps the government to monitor and keep track of property movement to prevent money laundering on real estate's (Joshi et al., 2018).

The deployed application is aimed to reduce fraudulence existing in our current system and eradicate the process of double spending by monitoring transactions. Digitalization along with blockchain makes the process convenient and secure for users, also improves security and authenticity as well as features effectiveness in time and energy consumption. The process of automation Solves the problem of inefficiency present in the Traditional system of land document registration, the assets are transferred and reissued with ease as there is no involvement of human interpretation, moreover, documents are stored virtually hence eliminating the need for large storage space. The decentralized land document storage system helps in maintaining immutable records, making the process of land forgery and money laundering merely impossible, making (Latifi et al., 2019). This helps the users and government in solving the problem faced by the existing system.

In the contemporary world, blockchain has become an emerging technology that is being implemented all around the globe, various and vast numbers of research are being regulated to deploy blockchain on different hoods. s (Ferrag et al., 2018) presented a complete survey on enduring blockchain consensus protocols, the research provided a juxtaposition of various modern methods with regards to the blockchain system, also discussed diverse challenges found and various feasible areas of interest to be studied in the domain internet of thing. Imam, Iftekher Toufique, et al discussed the benefits of implementing blockchain architecture for the storage of digital documents and provided a solution to eschew document forgery, the deployed system operates on Ethereum network and they ensured security and legibility even for users having a minimal idea about blockchain (Imam et al., 2021).

The economy faces loss from document forgery and Yadav and Kushwaha (2021) described the proposed method for decentralized documentation system using InterPlanetary File System could provide peer to peer transaction seamlessly, the proposed system consumes exceptionally less time than the proof-of-work mechanism. (Majumdar et al., 2020) developed an alternative blockchain system suitable for storing land registration documents, the approach was developed considering the registration process in Bangladesh, and the proposed system eliminates the necessity of solving computational puzzles using a delegated proof of stake mechanism. Proof-work algorithm used along with SHA-256 makes the transaction tamper proof and more secure, transactions are signed by owners and usage of elliptic curve algorithm verifies the authenticity of the transaction, the developed algorithm has been deployed into the application for purpose of testing where 200 transactions were initiated which were maintained and added to the blockchain network by 12 nodes (Krishnapriya & Sarath, 2020).

The new idea of implementing the periodical acquisition of blockchain consensus mechanism commencing with public and progressively consolidates bi-level of hybrid consensus blockchain mechanism was described and deployed by (Alam et al., 2020) the proposed solution is undoubtedly quicker and secure moreover convenient and foolproof.. The blockchain is being deployed in various sectors and is increasing rapidly, Andrian and Kurniawan (2018) explained about various hoods were the implementation of blockchain is emerging, the technology is not only bounded to cryptocurrencies but also used in financial, education and Forensic sectors. The main purpose of the work is to establish the fundamental objective of blockchain for analysts who aim at developing an application based on blockchain. Vulnerabilities are found in the present assets registration process which is used as a loophole to forge ownership, Khan et al. (2020) confer about fraud cases present in our current system and implemented a blockchain model built on Ethereum platform which can outperform the current document storage system and prevent fraud and forgery cases by pulling out midway salesperson which provides a safer and secure medium for transfer of asset ownership between citizens.

Shinde et al. (2019) stated that government will provide a printed copy of the registered property document to the owners and a soft copy of the documents are converted into hash values and stored in Ethereum blockchain network after they persuade certain requirements made by smart contracts. The disorganization present in our traditional asset maintenance system can be restrained by leading buyers, sellers and government authorities into a decentralized system to organize lucidity. Mukne et al. (2019) concluded that the proposed solution reduces fraudulence merely impossible, removal of the current assets maintenance system and shifting over to a new technology of decentralized networks would be an onerous process but it would result in a better and secure environment as an asset play an important role in the economy.

Shuaib et al. (2020) made a detailed explanation about various flaws and issues that make the current registration body a weaker system and also presented a case study of different nations implementing blockchain architecture and the status of the project respectively, also presented a scheme for different levels of asset registration which is implied by the concept of smart contract, automates the process by eliminating the need for more human capital and also provides potential benefits of maintaining a secure and authentic assist registration system. Many altercation cases are not solved legally by courts which leads to corruption in our country. Thakur et al. (2020) highlighted the presence and utilization of blockchain in the assets management system, discussed several privacy and security issues concerned with property enrolment, and implementation of blockchain architecture in the country would make it tamper proof and provide legible, authentic ownership details by defending against double spending, also explained the necessity for replacement of old asset registration system with blockchain in the modern era of technology.

Rajput et al. (2019) describes blockchain technology as being a backbone of bitcoin development, discussed the framework and various aces and cons of bitcoin, corporate financing and implementation of blockchain in IoT sectors, and concludes that there are a lot of opportunities and a greater level of advancement in professions related with electronic cash and it has proved that the need for trust is important. Zheng et al. (2017) discussed the overview of various architectures available, provided a comparison between consensus algorithms, described approaches and advances on consensus algorithms and also provided a brief overview of hindrance and that could probably raise the issue with the development of blockchain. Concluded that blockchain has the capacity to mutate and transform present industries into a promised land.

ARCHITECTURE

Blockchain

Blockchain is a highly potential and emerging technology that is right in its infancy, the idea of the smart contract which was implanted on ethereum gave an idea to unlock various aspects where blockchain can be applied. Blockchain is categorized based on the type of consortium chosen, Hybrid blockchain system is most suited for official government purpose. The transaction details along with timestamp, nonce, merle root and various parameter are made into a block, the blocks are mined by algorithm chosen miner then published into the network, the validator nodes present in the network evaluate the authenticity of the block, then the miners publish their decision in terms of the vote and once the number of votes required by the consortium is reached, the mined block is added to the blockchain network and ever nodes updates the chain (Joshi et al., 2018). Figure 1 explains the block header is hashed and the hash value is added to the header of the next block forming a series of blocks chained together.

Hashing plays an important role in maintaining authenticity, even a small change in the block could result in an entirely different hash value. Longer the chain, the probability of attack becomes impossible making the blockchain system tamper proof.

Figure 1. Blockchain

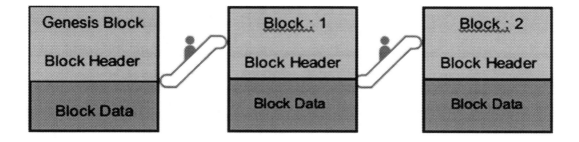

Inter Planetary File System

IPFS stands for Interplanetary file system which is mainly used for the storage of information or data, since certificates and documents occupy a vast space of memory and the size of a block in blockchain is limited considering efficiency, documents are stored in IPFS and only the hash of the file is attached to the block header (Nyaletey et al., 2019). IPFS is a peer to peer network for storage which means that certificates are available all around the world through peers and tracking back of certificates becomes a process of ease. The edge of using IPFS in this framework is the Storage is created from the blockchain's underlying architecture, so the data stored in the IPFS is immutable. IPFS system depends on cryptographic hashes to store on the blockchain and retrieve the data using the same hash. IPFS has a unique durability system, so the data is stored redundantly hashed across the chain, providing enhanced data security and availability. So the land details stored inside the IPFS node will remain untampered.

This will seriously help Government prevent land encroachment and various illegal real estate activities (Santhi et al., 2015).

Figure 2. Architecture

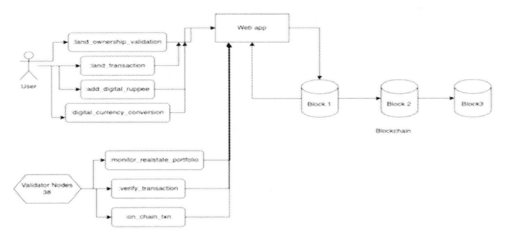

Figure 3. Blockchain asset details

Sparse Merle Trees

Sparse merle trees are similar to merle tree except for the fact that the data stored in the leaf nodes are indexed and key paired. The sparse merle tree is a great alternative to standard merle trees in terms of efficiency. This follows the same procedure as a standard merle tree but SMT stands out in the process of proving non-inclusion of data which is not possible in a standard merle tree (Dahlberg et al., 2016). In an SMT when data is not present in the leaf, the leaf node is filled with the null value. The valiant feature of a sparse merle tree is that the data points stored in leaves are represented by the key index pairs, this makes SMT stand elevated in terms of efficiency.

Lock Structure

Figure 2 shows the architecture and Figure 3 shows the blockchain asset details. The Blockchain is a series of connected blocks and these Blocks are custom designed considering the requirement to store and transfer the certificates of land registry. It imitates the standard block anatomy, but instead of a merle tree root, we have altered it to the sparse merle tree root. The Certificates are stored and maintained separately on IPFS to maintain the efficiency and robustness of the architecture.

Table 1. Framework of a block

Block Index	
Version	Version of the Blockchain
Validator	Detail of the Validator
Timestamp	Recorded Time of the Block
Merkle Tree Root	Root value of Merkle Tree
Previous Hash	Hash Value of Previous Block
Block Data	Transactions Detail

Table 2. Framework of block data

Block Data	
Transaction ID	Transaction Hash
Method	Type of Transfer
Age	Date and Time
From	Buyer ID
To	Seller Id
Fee	Transaction Fee

The version number and validator details are additional add-on details inside a Block header. The version number denotes the current version of the deployed blockchain system and the validator is the name of the validator node referring to the transactions in Block data verified by the respective validator node.

Consensus

The blockchain system deployed contains sensitive information, using a public blockchain mechanism would make the system secure and tamper proof but makes the information transparent to the users, at the same time private blockchain mechanism ensures limited visibility of information but comparatively making it less secure and vulnerable for single point failure (Desai et al., 2019). So, the implementation of a Hybrid consensus mechanism similar to the Delegated proof of stake would be a suitable consensus mechanism for the deployed project. There is a central authority but the nodes for validation and creation of blocks are chosen based on designed criteria from the pool after passing through the requirements. Each validator is provided with loyalty points based on the authenticity of the block created by them and the staked cryptocurrencies, if a validator node creates a malicious block, the loyalty point of the respective node is decremented and is removed from the electoral process for a certain period of time frame. The chosen hybrid consensus mechanism makes the information partially visible and also maintains the security and authenticity of the blockchain.

Working

The consensus protocol implemented is a hybrid protocol, there would be no need for a hard fork because a whenever hard fork is implemented the chain is broken into two versions (Khan et al., 2020). A soft fork is where we release updates similar to bug patches. A hard fork often needs a large amount of consultation with all miners present in the network as Blockchain networks size would be huge, sometimes a reasonable amount of miners would not be aware of the hard fork and would keep working on the previous chain, this may lead to confusion and wastage of resource and energy. The deployed project follows a hybrid consensus mechanism so that a soft fork would be fair enough to amend the changes required in the long run without affecting the nodes and users in the network, thus improving the scalability and solidness of the framework.

Wallet

Users can request a new wallet address, every user is provided with a unique wallet id which carries the cryptocurrencies transaction on their behalf, transaction is made through a deployed application making the process simpler and secure. In Figure 4, The wallet contains all the details including the cryptocurrency balance and details of the land record. If a user does not hold any Asset or Land the Asset value is denoted by zero. The deployed application interface is compatible with the mobile device, providing users to access the wallet instantly with ease.

Figure 4. Wallet

Node Hierarchy

The deployed model constitutes a three level Hierarchy, denoting the administrative control over the network.

Users are divided into three categories:

- **Central Node:** The node has administrative access to add a new member to the network. The node is provided with a feature to monitor the asset details of all the users.
- **State Node:** The node which verifies and validates the transaction and plays an important role in maintaining authenticity in the blockchain. Every state node has special permission on verifying the transaction and creating a block of the respective state. Working towards the blockchain network.
- **Users:** The nodes which take part in blockchain by making transactions and asset registration.

PROPOSED FRAMEWORK

Figure 5. Proposed system

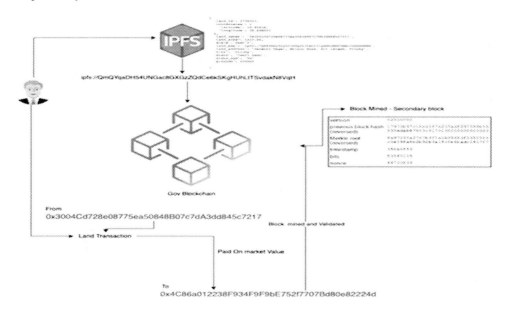

The proposed system is shown in Figure 5, aims to build authentic document storage and asset transfer platform. The paper is based on blockchain technology which is built by merging several encryptions and cryptographic algorithms, this ensures safety and security by preventing cyber-attacks and cuts the cost by reducing the need for a large building for storage of physical documents as well as avoiding or eliminating the possibilities of human error. The web interface is shown in Figure 8, Figure 6 and Figure 7 shows the frontend part has been developed using HTML, CSS, JavaScript, jQuery and ReactJs, the web technologies provide users an easy and convenient interface to interact with the blockchain making it easy to use for untrained users. The backend part has been implemented using python, Python flask which creates an API for interaction with blockchain and interaction between wallets, creation of web socket along with the implementation of real time data streaming protocol. Since storing certificates on blockchain makes the chain heavy and difficult to process.

Blockchain-Based Decentralized Documentation System

Figure 6. Plotting maps

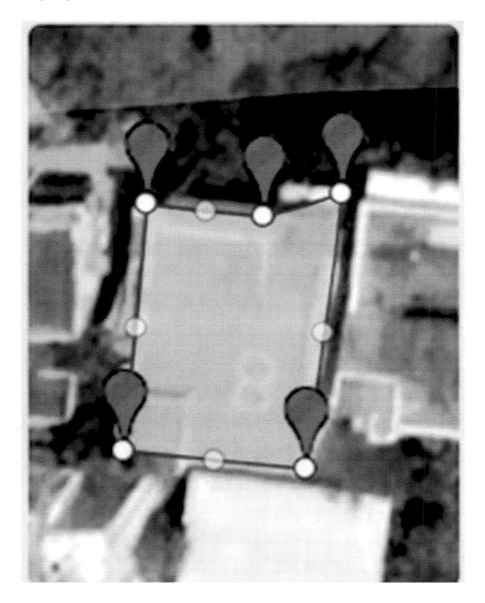

Blockchain-Based Decentralized Documentation System

Figure 7. JSON format

Figure 8. Web interface

IPFS is used to store certificates. Every user is provided with a wallet address which is used for identification, registered users carry out transactions using the wallet. There is an unlimited supply of coins so the created cryptocurrencies behave as a stablecoin. Whenever a user decides to make a transfer of property he needs to buy crypto coins for the equivalent amount of money, the properties are sold and bought at a government-fixed price. When the transfer of cryptocurrency is successfully done, the land document is transferred from the seller's wallet to buyer's wallet and added to the blockchain. The Land

Blockchain-Based Decentralized Documentation System

or the asset is virtually plotted using maps, the boundaries are marked across the perimeter to distinguish it from other plots, the marked plots describe the Perimeter, area and other details of the plot. The land document which is stored in IPFS contains several details about the plot or property which include address, city, state, pin-code, area size and coordinates. The coordinate of the plots are marked for representing the boundary in maps and these details are stored in JSON format. The developed system is a hybrid blockchain, the main reason behind choosing a hybrid consensus is to attain security by mandating scalability and efficiency there are three type of nodes, central, state and user nodes. The central node represents the central government having the central authority to monitor and deploy changes, the state and territory nodes are the validators and authenticators, every transaction happening in a state, territory is validated by the elected state or territory nodes, the block is created and established into the blockchain network, the remaining states nodes verifies the created block and poll their votes when a majority of the vote based on consensus is satisfied the block is added to the blockchain. The central node does not take part in the block validation and creation process. The central node has an exceptional access over the network, inorder to monitor the transaction for maintaining the tax and it behaves an administrative node, having access over creating wallets, adding and removing nodes, moreover has transparency over the transaction in the blockchain. The blocks are connected to each other by adding the hash of previous block to the current block and this process continuous for upcoming blocks making them immutable. The documents stored in IPFS are referenced through their hash value; whenever a file is uploaded in IPFS the user is given a hash value representation in return. When a user request an authentic transcript, it can be referenced through their provided hash value reference and easily downloaded in a moment. The deployed model makes it suitable maintaining authenticity in document storage; verification of document becomes undemanding process. The re-issue of lost document in current system is a very long process; the deployed model removes this barrier by providing us with an easy download of the document from the wallet. There is nearly no involvement of human intervention, therefore the possibility of unanticipated human error is merely possible making this system robust and secure.

PSEUDOCODE - ELECTION

```
TXN_THRESHOLD = 50
PRIORITY_BALANCE = 0.65
PRIORITY_FEES = 0.35
RELECTION_TIME = 21600000 #milliseconds FUNC validatorElection(chain):
validators = ["Rajasthan", "Madhya Pradesh", "Maharastra", "Uttar Pradesh",
"Gujarat", "Karnataka", "Andra Pradesh", "Odisha", "Chhattisgarh", "Tamil
Nadu", "Telangana", "Bihar", "West Bengal", "Arunachal Pradesh", "Jharkhand",
"Assam", "Himachal Pradesh", "Uttarkhand", "Punjab", "Haryana", "Jammu and
Kashmir", "Kerla", "Meghalaya", "Manipur", "Mizoram", "Nagaland", "Tripura",
"Andaman and Nicobar Islands", "Sikkim", "Goa", "Delhi", "Dadra & Haveli",
"Puducherry", "Chandigarh", "Lakshadweep"]
blocks = REVERSE(chain)
INITIALIZE TXNS empty array FOR i=0 to blocks length - 1:
FOR j=0 to blocks.data length - 1:
```

```
ADD blocks.data[j] to TXNS ENDFOR
ENDFOR
INITIALIZE validator_wallets empty array INITIALIZE min_txn_count = 0
FOR i=0 to self.validators_address length - 1:
INITIALIZE addr = self.validators_address.getKey(i)
INITIALIZE res = API.getWalletDetails(self.validators_address[addr]) ADD json.
loads(res) to validator_wallets[addr]
IF validator_wallets[addr]['txns'] length > self.TXN_THRESHOLD: SET min_txn_
count += 1
ENDIF ENDFOR
IF min_txn_count == validators length AND EPOCH_TIME - self.previousElection
>= self.RELECTION_TIME:
INITIALIZE election = {}
FOR i to validator_wallets length - 1:
INITIALIZE addr = validator_wallets.getKey(i)
INITIALIZE fees = API.getTransactionFees(validator_wallets[addr]['txns']) INI-
TIALIZE balance = validator_wallets[addr]["balance"]
INITIALIZE score = (balance * self.PRIORITY_BALANCE + fees * self.PRIORITY_
FEES) / 100
INITIALIZE election[addr] = score ENDFOR
INITIALIZE previousElectionWinner = random.choices(election, weight s= elec-
tion.values, k = len(election))
INITIALIZE previousElection = EPOCH_TIME return self.previousElectionWinner
ENDIF
ELSE IF time.time()-self.previousElection < self.RELECTION_TIME: return self.
previousElectionWinner
ENDIF ELSE
return self.validators[0]
```

Every validator node participates in the election and only one single node is selected for the creation of the block. We have a fixed period of six hours for reelection, when a node is elected it is the sole authority for the creation of the block until reelection. To increase their probability of winning the election, each node is expected to stake cryptocurrencies. The total gas fee or the transaction fees collected by the nodes are also taken into account for the evaluation of probability. More the total blocks mined by a node and the higher the staking amount greater the probability of winning the election. Once a node is elected it has the authority to into blocks, once the blocks are mined they are broadcasted to the network for verification when the majority of nodes approve the iced block it is then added to the blockchain. In case a node is corrupted and provides invalid details its authenticity is reduced which in turn directly affects the possibility of a node to contest and win in the upcoming elections. The timeframe for reelection is fixed so that there would not be a need for elections to be held for every block creation. Thus this mechanism enhances the light weightless of the deployed blockchain system.

Blockchain-Based Decentralized Documentation System

PSEUDOCODE - SPARSE MERKLE TREE

```
FUNC getMerkleTreeRoot(data) INITIALIZE TXNS_DATA array
FOR i=0 to data length - 1
ADD JSON(data[i]) to TXNS_DATA[i] ENDFOR
INITIALIZE TXNS_HASH array
FOR i=0 to TXNS_HASH length - 1
ADD data[i]['txn_hash'] to TXNS_HASH[i] ENDFOR
INITIALIZE TXN_HASH
WHILE TXNS_HASH length > 1
IF TXNS_HASH length % 2 == 1
ADD TXNS_HASH[TXNS_HASH length - 1]
ENDIF
INITIALIZE TEMP_TXN_HASH
FOR i=0 to TXNS_HASH length + 2
ADD KECCAK_256(TXNS_HASH[i], null) to TEMP_TXN_HASH[i] ENDFOR
TXNS_HASH = TEMP_TXN_HASH ENDWHILE
RETURN TXN_HASH
```

A sparse merle tree is made up of several layers of leaves, where leaves in the lower level are filled with the hash value of the transaction along with null values, the values in the leaves are hashed and added upon to the adjacent leaves, and this forms the second layer with half the population of the leaves in the lower level, this process is done on repetition until we derive with a single hash value and that has value is called the merle root hash. Figure 9 shows the body part of the mined block contains the list of translations and other details, the final root hash prepared from the Sparse merle tree hash is added to the block header for robustness because even a minor change to the list of the transaction will produce a different root hash. A sparse merle tree helps in easy verification of transaction than an ordinary merle tree; this contributes a greater part towards scalability and reliability making the developed system delicate and robust.

PSEUDOCODE - VALIDATE CHAIN

```
FUNC validateChain(CHAIN)
INITIALIZE PREVIOUS_BLOCK = CHAIN[0] INITIALIZE BLOCK_ID = 1
WHILE BLOCK_ID < CHAIN length
INITIALIZE BLOCK = CHAIN[BLOCK_ID]
IF BLOCK.merkleTreeRoot != BLOCK.getMerkleTreeRoot(PREVIOUS_BLOCK.DATA)
return FALSE
ENDIF
SET BLOCK_ID += 1 PREVIOUS_BLOCK = BLOCK
```

```
ENDWHILE
return TRUE
```

Figure 9. Transaction details

The chain is validated before adding a block to the blockchain system. Once a block is mined by the elected node and got its approval from the validators the validated chain function is called in order to verify the legibility of the chain, once the authenticity of the chain is validated, the approved block is then added to the blockchain network.

TRANSACTION POOL

```
FUNC transactionPool(RAW_TXN) INITIALIZE TXN = JSON(RAW_TXN)
INITIALIZE TRANSACTION = Transaction(TXN["from"], TXN["to"], TXN["value"]) SET
TRANSACTION.setTimestamp(TXN["timestamp"])
IF TRANSACTION.verifyTimestamp(TXN["sign"], TXN["txn_hash"]) ADD RAW_TXN to
POOL
BROADCAST TXN ADDED to POOL
ENDIF BROADCAST RECEIVER
INITIALIZE BLOCK_FEES = getTransactionPoolFees(POOL)
IF CALC_MIN() < BLOCK_FEES and self.previousElectionWinner != NULL INITIALIZE
RES = MINEBLOCK(POOL)
SET POOL empty array BROADCAST BLOCK MINED
```

Blockchain-Based Decentralized Documentation System

Figure 10. Transaction pool

When a user buys or sells an asset, the transaction is triggered in the blockchain system, the list of transactions keep getting added to the transaction pool which is shown in Figure 10, and once enough transaction list are collected the elected node starts mining the block, meanwhile the transaction happening during the process of mining is stored or collected in the transaction pool, a transaction is added to a ledger only after the block is validated and added to the network. This pooling of transactions reduces the need for more blocks to be mined, making the chain a light weighed network. The developed system and the mobile application interface are given in Figure 11 and Figure 12.

RESULT

We have created an application that works on its blockchain network, alliance with various cryptographic techniques made the blockchain system robust, secure, and immutable. The presented application eliminates the need for human resources and centralized storage; instead, all the details of the transaction are stored in distributed network creating a decentralized platform for maintenance.

Figure 11. Developed system

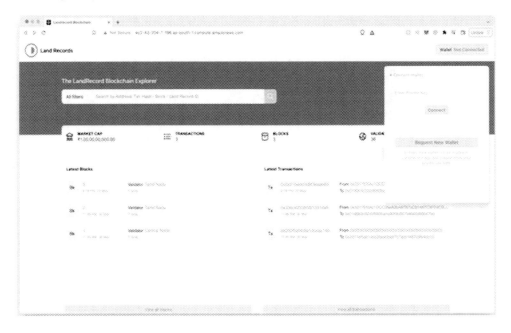

Blockchain-Based Decentralized Documentation System

Figure 12. Mobile application interface

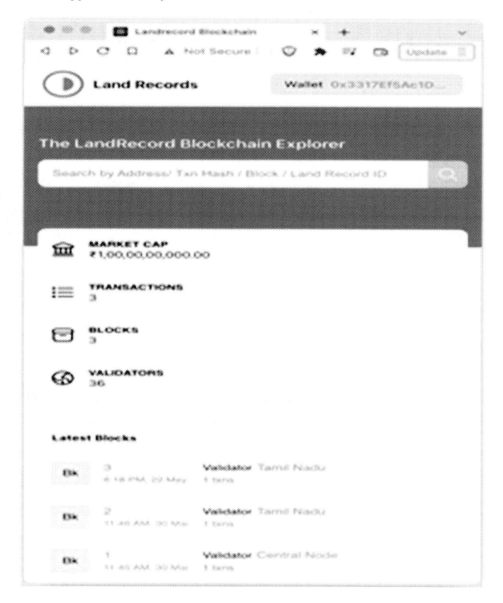

This would out-turn us the below mentioned perks:

- Time consumed for verification and transaction process is enormously reduced
- Details of proprietorship are authentic and accurate
- Problem with Re-issuing of documents becomes void as all the details are stored in blockchain.
- Prevents Forgery and money Laundering
- Updating or forking the Blockchain becomes a process of ease.

Table 3. Result comparison

	Public	**Private**	**Proposed**
Trade history recorded	Yes	Yes	Yes
Efficiency	Low	High	High
Forking	Hard	Easy	Easy
Centralised	No	Yes	Partial
Permission read	Public	Public	Restricted
Energy Consumption	High	Low	Low

The hybrid blockchain consensus makes the proposed system stand out in various aspects of comparison, the consensus stands midway between public and private blockchain giving it an advantage over both private and public blockchain. An elucidation was required to explain the fraudulence and forgery present in our present system, utilization of various cryptographic techniques makes the blockchain tamper- proof and immutable. The deployed blockchain application system creates a user friendly public platform for citizens and the government to store and authenticate registration documents.

The security is comparatively weaker than public blockchain architecture, because there may be cases where one or many of the nodes may get corrupted but keeping in mind the necessity to maintain the privacy of the asset details the Hybrid Blockchain system is implemented. The authenticity and security of blockchain increase along with the vast number of users, Transactions made by users contribute to the creation of blocks, the larger the number of blocks in blockchain networks harder the chance of intrusion. At present, the validators are assumed to be non- corrupted for the blockchain to survive at the start. So, the deployed project is assumed to have a large number of user entities and viable validators. Since Blockchain technology is in its infancy, a lot of improvement is needed to get it implemented in various sectors, but the technology has provided enough evidence to support that it is better than the present application system. The deployed system is just a skeletal product of how the implementation of a blockchain system could work in government sectors, improving the scalability could make it soon possible to be implemented in real time scenario.

CONCLUSION

As a result asset registration process become rapid, re-issuing of certificates are faster and easier, there is no need for physical documents to be stored and maintained, and double spending and money laundering on real estate become merely impossible. Digitalization of asset registration makes the process very transparent and simpler by providing security and preventing fraudulence. On comparing our deployed model with the existing land document system as well as with other blockchain mechanisms we have found that our model excels in efficiency, security, and scalability. But most substantial problem in IPFS networks is phishing. Phishing isn't a new problem, it is one of the most straightforward forms of hacking in the modern world of digitalization. It's common in the digital world, but its anonymous ability makes it lethal in the IPFS ecosystem. Hackers can easily scam users by uploading fake land details documents to public IPFS Node and pretend it to be legit. In the future implementation, we can build an IPFS Whitelisting portal where users can check the authenticity of the land records directly from the blockchain. Another way to counter phishing attacks is to use secure link validation using a secure hashing algorithm to hash a website and validate it to the orignal hash. In conclusion, the deployed project model is suitable to be implemented in any kind of organization and ensures security, authenticity and reliability. Since Blockchain technology is in its infancy, a lot of improvement is needed to get it implemented in various sectors, but the technology has provided enough evidence to support that it is better than the present application system. The deployed system is just a skeletal product of how the implementation of a blockchain system could work in government sectors, improving the scalability could make it soon possible to be implemented in real time scenario.

REFERENCES

Alam, K. M., Rahman, J. A., Tasnim, A., & Akther, A. (2020). A blockchain-based land title management system for Bangladesh. *Journal of King Saud University-Computer and Information Sciences.*

Andrian, H. R., & Kurniawan, N. B. (2018, October). Blockchain Technology and Implementation: A Systematic Literature Review. In *2018 International Conference on Information Technology Systems and Innovation (ICITSI)* (pp. 370-374). IEEE. 10.1109/ICITSI.2018.8695939

Dahlberg, R., Pulls, T., & Peeters, R. (2016). Efficient sparse Merkle trees: caching strategies and secure (non-) membership proofs. *Proceedings of the 21st Nordic Workshop on Secure Computer Systems (NORDSEC 2016).*

Desai, H., Kantarcioglu, M., & Kagal, L. (2019, July). A hybrid blockchain architecture for privacy-enabled and accountable auctions. In *2019 IEEE International Conference on Blockchain (Blockchain)* (pp. 34-43). IEEE. 10.1109/Blockchain.2019.00014

Ferrag, M. A., Derdour, M., Mukherjee, M., Derhab, A., Maglaras, L., & Janicke, H. (2018). Blockchain technologies for the internet of things: Research issues and challenges. *IEEE Internet of Things Journal*, 6(2), 2188–2204. doi:10.1109/JIOT.2018.2882794

Imam, I. T., Arafat, Y., Alam, K. S., & Aki, S. (2021, February). DOC-BLOCK: A Blockchain Based Authentication System for Digital Documents. In *2021 Third International Conference on Intelligent Communication Technologies and Virtual Mobile Networks (ICICV)* (pp. 1262-1267). 10.1109/ICICV50876.2021.9388428

Joshi, A. P., Han, M., & Wang, Y. (2018). A survey on security and privacy issues of blockchain technology. *Mathematical Foundations of Computing*, 1(2), 121–147. doi:10.3934/mfc.2018007

Khan, R., Ansari, S., Jain, S., & Sachdeva, S. (2020). Blockchain based land registry system using Ethereum Blockchain. *J. Xi'an Univ. Archit. Technol*, 3640-3648

Krishnapriya, S., & Sarath, G. (2020). Securing land registration using blockchain. *Procedia Computer Science*, 171, 1708–1715. doi:10.1016/j.procs.2020.04.183

Latifi, S., Zhang, Y., & Cheng, L. C. (2019, July). Blockchain-based real estate market: One method for applying blockchain technology in commercial real estate market. In *2019 IEEE International Conference on Blockchain (Blockchain)* (pp. 528-535). IEEE. 10.1109/Blockchain.2019.00002

Majumdar, M. A., Monim, M., & Shahriyer, M. M. (2020, June). Blockchain based land registry with delegated proof of stake (DPoS) consensus in Bangladesh. In *2020 IEEE Region 10 Symposium (TENSYMP)* (pp. 1756-1759). IEEE.

Mukne, H., Pai, P., Raut, S., & Ambawade, D. (2019, July). Land record management using hyperledger fabric and ipfs. In *2019 10th International Conference on Computing, Communication and Networking Technologies (ICCCNT)* (pp. 1-8). IEEE. 10.1109/ICCCNT45670.2019.8944471

Nakamoto, S. (2009). *Bitcoin: A Peer-to-Peer Electronic Cash System*. Academic Press.

Nyaletey, E., Parizi, R. M., Zhang, Q., & Choo, K. K. R. (2019, July). BlockIPFS-blockchain-enabled interplanetary file system for forensic and trusted data traceability. In *2019 IEEE International Conference on Blockchain (Blockchain)* (pp. 18-25). IEEE. 10.1109/Blockchain.2019.00012

Patel, K., Singh, N., Parikh, K., Kumar, K. S. S., & Jaisankar, N. (2014). Data security and privacy using data partition and centric key management in cloud. *International Conference on Information Communication and Embedded Systems (ICICES2014)*, 1-5. 10.1109/ICICES.2014.7033769

Rajput, S., Singh, A., Khurana, S., Bansal, T., & Shreshtha, S. (2019, February). Blockchain technology and cryptocurrenices. In 2019 Amity international conference on artificial intelligence (AICAI) (pp. 909-912). IEEE. doi:10.1109/AICAI.2019.8701371

Santhi, K., Zayaraz, G., & Vijayalakshmi, V. (2015). Resolving Aspect Dependencies for Composition of Aspects. *Arabian Journal for Science and Engineering*, 40(2), 475–486. doi:10.100713369-014-1454-3

Sendhil Kumar, K. S., Anbarasi, M., Shanmugam, G. S., & Shankar, A. (2020). Efficient Predictive Model for Utilization of Computing Resources using Machine Learning Techniques. *2020 10th International Conference on Cloud Computing, Data Science & Engineering (Confluence)*, 351-357. 10.1109/Confluence47617.2020.9057935

Shinde, D., Padekar, S., Raut, S., Wasay, A., & Sambhare, S. S. (2019, September). Land Registry Using Blockchain-A Survey of existing systems and proposing a feasible solution. In *2019 5th International Conference On Computing, Communication, Control And Automation (ICCUBEA)* (pp. 1-6). IEEE. 10.1109/ICCUBEA47591.2019.9129289

Shuaib, M., Daud, S. M., Alam, S., & Khan, W. Z. (2020). Blockchain-based framework for secure and reliable land registry system. *Telkomnika*, 18(5), 2560–2571. doi:10.12928/telkomnika.v18i5.15787

Thakur, V., Doja, M. N., Dwivedi, Y. K., Ahmad, T., & Khadanga, G. (2020). Land records on blockchain for implementation of land titling in India. *International Journal of Information Management*, 52, 101940. doi:10.1016/j.ijinfomgt.2019.04.013

Yadav, A. S., & Kushwaha, D. S. (2021). Digitization of land record through blockchain-based consensus algorithm. *IETE Technical Review*, 1–18.

Yadav, Shikha, Gupta, & Kushwaha. (2021). The efficient consensus algorithm for land record management system. In *IOP Conference Series: Materials Science and Engineering* (Vol. 1022, No. 1, p. 012090). IOP Publishing.

Zheng, Z., Xie, S., Dai, H., Chen, X., & Wang, H. (2017, June). *An overview of blockchain technology: Architecture, consensus, and future trends. 2017 IEEE international congress on big data (BigData congress).*

Chapter 21
Brain–Machine Interface and Blockchain in Avatar-Based Systems

Rinat Galiautdinov
Independent Researcher, Italy

ABSTRACT

The main purpose of this research is to provide a solution that allows neuroscientists and developers to keep the track of the neurosignals of live beings or biologically simulated neural networks and store them having the ability to guarantee that output of neurosignal translation was correct and can be reproduced later on any other biologically simulated neuron. Such a situation is especially important for the case when producers of different equipment, which are based on the biologically simulated neurons, can predict its behavior and guarantee that it will have accepted level of output deviations. Such a situation can be used for tracking live neurosignals of a beings and then reproduce them on avatars or different types of robots, neural networks, etc.

INTRODUCTION

Future producers of different equipment based on biologically simulated neurons will face with the problem where they have to be able: a) to predict the output of neurons based on their input b) reproduce such the output based on the well known inputs and consequently guarantee that deviation of output is in the acceptable range. And for such the purpose it will be necessary to provide a mechanism of storing the input signals providing guarantee that such the signals have never been altered. This approach could be applied not only in some neuron-based gadgets but also in Avatars where such the guarantee is extremely important. Thus as a saving mechanism we could consider blockchain. A blockchain is a data structure which guarantees that none of its element has never been altered and it can be confirmed by digital signatures and blocks' hashes. Currently blockchain is used mostly in crypto-currency sphere although there are some attempts of apply blockchain to the other spheres such as voting, bookkeeping documents, etc. The guaranteed backlog of neurosignals is going to be on demand soon because such

DOI: 10.4018/978-1-6684-7455-6.ch021

Brain-Machine Interface and Blockchain in Avatar-Based Systems

the data will be widely analyzed by Big Data and used in many sphere from scientific and medical researches to applied "templates" where certain set of the signals could be considered as a template and might be reused or spotted in the frame of another kind of research.

Over a decade a new term blockchain is known as a technology which is used as distributed database which keeps the track of financial transactions of different types of crypto-currencies, such as BTC, ETH, etc. All the payments or financial transactions go via peer-to-peer network which allows to decentralized the participants of the network granting them equal, from the network point of view, privileges and consequently such the network architecture is different from a regular client-server architecture where all the clients depend on the server: in the other words, if server is down then no client can connect to it and consequently make any type of transaction. Bitcoin officially was the first globally known crypto-currency, although the very first one appeared in the beginning of 90s. The Bitcoin blockchain contains only financial transactions and nothing else. However blockchain can be used for storing not only financially related data and thus it means blockchain can be applied and use in many different spheres. The typical structure of blockchain is represented by the number of the linked blocks where each block contains not only a useful data(in the case of bitcoin it could be the financial transactions) but also a reference to the previous block and a digital signature. This a very simple description of how blockchain looks like. In real world it's a bit more complicated and could even include some machine related instructions or smart contracts. The blockchain can be stored either on a single machine and this is the case for so called Scrooge coin, or it could be shared among multiple nodes where each node is represented by machine. The sharing of a blockchain could be useful when it is necessary to increase the trust level to some product/instrument: in the case of Bitcoin it is a financial instrument, so it makes sense to increase its trust level among the users. But this is not a must and in this case blockchain could be private serving as a special type of a database.

The Principals of Work of the Nervous System

Synapses are used to transfer a signal from one neuron to another neuron or a muscle's cell. During the time when information goes on a neuron it goes as an electric signal (action potential - AP) but when AP reaches the axon ending then axon emits neurotransmitter (NT), in ~80% it's either Acid – Glu or Gamma Aminobutyric acid –GABA, ~20% are covered by 20+ types of neurotransmitters. Then this neurotransmitter effects on the next neuron. The picture demonstrates it in Figure 1.

Figure 1. Demonstrates the work of neurotransmitters

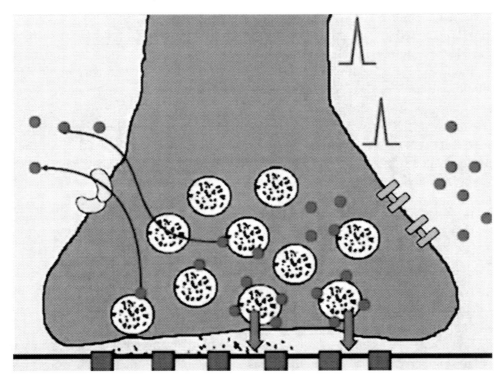

All this is called the synapse. And the work of synapse can be described in the following way:

Initially the AP goes along the surface of the membrane, then the AP starts the process of launching the vesicles with the neurotransmitters and they eject the neurotransmitters when they reach synaptic cleft (SC). This SC does not allow AP "to jump" to the next nerve-cell. And this is very important. So in the work of the neurons we do not have a pure electric signal, we have electrochemical signal.

AP lasts for about 1ms. Neurotransmitters effect on postsynaptic receptor proteins. These postsynaptic receptor proteins cause either irritation(in the case of ion input of Na+) or deceleration (in the case of ion input of Cl-) of the following nerve-cell. The irritation may lead to appearance of the AP and deceleration blocks or slows down the appearance of the AP.

Here we need to understand how the AP gets transformed into the movements of the neurotransmitters. There are ions of Ca^{2+} around the axon ending, demonstrating on Figure 2.

Figure 2. Demonstrates the work of neurotransmitters in the synaptic cleft and the work of vesicles

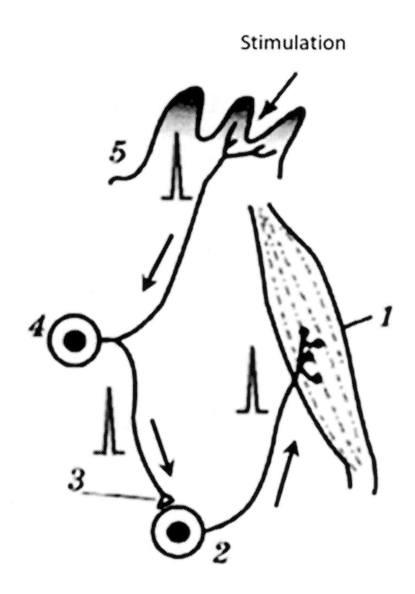

So when the AP comes, it opens (for the duration of 2-3ms) the special "calcium channels" (marked by green color on the picture), and then the ions of Ca^{2+} come inside of the axon ending and stick to the vesicles. The vesicles contain the neurotransmitters. In a normal situation there is no Ca inside of the axon ending, it goes inside only when the AP comes. The vesicles have special motor proteins and a vesicle starts moving when it catches 4 ions of Ca^{2+}. A vesicle will not move until it catches 4 ions of Ca^{2+}. The vesicle blow out when they reach the synaptic cleft after that the neurotransmitters get released and "jump" via the synaptic cleft on the synapses membrane of either dendrite(a regular case, when axon gets connected with dendrite) or axon(more rear case when axon is connected with another axon) or directly on another neuron(extremely rear case when axon is connected directly with another neuron). The vesicles with less caught number of Calcium's ions will start moving next time when they catch the missing number of them. However it is important to understand that once the ions of Calcium get inside of the axon ending the special pump-proteins (grey colored on the picture) start their work for throwing calcium ions back. Why it is important? Because if the calcium will not be removed then it will jump from one vesicle to another which will create the endless and increasing AP. In a practical situation this would lead either to epilepsy or death. All this gives us the understanding of the process called "Summation" which is necessary for understanding of the whole work-flow (Jin et al., 2018; Abbott & Kandel, 2019; Choi Yet al., 2020).

Let's imagine the situation when some weak AP comes: it's not necessary that such the signal will be transferred to the next nerve-cell. But if the nerve-cell catches the series of such the weak APs then it might reach the level when the signal will be transferred to another nerve-cell. It can be observed in Figure 3.

Figure 3. Demonstrates the workflow of a signal from the point of stimulation to the point of muscle reaction

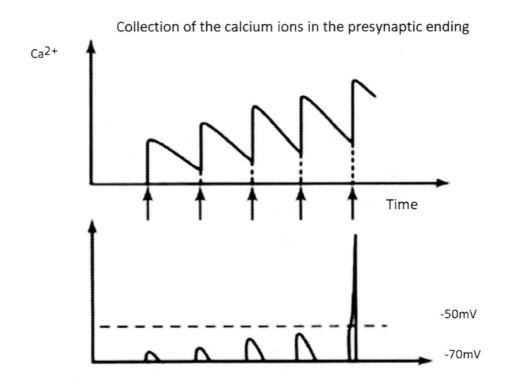

On this picture we can see the nerve system of the mollusk called aplysia. So when we stimulate the sensor (5) it sends the AP to the sensor neuron (4). The signal will not move to the next neuron in the neural circuit if the signal is weak. But if we send the series of such the weak signals (or if we send

Brain-Machine Interface and Blockchain in Avatar-Based Systems

a single strong signal) it will make the neuron(4) to transfer the signal to the next neuron(2 – which is a motor neuron) which will effect on the muscle making it to work. It's also important to note that the interval of time between several weak signals should not be too long, for example if we send a repeatable weak signal with the interval of 10 seconds it will eventually transfer the signal to the next neuron. The described mechanism depends on collecting of calcium ions in the presynaptic endings (Lee, 2020). It's shown in Figure 4.

Figure 4. Demonstrates the collection of the calcium ions in the presynaptic ending

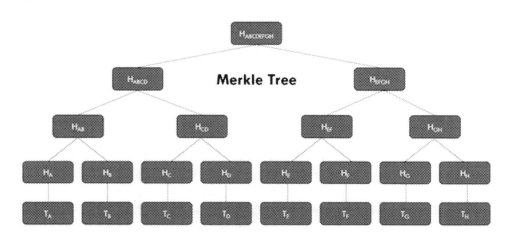

Here on the graph we can see that after we send a weak signal the calcium ions get inside of the synaptic ending, however the pump-proteins start their work which effects on reduction of the calcium ions. Then we can see the series of the weak signals which effect on increasing of the number of the calcium ions in the synaptic ending and eventually when the AP reaches the level of -50mV the signal gets generated and effects on the next neuron (The usual electric charge of the neuron is on the level of -70mV). The sudden growth of the AP happens because some vesicle already caught some calcium ions(and we remember that they need 4 of them to start moving) (Raeva et al., 2019).

The described above process can pass on any synapses, however there is another process called Long lasting potentiation which can pass only on the synapses with NMDA receptors (reacting on Glutamic Acid – Glu). Considering the synapses with the NMDA receptors we have to understand that if we send a weak signal it will not transfer it. It will start working only if we send a strong enough signal and after that the neuron would be able to react even on a weak signal. Such the state of the neuron could last for hours.

The principal of work of NMDA synapses is the following: the receptor protein contains the "tunnel" which is initially blocked by the ions of Mg^{2+}. So when we send a strong enough AP of at least -30mV(the max value is +30mV) and the neurotransmitters reach it, the receptor "spits out" the ion of Mg^{2+}. Starting from this moment the tunnel is free and the ions of Na^+ can pass. After this the neuron would react even on a weak signal until the ion of Mg^{2+} returns back, which could take hours (Galiautdinov & Mkrttchian, 2019a, 2019b; Galiautdinov, 2020).

Usually the ratio of NMDA to Non-NMDA receptors is 10: 1. However such the NMDA synapses do not exist everywhere in the brain, mostly in the special parts only. Most of all they exist in hippocampus where it's widely used in so called "the circle of Papez" (which is similar to the RAM of your PC).

RESEARCH AND SOLUTION BASED ON THE BRAIN MACHINE INTERFACE

Methods to Distinguish Glu and GABA (Used in the Major Experiments)

The most simple way would probably be the usage of litmus where the difference could be easily detected on the basis of carboxyl group's number. In the experiments the author used the following approach:

The method for assay determination of some amino acids in the joint presence of and in combination with natural bioactive components by high performance liquid chromatography (HPLC) in the reversed - phase variant with UV detection. The methodology is based on pre-derivatization of amino acids by phenylisothiocyanate (Smirnova et al., 2019). As an example, for detection of Glu, as the mobile phase a mixture of acetonitrile and ammonium acetate was used. The wave length of detection was 254 nm. It is established that the relative error of determination does not exceed 0.3% for glutamic acid. The content of the substance was detected by High performance liquid chromatography with the help of liquid chromatography Shi-madzu possessing fluorescence detector RF-10Axl.

For preparation of the mobile phase to detect GABA, it was used acetonitrile and a buffer system consisting of monosubstituted potassium phosphate 50tMol, pH 4.65 with the ratio 12:88. The substance was fixed at a wavelength of extinction of 210nm and the wave's length of the emission equal to 285nm. The identification of the test substance and calculation of its concentration was defined according to the method of absolute standards. The method of absolute calibration was used for quantity detection of the substance. The dependence of peak areas on the concentration of the GABA derivative was analyzed by regression analysis (Simonyan et al., 2020).

Blockchain Adopted for Neurosignals

To measure and store the input data first we need to identify the source where we are going to makes the measures and then to identity the blockchain structure used for storing the data.

The most obvious source of data measurement is a synaptic cleft which counts the passed neurotransmitters and the time when it happened.

Thus the data structure could be represented in the following way (in C#):

```
enum NeuroType { Glu, GABA };
class NeuroData {
      public Guid SourceId {get; set;}
      public DateTime DtAt {get; set;}
      public NeuroType NeuroType {get; set;}
      public int SignalCount  {get; set;}
      public byte[] Hash {get; set;}
}
```

And for every range of timestamp we will have the number of the instances of NeuroData.

Consequently we can name the range of timestamp as a Bucket. The structure of a bucket could be implemented in the following way:

```
classMerkleTree
{
privateNeuroData data;
privateint count;
private Tree left;
private Tree right;
}
class Bucket {
        public Guid Id {get; set;}
        public Guid PrevId {get; set;}
        public DateTime DtFormedAt {get; set;}
        public byte[] BucketHash {get; set;}
        public int Count  {get; set;}
        public MerkleTree Tree {get; set;}
        public byte[] Signature {get; set;}
        public byte[] PublicKey {get; set;}
}
```

The structure of the data is kept in so called Merkle Tree which is represented as a general Tree structure. The advantage of the provided structure reduces the time for calculation of a Tree hash because instead of iterating each node in the tree, we can iterate only the updated sub nodes and then update the Bucket Hash.

Figure 5. Demonstrates the Merkle tree

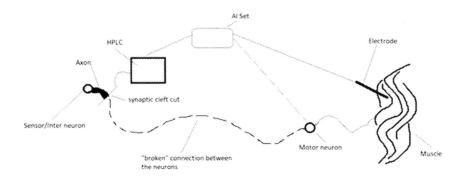

Every Neuro Data has its own Source Id which is basically an identified synaptic cleft from which we are going to collect the data.

The DateTime is a date/time stamp. The NeuroType is represented by the type of a neurotransmitter (for the given example we are considering only Glu and GABA, however this list can be easily increased). The SignalCount field collects the number of the neurotransmitters passed at the given timestamp. The Hash is a byte array (or it could also be represented as a string), which contains the calculated hash for the given data. In order to calculate a hash we can use any well known and reliable hash functions such as SHA256, etc.

Each bucket contains the Id, a reference to Id of a previous Bucket, the Merkle Tree which is based on the received instances of NeuroData. The DtFormedAt field (more exactly: a property in our case) contains the date/time when the Bucket was formed. The Count field represents the number of the elements in a tree. The BucketHash is a hash calculated based on the hashes of the MerkleTree's nodes. Finally each formed bucket contains a public key and a digital signature which signs the bucket's hash which is built on the basis of the Merkle Tree's hash and the fields of the bucket, such as: Id, PrevId, DtFormedAt. The result of this can be then stored as a serious of flat files on a drive.

Experiment of Neurotransmitter Detection and Analysis and Storing of the Data in a Blockchain and Repeating the Steps Using Blockchain

Here the author describes his own approach and the experimental part which proves that this is a working approach. Usually the reason of paralysis is that a signal of the neuron somewhere in the brain can't reach the motor-neuron which effects on the muscle. Strictly speaking the signal gets stopped somewhere because of the biological injury.

Consequently in order to resolve this problem it's necessary to catch the AP either in the source point or somewhere on its way to the destination and either simulate it effecting on the motor neuron or simulate directly the muscle based on the signal and type the neuron sent. However we can't just measure the electric charge somewhere and reproduce the same electric charge in the destination point: such the approach has a dead end, not accurate and will not work the way we need.

Before we make any kind of the signal interpretation it's necessary to understand the type of the neurotransmitters causing the signal (~80%: either Glu or GABA, ~20% the other types of neurotransmitters with the count of 20+), the strength of the signal (to distinguish the type of the running process: summation, long lasting potentiation) and the source point of the signal.

It's impossible to find out what kind of neurotransmitters are involved into the signal by checking only the AP of big enough and random areas of a brain. It is required to have some indicator within the synaptic cleft in order to find out this. This indicator would chemically evaluate the neurotransmitters types in the synaptic cleft and the time interval they get in. Another indication which is necessary for resolving the task is the detection of what kind of receptors are used: NMDA or Non-NMDA, but this could be resolved by the analysis of the caught transmitters.

For the experiment the author took aplysia (a mollusk) and considered the reflex chain of 24 sensor neurons leading to 6 motor neurons of the gills. However in this particular experiment it's not necessary to consider the whole chain, it would be enough to limit the consideration to only 2 linked neurons: one sensor neuron and one motor neuron. The difference of the author's experiment and the experiment of Professor Eric Kandel is enclosed in the following: the author's goal was not to research the process of summation, but to catch the emitted neurotransmitters and estimate whether the analysis of the neurotransmitters would allow to evaluate the running process and effect on the muscle.

Brain-Machine Interface and Blockchain in Avatar-Based Systems

However gathering the information about the neurotransmitters is something what could be quite difficult to do at the current level of technology. The most modern indicator has a width of around 80nm which is too much for a synaptic cleft which has a width of 10-50nm.

Thus taking into the account the current level of technology, we can't insert some indicator inside of a synaptic cleft of a working synapse. That's why the author decided to use another approach: instead of inserting the indicator inside of a synaptic cleft, the author cut the synapse on a level of its synaptic cleft and placed a piece of glass on a distance of 40nm from the cut, so that this piece of glass would simulate some kind of a postsynaptic membrane. Additionally, for the experimental part the author connected the neuron with the electrode in order to measure the AP. Then the author stimulated the sensor neuron effecting on the gills which led to emission of neurotransmitters on a glass playing the role of a postsynaptic membrane. The analysis of the chemical substance was then done with the help of HPLC described in (2.1).

This experiment allowed the author to catch the neurotransmitters of the synapse when it was working and detect the type of the emitted neurotransmitters. During the experiment the distance between the synaptic cut and the glass was varied between 10-40nm. The best result was achieved on a distance of 10-15nm.

In the initial sets of experiments the author's goal was to prove with the experiment that catching of the neurotransmitters could be done and the caught neurotransmitters could be defined. All this was proved by the experiment. The analysis showed the ability to distinguish the neurotransmitters and to define Glu ($C_5H_9NO_4$) in this particular experiment.

Catching the neurotransmitters allowed the author to assess the type of the neurotransmitters used and the approximate quantity. The further potential experiments with the quantity of neurotransmitters are quite useful and would allow to distinguish the running process: summation or long lasting potentiation.

The data was analyzed according to the described above method for assay determination of some amino acids in the joint presence of and in combination with natural bioactive components by high performance liquid chromatography (HPLC) in the reversed - phase variant with UV detection.

Then the data was automatically stored in the database and contained 3 fields for each experiment: the approximate quantity of the neurotransmitters, the type of the neurotransmitter and the value of the AP on the electrode. The running application allowed to find the correlation between the quantity and the AP and make prediction of the following result.

During the experiment the author was unable to measure directly the passed neurotransmitters in a synaptic cleft, so instead the author used some the approximate calculation based on the average number of the neurotransmitters passing per second. The result was written into a local blockchain using the following used methods:

This method is used to add a new data to the tree:

```
publicvoid Insert(NeuroData value)
        {
if (this.value == null)
this.value = value;
else
            {
if (this.value.CompareTo(value) == 1)
                {
```

```
if (left == null)
this.left = new Tree();
            left.Insert(value);
        }
elseif (this.value.CompareTo(value) == -1)
        {
if (right == null)
this.right = new Tree();
            right.Insert(value);
        }
else
thrownew Exception("Node already exists ");
    }
this.count = Recount(this);
    }
```
And this method is used to find the proper node:
```
public Tree Search(NeuroData value)
    {
if (this.value == value)
returnthis;
elseif (this.value.CompareTo(value) == 1)
        {
if (left != null)
returnthis.left.Search(value);
else
thrownew Exception("The node does not exist");
        }
else
        {
if (right != null)
returnthis.right.Search(value);
else
thrownew Exception("The node does not exist ");
        }
    }
```
And this method is used to recount the tree
```
privateint Recount(Tree t)
    {
int count = 0;
if (t.left != null)
            count += Recount(t.left);
        count++;
if (t.right != null)
            count += Recount(t.right);
```

Brain-Machine Interface and Blockchain in Avatar-Based Systems

```
        return count;
    }
```

The methods used for making and checking a digital signature depend on the used cryptography method, so the author used Elliptic Curves for this purpose. The advantage of such the method is enclosed in the fact that having the same or even more level of protection than RSA, the method uses shorter keys.

Below is the simplified version of the software code (written in Python and using Tensor Flow), based on Artificial Intelligence, where the author is able to find the correlation between the input data and where the author makes a prediction of the following result. Here's the simplified code:

```python
import tensorflow as tf
import numpy as np
import matplotlib.pyplot as plt
import xlrd
FILE_NAME = 'inputdata.xls'
#reading the data:
book = xlrd.open_workbook(FILE_NAME, encoding_override="utf-8")
sheet = book.sheet_by_index(0)
data = np.asarray([sheet.row_values(i) for i in range(1, sheet.nrows)])
#create placeholders for input X and Y:
X = tf.placeholder(tf.float32, name='X')
Y = tf.placeholder(tf.float32, name='Y')
#create weight and bias:
w = tf.Variable(0.0, name='Weights')
b = tf.Variable(0.0, name='Bias')
#model to predict Y:
Y_predicted = X * w + b
#square the error to calculate the loss:
loss = tf.square(Y - Y_predicted, name='Loss')
#train to minimize the loss:
optimizer = tf.train.GradientDescentOptimizer(learning_rate=0.001).minimize(loss)
with tf.Session() as sess:
    sess.run(tf.global_variables_initializer())
    #train the model 100 times
    for i in range(100):
        total_loss = 0
        for x, y in data:
            _, l = sess.run([optimizer, loss], feed_dict={X: x, Y: y})
            total_loss += l
        print ('Epoch {0}: {1}'.format(i, total_loss / sheet.nrows))
    #output weight and bias:
    w_value, b_value = sess.run([w, b])
#display the results:
```

```
X, Y = data.T[0], data.T[1]
plt.plot(X, Y, 'bo', label='Real data')
plt.plot(X, X*w_value+b_value, 'r', label='Predicted data')
plt.legend()
plt.show()
```

The collection of the data allowed the author to create another program which allows to estimate the AP based on the quantity of the caught neurotransmitter. And for this program we do not need any AP as an input parameter, it accepts only 2 parameters: the type of neurotransmitter and the quantity.

Experiment Effecting on Motor Neuron and Reproducing the Same Experiment on a Simulated Biological Neuron Using Blockchain

We know that in a calm situation the AP of a membrane is in the range of [-70, -90]mV. And it starts a "competition" between 2 major strengths (increasing or decreasing the AP) when the nerve circuit works.

In order to better understand this: let's presume that there are several oppositely directed forces effect on the neuron. As an example we might have 3 "exciting" neurons(Glu) and 2 "slowing down/stopping"(GAMMA) they all are connected to another neuron (S), in this case the neuron (S) would work only according to the principal "Aut Caesar aut nihil", which means: all the input signal will be summarized and the neuron (S) would behave only according to the received summarized signal, which means: if "exciting" neurons "win": the neuron (S) would send an "exciting" signal only if 3 input "exciting" signals "win", otherwise – no signal will be sent.

In the next set of experiments the author connected the electrode to the motor neuron and sent the series of APs with the goal to reach the level of -50ms and the muscle contraction was detected. Based on all the previously described experiment the author built the following architecture which is the solution against paralysis, shown in Figure 6.

Figure 6. Demonstrates the author's solution used against paralysis

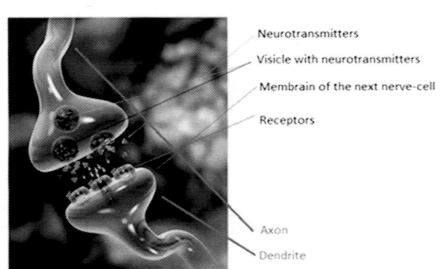

The picture shows the "initial" neuron (IN) (it could be either a sensor neuron or even some inter neuron) and there is a "broken" connection between this neuron and the motor neuron (due to disease or injury). The picture also shows the artificially made cut of the "wealthy" axon of the (IN) and adjusted glass on a distance of ~40nm from the cut. The HPLC is connected with the AI Set which collects the data from it, processes the data and based on the initially loaded data from the DB identifies:

1. The type of neurotransmitter (Glu, GABA)
2. The AP which should correspond to the received quantity of neurotransmitters

After that the AI Set decides whether it should send a signal or not and if yes it sends a signal to the electrode connected with the muscle. The muscle receives the signals and reacts. In the case if motor neuron (connected with the muscle) is still alive then the signal should be sent directly to the motor neuron instead of the muscle.

It's necessary to underline that the usage of HPLC is not the only way to achieve the same result. It's possible to use the other methods (even based on chemical reactions, etc) to distinguish the type of neurotransmitter. Thus the HPLC was used in this architecture as a replaceable block. Also the benefit of this architecture is that at the current stage it's obviously quite big and not mobile and takes time to get the results, however it can evolve with time: the replaceable block will surely become smaller and more mobile and the time used for neurotransmitters evaluation will be reduced.

It's also necessary to ad that during the experiment the cut of the synaptic cleft was 24 hours "fresh" and it was not tested how long it could be used: this is a goal of the following experiments.

The experiment showed and proved that with the specified architecture it's possible to:

- Distinguish the type of the signal based on the used neurotransmitters(Glu/GABA)
- Calculate the power of the AP which is required for the work of the muscle
- Make the muscle to properly work in the situation when there is no connection between a muscle and the sensor/inter neuron.

The solution takes into consideration 2 major neurotransmitters: Glu and GABA(and can potentially consider 20+ of them).

The experiment showed that such the architecture does not blindly send some unknown signal, it sends only the proper signal and only based on the results of neurotransmitters' analysis. To reproduce the experiment on a biologically simulated neuron, the author used his own neuron constructor app which allows to model simulated biological neurons and arrange the links between them and effect on them using different types of signals.

The constructed virtual model contained the same structure as a live one: 2 neurons (moto-neuron and sensor neuron) instead of the virtual muscle to generate the signals the author used the populated blockchain with the data from the previous experiment and sent its data to the virtual sensor neuron. The virtual sensor neuron processed the data and simulated summation process effecting on a virtual moto-neuron the same way it effected on a live moto-neuron.

As a result of this experiment the author found that the data from a live neuron can be digitized, stored in a blockchain and reproduced on unlimited number of virtually simulated models consuming biological neurons having the same result as it was noted during a physical experiment.

SUMMARY

In this article the author proved that based on analysis of the neurotransmitter, demonstrated in this research, it's possible to get the proper interpretation of a brain signal and effect on the muscle even in the situation when neural circuit is corrupted. After that the author provided a solution for gathering neurosignals in the synaptic cleft and storing them in a blockchain, after which the author demonstrated that collected data can't be altered and the neuron output can be then reproduced on any other biologically simulated neurons reducing the level of output deviations.

The purpose of this research to provide a solution which allows neuroscientists and developers to keep the track of the neurosignals of live beings or biologically simulated neural networks storing them and having the ability to guarantee that output of neurosignal translation was correct and can be reproduced later on any other biologically simulated neuron was proved during the number of the experiments. Such the situation is especially important for the case when producers of different equipment which are based on the biologically simulated neurons can predict its behavior and guarantee that it will have accepted level of output deviations. Such the situation can be used for tracking live neurosignals of a live being and then reproduced on Avatars or different types of robots, neural networks, etc. And this is also a future research path.

REFERENCES

Abbott, L. F., & Kandel, E. R. (2019). A computational approach enhances learning in Aplysia. *Nature Neuroscience*, *15*(2), 178–179. doi:10.1038/nn.3030 PMID:22281713

Choi, Y. B., Li, H. L., Kassabov, S. R., Jin, I., Puthanveettil, S. V., Karl, K. A., Lu, Y., Kim, J. H., Bailey, C. H., & Kandel, E. R. (2020). Neurexin-neuroligin transsynaptic interaction mediates learning-related synaptic remodeling and long-term facilitation in aplysia. *Neuron*, *70*(3), 468–481. doi:10.1016/j.neuron.2011.03.020 PMID:21555073

Galiautdinov, R. (2020). *Brain machine interface: the accurate interpretation of neurotransmitters' signals targeting the muscles. International Journal of Applied Research in Bioinformatics*. doi:10.4018/IJARB.2020010102

Galiautdinov, R., & Mkrttchian, V. (2019a). Math model of neuron and nervous system research, based on AI constructor creating virtual neural circuits: Theoretical and Methodological Aspects. In V. Mkrttchian, E. Aleshina, & L. Gamidullaeva (Eds.), *Avatar-Based Control, Estimation, Communications, and Development of Neuron Multi-Functional Technology Platforms* (pp. 320–344). IGI Global. doi:10.4018/978-1-7998-1581-5.ch015

Galiautdinov, R., & Mkrttchian, V. (2019b). Brain machine interface – for Avatar Control & Estimation in Educational purposes Based on Neural AI plugs: Theoretical and Methodological Aspects. In V. Mkrttchian, E. Aleshina, & L. Gamidullaeva (Eds.), *Avatar-Based Control, Estimation, Communications, and Development of Neuron Multi-Functional Technology Platforms* (pp. 345–360). IGI Global. doi:10.4018/978-1-7998-1581-5.ch016

Jin, I., Udo, H., Rayman, J. B., Puthanveettil, S., Kandel, E. R., & Hawkins, R. D. (2018). Spontaneous transmitter release recruits postsynaptic mechanisms of long-term and intermediate-term facilitation in Aplysia. *Proceedings of the National Academy of Sciences of the United States of America*, *109*(23), 9137–9142. doi:10.1073/pnas.1206846109 PMID:22619333

Lee, S. H., Kwak, C., Shim, J., Kim, J. E., Choi, S. L., Kim, H. F., Jang, D. J., Lee, J. A., Lee, K., Lee, C. H., Lee, Y. D., Miniaci, M. C., Bailey, C. H., Kandel, E. R., & Kaang, B. K. (2020). A cellular model of memory reconsolidation involves reactivation-induced destabilization and restabilization at the sensorimotor synapse in Aplysia. *Proceedings of the National Academy of Sciences of the United States of America*, *109*(35), 14200–14205. doi:10.1073/pnas.1211997109 PMID:22893682

Raeva, S. N., Vainberg, N. A., Dubynin, V. A., Tsetlin, I. M., Tikhonov, Y. N., & Lashin, A. P. (2019). Changes in the spike activity of neurons in the ventrolateral nucleus of the thalamus in humans during performance of a voluntary movement. Neuroscience and Behavioral Physiology, 29(5), 505-513.

Simonyan, E.V., Shikova, Y.V., & Khisamova, A.A. (2020). *Validation of assay method for certain amino acids in dosage forms by HPLC method.* Academic Press.

Smirnova, L.A., Riabuha, A.F., Kuznetsov, K.A., Suchkov, E.A., & Perfilova, V.N. (2019). *Development of method of quantitative determination of new GABA derivatives in biological samples.* Academic Press.

Chapter 22
The New Approach to the Architecture of Smart Contracts:
Its Impact on Performance, Vulnerability, Pollution, and Energy Saving Optimization

Rinat Galiautdinov
Independent Researcher, Italy

ABSTRACT

This research analyzes the problems of smart contracts and the whole concept of smart contracts and provides a solution that can resolve all such the issues in the current smart contract concept and additionally to this change the architecture used in smart contracts and blockchain. In this research, the author lists the issues, analyzes them, and provides the solution explaining how it will change the whole concept, performance, and what sort of positive impact it will have not only on the performance of smart contracts and their extensibility but also the impact on pollution and saving of energy.

INTRODUCTION

Over a decade a new term blockchain is known as a technology which is used as distributed database (Bernstein & Lange, 2016) which keeps the track of financial transactions of different types of cryptocurrencies (Brown, 2016), such as BTC, ETH, etc. All the payments or financial transactions go via peer-to-peer network which allows to decentralized the participants of the network granting them equal, from the network point of view, privileges and consequently such the network architecture is different from a regular client-server architecture where all the clients depend on the server: in the other words, if server is down then no client can connect to it and consequently make any type of transaction (Heuvel, 2014).

Blockchain technology introduced a new term: the smart contracts which were first proposed in 1990s by Nick Szabo (1997). The whole concept is quite simple: a smart contract is nothing but a computer program which checks different types of conditions and based on that decided which function(s) to run to perform the smart contract.

DOI: 10.4018/978-1-6684-7455-6.ch022

The New Approach to the Architecture of Smart Contracts

A typical schema of blockchain is shown in Figure 1.

Figure 1. A typical schema of blockchain

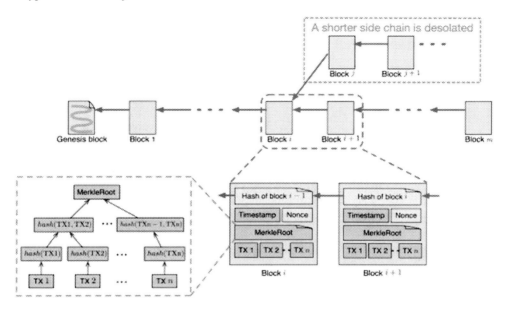

Bitcoin officially was the first globally known crypto-currency, although the very first one appeared in the beginning of 90s (Li et al., 2017). The Bitcoin blockchain contains only financial transactions and nothing else. The second well known cryptocurrency in this sphere was ETH which additionally introduced the term "smart contracts" into the blockchain world. A smart contract can be considered as a small program running on a blockchain when it receives a request (Nguyen, 2019). With the help of smart contracts the users could add additional logic not only to the financially related logic but also create very primitive games. At the same time, from the technical prospective, a smart contract is considered as a user who can receive and send transactions. This "user" has a record of different states, also known as variables and these variables stored in a blockchain can be changed and/or read. Reading a blockchain data is free for the users however is still very slow.

There are several reasons why reading data from a blockchain can be slow, one of them is the size of the blockchain itself. As the blockchain grows, the amount of data that needs to be processed and verified also grows. This can lead to longer transaction times and slower data retrieval.

Finally, the consensus mechanism used by the blockchain can also impact the speed of data retrieval. Some consensus mechanisms, such as proof-of-work, require complex mathematical calculations to be performed by the nodes in the network. These calculations can take time and slow down the overall performance of the blockchain.

Overall, reading data from a blockchain can be slow due to the decentralized nature of the technology, the size of the blockchain, and the consensus mechanism used. However, there are ongoing efforts to improve the scalability and speed of blockchain technology, such as the implementation of sharding and other scaling solutions.

However the change of variables (also called as a state change) is expensive (Zhang Rong, 2020). Why it's expensive: Every state change consumes funds (in Ether world known as gas), it also consumes quite a lot of time necessary for: a) making a transaction(a request for a state change), b) for processing such the transaction c) for building a transaction block which contains a new value for a smart contract. Thus in the Ether world, before the hard fork, the time for building a new block was 21 seconds, after the hard fork it still takes 12.5 seconds which is a lot in the world of IT (Mkrttchian et al., 2019).

Different crypto-currencies use different approaches to process the transactions.

Demonstrating acronyms of different types of transactions processing:

Proof of Work (PoW): A consensus algorithm that requires miners to solve complex mathematical equations to validate transactions and add them to the blockchain. It is energy-intensive and slow but provides high security.

Proof of Stake (PoS): A consensus algorithm that requires validators to hold a certain amount of cryptocurrency to validate transactions and add them to the blockchain. It is energy-efficient and faster than PoW but provides lower security.

Practical Byzantine-Fault Tolerance (PBFT): A consensus algorithm that allows a network of nodes to reach a consensus even if some of the nodes are malicious or faulty. It is fast and efficient but requires a high number of nodes.

Low Level Virtual Machine (LLVM): A compiler infrastructure that allows developers to write programs in high-level languages and compile them into machine code. It is widely used in the development of operating systems, programming languages, and other software.

Convolutional Neural Network (CNN): A type of deep learning algorithm that is used in image and video recognition, natural language processing, and other applications. It is designed to recognize patterns in data and learn from them.

Long Short-Term Memory (LSTM): A type of recurrent neural network that is used in speech recognition, language translation, and other applications. It is designed to remember long-term dependencies in data and avoid the problem of vanishing gradients.

Ether (ETH): The cryptocurrency used in the Ethereum blockchain. It is used to pay for transaction fees, smart contract execution, and other services on the network.

Bitcoin (BTC): The first and most well-known cryptocurrency. It is used as a store of value and a medium of exchange.

Ethereum Virtual Machine (EVM): A virtual machine that runs smart contracts on the Ethereum blockchain. It is designed to be Turing-complete, meaning that it can execute any program that can be written in any programming language.

Unspent Transaction Output (UTXO): A record of the unspent output of a transaction. It is used to prevent double-spending and ensure the integrity of the blockchain.

Internet of Things (IoT): A network of interconnected devices that are embedded with sensors, software, and other technologies. It allows for the exchange of data and communication between devices.

Distributed Autonomous Corporation (DAC): An organization that is run by smart contracts on a blockchain. It is designed to be decentralized, autonomous, and transparent.

Certificate Authority (CA): An entity that issues digital certificates that are used to verify the identity of users, devices, and organizations on the internet.

Delegated Proof of Stake (DPOS): A consensus algorithm that allows token holders to vote for delegates who will validate transactions and add them to the blockchain. It is faster than PoW and PoS but provides lower security.

WebAssembly (Wasm): A binary format that allows developers to write programs in any programming language and run them in web browsers. It is designed to be fast, efficient, and secure.

Border Gateway Protocol (BGP): A protocol that is used to exchange routing information between different networks on the internet. It is designed to ensure that data is transmitted efficiently and securely.

We can consider as an example a a smart contract between a buyer and a supplier. As demonstrated in Figure 2, a supplier first sends a product catalog to a buyer through the blockchain network. This catalog that includes product descriptions and all the other necessary details related to shipping and payment terms is stored and distributed in the blockchain so that a buyer can get the product information and verify the authenticity and reputation of the supplier at the same time. After that the buyer send the order with the specified quantity and payment date via the blockchain. This whole procedure forms a purchase contract (*i.e.*, *Contract 1*) enclosed in the blue box as shown in Figure 2. It is worth mentioning that the whole procedure is completed between the buyer and the supplier without the intervention of a third party.

The reasons of using smart contracts and their popularity were enclosed in the following:

- **Risks Optimization.** Due to conditional "immutability" of blockchains, smart contracts "cannot be" arbitrarily altered once they are issued (these issues will be discussed later on in the article). Moreover, all the transactions that are stored and duplicated throughout the whole distributed blockchain system are traceable and auditable. And finally, the result of all this: any malicious behaviors like financial frauds in theory can be greatly mitigated (however this is not always true).
- **Cutting Down Administration and Service Costs.** Block-chains assure the trust of the whole system by distributed consensus mechanisms without going through a central broker or a mediator. Smart contracts stored in blockchains can be automatically triggered in a decentralized way. Consequently, the administration and services costs due to the intervention from the third party can be significantly saved.
- **Improving the Efficiency of Business Processes.** The elimination of the dependence on the intermediary can significantly improve the efficiency of business process. Take the aforementioned supply-chain procedure as an example. The financial settlement will be automatically completed in a peer-to-peer manner once the predefined condition is met (*e.g.*, the buyer confirms the reception of the products). As a result, the turnaround time can be significantly reduced.
- **Transparency.** It happens by monitoring the transactions between the parties undertaking the contract in a blockchain. This ensures there is transparency between the transactions.
- **Manages Transactions.** As mentioned earlier, parties or companies cannot change the contract's agreement terms once it has gone live. This is useful in handling different transactions in the blockchain. Fast processing of transactions occurs since smart contracts utilize simple logic to perform that. Also, users are assured that their claims will be processed faster, leading to quick payouts.

- **Minimal paperwork.** Smart contracts ensure there will be less paperwork involved as it does not need the lawyers to set up an agreement. Also, less time is involved as no pre-contract talks are involved in the agreements.

Figure 2. Demonstrates an interaction between a buyer and a supplier using a smart contract

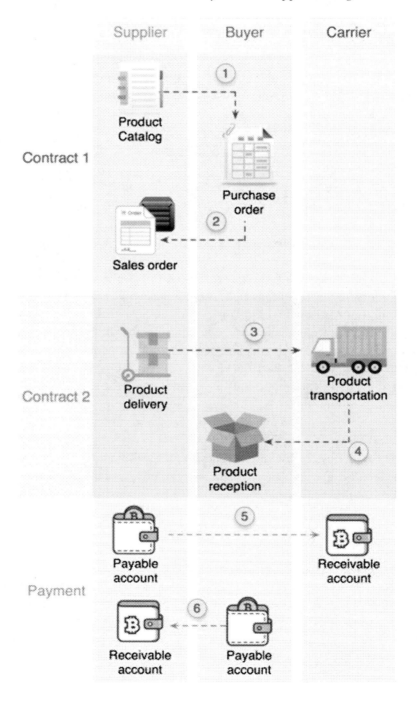

The New Approach to the Architecture of Smart Contracts

After *Contract 1* is done, the supplier will search for a carrier in the blockchain to complete the shipping phase. Like *Contract 1*, the carrier also publishes the shipping description (such as transportation fees, source, destination, capacity and shipping time) as well as shipping conditions and terms in the blockchain. If the supplier accepts the contract issued by the carrier, the products will be delivered to the carrier who will finally dispatch the products to the buyer. This whole procedure constructs *Contract 2* (enclosed in the pink box) as shown in Figure 2. Similarly, the whole procedure of *Contract 2* is also conducted without the intervention of a third party.

In addition to automatic execution of *Contract 1* and *Contract 2*, the payment procedures (including the payment from the supplier to the carrier and that from the buyer to the supplier) are also completed automatically. For example, once the buyer confirms the reception of the products, the payment between the buyer and the supplier will be automatically triggered as the predefined condition is met. The financial settlement from the buyer to the supplier is conducted via crypto currencies (*e.g.*, Bitcoin or Ether.1 .). In contrast to conventional transactions, the whole process is done in a peer-to-peer manner without the intervention of third parties like banks. As a result, the turnaround time and transactional cost can be greatly saved.

Figure 3. Shows the number of smart contracts created in Ethereum blockchain

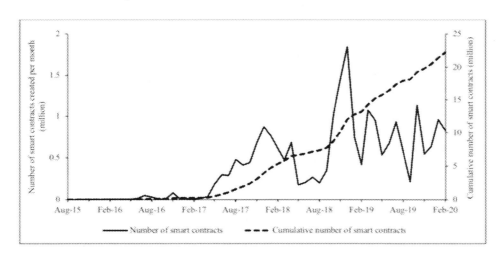

Smart contracts platforms:

Table 1. Comparison of smart contract platforms

	Ethereum	**Fabric**	**Corda**	**Stellar**	**Rootstock**	**EOS**
Execution environment	EVM	Docker	JVM	Docker	VM	WebAssembly
Language	Solidity, Serpent, LLL, Mutan	Java, Golang	Java, Kotlin	Python, JavaScript, Golang and PHP, etc.	Solidity	C++
Turing Completeness	Turing complete	Turing complete	Turing incomplete	Turing incomplete	Turing complete	Turing complete
Data model	Account-based	Key–value pair	Transaction-based	Account-based	Account-based	Account-based
Consensus	PoW	PBFT	Raft	Stellar Consensus Protocol (SCP)	PoW	BFT-DPOS
Permission	Public	Private	Private	Consortium	Public	Public

Smart contracts are also subjected to attacks, so in 2016 when the Decentralized Autonomous Organization (DAO) smart contract was manipulated to steal around 2 Million ETH (50 Million USD on the time) because of its re-entrancy vulnerability (Tasca Paolo, 2019). In addition to the vulnerability problem, smart contracts face several challenges including privacy, legal, and performance issues.

Below is one of the examples of re-entrancy attacks on a smart contract:

```
// SPDX-License-Identifier: MIT
pragma solidity ^0.8.0;
contract Auction {
    mapping(address => uint) public bidders;
    bool locked;
    function bid() external payable {
        bidders[msg.sender] += msg.value;
    }
    function refund() external {
        uint refundAmount = bidders[msg.sender];
        if (refundAmount > 0) {
            (bool success,) = msg.sender.call{value: refundAmount}("");
            require(success, "failed!");
            bidders[msg.sender] = 0;
        }
    }
    function currentBalance() external view returns(uint) {
        return address(this).balance;
    }
}
```

The New Approach to the Architecture of Smart Contracts

From the first glance at the smart contract the refund method has to get the value of the funds of a user and send him back his funds: *(bool success,) = msg.sender.call{value: refundAmount}(" ");*

After which the line *bidders[msg.sender] = 0;* marks that his current balance is 0.

And it seems to be ok and it was a regular application (not a smart contract of Etherium) it would work fine. But not in the world of Etherium.

Below is another smart contract which makes a re-entrancy attack on the Auction contract:

```
contract AuctionAttack {
    uint constant BID_AMOUNT = 1 ether;
    AuctionHacked auction;
    constructor(address _auction) {
        auction = AuctionHacked(_auction);
    }
    function proxyBid() external payable {
        require(msg.value == BID_AMOUNT, "incorrect");
        auction.bid{value: msg.value}();
    }
    function attack() external {
        auction.refund();
    }
    receive() external payable {
        if(auction.currentBalance() >= BID_AMOUNT) {
            auction.refund();
        }
    }
    function currentBalance() external view returns(uint) {
        return address(this).balance;
    }
}
```

What happens here is: an intruder first calls for a *proxyBid()* function to send some funds to the Action contract. Then the Action contract will receive this money and will make a record that a new user made a bid equal to some amount of the money. But then intruder calls for a *attack()* function which automatically calls a *refund()* function of the Action smart contract. The Action smart contract checks whether the user has the funds (yes) and tries to send them: *(bool success,) = msg.sender.call{value: refundAmount}(" ");* However in the world of smart contract of Etherium instead of making an update on the user's record making it 0, it will run the *receive()* function of an intruder which contains another request for the Action smart contract: *action.refund()* and as a result, the intruder will get all the money possessed by Auction smart contract.

This attack can be avoided if we make some changes in the Action smart contract:

```
modifier noReentrancy() {
    require(!locked, "no reentrancy!");
    locked = true;
```

477

```
        _;
        locked = false;
    }
    function refund() external noReentrancy {
        uint refundAmount = bidders[msg.sender];
        if (refundAmount > 0) {
            bidders[msg.sender] = 0;
            (bool success,) = msg.sender.call{value: refundAmount}("");
            require(success, "failed!");
        }
    }
}
```

However it's not obvious for the developers who came into the smart contracts world from the other spheres of software development.

There are a number of functional issues with incumbent smart contract platforms. We present several representative challenges:

1. Re-Entrancy. Means that the interrupted function can be safely recalled again. Malicious users may exploit this vulnerability to steal digital currency as indicated in (Li et al., 2017).

2. Block Randomness. Some smart contract applications such as lotteries and betting pools may require randomness of generated blocks. This can be achieved by generating pseudo-random numbers in a block timestamp or nonce. However, some malicious miners may fabricate some blocks to deviate from the outcome of the pseudo-random generator. In this way, attackers can control the probability distribution of the outcomes as shown in (Bonneau et al., 2015).

3. Overcharging. It is shown in recent work (Chen et al., 2017) that smart contracts can be overcharged due to the under-optimization of smart contracts. These overcharged patterns have the features like dead code, expensive operations in loops consisting of repeated computations.

Below are most often advances for functional issues.

- **Re-Entrancy:** Recently, several proposals attempt to solve some of the above challenges. Obsidian was proposed to address re-entrancy attacks and money leakage problems. In particular, Obsidian exploits *named* states to enable consistency checking on state transitions and verification so that re-entrancy vulnerability can be mended. Moreover, a data flow analytical method was proposed to prevent the illegal digital currency stealing from the leakage.
- **Block Randomness:** Blockchain is regarded as a promising technology to generate public and unpredictable random values. However, the random output might not be so random as people expect. Miners could control the block generation and release the block until they find it profitable. To address this issue, some approaches proposed to use the delay-function to generate randomness. It means that the random value will be only be known to others after a short time period since its generation. In this way, the blockchain moves on and the miners could not withhold their blocks to profit. But delay functions are not suitable for smart contracts as most of they require instance verification. To this end, the approach proposed the Sloth function to allow faster verification. Based on above propositions a multi-round protocol to verify delay functions using a refereed delegation model. It reduces the cost of verifying the output from $30 to $0.4 (S. Tessaro, 2016).

- **Overcharging:** Besides from caring the efficiency of their programs, developers of smart contract also need to pay attention to their execution costs. It's noticed that over 90% of real smart contracts suffer from gas-costly patterns in Ethereum (Zhang, Y., et al., 2019). A researcher proposed GasReducer, a tool used to detect gas-costly patterns. GasReducer can replace under-optimized byte code with efficient byte code.

However the problems with smart contracts are not limited by different types of attacks. Smart contracts have too many limitations which dramatically reduce their potential. Additionally to this smart contracts now are considered as a part of a payment system (for example in ETH blockchain) which is logically incorrect because logic on how exactly to process any financial transaction should have nothing to do with the blockchain where it stores the data. The current architecture negatively reflects on pollution, the cost of transaction, energy cost and all this could be easily changed.

LITERATURE REVIEW

Smart contracts have been a topic of discussion in the business world for several years, with proponents touting their potential benefits and critics pointing out their limitations. Smart contracts are self-executing contracts with the terms of the agreement between buyer and seller being directly written into lines of code. They have the potential to reduce transaction costs, increase efficiency, and reduce the potential for fraud. However, they may not be suitable for complex contracts that require human interpretation and discretion, and they may be vulnerable to hacking or programming errors.

The Harvard Business Review article suggests that smart contracts are best suited for simple, standardized agreements, such as those used in supply chain management. The article notes that smart contracts may require significant investment in technology infrastructure and expertise, which could limit their widespread adoption. The article also emphasizes the importance of legal and regulatory frameworks to support the use of smart contracts, particularly in areas such as contract enforcement and dispute resolution.

The TechRadar article discusses the potential benefits and drawbacks of smart contracts in more detail. The article notes that smart contracts have the potential to reduce transaction costs and increase efficiency by eliminating the need for intermediaries. However, the article also points out that smart contracts may be vulnerable to hacking or programming errors, which could lead to significant losses for parties involved in the contract. The article concludes that organizations should carefully consider the potential benefits and drawbacks of smart contracts before implementing them.

The CIO Dive article also emphasizes the limitations of smart contracts. The article suggests that smart contracts may not be suitable for all types of contracts, particularly those that require human interpretation and discretion. The article notes that smart contracts may be vulnerable to hacking or programming errors, which could lead to significant losses for parties involved in the contract. The article suggests that organizations should carefully consider the potential benefits and drawbacks of smart contracts before implementing them.

Overall, the articles suggest that while smart contracts have the potential to offer significant benefits, they may not be suitable for all types of contracts. Organizations should carefully consider the potential benefits and drawbacks of smart contracts before implementing them, and should ensure that legal and regulatory frameworks are in place to support their use. Additionally, organizations should invest in technology infrastructure and expertise to ensure that smart contracts are implemented correctly and securely.

PROBLEM

The existing approach to the architecture of the smart contracts provides lots of disadvantages, such as:

- Slow speed
- Unable to horizontally scale
- Can't have multiple run time environment for the running Smart contracts
- SOLID
- Can't use external services, databases, etc.
- Expensive to run a smart-contract
- Very limited number of the operation inside of a contract
- Limited types

Officially, the advantages of sand-box specify:

- A smart contract can't be modified.

However this is not fully true.

First of all we can recall the situation with Luna, ETH, BTC blockchain. Secondly, the developers can make add different versions of the final smart contracts and it's not obvious for non-professional user.

Since smart contracts in most cases (we all remember many cases where blockchains of ether and the other currencies were rolled back because it was not profitable for some of the groups) can't be modified, developers use a programming pattern which allows to switch between different versions of smart contracts. As an example, such the implementation could be done in the following way:

```
//SPDX-License-Identifier:MIT
pragma solidity ^0.8.13;
contract Proxy {
    address public implementation;
    uint public x;
    function setImplementation(address _imp) external {
        implementation = _imp;
    }
    receive() external payable {
    }
    function _delegate(address _imp) internal virtual {
        assembly {
            calldatacopy(0, 0, calldatasize())
            let result:= delegatecall(gas(), _imp, 0, calldatasize(), 0, 0)
            returndatacopy(0, 0, returndatasize())
            switch result
            case 0 {
                revert(0, returndatasize())
            }
```

The New Approach to the Architecture of Smart Contracts

```
            default {
                return (0, returndatasize())
            }
        }
    }
    fallback() external payable {
        _delegate(implementation);
    }
}
contract V1 {
    address public implementation;
    uint public x;
    function inc() external {
            x+=1;
    }
    function enc() external pure returns (bytes memory) {
        return abi.encodeWithSelector(this.inc.selector);
    }
    function encX() external pure returns (bytes memory) {
        return abi.encodeWithSelector(this.x.selector);
    }
}
contract V2 {
    address public implementation;
    uint public x;
    function inc() external {
            x+=10;
    }
    function dec() external {
            x-=1;
    }
    function enc1() external pure returns (bytes memory) {
        return abi.encodeWithSelector(this.inc.selector);
    }
    function enc2() external pure returns (bytes memory) {
        return abi.encodeWithSelector(this.dec.selector);
    }
    function encX() external pure returns (bytes memory) {
        return abi.encodeWithSelector(this.x.selector);
    }
}
```

Are there other advantages of placing the smart contracts to blockchain? Highly likely the answer is No. At the same time the list of disadvantages is quite big:

- Slow speed

A smart contract is running on a miner's machine and consequently is additionally limited by the speed of its computer.

- Unable to horizontally scale

A smart contract can't be horizontally scaled, which means a miner's machine can't create multiple instances of a smart contract to speed up its work and/or to accept multiple incoming requests. At the same time a smart contract can't be stateless (if it's doing something meaningful) and it also creates the additional issues because currently there is no way to split data from logic.

- Can't have multiple run time environment for the running Smart contracts

A smart contract does not support a situation where multiple smart contracts run in their own (isolated) runtime environments
A smart contract does not support creation of a separate processes and/or even threads which eventually have a negative effect on smart contract's performance.

- SOLID

SOLID is a very well known paradigm in software development where S stands for Single Responsibility, meaning that each service should be responsible only for its own business entity. However this approach should be applied to the crypto-currency sphere and it demonstrates that smart contracts should never be a part of blockchain.

- Can't use external services, databases, etc.

Smart contracts can't use any external services, databases, etc. and all this dramatically limits the abilities of smart contracts.

- Expensive to run a smart-contract

One of the critical issue related to smart contracts is enclosed in the fact that consumer of a smart contract (meaning that consumer makes some operation which lead to the state change of a smart contract and consequently makes a transaction) has to pay for every operation and it reflects on the complexity of the smart contracts: you can't really apply quite complex and extended logic also because of this limitation.

- Very limited number of the operation inside of a contract

Smart contract charges coins for operations and by default have lots of limitations on the number of the cycles inside of a smart contract, the number of operations, etc. All this limits the abilities of smart contracts.

The New Approach to the Architecture of Smart Contracts

- Limited types

Smart contracts have quite limited list of the allowed types.

Thus all these issues clearly demonstrate the poor side of smart contracts and the absence of any progress in this direction.

SOLUTION

Considering all such the issues we can come to conclusion that it's necessary to split smart contracts into 2 parts: the data and the services. In software development such the principal is used in several design patterns, for example in the Visitor pattern, where Visitor traverses the Data objects and performs some operations on them. The same is obviously required in the Smart Contract world: the contract should be split. However although this is a necessary part it's not the full solution (Galiautdinov & Mkrttchian, 2019a).

The next step in resolving the mentioned earlier issues related to smart contracts would be to get rid of smart contract logic from blockchain. This is a huge mistake and dead end from the technology prospective to store smart contract logic in blockchain (Galiautdinov & Mkrttchian, 2019b). The best option for this would be to store the logic in the cloud platforms, such as AWS, Azure, etc.

Finally we can introduce the new terms for the new smart contracts and some features:

A smart contract from now could be one of the following 2 types: Data Contract, Service Contract.

A service contract should be stateless which means it could not contain any state which has to be stored inside of a service contract and consequently reflect on its logic: the result of this will lead to ability to horizontally scale such the service contract in order to process multiple requests simultaneously.

Doing so we'll allow to resolve the following issues:

- Slow speed

Smart contract will become fast since it's running on a cloud platform.

- Unable to horizontally scale

A smart contract could easily become horizontally scaled, it will also make developers to make smart contract services stateless.

- Can't have multiple run time environment for the running Smart contracts

Each smart contract will have its own run time environment, there will be the possibilities to use threads or light threads (similar to Go Routins in Golang), separate processes, etc.

- SOLID

The extrapolation of SOLID principals will make blockchain and financial system more logical and stable.

- Can't use external services, databases, etc.

The Service contracts could easily use any type of external databases relational and/or non-relational. Which will allow to use big data and apply it to blockchain.

- Expensive to run a smart-contract

Running a smart contract will become cheap, it will cost the same as the cost of an ordinary request to a web service. The result of this will be a positive effect reflecting on natural environment and saving the energy.

- Very limited number of the operation inside of a contract

A Smart contract running on a cloud platform as a service will be able to extend its functionality and remove the limits on the number and the types of allowed operations.

- Limited types

Having a smart contract running on a cloud platform will also allow to introduce the new types which now can't be used.

The only type of disagreement with such the approach could be based on opinion that going this way will make smart contracts changeable and consequently there will be no guarantee that the logic was not changed (Galiautdinov, 2020). And that's true, however in the beginning of the article the author showed the pattern which is used by smart contract developers which allows to apply different logic depending on the version of a smart contract which means it does not make any difference. And as a result of such the approach a blockchain will contain only Data related to Data Contracts and the version number of a Service Contract used to process the data. The Service Contract will be located on a Cloud Platform, will have its own version and will work on the principals of Proof-of-Stake.

Proof-of-stake is a cryptocurrency consensus mechanism for processing transactions and creating new blocks in a blockchain. A consensus mechanism is a method for validating entries into a distributed database and keeping the database secure. In the case of cryptocurrency, the database is called a blockchain—so the consensus mechanism secures the blockchain.

Speaking of POS benefits:

- With proof-of-stake (POS), cryptocurrency owners validate block transactions based on the number of staked coins.
- Proof-of-stake (POS) was created as an alternative to Proof-of-work (POW), the original consensus mechanism used to validate a blockchain and add new blocks.
- While PoW mechanisms require miners to solve cryptographic puzzles, PoS mechanisms require validators to hold and stake tokens for the privilege of earning transaction fees.
- Proof-of-stake (POS) is seen as less risky regarding the potential for an attack on the network, as it structures compensation in a way that makes an attack less advantageous.
- The next block writer on the blockchain is selected at random, with higher odds being assigned to nodes with larger stake positions.

The New Approach to the Architecture of Smart Contracts

Additionally to this, as it was mentioned earlier: POS will have a positive impact on saving the energy and will surely reduce the pollution which is especially important nowadays.

Having POS concept it's necessary to compare it against the POW:

Both consensus mechanisms help blockchains synchronize data, validate information, and process transactions. Each method has proven to be successful at maintaining a blockchain, although each has pros and cons. However, the two algorithms have very differing approaches.

Under PoS, block creators are called validators. A validator checks transactions, verifies activity, votes on outcomes, and maintains records. Under PoW, block creators are called miners. Miners work to solve for the hash, a cryptographic number, to verify transactions. In return for solving the hash, they are rewarded with a coin.

To "buy into" the position of becoming a block creator, you need only own enough coins or tokens to become a validator on a PoS blockchain. For PoW, miners must invest in processing equipment and incur hefty energy charges to power the machines attempting to solve the computations.

The equipment and energy costs under PoW mechanisms are expensive, limiting access to mining and strengthening the security of the blockchain. PoS blockchains reduce the amount of processing power needed to validate block information and transactions. The mechanism also lowers network congestion and removes the rewards-based incentive PoW blockchains have.

Table 2.

Proof of Stake	Proof of Work
Block creators are called validators	Block creators are called miners
Participants must own coins or tokens to become a validator	Participants must buy equipment and energy to become a miner
Energy efficient	Not energy efficient
Security through community control	Robust security due to expensive upfront requirement
Validators receive transactions fees as rewards	Miners receive block rewards

However even this is not the end of the story as crypto-currencies contain the number of the other weak sides which sometimes are not obvious.

All the crypto-currency concept is based on the hash functions which, according to the number of testimonies, can't have collisions (or more exactly: almost no collisions during some obvious period of time). Unfortunately there is no publicly published theorem proving this concept.

But there is still another issue: most of the crypto-currencies, including BTC, have so called self-destroyed mechanism, represented by a special command or programming instruction. That could be the answer to the question how crypto-world will blow up.

CONCLUSION

In the article, the author conducted research and proposed a solution that can resolve the well-known issues in the current smart contract concept and completely change the architecture used in smart contracts and blockchain. The author listed the well-known issues related to smart contracts, analyzed them, and provided a solution explaining how it will change the situation and have a positive impact not only on the performance of smart contracts and their extensibility but also on the environment by reducing pollution and saving energy.

REFERENCES

Bernstein, D. J., & Lange, T. (2016). *SafeCurves: Choosing safe curves for elliptic-curve cryptography.* https://safecurves.cr.yp.to/

Bonneau, J., Clark, J., & Goldfeder, S. (2015). On bitcoin as a public randomness source. IACR Cryptol.

Chen, T., Li, X., Luo, X., & Zhang, X. (2017). Under-optimized smart contracts devour your money. *Proceedings of 24th International Conference on Software Analysis, Evolution and Reengineering, SANER,* 442–446. 10.1109/SANER.2017.7884650

Daniel, R. L. B. (2016). *SECG SEC 1: Elliptic Curve Cryptography* (Version 2.0). https://www.secg.org/sec1-v2.pdf

Galiautdinov, R. (2020). *Brain machine interface: the accurate interpretation of neurotransmitters' signals targeting the muscles. International Journal of Applied Research in Bioinformatics.* doi:10.4018/IJARB.2020010102

Galiautdinov, R., & Mkrttchian, V. (2019a). Math model of neuron and nervous system research, based on AI constructor creating virtual neural circuits: Theoretical and Methodological Aspects. In V. Mkrttchian, E. Aleshina, & L. Gamidullaeva (Eds.), *Avatar-Based Control, Estimation, Communications, and Development of Neuron Multi-Functional Technology Platforms* (pp. 320–344). IGI Global. doi:10.4018/978-1-7998-1581-5.ch015

Galiautdinov, R., & Mkrttchian, V. (2019b). Brain machine interface – for Avatar Control & Estimation in Educational purposes Based on Neural AI plugs: Theoretical and Methodological Aspects. In V. Mkrttchian, E. Aleshina, & L. Gamidullaeva (Eds.), *Avatar-Based Control, Estimation, Communications, and Development of Neuron Multi-Functional Technology Platforms* (pp. 345–360). IGI Global. doi:10.4018/978-1-7998-1581-5.ch016

Heuvel, S. (2014). *The demand for short-term, safe assets and financial stability: Some evidence and implications for central bank policies.* Academic Press.

Li, W., Andreina, S., Bohli, J.-M., & Karame, G. (2017). Securing Proof-of-Stake Blockchain Protocols. In J. Garcia-Alfaro, G. Navarro-Arribas, H. Hartenstein, & J. Herrera-Joancomartí (Eds.), *Data Privacy Management, Cryptocurrencies and Blockchain Technology* (pp. 297–315). Springer International Publishing., doi:10.1007/978-3-319-67816-0_17

Li, X., Jiang, P., Chen, T., Luo, X., & Wen, Q. (2017). A survey on the security of blockchain systems. *Future Generation Computer Systems.*

Mkrttchian, V., Gamidullaeva, L., & Galiautdinov, R. (2019). *Design of Nano-scale Electrodes and Development of Avatar-Based Control System for Energy-Efficient Power Engineering: Application of an Internet of Things and People (IOTAP) Research Center.* International Journal of Applied Nanotechnology Research. doi:10.4018/IJANR.2019010104

Nguyen, C. T., Hoang, D. T., Nguyen, D. N., Niyato, D., Nguyen, H. T., & Dutkiewicz, E. (2019). Proof-of-Stake Consensus Mechanisms for Future Blockchain Networks: Fundamentals, Applications and Opportunities. *IEEE Access : Practical Innovations, Open Solutions, 7*, 85727–85745. doi:10.1109/ACCESS.2019.2925010

Pearce, S. (2021, June). *Smart contracts: The good, the bad and the ugly.* TechRadar. https://www.techradar.com/news/smart-contracts-the-good-the-bad-and-the-ugly

Saleh, F. (2021). Blockchain without Waste: Proof-of-Stake. *The Review of Financial Studies, 34*(3), 1156–1190. doi:10.1093/rfs/hhaa075

Staff, H. B. R. (2021, July). Smart Contracts: Hype vs. Reality. *Harvard Business Review.* https://hbr.org/2021/07/smart-contracts-hype-vs-reality

Szabo, N. (1997). *The idea of smart contracts.* Nick Szabo's Papers and Concise Tutorials.

Tasca, P., & Tessone, C. J. (2019). *A Taxonomy of Blockchain Technologies: Principles of Identification and Classification.* doi:10.5195/ledger.2019.140

Tessaro, S. (2016). Sloth: A Lightweight Delay Function for ASIC-Resistant Proof-of-Work Based on Nakamoto's Consensus Algorithm. *Journal of Cryptology, 29*(2), 613–638.

Vogel, P. S. (2021, May). *Why smart contracts may not be smart after all.* CIO Dive. https://www.ciodive.com/news/smart-contracts-limitations/599279/

Zhang, R., & Chan, W. K. (2020). Evaluation of Energy Consumption in Block-Chains with Proof of Work and Proof of Stake. *Journal of Physics: Conference Series, 1584*(1). doi:10.1088/1742-6596/1584/1/012023

Zhang, Y., Sun, Y., Chen, J., & Liu, J. (2019). GasReducer: Detecting and Mitigating Gas-Costly Patterns in Ethereum Smart Contracts. *IEEE Transactions on Dependable and Secure Computing, 17*(2), 405–419. doi:10.1109/TDSC.2018.2863135

Compilation of References

Ab Talib, M. S., & Mohd Johan, M. (2012). Issues in halal packaging: A conceptual paper. *International Business Management*, 5(2), 94–98.

Abbott, L. F., & Kandel, E. R. (2019). A computational approach enhances learning in Aplysia. *Nature Neuroscience*, 15(2), 178–179. doi:10.1038/nn.3030 PMID:22281713

Aberer, K., Hauswirth, H., & Salehi, A. (2006). *Middleware Support for the Internet of Things*. Available: www.manfredhauswirth.org/research/papers/WSN2006.pdf

Abidin, N. Z., & Perdana, F. F. P. (2020). A Proposed Conceptual Framework for Blockchain Technology in Halal Food Product Verification. *Journal of Halal Industry and Services*, 3(Special Issue), 1–8. doi:10.36877/jhis.a0000079

Abrahams, L., & Burke, M. (2022). *Implementation Programme for the National Digital and Future Skills Strategy of South Africa, 2021 – 2025*. Retrieved from https://www.gov.za/sites/default/files/gcis_document/202203/digital-and-future-skillsimplementation-programmefinal.pdf

Abu-elezz, I., Hassan, A., Nazeemudeen, A., Househ, M., & Abd-alrazaq, A. (2020). "The benefits and threats of blockchain technology in healthcare: A scoping review", International Journal of Medical Informatics. *International Journal of Medical Informatics*, 142, 104246. doi:10.1016/j.ijmedinf.2020.104246 PMID:32828033

Adam, A. S. (2019, January 3). *An overview of Dell's supply chain strategy*. Dynamic Inventory. Retrieved September 18, 2022, from https://www.dynamicinventory.net/dell-supply-chain-strategy/

Adamkiewicz, W., & Jabbar, K. (2020). *Crossing the Chasm: Blockchain as an Innovation Driver in Broader Adoption of Carbon Offsetting Solutions* [Thesis]. CBS.

Ada, N., Ethirajan, M., & Kumar, A., Kek, V., Nadeem, S. P., Kazancoglu, Y., & Kandasamy, J. (2021). Blockchain technology for enhancing traceability and efficiency in automobile supply chain—A case study. *Sustainability*, 13(24), 13667. doi:10.3390u132413667

Adaptation Ledger Ltd. (2020). *Well Adapted Coffee Supply (WACS) an Adaptation Ledger Specific Application (ALSA) in the Adapt ITTM suite of climate adaptation tools*. https://www.adaptationledger.com/_files/ugd/621230_b41137a6a0524fd986184150308e22ad.pdf

Adat, V., & Gupta, B. B. (2017). A DDoS attack mitigation framework for Internet of things. *2017 International Conference on Communication and Signal Processing (ICCSP)*, 2036–2041. 10.1109/ICCSP.2017.8286761

Agrawal, K., Aggarwal, M., Tanwar, S., Sharma, G., Bokoro, P. N., & Sharma, R. (2022). An Extensive Blockchain Based Applications Survey: Tools, Frameworks, Opportunities, Challenges and Solutions. *IEEE Access : Practical Innovations, Open Solutions*, 10(November), 116858–116906. doi:10.1109/ACCESS.2022.3219160

Compilation of References

Agrawal, P., & Narain, R. (2018). Digital supply chain management: an overview. *IOP Conf. Ser.: Mater. Sci. Eng.* 10.1088/1757-899X/455/1/012074

Agrawal, T. K., Kumar, V., Pal, R., Wang, L., & Chen, Y. (2021). Blockchain-based framework for supply chain traceability: A case example of textile and clothing industry. *Computers & Industrial Engineering*, *154*, 154. doi:10.1016/j.cie.2021.107130

Ahemd, M. M., Shah, M. A., & Wahid, A. (2017). IoT security: a layered approach for attacks and defenses. *2017 International Conference on Communication Technologies (ComTech)*, 104–110. 10.1109/COMTECH.2017.8065757

Ahmad, R. W. (2021). Blockchain for aerospace and defense: Opportunities and open research challenges. *Computers & Industrial Engineering*, *151*, 106982. doi:10.1016/j.cie.2020.106982

Ahmad, R. W., Salah, K., Jayaraman, R., Yaqoob, I., Ellahham, S., & Omar, M. (2021). The role of blockchain technology in telehealth and telemedicine. *International Journal of Medical Informatics*, *148*, 104399. doi:10.1016/j.ijmedinf.2021.104399 PMID:33540131

Aich, S., Chakraborty, S., Sain, M., Lee, H., & Kim, H.-C. (2019). A Review on Benefits of IoT Integrated Blockchain based Supply Chain Management Implementations across Different Sectors with Case Study. In *Proceedings of the 2019 21st International Conference on Advanced Communication Technology (ICACT)* (pp. 138 - 141). 10.23919/ICACT.2019.8701910

Airehrour, D., Gutierrez, J. A., & Ray, S. K. (2019). Sectrust-rpl: A secure trust-aware rpl routing protocol for the Internet of things. *Future Generation Computer Systems*, *93*, 860–876. doi:10.1016/j.future.2018.03.021

Ajao, L. A., Agajo, J., Adedokun, E. A., & Karngong, L. (2019). Crypto hash algorithm-based blockchain technology for managing decentralized ledger database in oil and gas industry. *J*, *2*(3), 300-325.

Alaba, F. A., Othman, M., Hashem, I. A. T., & Alotaibi, F. (2017). Internet of things security: A survey. *Journal of Network and Computer Applications*, *88*, 10–28. doi:10.1016/j.jnca.2017.04.002

Alam, K. M., Rahman, J. A., Tasnim, A., & Akther, A. (2020). A blockchain-based land title management system for Bangladesh. *Journal of King Saud University-Computer and Information Sciences*.

Al-Asmari, A. M., Aloufi, R. I., & Alotaibi, Y. (2021). A Review of Concepts, Advantages and Pitfalls of Healthcare Applications in Blockchain Technology. *International Journal of Computer Science & Network Security*, *21*(5), 199–210.

Alccer, V., & Cruz-Machado, V. (2019). Scanning the industry 4.0: A literature review on technologies for manufacturing systems, Engineering Science and Technology. *International Journal (Toronto, Ont.)*, *22*(3), 899–919.

Alharbi, M., & Hussain, F. K. (2021). Blockchain-Based Identity Management for Personal Data: A Survey. In *International Conference on Broadband and Wireless Computing, Communication and Applications*. Springer.

Ali, M. S., Vecchio, M., Pincheira, M., Dolui, K., Antonelli, F., & Rehmani, M. H. (2019). Applications of blockchains in the Internet of things: a comprehensive survey. IEEE Commun. Surv. Tutorials.

Ali, M. H., Chung, L., Kumar, A., Zailani, S., & Tan, K. H. (2021). A sustainable Blockchain framework for the halal food supply chain: Lessons from Malaysia. *Technological Forecasting and Social Change*, *170*, 120870. doi:10.1016/j.techfore.2021.120870

Ali, O., Ally, M., Clutterbuck, & Dwivedi, Y. (2020). The state of play of blockchain technology in the financial services sector: A systematic literature review. *International Journal of Information Management*, *54*, 2020. doi:10.1016/j.ijinfomgt.2020.102199

Alkhudary, R., & Féniès, P. (2022). Blockchain and Trust in Supply Chain Management: A Conceptual Framework. *IFAC-PapersOnLine*, *55*(10), 2402–2406. doi:10.1016/j.ifacol.2022.10.068

Allen, D. W. E., Lane, A. M., & Poblet, M. (2019). The Governance of Blockchain Dispute Resolution. *SSRN*, *25*, 75–101. doi:10.2139srn.3334674

AlMendah, O. M. (2021). A Survey of Blockchain and E-governance applications: Security and Privacy issues. *Turkish Journal of Computer and Mathematics Education*, *12*(10), 3117–3125.

Alofi, A. (2021). *Selecting Miners within Blockchain-based Systems Using Evolutionary Algorithms for Energy Optimisation*. 10.1145/3449726.3459558

Al-Rakhami, M. S., & Al-Mashari, M. (2021). A blockchain-based trust model for the internet of things supply chain management. *Sensors (Basel)*, *21*(5), 1759. doi:10.339021051759 PMID:33806319

Al-Saqaf, S. (2017). Blockchain technology for social impact: opportunities and challenges ahead. *Journal of Cyber Policy*. doi:10.1080/23738871.2017.1400084

Alshamsi, M., Al-emran, M., & Shaalana, K. (2022). Systematic review on Blockchain adoption. *Applied Sciences (Basel, Switzerland)*, *2022*(12), 4245. doi:10.3390/app12094245

Al-Turjman, F., & Alturjman, S. (2018). Context-sensitive access in industrial Internet of things (IoT) healthcare applications. *IEEE Transactions on Industrial Informatics*, *14*(6), 2736–2744. doi:10.1109/TII.2018.2808190

Alvarado, U. Y., & Kotzab, H. (2001). Supply Chain Management. *Industrial Marketing Management*, *30*(2), 183–198. doi:10.1016/S0019-8501(00)00142-5

Aman, M. N., Chua, K. C., & Sikdar, B. (2017). A lightweight mutual authentication protocol for IoT systems. *GLOBECOM 2017 - 2017 IEEE Global Communications Conference*, 1–6.

Anagnostakis, A. (2019). Towards a blockchain architecture for cultural heritage tokens. In *Transdisciplinary Multispectral Modeling and Cooperation for the Preservation of Cultural Heritage: First International Conference, TMM_CH 2018, Athens, Greece, October 10–13, 2018, Revised Selected Papers, Part I* (pp. 541-551). Springer International Publishing. 10.1007/978-3-030-12957-6_38

Anand, M. V., & Vijayalakshmi, S. (2021). A Survey on Blockchain Adaptability in IoT Environments. In *2021 International Conference on Advance Computing and Innovative Technologies in Engineering (ICACITE)*. IEEE.

Andoni, M., Robu, V., Flynn, D., Abram, S., Geach, D., Jenkins, D., McCallum, P., & Peacock, A. (2019). Blockchain technology in the energy sector: A systematic review of challenges and opportunities. *Renewable & Sustainable Energy Reviews*, *100*, 143–174. doi:10.1016/j.rser.2018.10.014

Andrea, I., Chrysostomou, C., & Hadjichristofi, G. (2015). Internet of things: Security vulnerabilities and challenges. *2015 IEEE Symposium on Computers and Communication (ISCC)*, 180–187. 10.1109/ISCC.2015.7405513

Andrian, H. R., & Kurniawan, N. B. (2018, October). Blockchain Technology and Implementation: A Systematic Literature Review. In *2018 International Conference on Information Technology Systems and Innovation (ICITSI)* (pp. 370-374). IEEE. 10.1109/ICITSI.2018.8695939

Angeles, R. (2005). RFID technologies: Supply-chain applications and implementation issues. *Information Systems Management*, *22*(1), 51–65. doi:10.1201/1078/44912.22.1.20051201/85739.7

Angelis, J., & da Silva, E. R. (2019). Blockchain adoption: A value driver perspective. *Business Horizons*, *2019*(62), 307–314. doi:10.1016/j.bushor.2018.12.001

Compilation of References

Angelova, M. (2019). Application of Blockchain Technology in the Cultural and Creative Industries. In *2019 II International Conference on High Technology for Sustainable Development (HiTech)* (pp. 1-4). IEEE. 10.1109/HiTech48507.2019.9128267

Anuradha, J. (2015). A brief introduction on Big Data 5Vs characteristics and Hadoop technology. *Procedia Computer Science*, *48*, 319–324. doi:10.1016/j.procs.2015.04.188

Aouidef, Y., Ast, F., & Deffains, B. (2021). *Decentralized Justice: A Comparative Analysis of Blockchain Online Dispute Resolution Projects*. Retrieved November 14, 2022, from https://www.frontiersin.org/articles/10.3389/fbloc.2021.564551/full

Appelbaum, S. H. (1997). Socio-technical systems theory: An intervention strategy for organizational development. *Management Decision*, *35*(6), 452–463. doi:10.1108/00251749710173823

Araujo, J., Mazo, M., Anta, A. Jr, Tabuada, P., & Johansson, K. H. (2014, February). System Architecture, Protocols, and Algorithms for Aperiodic wireless control systems. *IEEE Transactions on Industrial Informatics*, *10*(1), 175–184. doi:10.1109/TII.2013.2262281

Arshinder, K., Kanda, A., & Deshmukh, S. G. (2011). A review on supply chain coordination: coordination mechanisms, managing uncertainty and research directions. *Supply chain coordination under uncertainty*, 39-82. doi:10.1007/978-3-642-19257-9_3

Asamoah, D., Agyei-Owusu, B., Andoh-Baidoo, F. K., & Ayaburi, E. (2021). Inter-organizational systems use and supply chain performance: Mediating role of supply chain management capabilities. *International Journal of Information Management*, *58*, 102195. doi:10.1016/j.ijinfomgt.2020.102195

Ashibani, Y., & Mahmoud, Q. H. (2017). An efficient and secure scheme for smart home communication using identity-based encryption. *2017 IEEE 36th International Performance Computing and Communications Conference (IPCCC)*, 1–7.

Asif, S. (2018). The halal and haram aspect of cryptocurrencies in Islam. *Journal of Islamic Banking and Finance*, *35*(2), 91–101.

Aslam, J., Saleem, A., Khan, N. T., & Kim, Y. B. (2021). Factors influencing blockchain adoption in supply chain management practices: A study based on the oil industry. *Journal of Innovation & Knowledge*, *6*(2), 124–134. doi:10.1016/j.jik.2021.01.002

Athey, S., Parashkevov, I., Sarukkai, V., & Xia, J. (2016). *Bitcoin pricing, adoption, and usage: Theory and evidence*. Academic Press.

Atlam, H. F., Alenezi, A., Alassafi, M. O., & Wills, G. B. (2018). Blockchain with Internet of things: Benefits, challenges, and future directions. *International Journal of Intelligent Systems and Applications*, *10*(6), 40–48. doi:10.5815/ijisa.2018.06.05

Attaran, M. (2020). Blockchain technology in healthcare: Challenges and opportunities. *International Journal of Healthcare Management*. doi:10.1080/20479700.2020.1843887

AtzoriM. (2017). Blockchain governance and the role of trust service providers: The TrustedChain® network. doi:10.2139/ssrn.2972837

Azam, M. S. E., & Abdullah, M. A. (2020). Global Halal Industry: Realities and Opportunities. *International Journal of Islamic Business Ethics*, *5*(1), 47. Advance online publication. doi:10.30659/ijibe.5.1.47-59

Azzi, R., Chamoun, R. K., & Sokhn, M. (2019). The power of a blockchain-based supply chain. *Computers & Industrial Engineering*, *135*, 582–592. doi:10.1016/j.cie.2019.06.042

Badhotiya, G. K., Sharma, V. P., Prakash, S., Kalluri, V., & Singh, R. (2021). Investigation and assessment of blockchain technology adoption in the pharmaceutical supply chain. *Materials Today: Proceedings*, *46*(20), 10776–10780. doi:10.1016/j.matpr.2021.01.673

Bag, S., Wood, L. C., Xu, L., Dhamija, P., & Kayikci, Y. (2020). Big data analytics as an operational excellence approach to enhance sustainable supply chain performance. *Resources, Conservation and Recycling*, *153*, 104559. doi:10.1016/j.resconrec.2019.104559

Baharmand, H., Maghsoudi, A., & Coppi, G. (2021). Exploring the application of blockchain to humanitarian supply chains: Insights from Humanitarian Supply Blockchain pilot project. *International Journal of Operations & Production Management*, *41*(9), 1522–1543. doi:10.1108/IJOPM-12-2020-0884

Bai, C., Quayson, M., & Sarkis, J. (2022). Analysis of Blockchain's enablers for improving sustainable supply chain transparency in Africa cocoa industry. *Journal of Cleaner Production*, *358*, 131896. doi:10.1016/j.jclepro.2022.131896

Bai, C., & Sarkis, J. (2020). A supply chain transparency and sustainability technology appraisal model for blockchain technology. *International Journal of Production Research*, *2020*(58), 2142–2162. doi:10.1080/00207543.2019.1708989

Baker, M., Dowling, C. & Proudfoot, C. (2021). Supply chain disputes: Avoidance, mitigation and resolution. *International arbitration report*. Norton Rose Fulbright.

Baker, T., & Smith, L. (2019). *Educ-AI-tion rebooted? Exploring the future of artificial intelligence in schools and colleges*. Retrieved from Nesta Foundation website: https://media.nesta.org.uk/documents/Future_of_AI_and_educat ion_v5_WEB.pdf

Balcilar, M., Bouri, E., Gupta, R., & Roubaud, D. (2017). Can volume predict Bitcoin returns and volatility? A quantiles-based approach. *Economic Modelling*, *64*, 74–81. doi:10.1016/j.econmod.2017.03.019

Ballou, R. H. (2007). *Business Logistics/supply Chain Management* (5th ed.). Pearson Education India.

Bamakan, S. M. H., Moghaddam, S. G., & Manshadi, S. D. (2021). Blockchain-enabled pharmaceutical cold chain: Applications, key challenges, and future trends. *Journal of Cleaner Production*, *302*, 127021. doi:10.1016/j.jclepro.2021.127021

Barnett, J., & Treleaven, P. (2018). Algorithmic Dispute Resolution—The Automation of Professional Dispute Resolution Using AI and Blockchain Technologies. *The Computer Journal*, *61*(3), 399–408. doi:10.1093/comjnl/bxx103

Baron, R. M., & Kenny, D. A. (1986). The moderator–mediator variable distinction in social psychological research: Conceptual, strategic, and statistical considerations. *Journal of Personality and Social Psychology*, *51*(6), 1173–1182. doi:10.1037/0022-3514.51.6.1173 PMID:3806354

Bathurst, T. F. (2012). The role of the courts in the changing dispute resolution landscape. *The University of New South Wales Law Journal*, *35*(3), 870–888. doi:10.3316/informit.075130696127938

Batwa, A., & Norrman, A. (2020). A Framework for Exploring Blockchain Technology in Supply Chain Management. *Operations and Supply Chain Management: An International Journal*, *13*(3), 294–306. doi:10.31387/oscm0420271

Baudie, V., & Chang, A. (2022). The impacts of blockchain on innovation management: Sectoral experiments. *Journal of Innovation Economics & Management*, *37*, 1-8.

Baur, D. G., Hong, K., & Lee, A. D. (2018). Bitcoin: Medium of exchange or speculative assets? *Journal of International Financial Markets, Institutions and Money*, *54*, 177–189. doi:10.1016/j.intfin.2017.12.004

Baxter, G., & Sommerville, I. (2011). Socio-technical systems: From design methods to systems engineering. *Interacting with Computers*, *23*(1), 4–17. doi:10.1016/j.intcom.2010.07.003

Compilation of References

Becker, J. (2013). Can we afford integrity by proof-of-work? Scenarios inspired by the Bitcoin currency. In *The economics of information security and privacy* (pp. 135–156). Springer. doi:10.1007/978-3-642-39498-0_7

Beck, R., Müller-Bloch, C., & King, J. L. (2018). Governance in the blockchain economy: A framework and research agenda. *Journal of the Association for Information Systems*, *19*(10), 1. doi:10.17705/1jais.00518

Behnke, K., & Janssen, M. F. W. H. A. (2020). Boundary conditions for traceability in food supply chains using blockchain technology. *International Journal of Information Management*, *52*, 101969. doi:10.1016/j.ijinfomgt.2019.05.025

Bekrar, A., Cadi, A. A. E., Todosijevic, R., & Sarkis, J. (2021). Digitalizing the closing-of-the-loop for supply chains: A transportation and blockchain perspective. *Sustainability (Basel)*, *13*(5), 2895. Advance online publication. doi:10.3390u13052895

Belchior, R., Vasconcelos, A., Guerreiro, S., & Correia, M. (2021). A survey on blockchain interoperability: Past, present, and future trends. *ACM Computing Surveys*, *54*(8), 1–41. doi:10.1145/3471140

Belk, R., Humayun, M., & Brouard, M. (2022). Money, possessions, and ownership in the Metaverse: NFTs, cryptocurrencies, Web3 and Wild Markets. *Journal of Business Research*, *153*, 198–205. doi:10.1016/j.jbusres.2022.08.031

Ben Slimene, S., & Lakhal, L. (2020). The moderating effect of Technological readiness and the exchange of information on supply chain performance: An empirical study in the Tunisian context. *Journal of Business and Management Research*, *13*, 258–270.

Bennouri, (2020). Study of the impact of digital technological innovations on the sustainable performance of a supply chain: case of the halio-industrial sector. *13th International Conference on Modeling, Optimization And Simulation (MOSIM2020)*.

Bentaher, C., & Rajaa, M. (2022). Supply Chain Management 4.0: A Literature Review and Research Framework. *European Journal of Business and Management Research*, *7*(1), 117–127. doi:10.24018/ejbmr.2022.7.1.1246

Bentov, I., Lee, C., Mizrahi, A., & Rosenfeld, M. (2014). Proof of activity: Extending bitcoin's proof of work via proof of stake [extended abstract]. *Performance Evaluation Review*, *42*(3), 34–37. doi:10.1145/2695533.2695545

Berdik, D. (2021). A survey on blockchain for information systems management and security. *Information Processing & Management*, *58*(1).

Berneis, M., Bartsch, D., & Winkler, H. (2021). Applications of Blockchain Technology in Logistics and Supply Chain Management—Insights from a Systematic Literature Review. *Logistics*, *5*(3), 43. doi:10.3390/logistics5030043

Berneis, M., & Winkler, H. (2021). Value proposition assessment of blockchain technology for luxury, food, and healthcare supply chains. *Logistics*, *5*(4), 85. doi:10.3390/logistics5040085

Bernstein, D. J., & Lange, T. (2016). *SafeCurves: Choosing safe curves for elliptic-curve cryptography*. https://safecurves.cr.yp.to/

Bessembinder, H., & Seguin, P. J. (1993). Price volatility, trading volume, and market depth: Evidence from futures markets. *Journal of Financial and Quantitative Analysis*, *28*(1), 21–39. doi:10.2307/2331149

Bhushan, B., Sinha, P., Sagayam, K. M., & J, A. (2021). Untangling blockchain technology: A survey on state of the art, security threats, privacy services, applications and future research directions. *Computers & Electrical Engineering*, *90*, 106897. doi:10.1016/j.compeleceng.2020.106897

Bhutta, M. N. M., Khwaja, A. A., Nadeem, A., Ahmad, H. F., Khan, M. K., Hanif, M. A., Song, H., Alshamari, M., & Cao, Y. (2021). A Survey on Blockchain Technology: Evolution, Architecture and Security. *IEEE Access : Practical Innovations, Open Solutions, 9*, 61048–61073. doi:10.1109/ACCESS.2021.3072849

Bi, R., Kam, B., & Smyrnios, K. X. (2011). IT Resources, Supply Chain Coordination Competency And Firm Performance: An Empirical Study. *PACIS 2011 Proceedings*, 27. https://aisel.aisnet.org/pacis2011/27

Bienhaus, F., & Haddud, A. (2018). Procurement 4.0: Factors influencing the digitisation of procurement and supply chains. *Business Process Management Journal, 24*(4), 965–984. doi:10.1108/BPMJ-06-2017-0139

Bin Dost, M. K., & Rehman, C. A. (2016). Significance of knowledge management practices effecting supply chain performance. *Pakistan Journal of Commerce and Social Sciences, 10*(3), 659–686. https://www.econstor.eu/handle/10419/188273

Biswas, S., & Sen, J. (2017). A Proposed Architecture for Big Data Driven Supply Chain Analytics. *The IUP Journal of Supply Chain Management, 13*(3), 7-33. https://doi.org//arXiv.1705.04958 doi:10.48550

Blockchain Partner. (2017). *Supply chain, traceability & blockchain.* Blockchain Partner Publications.

Blom, T. (2017). *Unplugging corruption at Eskom.* https://static.pmg.org.za/171018OUTA_report.pdf

Blossey, G., Eisenhardt, J., & Hahn, G. (2019). *Blockchain technology in supply chain management: An application perspective.* Academic Press.

Blossey, G., Eisenhardt, J., & Hahn, G. J. (2019). Blockchain technology in supply chain management: an application perspective. *Proceedings of the 52nd Hawaii International Conference on System Science.* 10.24251/HICSS.2019.824

Bodziony, N., Jemioło, P., Kluza, K., & Ogiela, M. R. (2021). Blockchain-Based Address Alias System. *Journal of Theoretical and Applied Electronic Commerce Research, 16*(5), 1280–1296. doi:10.3390/jtaer16050072

Böhme, R., Christin, N., Edelman, B., & Moore, T. (2015). Bitcoin: Economics, technology, and governance. *The Journal of Economic Perspectives, 29*(2), 213–238. doi:10.1257/jep.29.2.213

Bonneau, J., Clark, J., & Goldfeder, S. (2015). On bitcoin as a public randomness source. IACR Cryptol.

Bornholdt, S., & Sneppen, K. (2014). Do Bitcoins make the world go round? On the dynamics of competing cryptocurrencies. arXiv preprint arXiv:1403.6378. doi:10.1016/j.eswa.2020.114384

BorriN.LiuY.TsyvinskiA. (2022). The economics of non-fungible tokens. *Available at* SSRN.

Bosone, M., Nocca, F., & Fusco Girard, L. (2021). The Circular City Implementation: Cultural Heritage and Digital Technology. In *International Conference on Human-Computer Interaction* (pp. 40-62). Springer. 10.1007/978-3-030-77411-0_4

Bouoiyour, J., Selmi, R., & Tiwari, A. (2014). *Is bitcoin business income or speculative bubble? Unconditional vs. conditional frequency domain analysis.* Academic Press.

Bouoiyour, J., & Selmi, R. (2016). Bitcoin: A beginning of a new phase. *Economic Bulletin, 36*, 1430–1440.

Bouri, E., Das, M., Gupta, R., & Roubaud, D. (2018). Spillovers between bitcoin and other assets during bear and bull markets. *Applied Economics, 50*(55), 5935–5949. doi:10.1080/00036846.2018.1488075

Bouri, E., Gupta, R., Tiwari, A. K., & Roubaud, D. (2017). Does bitcoin hedge global uncertainty? evidence from wavelet-based quantile-in-quantile regressions. *Finance Research Letters, 23*, 87–95. doi:10.1016/j.frl.2017.02.009

Bouzembrak, Y., Klüche, M., Gavai, A., & Marvin, H. J. P. (2019). Internet of Things in food safety: Literature review and a bibliometric analysis. *Trends in Food Science & Technology, 2019*(94), 54–64. doi:10.1016/j.tifs.2019.11.002

Compilation of References

Bowen, G. A. (2009). Document Analysis as a Qualitative Research Method. *Qualitative Research Journal, 9*(2), 27–40. doi:10.3316/QRJ0902027

Bowman, P., Ng, J., Harrison, M., Lopez, S., & Illic, A. (2009). *Sensor based condition monitoring, Building Radio frequency IDentification for the Global Environment.* Euro RFID project.

Bowman, A. (2020). Parastatals and economic transformation in South Africa: The political economy of the Eskom crisis. *African Affairs, 119*(476), 395–431. doi:10.1093/afraf/adaa013

Boyes, H., Hallaq, B., Cunningham, J., & Watson, T. (2018). The industrial Internet of things (IoT): An analysis framework. *Computers in Industry, 101*, 1–12. https://dzone.com/articles/. doi:10.1016/j.compind.2018.04.015

Brailsford, T. J. (1996). The empirical relationship between trading volume, returns and volatility. *Accounting and Finance, 36*(1), 89–111. doi:10.1111/j.1467-629X.1996.tb00300.x

Brulhart, F. (2002). Le rôle de la confiance dans le succès des partenariats verticaux logistiques: Le cas des coopérations entre industriels agro-alimentaires et prestataires logistiques. *Finance Contrôle Stratégie, 5*(4), 51–77.

Buchwald, M. (2019). Smart Contract Dispute Resolution: The Inescapable Flaws of Blockchain-Based Arbitration. *University of Pennsylvania Law Review, 168*, 1369–1423. https://scholarship.law.upenn.edu/penn_law_review/vol168/iss5/3

Bufano, E. (2021). Blockchain e mercato delle opere di interesse artistico: Piattaforme, nuovi beni e vecchie regole. *Aedon*, (2), 100–110.

BushellC. (2022). *The Impact of Metaverse on Branding and Marketing.* doi:10.2139/ssrn.4144628

Buterin, V. (2014). A next-generation smart contract and decentralized application platform. *White Paper, 3*(37), 2-1.

Buterin, V. (2015). *On Public and Private Blockchains.* Ethereum Blog, Crypto Renaissance Salon.

Buvik, A., & John, G. (2000). When does vertical coordination improve industrial purchasing relationships? *Journal of Marketing, 64*(4), 52–64. doi:10.1509/jmkg.64.4.52.18075

Bux, C., Varese, E., Amicarelli, V., & Lombardi, M. (2022). Halal Food Sustainability between Certification and Blockchain: A Review. *Sustainability (Basel), 14*(4), 2152. https://www.mdpi.com/2071-1050/14/4/2152. doi:10.3390u14042152

Büyüközkan, G, (2018). *Digital Supply Chain: Literature review and a proposed framework for future research.* Elsevier.

Büyüköztürk, Ş., Çakmak, E. K., Akgün, Ö. E., Karadeniz, Ş., & Demirel, F. (2017). *Bilimsel araştırma yöntemleri.* Pegem Atıf İndeksi. doi:10.14527/9789944919289

CaiD.QianY.NanN. (2023). *Blockchain for Timely Transfer of Intellectual Property.* NBER Working Paper No. w30913. doi:10.2139/ssrn.4349546

Cai, Y., & Zhu, D. (2016). Fraud detection for online businesses: A perspective from blockchain technology. *Financial Innovation, 2*(1), 20. doi:10.118640854-016-0039-4

Calcaterra, C. (2018). On-chain governance of decentralized autonomous organizations: Blockchain organization using Semada. Available at SSRN 3188374.

Calluso, C., & D'Angelo, V. (2022). The impact of Digitalization on Organizational Change Catalysts in Museums. In *Handbook of Research on Museum Management in the Digital Era* (pp. 20–36). IGI Global. doi:10.4018/978-1-7998-9656-2.ch002

Calvaresi, D., Dubovitskaya, A., Calbimonte, J. P., Taveter, K., & Schumacher, M. (2018, June). Multi-agent systems and Blockchain: Results from a systematic literature review. In *International conference on practical applications of agents and multi-agent systems* (pp. 110-126). Springer. 10.1007/978-3-319-94580-4_9

Cambridge Center for Alternative Finance. (2019, July 2). *Cambridge Bitcoin Electricity Consumption Index - Methodology*. Retrieved on November 10, 2022 from https://ccaf.io/cbeci/index

Cao, B., Zhang, Z., Feng, D., Zhang, S., Zhang, L., Peng, M., & Li, Y. (2020). Performance analysis and comparison of PoW, PoS and DAG based blockchains. *Digital Communications and Networks*, *6*(4), 480–485. doi:10.1016/j.dcan.2019.12.001

Cao, Y., & Jiang, H. (2020, April). Dimension construction and test of dynamic capability of enterprise supply chain. In *2020 International Conference on E-Commerce and Internet Technology (ECIT)* (pp. 310-314). IEEE. 10.1109/ECIT50008.2020.00078

Caporale, G. M., & Plastun, A. (2019). The day of the week effect in the cryptocurrency market. *Finance Research Letters*, *31*, 31. doi:10.1016/j.frl.2018.11.012

Casado-Vara, R., Prieto, J., la Prieta, F. D., & Corchado, J. M. (2018). How blockchain improves the supply chain: Case study alimentary supply chain. *Procedia Computer Science*, *134*, 393–398. doi:10.1016/j.procs.2018.07.193

Catalini, C., & Gans, J. S. (2016). *Some simple Economics of the Blockchain*. National Bureau of Economic Research. doi:10.3386/w22952

Central Intelligence Agency. (2021). *The World Factbook: South Africa*. Retrieved 29 Nov. 2021 from https://www.cia.gov/the-world-factbook/countries/south-africa/#people-and-society

Cervantes, C., Poplade, D., Nogueira, M., & Santos, A. (2015). Detection of sinkhole attacks for supporting secure routing on 6lowpan for Internet of things. *2015 IFIP/IEEE International Symposium on Integrated Network Management (IM)*, 606–611. 10.1109/INM.2015.7140344

Ch'ng, E. (2018). The First Original Copy and the Role of Blockchain in the Reproduction of Cultural Heritage. *Presence (Cambridge, Mass.)*, *27*(1), 151–162. doi:10.1162/pres_a_00313

Chaabouni, A., & Ben Yahia, I. (2013). Application de la théorie de la structuration aux systèmes ERP: Importance de la gestion des connaissances. *Recherches en Sciences de Gestion*, *96*(96), 91–109. doi:10.3917/resg.096.0091

Chan, M., (2017). *Why Cloud Computing Is the Foundation of the Internet of Things*. Academic Press.

Chanchaichujit, J., Balasubramanian, S. & Charmaine, N.S.M. (2020). A systematic literature review on the benefit-drivers of RFID implementation in supply chains and its impact on organizational competitive advantage. *Cogent Bus. Manag.*

Chandra, C., & Grabis, J. (2007). *Supply Chain Configuration – Concepts, Solutions and Applications, Springer*. Springer Science Business Media.

Chandra, G. R., Liaqat, I. A., & Sharma, B. (2019). *Blockchain Redefining: The Halal Food Sector. 2019 Amity International Conference on Artificial Intelligence (AICAI)*, Dubai, UAE. 10.1109/AICAI.2019.8701321

Chang, S. E., & Chen, Y. (2020). When blockchain meets supply chain: A systematic literature review on current development and potential applications. *IEEE Access : Practical Innovations, Open Solutions*, *8*, 62478–62494. doi:10.1109/ACCESS.2020.2983601

Compilation of References

Chang, S. E., Chen, Y. C., & Lu, M. F. (2019). Supply chain re-engineering using blockchain technology: A case of smart contract based tracking process. *Technological Forecasting and Social Change*, *144*, 1–11. doi:10.1016/j.techfore.2019.03.015

Chang, S. E., Chen, Y.-C., & Wu, T.-C. (2019). Exploring blockchain technology in international trade: Business process re-engineering for letter of credit. *Industrial Management & Data Systems*, *119*(8), 1712–1733. doi:10.1108/IMDS-12-2018-0568

Chang, Y., Iakovou, E., & Shi, W. (2020). Blockchain in global supply chains and cross border trade: A critical synthesis of the state-of-the-art, challenges and opportunities. *International Journal of Production Research*, *58*(7), 2082–2099. doi:10.1080/00207543.2019.1651946

Charif, A., & Lemtaoui, M. (2022). The impact of the use of Blockchain on the performance of the supply chain. *International Review of Management Sciences*, *5*(1), 22–39.

Cha, S., Chen, J., Su, C., & Yeh, K. (2018). A blockchain connected gateway for ble-based devices in the Internet of things. *IEEE Access : Practical Innovations, Open Solutions*, *6*, 24639–24649. doi:10.1109/ACCESS.2018.2799942

Chatterjee, R., & Chatterjee, R. (2018). An Overview of the Emerging Technology: Blockchain. *Proceedings - 2017 International Conference on Computational Intelligence and Networks, CINE 2017*, 126–127. 10.1109/CINE.2017.33

Chaudhary, R., Aujla, G. S., Garg, S., Kumar, N., & Rodrigues, J. J. P. C. (2018). Sdn-enabled multi-attribute-based secure communication for smart grid in riot environment. *IEEE Transactions on Industrial Informatics*, *14*(6), 2629–2640. doi:10.1109/TII.2018.2789442

Chaudhry, N., & Yousaf, M. M. (2018). Consensus algorithms in blockchain: comparative analysis, challenges and opportunities. In *2018 12th International Conference on Open Source Systems and Technologies (ICOSST)* (pp. 54-63). IEEE. 10.1109/ICOSST.2018.8632190

Chekrouni, A. (2022). The potential impact of Blockchain on supply chain management: What applications and what perspectives? *French Review of Economics and Management*, *3*(8), 161–185.

Chen, G., & Ng, W. S. (2017). An efficient authorization framework for securing industrial Internet of things. TENCON 2017 - 2017 IEEE Region 10 Conference, 1219–1224. doi:10.1109/TENCON.2017.8228043

Chen, T., Li, X., Luo, X., & Zhang, X. (2017). Under-optimized smart contracts devour your money. *Proceedings of 24th International Conference on Software Analysis, Evolution and Reengineering, SANER*, 442–446. 10.1109/SANER.2017.7884650

Chen, G., Xu, B., Lu, M., & Chen, N.-S. (2018). Exploring blockchain technology and its potential applications for education. *Smart Learning Environments*, *5*(1), 1. doi:10.118640561-017-0050-x

Chen, I. J., & Paulraj, A. (2004). Towards a theory of supply chain management: The constructs and measurements. *Journal of Operations Management*, *22*(2), 119–150. doi:10.1016/j.jom.2003.12.007

Chen, L., Lee, W.-K., Chang, C.-C., Choo, K.-K. R., & Zhang, N. (2019). Blockchain-based searchable encryption for electronic health record sharing. *Future Generation Computer Systems*, *95*, 420–429. doi:10.1016/j.future.2019.01.018

Chetty, K., Qigui, L., Gcora, N., Josie, J., Wenwei, L., & Fang, C. (2018). Bridging the digital divide: measuring digital literacy. *Economics*, *12*(1).

Cheung, K.-F., Bell, M. G. H., & Bhattacharjya, J. (2021). Cybersecurity in logistics and supply chain management: An overview and future research directions. *Transportation Research Part E, Logistics and Transportation Review*, *146*, 102217. doi:10.1016/j.tre.2020.102217

Choi, J., & Kim, Y. (2016). An improved lea block encryption algorithm to prevent side-channel attack in the IoT system. *2016 Asia-Pacific Signal and Information Processing Association Annual Summit and Conference (APSIPA)*, 1–4. 10.1109/APSIPA.2016.7820845

Choi, S., Kim, B. H., & Noh, S. D. (2015). A diagnosis and evaluation method for strategic planning and systematic design of a virtual factory in smart manufacturing systems. *International Journal of Precision Engineering and Manufacturing*, *16*(6), 1107–1115. doi:10.100712541-015-0143-9

Choi, T. M. (2019). Blockchain-technology-supported platforms for diamond authentication and certification in luxury supply chains. *Transportation Research Part E, Logistics and Transportation Review*, *128*, 17–29. doi:10.1016/j.tre.2019.05.011

Choi, T. M., Cai, Y. J., & Shen, B. (2019). Sustainable Fashion Supply Chain Management: A System of Systems Analysis. *IEEE Transactions on Engineering Management*, *66*(4), 730–745. doi:10.1109/TEM.2018.2857831

Choi, Y. B., Li, H. L., Kassabov, S. R., Jin, I., Puthanveettil, S. V., Karl, K. A., Lu, Y., Kim, J. H., Bailey, C. H., & Kandel, E. R. (2020). Neurexin-neuroligin transsynaptic interaction mediates learning-related synaptic remodeling and long-term facilitation in aplysia. *Neuron*, *70*(3), 468–481. doi:10.1016/j.neuron.2011.03.020 PMID:21555073

Choon Tan, K., Lyman, S. B., & Wisner, J. D. (2002). Supply Chain Management: A strategic perspective. *International Journal of Operations & Production Management*, *22*(6), 614–631. doi:10.1108/01443570210427659

Choudhury, A., Behl, A., Sheorey, P. A., & Pal, A. (2021). Digital supply chain to unlock new agility: A TISM approach. *Benchmarking*, *28*(6), 2075–2109. doi:10.1108/BIJ-08-2020-0461

Chow, W. S., Madu, C. N., Kuei, C.-H., Lu, M. H., Lin, C., & Tseng, H. (2008). Supply Chain Management in the US and Taiwan: An empirical study. *Omega*, *36*(5), 665–679. doi:10.1016/j.omega.2006.01.001

Ciaian, P., Rajcaniova, M., & Kancs, A. (2016). The economics of bitcoin price formation. *Applied Economics*, *48*(19), 1799–1815. doi:10.1080/00036846.2015.1109038

Clark, C. E., & Greenley, H. L. (2019). *Bitcoin, blockchain, and the energy sector*. Congressional Research Service.

Clark, P. K. (1973). A subordinated stochastic process model with finite variance for speculative prices. *Econometrica*, *41*(1), 135–155. doi:10.2307/1913889

Clemons. Eric, K., & Row. Michael, C. (1992). Information Technology and Industrial Cooperation: The Changing Economics of Coordination and Ownership. *Journal of Management Information Systems*, *9*(2), 9–28. doi:10.1080/07421222.1992.11517956

Clerens. (2022). *Discover the Innovation Fund, one of the world's largest funding programmes, with €10 Billion funding*. https://www.euinnovationfund.eu/

Cocco, L., Concas, G., & Marchesi, M. (2017). Using an artificial financial market for studying a cryptocurrency market. *Journal of Economic Interaction and Coordination*, *12*(2), 345–365. doi:10.100711403-015-0168-2

Cohen, M. A., & Mallik, S. (1997). Global Supply Chains: Research and Applications. *Production and Operations Management*, *6*(3), 193–210. doi:10.1111/j.1937-5956.1997.tb00426.x

Colema, L. (2006). Frequency of man-made disasters in the 20th century. *Journal of Contingencies and Crisis Management*, *14*(1), 3–11. doi:10.1111/j.1468-5973.2006.00476.x

Cole, R., Stevenson, M., & Aitken, J. (2019). Blockchain technology: Implications for operations and supply chain management. *Supply Chain Management*, *24*(4), 469–483. doi:10.1108/SCM-09-2018-0309

Compilation of References

Collins, D., & Lindkvist, C. (2022, November). Block by block: Potential and challenges of the blockchain in the context of facilities management. *IOP Conference Series. Earth and Environmental Science*, *1101*(6), 062003. doi:10.1088/1755-1315/1101/6/062003

Cooper, M. C., Lambert, D. M., & Pagh, J. D. (1997). Supply Chain Management: More Than a New Name for Logistics. *International Journal of Logistics Management*, *8*(1), 1–14. doi:10.1108/09574099710805556

Copeland, T. E. (1976). A model of asset trading under the assumption of sequential information arrival. *The Journal of Finance*, *31*(4), 1149–1168. doi:10.2307/2326280

Coppola, M., Bifulco, F., Russo Spena, T., & Tregua, M. (2021). Value Propositions in Digital Transformation. In *Digital Transformation in the Cultural Heritage Sector* (pp. 69–92). Springer. doi:10.1007/978-3-030-63376-9_4

Corda. (2021). https://www.corda.net

Cornell, B. (1981). The relationship between volume and price variability in futures markets. *The Journal of Futures Markets*, *1*, 303.

Cosimato, S., Vona, R., Iandolo, F., & Loia, F. (2022). Digital Platforms for the Sustainability of Cultural Heritage: A Focus on Clickproject.eu. In Handbook of Research on Museum Management in the Digital Era (pp. 121-136). IGI Global.

CouchDB. (2021). https://www.couchdb.apache.org

Creswell, J. W., & Creswell, J. D. (2017). *Research design: Qualitative, quantitative, and mixed methods approaches.* Sage publications.

Crosby, M., Pattanayak, P., Verma, S., & Kalyanaraman, V. (2016). Blockchain technology: Beyond Bitcoin. *Appl. Innov.*, *2*, 6–10.

Crouch, R. L. (1970a). A nonlinear test of the random-walk hypothesis. *The American Economic Review*, *60*, 199–202.

Crouch, R. L. (1970b). The volume of transactions and price changes on the new york stock exchange. *Financial Analysts Journal*, *26*(4), 104–109. doi:10.2469/faj.v26.n4.104

Cryptonomica. (2018). *Cryptonomica Arbitration Rules*. Retrieved November 30, 2022, from https://github.com/Cryptonomica/arbitration-rules/blob/master/Arbitration_Rules/Cryptonomica/Cryptonomica-Arbitration-Rules.EN.clearsigned.md

Cryptonomica. (2022). *Cryptonomica Advanced Tools for Smart People*. Retrieved November 30, 2022, from https://www.cryptonomica.net/#!/

Cryptopedia. (2021). *Merkle trees and Merkle roots help make blockchains possible.* https://www.gemini.com/cryptopedia/merkle-tree-blockchain-merkle-root

Da Silveira, G., & Cagliano, R. (2006). The relationship between interorganisationnel information systems and operations performance. *International Journal of Operations & Production Management*, *26*(3/4), 232–253. doi:10.1108/01443570610646184

Dabbagh, M. (2021). A survey of empirical performance evaluation of permissioned blockchain platforms: Challenges and opportunities. *Computers & Security, 100*.

Dahlberg, R., Pulls, T., & Peeters, R. (2016). Efficient sparse Merkle trees: caching strategies and secure (non-) membership proofs. *Proceedings of the 21st Nordic Workshop on Secure Computer Systems (NORDSEC 2016)*.

Damianov, D. S., & Elsayed, A. H. (2020). Does bitcoin add value to global industry portfolios? *Economics Letters*, *191*, 108935. doi:10.1016/j.econlet.2019.108935

Daniel, R. L. B. (2016). *SECG SEC 1: Elliptic Curve Cryptography* (Version 2.0). https://www.secg.org/sec1-v2.pdf

Danzi, P., Kalor, A. E., Stefanovic, C., & Popovski, P. (2018). Analysis of the communication traffic for blockchain synchronization of IoT devices. In *2018 IEEE International Conference on Communications (ICC)*. IEEE. 10.1109/ICC.2018.8422485

Dasaklis, T. K., Voutsinas, T. G., Tsoulfas, G. T., & Casino, F. (2022). A systematic literature review of blockchain-enabled supply chain traceability implementations. *Sustainability (Basel)*, *14*(4), 2439. doi:10.3390u14042439

Daubechies, I. (1990). The wavelet transform, time-frequency localization and signal analysis. *IEEE Transactions on Information Theory*, *36*(5), 961–1005. doi:10.1109/18.57199

Davis, M. C., Challenger, R., Jayewardene, D. N., & Clegg, C. W. (2014). Advancing socio-technical systems thinking: A call for bravery. *Applied Ergonomics*, *45*(2), 171–180. doi:10.1016/j.apergo.2013.02.009 PMID:23664481

de Angelis, R., Howard, M., & Miemczyk, J. (2018). Supply chain management and the circular economy: Towards the circular supply chain. *Production Planning and Control*, *29*(6), 425–437. doi:10.1080/09537287.2018.1449244

De Bruyn, S., Ahdour, S., Bijleveld, M., de Graaff, L., Schep, E., Schroten, A., & Vergeer, R. (2018). Environmental Prices Handbook 2017: Methods and Numbers for Valuation of Environmental Impacts. CE Delft.

De Campos, M. G. S. (2021). Towards a Blockchain-Based Multi-UAV Surveillance System. *Frontiers in Robotics and AI*, *8*. PMID:34212007

De Filippi, P., & McMullen, G. (2018). *Governance of blockchain systems: Governance of and by Distributed Infrastructure* [PhD diss.]. Blockchain Research Institute and COALA.

De Giovanni, P. (2020). Blockchain and smart contracts in supply chain management: A game theoretic model. *International Journal of Production Economics*, *228*, 107855. doi:10.1016/j.ijpe.2020.107855

De Jong, F., & Rindi, B. (2009). *The microstructure of financial markets*. Cambridge University Press. doi:10.1017/CBO9780511818547

De Vaujany, F.-X. (2000). Use of information technologies and creation of value for the organization: proposal of a structuring analysis grid based on the key factors of success. *IXth international conference on strategic management (AIMS)*, 1-16.

de Vries, A. (2022a, April 21). *Bitcoin Energy Consumption Index*. Digiconomist. Retrieved November 3, 2022, from https://digiconomist.net/bitcoin-energy-consumption

de Vries, A. (2022b, September 25). *Ethereum Energy Consumption Index*. Digiconomist. https://digiconomist.net/ethereum-energy-consumption

De Vries, A. (2018). Bitcoin's growing energy problem. *Joule*, *2*(5), 801–805. doi:10.1016/j.joule.2018.04.016

de Vries, A., & Stoll, C. (2021). Bitcoin's growing e-waste problem. *Resources, Conservation and Recycling*, *175*, 105901. doi:10.1016/j.resconrec.2021.105901

de Wet, P. (2021). Eskom says it is now legally obliged to shut down one-third of its generating capacity. *Business Insider South Africa*. https://www.businessinsider.co.za/eskom-says-pollution-decision-will-cost-it-16000mw-of-capacity-if-implemented-2021-12

Compilation of References

De, S.J., & Ruj, S., (2017). Efficient decentralized attribute-based access control for mobile clouds. *IEEE Transactions on Cloud Computing.*

Decker, C., Berchtold, M. L., Chaves, W. F., Beigl, M., Roehr, D., & Riedel, T. (2008). Cost benefit model for smart items in the supply chain. In The Internet of Things. Springer. doi:10.1007/978-3-540-78731-0_10

Dede, S., Köseolu, M.C., & Yercan, F.H. (2021). Learning from Early Adopters of Blockchain Technology: A Systematic Review of Supply Chain Case Studies. *Technology Innovation Management Review, 11*(6).

Del Vacchio, E., & Bifulco, F. (2022). Blockchain in Cultural Heritage: Insights from Literature Review. *Sustainability (Basel), 14*(4), 2324. doi:10.3390u14042324

Department of Agriculture, Land Reform and Rural Development (DALRRD). (2020). *A profile of the South African beef market value chain.* https://www.dalrrd.gov.za/doaDev/sideMenu/Marketing/Annual\%20Publications/Beef\%20Market\%20Value\%20Chain\%20Profile\%202020.pdf

Desai, H., Kantarcioglu, M., & Kagal, L. (2019, July). A hybrid blockchain architecture for privacy-enabled and accountable auctions. In *2019 IEEE International Conference on Blockchain (Blockchain)* (pp. 34-43). IEEE. 10.1109/Blockchain.2019.00014

Deshmukh, A., Sreenath, N., Tyagi, A. K., & Eswara Abhichandan, U. V. (2022). Blockchain Enabled Cyber Security: A Comprehensive Survey. *2022 International Conference on Computer Communication and Informatics (ICCCI),* 1-6. 10.1109/ICCCI54379.2022.9740843

DeVries, P. D. (2016). An analysis of cryptocurrency, bitcoin, and the future. *International Journal of Business Management and Commerce, 1*(2), 1–9.

Dey, S., & Chatterjee, S. (2021). Blockchain Arbitration and Smart Contracts in India. *NyaayShastra Law Review, 2*(1), 1-14. doi:10.17613/ebks-ec42

Dhiba, H., & Alaoui, M. (2020). Blockchain and logistics risk management: What contribution? *International Review of the Researcher, 1*(3), 393–413.

Dibaei, M. (2021). Investigating the prospect of leveraging blockchain and machine learning to secure vehicular networks: A survey. *IEEE Transactions on Intelligent Transportation Systems.*

Digimarc. (2022). *A Blueprint for a Decentralized EU Digital Product Passport Model.* YouTube. https://www.youtube.com/watch?v=NfJ4yiyAriw

Dimitropoulos, G. (2022). The use of blockchain by international organizations: Effectiveness and legitimacy. *Policy and Society, 41*(3), 328–342. doi:10.1093/polsoc/puab021

Disastraa, G. M., Suryawardanib, B., Sastikac, W., & Hanifa, F. H. (2020). Religiosity, Halal Awareness, and Muslim Consumers' Purchase Intention in Non-Food Halal Products. *International Journal of Innovation, Creativity and Change,* 813-828.

Donlon, J. P. (1996). *Maximizing value in the supply chain.* The Free Library. Retrieved September 18, 2022, from https://www.thefreelibrary.com/Maximizingvalueinthesupplychain.-a018926696

Donoghue, D., Taylor, E., & Steffe, E. K. (2012). *Commercial disputes in the biotech and pharma sector.* Retrieved December 2, 2022, from https://www.financierworldwide.com/commercial-disputes-in-the-biotech-and-pharma-sector

DorriA.KanhereS. S.JurdakR.GauravaramP. (2019). *LSB: A Lightweight Scalable Blockchain for IoT Security and Privacy.* http://arxiv.org/ abs/1712.02969

Dorsala, M. R., Sastry, V. N., & Chapram, S. (2021). Blockchain-based solutions for cloud computing: A survey. *Journal of Network and Computer Applications*, *196*, 103246. doi:10.1016/j.jnca.2021.103246

Dos Santos, R. P. (2017). On the philosophy of Bitcoin/Blockchain technology: Is it a chaotic, complex system? *Metaphilosophy*, *48*(5), 620–633. doi:10.1111/meta.12266

Doshi & Commerce. (n.d.). *A Study of Opinions on Future of Crypto Currency in India*. Academic Press.

du Venage, G. (2020). South Africa comes to standstill with Eskom's load shedding. *Engineering and Mining Journal*, *221*(1), 18–18.

Dubey, R., Gunasekaran, A., Childe, S. J., Blome, C., & Papadopoulos, T. (2019). Big data and predictive analytics and manufacturing performance: Integrating institutional theory, resource-based view and big data culture. *British Journal of Management*, *30*(2), 341–361. doi:10.1111/1467-8551.12355

Dubois, A., & Gadde, L. E. (2002). Systematic combining: An abductive approach to case research. *Journal of Business Research*, *55*(7), 553–560. doi:10.1016/S0148-2963(00)00195-8

Dujak, D., & Sajter, D. (2019). Blockchain Applications in Supply Chain. In A. Kawa & A. Maryniak (Eds.), *SMART Supply Network* (pp. 21–46). Springer. doi:10.1007/978-3-319-91668-2_2

Duong, T., Fan, L., Katz, J., Thai, P., & Zhou, H. S. (2020, September). 2-hop blockchain: Combining proof-of-work and proof-of-stake securely. In *Computer Security–ESORICS 2020: 25th European Symposium on Research in Computer Security, ESORICS 2020, Guildford, UK, September 14–18, 2020, Proceedings, Part II* (pp. 697-712). Cham: Springer International Publishing.

Durach, C. F., Blesik, T., von Düring, M., & Bick, M. (2021). Blockchain applications in supply chain transactions. *Journal of Business Logistics*, *42*(1), 7–24. doi:10.1111/jbl.12238

Dutta, P., Choi, T. M., Somani, S., & Butala, R. (2020). Blockchain technology in supply chain operations: Applications, challenges and research opportunities. *Transportation Research Part E: Logistics and Transportation Review, 142*, 102067.

Dutta, P., Choi, T.-M., Somani, S., & Butala, R. (2020). Blockchain technology in supply chain operations: Applications, challenges and research opportunities. *Transportation Research Part E, Logistics and Transportation Review*, *142*, 102067. doi:10.1016/j.tre.2020.102067 PMID:33013183

Dwivedi, S. K., Roy, P., Karda, C., Agrawal, S., & Amin, R. (2021). Blockchain-based internet of things and industrial IoT: A comprehensive survey. *Security and Communication Networks*, *2021*, 2021. doi:10.1155/2021/7142048

Dyer, J. H., & Chu, W. (2000). The Determinants of Trust in Supplier-Automaker Relationships in the U.S., Japan and Korea. *Journal of International Business Studies*, *31*(2), 259–285. doi:10.1057/palgrave.jibs.8490905

Dyhrberg, A. H. (2016). Bitcoin, gold and the dollar–a garch volatility analysis. *Finance Research Letters*, *16*, 85–92. doi:10.1016/j.frl.2015.10.008

Dylag, M., & Smith, H. (2021). From cryptocurrencies to cryptocourts: Blockchain and the financialization of dispute resolution platforms. *Information Communication and Society*, *26*(2), 1–16. doi:10.1080/1369118X.2021.1942958

Eberhardt, J., & Heiss, J. (2018). Off-chaining models and approaches to off-chain computations. *Proceedings of the 2nd Workshop on Scalable and Resilient Infrastructures for Distributed Ledgers*, 7-12. 10.1145/3284764.3284766

Compilation of References

Efanov, D., & Roschin, P. (2018). The all-pervasiveness of the blockchain technology. *Procedia Computer Science*, *123*, 116–121. doi:10.1016/j.procs.2018.01.019

El Alaoui, M., Bouri, E., & Roubaud, D. (2019). Bitcoin price–volume: A multifractal cross-correlation approach. *Finance Research Letters*, 31.

El Bakkouri, A. (2021). Literature Review of the "Logistics Performance" Concept: A Synthesis Essay. *European Scientific Journal*, *17*(23), 210. doi:10.19044/esj.2021.v17n23p210

El Sobky, Gomaa, & Hassan. (n.d.). *A Survey of Blockchain from the Viewpoints of Applications, Challenges and Chances*. Academic Press.

Electronic Communications Network. (n.d.). *Telecommunications in South Africa*. Retrieved 2 March from https://www.ecn.co.za/telecommunications/

Eljazzar, M. M., Amr, M. A., Kassem, S. S., & Ezzat, M. (2018). Merging supply chain and blockchain technologies. arXiv preprint, arXiv:1804.04149. doi:10.3390/info12020070

Ellen MacArthur Foundation, (2016). *Intelligent assets: unlocking the circular economy potential*. Author.

Ennajeh, L. (2021). Blockchain Technology Diffusion and Adoption: Tunisian Context Exploration. In Digital Economy. Emerging Technologies and Business Innovation. ICDEc 2021. Springer. doi:10.1007/978-3-030-92909-1_6

Epps, T. W. (1975). Security price changes and transaction volumes: Theory and evidence. *The American Economic Review*, *65*, 586–597.

Epps, T. W., & Epps, M. L. (1976). The stochastic dependence of security price changes and transaction volumes: Implications for the mixture-of-distributions hypothesis. *Econometrica*, *44*(2), 305–321. doi:10.2307/1912726

Erbguth, J., & Morin, J.-H. (2018). Towards Governance and Dispute Resolution for DLT and Smart Contracts. In *Proceedings of the 2018 IEEE 9th International Conference on Software Engineering and Service Science (ICSESS)* (pp. 46-55). 10.1109/ICSESS.2018.8663721

Erol, I., Neuhofer, I. O., Dogru, T., Oztel, A., Searcy, C., & Yorulmaz, A. C. (2022). Improving sustainability in the tourism industry through blockchain technology: Challenges and opportunities. *Tourism Management*, *93*, 104628. doi:10.1016/j.tourman.2022.104628

Esfahani, A., Mantas, G., Matischek, R., Saghezchi, F. B., Rodriguez, J., Bicaku, A., Maksuti, S., Tauber, M. G., Schmittner, C., & Bastos, J. (2019). A lightweight authentication mechanism for m2m communications in industrial IoT environment. *IEEE Internet of Things Journal*, *6*(1), 288–296. doi:10.1109/JIOT.2017.2737630

Eskom. (n.d.). *What is load shedding?* Retrieved 17 Feb. from https://loadshedding.eskom.co.za/LoadShedding/Description

Etemadi, N., Gelder, P. V., & Strozzi, F. (2021). An ISM Modeling of Barriers for Blockchain/Distributed Ledger Technology Adoption in Supply Chains towards Cybersecurity. *Sustainability (Basel)*, *13*(9), 4672. doi:10.3390u13094672

Ethereum. (2021). https://www.ethereum.org

Evans, T. (2019). The Role of International Rules in Blockchain-Based Cross-Border Commercial Disputes. *Wayne Law Review*, *65*(1), 1–16. https://waynelawreview.org/role-of-international-rules-in-blockchain-based-cross-border-commercial-disputes/

Fairfield, J. A. (2022). Tokenized: The law of non-fungible tokens and unique digital property. *Industrial Law Journal*, *97*, 1261.

Fang, C., Liu, X., Pardalos, P. M., & Pei, J. (2016). Optimization for a three-stage production system in the Internet of Things: Procurement, production and product recovery, and acquisition. *International Journal of Advanced Manufacturing Technology*, *83*(5-8), 689–710. doi:10.100700170-015-7593-1

Fang, J., & Ma, A. (2020). IoT application modules placement and dynamic task processing in edge-cloud computing. *IEEE Internet of Things Journal*, *8*(6), 12771–12781.

Fang, J., Qu, T., Li, Z. G., Xu, G., & Huang, G. Q. (2013). Agent-based gateway operating system for RFID-enabled ubiquitous manufacturing enterprise. *Robotics and Computer-integrated Manufacturing*, *29*(4), 222–231. doi:10.1016/j.rcim.2013.01.001

Fan, J., Kwasnica, A. M., & Thomas, D. J. (2018). Paying for teamwork: Supplier coordination with endogenously selected groups. *Production and Operations Management*, *27*(6), 1089–1101. doi:10.1111/poms.12856

Fan, Z. P., Wu, X. Y., & Cao, B. B. (2020). Considering the traceability awareness of consumers: Should the supply chain adopt the blockchain technology? *Annals of Operations Research*, •••, 1–24. PMID:32836619

Farge, M. (1992). Wavelet transforms and their applications to turbulence. *Annual Review of Fluid Mechanics*, *24*(1), 395–458. doi:10.1146/annurev.fl.24.010192.002143

Fauzi, M. A., Paiman, N., & Othman, Z. (2020). Bitcoin and cryptocurrency: Challenges, opportunities and future works. *The Journal of Asian Finance, Economics, and Business*, *7*(8), 695–704. doi:10.13106/jafeb.2020.vol7.no8.695

Fawcett, S. E., Jones, S. L., & Fawcett, A. M. (2012). Supply chain trust: The catalyst for collaborative innovation. *Business Horizons*, *55*(2), 163–178. doi:10.1016/j.bushor.2011.11.004

Fedorova, E. P., & Skobleva, E. I. (2020). Application of Blockchain Technology in Higher Education. *European Journal of Contemporary Education*, *9*(3), 552-571. www.ejournal1.com doi:10.13187/ejced.2020.3.552

Fenwick, M., & Wrbka, S. (2016). The Flexibility of Law and its Limits in Contemporary Business Regulation. In M. Fenwick & S. Wrbka (Eds.), *Flexibility in Modern Business Law: A Comparative Assessment* (pp. 1–12). Springer. doi:10.1007/978-4-431-55787-6_1

Fernández-Caramés, T. M., Blanco-Novoa, O., Froiz-Míguez, I., & Fraga-Lamas, P. (2019). Towards an autonomous industry 4.0 warehouse: A UAV and blockchain-based system for inventory and traceability applications in big data-driven supply chain management. *Sensors (Basel)*, *19*(10), 2394. doi:10.339019102394 PMID:31130644

Fernandez, E. B., Yoshioka, N., Washizaki, H., & Yoder, J. (2022). Abstract security patterns and the design of secure systems. *Cybersecurity*, *5*(1), 7. doi:10.118642400-022-00109-w

Fernndez-Carams, T. M., & Fraga-Lamas, P. (2018). A review on the use of blockchain for the Internet of things. *IEEE Access : Practical Innovations, Open Solutions*, *6*, 32979–33001. doi:10.1109/ACCESS.2018.2842685

Ferrag, M. A., Derdour, M., Mukherjee, M., Derhab, A., Maglaras, L., & Janicke, H. (2018). Blockchain technologies for the internet of things: Research issues and challenges. *IEEE Internet of Things Journal*, *6*(2), 2188–2204. doi:10.1109/JIOT.2018.2882794

Ferran, M.A., Derdour, M., Mukherjee, M., Dahab, A., Maglaras, L., & Janicke, H., (2019). Blockchain technologies for the Internet of things: research issues and challenges. *IEEE Internet Things J*.

Ferreira da Silva, C., & Moro, S. (2021). Blockchain technology as an enabler of consumer trust: A text mining literature analysis. *Telematics and Informatics*, *60*(2), 101593. doi:10.1016/j.tele.2021.101593

Forbes. (2019). *Blockchain in healthcare: How it Could Make Digital Healthcare Safer and More Innovative*. Author.

Compilation of References

Fosso Wamba, S., Kala Kamdjoug, J. R., Epie Bawack, R., & Keogh, J. G. (2020). Bitcoin, Blockchain and Fintech: A systematic review and case studies in the supply chain. *Production Planning and Control*, *31*(2-3), 115–142. doi:10.1080/09537287.2019.1631460

Fosso Wamba, S., Queiroz, M. M., & Trinchera, L. (2020). Dynamics between blockchain adoption determinants and supply chain performance: An empirical investigation. *International Journal of Production Economics*, *229*, 107791. doi:10.1016/j.ijpe.2020.107791

Fosso, S., Maciel, W., & Queiroz, M. (2020). Industry 4.0 and the supply chain digitalization: A blockchain diffusion perspective. *Production Planning and Control*, *33*(2-3), 193–210. doi:10.1080/09537287.2020.1810756

Francati, D., Ateniese, G., Faye, A., Milazzo, A. M., Perillo, A. M., Schiatti, L., & Giordano, G. (2021). Audita: A blockchain-based auditing framework for off-chain storage. *Proceedings of the Ninth International Workshop on Security in Blockchain and Cloud Computing*, 5-10. 10.1145/3457977.3460293

Franceschet, M., Colavizza, G., Finucane, B., Ostachowski, M. L., Scalet, S., Perkins, J., ... Hernández, S. (2021). Crypto art: A decentralized view. *Leonardo*, *54*(4), 402–405. doi:10.1162/leon_a_02003

Fridgen, G., Lockl, J., Radszuwill, S., Rieger, A., Schweizer, A., & Urbach, N. (2018). A Solution in Search of a Problem: A Method for the Development of Blockchain Use Cases. *AMCIS*, *1*(1), 1-11.

Friedman, N., & Ormiston, J. (2022). Blockchain as a sustainability-oriented innovation?: Opportunities for and resistance to Blockchain technology as a driver of sustainability in global food supply chains. *Technological Forecasting and Social Change*, *175*, 121403. doi:10.1016/j.techfore.2021.121403

Frikha, T., Chaari, A., Chaabane, F., Cheikhrouhou, O., & Zaguia, A. (2021). Healthcare and fitness data management using the iot-based blockchain platform. *Journal of Healthcare Engineering*, *2021*, 2021. doi:10.1155/2021/9978863 PMID:34336176

Frustaci, M., Pace, P., Aloi, G., & Fortino, G. (2018). *Evaluating critical security issues of the IoT world: present and future challenges*. IEEE Internet Things.

Fulmer, N. (2019). Exploring the Legal Issues of Blockchain Applications. *Akron Law Review*, *52*(1), 162–191. https://ideaexchange.uakron.edu/akronlawreview/vol52/iss1/5/

Fuseini, A., Wotton, S. B., Knowles, T. G., & Hadley, P. J. (2017). Halal Meat Fraud and Safety Issues in the UK: A Review in the Context of the European Union. *Food Ethics*, *1*(2), 127–142. doi:10.100741055-017-0009-1

Fu, X., Wang, H., & Shi, P. (2021). A survey of Blockchain consensus algorithms: Mechanism, design and applications. *Science China. Information Sciences*, *64*(2), 1–15. doi:10.100711432-019-2790-1

Gabison, G. (2016). Policy considerations for the blockchain technology public and private applications. *SMU Sci. & Tech. L. Rev.*, *19*, 327.

Gai, J., Choo, K., Qiu, K. R., & Zhu, L. (2018). Privacy-preserving content-oriented wireless communication in internet-of-things. *IEEE Internet of Things Journal*, *5*(4), 3059–3067. doi:10.1109/JIOT.2018.2830340

Galaskiewicz, J. (2011). Studying supply chains from a social network perspective. *The Journal of Supply Chain Management*, *47*(1), 4–8. doi:10.1111/j.1745-493X.2010.03209.x

Galiautdinov, R. (2020). *Brain machine interface: the accurate interpretation of neurotransmitters' signals targeting the muscles*. International Journal of Applied Research in Bioinformatics. doi:10.4018/IJARB.2020010102

Galiautdinov, R., & Mkrttchian, V. (2019a). Math model of neuron and nervous system research, based on AI constructor creating virtual neural circuits: Theoretical and Methodological Aspects. In V. Mkrttchian, E. Aleshina, & L. Gamidullaeva (Eds.), *Avatar-Based Control, Estimation, Communications, and Development of Neuron Multi-Functional Technology Platforms* (pp. 320–344). IGI Global. doi:10.4018/978-1-7998-1581-5.ch015

Galiautdinov, R., & Mkrttchian, V. (2019b). Brain machine interface – for Avatar Control & Estimation in Educational purposes Based on Neural AI plugs: Theoretical and Methodological Aspects. In V. Mkrttchian, E. Aleshina, & L. Gamidullaeva (Eds.), *Avatar-Based Control, Estimation, Communications, and Development of Neuron Multi-Functional Technology Platforms* (pp. 345–360). IGI Global. doi:10.4018/978-1-7998-1581-5.ch016

Gandino, F., Montrucchio, B., & Rebaudengo, M. (2014). Key Management for Static Wireless Sensor Networks with Node Adding. *IEEE Transaction Industrial Informatics*.

Gao, T., & Tian, Y. (2014). Mechanism of supply chain coordination cased on dynamic capability framework-the mediating role of manufacturing capabilities. *Journal of Industrial Engineering and Management, 7*(5), 1250–1267. doi:10.3926/jiem.1266

Gawankar, S. A., Gunasekaran, A., & Kamble, S. (2020). A study on investments in the big data-driven supply chain, performance measures and organisational performance in Indian retail 4.0 context. *International Journal of Production Research, 58*(5), 1574–1593. doi:10.1080/00207543.2019.1668070

Gebka, B., & Wohar, M. E. (2013). Causality between trading volume and returns: Evidence from quantile regressions. *International Review of Economics & Finance, 27*, 144–159. doi:10.1016/j.iref.2012.09.009

Gharpure, C., & Kulyukin, V. (2008, Mar.). Robot-Assisted Shopping for the Blind: Issues in Spatial Cognition and Product Selection. *International Journal of Service Robotics*.

Ghisellini, P., Cialani, C., & Ulgiati, S. (2016). A review on circular economy: The expected transition to a balanced interplay of environmental and economic systems. *Journal of Cleaner Production, 114*, 11–32. doi:10.1016/j.jclepro.2015.09.007

Ghosh, A., Gupta, S., Dua, A., & Kumar, N. (2020). Security of Cryptocurrencies in blockchain technology: State-of-art, challenges and future prospects. *Journal of Network and Computer Applications, 163*, 102635. Advance online publication. doi:10.1016/j.jnca.2020.102635

Gibbon, J. (2018). *Introduction to Trusted Execution Environment: Arm's Trust zone*. Academic Press.

Giddens, A. (1987). *The Constitution of society - Elements of the theory of structuring*. PUF.

Gimenez-Aguilar, M. (2021). Achieving cybersecurity in blockchain-based systems: A survey. *Future Generation Computer Systems*.

Glaser, F., Hawlitschek, F., & Notheisen, B. (2019). *Blockchain as a Platform. InBusiness transformation through Blockchain*. Palgrave Macmillan.

Glaser, M., & Weber, M. (2009). Which past returns affect trading volume? *Journal of Financial Markets, 12*(1), 1–31. doi:10.1016/j.finmar.2008.03.001

Glissa, G., Rachedi, A., & Meddeb, A. (2016). A secure routing protocol based on rpl for Internet of things. *IEEE Global Communications Conference (GLOBECOM)*, 1–7. 10.1109/GLOCOM.2016.7841543

Goldberg, A. (2015). *The economic impact of load shedding: The case of South African retailers*. University of Pretoria.

Golosova, J., & Romanovs, A. (2018). *The Advantages and Disadvantages of the Blockchain Technology*. Elsevier Ltd. https://creativecommons.org/licenses/by/4.0/ doi:10.1109/AIEEE.2018.8592253

Compilation of References

Gomathi, S., Soni, M., Dhiman, G., Govindaraj, R., & Kumar, P. (2021). A survey on applications and security issues of blockchain technology in business sectors. *Materials Today: Proceedings*. Advance online publication. doi:10.1016/j.matpr.2021.02.088

Gomes, T., Salgado, F., Tavares, A., & Cabral, J. (2017). Cute mote, a customizable and trustable end-device for the Internet of things. *IEEE Sensors Journal*, *17*(20), 6816–6824. doi:10.1109/JSEN.2017.2743460

Gonczol, P., Katsikouli, P., Herskind, L., & Dragoni, N. (2020). Blockchain implementations and use cases for supply chains-a survey. *IEEE Access: Practical Innovations, Open Solutions*, *8*, 11856–11871. doi:10.1109/ACCESS.2020.2964880

Goodhart, C. A., & O'Hara, M. (1997). High frequency data in financial markets: Issues and applications. *Journal of Empirical Finance*, *4*(2-3), 73–114. doi:10.1016/S0927-5398(97)00003-0

Gope, P., & Sikdar, B. (2018). *Lightweight and privacy-preserving two-factor authentication scheme for IoT devices*. IEEE Internet Things.

Goranović, A., Meisel, M., Fotiadis, L., Wilker, S., Treytl, A., & Sauter, T. (2017, October). Blockchain applications in microgrids an overview of current projects and concepts. In *IECON 2017-43rd Annual Conference of the IEEE Industrial Electronics Society* (pp. 6153-6158). IEEE. 10.1109/IECON.2017.8217069

Govindan, K., Cheng, T. E., Mishra, N., & Shukla, N. (2018). Big data analytics and application for logistics and supply chain management. *Transportation Research Part E, Logistics and Transportation Review*, *114*, 343–349. doi:10.1016/j.tre.2018.03.011

Granville, K. (2018). *Facebook and Cambridge Analytica: What You Need to Know as Fallout Widens*. Academic Press.

Griggs, K. N., Osipova, O., Kohlios, C. P., Baccarini, A. N., Howson, E. A., & Hayajneh, T. (2018). Healthcare blockchain system using smart contracts for secure automated remote patient monitoring. *Journal of Medical Systems*, *42*(7), 1–7. doi:10.100710916-018-0982-x PMID:29876661

Guan, Z., Si, G., Zhang, X., Wu, L., Guizani, N., Du, X., & Ma, Y. (2018). Privacy-preserving and efficient aggregation based on blockchain for power grid communications in smart communities. *IEEE Communications Magazine*, *56*(7), 82–88. doi:10.1109/MCOM.2018.1700401

Gubbi, J., Buyya, R., Marusic, S., & Palaniswami, M. (2013). Internet of Things (IoT): A vision, architectural elements, and future directions. *Future Generation Computer Systems*, *29*(7), 1645–1660. doi:10.1016/j.future.2013.01.010

Guggenberger, T. (2021). A structured overview of attacks on blockchain systems. *Proceedings of the Pacific Asia Conference on Information Systems (PACIS)*.

Guillaume, F., & Riva, S. (2022). Blockchain Dispute Resolution for Decentralized Autonomous Organizations: The Rise of Decentralized Autonomous Justice. In A. Bonomi & M. Lehmann (Eds.), *Blockchain and Private International Law*. Brill Nijhoff. doi:10.2139srn.4042704

Guin, U., Singh, A., Alam, M., Caedo, J., & Skjellum, A. (2018). A secure low-cost edge device authentication scheme for the Internet of things. *31st International Conference on VLSI Design and 17th International Conference on Embedded Systems (VLSID)*, 85–90. 10.1109/VLSID.2018.42

Gupta, Kumari, & Tanwar. (2021). A taxonomy of blockchain envisioned edge-as-a-connected autonomous vehicles. *Transactions on Emerging Telecommunications Technologies, 32*(6).

Habib, M. A., Sardar, M. B., Jabbar, S., Faisal, C. M. N., Mahmood, N., & Ahmad, M. (2020). Blockchain-based Supply Chain for the Automation of Transaction Process: Case Study based Validation. *Proceedings of the 2020 International Conference on Engineering and Emerging Technologies, ICEET 2020*. 10.1109/ICEET48479.2020.9048213

HackiusN.PetersenM. (2017). Blockchain in logistics and supply chain: trick or treat? *Digitization in Supply Chain Management and Logistics*. Doi:10.15480/882.1444

Hakak, S. (2021). Recent advances in blockchain technology: A survey on applications and challenges. *International Journal of Ad Hoc and Ubiquitous Computing, 38*(1-3), 82-100.

Handfield, R. B., & Bechtel, C. (2002). The role of trust and relationship structure in improving supply chain responsiveness. *Industrial Marketing Management, 31*(4), 367–382. doi:10.1016/S0019-8501(01)00169-9

Hanekom, P. (2020). Covid-19 exposes South Africa's digital literacy divide. *The Mail & Guardian*. https://mg.co.za/opinion/2020-09-08-covid-19-exposes-south-africas-digital-literacy-divide/

Hang, L., & Kim, D. H. (2019). Design and implementation of an integrated iot blockchain platform for sensing data integrity. *Sensors (Basel), 19*(10), 2228. Advance online publication. doi:10.339019102228 PMID:31091799

Han, W., Huang, Y., Hughes, M., & Zhang, M. (2021). The trade-off between trust and distrust in supply chain collaboration. *Industrial Marketing Management, 98*, 93–104. doi:10.1016/j.indmarman.2021.08.005

Hao, J., Sun, Y. L., & Luo, H. (2018). *A Safe and Efficient Storage Scheme Based on BlockChain and IPFS for Agricultural Products Tracking*. Academic Press.

Haq, I., & Esuka, O. M. (2018). Blockchain technology in pharmaceutical industry to prevent counterfeit drugs. *International Journal of Computer Applications, 180*(25), 8–12. doi:10.5120/ijca2018916579

Hardwick, F. S., Akram, R. N., & Markantonakis, K. (2018). Fair and transparent blockchain based tendering framework-a step towards open governance. In *2018 17th IEEE International Conference On Trust, Security And Privacy In Computing And Communications/12th IEEE International Conference On Big Data Science And Engineering (TrustCom/BigDataSE)* (pp. 1342-1347). IEEE. 10.1109/TrustCom/BigDataSE.2018.00185

Harris, L., & Gurel, E. (1986). Price and volume effects associated with changes in the s&p 500 list: New evidence for the existence of price pressures. *The Journal of Finance, 41*(4), 815–829. doi:10.1111/j.1540-6261.1986.tb04550.x

Hasan, H., AlHadhrami, E., AlDhaheri, A., Salah, K., & Jayaraman, R. (2019). Smart contract-based approach for efficient shipment management. *Computers & Industrial Engineering, 136*, 2019. doi:10.1016/j.cie.2019.07.022

Hay, C., de Matos, A. D., Low, J., Feng, J., Lu, D., Day, L., & Hort, J. (2021). Comparing cross-cultural differences in perception of drinkable yoghurt by Chinese and New Zealand European consumers. *International Dairy Journal, 113*, 104901. doi:10.1016/j.idairyj.2020.104901

Hayes, A. F. (2013). *Introduction to mediation, moderation, and conditional process analysis: Methodology in the Social Sciences*. Kindle Edition.

He, Q., Guan, N., Lv, M., & Yi, W. (2018). On the consensus mechanisms of blockchain/dlt for internet of things. In *2018 IEEE 13th International Symposium on Industrial Embedded Systems (SIES)*. IEEE. 10.1109/SIES.2018.8442076

Heiskanen, A. (2017). The technology of trust: How the Internet of Things and blockchain could usher in a new era of construction productivity. *Construction Research and Innovation, 8*(2), 66–70. doi:10.1080/20450249.2017.1337349

Hei, X., Du, X., Wu, J., & Hu, F. (2010). Defending resource depletion attacks on implantable medical devices. *2010 IEEE Global Telecommunications Conference GLOBECOM 2010*, 1–5. 10.1109/GLOCOM.2010.5685228

Helo, P., & Hao, Y. (2019). Blockchains in operations and supply chains: A model and reference implementation. *Computers & Industrial Engineering, 136*, 242–251. doi:10.1016/j.cie.2019.07.023

Helo, P., & Shamsuzzoha, A. (2020). Real-time supply chain—A blockchain architecture for project deliveries. *Robotics and Computer-integrated Manufacturing*, *63*, 101909. doi:10.1016/j.rcim.2019.101909

Henderson, R. M., & Clark, K. B. (1990). Architectural innovation: The reconfiguration of existing product technologies and the failure of established firms. *Administrative Science Quarterly*, *35*(1), 9–30. doi:10.2307/2393549

Hepp, Sharinghousen, Ehret, Schoenhals, & Gipp. (2018). On-chain vs. off-chain storage for supply-and blockchain integration. *IT-Information Technology, 60*(5-6), 283-291.

Heuvel, S. (2014). *The demand for short-term, safe assets and financial stability: Some evidence and implications for central bank policies.* Academic Press.

Hewa, T. M., Hu, Y., Liyanage, M., Kanhare, S. S., & Ylianttila, M. (2021). Survey on blockchain based smart contracts: Technical aspects and future research. *IEEE Access : Practical Innovations, Open Solutions*, *9*, 87643–87662. doi:10.1109/ACCESS.2021.3068178

Hewa, T., Ylianttila, M., & Liyanage, M. (2021). Survey on blockchain based smart contracts: Applications, opportunities and challenges. *Journal of Network and Computer Applications*, *177*, 102857. doi:10.1016/j.jnca.2020.102857

Hew, J.-J., Wong, L.-W., Tan, G. W.-H., Ooi, K.-B., & Lin, B. (2020). The blockchain-based Halal traceability systems: A hype or reality? *Supply Chain Management*, *25*(6), 863–879. doi:10.1108/SCM-01-2020-0044

Higgs, P., Cunningham, S., & Bakhshi, H. (2008). *Beyond the creative industries: Mapping the creative economy in the United Kingdom.* Academic Press.

Hileman, G. (2016). *State of Bitcoin and Blockchain 2016: Blockchain Hits Critical Mass.* Retrieved from Coindesk Website: http://www. coindesk. com/state-of-bitcoin-blockchain-2016

Hippold, S. (2022, April 20). *How supply chain technology will evolve in the future.* Gartner. Retrieved September 18, 2022, from https://www.gartner.com/smarterwithgartner/gartner-predicts-the-future-of-supply-chain-technology

Hofman, A. (2014). *The Dawn of the National Currency–An Exploration of Country-Based Cryptocurrencies.* Retrieved from Bitcoin Magazine Website: https://bitcoinmagazine. com/articles/dawnnational-currency-exploration-country-based-cryptocurrencies-1394146138

Höllein, L., Kaale, E., Mwalwisi, Y. H., Schulze, M. H., & Holzgrabe, U. (2016). Routine quality control of medicines in developing countries: Analytical challenges, regulatory infrastructures and the prevalence of counterfeit medicines in Tanzania. *Trends in Analytical Chemistry*, *76*, 60–70. doi:10.1016/j.trac.2015.11.009

Holweg, M., Disney, S., Holmström, J., & Småros, J. (2005). Supply chain collaboration: Making sense of the strategy continuum. *European Management Journal*, *23*(2), 170–181. doi:10.1016/j.emj.2005.02.008

Howell, B. E., & Potgieter, P. H. (2019). Governance of Smart Contracts in Blockchain Institutions. SSRN *Electronic Journal.* doi:10.2139/ssrn.3423190

Howell, Potgieter, & Sadowski. (2019). *Governance of blockchain and distributed ledger technology projects.* Available at SSRN 3365519.

Howson, P. (2020). Building trust and equity in marine conservation and fisheries supply chain management with blockchain. *Marine Policy*, *115*, 103873. doi:10.1016/j.marpol.2020.103873

Huang, J., Kong, L., Chen, G., Wu, M., Liu, X., & Zeng, P. (2019b). Towards secure industrial IoT: blockchain system with credit-based consensus mechanism. IEEE Trans. Ind.

Huang, H., Kong, W., Zhou, S., Zheng, Z., & Guo, S. (2021). A survey of state-of-the-art on blockchains: Theories, modelings, and tools. *ACM Computing Surveys*, *54*(2), 1–42. doi:10.1145/3441692

Huang, W., & Dai, F. (2019). Research on digital protection of intangible cultural heritage based on Blockchain technology. *Information Management and Computer Science*, *2*(2), 14–18. doi:10.26480/imcs.02.2019.14.18

Huang, X., Zhang, Y., Li, D., & Han, L. (2019a). An optimal scheduling algorithm for hybrid EV charging scenario using consortium blockchains. *Future Generation Computer Systems*, *91*, 555–562. doi:10.1016/j.future.2018.09.046

Hughes, L., Dwivedi, Y. K., Misra, S. K., Rana, N. P., Raghavan, V., & Akella, V. (2019). Blockchain research, practice and policy: Applications, benefits, limitations, emerging research themes and research agenda. *International Journal of Information Management*, *49*, 114–129. doi:10.1016/j.ijinfomgt.2019.02.005

Huh, J.-H., & Seo, K. (2019). Blockchain-based mobile fingerprint verification and automatic log-in platform for future computing. *The Journal of Supercomputing*, *75*(6), 3123–3139. doi:10.100711227-018-2496-1

Huh, S.-K., & Kim, J.-H. (2019). The blockchain consensus algorithm for viable management of new and renewable energies. *Sustainability (Basel)*, *11*(3184), 3184. doi:10.3390u11113184

Huo, B., Zhang, C., & Zhao, X. (2015). The effect of IT and relationship commitment on supply chain coordination: A contingency and configuration approach. *Information & Management*, *52*(6), 728–740. doi:10.1016/j.im.2015.06.007

Imam, I. T., Arafat, Y., Alam, K. S., & Aki, S. (2021, February). DOC-BLOCK: A Blockchain Based Authentication System for Digital Documents. In *2021 Third International Conference on Intelligent Communication Technologies and Virtual Mobile Networks (ICICV)* (pp. 1262-1267). 10.1109/ICICV50876.2021.9388428

Islam, S. H., Khan, M. K., & Al-Khouri, A. M. (2015). Anonymous and provably secure certificateless multireceiver encryption without bilinear pairing. *Secure. Commun. Netw.*, *8*(13), 2214–2231. https://onlinelibrary.wiley.com/doi/abs/10.1002/sec.1165

Jabbar, S., Lloyd, H., Hammoudeh, M., Adebisi, B., & Raza, U. (2021). Blockchain-enabled supply chain: Analysis, challenges, and future directions. *Multimedia Systems*, *27*(4), 787–806. doi:10.100700530-020-00687-0

Jain, P. C., & Joh, G. H. (1988). The dependence between hourly prices and trading volume. *Journal of Financial and Quantitative Analysis*, *23*(3), 269–283. doi:10.2307/2331067

Jairam, S., Gordijn, J., Isaac da Silva, T., Kaya, F., & Makkes, M. (2021). A decentralized fair governance model for permissionless blockchain systems. *Proceedings of the International Workshop on Value Modelling and Business Ontologies*, 4-5.

Jakobsson, M., & Juels, A. (1999). Proofs of work and bread pudding protocols. In *Secure Information Networks: Communications and Multimedia Security*. Kluwer Academic Publishers. . doi:10.1007/978-0-387-35568-9_1

Jang, H., & Han, S. H. (2022). User experience framework for understanding user experience in blockchain services. *International Journal of Human-Computer Studies*, *158*, 102733. doi:10.1016/j.ijhcs.2021.102733

Jap, S. D. (1999). Pie-expansion efforts: Collaboration processes in buyer–supplier relationships. *JMR, Journal of Marketing Research*, *36*(4), 461–475. doi:10.1177/002224379903600405

Javaid, M., Haleem, A., Singh R. P., Khan, S., & Suman, R. (2021). Blockchain technology applications for Industry 4.0: A literature-based review. *Blockchain: Research and Applications*.

Jawab, F., & Bouami, D. (2004). La démarche Supply chain management enjeux et stratégies: Cas du commerce électronique. *La revue de sciences de gestion, Direction et Gestion Marketing, ABI/INFORM Global*, 208-209.

Compilation of References

Jayaram, J., Xu, K., & Nicolae, M. (2011). The direct and contingency effects of supplier coordination and customer coordination on quality and flexibility performance. *International Journal of Production Research*, *49*(1), 59–85. doi: 10.1080/00207543.2010.508935

Jeble, S., Dubey, R., Childe, S., Papadopoulos, T., Roubaud, D., & Prakash, A. (2018). Impact of big data and predictive analytics capability on supply chain sustainability. *International Journal of Logistics Management*, *29*(2), 513–538. doi:10.1108/IJLM-05-2017-0134

Jevremovic, N. (2020). Blockchain, Smart Contracts and ADR. SSRN *Electronic Journal*. doi:10.2139/ssrn.3699422

Jeyaraj, A., & Seth, B. (2010). Implementation of Information Systems Infrastructures for supply chain visibility. *Proceedings of the Southern Association for Information Systems Conference*.

Jiang, J., Li, Z., Tian, Y., & Al-Nabhan, N. (2020). A review of techniques and methods for IoT applications in collaborative cloud-fog environment. *Security and Communication Networks*, *2020*, 1–15. doi:10.1155/2020/8849181

Jiang, R., Kang, Y., Liu, Y., Liang, Z., Duan, Y., Sun, Y., & Liu, J. (2022). A trust transitivity model of small and medium-sized manufacturing enterprises under blockchain-based supply chain finance. *International Journal of Production Economics*, *247*, 108469. doi:10.1016/j.ijpe.2022.108469

Jin, I., Udo, H., Rayman, J. B., Puthanveettil, S., Kandel, E. R., & Hawkins, R. D. (2018). Spontaneous transmitter release recruits postsynaptic mechanisms of long-term and intermediate-term facilitation in Aplysia. *Proceedings of the National Academy of Sciences of the United States of America*, *109*(23), 9137–9142. doi:10.1073/pnas.1206846109 PMID:22619333

Johar, S. (2021). Research and applied perspective to blockchain technology: A comprehensive survey. *Applied Sciences*, *11*(14).

Jones, M. R., & Karsten, H. (2008). (2008(. « Giddens's structuration theory and information systems research. *Management Information Systems Quarterly*, *32*(1), 127–157. doi:10.2307/25148831

Joshi, A. P., Han, M., & Wang, Y. (2018). A survey on security and privacy issues of blockchain technology. *Mathematical Foundations of Computing*, *1*(2), 121–147. doi:10.3934/mfc.2018007

Jraisat, L., Jreissat, M., Upadhyay, A., & Kumar, A. (2022). Blockchain Technology: The Role of Integrated Reverse Supply Chain Networks in Sustainability. *Supply Chain Forum: An International Journal*. doi:10.1080/16258312.2022.2090853

Jung, Y. (2022). Current use cases, benefits and challenges of NFTs in the museum sector: Toward common pool model of NFT sharing for educational purposes. *Museum Management and Curatorship*, 1–17. doi:10.1080/09647775.2022.2132995

Kagermann, H. (2015). Change through digitization—Value creation in the age of Industry 4.0. In Management of Permanent Change. Springer.

Kahyaoğlu & Aksoy. (2021). Survey on blockchain based accounting and finance algorithms using bibliometric approach. *21st Century Approaches to Management and Accounting Research*.

Kamble, S. S., & Gunasekaran, A. (2020). Big data-driven supply chain performance measurement system: A review and framework for implementation. *International Journal of Production Research*, *58*(1), 65–86. doi:10.1080/00207543.2019.1630770

Kamble, S. S., Gunasekaran, A., & Gawankar, S. A. (2020). Achieving sustainable performance in a data-driven agriculture supply chain: A review for research and applications. *International Journal of Production Economics*, *2020*(219), 179–194. doi:10.1016/j.ijpe.2019.05.022

Kamble, S. S., Gunasekaran, A., & Sharma, R. (2020). Modeling the blockchain enabled traceability in agriculture supply chain. *International Journal of Information Management*, *52*, 101967. doi:10.1016/j.ijinfomgt.2019.05.023

Kamble, S., Gunasekaran, A., & Arha, H. (2019). Understanding the Blockchain technology adoption in supply chains-Indian Context. *International Journal of Production Research*, *57*(7), 2009–2033. doi:10.1080/00207543.2018.1518610

Kamboj, S., & Rana, S. (2021). Big data-driven supply chain and performance: a resource-based view. *The TQM Journal*. doi:10.1108/TQM-02-2021-0036

Kamilaris, A., Fonts, A., & Prenafeta-Boldύ, F. X. (2019). The rise of blockchain technology in agriculture and food supply chains. *Trends in Food Science & Technology*, *91*, 640–652. doi:10.1016/j.tifs.2019.07.034

Kamisah, S., Mokhtar, A., & Hafsah, A. (2018). Halal practices integrity and halal supply chain trust in Malaysian halal food supply chain. *International Food Research Journal*, *25*, S57–S62.

Kanda, A., & Deshmukh, S. G. (2006). A coordination-based perspective on the procurement process in the supply chain. *International Journal of Value Chain Management*, *1*(2), 117–138. doi:10.1504/IJVCM.2006.011181

Kanda, A., & Deshmukh, S. G. (2007). Supply chain coordination issues: An SAP-LAP framework. *Asia Pacific Journal of Marketing and Logistics*, *19*(3), 240–264. doi:10.1108/13555850710772923

Kanda, A., & Deshmukh, S. G. (2008). Supply chain coordination: Perspectives, empirical studies and research directions. *International Journal of Production Economics*, *115*(2), 316–335. doi:10.1016/j.ijpe.2008.05.011

Kane, E. (2017). *Is Blockchain a General Purpose Technology?* Academic Press.

Kang, J., Xiong, Z., Niyato, D., Ye, D., Kim, D. I., & Zhao, J. (2019a). Toward secure blockchain-enabled Internet of vehicles: Optimizing consensus management using reputation and contract theory. *IEEE Transactions on Vehicular Technology*, *68*(3), 2906–2920. doi:10.1109/TVT.2019.2894944

Kang, J., Yu, R., Huang, X., Maharjan, S., Zhang, Y., & Hossain, E. (2017). Enabling localized peer-to-peer electricity trading among plug-in hybrid electric vehicles using consortium blockchains. *IEEE Transactions on Industrial Informatics*, *13*(6), 3154–3164. doi:10.1109/TII.2017.2709784

Kang, J., Yu, R., Huang, X., Wu, M., Maharjan, S., Xie, S., & Zhang, Y. (2019b). Blockchain for secure and efficient data sharing in vehicular edge computing and networks. *IEEE Internet of Things Journal*, *6*(3), 4660–4670. doi:10.1109/JIOT.2018.2875542

Karacaoglu, Y., Mocan, S., & Halsema, R. A. (2018). The World Bank group's technology and innovation lab, from concept to development: A case study in leveraging an IT department to support digital transformation. *Innovations: Technology, Governance, Globalization*, *12*(1-2), 18–28. doi:10.1162/inov_a_00264

Karaesmen, F., Liberopoulos, G., & Dallery, Y. (2003). Production/inventory control with advance demand information. In *Stochastic Modeling and Optimization of Manufacturing Systems and Supply Chains* (pp. 243–270). Springer. doi:10.1007/978-1-4615-0373-6_10

Karati, A., Islam, S. H., & Karuppiah, M. (2018). Provably secure and lightweight certificateless signature scheme for IoT environments. *IEEE Transactions on Industrial Informatics*, *14*(8), 3701–3711. doi:10.1109/TII.2018.2794991

Katsiampa, P. (2017). Volatility estimation for bitcoin: A comparison of garch models. *Economics Letters*, *158*, 3–6. doi:10.1016/j.econlet.2017.06.023

Compilation of References

Katuk, N. (2019). The application of blockchain for halal product assurance: A systematic review of the current developments and future directions. *International Journal of Advanced Trends in Computer Science and Engineering, 8*(5), 1893–1902. doi:10.30534/ijatcse/2019/13852019

Kaur, S., Chaturvedi, S., Sharma, A., & Kar, J. (2021). A Research Survey on Applications of Consensus Protocols in Blockchain. *Security and Communication Networks, 2021*, 2021. doi:10.1155/2021/6693731

Kawaguchi, N. (2019). Application of blockchain to supply chain: Flexible blockchain technology. *Procedia Computer Science, 164*, 143–148. doi:10.1016/j.procs.2019.12.166

Kayikci, Y., Gozacan-Chase, N., Rejeb, A., & Mathiyazhagan, K. (2022). Critical success factors for implementing blockchain-based circular supply chain. *Business Strategy and the Environment, 31*(7), 3595–3615. doi:10.1002/bse.3110

Kayikci, Y., Usar, D. D., & Aylak, B. L. (2021). Using blockchain technology to drive operational excellence in perishable food supply chains during outbreaks. *International Journal of Logistics Management*.

Kazancoglu, I., Ozbiltekin-Pala, M., Kumar Mangla, S., Kazancoglu, Y., & Jabeen, F. (2022). Role of flexibility, agility and responsiveness for sustainable supply chain resilience during COVID-19. *Journal of Cleaner Production, 362*, 132431. doi:10.1016/j.jclepro.2022.132431

Kennedy, R. K. L., Khoshgoftaar, T. M., Villanustre, F., & Humphrey, T. (2019). A parallel and distributed stochastic gradient descent implementation using commodity clusters. *Journal of Big Data, 6*(1), 1–23. doi:10.118640537-019-0179-2

Kennett-Herbert, J. (2020). *Conceptualising trust as a data-driven attribute in a study of supply chain relationships* [Master's thesis]. Queensland University of Technology.

Ketchen, D.J., Rebarick, W., Hult, G.T.M., & Meyer, D. (2008). Best value supply chains: A key competitive weapon for the 21st century. *Business Horizons, 51*, 235–243.

Ketzenberg, M., Bloemhof, J., & Gaukler, G. (2015). Managing perishables with time and temperature history. *Production and Operations Management, 2015*(24), 54–70. doi:10.1111/poms.12209

Khan, Jung, & Hashmani. (2021). Systematic Literature Review of Challenges in Blockchain Scalability. *Applied Sciences, 11*(20).

Khan, R., Ansari, S., Jain, S., & Sachdeva, S. (2020). Blockchain based land registry system using Ethereum Blockchain. *J. Xi'an Univ. Archit. Technol*, 3640-3648

Khan, F. I., & Hameed, S. (2019). Understanding security requirements and challenges in the Internet of things (iots): A review. *Journal of Computer Networks and Communications*. doi:10.1016/j.future.2017.11.022

Khan, M. I., & Haleem, A. (2016). Understanding "Halal" and "Halal Certification & Accreditation System"- A Brief Review. *Saudi Journal of Business and Management Studies, 1*(1), 32–42. doi:10.36348jbms.2020.v05i01.005

Khan, S. N., Loukil, F., Ghedira-Guegan, C., Benkhelifa, E., & Bani-Hani, A. (2021). Blockchain smart contracts: Applications, challenges, and future trends. *Peer-to-Peer Networking and Applications, 14*(5), 1–25. doi:10.100712083-021-01127-0 PMID:33897937

Khanuja, A., & Jain, R.K. (2021). The conceptual framework on integrated flexibility: an evolution to data-driven supply chain management. *The TQM Journal*. doi:10.1108/TQM-03-2020-0045

Khatwani, S. (2018). *Explaining Hash Rate or Hash Power In Cryptocurrencies*. CoinSutra. https://coinsutra.com/hash-rate-or-hash-power/

Khosravi, M., Ali, N. I., Karbasi, M., Brohi, I. A., Shaikh, I. A., & Shah, A. (2018). Comparison between NFC/RFID and bar code systems for Halal tags identification: Paired sample T-test evaluation. *International Journal of Advanced Computer Science and Applications*, *9*(4). Advance online publication. doi:10.14569/IJACSA.2018.090435

Khoza, A. (2021). Load-shedding is here to stay, Cyril Ramaphosa tells parliament. *TimesLIVE*. https://www.timeslive.co.za/politics/2021-11-25-load-shedding-is-here-to-stay-cyril-ramaphosa-tells-parliament/

Kiefer, A. W., & Novack, R. A. (1999). An empirical analysis of warehouse measurement systems in the context of supply chain implementation. *Transportation Journal*, *38*(3), 18–27.

Kim, S. (2020). *Fractional ownership, democratization and bubble formation-the impact of Blockchain enabled asset tokenization*. Academic Press.

Kim, D., Cavusgil, S. T., & Calantone, R. J. (2006). Information System Innovations and Supply Chain Management: Channel Relationships and Firm Performance. *Journal of the Academy of Marketing Science*, *34*(1), 40–54. doi:10.1177/0092070305281619

Kim, J.-H., & Huh, S.-K. (1973). A study on the improvement of smart grid security performance and blockchain smart grid perspective. *Energies*, 11.

Kim, S.-K., Kim, U.-M., & Huh, H. J. (2017). A study on improvement of blockchain application to overcome vulnerability of IoT multiplatform security. *Energies*, *12*(402).

King, S., & Nadal, S. (2012). *PPCoin: Peer-to-Peer Crypto-Currency with Proof-of-Stake*. Self-published Paper.

Kocagil, A.E., Shachmurove, Y. (1998). Return-volume dynamics in futures markets. *The Journal of Futures Markets*, *18*, 399.

Köhler, S., Pizzol, M., & Sarkis, J. (2021). Unfinished paths—From Blockchain to sustainability in supply chains. *Frontiers in Blockchain*, *4*, 720347. doi:10.3389/fbloc.2021.720347

Konigsmark, S. T. C., Chen, D., & Wong, M. D. F. (2016). Information dispersion for trojan defense through high-level synthesis. *ACM/EDAC/IEEE Design Automation Conference (DAC)*, 1–6. 10.1145/2897937.2898034

Korpela, K., Hallikas, J., & Dahlberg, T. (2019). Digital supply chain transformation toward blockchain integration. *Hawaii International Conference on System Sciences (HICSS)*. 10.24251/HICSS.2017.506

Kosmarski, A. (2020). Blockchain adoption in academia: Promises and challenges. *Journal of Open Innovation*, *6*(4), 117. doi:10.3390/joitmc6040117

Kouhizadeh, M., Saberi, S., & Sarkis, J. (2021). Blockchain technology and the sustainable supply chain: Theoretically exploring adoption barriers. *International Journal of Production Economics*, *231*, 107831. doi:10.1016/j.ijpe.2020.107831

Kouhizadeh, M., & Sarkis, J. (2018). Blockchain practices, potentials, and perspectives in greening supply chains. *Sustainability (Basel)*, *10*(10), 3652. doi:10.3390u10103652

Kouicem, D. E., Bouabdallah, A., & Lakhlef, H. (2018). Internet of things security: A top-down survey. *Computer Networks*, *141*, 199–221. doi:10.1016/j.comnet.2018.03.012

Kreku, J., Vallivaara, V., Halunen, K., & Suomalainen, J. (2017). Evaluating the efficiency of blockchains in IoT with simulations. *IoTBDS 2017 - Proceedings of the 2nd International Conference on Internet of Things, Big Data and Security*, 216–223. https://doi.org/10.5220/0006240502160223

Compilation of References

Krishnapriya, S., & Sarath, G. (2020). Securing land registration using blockchain. *Procedia Computer Science, 171*, 1708–1715. doi:10.1016/j.procs.2020.04.183

Krönke, M. (2020). *Africa's digital divide and the promise of e-learning* [Policy Paper]. Academic Press.

Kshetri, N. (2018). Blockchain's roles in meeting key supply chain management objectives. *International Journal of Information Management, 39*(April), 80–89. doi:10.1016/j.ijinfomgt.2017.12.005

KshetriN.BhusalC. S.ChapagainD. (2021). BCT-AA: A survey of Blockchain Technology-based Applications in context with Agribusiness. doi:10.2139/ssrn.3834004

Kshetri, N., & Voas, J. (2019). Supply Chain Trust. *IT Professional, 21*(2), 6–10. doi:10.1109/MITP.2019.2895423

Kumar & Sharma. (2021). Leveraging blockchain for ensuring trust in IoT: A survey. *Journal of King Saud University-Computer and Information Sciences*.

Kumar Singh, R., Mishra, R., Gupta, S., & Mukherjee, A. A. (2023). Blockchain applications for secured and resilient supply chains: A systematic literature review and future research agenda. *Computers & Industrial Engineering, 175*, 108854. doi:10.1016/j.cie.2022.108854

Kumar, A. S., & Anusha, M. (2023). Blockchain Enabled Supply Chain Management. *SN Computer Science, 4*(2), 179. doi:10.100742979-022-01621-z PMID:36711045

Kumar, A., Abhishek, K., Ghalib, M. R., Nerurkar, P., Bhirud, S., Alnumay, W., & Ghosh, U. (2021). Securing logistics system and supply chain using Blockchain. *Applied Stochastic Models in Business and Industry, 37*(3), 413–428. doi:10.1002/asmb.2592

Kumari, L., Narsaiah, K., Grewal, M., & Anurag, R. (2015). Application of RFID in agri-food sector. *Trends in Food Science & Technology, 43*(2), 144–161. doi:10.1016/j.tifs.2015.02.005

Kumar, R., & Kumar Singh, R. (2017). Coordination and responsiveness issues in SME supply chains: A review. *Benchmarking, 24*(3), 635–650. doi:10.1108/BIJ-03-2016-0041

Laher, A., Van Aardt, B., Craythorne, A., Van Welie, M., Malinga, D., & Madi, S. (2019). 'Getting out of the dark': Implications of load shedding on healthcare in South Africa and strategies to enhance preparedness. *South African Medical Journal, 109*(12), 899–901. doi:10.7196/SAMJ.2019.v109i12.14322 PMID:31865948

Lambert, D., Emmehainz, M., & Gardner, J. (1996). Developing and implementing supply chain partnership. *International Journal of Logistics Management, 7*(2), 1–18. doi:10.1108/09574099610805485

Lam, C. Y., & Ip, W. H. (2019). An Integrated Logistics Routing and Scheduling Network Model with RFID-GPS Data for Supply Chain Management. *Wireless Personal Communications, 2019*(105), 803–817. doi:10.100711277-019-06122-6

Lansiti, M., & Lakhani, K. (2017). The truth about Blockchain. *Harvard Business Review*.

Larsen, T. S., Thernoe, C., & Andresen, C. (2003). Supply chain collaboration: Theoretical perspective and empirical evidence. *International Journal of Physical Distribution & Logistics Management, 33*(6), 531–549. doi:10.1108/09600030310492788

Lasi, H., Fettke, P., Kemper, H.-G., Feld, T., & Hoffmann, M. (2014). Industry 4.0. *Business & Information Systems Engineering, 6*(4), 239–242. doi:10.100712599-014-0334-4

Lasmoles O. & Diallo. (2022). Impacts of blockchains on international maritime. *Journal of Innovation Economics & Management*, 91 – 116.

Latif, S. (2021). Blockchain technology for the industrial Internet of Things: A comprehensive survey on security challenges, architectures, applications, and future research directions. *Transactions on Emerging Telecommunications Technologies, 32*(11).

Latifi, S., Zhang, Y., & Cheng, L. C. (2019, July). Blockchain-based real estate market: One method for applying blockchain technology in commercial real estate market. In *2019 IEEE International Conference on Blockchain (Blockchain)* (pp. 528-535). IEEE. 10.1109/Blockchain.2019.00002

Lawrence, A. (2020). Eskom and the Dual Character of the South African State. In *South Africa's Energy Transition* (pp. 59–83). Springer. doi:10.1007/978-3-030-18903-7_3

LawtechUK. (2022). *Digital representation and ownership of physical assets*. Retrieved December 7, 2022, from digital_representation_ownership_physical_assets.pdf

Lee, H. L. (2000). Creating value through supply chain integration. *Supply Chain Management Review, 4*(4), 30-36.

Lee, H. L., Padmanabhan, V., & Whang, S. (1997, April 15). The bullwhip effect in supply chains. *MIT Sloan Management Review*. Retrieved September 18, 2022, from https://sloanreview.mit.edu/article/the-bullwhip-effect-in-supply-chains

Lee, C. W., Kwon, I. W. G., & Severance, D. (2007). Relationship between supply chain performance and degree of linkage among supplier, internal integration, and customer. *Supply Chain Management, 12*(6), 444–452. doi:10.1108/13598540710826371

Lee, H., Kim, M. S., & Kim, K. K. (2014). Interorganizational information systems visibility and supply chain performance. *International Journal of Information Management, 34*(2), 285–295. doi:10.1016/j.ijinfomgt.2013.10.003

Lee, S. H., Kwak, C., Shim, J., Kim, J. E., Choi, S. L., Kim, H. F., Jang, D. J., Lee, J. A., Lee, K., Lee, C. H., Lee, Y. D., Miniaci, M. C., Bailey, C. H., Kandel, E. R., & Kaang, B. K. (2020). A cellular model of memory reconsolidation involves reactivation-induced destabilization and restabilization at the sensorimotor synapse in Aplysia. *Proceedings of the National Academy of Sciences of the United States of America, 109*(35), 14200–14205. doi:10.1073/pnas.1211997109 PMID:22893682

Leible, S., Schlager, S., Schubotz, M., & Gipp, B. (2019). A review on blockchain technology and blockchain projects fostering open science. *Frontiers in Blockchain*, 16.

Leonard-Barton. (1990). A Dual Methodology for Case Studies: Synergistic Use of a Longitudinal Single Site with Replicated Multiple Sites. *Organization Science, 1*(3).

Lesaege, C., Ast, F., & George, W. (2019). *Kleros Short Paper v1.0.7*. Kleros.

Lesueur-Cazé, M., Bironneau, B., Gulliver, L., &, Morvan, T. (2022). Reflections on the uses of blockchain for logistics and Supply Chain Management: a prospective approach. *French Review of Industrial Management*, 60-82.

Leveson, N. (2004). A new accident model for engineering safer systems. *Safety Science, 42*(4), 237–270. doi:10.1016/S0925-7535(03)00047-X

Lezoche, M., Panetto, H., Kacprzyk, J., Hernandez, J. E., & Alemany Díaz, M. M. E. (2020). Agri-food 4.0: A survey of the Supply Chains and Technologies for the Future Agriculture. *Computers in Industry, 2020*(117), 103187. doi:10.1016/j.compind.2020.103187

Li, A., Wei, X., & He, Z. (2020). Robust proof of stake: A new consensus protocol for sustainable blockchain systems. *Sustainability (Basel), 12*(7), 2824. doi:10.3390u12072824

Compilation of References

Liang, W., Fan, Y., Li, K. C., Zhang, D., & Gaudiot, J. L. (2020). Secure data storage and recovery in industrial Blockchain network environments. *IEEE Transactions on Industrial Informatics*, *16*(10), 6543–6552. doi:10.1109/TII.2020.2966069

Li, B., Yang, C., & Huang, S. (2014). Study on supply chain disruption management under service level dependent demand. *Journal of Networking*, *9*(6), 1432–1439. doi:10.4304/jnw.9.6.1432-1439

Li, C., & Palanisamy, B. (2019). Privacy in Internet of things: From principles to technologies. *IEEE Internet of Things Journal*, *6*(1), 488–505. doi:10.1109/JIOT.2018.2864168

Li, D. (2016). Perspective for smart factory in petrochemical industry. *Computers & Chemical Engineering*, *91*, 136–148. doi:10.1016/j.compchemeng.2016.03.006

Li, L., Lu, X., & Wang, K. (2022). Hash-based signature revisited. *Cybersecurity*, *5*(1), 13. doi:10.118642400-022-00117-w

Lim, M. K., Li, Y., Wang, C., & Tseng, M.-L. (2021). A literature review of blockchain technology applications in supply chains: A comprehensive analysis of themes, methodologies and industries. *Computers & Industrial Engineering*, *154*, 107133. doi:10.1016/j.cie.2021.107133

Lin, C., He, D., Huang, X., Choo, K.-K. R., & Vasilakos, A. V. (2018). Basin: A blockchain-based secure mutual authentication with fine-grained access control system for industry 4.0. *Journal of Network and Computer Applications*, *116*, 42–52. doi:10.1016/j.jnca.2018.05.005

Ling, Z., Liu, K., Xu, Y., Jin, Y., & Fu, X. (2017). An end-to-end view of IoT security and privacy. *IEEE Global Communications Conference*, 1–7. 10.1109/GLOCOM.2017.8254011

Lin, I., & Liao, T. (2017). A Survey of Blockchain Security Issues and Challenges. *International Journal of Network Security*, *19*, 653–659.

Lin, S. Y., Zhang, L., Li, J., Ji, L. L., & Sun, Y. (2022). A survey of application research based on blockchain smart contract. *Wireless Networks*, *28*(2), 635–690. doi:10.100711276-021-02874-x

Lin, Y.-P., Petway, J. R., Antony, J., Mukhtar, H., Lioa, S.-H., Chou, C.-F., & Ho, Y.-F. (2017). Blockchain: The Evolutionary Next Step for ICT E-Agriculture. *Environments (Basel, Switzerland)*, *2017*(4), 50. doi:10.3390/environments4030050

Li, Q., & Liu, A. (2019). Big data driven supply chain management. *Procedia CIRP*, *81*, 1089–1094. doi:10.1016/j.procir.2019.03.258

Li, R., Song, T., Mei, B., Li, H., Cheng, X., & Sun, L. (2019). Blockchain for large-scale Internet of things data storage and protection. *IEEE Transactions on Services Computing*, *12*(5), 762–771. doi:10.1109/TSC.2018.2853167

Li, S., Zhao, X., & Huo, B. (2018). Supply chain coordination and innovativeness: A social contagion and learning perspective. *International Journal of Production Economics*, *205*, 47–61. doi:10.1016/j.ijpe.2018.07.033

Liu, C., Cronin, P., & Yang, C. (2016). A mutual auditing framework to protect iot against hardware trojans. *2016 21st Asia and South Pacific Design Automation Conference (ASP-DAC)*, 69–74. 10.1109/ASPDAC.2016.7427991

Liu, T., Yuan, R., & Chang, H. (2012). Research on the internet of things in the automotive industry. ICMeCG 2012 international conference on management of e-commerce and e-Government, 230–3. doi:10.1109/ICMeCG.2012.80

Liu, C. H., Lin, Q., & Wen, S. (2019b). *Blockchain-enabled data collection and sharing for industrial IoT with deep reinforcement learning*. IEEE Transaction Industrial Informatics. doi:10.1109/TII.2018.2890203

Liu, C., Zhang, X., Chai, K. K., Loo, J., & Chen, Y. (2021). A survey on blockchain-enabled smart grids: Advances, applications and challenges. *IET Smart Cities*, *3*(2), 56–78. doi:10.1049mc2.12010

Liu, J., Zhang, C., & Fang, Y. (2018). Epic: A differential privacy framework to defend smart homes against internet traffic analysis. *IEEE Internet of Things Journal, 5*(2), 1206–1217. doi:10.1109/JIOT.2018.2799820

Liukkonen, M., & Tsai, T. N. (2016). Toward decentralized intelligence in manufacturing: Recent trends in automatic identification of things. *International Journal of Advanced Manufacturing Technology, 87*(9-12), 2509–2531. doi:10.100700170-016-8628-y

Liu, P., Xu, X., & Wang, W. (2022). Threats, attacks and defenses to federated learning: Issues, taxonomy and perspectives. *Cybersecurity, 5*(1), 4. doi:10.118642400-021-00105-6

Liu, X. F., Jiang, X.-J., Liu, S.-H., & Tse, C. K. (2021). Knowledge discovery in cryptocurrency transactions: A survey. *IEEE Access : Practical Innovations, Open Solutions, 9*, 37229–37254. doi:10.1109/ACCESS.2021.3062652

Liu, Y., Guo, W., Fan, C., Chang, L., & Cheng, C. (2019a). A practical privacy-preserving data aggregation (3pda) scheme for smart grid. *IEEE Transactions on Industrial Informatics, 15*(3), 1767–1774. doi:10.1109/TII.2018.2809672

Liu, Y., Lu, Q., Zhu, L., Paik, H. Y., & Staples, M. (2022). A systematic literature review on blockchain governance. *Journal of Systems and Software*, 111576.

Liu, Z., & Li, Z. (2020). A blockchain-based framework of cross-border e-commerce supply chain. *International Journal of Information Management, 52*, 102059. doi:10.1016/j.ijinfomgt.2019.102059

Li, W., Andreina, S., Bohli, J.-M., & Karame, G. (2017). Securing Proof-of-Stake Blockchain Protocols. In J. Garcia-Alfaro, G. Navarro-Arribas, H. Hartenstein, & J. Herrera-Joancomartí (Eds.), *Data Privacy Management, Cryptocurrencies and Blockchain Technology* (pp. 297–315). Springer International Publishing., doi:10.1007/978-3-319-67816-0_17

Li, X., Jiang, P., Chen, T., Luo, X., & Wen, Q. (2017). A survey on the security of blockchain systems. *Future Generation Computer Systems*.

Li, X., Niu, J., Bhuiyan, M. Z. A., Wu, F., Karuppiah, M., & Kumari, S. (2018a). A robust ECC-based provable secure authentication protocol with privacy-preserving for industrial Internet of things. *IEEE Transactions on Industrial Informatics, 14*(8), 3599–3609. doi:10.1109/TII.2017.2773666

Li, Z., Kang, J., Yu, R., Ye, D., Deng, Q., & Zhang, Y. (2018b). Consortium blockchain for secure energy trading in industrial Internet of things. *IEEE Transactions on Industrial Informatics, 14*(8), 3690–3700.

Llorente, G., Michaely, R., Saar, G., & Wang, J. (2002). Dynamic volume return relation of individual stocks. *Review of Financial Studies, 15*(4), 1005–1047. doi:10.1093/rfs/15.4.1005

Lom, M., Pribyl, O., & Svitek, M. (2016). Industry 4.0 as a Part of Smart Cities. In *Smart Cities Symposium Prague (SCSP)*. IEEE. 10.1109/SCSP.2016.7501015

Longo, F., Nicoletti, L., Padovano, A., d'Atri, G., & Forte, M. (2019). Blockchain-enabled supply chain: An experimental study. *Computers & Industrial Engineering, 136*, 57–69. doi:10.1016/j.cie.2019.07.026

Lund, J., & Wright, C. (2003). Building Union Power Through the Supply Chain Mapping Opportunities and Jurisdictional Boundaries in Grocery Distribution. *Labor Studies Journal, 27*(4), 59–75. doi:10.1353/lab.2003.0012

Lu, Y., & Li, J. (2016). A pairing-free certificate-based proxy re-encryption scheme for secure data sharing in public clouds. *Future Generation Computer Systems, 62*, 140–147. doi:10.1016/j.future.2015.11.012

Lycett, M. (2013). 'Datafication': Making sense of (big) data in a complex world. *European Journal of Information Systems, 22*(4), 381–386. doi:10.1057/ejis.2013.10

Compilation of References

Machado, C., & Frhlich, A. A. M. (2018). IoT data integrity verification for cyber-physical systems using blockchain. *2018 IEEE 21st International Symposium on Real-Time Distributed Computing (ISORC)*, 83–90. 10.1109/ISORC.2018.00019

Magnani, G. (2017). *Le aziende culturali: Modelli manageriali*. G Giappichelli Editore.

Mahmood, S., Chadhar, M., & Firmin, S. (2022). Cybersecurity challenges in blockchain technology: A scoping review. *Human Behavior and Emerging Technologies, 2022*, 2022. doi:10.1155/2022/7384000

Majumdar, M. A., Monim, M., & Shahriyer, M. M. (2020, June). Blockchain based land registry with delegated proof of stake (DPoS) consensus in Bangladesh. In *2020 IEEE Region 10 Symposium (TENSYMP)* (pp. 1756-1759). IEEE.

Makaci, M., Reaidy, P., Evrard-Samuel, K., Botta-Genoulaz, V., & Monteiro, T. (2017). Pooled warehouse management: An empirical study. *Computers & Industrial Engineering, 112*, 526–536. doi:10.1016/j.cie.2017.03.005

Makhdoom, I., Abolhasan, M., Abbas, H., & Ni, W. (2019). Blockchain's adoption in iot: The challenges, and a way forward. *Journal of Network and Computer Applications, 125*, 251–279. doi:10.1016/j.jnca.2018.10.019

Malik, S., Kanhere, S. S., & Jurdak, R. (2018, November). Productchain: Scalable blockchain framework to support provenance in supply chains. In *2018 IEEE 17th International Symposium on Network Computing and Applications (NCA)* (pp. 1-10). IEEE.

Malik, N., Wei, M. Y., Appel, G., & Luo, L. (2022). Blockchain Technology for Creative Industry: Current State and Research Opportunities. *International Journal of Research in Marketing*.

Malik, S., Chadhar, M., Vatanasakdakul, S., & Chetty, M. (2021). Factors Affecting the Organizational Adoption of Blockchain Technology: Extending the Technology–Organization–Environment (TOE) Framework in the Australian Context. *Sustainability (Basel), 2021*(13), 9404. doi:10.3390u13169404

Manditereza, K., (2017). *4 Key Differences between Scada and Industrial IoT*. Academic Press.

Mani, V., & Gunasekaran, A. (2021). Upstream complex power relationships and firm's reputation in global value chains. *International Journal of Production Economics, 237*, 108142. doi:10.1016/j.ijpe.2021.108142

Manzoor, A., Liyanage, M., Braeken, A., Kanhere, S. S., & Ylianttila, M. (2019). Blockchain-Based Proxy Re-encryption Scheme for Secure IoT Data Sharing. *Clinical Orthopaedics and Related Research*.

Marin-Dagannaud, G.(2017). The functioning of the blockchain. *Annales des Mines - Industrial Realities, 3*, 42-45.

Markmann, C., Darkow, I.-L., & von der Gracht, H. (2013). A Delphi-based risk analysis — Identifying and assessing future challenges for supply chain security in a multi-stakeholder environment. *Technological Forecasting and Social Change, 80*(9), 1815–1833. doi:10.1016/j.techfore.2012.10.019

Marsh, T. A., & Wagner, N. (2003). Return-Volume Dependence and Extremes in International Equity Markets. SSRN *Electronic Journal*. doi:10.2139/ssrn.424926

Martinez, V., Zhao, M., Blujdea, C., Han, X., Neely, A. & Albores, P. (2019). Blockchain-driven customer order management. *International Journal of Operations & Production Management, 39*(6-8), 993-1022. doi:10.1108/IJOPM-01-2019-0100

Marucheck, A., Greis, N., Mena, C., & Cai, L. (2011). Product safety and security in the global supply chain: Issues, challenges and research opportunities. *Journal of Operations Management, 29*(7-8), 707–720. doi:10.1016/j.jom.2011.06.007

Mastercard-Crescentrating. (2021). *Global Muslim Travel Index 2021*. https://www.crescentrating.com/halal-muslim-travel-market-reports.html

Mastercard-Crescentrating. (2022). *Global Muslim Travel Index 2022*. https://www.crescentrating.com/halal-muslim-travel-market-reports.html

Matharu, G. S., Upadhyay, P., & Chaudhary, L. (2014). The Internet of Things: Challenges & security issues. *Proceedings of the 2014 International Conference on Emerging Technologies, ICET 2014*. 10.1109/ICET.2014.7021016

Mathew, V. N., Abdullah, A. M. R. A., & Ismail, S. N. M. (2014). Acceptance on Halal Food among Non-Muslim Consumers. *Procedia: Social and Behavioral Sciences*, *121*, 262–271. doi:10.1016/j.sbspro.2014.01.1127

Maune, B. (2019). *Load shedding: Timeline of Eskom's battle to keep the lights on*. Retrieved 17 Feb. from https://www.thesouthafrican.com/news/eskom-load-shedding-timeline-since-2007/

McClellan, M. (2003). Collaborative manufacturing: A strategy built on trust and cooperation. *Instrumentation & Control Systems*, *76*(12), 27–31.

Medaglia, R., & Damsgaard, J. (2020). Blockchain and the United Nations Sustainable Development Goals: Towards an Agenda for IS Research. *24th Pacific Asia Conference on Information Systems: Information Systems (IS) for the Future, PACIS 2020*. doi:10.1080/10942912.2016.1203933

Meixell, M. J., & Gargeya, V. B. (2005). Global supply chain design: A literature review and critique. *Transportation Research Part E, Logistics and Transportation Review*, *41*(6), 531–550. doi:10.1016/j.tre.2005.06.003

Mele, C., Spena, T. R., & Kaartemo, V. (2022). Smart technologies in service provision and experience. In *The Palgrave Handbook of Service Management* (pp. 887–906). Palgrave Macmillan. doi:10.1007/978-3-030-91828-6_42

Menon, S., & Jain, K. (2021). Blockchain Technology for Transparency in Agri-Food Supply Chain: Use Cases, Limitations, and Future Directions. *IEEE Transactions on Engineering Management*.

Mentzer, J., DeWitt, W., Keebler, J., Min, S., Nix, N., Smith, C., & Zachria, Z. (2001). Defining supply chain management. *Journal of Business Logistics*, *22*(2), 1–26. doi:10.1002/j.2158-1592.2001.tb00001.x

Menzli, L. J., Smirani, L. K., Boulahia, J. A., & Hadjouni, M. (2022). Investigation of open educational resources adoption in higher education using Rogers' diffusion of innovation theory. *Heliyon Journal, 8*. www.cell.com/heliyon doi:10.1016/j.heliyon.2022.e09885

Merkle, R. C. (1980). Protocols for public key cryptosystems. *IEEE Symposium on Research in Security and Privacy*.

Mettler, T., & Rohner, P. (2009). Supplier relationship management: A case study in the context of health care. *Journal of Theoretical and Applied Electronic Commerce Research*, *4*(3), 58–71. doi:10.4067/S0718-18762009000300006

Metzger, J. (2019). The current landscape of blockchain-based, crowdsourced arbitration. *Macquarie Law Journal*, *19*, 81–101. doi:10.3316/informit.394273690449964

Mezquita, Y. (2021). Cryptocurrencies and Price Prediction: A Survey. In *International Congress on Blockchain and Applications*. Springer.

Mhugos. (2022, September 9). *Zara Clothing Company Supply Chain*. SCM Globe. Retrieved September 18, 2022, from https://www.scmglobe.com/zara-clothing-company-supply-chain/

Michael, J., Cohn, A., & Butcher, J. R. (2018). Blockchain technology. *The Journal*, *1*(7).

Michaelson, P. (2020). Arbitrating Disputes Involving Blockchains, Smart Contracts, and Smart Legal Contracts. *SSRN*, *74*(4), 89–133. doi:10.2139srn.3720876

Compilation of References

Michaelson, P., & Jeskie, S. A. (2021). A Guidebook to Arbitrating Disputes Involving Blockchains and Smart Agreements. *Alternatives to the High Cost of Litigation*, *74*(4), 89–133. doi:10.1002/alt.21887

Michalko, M. (2019). Blockchain 'Witness': A New Evidence Model in Consumer Disputes. *International Journal on Consumer Law and Practice, 7*, Article 3. https://repository.nls.ac.in/ijclp/vol7/iss1/3/

Mienye, I. D., Sun, Y., & Wang, Z. (2019). Prediction performance of improved decision tree-based algorithms: A review. *Procedia Manufacturing*, *35*, 698–703. doi:10.1016/j.promfg.2019.06.011

Min, H. (2019). Blockchain technology for enhancing supply chain resilience. *Business Horizons*, *62*(1), 35–45. doi:10.1016/j.bushor.2018.08.012

Min, S., & Mentzer, J. T. (2004). Developing and measuring supply chain management concepts. *Journal of Business Logistics*, *25*(1), 63–99. doi:10.1002/j.2158-1592.2004.tb00170.x

Mirabelli, G., & Solina, V. (2020). Blockchain and agricultural supply chains traceability: Research trends and future challenges. *Procedia Manufacturing*, *42*, 414–421. doi:10.1016/j.promfg.2020.02.054

Miraz, M. H., & Ali, M. (2018). Blockchain Enabled Enhanced IoT Ecosystem Security. *Proceedings of the International Conference on Emerging Technologies in Computing 2018*, 38-46. https://link.springer.com/chapter/10.1007/978-3-319-95450-9_3 doi:10.1007/978-3-319-95450-9_3

Mkrttchian, V., Gamidullaeva, L., & Galiautdinov, R. (2019). *Design of Nano-scale Electrodes and Development of Avatar-Based Control System for Energy-Efficient Power Engineering: Application of an Internet of Things and People (IOTAP) Research Center. International Journal of Applied Nanotechnology Research*. doi:10.4018/IJANR.2019010104

Mohammed, A. H., Abdulateef, A. A., & Abdulateef, I. A. (2021). Hyperledger, Ethereum and Blockchain Technology: A Short Overview. *Conference Paper*. 10.1109/HORA52670.2021.9461294

Mondal, S., & Samaddar, K. (2021). Reinforcing the significance of human factor in achieving quality performance in data-driven supply chain management. *The TQM Journal*. doi:10.1108/TQM-12-2020-0303

Mondal, S., Wijewardena, K. P., Karuppuswami, S., Kriti, N., Kumar, D., & Chahal, P. (2019). Blockchain inspired RFID-based information architecture for food supply chain. *IEEE Internet of Things Journal*, *6*(3), 5803–5813. doi:10.1109/JIOT.2019.2907658

Monrat, A., Schelén, O., & Andersson, K. (2019). A survey of blockchain from the perspectives of applications, challenges, and opportunities. *IEEE Access : Practical Innovations, Open Solutions*, *7*, 117134–117151. doi:10.1109/ACCESS.2019.2936094

Montecchi, M., Plangger, K., & Etter, M. (2019). It's real, trust me! Establishing supply chain provenance using blockchain. *Business Horizons*, *62*(3), 283–293. doi:10.1016/j.bushor.2019.01.008

Monteiro, M. (2018). *Blockchain: tecnologia da bitcoin está a chegar a múltiplas indústrias*. MaisTic.

Moosa, I. A. (2003). *International financial operations*. Arbitrage, Hedging, Speculation. doi:10.1057/9781403946034

Moosa, I., & Korczak, M. (1999). Is the price-volume relationship symmetric in the futures markets? *Journal of Financial Studies*, *7*, 1.

Morabito, V. (2017). *Business innovation through Blockchain*. Springer International Publishing.

Morawiec, P., & Sołtysik-Piorunkiewicz, A. (2022). Cloud computing, Big Data, and blockchain technology adoption in ERP implementation methodology. *Sustainability (Basel)*, *14*(7), 3714. doi:10.3390u14073714

Morgan, I. G. (1976). Stock prices and heteroscedasticity. *The Journal of Business*, *49*(4), 496–508. doi:10.1086/295881

Morgen, P. (2017). Reinforcing the links of the blockchain. *IEEE Future Directions Blockchain*.

Morkunas, V. J., Paschen, J., & Boon, E. (2019). How Blockchain technologies impact your business model. *Business Horizons*, *62*(3), 295–306. doi:10.1016/j.bushor.2019.01.009

Mosenia, A., & Jha, N. K. (2017). A comprehensive study of security of internet-of-things. *IEEE Transactions on Emerging Topics in Computing*, *5*(4), 586–602. doi:10.1109/TETC.2016.2606384

MosleyL.PhamH.GuoX.BansalY.HareE.AntonyN. (2022). Towards a systematic understanding of blockchain governance in proposal voting: A dash case study. *Blockchain: Research and Applications, 100085*.

Mostaghel, R., Oghazi, P., Patel, P. C., Parida, V., & Hultman, M. (2019). Marketing and supply chain coordination and intelligence quality: A product innovation performance perspective. *Journal of Business Research*, *101*, 597–606. doi:10.1016/j.jbusres.2019.02.058

Mounir, Y., & Naji, M. (2021). *De la mesure de performance des chaines logistiques*. Academic Press.

Mucchi, L., Milanesi, M., & Becagli, C. (2022). Blockchain technologies for museum management. The case of the loan of cultural objects. *Current Issues in Tourism*, *25*(18), 1–15. doi:10.1080/13683500.2022.2050358

Mukne, H., Pai, P., Raut, S., & Ambawade, D. (2019, July). Land record management using hyperledger fabric and ipfs. In *2019 10th International Conference on Computing, Communication and Networking Technologies (ICCCNT)* (pp. 1-8). IEEE. 10.1109/ICCCNT45670.2019.8944471

Muneeb, M., & Raza, Z. (2021). Tree-based blockchain architecture for supply chain. *International Journal of Blockchains and Cryptocurrencies*, *2*(2), 143–160. doi:10.1504/IJBC.2021.118113

Munirathinam, S. (2019). Industry 4.0: Industrial Internet of Things (IIOT). *Advances in Computers*, *117*(1), 129–164.

Musamih, A., Jayaraman, R., Salah, K., Hasan, H. R., Yaqoob, I., & Al-Hammadi, Y. (2021). Blockchain-based solution for distribution and delivery of COVID-19 vaccines. *IEEE Access : Practical Innovations, Open Solutions*, *9*, 71372–71387. doi:10.1109/ACCESS.2021.3079197 PMID:34812393

Myllyvitra, L. (2021). *Eskom is now the world's most polluting power company*. https://energyandcleanair.org/wp/wp-content/uploads/2021/10/Eskom-is-now-the-worlds-most-polluting-power-company.pdf

Naeem, H., Guo, B., & Naeem, M. R. (2018). A lightweight malware static visual analysis for IoT infrastructure. *International Conference on Artificial Intelligence and Big Data (ICAIBD)*, 240–244.

Najand, M., & Yung, K. (1991). A garch examination of the relationship between volume and price variability in futures markets. *Journal of Futures Markets*, *11*(5), 613–621. doi:10.1002/fut.3990110509

Nakamoto, S. (2008). *Bitcoin: A Peer-to-Peer Electronic Cash System*, Retrieved December 10, 2022, from https://bitcoin.org/bitcoin.pdf

Nakamoto, S. (2008). *Bitcoin: A peer-to-peer electronic cash system*. Academic Press.

Nakamoto, S. (2008). *Bitcoin: A Peer-to-Peer Electronic Cash System*. bitcoin.org

Nakamoto, S. (2008). Bitcoin: A peer-to-peer electronic cash system. *Decentralized Business Review*, 21260.

Nakamoto, S. (2009). *Bitcoin: A Peer-to-Peer Electronic Cash System*. Academic Press.

Compilation of References

Nandi, M. L., Nandi, S., Moya, H., & Kaynak, H. (2020). Blockchain technology-enabled supply chain systems and supply chain performance: A resource-based view. *Supply Chain Management, 25*(6), 841–862. doi:10.1108/SCM-12-2019-0444

Narasimhan, R., & Nair, A. (2005). The antecedent role of quality, information sharing and supply chain proximity on strategic alliance formation and performance. *International Journal of Production Economics, 96*(3), 301–313. doi:10.1016/j.ijpe.2003.06.004

Narayanan, A. (2015). *'Private Blockchain' is just a confusing name for a shared database*. Available:https://freedom-to-tinker.com/2015/09/18/private-blockchainis-just-a-confusing-name-for-a-shared-database/

Narayanan, A., & Clark, J. (2017). Bitcoin's academic pedigree. *Communications of the ACM, 60*(12), 36–45. doi:10.1145/3132259

National Research Council. (2000). *Surviving supply chain integration: Strategies for small manufacturers*. National Academies Press.

Nelson, M. (2001). Sustainable Competitive Advantage from Information Technology: Limitations of the Value Chain. In R. Papp (Ed.), *Strategic Information Technology: Opportunities for Competitive Advantage* (pp. 40–55). Idea Group Publishing. doi:10.4018/978-1-878289-87-2.ch002

Nerurkar, P., Patel, D., Busnel, Y., Ludinard, R., Kumari, S., & Khan, M. K. (2021). Dissecting bitcoin blockchain: Empirical analysis of bitcoin network (2009–2020). *Journal of Network and Computer Applications, 177*, 102940. doi:10.1016/j.jnca.2020.102940

Ng, I. C., & Wakenshaw, S. Y. (2017). The Internet-of-Things: Review and research directions. *International Journal of Research in Marketing, 34*(1), 3–21. doi:10.1016/j.ijresmar.2016.11.003

Nguyen, T., Katila, R., & Gia, T. N. (2021). A Novel Internet-of-Drones and Blockchain-based System Architecture for Search and Rescue. In *2021 IEEE 18th International Conference on Mobile Ad Hoc and Smart Systems (MASS)*. IEEE. 10.1109/MASS52906.2021.00044

Nguyen, C. T., Hoang, D. T., Nguyen, D. N., Niyato, D., Nguyen, H. T., & Dutkiewicz, E. (2019). Proof-of-stake consensus mechanisms for future blockchain networks: Fundamentals, applications and opportunities. *IEEE Access : Practical Innovations, Open Solutions, 7*, 85727–85745. doi:10.1109/ACCESS.2019.2925010

Norris, G., Hurley, J. R., Hartley, K. M., Dunleavy, J. R., & Balls, J. D. (2000). *E-business and ERP: Transforming the Enterprise*. John Wiley & Sons.

Nyaletey, E., Parizi, R. M., Zhang, Q., & Choo, K. K. R. (2019, July). BlockIPFS-blockchain-enabled interplanetary file system for forensic and trusted data traceability. In *2019 IEEE International Conference on Blockchain (Blockchain)* (pp. 18-25). IEEE. 10.1109/Blockchain.2019.00012

O'Dwyer, R. (2020). Limited edition: Producing artificial scarcity for digital art on the Blockchain and its implications for the cultural industries. *Convergence (London), 26*(4), 874–894. doi:10.1177/1354856518795097

ObserveIT. (2018). *5 Examples of Insider Threat-Caused Breaches that Illustrate the Scope of the Problem*. Author.

Okorie, O., Turner, C., Charnley, F., Moreno, M., & Tiwari, A. (2017). A review of data-driven approaches for circular economy in manufacturing. *Proceedings of the 18th European Roundtable for Sustainable Consumption and Production*.

Oliveira-Dias, D., Moyano-Fuentes, J., & Maqueira-Marín, J. M. (2022). Understanding the relationships between information technology and Lean and Agile Supply Chain Strategies: A systematic literature review. *Annals of Operations Research, 312*(2), 973–1005. doi:10.100710479-022-04520-x

Olivier, L., Skema, O-L., Mamadou, T., & Diallo, M-T. (2022). Impacts of Blockchains on International Maritime Trade. *Journal of Innovation Economics & Management, 1*(31), 91-116.

Olson, L. D. (2012). Supply Chain Information Technology. In S. Nahmias (Ed.), *The Supply and Operations Management Collection*. Business Expert Press.

Olukanmi, P., Nelwamondo, F., & Marwala, T. (2019). Rethinking k-means clustering in the age of massive datasets: A constant-time approach. *Neural Computing & Applications, 0*, 19–27. doi:10.100700521-019-04673-0

Omar, A. A., Bhuiyan, M. Z. A., Basu, A., Kiyomoto, S., & Rahman, M. S. (2019). Privacy-friendly platform for healthcare data in cloud-based on blockchain environment. *Future Generation Computer Systems, 95*, 511–521. doi:10.1016/j.future.2018.12.044

Orlikowski, W. (2000). Using Technology and Constituting Structures: A Practice Lens for Studying Technology in Organizations. *Organization Science, 11*(4), 149–160. doi:10.1287/orsc.11.4.404.14600

Orlikowski, W. J., & Yates, J. (1994). Genre Repertoire: The Structuring of Communicative Practices in Organizations. *Administrative Science Quarterly, 39*(4), 541–574. doi:10.2307/2393771

Ozer, K., Sahin, M. A., & Cetin, G. (2022). Integrating Big Data to Smart Destination Heritage Management. In *Handbook of Research on Digital Communications, Internet of Things, and the Future of Cultural Tourism* (pp. 411–429). IGI Global. doi:10.4018/978-1-7998-8528-3.ch022

Oztemel, E., & Gusev, S. (2018). Literature review of industry 4.0 and related technologies. *Journal of Intelligent Manufacturing*.

Paksoy, T., Karaoğlan, I., Gökçen, H., Pardalos, P. M., & Torğul, B. (2016). Experimental research on closed loop supply chain management with internet of things. *Journal of Economics Bibliograph., 15*(3), 1–20.

Pal, K. (2017). Building High Quality Big Data-Based Applications in Supply Chains. IGI Global.

Pal, K. (2017). Supply Chain Coordination Based on Web Services. In Supply Chain Management in the Big Data Era. IGI Global.

Pal, K. (2018). A Big Data Framework for Decision Making in Supply Chain. In Predictive Intelligence Using Big Data and the Internet of Things. IGI Global.

Pal, K. (2018). *Ontology-Based Web Service Architecture for Retail Supply Chain Management*. The 9th International Conference on Ambient Systems, Networks and Technologies, Porto, Portugal.

Pal, K. (2019). Algorithmic Solutions for RFID Tag Anti-Collision Problem in Supply Chain Management. *Procedia Computer Science*, 929-934.

Pal, K. (2019). Quality Assurance Issues for Big Data Applications in Supply Chain Management. In Predictive Intelligence Using Big Data and the Internet of Things. IGI Global.

Pal, K. (2021). Applications of Secured Blockchain Technology in Manufacturing Industry. In Blockchain and AI Technology in the Industrial Internet of Things. IGI Global.

Pal, K. (2021a). Applications of Secured Blockchain Technology in Manufacturing Industry. In Blockchain and AI Technology in the Industrial Internet of Things. IGI Global.

Pal, K. (2023). Security Issues and Solutions for Resource-Constrained IoT Applications Using Lightweight Cryptography. In Cybersecurity Issues, Challenges, and Solutions in the Business World. IGI Global.

Compilation of References

Pal, A., Tiwari, C. K., & Haldar, N. (2021). Blockchain for business management: Applications, challenges and potentials. *The Journal of High Technology Management Research*, *32*(2), 100414. doi:10.1016/j.hitech.2021.100414

Pal, K. (2017). Supply Chain Coordination Based on Web Services. In H. K. Chan, N. Subramanian, & M. D. Abdulrahman (Eds.), *Supply Chain Management in the Big Data Era* (pp. 137–171). IGI Global Publication. doi:10.4018/978-1-5225-0956-1.ch009

Pal, K. (2019). Algorithmic Solutions for RFID Tag Anti-Collision Problem in Supply Chain Management. *Procedia Computer Science*, *151*, 929–934. doi:10.1016/j.procs.2019.04.129

Pal, K. (2020). *Information sharing for manufacturing supply chain management based on blockchain technology*. In I. Williams (Ed.), *Cross-Industry Use of Blockchain Technology and Opportunities for the Future* (pp. 1–17). IGI Global.

Pal, K. (2020). Internet of Things and Blockchain Technology in Apparel Supply Chain Management. In H. Patel & G. S. Thakur (Eds.), *Blockchain Applications in IoT Security*. IGI Global Publication.

Pal, K. (2021). Applications of secured blockchain technology in the manufacturing industry. In *Blockchain and AI Technology in the Industrial Internet of Things* (pp. 144–162). IGI Global. doi:10.4018/978-1-7998-6694-7.ch010

Pal, K. (2021b). Privacy, Security and Policies: A Review of Problems and Solutions with Blockchain-Based Internet of Things Applications in Manufacturing Industry. *Procedia Computer Science*, *191*, 176–183. doi:10.1016/j.procs.2021.07.022

Pal, K., & Yasar, A. (2020). Internet of Things and blockchain technology in apparel manufacturing supply chain data management. *Procedia Computer Science*, *170*, 450–457. doi:10.1016/j.procs.2020.03.088

Pal, O., Alam, B., Thakur, V., & Singh, S. (2021). Key management for blockchain technology. *ICT Express*, *7*(1), 76–80. doi:10.1016/j.icte.2019.08.002

Panayides, P. M., & Venus Lun, Y. H. (2009). The impact of trust on innovativeness and supply chain performance. *International Journal of Production Economics*, *122*(1), 35–46. doi:10.1016/j.ijpe.2008.12.025

Papp, R. (2001). *Strategic Information Technology: Opportunities for Competitive Advantage Hershey*. Idea Group Publishing. doi:10.4018/978-1-87828-987-2

Park, A., & Li, H. (2021). The effect of blockchain technology on supply chain sustainability performances. *Sustainability (Basel)*, *13*(4), 1726. Advance online publication. doi:10.3390u13041726

Park, N., & Kang, N. (2015). Mutual authentication scheme in secure Internet of things technology for comfortable lifestyle. *Sensors (Basel)*, *16*(1), 20. doi:10.339016010020 PMID:26712759

Pasdar, A., Lee, Y. C., & Dong, Z. (2023). Connect api with blockchain: A survey on blockchain oracle implementation. *ACM Computing Surveys*, *55*(10), 1–39. doi:10.1145/3567582

Patel, S. S., & Quazi, T. (2022). A multiple-input, multiple-output broadcasting system with space, time, polarization, and labeling diversity. *Transactions on Emerging Telecommunications Technologies,* e4663. https://doi.org/https://doi.org/10.1002/ett.4663

Patel, K., Singh, N., Parikh, K., Kumar, K. S. S., & Jaisankar, N. (2014). Data security and privacy using data partition and centric key management in cloud. *International Conference on Information Communication and Embedded Systems (ICICES2014)*, 1-5. 10.1109/ICICES.2014.7033769

Patnayakuni, R., Rai, A., & Seth, N. (2006). Relational antecedents of information flow integration for supply chain coordination. *Journal of Management Information Systems*, *23*(1), 13–49. doi:10.2753/MIS0742-1222230101

Paton, C. (2021). Eskom: Massive maintenance delays on the back of worst load shedding year ever. *News24*. https://www.news24.com/fin24/Economy/eskom-massive-maintenance-delays-on-the-back-of-worst-load-shedding-year-ever-20220127

Patrickson, B. (2021). What do Blockchain technologies imply for digital creative industries? *Creativity and Innovation Management*, *30*(3), 585–595. doi:10.1111/caim.12456

Paul, T., Mondal, S., Islam, N., & Rakshit, S. (2021). The impact of blockchain technology on the tea supply chain and its sustainable performance. *Technological Forecasting and Social Change*, *173*, 121163. doi:10.1016/j.techfore.2021.121163

Pearce, S. (2021, June). *Smart contracts: The good, the bad and the ugly*. TechRadar. https://www.techradar.com/news/smart-contracts-the-good-the-bad-and-the-ugly

Pearce, D. W., & Turner, R. K. (1990). *Economics of Natural Resources and the Environment*. JHU Press.

Pearson, S. (2019, October 14). *Growing adoption of Supply Chain Analytics*. Deloitte United States. Retrieved September 20, 2022, from https://www2.deloitte.com/us/en/pages/operations/articles/digital-disruption-supply-chain-analytics.html

Peng, C., Liu, Z., Wen, F., Lee, J. Y., & Cui, F. (2022). Research on Blockchain Technology and Media Industry Applications in the Context of Big Data. *Wireless Communications and Mobile Computing*, *2022*, 1–8. Advance online publication. doi:10.1155/2022/3038436

Peng, L., Feng, W., Yan, Z., Li, Y., Zhou, X., & Shimizu, S. (2021). Privacy preservation in permissionless blockchain: A survey. *Digital Communications and Networks*, *7*(3), 295–307. doi:10.1016/j.dcan.2020.05.008

Perboli, G., Musso, S., & Rosano, M. (2018). Blockchain in logistics and supply chain: A lean approach for designing real-world use cases. *IEEE Access : Practical Innovations, Open Solutions*, *6*, 62018–62028. doi:10.1109/ACCESS.2018.2875782

Pierce, F. (2020). *Consignment theft dispute ruling has implications for logistics industry*. Retrieved December 12, 2022, from https://www.supplychaindigital.com/supply-chain-2/consignment-theft-dispute-ruling-has-implications-logistics-industry

Platanakis, E., & Urquhart, A. (2020). Should investors include bitcoin in their portfolios? a portfolio theory approach. *The British Accounting Review*, *52*(4), 100837. doi:10.1016/j.bar.2019.100837

Porambage, P., Schmitt, C., Kumar, P., Gurtov, A., & Ylianttila, M. (2014). Pauthkey: A pervasive authentication protocol and key establishment scheme for wireless sensor networks in distributed IoT applications. *International Journal of Distributed Sensor Networks*, *10*(7), 357430. doi:10.1155/2014/357430

Pournader, M., Shi, Y., Seuring, S., & Koh, S. C. L. (2020). Blockchain applications in supply chains, transport, and logistics: A systematic review of the literature. *International Journal of Production Research*, *2020*(58), 2063–2081. doi:10.1080/00207543.2019.1650976

Prause, G. (2019). Smart Contracts for Smart Supply Chains. *IFAC-PapersOnLine*, *52*(13), 2501–2506. doi:10.1016/j.ifacol.2019.11.582

Prendeville, S., Cherim, E., & Bocken, N. (2017). Circular cities: Mapping six cities in transition. *Environmental Innovation and Societal Transitions*.

Compilation of References

Prewett, K. W., Prescott, G. L., & Phillips, K. (2020). Blockchain adoption is inevitable—Barriers and risks remain. *Journal of Corporate Accounting & Finance*, *31*(2), 21–28. doi:10.1002/jcaf.22415

Print, D. (2015). *Supply Chain Performance and Evaluation Models*. ISTE.

Priyadarshini, I. (2019). Introduction to blockchain technology. *Cyber security in parallel and distributed computing: Concepts, techniques, applications and case studies,* 91-107.

Pu, C., & Hajjar, S. (2018). Mitigating forwarding misbehaviors in rpl-based low power and lossy networks. *2018 15th IEEE Annual Consumer Communications Networking Conference (CCNC)*, 1–6. 10.1109/CCNC.2018.8319164

Pundir, A. K., Jagannath, J. D., Chakraborty, M., & Ganpathy, L. (2019). Technology integration for improved performance: a case study in digitization of supply chain with integration of Internet of Things and blockchain technology. *IEEE 9th Annual Computing and Communication Workshop and Conference (CCWC)*, 170-176. 10.1109/CCWC.2019.8666484

Queiroz, M. M., Fosso Wamba, S., De Bourmont, M., & Telles, R. (2021). Blockchain adoption in operations and supply chain management: Empirical evidence from an emerging economy. *International Journal of Production Research*, *59*(20), 6087–6103. doi:10.1080/00207543.2020.1803511

Queiroz, M., Telles, R., & Bonilla, S. (2019). Blockchain and supply chain management integration: A systematic review of the literature. *Supply Chain Management*, *25*(2), 241–254. Advance online publication. doi:10.1108/SCM-03-2018-0143

Rabinovich-Einy, O., & Katsch, E. (2019). Blockchain and the Inevitability of Disputes: The Role for Online Dispute Resolution. *Journal of Dispute Resolution*, *2019*(2), 47–75. https://ssrn.com/abstract=3508461

Radikoko, I., & Ndjadingwe, E. (2015). Investigating the effects of dividends pay-out on stock prices and traded equity volumes of bse listed firms. *International Journal of Innovation and Economic Development*, *1*(4), 24–37. doi:10.18775/ijied.1849-7551-7020.2015.14.2002

Raeva, S. N., Vainberg, N. A., Dubynin, V. A., Tsetlin, I. M., Tikhonov, Y. N., & Lashin, A. P. (2019). Changes in the spike activity of neurons in the ventrolateral nucleus of the thalamus in humans during performance of a voluntary movement. Neuroscience and Behavioral Physiology, 29(5), 505-513.

Rafudeen, A. (2013). The Orion Cold Storage Saga: Debating 'Halaal' in South Africa. *Alternation Journal, 11*, 134-162. https://journals.ukzn.ac.za/index.php/soa/article/view/406

Rahulamathavan, Y., Phan, R. C., Rajarajan, M., Misra, S., & Kondoz, A. (2017). Privacy-preserving blockchain-based IoT ecosystem using attribute-based encryption. *IEEE International Conference on Advanced Networks and Telecommunications Systems (ANTS)*, 1–6. 10.1109/ANTS.2017.8384164

Rajput, S., Singh, A., Khurana, S., Bansal, T., & Shreshtha, S. (2019, February). Blockchain technology and cryptocurrenices. In 2019 Amity international conference on artificial intelligence (AICAI) (pp. 909-912). IEEE. doi:10.1109/AICAI.2019.8701371

Rambus. (n.d.). *Industrial IoT: Threats and countermeasures*. https://www.rambus.com/iot/ industrial-IoT/

Rashideh, W. (2020). Blockchain technology framework: Current and future perspectives for the tourism industry. *Tourism Management*, *80*, 104125. doi:10.1016/j.tourman.2020.104125

Rasmussen, J. (1997). Risk management in a dynamic society: A modelling problem. *Safety Science*, *27*(2), 183–213. doi:10.1016/S0925-7535(97)00052-0

Rathke, S. K. (2015). *Supply Chain Dispute Resolution in the US*. Retrieved November 28, 2022, from https://www.globalsupplychainlawblog.com/wp-content/uploads/sites/22/2015/07/Supply-Chain-Dispute-Resolution-in-the-US.pdf

Rauniyar, K., Wu, X., Gupta, S., Modgil, S., & Lopes de Sousa Jabbour, A. B. (2022). Risk management of supply chains in the digital transformation era: Contribution and challenges of blockchain technology. *Industrial Management & Data Systems*, *123*(1), 253–277. doi:10.1108/IMDS-04-2021-0235

Reddy, K. R. K., Gunasekaran, A., Kalpana, P., Sreedharan, V. R., & Kumar, S. A. (2021). Developing a blockchain framework for the automotive supply chain: A systematic review. *Computers & Industrial Engineering*, *157*, 107334. doi:10.1016/j.cie.2021.107334

Rehman, W., Zainab, H., Imran, J., & Bawany, N. Z. (2021, December). NFTs: Applications and challenges. In *2021 22nd International Arab Conference on Information Technology (ACIT)* (pp. 1-7). IEEE.

Rejeb, A., Keogh, J. G., & Treiblmaier, H. (2020). How Blockchain technology can benefit marketing: Six pending research areas. *Frontiers in Blockchain*, 3.

Rejeb, A., Keogh, J.G., Simske, S.J., Stafford, T., & Treiblmaier, H. (2021). Potentials of Blockchain technologies for supply chain collaboration: a conceptual framework. *The International Journal of Logistics Management*. doi:10.1108/IJLM-02-2020-0098

Rejeb, A., Rejeb, K., Zailani, S., Treiblmaier, H., & Hand, K. J. (2021). Integrating the Internet of Things in the halal food supply chain: A systematic literature review and research agenda. *Internet of Things, 13*, 100361. https://doi.org/https://doi.org/10.1016/j.iot.2021.100361

Rejeb, A. (2018). Halal Meat Supply Chain Traceability based on HACCP, Blockchain and Internet of Things. *Acta Technica Jaurinensis*, *11*(4), 218–247. doi:10.14513/actatechjaur.v11.n4.467

Rejeb, A., Keogh, J. G., & Treiblmaier, H. (2019). Leveraging the internet of things and blockchain technology in supply chain management. *Future Internet*, *11*(7), 161. doi:10.3390/fi11070161

Reyna, A., Martn, C., Chen, J., Soler, E., & Daz, M. (2018). On blockchain and its integration with iot. challenges and opportunities. *Future Generation Computer Systems*, *88*, 173–190. doi:10.1016/j.future.2018.05.046

Ripsal. (2002). *The case method, application to management research*. De Boeck University Edition.

Robinson, D. (2020). *NB-IoT (LTE Cat-NB1/narrow-band IoT) performance evaluation of variability in multiple LTE vendors, UE devices and MNOs*. Stellenbosch University.

Rogalski, R. J. (1978). The dependence of prices and volume. *The Review of Economics and Statistics*, *60*(2), 268–274. doi:10.2307/1924980

Rogers, E. M. (1995). *Diffusion of Innovations* (4th ed.). Free Press.

Rong, S., & Bao-Wen, Z. (2018). The research of regression model in machine learning field. *MATEC Web of Conferences, 176*, 8–11. 10.1051/matecconf/201817601033

Ruby, D., (2023). *Blockchain statistics: How many people use bitcoin?* demandesage.com

Ruslan, A. A. A., Kamarulzaman, N. H., & Sanny, M. (2018). Muslim consumers' awareness and perception of Halal food fraud. *International Food Research Journal*, *25*, S87–S96.

Compilation of References

Russo-Spena, T., Mele, C., & Pels, J. (2022). Resourcing, sensemaking and legitimizing: blockchain technology-enhanced market practices. *Journal of Business & Industrial Marketing*.

Saadatfar, H., Khosravi, S., Joloudari, J. H., Mosavi, A., & Shamshirband, S. (2020). A new k-nearest neighbors classifier for big data based on efficient data pruning. *Mathematics*, *8*(2), 1–12. doi:10.3390/math8020286

Saberi, S., Kouhizadeh, M., Sarkis, J., & Shen, L. (2019). Blockchain technology and its relationships to sustainable supply chain management. *International Journal of Production Research*, *57*(7), 2117–2135. doi:10.1080/00207543.2018.1533261

Sagan, A., Liu, Y., & Bernstein, A. (2021). Decentralized low-rank state estimation for power distribution systems. *IEEE Transactions on Smart Grid*, *12*(4), 3097–3106. doi:10.1109/TSG.2021.3058609

Sahay, B. S. (2003). Understanding trust in supply chain relationships. *Industrial Management & Data Systems*, *103*(8), 553–563. doi:10.1108/02635570310497602

Sajja, G. S., Rane, K. P., Phasinam, K., Kassanuk, T., Okoronkwo, E., & Prabhu, P. (2021). Towards applicability of blockchain in agriculture sector. *Materials Today: Proceedings*. Advance online publication. doi:10.1016/j.matpr.2021.07.366

Salcedo, E., & Gupta, M. (2021). The effects of individual-level espoused national cultural values on the willingness to use Bitcoin-like blockchain currencies. *International Journal of Information Management*, *60*, 102388. doi:10.1016/j.ijinfomgt.2021.102388

Saleh, F. (2021). Blockchain without Waste: Proof-of-Stake. *The Review of Financial Studies*, *34*(3), 1156–1190. doi:10.1093/rfs/hhaa075

Sambasivan, R., Das, S., & Sahu, S. K. (2020). A Bayesian perspective of statistical machine learning for big data. *Computational Statistics*, *35*(3), 893–930. Advance online publication. doi:10.100700180-020-00970-8

Sanders, N. R. (2014). *Big Data Driven Supply Chain Management: A Framework for Implementing Analytics and Turning Information Into Intelligence*. Pearson Education.

Sanders, N. R., & Wagner, S. M. (2011). Multidisciplinary and Multimethod Research for Addressing Contemporary Supply Chain Challenges. *Journal of Business Logistics*, *32*(4), 317–323. doi:10.1111/j.0000-0000.2011.01027.x

Sangari, M. S., & Mashatan, A. (2022). A data-driven, comparative review of the academic literature and news media on blockchain-enabled supply chain management: Trends, gaps, and research needs. *Computers in Industry*, *143*, 103769. doi:10.1016/j.compind.2022.103769

Sanka, A. I., Irfan, M., Huang, I., & Cheung, R. C. C. (2021). A survey of breakthrough in blockchain technology: Adoptions, applications, challenges and future research. *Computer Communications*, *169*, 179–201. doi:10.1016/j.comcom.2020.12.028

Santhi, K., Zayaraz, G., & Vijayalakshmi, V. (2015). Resolving Aspect Dependencies for Composition of Aspects. *Arabian Journal for Science and Engineering*, *40*(2), 475–486. doi:10.100713369-014-1454-3

Sarote, P., & Shukla, O. J. (2021). Blockchain Technology Adoption in Healthcare Sector for Challenges Posed by COVID-19. In Recent Advances in Smart Manufacturing and Materials. Springer. doi:10.1007/978-981-16-3033-0_34

Sashi, C. M. (2021). Digital communication, value co-creation and customer engagement in business networks: A conceptual matrix and propositions. *European Journal of Marketing*, *55*(6), 1643–1663. doi:10.1108/EJM-01-2020-0023

Savelyev, A. (2018). Copyright in the Blockchain era: Promises and challenges. *Computer Law & Security Report*, *34*(3), 550–561. doi:10.1016/j.clsr.2017.11.008

Schatsky, D., Arora, A., & Dongre, A. (2018). *Blockchain and the five vectors of progress*. Recuperado de https://www2.deloitte.com/us/en/insights/focus/signals-for-strategists/value-of-blockchain-applications-interoperability.html

Schlund, J., Ammon, L., & German, R. (2018). ETHome: Open-source blockchain based energy community controller. *e-Energy '18, International Conference on Future Energy Systems*.

Schmitz, A. J. (2020). *Making Smart Contracts "Smarter" with Arbitration*. University of Missouri School of Law Legal Studies Research Paper Series, Paper No. 2020-18. https://scholarship.law.missouri.edu/facpubs/726/

Schmitz, A., & Rule, C. (2019). Online Dispute Resolution for Smart Contracts. *Journal of Dispute Resolution, 2019*(2), 103–125. https://papers.ssrn.com/sol3/papers.cfm?abstract_id=3647573

Schönhals, A., Hepp, T., & Gipp, B. (2018, June). Design thinking using the blockchain: enable traceability of intellectual property in problem-solving processes for open innovation. In *Proceedings of the 1st Workshop on Cryptocurrencies and Blockchains for Distributed Systems* (pp. 105-110). 10.1145/3211933.3211952

SDG. (2023). https://www.un.org/sustainabledevelopment/sustainable-development-goals

Sedlmeir, J., Buhl, H. U., Fridgen, G., & Keller, R. (2020). The energy consumption of blockchain technology: Beyond myth. *Business & Information Systems Engineering, 62*(6), 599–608. doi:10.100712599-020-00656-x

Seebacher, G., & Winkler, H. (2015). A capability approach to evaluate supply chain flexibility. *International Journal of Production Economics, 167*, 177–186. doi:10.1016/j.ijpe.2015.05.035

Seebacher, S., & Schüritz, R. (2017). Blockchain Technology as an Enabler of Service Systems: A Structured Literature Review. In W. Van der Aalst, J. Mylopoulos, S. Ram, M. Rosemann, & C. Szyperski (Eds.), *Exploring Services Science. IESS 2017. Lecture Notes in Business Information Processing* (pp. 12–23). Springer. doi:10.1007/978-3-319-56925-3_2

Sendhil Kumar, K. S., Anbarasi, M., Shanmugam, G. S., & Shankar, A. (2020). Efficient Predictive Model for Utilization of Computing Resources using Machine Learning Techniques. *2020 10th International Conference on Cloud Computing, Data Science & Engineering (Confluence)*, 351-357. 10.1109/Confluence47617.2020.9057935

Seyednima Khezr, S., Moniruzzaman, M., Yassine, A., & Benlamri, R. (2019). Blockchain Technology in Healthcare: A Comprehensive Review and Directions for Future Research. *Applied Sciences, 9*(1736). www.mdpi.com/journal/applsci doi:10.3390/app9091736

Sfar, A. R., Natalizio, E., Challal, Y., & Chtourou, Z. (2018). A roadmap for security challenges in the Internet of things. *Digital Communications and Networks, 4*(2), 118–137. doi:10.1016/j.dcan.2017.04.003

Shahid, A., Almogren, A., Javaid, N., Al-Zahrani, F. A., Zuair, M., & Alam, M. (2020). Blockchain-based agri-food supply chain: A complete solution. *IEEE Access : Practical Innovations, Open Solutions, 8*, 69230–69243. doi:10.1109/ACCESS.2020.2986257

Shaik, M. N., & Abdul-Kader, W. (2013). Interorganizational Information Systems Adoption in Supply Chains: A Context-Specific Framework. *International Journal of Information Systems and Supply Chain Management, 6*(1), 24–40. doi:10.4018/jisscm.2013010102

Shankar, C. G. (2021). A survey on blockchain applications. *Information Technology in Industry, 9*(3), 635–639.

Sharma, P. K., Moon, S. Y., & Park, J. H. (2017). Block-VN: A distributed Blockchain based vehicular network architecture in smart city. *Journal of Information Processing Systems, 13*(1), 84.

Compilation of References

Shehata, I. (2018). Smart Contracts & International Arbitration. SSRN *Electronic Journal*. doi:10.2139/ssrn.3290026

Shen, M., Tang, X., Zhu, L., Du, X., & Guizani, M. (2019). Privacy-preserving support vector machine training over blockchain-based encrypted IoT data in smart cities. *IEEE Internet of Things Journal*, *6*(5), 7702–7712. doi:10.1109/JIOT.2019.2901840

Shields, N. (2019). *Amazon is Rolling Out New Warehouse Robots*. Business Insider. Retrieved September 20, 2022, from https://www.businessinsider.com/amazon-introduces-new-warehouse-robots-2019-5?IR=T

Shi, N. (2016). A new proof-of-work mechanism for bitcoin. *Financial Innovation*, *2*(1), 31. doi:10.118640854-016-0045-6

Shinde, D., Padekar, S., Raut, S., Wasay, A., & Sambhare, S. S. (2019, September). Land Registry Using Blockchain- A Survey of existing systems and proposing a feasible solution. In *2019 5th International Conference On Computing, Communication, Control And Automation (ICCUBEA)* (pp. 1-6). IEEE. 10.1109/ICCUBEA47591.2019.9129289

Shinde, R. (2021). Blockchain for securing ai applications and open innovations. *Journal of Open Innovation: Technology, Market, and Complexity*, *7*(3).

Shin, H., Collier, D. A., & Wilson, D. D. (2000). Supply Management Orientation and supplier/buyer performance. *Journal of Operations Management*, *18*(3), 317–333. doi:10.1016/S0272-6963(99)00031-5

Shin, T. H., Chin, S., Yoon, S. W., & Kwon, S. W. (2011). A service-oriented integrated information framework for RFID/WSN-based intelligent construction supply chain management. *Automation in Construction*, *20*(6), 706–715. doi:10.1016/j.autcon.2010.12.002

Shin, W. S., Dahlgaard, J. J., Dahlgaard-Park, S. M., & Kim, M. G. (2018). A Quality Scorecard for the era of Industry 4.0. *Total Quality Management & Business Excellence*, *29*(9-10), 959–976. doi:10.1080/14783363.2018.1486536

Shiralkar, K., Bongale, A., Kumar, S., Kotecha, K., & Prakash, C. (2021). Assessment of the benefits of information and communication technologies (ICT) adoption on downstream supply chain performance of the retail industry. *Logistics*, *5*(4), 80. doi:10.3390/logistics5040080

Shi, X., Yao, S., & Luo, S. (2021). Innovative platform operations with the use of technologies in the blockchain era. *International Journal of Production Research*, 1–19. Advance online publication. doi:10.1080/00207543.2021.1953182

Shrestha, R., Bajracharya, R., Shrestha, A. P., & Nam, S. Y. (2019). A new type of blockchain for secure message exchange in vanet. *Digital Communications and Networks*.

Shuaib, M., Daud, S. M., Alam, S., & Khan, W. Z. (2020). Blockchain-based framework for secure and reliable land registry system. *Telkomnika*, *18*(5), 2560–2571. doi:10.12928/telkomnika.v18i5.15787

Shukla, P. (2017). Ml-ids: A machine learning approach to detect wormhole attacks in the Internet of things. Intelligent Systems Conference (IntelliSys), 234–240. doi:10.1109/IntelliSys.2017.8324298

Sicari, S., Rizzardi, A., Miorandi, D., & Coen-Porisini, A. (2018). Reatoreacting to denial-of-service attacks in the Internet of things. *Computer Networks*, *137*, 37–48. doi:10.1016/j.comnet.2018.03.020

Sidarto, L. P., & Hamka, A. (2021). Improving Halal Traceability Process in the Poultry Industry Utilizing Blockchain Technology: Use Case in Indonesia. *Frontiers in Blockchain*, *4*(27), 612898. Advance online publication. doi:10.3389/fbloc.2021.612898

Simatupang, T. M., Wright, A. C., & Sridharan, R. (2002). The knowledge of coordination for supply chain integration. *Business Process Management Journal*, *8*(3), 289–308. doi:10.1108/14637150210428989

Simonnot, B. (2012). *Access to online information: Engines, devices and mediations*. Hermès Lavoisier.

Simonyan, E.V., Shikova, Y.V., & Khisamova, A.A. (2020). *Validation of assay method for certain amino acids in dosage forms by HPLC method*. Academic Press.

Singh, M., Rajan, M. A., Shivraj, V. L., & Balamuralidhar, P. (2015). Secure MQTT for the Internet of things (IoT). *5th International Conference on Communication Systems and Network Technologies*, 746–751. 10.1109/CSNT.2015.16

Smirlock, M., & Starks, L. (1985). A further examination of stock price changes and transaction volume. *Journal of Financial Research*, *8*(3), 217–226. doi:10.1111/j.1475-6803.1985.tb00404.x

Smirnova, L.A., Riabuha, A.F., Kuznetsov, K.A., Suchkov, E.A., & Perfilova, V.N. (2019). *Development of method of quantitative determination of new GABA derivatives in biological samples*. Academic Press.

Soares, M. J., & Aguiar-Conraria, L. (2006). *The continuous wavelet transform: A primer*. Academic Press.

Sommanawat, K., Vipaporn, T., & Joemsittiprasert, W. (2019). Can Big Data Benefits Bridge Between Data Driven Supply Chain Orientation and Financial Performance? Evidence from Manufacturing Sector of Thailand. *International Journal of Supply Chain Management*, *8*(5), 597.

Song, J. M., Sung, J., & Park, T. (2019). Applications of Blockchain to Improve Supply Chain Traceability. *Procedia Computer Science*, *162*, 119–122. doi:10.1016/j.procs.2019.11.266

Song, T., Li, R., Mei, B., Yu, J., Xing, X., & Cheng, X. (2017). A privacy-preserving communication protocol for IoT applications in smart homes. *IEEE Internet of Things Journal*, *4*(6), 1844–1852. doi:10.1109/JIOT.2017.2707489

Sony, M., & Naik, S. (2020). Industry 4.0 integration with socio-technical systems theory: A systematic review and proposed theoretical model. *Technology in Society*, *61*, 101248. Advance online publication. doi:10.1016/j.techsoc.2020.101248

Sookhak, M., Jabbarpour, M. R., Safa, N. S., & Yu, F. R. (2021). Blockchain and smart contract for access control in healthcare: A survey, issues and challenges, and open issues. *Journal of Network and Computer Applications*, *178*, 102950. doi:10.1016/j.jnca.2020.102950

SOPHOS. (2015). *49 Busted in Europe for Man-In-The-Middle Bank Attacks*. https://nakedsecurity.sophos.com/2015/06/11/49-busted-in-europe-for-man-in-themiddle-bank-attacks/

Soppé, F. (2005). Containerized maritime transport and globalization. *Annals of Geography*, *2*(642), 187 – 200.

South African Government News Agency. (2022). *Radio spectrum auction a catalyst for digital development*. Retrieved 23 March from https://www.sanews.gov.za/south-africa/radio-spectrum-auction-catalyst-digital-development

Sreamr. (2017). *Streamr White Paper v2.0*. https://s3.amazonaws.com/streamr-public/ streamr-datacoin-whitepaper-2017-07-25-v1_0.pdf

Srinivas, J., Das, A. K., Wazid, M., & Kumar, N. (2018). Anonymous lightweight chaotic map-based authenticated key agreement protocol for industrial Internet of things. *IEEE Trans. Dependable Secure Comput.*

Staff Writer. (2022). *New data reveals ugly truth about load shedding in South Africa*. *BusinessTech*. https://businesstech.co.za/news/energy/632229/new-data-reveals-the-ugly-truth-about-load-shedding-in-south-africa/

Staff, H. B. R. (2021, July). Smart Contracts: Hype vs. Reality. *Harvard Business Review*. https://hbr.org/2021/07/smart-contracts-hype-vs-reality

Compilation of References

Stank, T., Esper, T., Goldsby, T. J., Zinn, W., & Autry, C. (2019). Toward a Digitally Dominant Paradigm for twenty-first century supply chain scholarship. *International Journal of Physical Distribution & Logistics Management*, *49*(10), 956–971. doi:10.1108/IJPDLM-03-2019-0076

Statista. (2021). *African countries with the highest Gross Domestic Product (GDP) in 2021*. Retrieved 29 November from https://www.statista.com/statistics/1120999/gdp-of-african-countries-by-country/

Statistics South Africa. (2018). *How important is tourism to the South African economy?* Department: Statistics South Africa. Retrieved 6 March from http://www.statssa.gov.za/?p=11030

Statman, M., Thorley, S., & Vorkink, K. (2006). Investor overconfidence and trading volume. *Review of Financial Studies*, *19*(4), 1531–1565. doi:10.1093/rfs/hhj032

Steinmetz, F., von Meduna, M., Ante, L., & Fiedler, I. (2021). Ownership, uses and perceptions of cryptocurrency: Results from a population survey. *Technological Forecasting and Social Change*, *173*, 121073. doi:10.1016/j.techfore.2021.121073

Sternberg, H. S., Hofmann, E., & Roeck, D. (2021). The struggle is real: Insights from a supply chain blockchain case. *Journal of Business Logistics*, *42*(1), 71–87. doi:10.1111/jbl.12240

Stock, T., & Seliger, G. (2016). Opportunities of sustainable manufacturing in industry 4.0. *Procedia CIRP*, *40*, 536–541. doi:10.1016/j.procir.2016.01.129

Su, J., Vasconcellos, V.D., Prasad, S., Daniele, S., Feng, Y., & Sakurai, K. (2018). Lightweight classification of IoT malware based on image recognition. *IEEE 42nd Annual Computer Software and Applications Conference (COMPSAC)*, *2*, 664–669.

Su, J., Li, C., Zeng, Q., Yang, J., & Zhang, J. (2019). A green closed-loop supply chain coordination mechanism based on third-party recycling. *Sustainability (Basel)*, *11*(19), 5335. doi:10.3390u11195335

Sukati, I., Abdul Hamid, A. B., Tat, H. H., & Said, F. (2012). A study of Supply Chain Management Practices: AN Empirical Investigation on consumer goods industry in Malaysia. *International Journal of Business and Social Science*, *2*(17), 166–176.

Sun, X., Chen, M., Zhu, Y., & Li, T. (2018, October). Research on the application of blockchain technology in energy internet. In *2018 2nd IEEE Conference on Energy Internet and Energy System Integration (EI2)* (pp. 1-6). IEEE. 10.1109/EI2.2018.8582599

Sundarakani, B., Ajaykumar, A., & Gunasekaran, A. (2021). Big data driven supply chain design and applications for blockchain: An action research using case study approach. *Omega*, *102*, 102452. doi:10.1016/j.omega.2021.102452

Sun, J., Yan, J., & Zhang, K. Z. (2016). Blockchain-based sharing services: What blockchain technology can contribute to smart cities. *Financial Innovation*, *2*(1), 1–9. doi:10.118640854-016-0040-y

Sunny, J., Undralla, N., & Pillai, V. M. (2020). Supply chain transparency through blockchain-based traceability: An overview with demonstration. *Computers & Industrial Engineering*, *150*, 106895. doi:10.1016/j.cie.2020.106895

Surjandari, I., Yusuf, H., Laoh, E., & Maulida, R. (2021). Designing a Permissioned Blockchain Network for the Halal Industry using Hyperledger Fabric with multiple channels and the raft consensus mechanism. *Journal of Big Data*, *8*(1), 10. Advance online publication. doi:10.118640537-020-00405-7

Swan. (2015). Blockchain-Based Equity and STOs: Towards a Liquid Market for SME Financing? *Theoretical Economics Letters*, *9*(5).

Swatman. (1994). Efficient Consumer Response (ECR): A Survey of the Australian Grocery Industry. *ACIS'97 8th Australasian Conference on Information Systems*, 137-148.

Sylvester, G. (2019). *E-agriculture in action: blockchain for agriculture. Opportunities and challenges*. Academic Press.

Szabo, N. (1996). *Smart Contracts: Building Blocks for Digital Markets*. Retrieved December 2, 2001, from http://www.truevaluemetrics.org/DBpdfs/BlockChain/Nick-Szabo-Smart-Contracts-Building-Blocks-for-Digital-Markets-1996-14591.pdf

Szabo, N. (1997). *The idea of smart contracts*. Nick Szabo's Papers and Concise Tutorials.

Tabachnick, B., & Fidell, L. (2013). *Using multivariate statistics* (6th ed.). Pearson.

Tadejko, P. (2015). Application of Internet of Things in logistics-current challenges. Ekonomia i Zarzadzanie, 7(4), 54–64.

Tan, A., Gligor, D., & Ngah, A. (2020). Applying Blockchain for Halal food traceability. *International Journal of Logistics Research and Applications*, 1-18. doi:10.1080/13675567.2020.1825653

Tang, C. S., & Veelenturf, L. P. (2019). The strategic role of logistics in the industry 4.0 era. Transp. Res. Part E Logist. *Transport Reviews, 2019*(129), 1–11.

Tanha, F. E., Hasani, A., Hakak, S., & Gadekallu, T. R. (2022). Blockchain-based cyber physical systems: Comprehensive model for challenge assessment. *Computers & Electrical Engineering*, *103*, 108347. doi:10.1016/j.compeleceng.2022.108347

Tan, J., & Koo, S. (2014). A survey of technologies in internet of things, in IEEE. *Computers & Society*, 269–274.

Tan, K. C., Kannan, V. R., Handfield, R. B., & Ghosh, S. (1999). Supply Chain Management: An empirical study of its impact on performance. *International Journal of Operations & Production Management*, *19*(10), 1034–1052. doi:10.1108/01443579910287064

Tan, W. C., & Sidhu, M. S. (2022). Review of RFID and IoT integration in supply chain management. *Operations Research Perspectives*, *9*, 100229. doi:10.1016/j.orp.2022.100229

Tasatanattakool, P., & Techapanupreeda, C. (2018). Blockchain: Challenges and applications. *International Conference on Information Networking*, 473–475. 10.1109/ICOIN.2018.8343163

Tasca, P., & Tessone, C. J. (2017). *Taxonomy of blockchain technologies. Principles of identification and classification*. arXiv preprint arXiv:1708.04872.

Tasca, P., & Tessone, C. J. (2019). *A Taxonomy of Blockchain Technologies: Principles of Identification and Classification*. doi:10.5195/ledger.2019.140

Tauchen, G. E., & Pitts, M. (1983). The price variability-volume relationship on speculative markets. *Econometrica*, *51*(2), 485–505. doi:10.2307/1912002

Tayob, S. (2016). 'O You who Believe, Eat of the Tayyibāt (pure and wholesome food) that We Have Provided You'— Producing Risk, Expertise and Certified Halal Consumption in South Africa. *Journal of Religion in Africa. Religion en Afrique*, *46*(1), 67–91. doi:10.1163/15700666-12340064

Tayob, S. (2020). Trading Halal: Halal Certification and Intra-Muslim Trade in South Africa. *Sociology of Islam*, *8*(3-4), 322–342. doi:10.1163/22131418-08030003

Compilation of References

Team, V. (2018). *Vechain White Paper*. https://cdn.vechain.com/vechain_ico_ideas_of_ development_en .pdf

Teece, D. J. (2007). Explicating dynamic capabilities: The nature and microfoundations of (sustainable) enterprise performance. *Strategic Management Journal*, *28*(13), 1319–1350. doi:10.1002mj.640

Terzi, S., Terresan, S., Schneiderbauer, S., Critto, A., Zebisch, M., & Marcomini, A. (2019). Multi-risk assessment in mountain regions: A review of modelling approaches for climate change adaptation. *Journal of Environmental Management*, *232*, 759–771. doi:10.1016/j.jenvman.2018.11.100 PMID:30529418

Tessaro, S. (2016). Sloth: A Lightweight Delay Function for ASIC-Resistant Proof-of-Work Based on Nakamoto's Consensus Algorithm. *Journal of Cryptology*, *29*(2), 613–638.

Thakur, V., Doja, M. N., Dwivedi, Y. K., Ahmad, T., & Khadanga, G. (2020). Land records on blockchain for implementation of land titling in India. *International Journal of Information Management*, *52*, 101940. doi:10.1016/j.ijinfomgt.2019.04.013

The Government of South Africa. (2020). *Building a new economy: Highlights of the reconstruction and recovery plan* [Economic Recovery Action Plan]. https://www.gov.za/sites/default/files/gcis_document/202010/building-new-economy-highlights-reconstruction-and-recovery-plan.pdf

The MTN Group. (2015). *MTN Business unveiles Internet of Things (IoT) platform* https://www.mtnbusiness.co.za/en/Pages/Press-detail.aspx?queryString=mtnbusinesslaunchesfirsttrulypanafricaninternetofthingsplatform

The Muslim Judicial Council Halaal Trust. (n.d.). *MJC Halaal Trust: Certification Process Flowchart*. Retrieved 12 January from https://mjchalaaltrust.co.za/halal-certification-process/

The United Nations General Assembly. (2015). *Transforming Our World: The 2030 Agenda for Sustainable Development*. Author.

Thekkoote, R. (2021). Understanding big data-driven supply chain and performance measures for customer satisfaction. *Benchmarking: An International Journal*. doi:10.1108/BIJ-01-2021-0034

Thiétart, R.A.(1999). *Méthodes de Recherche en Management*. Dunod edition.

Thorelli, H. B. (1986). Networks: Between markets and hierarchies. *Strategic Management Journal*, *7*(1), 37–51. doi:10.1002mj.4250070105

Tian, F. (2017, June). A supply chain traceability system for food safety based on HACCP, blockchain & Internet of things. In *2017 International conference on service systems and service management* (pp. 1-6). IEEE.

Tijan, E., Aksentijević, S., Ivanić, K., & Jardas, M. (2019). Blockchain technology implementation in logistics. *Sustainability (Basel)*, *11*(4), 1185. doi:10.3390u11041185

Tokkozhina, U., Ferreira, J. C., & Martins, A. L. (2021, November). Wine Traceability and Counterfeit Reduction: Blockchain-Based Application for a Wine Supply Chain. In *International Conference on Intelligent Transport Systems* (pp. 59-70). Springer.

Torrence, C., & Compo, G. P. (1998). A practical guide to wavelet analysis. *Bulletin of the American Meteorological Society*, *79*(1), 61–78. doi:10.1175/1520-0477(1998)079<0061:APGTWA>2.0.CO;2

Torrence, C., & Webster, P. J. (1999). Interdecadal changes in the enso–monsoon system. *Journal of Climate*, *12*(8), 2679–2690. doi:10.1175/1520-0442(1999)012<2679:ICITEM>2.0.CO;2

TOSBOL. (2022). *Trabzon-Arsin Organize Sanayi Bölgesi Yönetim Kurulu Başkanlığı*. Retrieved from https://www.tosbol.org.tr/

Toufaily, E., Zalan, T., & Dhaou, S. B. (2021). A framework of blockchain technology adoption: An investigation of challenges and expected value. *Information & Management*, *58*(3), 103444. doi:10.1016/j.im.2021.103444

Tran, Q. N., Turnbull, B. P., Wu, H.-T., de Silva, A. J. S., Kormusheva, K., & Hu, J. (2021). A Survey on Privacy-Preserving Blockchain Systems (PPBS) and a Novel PPBS-Based Framework for Smart Agriculture. *IEEE Open Journal of the Computer Society*, *2*, 72–84. doi:10.1109/OJCS.2021.3053032

Treiblmaier, H. (2018). The impact of the blockchain on the supply chain: A theory-based research framework and a call for action. *Supply Chain Management*, *23*(6), 545–559. doi:10.1108/SCM-01-2018-0029

Treleaven, P., Brown, R. G., & Yang, D. (2017). Blockchain technology in finance. *Computer*, *50*(9), 14–17. doi:10.1109/MC.2017.3571047

Tresise, A., Goldenfein, J., & Hunter, D. (2018). *What blockchain can and can't do for copyright*. Academic Press.

Tripoli, M., & Schmidhuber, J. (2020). *Emerging opportunities for the application of blockchain in the agri-food industry*. https://policycommons.net/artifacts/1422549/emerging-opportunities-for-the-application-of-blockchain-in-the-agri-food-in dustry/

Tsai, C. W., Lai, C. F., Chao, H. C., & Vasilakos, A. V. (2015). Big data analytics: A survey. *Journal of Big Data*, *2*(1), 1–32. doi:10.118640537-015-0030-3 PMID:26191487

Tsang, Y. P., Choy, K. L., Wu, C. H., Ho, G. T. S., & Lam, H. Y. (2019). Blockchain-Driven IoT for Food Traceability With an Integrated Consensus Mechanism. *IEEE Access : Practical Innovations, Open Solutions*, *7*, 129000–129017. doi:10.1109/ACCESS.2019.2940227

Tsao, Y. C., Thanh, V. V., & Wu, Q. (2021). Sustainable microgrid design considering blockchain technology for real-time price-based demand response programs. *International Journal of Electrical Power & Energy Systems*, *125*, 106418. doi:10.1016/j.ijepes.2020.106418

Turek, B. (2013). *Information systems in supply chain integration and management*. Retrieved from https://www.ehow.com/info_8337099_information-supply-chain-i ntegration-management.html

Ullah, N., Mugahed Al-Rahmi, W., Alzahrani, A. I., Alfarraj, O., & Alblehai, F. M. (2021). Blockchain Technology Adoption in Smart Learning Environments. *Sustainability (Basel)*, *2021*(13), 1801. doi:10.3390u13041801

Urquhart, A. (2017). Price clustering in bitcoin. *Economics Letters*, *159*, 145–148. doi:10.1016/j.econlet.2017.07.035

Van Alstyne, M. (2014). Why Bitcoin has value. *Communications of the ACM*, *57*(5), 30–32. doi:10.1145/2594288

Van Haaften-Schick, L., & Whitaker, A. (2022). From the artist's contract to the blockchain ledger: New forms of artists' funding using equity and resale royalties. *Journal of Cultural Economics*, *46*(2), 287–315. doi:10.100710824-022-09445-8

van Pelt, R., Jansen, S., Baars, D., & Overbeek, S. (2021). Defining blockchain governance: A framework for analysis and comparison. *Information Systems Management*, *38*(1), 21–41. doi:10.1080/10580530.2020.1720046

Compilation of References

Vanany, I., Rakhmawati, N. A., Sukoso, S., & Soon, J. M. (2020, 17-18 Nov. 2020). Indonesian Halal Food Integrity: Blockchain Platform. *2020 International Conference on Computer Engineering, Network, and Intelligent Multimedia (CENIM).*

Vanichchinchai, A. (2019). The effect of lean manufacturing on a supply chain relationship and performance. *Sustainability (Basel)*, *11*(20), 5751. doi:10.3390u11205751

Vanichchinchai, A. (2021). The linkages among supplier relationship, customer relationship and supply performance. *Journal of Business and Industrial Marketing*, *36*(8), 1520–1533. doi:10.1108/JBIM-01-2020-0033

Varga, P., Plosz, S., Soos, G., & Hegedus, C. (2017). Security Threats and Issues in Automation IoT. *2017 IEEE 13th International Workshop on Factory Communication Systems (WFCS)*, 1–6. 10.1109/WFCS.2017.7991968

Verdouw, C. N., Wolfert, J., Beulens, A., & Rialland, A. (2016). Virtualization of food supply chains with the internet of things. *Journal of Food Engineering*, *176*, 128–136. doi:10.1016/j.jfoodeng.2015.11.009

Verhoeven, P., Sinn, F., & Herden, T. T. (2018). Examples from blockchain implementations in logistics and supply chain management: Exploring the mindful use of a new technology. *Logistics*, *2*(3), 20. doi:10.3390/logistics2030020

Verma, N., Jain, S., & Doriya, R. (2021, February). Review on consensus protocols for blockchain. In 2021 international conference on computing, communication, and intelligent systems (ICCCIS) (pp. 281-286). IEEE. doi:10.1109/ICCCIS51004.2021.9397089

Verma, V., Priya, S., Mishra, S., & Priyadarshini, R. (2019). Property Fraud Detection and Prevention Using Blockchain. *International Conference on Intelligent Computing and Remote Sensing (ICICRS).*

Verny, J. (2018). The blockchain at the service of improving the competitiveness of companies and the attractiveness of territories. Application to the pharmaceutical sector of the Seine Valley. Annals of Geography, 723-724.

Veza, I., Mladineo, M., & Gjeldum, N. (2015). Managing innovative production network of smart factories. *IFAC-PapersOnLine*, *48*(3), 555–560. doi:10.1016/j.ifacol.2015.06.139

Viriyasitavat, H., & Hoonsopon, D. (2019). Blockchain Characteristics and Consensus in Modern Business Processes. *Journal of Industrial Information Integration*, *13*, 32–39. doi:10.1016/j.jii.2018.07.004

Viriyasitavat, W., Xu, L. D., Sapsomboon, A., Dhiman, G., & Hoonsopon, D. (2022). Building trust of Blockchain-based Internet-of-Thing services using public key infrastructure. *Enterprise Information Systems*, *16*(12), 2037162. doi:10.1080/17517575.2022.2037162

Vishnubhotla, A. K., Pati, R. K., & Padhi, S. S. (2020). Can Projects on Blockchain Reduce Risks in Supply Chain Management?: An Oil Company Case Study. *IIM Kozhikode Society & Management Review*, *9*(2), 189–201. doi:10.1177/2277975220913370

Vodacom. (n.d.). *The Internet of Things (IoT) is transforming assets into intelligent devices.* Retrieved 2 March 2022 from https://www.vodacom.com/internet-of-things.php

Vogel, P. S. (2021, May). *Why smart contracts may not be smart after all.* CIO Dive. https://www.ciodive.com/news/smart-contracts-limitations/599279/

Vogel-Heuser, B., & Hess, D. (2016). Guest editorial Industry 4.0–prerequisites and visions. *IEEE Transactions on Automation Science and Engineering*, *13*(2), 411–413. doi:10.1109/TASE.2016.2523639

Vosooghidizaji, M., Taghipour, A., & Canel-Depitre, B. (2020). Supply chain coordination under information asymmetry: A review. *International Journal of Production Research*, *58*(6), 1805–1834. doi:10.1080/00207543.2019.1685702

Vranken, H. (2017). Sustainability of bitcoin and blockchains. *Current Opinion in Environmental Sustainability*, *28*, 1–9. doi:10.1016/j.cosust.2017.04.011

Vu, N., Ghadge, A., & Bourlakis, M. (2022). Evidence-driven model for implementing Blockchain in food supply chains. *International Journal of Logistics Research and Applications*, 1-21.

Waller, M. A., & Fawcett, S. E. (2013). Data science, predictive analytics, and big data: A revolution that will transform supply chain design and management. *Journal of Business Logistics*, *34*(2), 77–84. doi:10.1111/jbl.12010

Walsh, C., O'Reilly, P., Gleasure, R., McAvoy, J., & O'Leary, K. (2021). Understanding manager resistance to blockchain systems. *European Management Journal*, *39*(3), 353–365. doi:10.1016/j.emj.2020.10.001

Waltonchain. (2021). *Waltonchain white paper v2.0.* https://www.waltonchain.org/en/ Waltonchain_White_Paper_2.0_EN.pdf

Wamba, S. F., Gunasekaran, A., Akter, S., Ren, S. J. F., Dubey, R., & Childe, S. J. (2017). Big data analytics and firm performance: Effects of dynamic capabilities. *Journal of Business Research*, *70*, 356–365. doi:10.1016/j.jbusres.2016.08.009

Wan, J., Li, J., Imran, M., Li, D., & e-Amin, F. (2019). A blockchain-based solution for enhancing security and privacy in smart factory. *IEEE Transaction*.

Wang & Nixon. (2021). Intertrust: Towards an efficient blockchain interoperability architecture with trusted services. *Cryptology ePrint Archive*.

Wang, J., Zhou, H., & Jin, X. (2021). Risk transmission in complex supply chain network with multi-drivers. *Chaos, Solitons, and Fractals*, *143*, 110259. doi:10.1016/j.chaos.2020.110259

Wang, L., Laszewski, G. V., Young, K. M., & Tao, J. (2010). Cloud Computing: A Perspective Study. *New Generation Computing*, *28*(2), 137–146. doi:10.100700354-008-0081-5

Wang, M. (2011). *Multi-channel peer-to-peer streaming systems as resource allocation problems*. The University of Nebraska-Lincoln.

Wang, M., Wu, Y., Chen, B., & Evans, M. (2020). Blockchain and supply chain management: A new paradigm for supply chain integration and collaboration. *Operations and Supply Chain Management: An International Journal*, *14*(1), 111–122. doi:10.31387/oscm0440290

Wang, Q., Zhu, X., Ni, Y., Gu, L., & Zhu, H. (2019b). *Blockchain for the IoT and industrial IoT: a review*. Internet Things.

Wang, T., Zhang, Y., & Zang, D. (2016). Real-time visibility and traceability framework for discrete manufacturing shopfloor. *Proceedings of the 22nd International Conference on Industrial Engineering and Engineering Management*, 763–772. 10.2991/978-94-6239-180-2_72

Wang, X., Zha, X., Ni, W., Liu, R. P., Guo, Y. J., Niu, X., & Zheng, K. (2019a). Survey on blockchain for Internet of things. *Computer Communications*, *136*, 10–29. doi:10.1016/j.comcom.2019.01.006

Wang, Y., Chen, C. H., & Zghari-Sales, A. (2021). Designing a blockchain enabled supply chain. *International Journal of Production Research*, *59*(5), 1450–1475. doi:10.1080/00207543.2020.1824086

Wang, Y., Han, J. H., & Beynon-Davies, P. (2019). Understanding blockchain technology for future supply chains: A Systematic Literature Review and Research Agenda. *Supply Chain Management*, *24*(1), 62–84. doi:10.1108/SCM-03-2018-0148

Compilation of References

Wang, Z., Jin, H., Dai, W., Choo, K.-K. R., & Zou, D. (2021). Ethereum smart contract security research: Survey and future research opportunities. *Frontiers of Computer Science*, *15*(2), 1–18. doi:10.100711704-020-9284-9

Wan, J., Tang, S., Shu, Z., Li, D., Wang, S., Imran, M., & Vasilakos, A. V. (2016). Software-defined industrial Internet of things in the context of industry 4.0. *IEEE Sensors Journal*, *16*(20), 7373–7380. doi:10.1109/JSEN.2016.2565621

Wan, P. K., Huang, L., & Holtskog, H. (2020). Blockchain-enabled information sharing within a supply chain: A systematic literature review. *IEEE Access : Practical Innovations, Open Solutions*, *8*, 49645–49656. doi:10.1109/ACCESS.2020.2980142

Waters, D. (Ed.). (2003). *Logistics: An Introduction to Supply Chain Management*. Palgrave Macmillan.

Weidema, B. P. (2015). Comparing three life cycle impact assessment methods from an endpoint perspective. *Journal of Industrial Ecology*, *19*(1), 20–26. doi:10.1111/jiec.12162

Weinstein, S. (1988). *Secrets for profiting in bull and bear markets*. Irwin.

Werbach, K. (2018). Trust, but verify: Why the blockchain needs the law. *Berkeley Technology Law Journal*, *33*(2), 487–550.

Werner, F., Basalla, M., Schneider, J., Hays, D., & Vom Brocke, J. (2021). Blockchain adoption from an interorganizational systems perspective–a mixed-methods approach. *Information Systems Management*, *38*(2), 135–150. doi:10.1080/10580530.2020.1767830

Westerfield, R. (1977). The distribution of common stock price changes: An application of transactions time and subordinated stochastic models. *Journal of Financial and Quantitative Analysis*, *12*(5), 743–765. doi:10.2307/2330254

Whitaker, A. (2019). Art and blockchain: A primer, history, and taxonomy of blockchain use cases in the arts. *Artivate*, *8*(2), 21–46. doi:10.1353/artv.2019.0008

Whitaker, A., Bracegirdle, A., de Menil, S., Gitlitz, M. A., & Saltos, L. (2021). Art, antiquities, and Blockchain: New approaches to the restitution of cultural heritage. *International Journal of Cultural Policy*, *27*(3), 312–329. doi:10.1080/10286632.2020.1765163

Wiegmann, D. A., & Shappell, S. A. (2017). *A human error approach to aviation accident analysis: The human factors analysis and classification system*. Routledge. doi:10.4324/9781315263878

Wieland, A., & Wallenburg, C. M. (2012). Dealing with supply chain risks. *International Journal of Physical Distribution & Logistics Management*, *42*(10), 887–905. doi:10.1108/09600031211281411

Wognum, P. M., Bremmers, H., Trienekens, J. H., Van Der Vorst, J. G. A. J., & Bloemhof, J. M. (2011). Systems for sustainability and transparency of food supply chains—Current status and challenges. *Advanced Engineering Informatics*, *2011*(25), 65–76. doi:10.1016/j.aei.2010.06.001

Wolf, F., & Pickler, L. (2010). Supply Chain Dispute Resolution: A Delphi Study. *International Journal of Information Systems and Supply Chain Management*, *3*(3), 50–65. doi:10.4018/jisscm.2010070104

Wood, R. A., McInish, T. H., & Ord, J. K. (1985). An investigation of transactions data for nyse stocks. *The Journal of Finance*, *40*(3), 723–739. doi:10.1111/j.1540-6261.1985.tb04996.x

Wu, C., Xiong, J., Xiong, H., Zhao, Y., & Yi, W. (2022). A review on recent progress of smart contract in blockchain. *IEEE Access : Practical Innovations, Open Solutions*, *10*, 50839–50863. doi:10.1109/ACCESS.2022.3174052

Wu, F., Yeniyurt, S., Kim, D., & Cavusgil, S. T. (2006). The impact of information technology on supply chain capabilities and firm performance: A resource-based view. *Industrial Marketing Management*, *35*(4), 493–504. doi:10.1016/j.indmarman.2005.05.003

Wu, H., Han, X., Yang, Q., & Pu, X. (2018). Production and coordination decisions in a closed-loop supply chain with remanufacturing cost disruptions when retailers compete. *Journal of Intelligent Manufacturing*, *29*(1), 227–235. doi:10.100710845-015-1103-z

Wurm, J., Hoang, K., Arias, O., Sadeghi, A., & Jin, Y. (2016). Security analysis on consumer and industrial IoT devices. *21st Asia and South Pacific Design Automation Conference (ASP-DAC)*, 519–524. 10.1109/ASPDAC.2016.7428064

Wüst, K., & Gervais, A. (2017). Do you need blockchain? *Conference: 2018 Crypto Valley Conference on Blockchain Technology (CVCBT)*.

Xiao, H., Wang, L., & Chang, J. (2022). The differential fault analysis on block cipher FeW. *Cybersecurity*, *5*(1), 28. doi:10.118642400-022-00130-z

Xing, B., Gao, W. J., Battle, K., Nelwamondo, F. V., & Marwala, T. (2012). e-RL: the Internet of things supported reverse logistics for remanufacture-to-order. *International Conference in Swarm Intelligence: Advances in Swarm Intelligence*, 519–526.

Xiong, H., Dalhaus, T., Wang, P., & Huang, J. (2020). Blockchain Technology for Agriculture: Applications and Rationale [Mini Review]. *Frontiers in Blockchain*, *3*, 7. Advance online publication. doi:10.3389/fbloc.2020.00007

Xiong, Z., Zhang, Y., Niyato, D., Wang, P., & Han, Z. (2018). When mobile blockchain meets edge computing. *IEEE Communications Magazine*, *56*(8), 33–39. doi:10.1109/MCOM.2018.1701095

Xu, C., McDowell, N. G., Fisher, R. A., Wei, L., Sevanto, S., Christoffersen, B. O., Weng, E., & Middleton, R. S. (2019). Increasing impacts of extreme droughts on vegetation productivity under climate change. *Nature Climate Change*, *9*(12), 948–953. doi:10.103841558-019-0630-6

Xu, L. D., He, W., & Li, S. (2014). Internet of things in industries: a survey. *IEEE Trans. Ind. Inf.*, *10*(4), 2233–2243. doi:10.1080/00207543.2018.1444806

Xu, L., & Beamon, B. M. (2006). Supply chain coordination and cooperation mechanisms: An attribute-based approach. *The Journal of Supply Chain Management*, *42*(1), 4–12. doi:10.1111/j.1745-493X.2006.04201002.x

Xu, M., Chen, X., & Kou, G. (2019). A systematic review of blockchain. *Financial Innovation*, *5*(1), 27. doi:10.118640854-019-0147-z

Xu, W., Hu, D., Lang, K. R., & Zhao, J. L. (2022). Blockchain and digital finance. *Financial Innovation*, *8*(1), 97. Advance online publication. doi:10.118640854-022-00420-y PMID:36465063

Xu, Y., Ren, J., Wang, G., Zhang, C., Yang, J., & Zhang, Y. (2019). *A blockchain-based non-repudiation network computing service scheme for industrial IoT*. IEEE Transaction Industrial Informatics.

Yadav, Shikha, Gupta, & Kushwaha. (2021). The efficient consensus algorithm for land record management system. In *IOP Conference Series: Materials Science and Engineering* (Vol. 1022, No. 1, p. 012090). IOP Publishing.

Yadav, A. S., & Kushwaha, D. S. (2021). Digitization of land record through blockchain-based consensus algorithm. *IETE Technical Review*, 1–18.

Yadav, S. V., & Singh, A. R. (2019). A Systematic Literature Review of Blockchain Technology in Agriculture. *Proceedings of the International Conference on Industrial Engineering and Operations Management Pilsen*.

Compilation of References

Yadav, S., & Singh, S. P. (2020). Blockchain critical success factors for sustainable supply chain. *Resources, Conservation and Recycling, 152*, 104505. doi:10.1016/j.resconrec.2019.104505

Yaga, D., Mell, P., Roby, N., & Scarfone, K. (2019). *Blockchain technology overview.* arXiv preprint arXiv:1906.11078.

Yakovenko, A. (2018). *Solana: A new architecture for a high performance blockchain v0. 8.13.* Whitepaper.

Yan, B., & Huang, G. (2009). Supply chain information transmission based on RFID and internet of things in Computing. *Communication, Control, and Management, ISECS International Colloquium on,* 166–169.

Yan, C., Zhang, C., Lu, Z., Wang, Z., Liu, Y., & Liu, B. (2022). Blockchain abnormal behavior awareness methods: A survey. *Cybersecurity, 5*(1), 5. doi:10.118642400-021-00107-4

Yang, C.-S. (2019). Maritime shipping digitalization: Blockchain-based technology applications, future improvements, and intention to use. *Transportation Research Part E, Logistics and Transportation Review, 131*, 108–117. doi:10.1016/j.tre.2019.09.020

Yang, F., Han, Y., Ding, Y., Tan, Q., & Xu, Z. (2022). A flexible approach for cyber threat hunting based on kernel audit records. *Cybersecurity, 5*(1), 11. doi:10.118642400-022-00111-2

Yang, W., Wang, S., Huang, X., & Mu, Y. (2019a). On the Security of an Efficient and Robust Certificateless Signature Scheme for IIoT Environments. *IEEE Access : Practical Innovations, Open Solutions, 7*, 91074–91079. doi:10.1109/ACCESS.2019.2927597

Yang, Y., Wu, L., Yin, G., Li, L., & Zhao, H. (2017). A survey on security and privacy issues in internet-of-things. *IEEE Internet of Things Journal, 4*(5), 1250–1258. doi:10.1109/JIOT.2017.2694844

Yang, Z., Yang, K., Lei, L., Zheng, K., & Leung, V. C. M. (2019b). Blockchain-based decentralized trust management in vehicular networks. *IEEE Internet of Things Journal, 6*(2), 1495–1505. doi:10.1109/JIOT.2018.2836144

Yanjing, J. (2009). Integration of ERP and CRM in an E-commerce environment. *Proceedings of the International Conference on Management and Service Science,* 1–9.

Yan, Q., Huang, W., Luo, X., Gong, Q., & Yu, F. R. (2018). A multi-level DDoS mitigation framework for the industrial Internet of things. *IEEE Communications Magazine, 56*(2), 30–36. doi:10.1109/MCOM.2018.1700621

Yao, X., Kong, H., Liu, H., Qiu, T., & Ning, H., (2019). An attribute credential-based public-key scheme for fog computing in digital manufacturing. *IEEE Trans. Ind. Inf.*

Yaşlıoğlu, M. M. (2017). Sosyal bilimlerde faktör analizi ve geçerlilik: Keşfedici ve doğrulayıcı faktör analizlerinin kullanılması. *İstanbul Üniversitesi İşletme Fakültesi Dergisi, 46*, 74-85.

Yeoh, P. (2017). Regulatory issues in blockchain technology. *Journal of Financial Regulation and Compliance.*

Yildirim, U., Toygar, A., & Çolakoğlu, C. (2022). Compensation effect of wages on decent work: A study on seafarers attitudes. *Marine Policy, 143*, 105155. doi:10.1016/j.marpol.2022.105155

Yin, D., Zhang, L., & Yang, K. (2018). A DDoS attack detection and mitigation with software-defined Internet of things framework. *IEEE Access : Practical Innovations, Open Solutions, 6*, 24694–24705. doi:10.1109/ACCESS.2018.2831284

Ying, C. C. (1966). Stock market prices and volumes of sales. *Econometrica, 34*(3), 676–685. doi:10.2307/1909776

Yin, R. K. (2018). Case study research and applications. *Sage (Atlanta, Ga.).*

Yli-Huumo, J., Ko, D., Choi, S., Park, S., & Smolander, K. (2016). Where is current research on blockchain technology? A systematic review. *PLoS One, 11*(10), e0163477. doi:10.1371/journal.pone.0163477 PMID:27695049

Yue, K., Zhang, Y., Chen, Y., Li, Y., Zhao, L., Rong, C., & Chen, L. (2021). A Survey of Decentralizing Applications via Blockchain: The 5G and Beyond Perspective. *IEEE Communications Surveys and Tutorials*, *23*(4), 2191–2217. doi:10.1109/COMST.2021.3115797

Yuvaraj, S., & Sangeetha, M. (2016). Smart supply chain management using internet of things (IoT) and low power wireless communication systems. *Wireless Communication, Signal Processing and Networking, International Conference*, 555-558.

Yu, W., Chavez, R., Jacobs, M. A., & Feng, M. (2018). Data-driven supply chain capabilities and performance: A resource-based view. *Transportation Research Part E, Logistics and Transportation Review*, *114*, 371–385. doi:10.1016/j.tre.2017.04.002

Yu, W., Jacobs, M. A., Chavez, R., & Feng, M. (2019). Data-driven supply chain orientation and financial performance: The moderating effect of innovation-focused complementary assets. *British Journal of Management*, *30*(2), 299–314. doi:10.1111/1467-8551.12328

Yu, Y., Huo, B., & Zhang, Z. J. (2020). Impact of information technology on supply chain integration and company performance: Evidence from cross-border e-commerce companies in China. *Journal of Enterprise Information Management*, *34*(1), 460–489. doi:10.1108/JEIM-03-2020-0101

Zasemkova, O. (2019). Dispute resolution by means of blockchain technology. *Actual Problems of Russian Law*, *4*(4), 160–167. doi:10.17803/1994-1471.2019.101.4.160-167

Zasemkova, O. (2020). Methods of Resolving Disputes Arising from Smart Contracts. *Lex Russica*, *2020*(4), 9–20. doi:10.17803/1729-5920.2020.161.4.009-020

Zawadzki, P., & Zywicki, K. (2016). Smart product design and production control for effective mass customization in the industry 4.0 concept. *Management of Production Engineering Review*, *7*(3), 105–112. doi:10.1515/mper-2016-0030

Zhang, H., Nakamura, T., & Sakurai, K. (2019). Security and trust issues on digital supply chain. *IEEE Intl Conf on Dependable, Autonomic and Secure Computing*, 338-343. . doi:10.1109/DASC/PiCom/CBDCom/CyberSciTech.2019.00069

Zhang, N., Mi, X., Feng, X., Wang, X., Tian, Y., & Qian, F. (2018). *Understanding and Mitigating the Security Risks of Voice-Controlled Third-Party Skills on Amazon Alexa and Google Home*. Academic Press.

Zhang, R., & Chan, W. K. (2020). Evaluation of Energy Consumption in Block-Chains with Proof of Work and Proof of Stake. *Journal of Physics: Conference Series, 1584*(1). doi:10.1088/1742-6596/1584/1/012023

Zhang, H., Wang, J., & Ding, Y. (2019b). Blockchain-based decentralized and secure keyless signature scheme for smart grid. *Energy*, *180*, 955–967. doi:10.1016/j.energy.2019.05.127

Zhang, J. (2017). Multivariate analysis and machine learning in cerebral palsy research. *Frontiers in Neurology*, *8*, 1–13. doi:10.3389/fneur.2017.00715 PMID:29312134

Zhang, W., & Gao, F. (2011). An improvement to naive bayes for text classification. *Procedia Engineering*, *15*, 2160–2164. doi:10.1016/j.proeng.2011.08.404

Zhang, X., & Yousaf, H. A. U. (2020). Green supply chain coordination considering government intervention, green investment, and customer green preferences in the petroleum industry. *Journal of Cleaner Production*, *246*, 118984. doi:10.1016/j.jclepro.2019.118984

Zhang, Y., Deng, R., Zheng, D., Li, J., Wu, P., & Cao, J. (2019a). *Efficient and Robust Certificateless Signature for Data Crowdsensing in Cloud-Assisted Industrial IoT*. IEEE Transaction Industry. doi:10.1109/TII.2019.2894108

Compilation of References

Zhang, Y., & Kitsos, P. (2016). *Security in RFID and Sensor Networks* (1st ed.). Auerbach Publications.

Zhang, Y., Montenegro-Marin, C. E., & Díaz, V. G. (2021). Holistic cognitive conflict chain management framework in supply chain management. *Environmental Impact Assessment Review*, *88*, 106564. doi:10.1016/j.eiar.2021.106564

Zhang, Y., Sun, Y., Chen, J., & Liu, J. (2019). GasReducer: Detecting and Mitigating Gas-Costly Patterns in Ethereum Smart Contracts. *IEEE Transactions on Dependable and Secure Computing*, *17*(2), 405–419. doi:10.1109/TDSC.2018.2863135

Zhao, G., Liu, S., Lopez, C., Lu, H., Elgueta, S., Chen, H., & Boshkoska, B. M. (2019). Blockchain technology in agri-food value chain management: A synthesis of applications, challenges and future research directions. *Computers in Industry*, *109*, 83–99. doi:10.1016/j.compind.2019.04.002

Zheng, D., Wu, A., Zhang, Y., & Zhao, Q. (2018). Efficient and privacy-preserving medical data sharing in the Internet of things with limited computing power. *IEEE Access : Practical Innovations, Open Solutions*, *6*, 28019–28027. doi:10.1109/ACCESS.2018.2840504

Zheng, Z., Xie, S., Dai, H., Chen, X., & Wang, H. (2017, June). *An overview of blockchain technology: Architecture, consensus, and future trends. 2017 IEEE international congress on big data (BigData congress)*.

Zheng, Z., Xie, S., Dai, H.-N., Chen, X., & Wang, H. (2018). Blockchain challenges and opportunities: A survey. *International Journal of Web and Grid Services*, *14*(4), 352–375. doi:10.1504/IJWGS.2018.095647

Zhou, K., Liu, T., & Zhou, L. (2015). Industry 4.0: towards future industrial opportunities and challenges. In *2015 12th International Conference on Fuzzy Systems and Knowledge Discovery (FSKD)*. IEEE.

Zhou, R., Zhang, X., Du, X., Wang, X., Yang, G., & Guizani, M. (2018). File-centric multi-key aggregate keyword searchable encryption for industrial Internet of things. *IEEE Transactions on Industrial Informatics*, *14*(8), 3648–3658. doi:10.1109/TII.2018.2794442

Živković, P., McCurdy, D., Zou, M., & Raymond, A. H. (2021). Mind the gap: Tech-based dispute resolutions in global supply blockchains. *Business Horizons*, *66*(1), 13–26. doi:10.1016/j.bushor.2021.10.008

Zuo, Y. (2021). Making smart manufacturing smarter–a survey on blockchain technology in Industry 4.0. *Enterprise Information Systems*, *15*(10), 1323–1353. doi:10.1080/17517575.2020.1856425

Zwitter, A., & Hazenberg, J. (2020). Decentralized network governance: Blockchain technology and the future of regulation. *Frontiers in Blockchain*, *3*, 12. doi:10.3389/fbloc.2020.00012

About the Contributors

Tharwa Najar (Ph.D., University of Gafsa, Tunisia) is an associate professor in Business Administration and a Doctor in Management Sciences at the University of Gafsa, Tunisia. She's a member of RIGUEUR laboratory. Her works have been published in management journals and supply chain journals. Her research interest includes supply chain management, information systems use, and interorganizational relationships in B2B environment in the automotive industry. She currently investigates Knowledge Management, open innovation, and open business models in large companies and SME's.

Najar Yousra has an engineering degree in Industrial Computer Systems (INSAT, Tunisia) and a Ph.D in Computer Systems (FST, Tunisia). She is an assistant professor in Computer Systems at the UTM University (ISI, Tunisia). Her research concerns artificial intelligence, multiprocessor computer systems, deep learning and energy consumption. She is also a professional certified trainer in big data, cloud computing, data analysis and blockchain.

Adel Aloui has a PhD in management and in industrial engineering. He is associate professor of management at EM Normandie Business School. Aloui's research interests are in supply chain management, organization, design, and innovation.

* * *

Jean Babei aggregated (Master of Conferences) of Universities in Management Sciences Specialty: Logistics and Information Systems. Research teacher at the University of Douala - Cameroun. Associate researcher at CRETLOG, Aix Marseille University - France. He has been teaching logistics, operations management, information systems management and statistics for more than a decade. He is the author of several articles and book contributions.

Vishesh Bansal is a third-year undergraduate student at Vellore Institute of Technology majoring in Computer Science and Engineering. He has an interest in Cyber Security, Artificial Intelligence and Blockchain Technologies.

Francesco Bifulco is Full Professor in Management at University of Naples Federico II. His main areas of interest are focused on cultural heritage (branding enhancement, phygital journey, sustainable business models, innovation ecosystem). He published papers and books about these themes on top journal and publisher. He chaired and participated sessions in international conferences. He led, as Scientific

About the Contributors

coordinator (University of Naples Federico II) in projects PON Research & Competitiveness Program (High-tech districts and related networks).

Serge Guy Biloa is a PhD student from the University of Douala, his research topic is: the digitalization of the supply chain and commercial performance of companies in the agri-food retail sector (GMS) in Cameroon, he also gives courses monitoring and evaluation of logistics performance, logistics risks and coverage and introduction to logistics and foreign trade.

Najeh Chaâbane is a Ph.D. in Quantitative Economics from the University of Sousse. Member of the Quantitative Analysis Research Group (QuARG), Campus University of Manouba, Tunisia, and Assistant Professor in the Economics and Quantitative Methods Department, Higher Institute of Business Administration, University of Gafsa. His dissertation and subsequent research have focused on financial time series analysis, computational statistics, and econometrics (). Najeh is a Statistician, with expertise spanning various fields in Econometrics, Theoretical, and Applied Statistics, as pertaining to applications in the areas of Business, Finance, and Economics.

Laura Clemente is a PhD student in Heritage Science at the Department of Sciences of Antiquity at Sapienza University of Rome. She earned a Master's degree in Cultural Heritage Management at University of Naples Federico II and her fields of specialisation concern digitalization of cultural heritage, management of cultural and creative industries, cultural innovation, digital strategies and blockchain technologies.

Åsa Dahlborn works as a Project Manager at the IOTA Foundation. An active member of INABTA's Social Impact and Sustainability Working Group, she has contributed to the recent achievements of the working group such as the report "Blockchain for Social Impact". She holds a Bachelor of Arts in Economics, Politics and Social Thought and her focus of interest lies in exploring how DLT can be used to promote sustainability, equality and economic empowerment.

Mariana de la Roche started as Social Impact project Manager in 2018 and currently is the Regulatory Affairs Manager of the IOTA Foundation and; since 2021, she is the co-chair of the INABTA Social Impact and Sustainability Working Group. She is a Colombian human rights lawyer with a law degree obtained with academic excellence, a specialization in human rights and humanitarian law, and a master's degree in public administration. She has over 9 years of experience as a project manager and legal and regulatory advisor for different NGOs and social businesses in Colombia and Germany. Mariana has been leading the actions of the social impact and climate of INATBA, raising awareness and advocating for blockchain for good at the global level. She spoke and presented blockchain use cases for good in COP26, the EU blockchain week, and the Environment Ministerial For Europe Conference, among other relevant international spaces. Mariana is also part of the leading team coordinating Blockchcain 100+, an initiative supported by the UN's General Assembly to create a charter for blockchain and the UN Values.

Anas Elmalkli, Ph.D. in financial management, was previously Dean of High institution of Arts and Crafts Gafsa University, Actually Master coordinator Accounting Control Audit. Member of the local organization of Research Business and Development of Gafsa. Scientific interests: Contract Theory; Islamic Finance, Fintech, behavioral finance (). Awards: 2015 Second Prize of Zitouna Islamic Bank for the Best Thesis in the Maghreb Arab (Tunisia, Algeria, and Morocco). Independent Consultant in project Management and development. Member of Scientific Committee Research and Applications in Islamic Finance (RAFI). Contributed as a "reviewer" in the International Journal of Islamic and Middle Eastern Finance and Management.

Rinat Galiautdinov is a Principal Software Developer and Software Architect having the expertise in Information Technology and Computer Science. Mr. Galiautdinov is also an expert in Banking/Financial industry as well as in Neurobiological sphere. Mr. Rinat Galiautdinov works on the number of highly important researches (including such the spheres as: Drones, Financial Systems and Private Money, Brain interface and neuro-biology) as an independent researcher and projects holder and developer.

Louis Helmer is a student in the Faculty of Economics and Business at the University of Amsterdam. He is a former employee of the IOTA Foundation, where he has authored a research report on the energy consumption profile of the novel IOTA protocol.

Martial Tangui Kadji Ngassam is a holder of a PhD in management science in business strategy obtained at the University of Versailles Saint Quentin-en-Yvelines in France, Martial Kadji Ngassam is a lecturer at ESSEC Douala / University of Douala and Associate Researcher at the University of Versailles Saint Quentin-en-Yvelines. His research focuses on the sustainability of free software business models. He also works on the digital transformation of companies, mainly on subjects related to the appropriation of Information Technologies (IT). In addition, his teaching at ESSEC Douala and Paris Saclay University focuses on the management of information systems, digital marketing and strategy.

Laura Kajtazi is working as Project Manager at the IOTA Foundation and is an active Member of the SISWG of INATBA. Before working full time as a Project Manager for the IOTA Foundation Laura studied and completed her Master Programm in International Economics and Management at the University of Paderborn (Germany). In her studies she discovered her passion for Entrepreneurship and Macroeconomics and began to more closely deal with the crypto area from an entrepreneurial and monetary policy perspective. During her Master studies she has already started working as a working student for the IOTA Foundation and gained increasing insights on the benefits of Distributed Ledger Technologies for different sectors like health tech, sustainability and global trade and supply chain.

Dulal Chandra Kar is an experienced educator in computer science and electrical engineering, with over 30 years of teaching experience across various institutions such as Texas A&M University-Corpus Christi, Virginia Tech, Mountain State University, North Dakota State University, and Bangladesh University of Engineering and Technology. He obtained his BS degree in Electrical and Electronic Engineering from Bangladesh University of Engineering and Technology in 1982. He went on to complete his MS in Electrical and Electronics Engineering in 1991, followed by a PhD in Engineering with a specialization in Computer Engineering in 1994, both from North Dakota State University. Currently, Dr. Kar holds the position of full professor in the Department of Computing Sciences at Texas A&M University-Corpus Christi. He recently served as the Interim Chair of the Department of Computing Sciences at TAMUCC from August 2020 to August 2021. During this time, he managed five programs, including one PhD program in Geospatial Computer Science, one MS program in Computer Science, and one BS program in Computer Science. Dr. Kar has directed several projects funded by the National

About the Contributors

Science Foundation (NSF), including NSF REU, NSF S-STEM, NSF CRI, and NSF MRI grants. His areas of research interests include information security, network security, unmanned aerial systems, and sensor networks. He has published over 75 papers in peer-reviewed journals and conference proceedings. He also edited a book titled "Network Security, Administration and Management: Advancing Technology and Practice," which was published by IGI Global in 2011. Dr. Kar is a senior member of the Institute of Electrical and Electronics Engineers (IEEE).

Karahan Kara was born on August 1, 1987, in Artvin, Turkey. He graduated from Land Forces Academy, Department of Electrical and Electronics Engineering. He completed his master's at Okan University Department of Logistics Management and doctorate studies at Çanakkale Onsekiz Mart University, Department of Business Management. He works as an assistant professor in Artvin Çoruh University, Vocational School of Hopa, logistics Program and continues his academic studies in the same field.

A.V. Senthil Kumar is working as a Director & Professor in the Department of Research and PG in Computer Applications, Hindusthan College of Arts and Science, Coimbatore since 05/03/2010. He has to his credit 11 Book Chapters, 265 papers in International and National Journals, 25 papers in International Conferences, 5 papers in National Conferences, and edited Nine books (IGI Global, USA). He is an Editor-in-Chief for various journals. Key Member for India, Machine Intelligence Research Lab (MIR Labs). He is an Editorial Board Member and Reviewer for various International Journals. He is also a Committee member for various International Conferences. He is a Life member of International Association of Engineers (IAENG), Systems Society of India (SSI), member of The Indian Science Congress Association, member of Internet Society (ISOC), International Association of Computer Science and Information Technology (IACSIT), Indian Association for Research in Computing Science (IARCS), and committee member for various International Conferences.

Sunita Kumar is a passionate educationist with 17+ years of experience (Industry: 5+ years and Teaching: 12+ years) experience. Dr Sunita area of expertise/ specialization including advertising, branding, digital Marketing, consumer behaviour, Marketing Analytics. Over the last 12 years, she has taught and received positive evaluations for many marketing units, including Brand Management, Marketing Research, International Marketing, Fundamental of Marketing, Consumer Behaviour, Marketing Management, Social Media and Digital Marketing, Data Analysis using SPSS both postgraduate and undergraduate level. She has also been actively supervising master's and Ph.D. candidates from Christ university in Bangalore. Dr Sunita also often shares her industry experience and research findings with different audiences and stakeholders, both locally and internationally. she has been actively leading and involved in numerous research project and consultancies projects, as well as published numerous indexed journals/ articles, book, chapters in a book, conference proceedings, and industry reports.

Lakhal Lassaad is Professor of Management at the University of Sousse (Tunisia). He holds a doctorate from the Higher Institut of Management of Tunis. His areas of research are in strategic management, quality management, entrepreneurship, Human research management and performance measurement. He has published in various journals such as Journal of the Operational Research Society, International Journal of Quality and Reliability Management, Total Quality and Business Excellence Journal, Managerial

Finance, Revue Française de Gestion Industrielle, Journal of High Technology Management Research, Journal of Enterprising Culture and Journal of Management Development.

Abirami Manoharan, Ph.D., is currently working as an Assistant Professor in the Department of Electrical and Electronics Engineering, Government College of Engineering, Srirangam. Her research contributions include 10 SCI articles. She is a Senior Member in IEEE (SM 93333628) and also a Member in Institution of Engineers (India) (M 1558689).

Hariprasath Manoharan is working as Associate Professor in the Department of Electronics and Communication Engineering, Panimalar Engineering College, Poonamallee, Chennai. He has published 70 research articles in well indexed Journals. He has also published a book entitled 'Computer Aided State Estimation for Electric Power Networks' and published more than 15 Patents.

Ana Lúcia Martins is an Assistant Professor at ISCTE-IUL and an integrated researcher at BRU-Iscte (Business Research Unt). She holds a Ph.D. in Management, with a specialization in Operations Management and Technology, and an MSc in Management, with a specialization in Strategy. She currently serves as Iscte Business School Vice-dean for Teaching and Innovation, and as Vice-President of Iscte's Pedagogical Council. She also serves as director of the Master in Humanitarian Action, and in the past served as director of the bachelor's degree in Industrial Management and Logistics. Ana teaches Operations Management, Logistics Management, Service Operations Management, and Supply Chain Management. Ana authored more than 85 scientific articles and authored book chapters in logistics management and lean management in the justice systems. Her current main research topics are operations management in humanitarian settings, logistics management, supply chain management, and lean management in the services area, mainly in judicial and healthcare systems.

Shadi R. Masadeh is a Full Professor in the Cyber Security Department at Isra University, Amman (Jordan). He got his M.Sc. and Ph.D. degrees in computer information systems /Information Security from the Arab Academy of Banking and Financial Sciences in 2003 and 2009 respectively, He worked as a professor at various universities including Applied Science University, Al-Hussein bin Talal |University (Jordan),. His research interests include Cryptography, Steganography, Information and Computer Network Security, Authentication, Digital Signature, Artificial Intelligence, E-learning Management, and Robotics.

Anbarasi Masilamani is an Assistant Professor (Grade 2) in the School of Computer Science and Engineering at Vellore Institute of Technology, Vellore, India. She received Ph. D in Computer Science and Engineering from the Vellore Institute of Technology in 2020. She has 19 years of experience in teaching and research. She has published more than 25 research papers in international journals and conferences. Her research interest includes Soft Computing, Data Mining and Bio Informatics.

Varun Murpani is a third-year undergraduate student at Vellore Institute of Technology, India, majoring in computer science engineering. He enjoys combining his curiosity about modern technology with his passion for management and operations.

About the Contributors

Abdullah Önden has 15+ years of experience in software development and business management. 250+ delivered tech projects. Main focus is digital entrepreneurship and next generation internet solutions. Developed in both academical and business way, completed his PhD on big data and digital marketing and mainly works on these research areas.

Kamalendu Pal is with the Department of Computer Science, School of Science and Technology, City, University of London. Kamalendu received his BSc (Hons) degree in Physics from Calcutta University, India, Postgraduate Diploma in Computer Science from Pune, India, MSc degree in Software Systems Technology from the University of Sheffield, Postgraduate Diploma in Artificial Intelligence from Kingston University, MPhil degree in Computer Science from the University College London, and MBA degree from the University of Hull, United Kingdom. He has published over hundred international research articles (including book chapters) widely in the scientific community with research papers in the ACM SIGMIS Database, Expert Systems with Applications, Decision Support Systems, and conferences. His research interests include knowledge-based systems, decision support systems, teaching and learning practice, blockchain technology, software engineering, service-oriented computing, sensor network simulation, and supply chain management. He is on the editorial board of an international computer science journal and is a member of the British Computer Society, the Institution of Engineering and Technology, and the IEEE Computer Society.

Sulaiman Saleem Patel completed his PhD in Electronic Engineering at the University of Kwa-Zulu Natal in 2019, and was heralded as the university's youngest ever Doctoral graduate in this field. He is currently a Lecturer in the Department of Information Systems at the Durban University of Technology, as well as the Postgraduate Coordinator for the Department. Sulaiman as previously worked as in cross-industry digital consulting with KPMG and quantitative analyst at Nedbank.

Pawar Pratap is a seasoned Technical Writer, based out of Solapur, India. With strong academic background in Computer Science Engineering, working on Blockchain Technology, Internet of Things, Artificial Intelligence & Machine Learning. He aspires to continue his research work along with the software development tasks.

Bharathi Putta graduated with a B.S. in computer science in 2021 from Amrita Vishwa Vidhyapeetham University in India. Currently, she is completing her M.S. in computer science at Texas A&M University in the United States in 2023. In 2021, she published her first article on the use of hybrid cryptography encryption to improve security. Her current areas of focus in research are cloud computing, blockchain, forensics, network security, and cyber security.

Tahmid Quazi has been a researcher in wireless communications since 2002. He obtained his MSc in 2003 for his research and development work in mobile ad-hoc networks for tactical communications. He began his Ph.D. in the area of Cross-Layer Design (CLD) in wireless communications in 2005, which he completed in 2009. Since then, he has published many works in international journals in multimedia traffic transmission using various techniques, including CLD and hierarchical modulation. More recently, his work has focused on research into a variety of diversity systems, including space, time, signal, labelling, and polarization diversity, to improve the error rate performance of wireless links. Dr. Quazi is passionate about using technology for the betterment of mankind, and channels his research accordingly.

In addition to his research in the field of advanced telecommunication systems to help bridge the digital divide, he runs numerous R&D projects in IoT, embedded systems and signal processing systems.

Paul Reaidy is Associate Professor of Management Sciences at the University Grenoble Alpes, France. He has a PhD in Industrial Engineering from the University of Savoie Mont Blanc and M.S. in Computer Science from the University of Strasbourg. He worked before as consultant in logistic and supply chain domains at Capgemini consulting group and Michelin Industry. He is a researcher at CERAG (Centre for Studies and Research Applied in Management). His research interests include Supply Chain Integration, Supply Chain Resilience, Industry 4.0, and Blockchain Arbitration.

Marianna Riabova is a PhD student in Management Science at the University Grenoble Alpes, CERAG (Centre for Studies and Research Applied in Management), France. She has a master's degree in Management of Information Systems from IAE Grenoble (Grenoble INP - University Grenoble Alpes) and a bachelor's degree in Management from the Russian Foreign Trade Academy. Considering the professional experience in supply chain and logistics and educational expertise that she aquired, her research interests are directed towards blockchain technology adoption for the Supply Chain Dispute Resolution process digitalization and enhancement.

Shitharth S. received his B.Tech. degree in Information Technology from Kgisl Institute of Technology, Coimbatore, India, in affiliation with Anna University, Chennai, India in 2012; and his M.E. degree in Computer Science & Engineering from Thiagaraja College of Engineering, Madurai, India, in affiliation with Anna University, Chennai, India in 2014. He completed his Ph.D. degree in the Department of Computers Science &Engineering, Anna University. He is currently working as Assistant Professor in Vardhaman College of Engineering, Hyderabad. He has published more than 10 International Journals along with 12 International & National conferences. He has even published 3 patents in IPR. He is also an active member in IEEE Computer society and in 5 more professional bodies. His current research interests include Cyber Security, Critical Infrastructure & Systems, Network Security & Ethical Hacking. He is an active researcher, reviewer and editor for many international journals.

Ben Slimene Samar is a Doctor in Management of information system; a post-doc position at the University of Nabeul (Tunisia). She holds a doctorate from the Hight institute of management of Sousse. Her areas of research are in supply chain management, strategic scanning, entrepreneurial university, organizational agility, and organizational performance. She has published in Journal of Business and Management Research, International Journal of Advanced Research.

Ramani Selvanambi is an Associate Professor in the School of Computing Science and Engineering at Vellore Institute of Technology (VIT), Vellore, India. He received his B.E in Computer Science and Engineering from Madras University and M. Tech Computer Science and Engineering from Bharathidasan University and Ph.D. in Computer Science and Engineering from Vellore Institute of Technology (VIT), Vellore. He has 13+ years of experience in teaching and 2 years of experience in the Consultancy and Software Industry. He has published about 40 research papers in International Journals on Machine Learning, Nature-Inspired Algorithms, Cyber Security and Health Care. His research interest includes Data Mining, Machine learning, Database Systems, Optimization Techniques and Cyber Security. He is a senior member in an IEEE and also a member in other technical societies.

About the Contributors

Chellatamilan T. is an Associate Professor (Senior) in School of Computer Science and Engineering, Vellore Institute of Technology (VIT), Vellore, India. He received Ph. D (Computer Science and Engineering) from Anna University, Chennai, India, in 2014, M. Tech (Computer Science and Engineering) from Manipal University, India, in 2003. His research interests include Artificial Intelligence, Machine Learning, Software Architecture, Data Mining, Cloud Computing and Big data Analytics. He has published many national and international journal papers. He is an active member in various professional bodies -CSI, ISTE, IEEE and IAENG.

Amit Kumar Tyagi is Assistant Professor (Senior Grade), and Senior Researcher at Vellore Institute of Technology (VIT), Chennai Campus, India. He received his Ph.D. Degree in 2018 from Pondicherry Central University, India. He joined the Lord Krishna College of Engineering, Ghaziabad (LKCE) for the periods of 2009-2010, and 2012-2013.

Galip Yalçın was born on October 16, 1987, in Ankara, Turkey. He graduated from Land Forces Academy, Department of Electrical and Electronics Engineering. He completed his master's at Kırıkkale University Department of Statistics. He continues doctorate studies at Kırıkkale University, Department of Mathematics. He works as an officer in Turkish Armed Forces and continues his academic studies in the same field.

Index

A

Adopters 40-42, 44-46, 49-54, 56, 273, 275-276, 278, 280-281
Adoption Curve 40-42, 45-46, 49, 52-54, 56
Adoption Decision Process 40-42, 44-45, 49-50, 53, 56
AI 19, 32, 35-36, 127, 161, 250, 284, 312, 320, 389, 393, 396, 467-468, 486
Alternative Dispute Resolution (ADR) 134
Art Market 310-312, 316-319, 321
Artificial Intelligence 15, 19, 21, 28, 33, 35-36, 161, 201, 304, 312, 318-319, 407, 409, 411, 452, 454, 465
Asset Management 99, 194
Authenticity 57, 69, 88, 112, 116, 121, 145, 152, 166, 172, 186, 189, 195, 198-199, 221, 275, 290, 312-315, 317-318, 320, 326, 331, 432-433, 435, 438-439, 443-444, 446, 450-451, 473
Autonomous Operations 399
Avatar 454, 468, 486

B

B2B 44, 166
Block 41-42, 50, 58, 66-72, 78, 86-94, 96-97, 99-102, 104-108, 111-112, 141, 144-146, 154, 157, 164-165, 169-170, 185-194, 198-199, 201, 219, 224, 239, 241, 252, 280, 313, 322, 325, 328, 331, 334-340, 343, 365-366, 368-369, 371, 373-374, 376, 382-384, 386, 400-406, 408, 424-425, 427-428, 432, 435, 437-439, 443-447, 455, 467, 472, 478, 484-485
Blockchain 15, 31-32, 37-38, 40-68, 70-84, 86-94, 96-102, 104-106, 111-114, 116-134, 137-149, 151-163, 165-167, 169-184, 186-205, 208-209, 211-230, 233, 239-252, 256, 270, 273-279, 282-311, 313-333, 336-344, 347, 364-367, 369-383, 385-397, 399, 405, 408, 429, 431-440, 442-444, 446-447, 449, 451-455, 460, 462-463, 466-468, 470-473, 475, 478-487
Blockchain Arbitration 113-114, 118-126, 128, 134
Blockchain Technology 38, 40-61, 63-66, 71, 77, 79, 81-84, 86-87, 91-92, 99, 111-114, 116-119, 121-134, 137-139, 141-144, 146-153, 155-156, 161, 167, 169, 173, 175-184, 189, 194-196, 198-205, 207, 212-213, 215-217, 219-221, 223, 225-226, 228-230, 233, 239-242, 244-251, 273-274, 282-284, 286, 288-290, 292, 294-296, 300-301, 303-304, 307-308, 311, 313-319, 322-325, 331-333, 336, 339-340, 342, 347, 365-367, 370, 374-377, 386-387, 389, 392-397, 405, 408, 429, 433-434, 440, 450-453, 470-471, 486
Brain 454, 460, 462, 468, 486
Business Sustainability 228

C

Cameroon 327-329, 334, 336-340, 343
Cloud Platform 470, 483-484
Communication Systems 1-2, 5, 7, 12, 155, 162-163, 251
Comovement 346, 356
Consensus 5, 48, 57-59, 61-62, 64-66, 72, 75, 78, 80, 82, 86, 88-90, 92, 100-101, 104-107, 111, 116-117, 144-148, 150-151, 153-154, 158-159, 170-171, 188-189, 191-192, 195, 205, 211-212, 215, 217-219, 223, 240-241, 243, 248, 275, 285, 291, 297, 307-308, 313, 318-319, 323, 342, 366-367, 374, 377, 379, 383, 391, 393-395, 432-434, 438, 443, 450, 452-453, 471-473, 484-485, 487
Consensus Modal 86
Corporate 92, 149, 166, 174, 229, 233, 324, 366, 434
Crypto Art 312, 315, 317, 323, 325
Crypto Currency 87, 112, 394
Cryptocurrencies 40, 43, 47, 55, 116, 129, 155, 173-175, 179, 218-219, 240-241, 295, 303, 315, 322, 325, 330, 346-349, 351, 356, 359, 364-369, 372, 374-376, 378-379, 381-383, 385-386, 389, 391, 395, 432, 434, 438, 442, 444, 486

Index

Cryptocurrency 41, 43, 46, 53, 72-74, 92, 112, 144, 151, 167, 170, 173-175, 189, 193, 239, 274, 336, 338, 346-347, 354, 359-360, 364-368, 370, 372, 374-376, 378-386, 389, 391, 393-396, 432, 438, 442, 471-472, 484

Cryptography 46-47, 87, 90, 101-102, 112, 120, 146, 148, 151-153, 165, 180, 185-186, 189, 196, 239, 250, 252, 310, 325, 371, 373, 379, 382, 388, 432, 465, 486

Cultural and Creative Industry 310-312, 314

Cultural Heritage 310-312, 314-318, 320-323, 325

Cyber Security 35, 83, 86-87, 97, 201, 393

D

Data Integrity 77, 138, 155, 160, 167, 174, 195, 207, 239, 297, 330, 379, 429

Data Transparency 44, 168, 207, 211-212

Data-Driven Supply Chain 254-256, 268-272

Decentralizations 86

Decentralized Computing Infrastructure 165, 252

Digital Signature 58, 67, 72, 93-94, 98, 102, 154, 180, 186-187, 381, 402, 455, 462, 465

Dispute 113-115, 117-123, 125-129, 132-134, 165, 193, 252, 479

Dispute Resolution 113-114, 117-129, 132-134, 479

Distributed Ledger Systems 364

Distributed Ledger Technology 40, 42-44, 53, 56, 83, 96, 141, 144, 148, 151, 186, 202-203, 207, 211, 226, 288, 310, 325

Driverless Vehicles 15, 33-34

E

Economic Sectors 40-42, 45-46, 50-54, 56

Encryption 47, 58, 93, 97, 99-100, 102-103, 107-109, 111-112, 116, 144, 150, 153-154, 156-157, 159, 162, 164, 186, 368, 374, 381, 391, 400, 432

Energy 41, 45, 49, 51, 56, 82, 105, 146, 156, 160, 164, 171, 173, 175, 178-179, 189, 192, 207-210, 215-219, 222-225, 231, 237, 243, 297-298, 305, 307, 313, 318-319, 325, 333, 336, 350, 365, 383-384, 390-392, 427-428, 431-433, 438, 470, 479, 484-487

Energy Consumption 105, 146, 207, 209-210, 215-219, 222-225, 231, 313, 318-319, 325, 384, 428, 433, 487

E-Waste 207, 218, 224-225

Experience Feedback 273

F

Fractional Ownership 311, 315, 323, 325

G

Generative Art 312, 318, 326

Governance 41, 45, 58-66, 75, 78-84, 96, 127, 129-130, 148, 173-174, 179, 183, 199, 297, 393

Gross Domestic Product 289, 307, 431

H

Halaal 287-290, 292-303, 306, 308

Halaal Accreditation 287-288, 291-292, 294, 296, 301-302, 308

Halaal Blockchain System 287-303, 308

Halaal Supply Chain 287-288, 292, 294-295, 299, 301-302, 308

Hashing 86, 91, 101-102, 112, 144-145, 180, 186-187, 189, 339, 366, 384, 432, 435, 451

I

Immutability 41, 53, 57, 59, 61, 90-91, 116, 123-124, 126, 146, 155, 165, 180, 185, 195-196, 219, 221, 239-240, 252, 280, 291, 310-311, 313, 318, 330, 366, 473

Immutable-Ledger 86

INATBA 207

Information Systems 1-2, 4, 6, 8, 12-14, 28, 37-38, 49, 82, 84, 133, 138-141, 143, 147-150, 153, 155, 167, 226, 229, 235, 239, 246, 249, 269-270, 285, 306, 325, 341, 367, 393-394, 397

Information Systems and Information Technologies 13

Innovation 1, 15, 40-42, 44-45, 50-52, 54-56, 83, 111-112, 122, 127, 129-130, 146, 179, 202, 208-209, 224-225, 232, 235-236, 241, 250, 270, 276, 280, 304, 310-312, 317, 321, 323-325, 328-329, 339-341, 344, 362, 365, 368, 378, 387, 390, 396, 429, 451

Innovation Diffusion Theory (IDT) 40, 56

Inter Planetary File System 431, 435

Internet of Things 16, 31, 37-38, 52, 130, 137-138, 140, 149-150, 155-165, 167, 183, 199-201, 205, 228-229, 232, 245-252, 275, 282, 284-285, 287, 290, 306-308, 314, 324, 330, 341, 394-395, 399-400, 429, 431, 451, 472, 487

Internet of Things (IoT) 31, 52, 137-138, 140, 149, 156-157, 162, 165, 183, 201, 228-229, 248, 251-252, 275, 287, 290, 307-308, 314, 330, 400, 472

Inter-Organizational Information Systems 4, 28

Inventory Management 9, 11-12, 17, 20, 23, 27, 30,

32, 166, 171, 181, 229, 245
IOTA 207, 213, 216-221, 223, 225-226

L

Ledger 31, 40, 42-44, 46, 48, 53, 56, 58, 67-68, 71, 76-78, 80, 83, 87-88, 90, 96, 98, 100, 116, 134, 138, 141, 144, 148, 150-152, 165-167, 169-170, 184-186, 188, 195, 197-203, 207, 211-212, 216, 221-223, 226, 230, 239-240, 246, 252, 274-275, 279-280, 282, 288, 291, 297-299, 308, 312-313, 316, 320, 325, 330, 364-366, 371, 376, 382, 389, 432, 447, 487

M

Machine Learning 15, 19, 28, 32, 92, 162, 201, 234, 320, 393, 399, 406-409, 411-412, 415, 421, 424-430, 452
Manufacturing Industry 45, 137-141, 146, 149, 155, 161, 250, 258, 266, 284
Merkle Tree 145, 169, 180, 189-191, 401-402, 432, 445, 461-462
MiCAR 219
ML 32, 35
Moderator Effect 254, 264-266

N

Neural Circuit 454, 458, 468
Neuron 454-455, 458-459, 462-463, 466-468, 486
Neuron Signals 454
Neurotransmitters 454-457, 459-460, 462-463, 467-468, 486
NFT 310, 315, 317-318, 323, 432
Nonce 69-70, 105, 164, 169, 188-189, 191-192, 252, 384, 435, 478
Non-Fungible Token 326

O

Off-Chain Governance 57, 80-81
On-Chain Governance 60, 79, 82
Online Dispute Resolution (ODR) 134
Organizational Performance 1, 13

P

Performance 1, 3-4, 7-9, 12-13, 16, 19, 32, 34-35, 38, 79, 91, 96, 114-115, 117, 121, 125-126, 129, 131-132, 135, 148, 155-156, 159, 178-179, 205, 213, 234-236, 248, 257-259, 266-272, 275, 280, 285, 299, 306, 319, 327-330, 332-341, 343-344, 385, 392-393, 406, 419, 423-424, 426, 429, 460, 463, 469-471, 476, 482, 486
Pollution 218, 229, 297, 470, 479, 485-486
Price Index 346
Private Key 72, 86, 102, 106, 148, 150, 152-153, 186-187, 241, 374, 379, 388, 432
Proof-of-Stake 170-171, 178, 192, 204-205, 484, 486-487
Proof-of-Work 67, 146, 170-171, 178, 191-192, 275, 371, 374, 379, 392, 396, 433, 471, 484, 487
Provenance 31, 90, 115, 117, 121, 165, 185, 200, 252, 273-275, 284, 314, 317-318, 320, 377, 389
Public Key 47, 72, 86, 93, 102-103, 116, 180, 186, 205, 275, 285, 374, 379, 432, 462
Public Key Cryptography 180, 186

R

Radio Frequency Identification 17, 137, 140, 229, 236, 246
Regulatory Issues 52, 166, 173, 178-179
RFID 15, 19, 21, 29-31, 35, 82, 133, 137-138, 140, 161, 177, 229-230, 236, 246-247, 250-252, 275, 296, 299, 305

S

Scalability 57, 65, 82, 91, 105, 111, 124-125, 138, 141, 182-183, 192, 236, 239, 242, 273, 276, 279, 281, 395, 438, 443, 445, 450-451, 471
Security Issues 87, 92, 115, 139, 158, 204, 230, 249-250, 394, 406, 434
Smart Contracts 46, 58, 61-62, 65, 72, 74-75, 77, 79, 98, 113-114, 116-126, 128-134, 147, 153, 155, 158, 167, 176, 178, 181-182, 184-185, 196-197, 199-202, 211, 213, 224, 226, 230, 243, 245, 275-276, 291, 319-320, 366, 370, 374, 390, 394-395, 434, 455, 470-476, 478-487
Smart Era 364
Socio-Technical Systems Thinking 292, 296, 304, 309
Software Architecture 470
Software Packages 5-6
Supplier Coordination 254-255, 257-259, 263, 265-266, 268-269
Supply Chain 2-13, 15-38, 41-45, 49, 52-55, 61, 74, 82, 98-99, 113-118, 121-135, 137-138, 155, 157, 160-161, 165-168, 171-173, 175-186, 189, 193-205, 207-215, 217, 219-226, 228-230, 232-233, 235-239, 241-242, 244-252, 254-260, 263, 266-

Index

275, 282-292, 294-299, 301-306, 308, 314, 320, 323-324, 327-330, 333-334, 336-341, 343-344, 377, 389, 432, 479

Supply Chain and Supply Chain Management 13

Supply Chain Communication Systems 5

Supply Chain Coordination Capability 254-255, 257

Supply Chain Management 1-3, 7-8, 12-13, 15-24, 26-28, 30-38, 43, 61, 82, 99, 113-115, 125, 127-128, 131-135, 137, 161, 165-168, 177-184, 186, 194-197, 199, 202-205, 207, 209, 219, 224-226, 228-230, 235, 237, 241, 244, 246-252, 255-257, 267-271, 273-275, 282-285, 305, 324, 328-329, 333, 337, 340-341, 377, 479

Supply Chain Partners 13, 118, 210, 212-213, 338

Supply Chain Performance 7, 12, 34, 113, 129, 131-132, 135, 257, 259, 266-267, 269, 285, 338, 341, 343-344

Supply Demand Network 15, 18

T

Technology 7, 12-13, 15-19, 21, 24-25, 27-35, 37-38, 40-44, 46-61, 63-66, 71, 77, 79, 81-84, 86-87, 91-94, 96, 99, 101, 111-119, 121-134, 137-144, 146-153, 155-156, 159, 161, 165-169, 173-186, 189, 194-196, 198-205, 207-209, 211-213, 215-223, 225-226, 228-230, 233-252, 256-258, 266-268, 271-284, 286-297, 299-305, 307-309, 311-325, 327-328, 330-333, 336-342, 344, 347, 364-368, 370, 374-378, 382, 386-387, 389, 391-397, 399-406, 408-409, 424, 427-429, 431, 433-435, 440, 450-453, 455, 463, 468, 470-471, 478-479, 483, 486

Technology Adoption 19, 40, 50, 55-56, 127, 177, 203, 248, 274, 276, 280, 284, 291, 325

Token 64-65, 75, 77, 79, 145, 148, 176, 194, 212, 315, 326, 473

Tokenization 95, 148, 194, 211, 314-315, 317-318, 320, 323, 326

Trading Volume 346, 348-349, 351-358, 360-362

Traditional Supply Chain 1, 3, 10, 27, 177, 185, 256

Transaction 4-5, 12, 27, 42, 50-51, 58, 61-63, 65-67, 69-72, 74-75, 78, 82, 86-102, 104-106, 108-112, 114, 116-118, 120, 143-146, 148, 152-154, 158, 160, 163-165, 167, 171, 175, 177, 182, 188-190, 192-197, 199, 211-213, 219, 226, 239, 241-242, 244, 246, 248, 252, 275, 291, 330-331, 337-338, 361-362, 364, 366, 368, 371-374, 376-378, 380-383, 391, 401-402, 404-405, 424-425, 432-433, 435, 438-439, 443-447, 449, 455, 470-472, 479, 482, 484

Triple Bottom Line 209-210

W

Warehouse 6, 21, 29, 31-33, 38, 130, 141, 165, 177, 184, 229, 252, 260, 268, 341

Wavelet Coherence 346-347, 350-351, 356-358

Recommended Reference Books

IGI Global's reference books are available in three unique pricing formats:
Print Only, E-Book Only, or Print + E-Book.

Order direct through IGI Global's Online Bookstore at
www.igi-global.com or through your preferred provider.

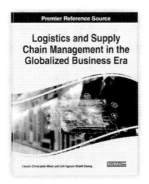

ISBN: 9781799887096
EISBN: 9781799887119
© 2022; 413 pp.
List Price: US$ **250**

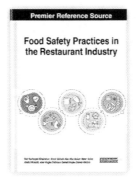

ISBN: 9781799874157
EISBN: 9781799874164
© 2022; 334 pp.
List Price: US$ **240**

ISBN: 9781668440230
EISBN: 9781668440254
© 2022; 320 pp.
List Price: US$ **215**

ISBN: 9781799889502
EISBN: 9781799889526
© 2022; 263 pp.
List Price: US$ **240**

ISBN: 9781799885283
EISBN: 9781799885306
© 2022; 587 pp.
List Price: US$ **360**

ISBN: 9781668455906
EISBN: 9781668455913
© 2022; 2,235 pp.
List Price: US$ **1,865**

Do you want to stay current on the latest research trends, product announcements, news, and special offers?
Join IGI Global's mailing list to receive customized recommendations, exclusive discounts, and more.
Sign up at: **www.igi-global.com/newsletters**.

Publisher of Timely, Peer-Reviewed Inclusive Research Since 1988

www.igi-global.com   Sign up at www.igi-global.com/newsletters   facebook.com/igiglobal   twitter.com/igiglobal   linkedin.com/igiglobal

Ensure Quality Research is Introduced to the Academic Community

Become an Evaluator for IGI Global Authored Book Projects

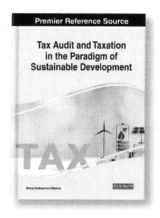   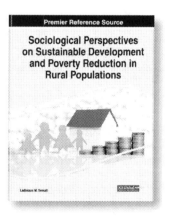

The overall success of an authored book project is dependent on quality and timely manuscript evaluations.

Applications and Inquiries may be sent to:
development@igi-global.com

Applicants must have a doctorate (or equivalent degree) as well as publishing, research, and reviewing experience. Authored Book Evaluators are appointed for one-year terms and are expected to complete at least three evaluations per term. Upon successful completion of this term, evaluators can be considered for an additional term.

If you have a colleague that may be interested in this opportunity, we encourage you to share this information with them.

Easily Identify, Acquire, and Utilize Published
Peer-Reviewed Findings in Support of Your Current Research

IGI Global OnDemand

Purchase Individual IGI Global OnDemand Book Chapters and Journal Articles

For More Information:
www.igi-global.com/e-resources/ondemand/

Browse through 150,000+ Articles and Chapters!

Find specific research related to your current studies and projects that have been contributed by international researchers from prestigious institutions, including:

- Accurate and Advanced Search
- Affordably Acquire Research
- Instantly Access Your Content
- Benefit from the InfoSci Platform Features

"*It really provides* an excellent entry into the research literature of the field. *It presents a manageable number of* highly relevant sources *on topics of interest to a wide range of researchers. The sources are* scholarly, but also accessible *to 'practitioners'.*"

– Ms. Lisa Stimatz, MLS, University of North Carolina at Chapel Hill, USA

Interested in Additional Savings?

Subscribe to
IGI Global OnDemand *Plus*

Learn More

Acquire content from over 128,000+ research-focused book chapters and 33,000+ scholarly journal articles for as low as US$ 5 per article/chapter (original retail price for an article/chapter: US$ 37.50).

7,300+ E-BOOKS.
ADVANCED RESEARCH.
INCLUSIVE & AFFORDABLE.

IGI Global e-Book Collection

- **Flexible Purchasing Options** (Perpetual, Subscription, EBA, etc.)
- Multi-Year Agreements with **No Price Increases** Guaranteed
- **No Additional Charge** for Multi-User Licensing
- No Maintenance, Hosting, or Archiving Fees
- Continually Enhanced & Innovated **Accessibility Compliance Features** (WCAG)

Handbook of Research on Digital Transformation, Industry Use Cases, and the Impact of Disruptive Technologies
ISBN: 9781799877127
EISBN: 9781799877141

Handbook of Research on New Investigations in Artificial Life, AI, and Machine Learning
ISBN: 9781799886860
EISBN: 9781799886877

Handbook of Research on Future of Work and Education
ISBN: 9781799882756
EISBN: 9781799882770

Research Anthology on Physical and Intellectual Disabilities in an Inclusive Society (4 Vols.)
ISBN: 9781668435427
EISBN: 9781668435434

Innovative Economic, Social, and Environmental Practices for Progressing Future Sustainability
ISBN: 9781799895909
EISBN: 9781799895923

Applied Guide for Event Study Research in Supply Chain Management
ISBN: 9781799889694
EISBN: 9781799889717

Mental Health and Wellness in Healthcare Workers
ISBN: 9781799888130
EISBN: 9781799888147

Clean Technologies and Sustainable Development in Civil Engineering
ISBN: 9781799898108
EISBN: 9781799898122

Request More Information, or Recommend the IGI Global e-Book Collection to Your Institution's Librarian

For More Information or to Request a Free Trial, Contact IGI Global's e-Collections Team: eresources@igi-global.com | 1-866-342-6657 ext. 100 | 717-533-8845 ext. 100

Are You Ready to Publish Your Research?

IGI Global offers book authorship and editorship opportunities across 11 subject areas, including business, computer science, education, science and engineering, social sciences, and more!

Benefits of Publishing with IGI Global:

- Free one-on-one editorial and promotional support.
- Expedited publishing timelines that can take your book from start to finish in less than one (1) year.
- Choose from a variety of formats, including Edited and Authored References, Handbooks of Research, Encyclopedias, and Research Insights.
- Utilize IGI Global's eEditorial Discovery® submission system in support of conducting the submission and double-blind peer review process.
- IGI Global maintains a strict adherence to ethical practices due in part to our full membership with the Committee on Publication Ethics (COPE).
- Indexing potential in prestigious indices such as Scopus®, Web of Science™, PsycINFO®, and ERIC – Education Resources Information Center.
- Ability to connect your ORCID iD to your IGI Global publications.
- Earn honorariums and royalties on your full book publications as well as complimentary content and exclusive discounts.

Join Your Colleagues from Prestigious Institutions, Including: Australian National University, MIT Massachusetts Institute of Technology, Johns Hopkins University, Harvard University, Tsinghua University, Columbia University in the City of New York

Learn More at: www.igi-global.com/publish
or Contact IGI Global's Aquisitions Team at: acquisition@igi-global.com

Individual Article & Chapter Downloads
US$ 29.50/each

 Easily Identify, Acquire, and Utilize Published Peer-Reviewed Findings in Support of Your Current Research

- Browse Over **170,000+ Articles & Chapters**
- **Accurate & Advanced** Search
- Affordably Acquire **International Research**
- **Instantly Access** Your Content
- Benefit from the **InfoSci® Platform Features**

THE UNIVERSITY of NORTH CAROLINA at CHAPEL HILL

"*It really provides an excellent entry into the research literature of the field. It presents a manageable number of highly relevant sources on topics of interest to a wide range of researchers. The sources are scholarly, but also accessible to 'practitioners'.*"

- Ms. Lisa Stimatz, MLS, University of North Carolina at Chapel Hill, USA

Interested in Additional Savings?

Subscribe to **IGI Global OnDemand Plus**

Learn More

Acquire content from over 137,000+ research-focused book chapters and 33,000+ scholarly journal articles for as low as US$ 5 per article/chapter (original retail price for an article/chapter: US$ 29.50).

Printed in the United States
by Baker & Taylor Publisher Services